Ocean

East
Siberian Sea

EVERNAYA
ZEMLYA

NEW
SIBERIAN
ISLS.

Kolima R.

ARCTIC CIRCLE

Sea

Laptev Sea

Indigirka R.

Kamchatka

Taimyr
Pen.

Lena R.

Magadan

Sea of

Olhotsk

SAKHALIN

B   E   R   I   A

Vilyuy R.

Yakutsk

Aldan R.

SOCIALIST REPUBLIC

REPUBLICS

KURILE ISLANDS

ower Tunguska R.

RATED

SOCIALIST

SOCIALIST

Angara R.

Lena R.

Khabarovsk

Amur R.

Sea of

Krasnoyarsk

Lake
Baikal

Argun R.

Amur R.

Japan

JAPAN

Irkutsk

UlanUde

Chita

Vladivostok

NORTH
KOREA

MONGOLIA

SOUTH
KOREA

East
China
Sea

C H I N A

C. E. MC DONNELL – D. BROWNSTEIN   N. Y. TIMES MAP DEPT.

THE SOVIET UNION: THE FIFTY YEARS

The
Soviet Union:
The Fifty Years

EDITED BY

Harrison E. Salisbury

A NEW YORK TIMES BOOK

HARCOURT, BRACE & WORLD, INC.

NEW YORK

Contents

Illustrations are between pages 104 and 105, 200 and 201, 296 and 297, and 392 and 393.

A SOVIET CHRONOLOGY 1917–1967

»

Compiled by Lee Foster

1917

March 6	Bread riots erupt in Petrograd, Russia's capital.
March 10	Troops mutiny in Petrograd.
March 12–14	Provisional Government is organized with Prince Georgi Y. Lvov as its head.
March 15	Czar Nicholas II abdicates for himself and his son in favor of Grand Duke Michael, his brother.
March 16	Grand Duke Michael in effect abdicates in favor of the Provisional Government.
April 16	Lenin and other Bolshevik leaders arrive in Petrograd from Switzerland after a trip through Germany in a sealed railway carriage. The Germans permitted the trip on the ground that these radicals would undermine the Provisional Government, which had pledged to continue fighting on the Allied side in World War I.
July 16–18	Bolsheviks fail in an attempt to seize power in Petrograd. Lenin goes into hiding in Finland. Trotsky is arrested.
July 20	Prince Lvov resigns as head of the Provisional Government. Alexander Kerensky takes his place.
Nov. 7	The Bolshevik Revolution. The Provisional Government is overthrown and its members arrested. Kerensky escapes and eventu-

1917 *(cont.)*

ally goes into exile. A new regime is organized, headed by Lenin and including Trotsky and Stalin.

Dec. 9   The Don Cossacks rebel. This is sometimes regarded as marking the beginning of the great civil war, which continued through 1920. The counterrevolution against the Bolsheviks was supported by the United States, Britain, France, and Japan.

1918

March 3   With World War I still raging, the Bolshevik government signs the Treaty of Brest-Litovsk, a separate peace accord with the Central Powers. The treaty's terms deprive the Russians of vast territories, including the Ukraine.

March 9   The Bolshevik regime announces the transfer of the capital from Petrograd (the present Leningrad) back to Moscow.

July 10   A Soviet constitution is promulgated.

July 16   Former Czar Nicholas II and his family are murdered in a cellar at Yekaterinburg (the present Sverdlovsk) by local Bolsheviks.

1919

March 2   The Communist International, known as the Comintern, is founded, with the ultimate aim of bringing about world revolution.

1920

April 25   War with Poland, followed by the Treaty of Riga (March 18,
–Oct. 12   1921), which defines the Russian-Polish border.

Nov. 14   The anti-Bolshevik forces of General P. N. Wrangel are evacuated from the Crimea to Turkey. Subsequently the great civil war flickers out.

1921

March 17   Lenin initiates the New Economic Policy (NEP), described as a "temporary retreat" from Communism in the interests of economic rehabilitation.

1922

April 3   Stalin becomes General Secretary of the Central Committee of the Communist party.

April 16   Treaty of Rapallo is signed. A pact with Germany, it provides for mutual economic assistance and establishes a framework for political collaboration.

Dec. 30   The U.S.S.R. is organized, bringing together the Russian, Ukrainian, and Byelorussian Soviet Socialist republics and Transcaucasia, with political control exercised from Moscow. Other republics are added later.

1924

Jan. 21   Lenin dies, and a struggle for power begins within the government and Communist party. The chief antagonists are Stalin and Trotsky.

1925

May 12   A revised constitution for the U.S.S.R. is ratified.

1927

Dec. 27   Stalin and his followers score a decisive victory over the Trotsky-ites as the Fifteenth All-Union Congress of the Communist party denounces deviations from the Stalinist line. Trotsky and his allies are expelled from the party and banished to the provinces.

1928

Oct. 1   The first of the five-year plans is introduced by Stalin, replacing the N.E.P. with a Communist program to speed industrialization and collectivize agriculture. The kulaks, prosperous landholding peasants, are eventually wiped out, many through terror tactics, slaughter, and starvation.

1929

Feb. 10   Trotsky is put aboard a ship and expelled from the Soviet Union.
Nov. 17   Bukharin and others who had urged concessions to the peasants are ousted from the Politburo. Stalin's dictatorial sway is complete.

1933

During the year approximately one-third of the members of the Communist party, about a million people, are expelled from its ranks.
Nov. 17   The United States accords diplomatic recognition to the Soviet Union.

1934

Sept. 18   The Soviet Union joins the League of Nations.
Dec. 1   Sergei Kirov, Leningrad party leader, is assassinated, possibly with Stalin's complicity. The first of the purges begins.

1935

May 2   A mutual assistance treaty is signed by the Soviet Union and France.
July 25   In view of the growing fascist threat, the Comintern, meeting in
–Aug. 20   Moscow, orders Communist parties in the West to support the "bourgeois" governments of the democracies and form popular fronts with non-Communist leftists.

A *Soviet Chronology, 1917–1967*

1936

July 18   The Spanish Civil War breaks out. The Soviet Union supports the ultimately defeated Loyalists. The war ends March 28, 1939.

Aug. 19–23   Zinoviev, Kamenev, and others are tried, convicted, and executed as Trotskyite plotters. The period 1936–39 is one of great purges and numerous trials, with Stalin liquidating many prominent Bolsheviks and military men.

Dec. 5   A new constitution is adopted, altering the composition of the U.S.S.R.

1938

March 2–15   Bukharin, Rykov, Yagoda, and other Bolsheviks are tried as conspirators, convicted, and executed.

1939

Aug. 23   The Soviet Union and Nazi Germany conclude a nonaggression pact.

Sept. 1   Germany invades Poland, triggering World War II. The Soviet Union subsequently invades Poland, and the two once again partition that country.

Sept. 29 –Oct. 10   The Soviet Union concludes treaties with Estonia, Latvia, and Lithuania under which it acquires military bases in those countries.

Nov. 30   The Soviet Union invades Finland, which refused to sign a military pact with the U.S.S.R.

Dec. 14   The League of Nations expels the Soviet Union for aggression against Finland.

1940

March 12   The Soviet-Finnish War ends. Finland is forced to cede territory to the Soviet Union.

Aug. 3–6   Lithuania, Latvia, and Estonia are incorporated into the U.S.S.R.

Aug. 20   Trotsky is mortally wounded by an assassin in Mexico City and dies the next day.

1941

April 13   The Soviet Union concludes a neutrality treaty with Japan.

June 22   Germany invades the Soviet Union.

1942

June 11   Accord on Lend-Lease. Before the end of the war, the Soviet Union will receive billions in United States aid.

Aug. 22   Battle of Stalingrad (the present Volgograd) begins.

1943

Feb. 2   Battle of Stalingrad ends in a crushing defeat for the Germans.

May 23   The Comintern is dissolved.

1943 *(cont.)*

Nov. 28
–Dec. 1
The Teheran Conference. Roosevelt, Churchill, and Stalin concert war plans.

1945

Feb. 7–12
The Yalta Conference. Roosevelt, Churchill, and Stalin plan postwar occupation of Germany, arrange for the Soviet Union to declare war on Japan after Germany is defeated, pledge assistance to the liberated nations of Europe, and support the formation of a world organization (the United Nations) for peace and security.

April 15
The Soviet Union denounces its neutrality treaty with Japan.

May 7
Germany surrenders.

July 17
–Aug. 2
The Potsdam Conference. Truman, Stalin, and Churchill, who is later replaced by Attlee, decide on basic principles for the administration of occupied Germany.

Aug. 6
The United States drops an atomic bomb on Hiroshima.

Aug. 8
The Soviet Union declares war on Japan.

Aug. 9
The United States drops an atomic bomb on Nagasaki.

Aug. 14
Japan surrenders, ending World War II. The formal terms of surrender are signed aboard the U.S.S. *Missouri* in Tokyo Bay on Sept. 2. The Soviet Union gets southern Sakhalin and the Kurile Islands.

Oct. 24
The United Nations is formally established, with the Soviet Union as a charter member.

1947

March 10
–April 24
The foreign ministers of the United States, the Soviet Union, Britain, and France meet in Moscow. The conference discloses disagreements on Germany between the three Western powers and the U.S.S.R. and dashes hopes for Big Four co-operation.

July 2
At a foreign ministers' meeting with Britain and France, the Soviet Union refuses to participate in the Marshall Plan program of United States aid for European economic reconstruction, thus forcing its satellites to follow suit.

Oct. 5
The founding of the Communist Information Bureau, or Cominform, is announced. Successor to the Comintern, it aims to co-ordinate the activities of the Communist parties of the Soviet Union, its East European satellites, France, and Italy.

1948

April 1
The Soviet Union, in growing disagreement with the United States, Britain, and France over the quadripartite administration of Germany, begins to interfere with surface traffic to Berlin. By late July the blockade is completely in effect and is regarded as an attempt to force the Western allies to yield their rights in

1948 *(cont.)*

	the city. They respond with a massive and sustained airlift of vital supplies to Berlin.
June 28	The Cominform expels Yugoslavia, accusing that country's Communist leadership of hostility toward the Soviet Union and deviations from Marxist-Leninist doctrine.

1949

Jan. 25	The Council for Mutual Economic Assistance, often referred to as Comecon, is formed as a Communist riposte to the Marshall Plan. The initial members are the Soviet Union, Poland, Czechoslovakia, Hungary, Rumania, and Bulgaria.
May 12	The Berlin blockade is terminated by the Soviet Union.
Sept. 23	Truman announces that an atomic explosion has taken place in the Soviet Union. This event signals the end of the United States monopoly of atomic weapons.
Oct. 1	The People's Republic of China (Communist China) comes into existence. Before the end of the year the Nationalist government retreats from the Chinese mainland to Taiwan.

1950

Jan. 10	The Soviet Union, objecting to the continued seating of Nationalist China, begins what proves to be a six-month boycott of the United Nations.
Feb. 14	The Soviet Union and Communist China sign a treaty of alliance.
June 25	The Korean War erupts as North Korea invades South Korea. The United Nations Security Council calls in vain for a cessation of hostilities and the withdrawal of North Korean troops.
July 7	The Security Council establishes a United Nations military command for South Korea in which the United States is to have the dominant role. It is able to do this because the Soviet Union, boycotting the session, cannot cast a veto.

1952

Oct. 5–14	The Nineteenth Congress of the Communist party of the U.S.S.R. is held. The Central Committee's report states that Soviet policy is based on the premise that peaceful coexistence between capitalism and Communism is quite possible.

1953

Jan. 13	The U.S.S.R. announces the arrest of nine physicians, six of them of Jewish origin, charging that they caused the death of two Soviet leaders in the 1940's and conspired to kill others by means of improper medical treatment. The announcement of this so-called "doctors' plot" is coupled with Soviet press attacks on Zionism.

1953 *(cont.)*

March 5   Stalin dies. His death leads to a new struggle for power in the Soviet Union.

March 6   Malenkov succeeds Stalin as Premier and First Secretary of the Communist party.

March 14   Malenkov resigns as First Secretary and is succeeded by Khrushchev.

April 3   The Soviet Union announces that all the physicians who were arrested in the so-called "doctors' plot" have been exonerated and released.

June 15   Yugoslavia announces acceptance of a Soviet proposal to exchange ambassadors and thus normalize diplomatic relations, which were severed in the wake of Yugoslavia's expulsion from the Cominform in 1948.

July 10   The Soviet Union discloses the arrest of Beria, the secret-police chief, and many of his top aides on charges of falsifying arrests and executing thousands of innocent citizens.

July 27   The Korean War ends with the signing of an armistice agreement. In a message to North Korea the Soviet Union hails the accord.

Aug. 12   The Soviet Union explodes a hydrogen bomb.

Dec. 23   The trial and execution of Beria and six of his associates as traitors is announced.

1954

Jan. 25   The foreign ministers of the United States, the Soviet Union,
–Feb. 18   Britain, and France confer in Berlin. No progress is made on German reunification or a Big Four accord on Austria.

April 26   The Geneva conference on Far Eastern problems opens. Among the nations attending are the United States, the Soviet Union, Communist China, Britain, and France, which is embroiled in war in Indochina.

July 21   Vietnam is partitioned at the Geneva conference pending elections to unify the country. Subsequently, French forces withdraw from Indochina.

Oct. 12   Moscow and Peking announce an accord in which the Soviet Union makes important economic and political concessions to Communist China. The agreement was negotiated in Peking by a top-level Soviet delegation that included Khrushchev.

1955

Feb. 8   Malenkov, admitting "fault and responsibility" for Soviet agricultural shortcomings, resigns as Premier and is succeeded by Bulganin, Khrushchev's nominee. Malenkov becomes a Deputy Premier and Minister for Electric Power Stations.

1955 *(cont.)*

May 14   The Warsaw Treaty, establishing a Communist counterpart to NATO, is signed by the Soviet Union, Poland, Czechoslovakia, East Germany, Hungary, Rumania, Bulgaria, and Albania.

May 15   The Austrian State Treaty is signed by the United States, the Soviet Union, Britain, and France, which have been occupying Austria since World War II. The treaty, on which the Western allies and the Soviet Union were previously unable to agree, ends the occupation. The Austrians pledge permanent neutrality.

May 26 –June 3   Khrushchev and Bulganin visit Yugoslavia in the interests of Soviet-Yugoslav *rapprochement*. Khrushchev blames Beria for the bitterness that existed between the two countries.

July 18–23   Bulganin, accompanied by Khrushchev, meets in Geneva with Eisenhower, Eden, and Faure, the heads of government of the United States, Britain, and France. The conferees instruct their foreign ministers to propose ways to solve the problems of German reunification, European security, disarmament, and East-West contacts.

Oct. 27 –Nov. 16   The foreign ministers of the United States, the Soviet Union, Britain, and France meet in Geneva to carry out the instructions of the Geneva summit conference of July 18–23. No agreement is reached on any of the items on the agenda.

1956

Feb. 14–25   The Twentieth Congress of the Communist party of the U.S.S.R. is held. In a secret session on Feb. 24–25, Khrushchev delivers his now-famous speech attacking Stalin. He denounces the late dictator for megalomania, self-glorification, repressions, and cruelties, and derides his World War II leadership. He also says that Stalin and Beria fabricated the so-called "doctors' plot." This speech becomes a keystone in the de-Stalinization process.

April 18   The dissolution of the Cominform is announced.

June 28–30   Strikes and riots of an anti-Soviet nature take place in Poland. This Polish uprising leads to liberalizing measures within the country.

Oct. 23   The Hungarian revolution begins.

Nov. 4   The Hungarian revolution is crushed by Soviet troops.

1957

July 3   Moscow announces that Malenkov and the other members of a so-called "anti-party" group have been expelled from the Presidium and Central Committee of the Soviet Communist party.

July 4   Malenkov's ouster as a Deputy Premier and Minister of Electric Power Stations is announced. Shortly thereafter he is appointed manager of a power plant in Ust-Kamenogorsk.

1957 *(cont.)*

Aug. 26   The Soviet Union announces that it has successfully tested an intercontinental ballistic missile.

Oct. 4   The first man-made space satellite, dubbed Sputnik, is launched by the Soviet Union. It is a sphere weighing 184 pounds.

Nov. 3   A second satellite is launched by the Soviet Union. It weighs 1,120 pounds and carries scientific instruments and a live dog, which thus becomes the world's first voyager in space.

1958

March 27 Khrushchev replaces Bulganin as Premier. In addition to becoming Premier, he continues as First Secretary of the Communist party. Thus, like Stalin before him, he now occupies the Soviet Union's two top posts simultaneously.

Sept. 5   Bulganin's ouster from the party's Presidium is announced.

Nov. 13   Khrushchev calls Bulganin a member of the "anti-party" group. In December, at a session of the party's Central Committee, Bulganin confesses guilt.

1959

Jan. 1   Castro topples the Batista regime and comes to power in Cuba.

Jan. 2   The Soviet Union launches a rocket that goes into orbit around the sun, becoming its first man-made "planet."

Jan. 27   The Twenty-first Congress of the Communist party of the
–Feb. 5   U.S.S.R. is held. Its effect is to acknowledge Khrushchev's victory in the post-Stalin power struggle.

May 11   The foreign ministers of the United States, the Soviet Union, Britain, and France begin conferring in Geneva on the future of Berlin and Germany.

July 24   The Nixon-Khrushchev "kitchen debate" takes place as the Vice-President, in Moscow to open an American exhibition, carries on a heated exchange of views with the Soviet Premier in front of a model kitchen.

Aug. 3   The United States and the Soviet Union announce that their heads of government will exchange visits, with Khrushchev coming to the United States in the fall and Eisenhower subsequently going to the Soviet Union.

Aug. 5   The Geneva conference of foreign ministers ends. No substantive agreements are reached.

Sept. 14 A Soviet rocket hits the moon.

Sept. 15–27 Khrushchev visits the United States. During his trip he addresses the United Nations General Assembly and tours the country. Some of his talks with Eisenhower are held at Camp David, Md., and the aura of good will generated there comes to be known as the "spirit of Camp David."

1959 *(cont.)*

Oct. 4   The Soviet Union launches a rocket that circles the moon and transmits the first photographs of its far side.

Dec. 1   The United States, the Soviet Union, and ten other countries sign a treaty banning military activities in Antarctica.

Dec. 19–21   The Western Big Four heads of government—Eisenhower, de Gaulle, Macmillan, and Adenauer—meet in Paris. Khrushchev is invited to attend a summit conference in the French capital in the spring of 1960.

1960

Jan. 17   The United States announces that Eisenhower will visit the Soviet Union from June 10 to 19.

May 1   A United States U-2 reconnaissance plane is shot down over the Soviet Union and its pilot, Francis Gary Powers, is taken alive.

May 4   Kosygin becomes one of the two First Deputy Premiers of the Soviet Union.

May 5   Khrushchev, in announcing the shooting down of the U-2, terms its flight over the Soviet Union a "direct provocation" and "aggressive act" by the United States.

May 7   Brezhnev becomes the Soviet Union's chief of state. This is a less important post than the ones held by Khrushchev, who as Premier and First Secretary is head of both the government and the party.

May 16   The Paris summit conference of Eisenhower, Khrushchev, de Gaulle, and Macmillan breaks up at what was to have been its first session after Khrushchev cancels Eisenhower's visit to the Soviet Union and demands that Eisenhower apologize for the U-2 flight.

Aug. 19   Powers, the U-2 pilot, is convicted of espionage by a Soviet military tribunal and given a ten-year sentence.

Sept. 19   Khrushchev is in New York for the fifteenth United Nations
–Oct. 13   General Assembly session, which is attended by a number of heads of state and heads of government, including Castro. In the United Nations, Khrushchev attacks colonialism and presses unsuccessfully for a Soviet disarmament plan and replacement of the secretary general of the world organization with a three-man directorate representing the Eastern, Western, and nonaligned blocs. He engages in shouting, fist-pounding, and bangs his shoe on the desk.

Nov. 9   Khrushchev, in a telegram, congratulates Kennedy on his election as President of the United States and voices hope of better Soviet-American relations.

Dec. 6   The Soviet Union publishes a manifesto adopted by an international conference of Communist parties in Moscow. The manifesto represents a compromise between Moscow's and Peking's

1960 *(cont.)*

ideological views in a rift that has been building since the latter part of the 1950's.

1961

April 12   The Soviet Union, orbiting an astronaut around the earth, achieves history's first manned space flight.

April 17   The U.S.-backed "Bay of Pigs" invasion of Cuba begins and is swiftly crushed by Castro's forces.

June 3–4   Khrushchev and Kennedy confer in Vienna. They reach no agreement on the key issues of Germany and disarmament.

Aug. 13   East Germany seals the border between East and West Berlin with barricades and barbed wire. In succeeding months the East Germans erect the Berlin Wall.

Sept. 1   The Soviet Union resumes nuclear-weapons testing, breaking an unofficial Soviet–United States–British moratorium of about three years' duration. In October it sets off the largest nuclear blast the world has ever experienced.

Oct. 17–31   The Twenty-second Congress of the Communist party of the U.S.S.R. is held. It approves a long-range program for the Soviet Union and reaffirms the view that major wars are not necessary for Communism to triumph in the world. Albania, which has been siding with Communist China against the Soviet Union in ideological disputes, is attacked during the debates.

Dec. 10   The Soviet Union severs diplomatic relations with Albania.

1962

Feb. 10   Powers, the U-2 pilot, is freed by the Soviet Union in exchange for Rudolf Abel, sentenced to thirty years' imprisonment by the United States in 1957 as a Soviet spy.

Aug. 12–15   Two Soviet astronauts, in separate spacecraft, orbit the earth simultaneously—another first for the U.S.S.R.

Oct. 22
–Nov. 2   The Cuban missile crisis. On Oct. 22 Kennedy declares that the Soviet Union has put missiles in Cuba that are capable of striking a large part of the United States. He announces a naval blockade to intercept any further shipments of offensive weapons to Cuba and calls on the U.S.S.R. to withdraw the missiles already there. On Oct. 28 Khrushchev says that the Soviet missiles will be withdrawn. On Nov. 2 Kennedy announces that aerial reconnaissance has shown that the Soviet missile bases in Cuba are being dismantled and the missiles crated for return to the U.S.S.R.

Oct. 31   Peking publishes the first of many editorials criticizing Khrushchev's withdrawal of the Soviet missiles from Cuba.

Nov. 20   Khrushchev announces the lifting of the United States naval blockade of Cuba.

1962 *(cont.)*

Dec. 1   Khrushchev delivers a speech in which he attempts to justify his withdrawal of the missiles from Cuba. He attacks Albania and, by unmistakable implication, Communist China for the "Trotskyist position" of seeking a global war to make the world Communist.

1963

June 16–19   The Soviet Union sends the first woman into space. She orbits the earth forty-eight times.

June 20   To reduce the risk of war by miscalculation or accident, the United States and the Soviet Union sign an agreement to set up a "hot line"—an emergency communications channel between Washington and Moscow.

July 5–21   The Soviet Union and Communist China hold a high-level ideological conference in Moscow. It follows Chinese accusations during the year that Khrushchev and the Soviet Communist party have abandoned Marxist-Leninist policies, have erroneously espoused "peaceful coexistence" at the expense of "revolutionary struggle," and have abrogated hundreds of agreements with China. These accusations have drawn Soviet countercharges. The ideological conference ends in failure, being recessed indefinitely.

July 25   The United States, the Soviet Union, and Britain agree on a treaty banning nuclear tests in the atmosphere, in space, and under water. The only tests not banned are those carried out underground.

July 31   Peking denounces the test-ban treaty, and Moscow condemns
–Aug. 3   Peking's denunciation of it. Subsequently, Chinese-Soviet polemics continue, with Peking castigating "de-Stalinization" and Khrushchev's "filthy" attacks on Stalin.

1964

July 15   Brezhnev is relieved of the post of head of state so that he may concentrate on Communist party affairs.

Sept. 2   With the Chinese-Soviet quarrel continuing unabated, Moscow declares that Peking has made claims to hundreds of thousands of square miles of Soviet territory and warns that any attempt to enforce those claims will be dangerous.

Oct. 12–13   The Soviet Union orbits the world's first spacecraft containing more than one person. It contains three.

Oct. 14   Khrushchev is toppled from power. He is succeeded as First Secretary of the Communist party of the U.S.S.R. by Brezhnev, and as Premier by Kosygin. He also loses his membership in the party's Presidium. Important factors contributing to Khrushchev's downfall are the Chinese-Soviet rift, the U.S.S.R.'s agri-

1964 *(cont.)*

cultural shortcomings, and his apparent violations of the principle of Soviet "collective leadership."

Oct. 16   Communist China conducts its first atomic test explosion. On the same day it congratulates Brezhnev and Kosygin on their takeover.

Oct. 20   The Soviet Union announces that one-third of its clothing and shoe factories will be converted from a system of rigid central planning to a pattern of consumer orientation, with plants planning production in relation to demand and measuring performance by the yardstick of goods actually sold. This represents a massive turn toward the theories of Yevsei G. Liberman, a Soviet professor, whose advocacy of certain market-oriented devices to increase industrial efficiency within the over-all framework of a state-planned society has come to be known as "Libermanism."

Nov. 5–13   Premier Chou of Communist China is in the Soviet Union for talks with the new leadership.

Nov. 20   Peking publishes a lengthy article that speaks of "Khrushchevism without Khrushchev" and attacks the policies of his successors.

Dec. 6   Moscow prints an editorial rejecting Peking's criticism of the policies of the Soviet Union's new leadership.

1965

March 18   A Soviet astronaut, leaving his orbiting vehicle, takes man's first "walk in space."

July 24   A United States jet plane is shot down over North Vietnam by a Soviet missile. This incident occurs after a U.S. announcement that the U.S.S.R. has been installing missile sites around Hanoi.

Oct. 1–2   Further and wider industrial changes along the lines of "Libermanism" are decreed in the Soviet Union.

1966

Feb. 3   An unmanned Soviet spacecraft achieves the first soft landing on the moon.

March 1   An unmanned Soviet spacecraft strikes Venus, becoming man's first artifact to reach another planet.

March 29 –April 8   The Twenty-third Congress of the Communist party of the U.S.S.R. is held. It endorses the general policies of Khrushchev's successors and a five-year plan with features that constitute an approval of "Libermanism." The Presidium of the party reverts to its old name, the Politburo.

April 3   In another first, an unmanned Soviet spacecraft achieves a lunar orbit.

Nov. 6–7   At celebrations in Moscow for the forty-ninth anniversary of the

1966 *(cont.)*

Bolshevik Revolution, Communist China is repeatedly denounced. These denunciations follow a worsening of Chinese-Soviet relations during the year.

1967

Jan. 27   The United States, the Soviet Union, and a host of other countries sign a treaty outlawing nuclear weapons in space and prohibiting the use of the moon and other celestial bodies for military purposes.

April 21   Having quit her homeland, Svetlana Alliluyeva, Stalin's daughter, arrives in the United States "to seek the self-expression that has been denied me for so long in Russia."

April 24   A Soviet astronaut is killed during a mission, becoming the world's first known casualty in space.

June 17–26 Kosygin is in the United States to attend the United Nations General Assembly session called by the Soviet Union following the Arab-Israeli war of early June. On June 23 and 25 he confers with Johnson in Glassboro, N.J., and the two leaders agree that their talks on world problems should be continued at the ministerial level.

Nov. 7   The fiftieth anniversary of the Bolshevik Revolution.

THE SOVIET UNION: THE FIFTY YEARS

FIFTY YEARS THAT SHOOK THE WORLD

»

Harrison E. Salisbury

At first people said it was only a squabble among the women in the *khvosti,* or queues, which had for months been forming at 4:00 A.M. before the Petrograd bakeshops. Now on this gray and bitter winter morning the bakers scrawled on bits of cardboard: KHLEBA NYET, No Bread, and stuck the signs on the locked doors. In the tallow and kerosene shops similar signs appeared: KEROSINA NYET.

That was March 6, 1917.* Nikolai Sukhanov, working in the Turkestan irrigation offices at the end of Kamenno-Ostrovsky Prospekt (Stony Island Boulevard), heard two typists talking. One girl was telling the other about the queues, how angry the women were, how they had tried to smash into the bakeries. "You know," the girl said, "if you ask me, it's the beginning of the revolution." Sukhanov, a radical, a man of the world, laughed to himself. A fine lot these girls knew about revolutions!

At that moment Vladimir Ilyich Ulyanov, fervent factionalist of Russian radical politics, was sitting, disheartened, in a Zurich library, wondering if

---

* February 21, 1917, by the Julian, or Old Style, calendar. Russia did not adopt the Gregorian, or New Style, calendar, already in use in the Western world, until 1918. I have used New Style dates throughout.

indeed he would live to see a revolution in Russia in his lifetime. Leon Bronstein, who wrote under the name Trotsky, was arguing dialectical points with fellow exiles in a Yiddish café in New York's lower East Side; what else was there to do? A dark-haired, slow-speaking Georgian named Dzhugashvili, better known to history as Stalin, was whiling away endless hours of exile in a dreary whistle stop on the Trans-Siberian Railroad called Achinsk.

Czar Nicholas II, separated from his beloved Czarina Alexandra and still grieving over the murder of "Our Friend," the sinister monk Rasputin, was at his army headquarters at Mogilev, brooding on the disastrous war with Germany. If anyone had told him that the Russian Revolution was about to emerge from beneath the gray wool shawls and drab cloth coats of thousands of angry women wearily waiting in front of the Petrograd bread-shops he would have thought them mad.

No one in Petrograd, no one in Russia, not the revolutionaries who had conspired and dreamed for a century, not the exiled enemies of the Czar in Siberia, not the plotters in Switzerland and New York—no one in those murky March days had a notion that the fall of the three-hundred-year-old House of Romanov was imminent, that Russia would soon be moving relentlessly on a new course which would transform the ancient land of the Slavs and set off shock waves affecting all of humanity.

Never again would the world be the same. Fifty years hence it would still be vibrating from the explosion whose fuse was lit in the bread lines of Petrograd. Fifty years later statesmen would struggle endlessly with the consequences of that explosion and the events that followed. The content of almost every great international problem would be influenced by Russia's revolution. Philosophy and political thought would assume new shapes. The social fabric of Western Europe, the life of painted warriors in Africa, the aspirations of men and women in the rice fields of Asia would be metamorphosed. The world of kings, emperors, czars would vanish. Millions would die. New hopes, new fears would possess the world's peoples. Russia itself would be transformed—changed from a shapeless mass of backward peasantry into a powerful nation sending the first men into space and matching missiles and Armageddonian nuclear might with the United States. Science and enlightenment would stalk the Russian streets and steppes.

So would terror.

Fifty years have passed. The Union of Soviet Socialist Republics has arisen, powerful, successful, second only to the United States in prestige and strength. What have the events of 1917 brought to the people of Russia and to the world? What are the gains and what are the losses? What is the good and what is the bad? Who paid the price? Who reaped the consequences? Is the world the better or the worse? There are a thousand questions. Not all can be answered. And to many questions there are many answers, as many as there are people to be asked.

For several months in 1967 a dozen correspondents of *The New York Times* pondered these problems. They traveled tens of thousands of miles across the Soviet Union. They penetrated remote Siberia. They visited the villages of Central Asia and the vineyards of the Caucasus. They spoke with nuclear physicists in laboratories never before opened to journalists. They sat in student bull sessions through Leningrad's white nights. They attended Russian pot parties and listened to young Soviet composers play aleatory music. They talked to Soviet women about the cost of abortions and the problems of miniskirts. They sought out aging diplomats who had survived Stalin's concentration camps. They talked with men who had escaped death by a hairsbreadth in the Russian civil war and with some who had come even closer to destruction in the black purges of the 1930's, 1940's, and early 1950's. They talked with the men who are creating the "new" economy and with those who spent their lives building Stalin's steel plants. They took part in conversations in a dozen languages with men and women of a dozen nationalities. They experienced the burning anger of young poets at the backwardness of contemporary Russia. They listened to the plaint of aging Stalinists who fear that all they created is vanishing. They examined documents from ancient files never before opened. They inspected plans for a future that is still classified as "top secret."

No neat, categorical answers emerged. The problems are too great, the evidence too contradictory, the balance of gains and losses too mixed, too controversial. It is easier to determine what happened than why it happened, easier to record hopes than to plot scientific projections.

A revolution, after all, is a social hurricane. It destroys, it transposes, it sweeps aside the old so that the seeds of the new can take root. It smashes the past, transforms the present, and dreams of what is to come. But ghosts of history persist into the present and haunt the visions of tomorrow. The past is, inevitably, the matrix of the future.

Contemplating his country in the fiftieth year of the revolution, a brilliant young Soviet economist sighed deeply and said to me: "You know, perhaps after all Marx was right!"

He did not mean that the Soviet Union as it stands today is a monument to Marxian vision. He meant the contrary. Karl Marx thought that the Communist Revolution would come to industrialized Western Europe, to Germany. Subconsciously, he shaped his doctrine to fit the pattern of what he hoped and dreamed for his fatherland. He never thought an advanced socialist society might emerge in Russia. Russia was too backward, too remote, too illiterate. It possessed only the beginnings of modern industry. Its working class, or proletariat, was rudimentary. It was only emerging from what Marx called "feudalism." Ahead of Russia, he thought, lay a century of intensive industrialization, of private enterprise and proliferating commerce. Only when the industrial and social foundations had been completed, only when Russia had assumed the aspect of a contemporary bourgeois society, would it be ready, in Marx's view, for Communism. Communism was not a doctrine for backward or primitive nations. Marx conceived it as a flowering of human society which would occur first and foremost in the advanced West.

It was this thought the young economist was expressing. Perhaps, he was saying, it would have been better had Russia not attempted to leap directly from semifeudalism into the complex, never-before-tried Marxian system of a totally organized, totally theorized, totally directed state.

Perhaps this was why the new Soviet society had been born in such pain and had evolved through decades of such suffering, war, agony. No one in 1917 would have raised such a question. No one would have understood it. In 1917 the future lay open, inviting, a blank page ready to receive what men would write upon it. Generations of young Russians had been waiting for this day; generations had given their lives and their manhood to the cause of freeing Russia from czarist despotism. Now they were ready to write upon the white page of the future, and the most eager among them was the balding, sharp-eyed Vladimir Ilyich Ulyanov, the man whose signature "N. Lenin" was still unknown to most of the world and to the mass of his countrymen—but only too familiar to the worried agents of the Okhrana, the Czar's secret police.

On the morning of March 12, 1917, an eleven-year-old youngster named Georgi Lozgachev started off for school in Petrograd. Georgi, or Gora, as he was nicknamed, was an adopted boy. He lived with his adopted parents, the Yelizarovs, in what they called a "steamship" flat, six oddly arranged rooms on the third floor of an apartment house at the corner of Shiroky and Gazovy streets. Gora's adopted mother was Anna Ilyinichna Yelizarova-Ulyanova, sister of Vladimir.

Every morning Gora caught a streetcar to the Commercial School on Bolshoi Grebetzky Street, just across from the Vladimirsky Cadet Academy. On this morning his streetcar was halted after a couple of blocks by a crowd carrying red flags. Some had banners saying DOWN WITH WAR! DOWN WITH AUTOCRACY! They were singing a song Gora had never heard before. Later on he learned that it was the "Internationale."

A revolution means different things to different people. A few days earlier, the czarist political police had appeared at the apartment and led Gora's mother, Anna Ilyinichna, away. To Gora the revolution meant that his mother burst into the apartment that evening crying: "The revolution has freed me!" But then Gora burst into tears. He had opened the door for his mother, but in her excitement she had rushed right past him, not even noticing that he was standing there.

Today Georgi Lozgachev is a slender, handsome, reserved man of sixty-one, retired from work, devoting himself to writing and research about the Ulyanov family, of which he is the closest living link to the past.

"You can imagine how exciting it was for an eleven-year-old," he recalls quietly. "Mother, Anna Ilyinichna, didn't want me out on the streets because of the shooting. But, of course, I was a boy and I wanted to see what was happening."

Finally his mother bowed to the inevitable. Gora was permitted to go out, but only if he would buy as many newspapers as he could—all the newspapers, whatever their politics. Because, as Anna well knew, Lenin soon would be returning to Russia. And first of all he would need the papers to familiarize himself with what had been happening, with the political lines of the dozen competing parties. "It was," Lozgachev says shyly, "my first service to the revolution."

Again and again Gora went out. He brought back stacks of papers—the *People's Cause,* the *Novaya Zhizn,* or *New Life,* the *Novoye Vremya,* or *New Times, Rech (Speech), Birzheviye Vedomosti,* the organ of the Stock Exchange, *Izvestia, Ogonyok,* and, of course, *Pravda*—the organ of Lenin's own Bolsheviks.

Events raced past. The Czar abdicated, Lenin returned, preceded by a telegram which arrived at the "steamboat" April 16. It said: "Arriving Monday night 11 P.M. Tell Pravda. [Signed] Ulyanov."

Gora wasn't permitted to go down to the Finland Station for Lenin's arrival. But at 4:00 A.M. he awoke. Lenin and his wife, Nadezhda Krupskaya, had arrived at the "steamboat," where they were to make their home. An hour later, on the morning of April 17, 1917, the Ulyanov family, with Lenin at the head of the table and Gora on his right-hand side, sat down for breakfast. Russia and the world did not yet know it, but the second act of the revolution was about to begin.

Looking back over fifty years, the survivors (and the scholars) agree that it was Lenin who gave to the Russian Revolution its special character. He it was who insisted—over the objections of most of his radical Bolshevik associates—on going for broke, on moving straight ahead into the Communist era, on striving to smash the moderate government coalition, which was precariously headed first by Prince Lvov and then by Alexander Kerensky, on setting up a Bolshevik dictatorship and driving headlong into the proletarian revolution dreamed of by Marx.

That morning, as the Ulyanov family sat around the breakfast table drinking tea, eating bread, butter, cheese, and sausage, this audacious program was full-blown in Lenin's mind. Already he had astounded his opponents and dismayed his associates by his uncompromising address a few hours before at the Finland Station. The die was cast. But perhaps only Lenin comprehended this. Certainly not wide-eyed Gora, listening as his uncle laughed and joked, regaling the family with stories of his trip on the famous sealed train through Germany, leaning back happily in his chair, his eyes sparkling. It was only beginning to grow light when a knock came at the door. Gora ran to answer it. Robert Matisovich Gabalin, a chauffeur who later became chief of Lenin's personal bodyguard, had come to report that a car had been placed at Lenin's disposal and awaited him on the street below.

"Come on and take a ride with me," Lenin told Gora gaily. As dawn broke over the steel-gray city, its boulevards swept by winds from the Baltic, the snow still deep in the parks, Gora had the first automobile ride of his life, with the man who was to take Russia out of the troika and put her on the way to the Sputnik. The car that sped through the streets of the capital built by Peter the Great—St. Petersburg, now Petrograd, one day to become Leningrad—was a four-passenger Renault sedan, painted gray.

History is fond of strange quirks. None of the men who helped Lenin make *his* revolution survived to mark its fiftieth anniversary. Lenin himself died on January 21, 1924. Trotsky, driven into exile by Stalin, was assassinated, and died on August 21, 1940. Stalin died March 5, 1953. Lev Kamenev and Grigory Zinoviev—and many, many more Old Bolsheviks—went to their deaths in Stalin's purges. Of the major actors on the Russian stage at the time of the Bolshevik Revolution of November 7, 1917, only their most hated, most reviled, most despised rival lived to witness the golden jubilee of Bolshevik power—Alexander F. Kerensky, head of the Provisional Government, the man whom Lenin thrust aside in order to set Russia's history onto new Communist tracks. Lenin did not live to write his memoirs. Most of his closest associates were killed by Stalin. If they put down any impressions, the documents have not yet come to light. Stalin had his scribes write his own version of the revolution and personally edited it so that his role emerged grander than life, as large as that of Lenin himself. Trotsky wrote endlessly, but he wrote polemics, not history. Kerensky recorded the story, but as it seemed to him—the loser.

There are still survivors in Russia of the political events of fifty years ago. But none who played a major role except for Vyacheslav M. Molotov, the man who so faithfully served Stalin and who as a nineteen-year-old fledgling edited the party newspaper, *Pravda,* in Petrograd until his senior Bolshevik associates Stalin, Kamenev, and Zinoviev made their way back from Siberian exile. But Molotov's memoirs are not yet publicly accessible. Other survivors whose careers date back to the revolution—Marshals Semyon M. Budenny and Kliment Y. Voroshilov, Anastas I. Mikoyan, Andrei A. Andreyev—were too junior, too remote on the periphery, too young, too far from the levers of power to make a contribution. The Ulyanov family is dead. The sisters, Anna and Mariya, died in 1935 and 1937. Lenin's wife, Nadezhda Krupskaya, sorely harassed by Stalin, lived until February, 1939. Lenin's younger brother, Dmitri, died in 1943.

One of Lenin's secretaries, Yelena Stasova, died in 1966. Another, Lidiya Fotiyeva, was still living in 1967, in a sanatorium near Moscow, eighty-six years old and in poor health. A third, Mariya Volodicheva, joined him after the revolution. The ranks of the Old Bolsheviks were so savagely thinned by Stalin's purges that today only a hundred or so survive, most of them feeble pensioners, living out their last days in rest homes or hospitals.

No event of the twentieth century possessed more drama than the Bolshevik seizure of power in 1917. No event cast longer shadows. No event so called for study, analysis, retrospection. Yet few historical occurrences are more difficult to grasp. No good Soviet history has yet been written. For years Stalin and Stalin's opponents, the friends and foes of Bolshevism, recast the story to suit their political purposes. Each turn of the party line caused past versions to be suppressed and new ones to be written. Only with the approach of the golden-jubilee year of the Bolshevik Revolution and the self-conscious effort of the post-Stalin era to seek at least a measure of historical truth have the archives begun to be searched with scholarly care.

Fifty years after the storming of the Winter Palace in Petrograd no one has come closer to capturing the spirit of the moment in which Soviet society was born than did a radical young Harvard graduate named John Reed, attracted to Petrograd by the revolutionary events. He it was who etched his impressions unforgettably in *Ten Days That Shook the World.*

In the summer of 1967 throngs of young Moscow people gathered two or three evenings a week on the narrow sidewalk, seeking admission to a little theater not far from the site of the old Khitrov market, once the home of half of Moscow's thieves and prostitutes. At the doors of the theater stood soldiers wearing the cloth-peaked caps with red stars that were the emblem of the Red Guards of 1917. They jammed the ticket stubs down the long bayonets of ancient rifles. Inside the theater pretty girls pinned revolutionary-red cockades on the breasts of spectators. The walls were plastered with red banners and strident posters: *"Doloi!* Down with the Provisional Government! All Power to the Soviets of Workers' and Soldiers' Deputies!" A file of sailors in blue-striped jerseys, carbines strapped to their backs, wandered through the lobby, chanting *chastushki,* or impromptu revolutionary songs, to an accordion's tune. *Ten Days That Shook the World* had come to life again. On the stage of the Taganka Theater, John Reed, with white starched collar, easy air, notebook in hand, and *propusk,* or pass, signed by Felix Dzerzhinsky (first chief of the dread Bolshevik Cheka), wandered once more through revolutionary Petrograd. He talked his way into the Winter Palace, where a handful of junkers, or cadets, held out even after Kerensky had made his escape in a woman's dress and a car flying an American flag. He talked to the frightened girls of the Women's Battalion of Death. He walked down the Nevsky Prospekt and saw the field guns lumbering into position. He heard the thunder when the cannon of the battleship *Aurora,* standing in the Neva River, opened fire on the Winter Palace. Neither he nor the frightened junkers, girl soldiers, and holdout ministers knew the dreadnaught was firing blanks. He elbowed his way into the old school for girls of the nobility, the Smolny Institute, and there, on the evening of November 8, 1917, he was at the press table in the big hall. Kamenev was speaking—reading a report of the Military Revolutionary Committee recommending abolition of the death penalty in the army, release of soldiers and officers arrested for political crimes, and an order to arrest Kerensky. The time was 8:40 P.M., and the hall suddenly burst into pandemonium as the Presidium entered, among them a short man with a stocky figure and a big head. His nose was snubbish and his chin heavy. He was clean-shaven, and his trousers seemed too long. The debate continued. The representative of the Jewish Bund rose and denounced the Bolsheviks. Then he walked out. Some Mensheviks complained but did not walk out. Soldiers took the tribune to read greetings from the front. Finally the floor was given to the short man with the big head—Lenin. He moved forward to the podium and, as John Reed noted, grasped it with both hands, letting his eyes range over the crowd as he waited for the ovation to die down. When it was quiet—comparatively—Lenin began to speak: "We shall now proceed to construct the Socialist order!"

The Bolshevik Revolution was one day old. Ahead lay bitter years of war against the White Russian armies which hoped to restore the monarchy or, perhaps, a democratic rule. Ahead lay war against the intervening troops of Britain, France, Japan, and the United States. Ahead lay famine, starvation, destruction, and death. Ahead lay tragedy untold. But on that night when Lenin set his nation forward on the great adventure which is still unfolding his first words were of peace, of an end to the war that gripped the world, of a peace without conquests, without annexations, without indemnities, a universal peace to be shared by all, great countries and small, rich and poor, backward and advanced—a peace without privilege, without secret deals, without hidden diplomacy. He concluded with the words: "The revolution of November 6th and 7th has opened the era of the Social Revolution. . . . The labor movement, in the name of peace and Socialism, shall win and fulfill its destiny." To John Reed, starry-eyed, choked with emotion, enthusiastic for the overturn of capitalism and the victory of his ideals, Lenin's words sounded "quiet and powerful." He felt they "stirred the souls" of the listening men.

Another observer sat in the hall of the Smolny Institute that night—in one of the back seats. He was Nikolai Sukhanov. Until that evening he had been part of the revolution, a member of the ruling Soviet. Now he was out. He listened to Lenin speak. He watched the reaction—hails for Lenin, shouts, caps flung in the air, a solemn funeral oratorio for the revolution's martyrs, Lenin and his associates on the platform, eyes blazing, faces exalted.

But Sukhanov's heart was heavy. He did not believe in the success, the rightfulness, the historic mission of the Bolsheviks. He watched with growing concern as Lenin presented his decree on the land. A short recess was called. Sukhanov went to the buffet. There he found Kamenev gulping down a glass of tea. Kamenev was bragging about the success of the Bolshevik *coup d'état*. Kerensky had been routed. But another thought was in Sukhanov's mind—the decision of Lenin to go it alone, to govern not with a coalition of parties but with his Bolsheviks, concentrating all power into their hands. He challenged Kamenev on the Bolshevik monopoly of power.

"I think it's absolutely scandalous," Sukhanov said. "I'm afraid that when you've made a mess of it it will be too late to go back."

"Yes, yes," Kamenev muttered vaguely, and then added, "Although why should we make a mess of it?"

There was no answer to that question on the evening of November 8, 1917. And fifty years later the question still dangled in the air, unanswered, possibly unanswerable.

One hot summer afternoon in 1967 Anastas I. Mikoyan sat in his sun-drenched office on the third floor of the Presidium building within the Kremlin. On the door a neat sign said: MEMBER OF THE PRESIDIUM OF THE SUPREME SOVIET OF THE U.S.S.R. The sign was a token of the fact that Anastas Mikoyan, at seventy-one, a Bolshevik since 1915 and a member of the Central Committee of the Communist party since two years before Lenin's death, no longer took an active part in the Soviet government.

Mikoyan was in a reminiscent mood. His mind went back to the days of the first five-year plan, the Stalin program for crash industrialization of the Soviet Union. The year was 1928.

"I was Commissar of Foreign and Domestic Trade at that time," Mikoyan recalled. "Steel production had been 4,000,000 tons in Russia before the revolution. In Lenin's time it had dropped as low as 200,000 tons."

With Russia flat on its back, with the country devastated by civil war, famine, starvation, there had been little Lenin could do to get industry going again. He had had to retreat from socialism back toward private enterprise, launching what he called his New Economic Policy (NEP), a program of encouraging private trade, entrepreneurs, and foreign concessions in order to get Russia's crippled economy on its feet. Of one thing Lenin dreamed: electrification. In fact, he once defined Communism as "electrification—plus Soviet power."

That dream of Lenin's had been given form in what he called the Goelro plan for electrification of Russia, which he spelled out in December, 1920, but had no time to complete before his death. Goelro was in Mikoyan's mind as he recalled the story of Soviet industrialization. Lenin had said that in ten to fifteen years electric-power capacity should be brought up to 1,750,000 kilowatts and output to 8.5 billion kilowatt-hours. At the time Lenin spoke, Russia had an output of about 500,000,000 kilowatt-hours, not enough for one small power grid today. And total production under the czars had been 2 billion kilowatt-hours. "That's less than we produce in Turkmenia today," Mikoyan said wryly.

"If anyone had told me when the first five-year plan was presented that we would produce in my lifetime—in 1967, to be specific—102,000,000 tons of steel," Mikoyan said, "I would not have believed it."

He opened a slim folder and showed me a sheet on which the latest Soviet production figures had been typed out. "This year we will have an output of 590 billion kilowatt-hours of electricity," he said. "That is more than six times what we produced in 1950, when output was 90 billion kilowatt-hours."

He ticked off the figures, item by item: textiles, 3,300,000 meters in 1950, 8,900,000 in 1967; television sets, 11,900 in 1950, 4,900,000 in 1967; washing machines, 300 in 1950, 4,200,000 in 1967; refrigerators, 1,200 in 1950, 2,800,000 in 1967. ("Soon it will be 5,000,000," he interjected.) Most of Mikoyan's career was devoted to consumer-goods production, and he chose to measure Soviet industrial achievement in terms of television sets, refrigerators, and other "big ticket" items.

Mikoyan recalled how he went to America in 1937 and for the first time saw electric refrigerators being turned out by the hundred thousand at a General Electric plant. "I came back and said we must also produce refrigerators," he said. "I think my colleagues thought I was drunk. 'Refrigerators,' they said; 'first you have to have something to put in them. Besides, who needs refrigerators in a cold climate like Russia's?' "

But Mikoyan stuck to his guns. After the war, in 1949, he got Stalin's agreement to begin to make refrigerators on a small scale. He had authorization to turn out 100,000, "although everybody thought 50,000 would be too many."

He went ahead, and succeeded in making 150,000 by placing his orders with defense plants and automobile plants—"our most advanced industries." But when he got the refrigerators, the Russian housewives didn't want them. They weren't used to refrigerators. The prices were too high. The prices were cut, and today, with the enormous new housing program under way, production cannot keep up with demand; there are long queues at the refrigerator stores and waits for delivery.

"Yes," mused Mikoyan, "I think we have made great progress. Formerly, we were a backward nation. Perhaps the shoes we turn out are still not up to quality. But we have scientists and intelligentsia now even in Central Asia, where the literacy rate was only seven per thousand at the time of the revolution."

He paused and looked out the window of his Kremlin office. "I think," he resumed, "that the policy of our state deserves respect. All those who intimately assess it cannot but find that we have achieved a high level of culture. We must take pride in our attainments."

Mikoyan's pride in Soviet accomplishments is matched by that of most Russians. When they turn to the period of nearly thirty years that Stalin ruled their land they grant his cruelty and his terror. Still, they say, he built our industry, he transformed agriculture, he created the modern foundations of the state. Without him, Russia would not have survived the war with Germany. He brought Russia into the nuclear age. It was his policies that opened the path to Sputnik, to the Soviet space age, to Soviet intercontinental missiles, to H-bombs, to all the accouterments that mark Russia's emergence as one of the world's two superpowers.

That Stalin was acutely conscious of the necessity to build and strengthen the Russian economy there is no doubt. He best expressed this feeling in a February, 1931, speech when he said: "No comrades, the pace must not be slackened. . . . To slacken the pace would be to lag behind; and those who lag behind are beaten. We do not want to be beaten. The history of old Russia was that she was ceaselessly beaten for her backwardness. She was beaten by the Mongol Khans, she was beaten by the Turkish Beys, she was beaten by the Swedish feudal lords, she was beaten by the Polish-Lithuanian Pans, she was beaten by Anglo-French capitalists, she was beaten by Japanese barons, she was beaten by all for her backwardness. . . . We are fifty or a hundred years behind the advanced countries. We must make good this lag in ten years. Either we do it or they crush us."

No one in or out of Russia ever doubted the need for bringing Russia's economy into the twentieth century. The question that has arisen persistently over the years has not related to Stalin's goals, but to Stalin's methods.

Between 1928 and 1940 Stalin carried out two crash programs. The first was in the field of agriculture. At enormous cost, in a campaign of frenzy, utilizing violence, expropriation, exile, execution, he "collectivized" Soviet agriculture in the years 1928, 1929, and 1930. Possibly 10,000,000 peasants were driven from their homes and into hungry exile in Siberia and Central Asia. How many died, either in random violence or in quasi-formal executions, how many starved, how many perished of deprivation no one has ever been able to estimate. Cattle, livestock, horses, pigs, even chickens and ducks died as well. The peasants slaughtered their animals and fowl rather than turn them over to the collective farms—Stalin's state-enforced, state-dictated, state-dominated co-operatives. The country was turned upside down. Famine swept the Ukraine and the lower Volga. Millions died. When the fever abated in 1934, the pool of Soviet animals had been decimated: 15.4 million horses compared with 32.1; 33.5 million cattle compared with 60.1; 11.5 million hogs compared with 22; 32.9 million sheep compared with 97.3. The consequences were inscribed indelibly on the Russian countryside. Never, after 1934, did Stalin travel into rural Russia. And in 1953, a few months after Stalin's death, Nikita S. Khrushchev revealed the grim truth: in Stalin's last years, nearly four decades after the Bolshevik Revolution, the grain harvest was averaging almost 10 per cent below the totals reached in prewar czarist Russia in 1913. And the census of farm animals—cows, pigs, horses, sheep, and mules—was not equal to that of 1916, the last year of the Romanovs.

Small wonder that Stalin himself, in a burst of candor, told Winston Churchill during World War II that the collectivization drive was worse than the war against the Nazis. He implied that had he to do it over again, he might not do it.

Stalin's farm policy bequeathed to his successors one of their most stubborn problems—that of creating an agricultural base productive enough and reliable enough to support the urban technological society of the late twentieth century.

In the U.S.S.R.'s golden-jubilee year some of the most optimistic Soviet commentators were proclaiming the farm-food problem solved. By heavily subsidizing the farmers, by radically increasing investment in fertilizers, irrigation systems, electrification, and machinery, the government had increased yields, and, they felt, the new gains could be maintained in contrast to the erratic gambles of Khrushchev on virgin-lands grain production, universal corn cultivation, and *agrogorods,* or urbanized agricultural centers.

But more skeptical observers crossed their fingers. True, the Soviet Union for the first time since before the revolution was now producing a surplus of butter and serious questions of storage capacity had arisen. But butter prices had not been reduced. True, meat and dairy products were now reaching the cities in quantities ample to meet demands. But substantial imports of foodstuffs continued to enter the Soviet Union from a multitude of sources—Eastern Europe, Asian countries, and Western food-producing nations.

It was far too soon to be certain whether, after fifty years of Communism, Russia, one of the great food-exporting lands before World War I, had finally organized its agriculture on a basis efficient, economical, and profitable enough to insure that fundamental requirement of any nation, advanced or primitive: enough food to keep its people from going hungry. After all, as recently as 1965 Moscow had been buying quantities of grain in the international market to make up for deficits in production in Siberia, in the Volga region, and in the Ukraine.

In industry no one could gainsay Soviet achievements. Russia was a laggard country when Stalin came to the helm. Today it is not only capable of competing with the most advanced states, but it *is* one of the most advanced nations. However, there were cautious critics who invited a second look at the Soviet industrial achievements. True, Russia was backward when Bolshevism came to power. But it was developing at a pace more rapid than any other country in Europe. It had started behind, but was speeding ahead at a violent tempo—equaled only by that other latecomer, Japan. Russia had been tardy in entering the modern world of steel-and-coal technology. But because of this very lateness its mills in 1914 were the best in Europe—few in number but high in quality. The same was true of its new metallurgical works, its new chemical plants, its new and rapidly growing railroad system. Its oil industry was the most advanced in the world. Russia in 1916 was not just the dim, feudal world that it appears to be in the caricatures drawn by the Bolsheviks. In later years, painting a picture of life in the industrial Donbas, where he grew up, Khrushchev told of the heavy involvement of foreign capital—the Belgian, French, German, and English firms that owned the mines and factories. The town in which he first worked was called Yuzovka (Hughes-town) for the Scot who owned the steel mill there. There were large foreign investments in Russia —in mining, manufacturing, textiles, and oil—attracted by the extraordinarily rapid expansion of the Russian economy. But Russia by no means was entirely in the hands of rapacious foreign or domestic capitalists—as the Bolsheviks liked to contend. Much of the industry was state-subsidized or state-owned, and there was, long before the revolution, more state participation and direction of the economy than in any other European country. In fact, when Stalin turned to his economists to devise a blueprint for the first Soviet five-year plan, they, in turn, dug out of the files a czarist industrial plan drafted on the eve of the war and designed to be launched in 1916. It was on a revision of this czarist program for the planned expansion of the Russian economy that the first Bolshevik five-year plan was based.

That five-year plan was initiated in 1928. Plan succeeded plan with bewildering rapidity. Three had been put into operation before World War II interrupted the sequence. At the end of the war, with steel production knocked down by Nazi destruction to 12,000,000 tons, the level of the middle 1930's, new sequences were invoked—to repair the damage of the war and push the country up to new levels of achievement. In fifteen years, Stalin postulated, he would lift steel production to 60,000,000 tons a year. More—always more. There never was to be any relaxation in his insatiable demands for more steel, more coal, more oil, more electricity. Housing made no difference. Comfort made no difference. Consumer goods were neglected. Farm investment was nonexistent. People sweated, froze, went hungry and threadbare. Everything was sacrificed to the expansion of heavy industry, to the creation of a base of technology, industrial capacity, and science on which Soviet armed might could rely.

When the country, dazed, exhausted, sullen, dispirited, sodden with hardship, sacrifice, and violence, staggered to its feet after Stalin's death in 1953, it found itself possessed of nuclear weapons, H-bombs, long-range missiles, space technology, and a steel industry that not only reached the 60,000,000-ton mark by 1960, but surpassed it. It had a standard of living that had radically declined from a high set in 1938. In spirit Russia resembled a badly run prison camp.

Was this necessary? Was Stalin's way the only one that could enable Russia to catch up to and exceed the levels of the most advanced industrial nations? Was Russia compelled to sacrifice three or four generations of its best people in order to enter the twentieth century?

Fifty years after November 7, 1917, more and more persons, inside and outside Russia, were inclined to think the answer to these questions was No.

Galina Serebryakova is a handsome woman of sixty-two. Her grayish hair is stylishly coiffed. She wore a dark dress that could have come from Paris. In her arms was a cluster of deep-red roses, peonies, and fragrant jasmine, picked that morning in the gardens of her country house. Beside the crystal and silver on the table in the smart dining room of the Hotel National lay a book by Bernard Shaw, leather-bound in an edition of a single copy, a gift to her from the author in 1929 when she was the beautiful young wife of the first Soviet ambassador to London, Grigory Y. Sokolnikov.

The dining room was filled with people chatting gaily, and at first Madame Serebryakova's remarks were reminiscent. She remembered when she had been in the room for the first time—back in 1919. Then, it was a commissary for high party officials. They got their daily ration there—two hundred grams of bread and a little watery soup, served in tin plates. There was no electricity, little heat, no linen. In those days droshkies stood outside and streetcars whined through Red Square. Times had changed.

Yes, she said, it was true that she had spent twenty years in Stalin's concentration camps, many of the years in the terrible "isolators," the solitary-detention prisons in Yaroslavl, Suzdal, and Verkhne-Uralsk. She had been married twice before her arrest, first to Sokolnikov and later to L. P. Serebryakov. Both her husbands had been arrested, both had been shot. She herself had been a staunch Bolshevik. She believed that her husbands had really been guilty. It was only after years in prison that the truth began to dawn, that she began to realize that not only were they not guilty, but that none of the thousands upon thousands trapped in the nightmare of the purges were guilty; that it was all a phantasmagoria.

"I believed in Stalin," she said. "My mother was an old Bolshevik, a friend of Lenin, a friend of his wife, Madame Krupskaya. She believed, too. We thought it was all my husbands' fault, that they had gotten me mixed up in their dirty dealings."

In this belief in Stalin, Galina Serebryakova was indistinguishable from thousands of Soviet citizens—particularly staunch Communists, Old Bolsheviks, who went to their deaths with the name of Stalin on their lips; who, like the famous Red Army commander Iona E. Yakir, faithfully wrote final letters which they pathetically hoped might find their way to Stalin so that he might finally learn what crimes were being committed by the men under him.

The story of the purges runs like a bloody stain through the Stalin years. No aspect of Soviet life has been more written about abroad and few subjects have been more intensively examined within the Soviet Union since the speech at the Twentieth Congress of the Communist party by Nikita Khrushchev on February 24–25, 1956, in which for the first time a Soviet spokesman conveyed some notion of the depth and breadth of Stalin's crimes.

It has been sometimes suggested that this was an impulsive act by Khrushchev, that his associates did not know or approve of what he did. But this interpretation is challenged by Anastas I. Mikoyan. Actually, he pointed out to me, the first attack on Stalin was leveled by himself at a public session of the Twentieth Congress two days before Khrushchev spoke in private session. "Those speeches were no accident," Mikoyan recalled. "They were carefully planned. We fought and fought for that. For three years we carried out a quiet, meticulous investigation—analyzing everything. That's why the Twentieth party Congress is so important. That is why every party congress since then and, now, the fiftieth-anniversary declaration reiterate the same principle—the Leninist principle of intraparty democracy."

There was fire in Mikoyan's eyes as he spoke. Well might there be. For on the infinite list of Stalin's victims and prospective victims his name held a high place on the final tabulation, the purge to end all purges, the one Stalin was preparing just before his death on March 5, 1953.

The fifty years of Bolshevik power cannot be assessed in human and psychological terms without considering the purges. They conditioned two or three Russian generations. The scars of the terror mark the Russian character as though made with a branding iron. They are still to be seen in the sudden drop of voice to a conspiratorial level, the quick look over the shoulder for sign of a telltale shadow, the frequent conversational lapses into elliptical or Aesopian language.

Why did it happen? There is a tendency in Russia to blame it on the personality of Stalin. Leonid Leonov, the great Russian author, calls it Russia's tragedy that the country was ruled by a Georgian who was afraid of the nation he ruled. Fear of Russia, thus, bred terror at the order of its ruler. Others find in Stalin a deep psychological malaise, a chronic paranoia, with the characteristic delusions of persecution and conspiracy growing stronger (in Khrushchev's opinion) as he grew older. Some cite the long history of tyranny in Russia and the Russian tradition of rule by terror and bloodshed.

Whatever the cause, the results were beyond the capacity of the mind to comprehend. The scent of terror and conspiracy haunted Stalin's career from the earliest times. Trotsky hinted that Stalin may have brought on Lenin's fatal illness deliberately by his intemperate conduct, knowing that his rough words would aggravate the precarious balance of Lenin's health. The daybooks of Lenin's secretaries, the minutes of his last lucid days, only now revealed in detail, lend some support to Trotsky's view. Stalin was rude and vulgar toward Lenin's wife. "If you don't behave yourself we'll get another widow for Lenin," he is said to have told her. His attitude toward the surviving members of Lenin's family after Lenin's death was openly hostile. Even Georgi Lozgachev, the adopted son, did not escape the effects. World War II found him in Central Asia, either in exile or deliberately dispatched to a remote region on Stalin's orders. As early as 1925 rumors circulated in Moscow that Stalin caused the death of Mikhail Frunze, first commander of the Red Army, and an adherent of Trotsky, by compelling him to submit to a dangerous operation against Frunze's wishes.

These incidents antedate the documented Stalinist purges by ten years. Whatever Stalin's conduct may have been in 1924 and 1925, no doubt remained of its nature in the 1930's, 1940's, and early 1950's. In those years he was using terror, the secret police, fabricated charges, false accusations of conspiracy and treason against his countrymen, and particularly against his fellow members of the Communist party, on a scale that made the outbursts of dictatorial terror by Nero in Rome, Ivan the Terrible in medieval Russia, and Hitler in Nazi Germany look like Sunday-school exercises.

The terror started on December 1, 1934, when the Leningrad party leader, Sergei M. Kirov, was assassinated by an obscure young Communist named Leonid Nikolayev. If Stalin did not order Kirov shot, his police knowingly acquiesced in the killing. Nikita Khrushchev has publicly speculated on the possibility of Stalin's direct complicity in the affair.

After that, Stalin arrested and executed practically every important living Bolshevik participant in the revolution. His police caught tens of thousands of lesser party members in their net. Thousands were killed, thousands died of police brutality, hundreds of thousands were sent into the cruelest exile in Siberia. Each year the total grew, but always the most savage penalties were applied to the most prominent party members and, as time went on, to persons close to Stalin. In those days there was wonder and mystification at the "confessions" of the victims. Today the mystery has vanished. They were beaten, tortured, twisted into submission. The formula, Khrushchev once said, was: "Beat, beat and again beat."

There are no reliable statistics on the number of Stalin's victims. But some figures have been brought to light. For example, of the participants in the Seventeenth party Congress—the so-called Victors Congress, held in

1934 by supporters of Stalin to memorialize his triumph in winning full control of the party—1,108 of 1,966 delegates and 98 out of 139 members of the Central Committee were arrested. Most of them were killed or died in concentration camps. When the purge extended to the Red Army in 1937 and 1938, it wiped out three marshals—including the chief of the Red Army, Mikhail N. Tukhachevsky—every officer who commanded a military district, two of the four fleet commanders, every commander of an army corps, almost every division commander, and half the regimental commanders, members of military councils, and chiefs of political work. Between one-third and one-half of the 75,000 officers in the Red Army were arrested and sent to prison camp or shot.

The turnover of personnel in industry was so great that Soviet production declined badly and sorely handicapped efforts to prepare the country for World War II. The Communist party fell into the hands of junior untested members or local police chiefs. And after each round of purges the police chiefs would be shot and a new set brought in.

World War II only slightly interrupted the process. It was renewed with a vengeance after the war, acquiring an anti-Semitic bias. Most of Russia's leading Jewish writers were arrested in the late 1940's and shot in 1952, along with many Jewish diplomats. The whole party leadership of Leningrad was wiped out in 1949–50. At the time of his death, Stalin had set in train a fantastic new plot; he contended that the Kremlin physicians (most of them Jewish) were involved in a conspiracy directed by Jewish, American, and British intelligence agents to wipe out the Soviet political and military leadership. Not only Jews were to be swept up in his net. There is evidence that he planned to liquidate Mikoyan, Molotov, Voroshilov, Police Chief Lavrenti Beria, and quite possibly many more of his intimate associates. He was weighing plans for sending all the Jews in Russia—possibly as many as 3,000,000—into exile in Siberia and Central Asia, where he had already sent millions of Soviet citizens—almost all returning prisoners of war, or victims of Hitler's slave-labor camps, hundreds of thousands of residents of the Baltic states, the total populations of the Volga German Republic, the Crimean Tatar republic, the Kalmyk Republic, and several mountainous districts in the Caucasus. Indeed, if Khrushchev is to be believed, Stalin would have exiled the whole population of the Ukraine, but there was not room in Siberia where they could be settled.

The role of the police by this time had grown so large in the Soviet Union that possibly 25 per cent of Soviet industrial production was in the hands of the "industrial department" of the secret police. The vast reaches of Siberia and its enormous resources of forests, its mines and manufacturing enterprises were directed and managed by the secret police, using slave labor or persons in forced residence. Whole categories of industry were run by the police. The construction of major public works, railroads, dams, waterways, and harbor facilities was a police operation. So were the whole Soviet nuclear-energy, A-bomb, and H-bomb programs. Much of the Soviet aviation industry was dominated by the secret police, which by 1953 operated advanced scientific laboratories and design establishments, staffed almost entirely by prisoners. The police possessed its own armed forces, tank corps, artillery units, and air force. By 1953 Russia was a country-within-a-country, the essential core of which was the secret-police apparatus. The effect of the terror was slowly grinding the economic and technological advancement of the nation to a halt.

So pervasive was the legacy of the purges that, visiting the Soviet Union in the 1967 jubilee year, I found myself in the space of one day talking with a distinguished diplomat who had been arrested not long before Stalin's death, an editor who did not return from concentration camp until 1956, a high political figure who had been told by Stalin that he was to be executed in the epilogue to the "doctors' plot," and a movie actress who had spent five years in prison. It was not an unusual day. The unusual day was when I met no one who had suffered under Stalin.

The full story of Stalin's terror probably will never be known. Many secrets died with him. Many more perished with the death of the sinister man who managed Stalin's Grand Guignol in the last years—General Aleksandr N. Poskrebyshev, chief of Stalin's personal secretariat. Poskrebyshev vanished from the public eye the day after Stalin's death. But, I learned, he lived on until the autumn of 1966, when he died at the Kremlin hospital where he had been a patient for several years.

"His memory was absolutely infallible," Madame Serebryakova told me. She met him in the hospital in 1962, and they had several long talks. He knew everything, but apparently did not write his memoirs. He talked freely of Stalin, of Stalin's crimes. He seemed to have no conscience.

"He was absolutely the perfect man for Stalin," Madame Serebryakova remarked. Poskrebyshev had chanced to be sent to the Kremlin in 1925, as a young duty officer. Stalin found in him an ideal tool for his devices. Poskrebyshev was married to a fine woman, an Old Bolshevik, a long-time member of the Communist party. Stalin had her shot. Poskrebyshev never raised a finger in protest.

"Stalin," Madame Serebryakova said, "was like a Chinese god. First he said, 'Give me your eye.' You gave it. Then he said, 'Give me your father's head.' You gave it. Then, 'Give me your son's body.' You gave it.

You remember the fairy story? Finally the god said: 'Give me your gold-fish.' Only then did his victim turn upon the god and kill him."

Poskrebyshev never turned on his god, Stalin. In his Kremlin hospital refuge he showed no remorse for the thousands upon thousands of deaths in which he had a hand. He had a favorite story about Police Chief Beria. He had once asked Beria if a certain prominent Communist now "sat" in prison (the Russian phrase for being in jail is to "sit"). Beria laughed loudly. No, said the Police Chief. He isn't sitting any more. He's lying flat on the floor. Each time Poskrebyshev told the story he roared with laughter.

Madame Serebryakova asked Poskrebyshev about a friend of hers, a party worker who had vanished. She knew her friend was dead, but she had never heard what was the cause. Was it possible that he had been poisoned? Poskrebyshev screwed up his face. What year was that? he asked. She told him it was 1937 or possibly 1938. "Must have been shot," he said. "We didn't start using poison until 1940 or thereabouts."

Why, after his loyal service to Stalin, after his hand in so many deaths, was Poskrebyshev permitted by Stalin's heirs to live out his natural days? Possibly they utilized his prodigious memory to help unravel thousands of complicated, obscure, fabricated "plots" which sent so many loyal and decent men and women to the execution chamber or to death from beatings and starvation in the slave camps. Possibly Poskrebyshev's life was spared out of some strange sense of propriety, some sense of his being merely an unthinking servant of a cruel and tortured master.

Fifty years from the Bolshevik Revolution's golden jubilee the full answer to the mystery of the purges may still elude historians and political psychologists. But many believe that the central cause lay in the decision taken by Lenin on November 7, 1917, to go it alone. On that date he set up his Bolshevik party as the dictator of the country, to brook no effective opposition, to create an apparatus which could be turned against itself by a paranoid or fearful tyrant. Sukhanov's comment to Kamenev on the night of November 8, 1917, at the Smolny Institute may hold the essential key; once the Bolsheviks "made a mess of it" it was too late to go back, and they had left themselves no open path for change of policy, change of program, or change of leadership. In 1967 the essential problem persisted: there was still no established medium through which a critical or opposition policy could be voiced; there was no simple, recognized method for changing leadership, for replacing a Stalin with a Khrushchev or replacing a Khru-shchev with a Brezhnev, save death or a *coup d'état*. In its fiftieth year the Soviet Union was still governed by what, essentially, was a conspiratorial oligarchy—albeit a much less sinister oligarchy than the Byzantine clique created by Stalin.

:

One bright July day I went to the gray stone gothic mansion on Kalinin Prospekt which was built in the early 1900's by one of the wealthy Morozovs of Moscow. There I found Marshal Semyon M. Budenny waiting in the fumed-oak dining room of the old house, sitting erect despite his eighty-four years, his broad chest covered with eight rows of military ribbons, the first won for bravery during the Russo-Japanese war of 1904–05.

"I'm still on active service," he told me proudly. "Active service in the cavalry. Cavalry played the decisive role in World War II."

"And if there is another war," I said, "will cavalry still play a role?"

Marshal Budenny was appalled. "A role?" he said in indignation. "The *decisive* role!"

Despite his passionate dedication to cavalry and the mounted soldier, Marshal Budenny is a military man of vast experience and intimate knowledge of Soviet defense strategy and tactics. He began to talk about World War II, about how it started, about why the Germans had achieved such tactical surprise on June 22, 1941.

I asked whether Stalin expected the attack. Many Soviet historians have contended that Stalin did not believe the Nazis would actually go to war.

"I don't believe Stalin could have been surprised by Hitler's attack," Budenny said, explaining that late in the afternoon of June 21, 1941, Stalin summoned a meeting of the Politburo and invited in some of his top military leaders. The meeting was called to consider the possibility that Hitler might attack Russia either that night or sometime during the weekend.

The fact that Stalin for months had received warning after warning from his professional intelligence network in Germany, from the archspy Richard Sorge in the German Embassy in Tokyo, from Winston Churchill, from Sumner Welles, from Soviet Ambassador Ivan M. Maisky in London, from almost every Soviet military commander on the western frontier, from Soviet naval and air patrols in the Baltic and in the Arctic, and had until June 21 resolutely ignored this mountain of information—indeed, had ordered the arrest of some of those sending in the reports on charges of treason—none of this seemed to bulk very large with the elderly cavalryman.

"We were asked to give our ideas of what to do in the emergency," Budenny said. It was obvious, he continued, that urgent measures had to be taken. Some preliminary moves had been under way to improve Soviet defenses in the west, but the preparations were only half-complete. The task of erecting new fortifications on the western frontiers acquired by the division of Poland with Hitler, the annexation of the Baltic states, and the occupation of Bessarabia had largely been in the hands of the security

[23]

authorities and their prison labor battalions. The new lines along the Bug and the Prut were not yet ready, and the old lines had been semidemolished, much of their armament cannibalized, Budenny said, to equip the new positions. Many troops had been ordered west from Siberia and north from the Caucasus to strengthen the western areas, but they were still far from their destinations and, so fearful had Stalin been of provoking action by Hitler, he had forbidden his armies to move up to advanced defense positions or to shoot down the dozens of Nazi reconnaissance planes which daily flew over the Soviet Union.

It was in this situation, at the eleventh hour, that the Politburo meeting had been summoned.

When Budenny was called upon to speak, he offered two ideas. First, because of the likelihood a Nazi attack would quickly overrun the new western frontiers, he proposed that a new reserve line should be thrown up along the Dnieper. It would run north through Kiev to Riga. He proposed that the Dnieper be turned into a barrier against Nazi tanks by mobilizing hundreds of thousands of men and women to shear off the western banks. This, he said, would confront the Nazi *Panzers* with a formidable moat which they could not cross. Behind this wall the Soviet armies would have time to mass and repel the German assault.

"I also proposed that we take the ropes off our planes," the Marshal said. He explained that the Soviet aircraft at their bases in the west ordinarily were tied down by ropes and cables, to prevent a sudden gust of wind from overturning them. "I said," the Marshal recalled, "let's untie the planes and put our pilots in a state of alert." His suggestion was that the airmen be ordered to sit in their cockpits, ready to take off.

"Stalin said: 'Well, Budenny seems to know what he thinks should be done. Let's put him in charge.' " Budenny smiled and caressed his broad mustaches. "That's how I happened to be put in command of the Reserve Army. I got my orders nine hours before Hitler attacked."

When the Germans struck at 3:30 on the morning of June 22, Marshal Budenny was in the People's Commissariat for Defense in Moscow, working furiously. He was Commander of Reserve Armies. But he had no armies, no staff, no equipment, nothing. Needless to say, the planes were still staked down, and 90 per cent of them were destroyed in the first Nazi strikes. "Georgi Malenkov was my commissar," Budenny recalled. "I told him to get some sleep. I would put together a staff. We were supposed to leave in the morning for the western districts."

The haphazard last-minute order to Budenny was typical of the disarray in which the Nazis caught Moscow. Despite Budenny's conviction that the attack could not have taken Stalin by surprise, other high Soviet commanders found that as late as 6:00 A.M. and 7:00 A.M. on June 22—two or three hours after the German planes, tanks, and artillery had begun their assault—Stalin seemed incapable of belief that war had begun.

"The tragedy of it," said Maisky, now eighty-three, who sent Stalin warning after warning from London of the oncoming war, "was that Stalin believed in nobody—except Hitler. He believed Hitler. He thought he could outmaneuver Hitler. It was a question of psychology." It was five days after the outbreak of war before Maisky got any instructions from Moscow. He attributed this to the chaos brought on by the Nazi attack and the fact that Stalin, certain that all was lost, had locked himself in his study and refused to give any orders.

Stalin's "psychology" cost Russia dearly. The Russian disaster made the results of the Japanese surprise attack on Pearl Harbor look like a child's game. In Russia not only were hundreds of warnings of the attack put aside, but also for hours after the Germans launched their offensive dozens of Soviet units had no orders at all; many were not even authorized to defend themselves.

All the disasters of the war, in the opinion of Marshal Budenny, could have been averted had appropriate steps been taken in time, had the country not moved up to the final hours firmly believing war would not occur. The disasters were of a magnitude that would affect Russian life for at least another generation: 20,000,000 to 25,000,000 men killed in a population of about 195,000,000; a net population loss of upward of 40,000,000 from war deaths, increased civilian mortality, and the net loss in births; the devastation of European Russia; the reduction of production levels to those of the early 1920's. Leningrad, a city of more than 3,000,000 people, was besieged for nearly nine hundred days and suffered 1,300,000 civilian deaths from starvation, cold, and disease. In one Leningrad ceme- tery alone—the Piskarevsky—500,000 persons are interred in mass graves. Kiev, the ancient Russian capital in the Ukraine, fell with a loss of nearly 2,000,000 troops, most of them by encirclement. Moscow was almost lost. In the opinion of many Russians, it could have been taken by the Germans had they driven on to the city in the first week of October, 1941, when the way lay open and Moscow was virtually undefended. Marshal Budenny did not agree with this assessment. When the Nazis failed to overpower Russia in July and August, he became confident Russia would survive. "I knew we would never lose Leningrad and Moscow," he said. Not all his military colleagues were so confident.

Russia won the war. But it remained the disaster of a century. The cost of Stalin's victory in World War II dwarfed the losses from Napoleon's in- vasion in 1812 and the burning of Moscow. Only the Mongol incursions of the thirteenth century cost Russia so much. The consequences of the war's toll were still to be seen and felt everywhere in the Soviet Union's jubilee year—in the armies of widows, the regiments of middle-aged spinsters whose husbands-to-be perished between 1941 and 1945, in the gaps in the labor force caused by those lost from 1941 through 1945. The effects of the population decimation persisted long after war ended, in the over-all imbalance that gives Russia three women for every two men in the age bracket forty to sixty, in the rural areas where women still outnumber men by five to three or even five to two, in the millions of women who lost all male relatives—husband, father, brother, son. There was not a Russian family without lost dear ones.

"You wonder why we Russians fight so strongly for peace," a middle-aged woman said. "You see, we know what war is. What it really is. No one knows so well."

"One thing you can be sure of," a young Russian newspaperman said. "No Russian leader for a long time is going to get Russia to go to war. We want peace. We must have peace. We will not tolerate any other policy."

A middle-aged father told his thirty-year-old son: "The younger generation thinks it knows what war is. But it is too young to know." The son replied: "Papa, you don't know the younger generation. We know the war in a way which you of the older generation can't understand."

"I was a little boy during the days of the blockade," a Leningrad man told me. "My grandmother had put some crusts of bread in a tin box. It was all the food we had left."

One day the youngster heard a noise in the box. A mouse had gotten in and was devouring the family's last food reserve.

"I opened the box, and there was the mouse," the man said. "I had the greatest moral struggle of my life. Should I kill the mouse? Should I eat it? After all, it had been eating our food. And, of course, we had eaten dogs and cats. Some people had eaten rats."

Finally the boy came to his decision. He killed the mouse but did not eat it.

Not all Russians underwent wartime experiences so traumatic. But no Russian emerged without trauma. The consequences of the years 1941–45 are ground into the Soviet Union's social and political fabric. They condition the government's response to domestic problems and they limit its ability to maneuver on the international front. One thing still strongly held by many Russians against former Premier Khrushchev was his recklessness in leading them to the brink in the Cuban missile crisis. It will be a long, long time before many Russians will hail with enthusiasm a program or policy likely once again to engage their country in general war.

:

When Lenin and his Bolsheviks came to power, their objective was to create a kind of heaven on earth, according to the prescription worked out by Marx. Marx thought that the ills of mankind were economic in origin and that they stemmed from the exploitation of man by man. Remove greed, remove the motivation for one man's bettering himself at the expense of others, and paradise would ensue. Governments, social systems, armies, police, courts—the whole apparatus of society—were seen by Marx as having been developed to protect the exploiting class in society, those who had by inheritance, cunning, energy, imagination, evil, or sheer luck come to be haves as contrasted with have-nots.

Shatter the old system, Marx and Lenin believed, and a new society, devoid of poverty and suffering, purged of hate, envy, and want, dedicated to the humane relationship of man to man, would arise. Government would wither away. Each man and woman would contribute of his or her talent, labor, and creative energy. Each would be rewarded according to his or her needs. Money would vanish. Crime would disappear. War would be forgotten.

This dream had possessed the imagination of generations of social reformers and radicals. It underlay the frenzy of the French Revolution, it motivated the violent uprisings all over Europe in 1848, and it became an *idée fixe* among young Russians, locked in hopeless struggle with the most backward and brutal autocracy on earth.

It was this vision that motivated Lenin and his Bolsheviks when they seized power in Petrograd. Lenin answered every challenge to his methods by referring to the wondrous and shining goal which now lay within grasp.

True, neither he nor Trotsky nor Kamenev nor Zinoviev nor Bukharin nor, perhaps, even Stalin really believed this would occur first in Russia. The fact that the Bolsheviks had come to power seemed to Lenin to be an accident of history. On the seventy-first day after November 7 Lenin told his associates they should dance in the streets—they had surpassed the life of the Paris Commune. What he was waiting for was the end of World War I, the collapse of the bourgeois states in Western Europe, and the coming to power of Socialists (as they were then called) or Communists (as we now call them) in those advanced countries. Then, thought Lenin, he and his Bolsheviks would march arm in arm with their Western comrades toward the Marxian nirvana.

When the revolutions did not come in the West, Lenin was bitterly disheartened. He was not sure that Bolshevism could survive in one backward country like Russia. When Stalin came to power he harshly revised the Bolshevik dream. Russia, he said, must make Communism work in one country, one backward country, a country surrounded by capitalist states which, like wolves, were ready to tear the new Communist society limb from limb. Many Old Bolsheviks thought Stalin's vision was too limited. They went to their deaths under Stalin certain that he was wrong, that only on an international basis could the revolution survive.

After fifty years of Bolshevism there were many in Russia who began to perceive that life had not produced the utopia dreamed of by Marx and Lenin. Revolution never came to the West, and the Communism that survived in Russia bore little resemblance to the bright dream of 1917. Under Stalin the state had not withered away. It became all-pervasive. Man's inhumanity to man had not ended with the abolition of private ownership, private business, private profit. The state became a master more greedy, more brutal, more ruthless, more terrible than any bourgeois exploiter.

With Stalin's death, his heirs, trying to revitalize the monstrous state apparatus they had inherited, turned to the West, to the surviving, thriving capitalist system for ideas, methods, mechanisms, incentives with which to attempt to reform the hideous Goliath which had been created in the name of Marx.

True, by 1967 Russia had become the world's number-two power. True, by 1967 it possessed the world's second-greatest industrial system. True, by 1967—at long last—the standard of living, comfort, and ease in Russia had begun to move toward Western European levels in the principal cities. In education, in the arts, in science, Russia had demonstrated brilliance and leadership.

Yet the gap between 1967's reality and the early Bolshevik dream was so wide that in the jubilee declarations and programmatic statements there was a calculated reticence that masked it. The new Soviet man was not a gentle utopian knight, motivated by a desire to better his brother's lot, but a hard-working, harassed citizen with simple wants: a decent two-room flat, a bit of leisure away from the dirty, noisy factory, a chance to bring up the kids (not more than one or two children, certainly, in those cramped quarters) to a little better life, and maybe a car—such a machine as was the commonplace possession of the "oppressed" capitalist worker in Italy and Sweden, New York and Barcelona. When the Soviet man spoke frankly, he left no doubt of his disinterest in the cause of world revolution. He thought the Chinese Communists were insane. Vietnam left him cold. He admired Moshe Dayan—he was really a Russian, wasn't he? What he liked about the Eastern European Communist countries was their higher standard of living and greater ease. But, given a chance, he would prefer France or the Netherlands. America—well, that was beyond his dreams. But he hoped that his son and daughter might go there. And if he envisaged the future of Bolshevism after another fifty years, he spoke of it in terms that made it sound like life in the suburbs of Los Angeles or New York.

At age fifty, it was more and more apparent that the Bolshevik Revolution was middle-aged, a bit wheezy, inclined to sit back in an easy chair, turn on the TV and watch a good light program. No speeches, please. No party exhortations! If there was any complaint about the fiftieth year, it was that there had been so much printed and spoken about the anniversary, about the great achievements of the golden half-century, that everyone was bored stiff long before the magic date of November 7, 1967.

And underlying all this there were in many minds gnawing anxieties. They emerged in talks with ordinary men and women as well as high officials.

Fifty years of Bolshevism did not eradicate every vestige of superstition in Russia. There were still gypsies in Moscow, particularly around the Luzhniki summer fairgrounds, who would tell your fortune if their palms were crossed with silver. Old women would read a girl's horoscope with a candle and a mirror and predict what kind of marriage she would make. And there were soothsayers of dubious identity who, having seen how many mushrooms sprouted under the white birches and dark green pines, would say whether or not there would be war by autumn. Many mushrooms was a sign of war, few mushrooms a sign of peace. In 1967 they fell in between plenty and paucity, war and peace.

In the spring of 1967, just after the disaster that took the life of Soviet Cosmonaut Vladimir Komarev, a rumor spread through Moscow that a soothsayer had predicted that the Bolshevik Revolution would not live to celebrate its fiftieth anniversary. Of course, not many Muscovites actually believed in this prediction. But it had a sour effect upon the preparations for the great jubilee. It seemed to many Russians that fate was treating the anniversary with great lack of kindness. The loss of the cosmonaut jeopardized the elaborate plans that had been made to celebrate the Golden Year with other space achievements, which would bring new glory to Soviet science, Soviet technology, and the Soviet state. And there were other worries. Every effort had been made by the party to create a bright and positive atmosphere for the anniversary. Writers were ordered to avoid controversial topics. Diplomats were instructed to try to play down conflict and crises. Editors were told to keep the tone of the press festive and bland. Difficult themes were to be put aside until after November 7. Quarrels over the past, exposés of Stalin's crimes, rows between literary factions, polemics between East and West, intraparty quarrels—all of these were to be laid aside. The watchword was: Keep Smiling.

But the turbulent world of the late 1960's did not seem capable of providing an appropriate atmosphere. The death of the cosmonaut followed an event even more embarrassing, inappropriate, and jarring: Svetlana Alliluyeva, Stalin's daughter, picked this moment to abandon her motherland and flee to America, where she announced she would publish her memoirs, exposing many a hitherto untold and unpleasant aspect of Soviet life in the era of her father. Even though many Russians, both ordinary citizens and high officials, managed to convince themselves that Svetlana's defection to the United States was the product of an elaborate plot by the Central Intelligence Agency and the American propaganda apparatus, designed deliberately to spoil the golden anniversary, this did not change the atmosphere. It remained sour, dyspeptic, and uncertain.

Moscow's mood was not improved by many things. One was the intractable, irresolvable quarrel with China, which had gone far beyond the point of any effective resolution. Here, too, it was not just a matter of reading the Chinese out of the Communist family. The quarrel nagged and irritated. It had its dangerous aspects.

"The root of the problem is their population," said a writer who had spent two months in China before the great split. Even then, some two or three years before relations had been irreparably damaged, he professed to have seen the handwriting on the wall. "I knew something was wrong," he said, "when I saw they had English cars to drive us around, not Russian. I asked them why and they said that Russians made good trucks but the English made better cars."

The question that festered in Russian minds was that somehow, somewhere, the Chinese quarrel might turn into war; they didn't know where, they didn't know how. But it worried them, and they worried equally over the position of the United States. If there was going to be war with China, they wanted the United States on their side, not on China's.

"We know all about those private conversations in the back room of that bar in Hong Kong," one young Russian said.

"How are we to understand the reports we get that the United States is seriously seeking a *rapprochement* with Mao Tse-tung?" a Foreign Ministry man asked me. The U.S.-China talks in Warsaw and statements by President Johnson and the State Department indicating a desire for better relations with China sorely troubled Moscow. In the fiftieth year of Bolshevism it did not seem incongruous to them to prefer capitalist America to Communist China.

In general, Moscow was concerned about the state of relations with the United States. It was not only the problem of Vietnam that stood like a roadblock in the path of the return to the quasi-*détente* that had flowered under Khrushchev. This, of course, was in many official minds, although seldom prominent in the consciousness of ordinary citizens. "After all," said one veteran Soviet propagandist, "Washington certainly must know that it is Soviet missiles which are shooting down American planes. It is Soviet MIG's which are battling American bombers. And if you invade the North you will find that you are fighting us directly. There can be no mistake about that."

There was beginning to be heard from some Soviet political figures a challenge to the whole idea of *détente* with the United States—a challenge not advanced since the early post-Stalin years. It was based on the contention that Washington was taking undue, unfair advantage of Moscow's desire to maintain a basically nonhostile attitude. The United States, it was contended, had embarked upon a deliberate offensive designed to shift the balance of power strongly in its favor.

The Vietnam war was seen as part of this strategy. So were the Greek right-wing *coup d'état* and the Israeli blitz of the Arabs. The hand of the United States was detected in both events.

Moscow had its hawks and doves, and the hawks grew in strength with the stalemate in Vietnam, the cul-de-sac in relations with China, the Soviet defeats in the Middle East. The hawks were set back when they overplayed their hand at a plenary session of the Central Committee in June, 1967. A hard-line faction, headed by Aleksandr N. Shelepin, a one-time Komsomol and Security Committee chief, was sharply rebuffed. Several hawks lost their jobs. But the threat remained, and some thought it might be renewed again, even before the November 7 anniversary.

An ominous note was struck by one prominent hawk, a hard-line propagandist who had been relegated to the Foreign Ministry after the downfall of Premier Khrushchev. Once again, after a lapse of several years, he began to talk publicly and aggressively about the "positive achievements of Stalin," about the necessity of looking to the good Stalin instead of concentrating so much on the bad. "After all," said this man, "where would we be without Stalin? We must give him due credit."

The fiftieth anniversary was being celebrated in the fourteenth year after Stalin's death. But, as the poet Yevgeny Yevtushenko had warned five years earlier, his spirit was far from dead. "Guard well the tomb," Yevtushenko had warned, lest Stalin's spirit emerge and once more stalk the Russian land. Since then Stalin's body had been removed from the Mausoleum. No longer did he lie beside Lenin. Now his grave was a simple stone lying flat on the ground beside the Kremlin wall. But his heirs were still abroad.

As the memorable day of November 7 approached, there was in Russia some feeling of time lost, of events moving in unpredictable and possibly adverse directions, a feeling of *déjà vu* and of faint unease. There were within Russia and in the world at large too many uncertain and possibly hostile forces. Fifty years after the event, the revolution and its goals seemed, to many, more like the first scene in a badly articulated Shakespearean drama than the opening act of a new adventure in constructing a humane society.

There was a note of pathos in the talk of Russians as they viewed their world and the world around them. Perhaps it was not entirely accidental that many of them, young men in the university, an artist in his Leningrad studio, an elderly diplomat, a middle-aged woman who lost her husband in World War II, turned in nostalgia to the memory of President John F. Kennedy.

"You do not know how we miss him," they said again and again, not realizing they were repeating each other's thought. "What a man he was! He understood the world. We admired him. If only he had lived—things would not be in this shape." And then the man or woman would add: "I will tell you openly. I wept when I heard of President Kennedy's death. I could not believe it was true."

Nor was there any Russian, so speaking, who seemed to feel the slightest anomaly in the fact that a loyal heir to the tradition of 1917 was mourning and glorifying the man who had headed the citadel of world capitalism.

Russia in 1967 was far, far from being the United States. But it was far closer in the spirit of its people than Lenin or any of the men who made 1917 would have believed possible.

THE WAY PEOPLE LIVE

» *Charlotte Curtis*

The Soviet woman, tardily but with that special gusto she gives to all her enthusiasms, has arrived at a view long held by Western women. The ideal feminine status, she has decided, is one equal but separate: one that combines all the benefits of equality with all the special privileges of femininity.

Fifty years after the Bolshevik Revolution she is rejecting the masculinity of those serious women of an earlier generation who answered the call of an ideal and the need of a nation by abandoning hearth and home for the dubious satisfaction of the pickax and shovel. After years of working side by side with men in industry, construction, mining, and shipping, she is increasingly distracted by food, family, furnishings, and fashion.

The new Soviet woman still is fired by visions of a better world, but she has no intention of building it, as her predecessors did, brick by brick.

One who has played both roles, fifty-year-old Tatyana Fyodorova, a buxom blonde, can look today on the terrible times of the past with warmth and some humor. "In 1931 the Central Committee and the government decided Moscow needed a subway," she told me. "So we built one. It didn't matter that we didn't know what a subway was—someone had to tell us that it was an underground railway. It didn't matter that we didn't know how to build one. We were young Komsomols [Young Communists] and we had this great desire to build. We knew how to dig. I remember they told us to go out and look for a 'mine,' but there wasn't any 'mine,' so we started digging a big hole in the frozen ground. There were no machines. It was hard work."

Mrs. Fyodorova worked as a miner and a day laborer. Today she is the fashion-conscious deputy chief of the Moscow subway construction agency, a thoroughly feminine executive who indulges her passion for flowers by buying bouquets in the streets and keeping her office window sill full of potted plants. "I love lilacs," she said as she poured us cups of coffee. "If I were weak, I could faint when I see them."

Her big hands, which once held a pickax, are soft and smooth, and she wears pale-pink nail polish. At least once a week she has her neat blond hair done. "I use cold cream," she said laughingly, touching her fingers to her cheeks. "Not because I believe it will do any good but because it's harmless."

The Tatyanas of the Soviet Union built the railroads and mixed the concrete. They harvested the wheat by hand and they served with their men on the battlefield. And at the time they thought this was what they wanted. But they now have a better explanation. "We had to do the hard work," said Valentina Tsyslyak, vice chairman of the Women's Commission of the All-Union Council of Trade Unions of the U.S.S.R. "Everybody had to help after the revolution. It was not what we wanted to do at all."

Besides hard work, the Soviet woman has also rejected the shapeless, long, drab dresses and men's shoes of her predecessors and the way they pulled their hair into knots at the back of their heads. The revolutionaries went about like that to express their freedom from all that was old, bourgeois, and decadent about women's role in society. The new woman does not want to be that equal.

She is concerned, instead, about where she lives and how she lives and what she looks like. She has decided that she looks better in high-heeled shoes, lipstick, and brightly colored clothes and that her hair should be soft and feminine whether she dyes it or not. She spends a lot more time in front of the mirror these days, playing with eye liner and the idea of false eyelashes, and she is even seriously thinking of doing something about the bulky, lumpy shape for which she is famous.

Now that she has had a chance to think about it, she wants the man she loves to pursue her, marry her, and give her security, rather than to live with her in the old, casual, free way. She wants contraceptives (the pill is not available) so she can decide when she will have children and not have to resort to the old system of legal abortion, which takes more time and money. But she wants abortions to remain legal, just in case.

No matter what the condition of her apartment, she is ready to re-decorate if only she could get her hands on some extra money or her government would offer her new designs. She is just as ready to move if larger, airier quarters should become available, and she aspires to a thoroughly modern kitchen, pretty chairs, sofas, curtains, tablecloths, and maybe even a piano.

Now that she wears high heels, she does not want to walk as far as she used to. She wants buses and subways that come to her front door and wages that allow her to take taxis. What she really wants is an automobile and a dacha. It doesn't matter which comes first. Once she has one her next project will be to get the other.

She wants more and better nurseries and kindergartens so she can have her children and her career, too. But she is coming more and more to the view that maybe her place is in the home—for at least part of the time during her children's formative years—and that maybe part-time jobs are the answer. In the meantime she is calling for more services and a shorter, better-paid work week.

"There are not enough kindergartens," said Galina Andreyeva, Professor of Sociology at Moscow State University. "We have those that board children overnight and those for the daytime. In my opinion, the day kindergartens are better because they allow the mother more time with the child."

The Soviet woman wants to keep right on being equal, but she no longer thinks equality involves opening doors for herself, lighting her own cigarettes, pulling out her own chair at a table, being slapped on the back, fighting a man for a seat on the subway, or generally being expected to fend completely for herself. She neither wants nor tries to be coy, helpless, or fragile. In fact, she probably is one of the least scheming and most straight-forward women in the world—but she wants everyone to remember that she is a woman and that being a woman is a lot different from being a man.

At this stage in history women play the most active role they have ever played in Soviet society. Ninety per cent of the city women are believed to have jobs outside their homes. Women outnumber men considerably, and might have been expected to make something out of that politically. But they have not, and there are no signs that they are going to. Even in their most "equal" days women did not dominate or attempt to control either the Communist party or the power structure of the government.

Today less than 20 per cent of the party membership is female. Fewer than a dozen women belong to the party's three-hundred-and-sixty-member Central Committee. Women account for only 27 per cent of the membership of the Supreme Soviet of the U.S.S.R., the country's legislature, whereas fifteen years ago they accounted for 20 per cent. Two women are the most who have ever served together on a single Presidium, the Supreme Soviet's thirty-three-member governing body. And the number of women who have served as ambassadors or foreign correspondents is low.

The Soviet woman's reticence or sheer indifference to the topmost political and economic jobs, especially in recent years, has been such that *Pravda* has had to chide her repeatedly. In 1965 *Pravda* gently placed the blame on the men for the decreasing number of women in important positions. When it came time to appoint or elect someone to a higher position, the newspaper reported, women were being ignored. The paper, which has yet to find any real improvement in the situation, made the same pitch again in 1966—without significant encouragement from women. There probably is some truth to the complaints that party branches and some segments of industry and agriculture are not pushing their women into the best jobs, even where women have more than enough education and experience for the posts and far outnumber their male co-workers.

But women, except for those who are actively seeking "softer" work with either the same or higher pay, are so sure of themselves they rarely make such complaints. And the truth is that not many women seem to want the responsibilities (or the vulnerability to criticism) the top jobs usually entail. Such jobs would take too much time away from their families. They would interfere with their increasingly treasured leisure. And most women intend to hold on to the shorter work week a less demanding job affords. It is time, many serious-minded middle-aged women have said, to have some fun. But this does not mean they do not want jobs, and jobs that interest them. Even discounting their need for money from a job, they cannot imagine being nothing more than a housewife. They argue that that would be a boring, one-sided life that made little if any contribution to society. Sometimes they cite their Constitution, which gives them the right to work. And sometimes they say that in their society it is immoral not to work. "The older generation may be happy being housewives," Mrs. Andreyeva said, referring to the women who did not leave home after the revolution. "But our generation has to be out working and doing to be happy."

In Moscow there are such strong feelings against being "only a housewife" that the term is rarely used in any but a disparaging way. Georgian and Uzbek women are more tolerant, for very different reasons.

The Georgians are a romantic, cultivated people who tend to idealize women. Their favorite ruler was Queen Tamara, and their national symbol is a woman. They have allowed their wives, sisters, and mothers to play a significant role in their culture for centuries.

Uzbek women, by contrast, were second-class citizens until well into the twentieth century. They were Moslems. They were bought and sold like slaves, expected to cover themselves from head to toe in concealing robes called *paranjas,* to share their husbands with other wives, and to seclude themselves from men and from everything the outside world represented. In this culture it took two women to equal one male witness in any judicial proceeding. If a man was killed, someone had to pay or be punished for taking his life. It did not matter so much about a woman. The recently "emerged" Uzbeks, therefore, are proud today to be hyphenated women: housewife-government officials, housewife-professors, and housewife-writers. "Each woman thinks she should be a good housewife as well as a worker," said Saida Zununova, one of Uzbekistan's leading housewife-writers. "As far as I'm concerned, the problem is not just of work but how to do my housework and look after my family while finding time for my creative work."

Despite her disinterest in life at the top, the Soviet woman likes and seeks the prestige (and the money) associated with middle management or the running of medium-sized things, whether it be a state farm, the chairmanship of an academic specialty at a major educational institution, a city Soviet, or council, or the Moscow subway. She is even more enthusiastic about the well-paid professions, particularly what she calls "humanitarian" work. She accounts for 75 per cent of the doctors, 70 per cent of the teachers, and 40 per cent of the Moscow lawyers.

Like her predecessors, she is passionately outspoken in her insistence that she and all Soviet women are "more equal" than any other women in the world, although only an exceptional few have had an opportunity to see Western women in their native habitat.

But when it comes to the old thinking that a woman is up to any job in the Soviet economy (regardless of whether she wants to do some of the jobs or not), or that the only real "women's work" is that of having babies, the new woman parts company with the past. "Equality," Mrs. Andreyeva said dryly, "doesn't mean physiological equality. It's quite all right for men to do harder work. Everything is pointing to a time when there will be no hard work for anyone." Or, as Mrs. Tsyslyak, the trade-union official, put it: "Of course we want to make work easier for women—without lowering their wages. The problem is one of advancing their skills so they don't have to do hard work. Men now say they are the ones who are being discriminated against. But they understand. It's obvious that they should do the harder work. Eventually everything will be mechanized."

What this means, among other things, is that women are going to get to the promised land of Communism faster than the men, that men are going to be doing increasingly more of what formerly was accepted as "women's work," and that, in the meantime, everyone is going to be a good sport about it—particularly the women.

But there is some consolation for the men. They are generally accepted as the heads of their households. They may turn the management of the family's finances over to their wives, who then give them an allowance for such things as cigarettes and bus fare, but when it comes to important decisions, the men usually get their way.

For eight years pretty, dark-haired Olga Butuzova, administrator of the Minsk Hotel in Moscow, and her husband have gone to the Black Sea for their vacation. But Mrs. Butuzova is tired of the sea. She told me she would like to go somewhere else—anywhere else. And what will she do? "My husband loves the sea," she said, toying with the new Kelly-green telephone in her office. "I think we shall go to the sea."

There was no rancor in Mrs. Butuzova's voice, only a softness. It was a few minutes before she looked away from the telephone. I asked her if husbands were ever dominated by their wives. "Oh, never," she said, smiling broadly. "My husband says he's afraid of me, but he's not. He's teasing."

When pressed, the Soviet woman also admits—all things being equal—that she would prefer to work with and for men rather than for women or in a situation involving only women. She subscribes to this philosophy, a handsome Georgian woman government official explained, because "Woman is still woman, and when she works with a man, she always works harder and better. She tries to prove she's as capable as he is. This makes her more valuable."

The Soviet woman also admits, albeit reluctantly, that "other women" (herself never included) are generally not very good about supporting each other's aspirations for better jobs. And she is likely to ascribe this not to women's distrust of one another but to their great respect for men.

And when it comes to housework, the Soviet woman, regardless of age, education, environment, nationality, job, or position in the social system, believes that it is her responsibility, not her husband's, to attend to the myriad details of making the home run efficiently and pleasantly.

Housing is one of the Soviet Union's most pressing problems. It ranges from highly prized but not very luxurious "personal" dachas (that are only semantically different from illegal, capitalist "private" country houses) to rickety, antiquated log cabins or mud huts built before the revolution. In between, there are "personal" houses on the state-owned land of the collective farms and a small number of modern "personal" houses on the outskirts of such faraway cities as Tashkent, Alma-Ata, and Tbilisi.

But for the overwhelming number of Soviet women and their families, home is a cramped, dimly lighted, and inadequately furnished "modern" apartment that rents for between five and ten rubles ($5.55 and $11.10) a month.

It is here, in a universally small kitchen she often has to share with at least one other family, that the Soviet woman prepares her family's meals. If she is extremely lucky, her kitchen is equipped with a refrigerator—but a tiny one.

Her husband, a retired relative, her children, or a neighbor may help her with her shopping (which must be done daily in the summer if she has no refrigerator). Only in the best urban neighborhoods may she order some of her groceries by telephone and have them delivered. There are no supermarkets where she can buy under one roof everything she needs. She has to wait in long lines and she is always plagued by shortages of foods she says she wants or can afford. A city family of three or four persons has an average monthly budget of one hundred and eighty rubles ($199.80). More than half of this amount goes for food. A loaf of bread costs the equivalent of eighteen cents; a liter of milk, thirty-three cents; meat, a dollar a pound; fish, fifty cents a pound; poultry, $1.30 a pound, and butter, $1.50 a pound.

The quality of fresh meats, vegetables, and fruits that the collective-farm workers have raised on their "personal" plots to be sold—at a "personal" profit—in what amounts to giant farmers' markets is far superior to what is sold in most state stores. The prices are higher, for a collective-farm worker may charge what the traffic will bear, but the Soviet woman is usually willing to pay. However, this means she has to find the time to go to market.

Once she has been there, she may have to go on to a department store before finding the Cyprian canned orange juice her family likes, a specialty shop for a precooked hot dish, a state store for a canned Polish ham, a baked-goods shop for bread, and on and on in seemingly endless rounds not necessarily in the vicinity of either her home or her job.

Yet despite all this, cooking dinner is the one household chore the Soviet woman seems to enjoy—even if she cooks only one big dinner on the weekend. The emphasis on work outside the home has resulted in few city women knowing as much about cooking as their mothers and grandmothers did. But when they go at it, they cook with an intensity motivated by a great desire to please.

"I cook a good dinner so my family will praise me," a nuclear physics professor at the University of Moscow said only half-jokingly.

"I like to cook for my Aram because he likes it," composer Aram Khachaturian's wife said more seriously.

The Soviet woman also has to wash dishes (sometimes with water she has had to heat on the stove, always without a dishwasher), dust and clean (frequently without a sweeper, almost invariably without a vacuum cleaner), clean and polish floors (without long-handled mops, waxers, and polishers), and do the family laundry (without a washer, wringer, or dryer). She hates these jobs and does not hesitate to say so.

Until recently the city woman could count on her mother, her husband's mother, or some other older female relative, including her grandmother, to be at home and help with the housework. Thus it was that the *babushka,* or grandmother, in an institutional role she had played for centuries, was the real mother figure in Soviet households. It was the *babushka,* rather than the working mother, who looked after the little children before and after school or at home if they were not enrolled in kindergartens or nurseries. And it was the aging, home-bound *babushka,* in her head scarf, her nondescript clothes, and her sloppy flat-heeled slippers, who was regularly accused of spoiling the children and encouraging them in old-fashioned ways.

Her fault, perhaps, was that she had never read Marx or Lenin, or if she had she did not seem to understand that one was not supposed to believe in God any more and that there was a brave new world to build. She may or may not have gone to church, but even if she did not she could not seem to push, shove, and condition children to the new life. And, almost inevitably, she was somebody's mother-in-law.

"In ten years there may be no more *babushkas* as we knew them," said Lyudmila Yakovenko, one of Moscow's leading lawyers. "Grandmothers are educated now. They are professors and doctors. They don't want to stay home." Mrs. Yakovenko, whose mother was a judge, was speaking about the situation in Moscow. The traditional *babushka* thrives in the rural areas and is greatly loved and respected all along the Black Sea and in Central Asia. And although there is talk of the generation gap, few families want her to move, assuming she had the chance, into an apartment of her own. "Our *babushkas* are very advanced people now that they read newspapers and see television," said Zinaida Kvachadze, secretary of the Presidium of Georgia's Supreme Soviet. "They all help us with our housework."

If the Soviet woman has the money, and not many women do, she can afford household help. What she wants is a cleaning woman, whom the Russians call an "in-comer" (*prikhodyashchaya*). It is ideologically all right to hire such help, it is argued, because the helper does not produce material values, so her labor does not serve as a means of enriching her employer. Well, not according to Marx and Engels.

But having the money for an in-comer and finding one are two different things now that all women are supposed to be educated and do not want to do housework. "It's a serious matter," Mariya Blagovolina, an actress turned successful criminal lawyer, told her friend Mrs. Yakovenko. "I'm so lucky. I have a woman who comes in three days a week. She does everything. When she isn't there, I have to wash the dishes." "It's the same with me," Mrs. Yakovenko answered. "It's our obligatory eight years of education."

Mrs. Blagovolina and Mrs. Yakovenko, whose offices are in the Moscow Collegium of Lawyers building, are middle-aged women whose children are grown. They are both divorced from architects, seriously devoted to their careers, and rich by Soviet standards. They pay their in-comers a few rubles a day.

Soviet women who have in-comers have to pay top wages to compete with industry, and this can mean fifty rubles ($55.50) a month and up for full-time work. The helper's hours, vacations, and sick pay are covered by law. But most employers think of such cleaning women as equals and often introduce them to their visitors. In some instances, full-time helpers are invited to sit with the family at dinner.

Whether she is among the few who are reasonably well-to-do or the many poor, the Soviet woman wishes her government would do more— much, much more—to provide her with the food, the furnishings, the clothes, the labor-saving devices, and the services she has decided she wants and needs.

Her first wish is for a refrigerator if she does not already have one. Then comes a vacuum cleaner. Both are in short supply. She does not care if they are her "personal" possessions or not. All she really wants is to be able to rent one in her own neighborhood. Such rental services, sometimes organized as part of what the Russians call "bureaus of good services," apparently are on the way.

But such establishments, still a luxurious rarity, are expected to be more than rental agencies. They are to have a variety of services—say, everything needed for a birthday celebration, a shoe-repair center, a counter at which a homemaker could set a time and a day for floor polishers to come to her apartment, engage college students interested in extra money as temporary household help, or arrange for a "capital cleaning."

The Soviet woman who can afford the service likes to have a "capital cleaning" four times a year—in the spring, summer, fall, and winter. In the process everything in an apartment that needs it gets repaired, scrubbed, washed, polished, cleaned, shined, or scoured.

There also is an increasing number of neighborhood laundries, dry cleaners, and repair shops, clothing stores, cafeterias, and food stores. But the next most important service the Soviet woman wants, and most vociferously demands, is a good house kitchen—a prepared-food center in her own apartment building. She wants to be able to walk in and buy a ready-to-serve dinner—everything from freshly sliced tomatoes, scallions, and cucumbers for a salad to the hot meat entrée and the gooey dessert cake. Great house kitchens do not exist, but there are some reasonably good ones by Soviet standards. The selection of food is meager. The menu does not change much from day to day, and the kitchen hours often are at variance with the workers' schedules. But women who frequent them seem to like them, if for no other reason than that they save a great deal of time and energy.

Next to a good house kitchen, nothing in the homemaking line seems to delight a Soviet woman more than the growing number of "culinarias." They are expensive "gourmet" food shops that sell "half-fabricated" delicacies—Uzbek, Russian, or Armenian specialities that have only to be put in the oven before serving. Some are made from recipes supplied by the better restaurants. These stores, most of which are in such vast urban centers as Moscow and Leningrad, also carry baked goods, hors d'oeuvres such as hard-boiled eggs stuffed with *pâté* and smeared with thick mayonnaise, casseroles, meat-stuffed pastry piroshki, and hearty, freshly made soups.

"I cannot tell you what culinarias mean to me," an exuberant, well-dressed woman executive said. "I used to make chicken soup from the beginning. A meal is an occasion now. Afterward, I watch television."

Nothing in recent social history, not even the coming of the automobile, has done more to change Soviet living patterns than the advent and increasing availability of the television set, and the more cosmopolitan Russia of the European west is in as much of a tizzy about it as the Central Asian deserts of the east. Antennas spring from the roofs of wood or mud houses that have no running water, from the tops of newly constructed apartment buildings, and from the palaces within the Kremlin walls. Tour leaders on sight-seeing buses point with as much pride to the new television towers in city after city as they do to the historic sites. Big city hotels, which have not yet come to terms with the mechanics of the flush toilet, are quick to announce that guests may rent television sets for their rooms. But for most families the first problem in crowded living quarters was where to put this marvelous new people's toy.

For centuries life has revolved around the kitchen—even when it was a shared kitchen. Dining rooms were, and generally are, nonexistent, and parlors, when they were to be had, were for family celebrations and the entertainment of guests. At night most of these parlors became bedrooms.

The only other rooms were bedrooms for two or more, bathrooms where one washed, and toilets. Meals, therefore, were served in the kitchen, and that is where the dining table was kept. So some television sets went immediately into the kitchen. "Everybody I know gathers in the kitchen," a well-heeled Moscow journalist said, "because the television and the refrigerator are there."

But the television set, a major purchase for any family and a piece of furniture to be proud of, also went into what passed for the living room. And when it did, a second dining table and some of the meals went with it. After a while *babushkas* had to be reminded that in such close quarters their evening television-watching stints were disturbing the children's homework. Fathers complained about mothers who appeared to care more for television than they did about the upkeep of the household.

Women, who may or may not have succeeded in parting their men—particularly the better-educated ones—from the inexpensive socialist newspapers, magazines, and books they liked to read far into the night, found that they had a newer, even more fascinating, rival. Youngsters arranged their lives so they could see "Good Night, Children," an evening telecast of fairy tales and entertainment that usually conflicted with the adult program the rest of the family wanted to see.

In Moscow, a thoroughly competent woman hotel administrator said she stopped reading (a common complaint) after she and her husband got their television set and that they are now forcing themselves to leave their apartment for walks just to escape it.

A former representative to the U.S.S.R.'s Supreme Soviet—a vigorous athlete who plays volleyball, skis, and ice skates—used to join the thousands of spectators at sports events. Sometimes she still does. But she is far more likely to stay home and watch them from her easy chair. "Why should I go out," she asked rhetorically, "when I can see them at home?"

In Tbilisi a serious discussion of Georgian family life dissolved into laughter when the subject of television came up. That distinguished old city's leading women's news editor and writer, an intelligent grandmother with a keen sense of humor, said she saw only one solution to the problem: "Turn off the set."

"That is easier to say than to do," answered the beautiful young Georgian deputy premier. "Who is going to turn it off when her *babushka* is watching?"

"The solution," said a third woman, secretary of the Presidium of the Supreme Soviet, "is for the *babushka* to watch television after the children have gone to bed."

"Again," said the deputy premier, "that is easy to say."

"Well, I know what I do," answered the secretary, herself a grand-mother. "I switch off the television in front of my grandson and go over to a neighbor's to watch. Then he doesn't see television or me watching it."

Moscow has two news and entertainment channels and one devoted to education. The stations are on the air for about two hours around noon and off again until 5:00 P.M. Then the broadcasts begin once more and last until midnight. Other cities have only one channel.

Television programs are state-controlled. Like newspapers and maga-zines, they report the important political and economic news as the leaders and a few well-chosen reporters and commentators, having access only to socialist and other sympathetic news sources, see it. Soviet television also covers sports events, takes viewers into restaurants for interviews, and features movies and drama. Programs take up the problems of the family, youth, home, and health, and teach foreign languages.

But despite the Soviet citizens' attachment to such fare, no one raves much about the quality. They do, however, clamor for more television sets, and they may get them, along with other highly prized consumer goods.

At the Twenty-third party Congress in Moscow in 1966, Soviet leaders introduced a new five-year plan, promising that by 1970 twice as many tele-vision sets would be produced a year as were produced in 1965 (the goal is 4,000,000 new sets a year), four times as many refrigerators, and nearly twice as many washing machines. The leaders also promised higher wages and lower prices, more consumer goods generally, and fewer taxes, ex-panded housing, and a five-day work week. Similar promises have been made before, particularly since World War II, and some of them have been kept. The Soviet homemaker believes these promises.

And when her leaders cite the Vietnam war as one of the reasons why production of consumer goods has had to be limited, she believes that, too. It is the United States and its policy in Vietnam, she is likely to think, that keeps her from getting her new refrigerator. She may or may not have the Russians' pathological fear of war, but almost inevitably she has what she considers strong moral feelings against the war. "It is evil to keep a people from the kind of government they want," a Georgian educator said. "If the United States wasn't there, they could be Communists."

The educator is not typical. She has gone a step beyond the average woman's reaction to the war, although she subscribes to what the Soviet Union considers an acceptable analysis of Vietnam these days. That analysis goes like this: A "capitalistic" and therefore anathematic United States government (as distinct from the mass of the American people, who are generally believed to be "oppressed," "exploited," or merely "duped") is waging an "aggressive" war against "downtrodden peasants and workers" because of its "imperialistic" designs upon a portion of Asia.

The more typical Soviet woman's first thoughts are not about Vietnam itself but about war in general. All wars are immoral, she says, and they should be stopped—not just by powerful men but by ordinary women. Of course, *her* leaders are working very hard to keep the peace, and Westerners, particularly American leaders, are not. "If we worked together to achieve peace we could have it," a state farm official in Batumi said, raising a glass of rose-flavored liqueur. "We must do this. We must work for peace."

Such toasts, and toasts to the memory of John F. Kennedy, the only American President since Franklin D. Roosevelt that they seem to have admired, are common to Soviet women in the presence of Americans. And if given a chance, the women usually will explain why peace and internal stability—besides allowing them their refrigerators—are important to them.

"During the Great Patriotic War [World War II] I was chief of a military hospital and I remember all the amputations I had to do," said Dr. Agnessa Bazhenova, surgical department chief of Moscow's Herzen Cancer Institute. "It seemed like thousands. We lost millions. I should never want us to go through war again."

Dr. Bazhenova, an auburn-haired woman with big capable hands and delicate little gold jewels in her pierced ears, is an orphan. She was born in 1914 when her country was embroiled in the Balkan disputes that led to World War I. Her earliest memories are of suffering and deprivation in the orphanage where she grew up. "There were no nurses to look after us," she said simply. "We children had to depend on each other." She was ten when Lenin died and she remembers his funeral in Moscow because the orphanage was nearby. She remembers weeping and not having enough to eat. Life was only slightly better in the 1930's, when she was a medical student in Moscow. "The times were hard," she recalled matter-of-factly. "I lived in student hostels. It was much better than the orphanage, because we had a place to eat and clean sheets." And then came World War II.

Between four o'clock in the morning on June 22, 1941, when the Germans invaded Russia, and November of 1942, when the tide began to turn against the invaders, Minsk, Smolensk, Kiev, Kharkov, and Orel were captured. Between 300,000 and 800,000 people starved to death in the two and a half years Leningrad was shelled and besieged. Stalingrad was the scene of one of the bloodiest battles in history. By 1945, when the Russians had succeeded in pushing the Germans back to the Oder River, the Soviet

Union was in a shambles. It had suffered upward of 20,000,000 casualties. To all intent, a generation of men had disappeared.

"It is hard to say now whether we [women] wanted to fight or we thought we had to fight," said Irina Rokambolskaya. "We were very young." Mrs. Rokambolskaya, a nuclear physics professor and researcher at the University of Moscow, was a college student when the war began. When a women's air unit was formed, she joined it and became a specialist in navigation. She was just twenty. By the time she was twenty-one she was flying a two-seat single-engine plane with an open cockpit over the German lines. It was her job to see to it that the bombs, which she and her woman co-pilot had trouble lifting into the plane, hit their mark.

"We were night bombers," she said. "The sound of the plane was not much louder than a motorcycle. We flew very low. I was frightened. A good friend of mine was shot down in fire."

Mrs. Rokambolskaya, now the mother of two sons—aged sixteen and nineteen—was still twenty-one when she was made a high-ranking officer. The other women in her regiment were between seventeen and twenty-three. "Our chief was twenty-six," she said, "and we considered her very old. I look at my older son now. He wants to be a physicist. He is almost the age I was when I went to the front. I do not want him to have to fight a war."

Nearly everyone's life has been seriously affected, not just by World War II, but also by the social, economic, and political upheavals of the last fifty years. The revolution—coming as it did during World War I, which had already given rise to famine and epidemics—produced a civil war that disrupted and nearly paralyzed both the industrial machine and the agricultural economy. Industry was not modernized for years. It was only after World War II that many families, particularly in the big cities, had enough to eat. It was only after 1953, when Stalin died, that people began to feel a sense of security. And it is only in the last ten years that women have begun to have the time, money, and desire to think about such a frivolous matter as how they look.

Now that they do, however, women are going at fashion with a child-like enthusiasm. They are enraptured by such things as fake alligator shoes, printed nylon dresses, and washable plastic handbags. And they flock to fashion shows to see what is new and exciting. Such showings, usually held in somber rooms, are often run by slim, well-dressed women, who describe each garment in great detail. The women in the audience write down the numbers of the designs. Afterward, they may buy patterns for about thirty-six kopecks (forty cents), select the fabrics they like, and then turn the whole project over to a seamstress.

The Soviet woman has to go through this drawn-out procedure because the Soviet Union has so little ready-to-wear. The garment industry is grow-ing, but at a snail's pace. The best styles are either imported or custom-made. And everybody who is anybody has either a special seamstress or a good relationship with an atelier.

"I have two seamstresses," said Medea Dzhaparidze, one of Georgia's most beautiful and celebrated actresses. "One is very good but she lives very far away. So I use the second, who's nearer. We have the car, but psychologically it's hard to go so far. It takes so much time. I don't like what the second seamstress does for me, but I go again. Sometimes I say I never will, but I do."

Bella Akhmadulina, the Soviet Union's leading young poetess, has similar problems, although she is equally rich by Soviet standards. A baby-faced Tatar, she was first married to the poet Yevgeny Yevtushenko. Her present husband, Yuri Nagibin, to whom she says she intends to stay mar-ried because she thinks "two marriages are enough," is the wealthy author of short stories and screenplays.

When Yevtushenko was in the United States for the first time, he bought Bella the fitted black silk Jonathan Logan dress she wears on festive occasions. Her hair, the color of Burgundy wine, is up-to-the-minute, too. She uses German dye. "It is not my natural color," she hastened to explain. "Nobody's hair really looks like that."

The question of whether a woman does or does not dye her hair rarely comes up in the Soviet Union. The answer is obvious. No natural hair looks even vaguely like the bright colors that come out of the available dye bottles. A decade ago the brassy blondes were the avant-garde. Today one must have some shade of red—the brighter the better.

"We have more hair colors—many more—in the last five years than we ever had before," said Yelena Ryabinkina, one of the Bolshoi's up-and-coming young ballerinas. "Even older women dye their hair. Everybody wants to look young."

Miss Ryabinkina and her younger sister, Ksana, do not dye their long, light-brown hair. But they have lightened their nail polish ("It used to be the fashion to wear very red nails"), shortened their skirts to just above their knees ("We do not like miniskirts"), added pale-blue eye shadow above their neatly outlined brown eyes, and given up lipstick. "We don't like lipstick," Yelena said. "It is for the stage."

The Ryabinkinas are what most Russian women would like to be—beautiful, young, fashionable, and successful. The sisters wear imported little A-line knit dresses with slightly flared skirts. They dance the shake and the bossa nova (rock 'n' roll is considered neither bourgeois nor decadent—simply old-fashioned), adore caviar, when they can get it, and vodka. "Champagne," Yelena said wearily, "is for when it is very hot."

The girls dream of owning mink coats like those they have seen on the richest women in Paris, New York, and Moscow ("I have a karakul coat and another of very short hair") and think it is not chic to pierce their ears as their female ancestors did and the older generation does. "Not when you're young," Yelena said. "Clip earrings are better. The newest ones are big and long."

Both sisters love colored textured stockings that match their dresses and insist upon low-heeled shoes. Miss Akhmadulina, like most Soviet women, wears *shpilki*—spike-heeled shoes—although they are on the way out of Soviet fashion.

Ten years ago the Soviet woman—who had progressed from men's shoes—wore clumsy low-heeled shoes and stared admiringly at Western women in their trim high heels. Now it's the other way around. Westerners and the Soviet Union's bright young fashionables wear low heels, with or without buckles—the absolute last word—and the typical woman is in high, spiky heels with metal taps. Such are the perversities of fashion.

The Soviet woman can take jewelry or leave it alone. She is just as content with plastic, rhinestones, or other fake ornaments. Only a few women have any real jewelry—a pair of earrings or a brooch that belonged to somebody's grandmother. In the past most women were afraid to wear anything showy.

If she has one, a Russian woman usually wears her wedding ring on her right hand, on her second or third finger. Uzbeks wear theirs on their left hands. Such rings are gold or gold plated. If they are plated they eventually make dark-green marks on the wearer's fingers. It is a common sight.

Silver rings set with colored glass are not unusual, nor are gold-plated rings with simulated pearls. The Soviet woman cannot distinguish between glass and diamonds, and she has no idea whether the pearls she bought for a few rubles are real or fake. The Ryabinkinas, like other women in the hazily defined upper class of accomplishment the Soviet sociologists call "the intelligentsia," have rings they wear most of the time. Ksana's is silver with turquoise. Yelena's, which belonged to her grandmother, is fine gold with rose-cut diamonds and sapphires. The girls seem to think the rings are of equal value.

"We are not interested in jewels," Khachaturian's plump black-haired wife said heatedly. "I know artists who love diamonds. My mother had them. Me? I don't care!"

Mrs. Khachaturian, who considers herself "a good Communist" although she is not a member of the party, is a composer, too. She writes operas, ballads, and concertos under her maiden name, Nina Makarova. All her music, including *Zoya,* an opera about a sixteen-year-old partisan who was hanged by the Germans, promotes the socialist cause. She is particularly proud of a passage in her First Symphony that re-creates the sounds of whistles on the Volga River. And she is so upset about the Vietnam war that she is thinking of writing a song about it. "It's quite impossible to separate creative work from politics," she said. "Politics is life. I cannot just ignore what's happening in Vietnam. I'm saving clippings and information so when the time comes I will be inspired. The music must have beautiful verses."

The Spanish Civil War had much the same effect on Mrs. Khachaturian, and she wrote a musical play about it. Aside from Vietnam, her most serious political interest at the moment concerns the Soviet Union's old-age pension laws. She wants them changed so all women get their full pensions at fifty instead of fifty-five. And although she is nearing retirement age, she doesn't intend to retire or get musical about pensions.

"I wear this bracelet," she said, indicating a circlet of gold, "because it reminds me of my childhood. It was my mother's." She regularly wears a real gold link necklace as well as the bracelet, whether she's decked out for some grand event or dressed in her black sweater and skirt. She is of the generation that had little use for lipstick. But she wears it when she remembers it. And sometimes she ties her hair up with a black velvet ribbon. "I don't care about my face too much," she said. "But I do love steam baths. When you go to the steam bath you do not become old."

When Ilya Selvinsky, a Soviet poet, called last spring for a new awareness of women's beauty and criticized his country's unkempt female intellectuals, it made headlines around the Western world. It need not have.

Soviet women, including intellectuals, are much better groomed and dressed than Selvinsky's words implied. The city Russians, Ukrainians, and Byelorussians who accounted for most of the stereotype women commissars of the past were among the first to opt for a more modern, Western look. These women, partly because of the fashion experimenting among the young, have been arranging and rearranging and dying their hair for ten years. They exercise. They complain when they cannot find shoes to match their new red Hungarian handbags or handbags to match their brown Czechoslovak shoes.

And they shop incessantly—each woman in the hope that she will be in the right store on the right day. If her timing is right, she will be one of the lucky few to come upon some exciting fashion prize: a dress, skirt, pair of shoes, or carryall she can show to all her neighbors.

City women outside Moscow and Leningrad are not slouches either. Georgians and Armenians have always seemed to have a sense of style and a way with their great manes of naturally curly black hair. The Kurds may be "backward" people by Soviet standards, but they are a dazzling array of brightly colored scarves, blouses, and skirts, with dangling gold earrings and gaudy gold necklaces. And the Uzbeks, particularly the ones who have not allowed themselves to get fat, are as trimly put together as any of their sisters in the sophisticated cities of Russia.

When the Russians "equalized" the Uzbeks they found brightly colored dresses under the *paranjas* and strong, handsome faces with delicately painted eyelids and neatly darkened brows. Such women would no more leave their apartments without their eye make-up than without their clothes. But in Uzbekistan eye make-up is no simple matter. "What you do," said Mrs. Zununova, the housewife-writer, "is to take these leaves and put them out in the sun until they wither. Then you press the leaves for a green juice. It turns black. You apply it with a matchstick and cotton. It goes above and below your eyes. If it gets into your eyes it hurts."

Country women, whether in the European or Asian area of the Soviet Union, have a lot less style and a much more rigorous life. They are still "equal" in the old sense. They are agricultural workers, and their role, although changed from the time of the czars, is that of the peasant.

They have learned to read and write since the revolution. Such diseases as malaria have been all but stamped out, and there are reasonably modern hospitals where they may have their babies. And like women everywhere in the Soviet Union they make equal pay with men for equal work, but nobody makes very much.

The only advantage collective-farm women have is a "personal" house and the opportunity of making a "personal" profit on what they raise on their "personal" plots. The houses usually contain slightly more space per person than apartments. But the women have little access to what is new in the home-furnishings and fashion worlds, fewer conveniences and services than their city sisters, and a lot less money.

In the warm, sweet-smelling countryside outside Batumi, the chairman of a tea collective proudly announced that one of his farm families had made 9,000 rubles ($9,990) last year. That's more than twice what an experienced writer-editor makes in Moscow. But then the chairman described the family. "There are three adults and five children," he said. "One of the children is eighteen." That's 9,000 rubles divided among four adult workers, or an average of 2,250 rubles per person. And the average gross annual pay for an adult worker, the chairman later said, is 850 rubles ($943.50).

Women, rather than men, pick the tea in Georgia, and tea-picking is stoop labor. Women are assigned this work, according to the chairman, "because they are good at it. It takes a sensitive, practiced hand." It also frees the men for the "hard" work.

A new tea-picking machine should eventually release women from this toil. But there are not many machines yet, and those available cannot climb up and down the hills where much of the tea is raised. Similar problems plague the cotton, wheat, and corn industries.

The only thing the peasant woman tends to have in abundance is children—many more than her city sister. The one-child family is common in urban areas. The family with ten children is not uncommon in the country. This is partly because the country woman knows little if anything about birth-control practices and not much about legal abortions. If she does know about abortions, she's against them, either because they're "immoral" or because they mean a trip to a hospital, and any hospital stay is something to be avoided. The country woman is used to big families, and she looks at her situation quite realistically. The extra hands are helpful. The extra mouths are not that difficult to feed in an agricultural situation. And, most important of all, her government has made motherhood what amounts to a paid profession.

Since the 1930's the Soviet Union has been trying to increase its lagging birth rate, and although the money paid to mothers has varied through the years, the government has used these cash rewards as incentives as well as maternal benefits. The highest honor (and the most money) goes to the Heroine Mother, a woman who has borne and reared ten or more children. Most Heroine Mothers are country women. Evidently city women would rather make their money in other ways.

A mother of six or more children has a "profession" in that she is not expected to have an additional job. She is thought of not as a "housewife," but as a "mother." But even with the government subsidies, she may like or need an outside job and often has one. If she does, she is known as whatever kind of worker she chooses to become.

When the Soviet Union gets around to eliminating what its various ideologists call "the differences," it will have at last achieved the "classless society." In the meantime, it is struggling along with what it calls two classes—the peasants and the workers—and a single "stratum"—the intelligentsia. Soviet sociologists like to compare the existing class structure with a popular Russian dessert that has cake on the bottom, cake on the top, and a thin layer of jam or icing in the middle. The peasants and the workers are the cake. The intelligentsia is the icing.

They also like to say how equal all the classes are, and to prove it they frequently resort to horizontal pictures of the class structure rather than vertical ones. But no matter what they do, it is increasingly evident that although class antagonisms may be fading, class differences are not.

The intelligentsia, which by Soviet definition consists of the achievers—virtually everyone who has an advanced education or who works in the country's highest echelons—is the rapidly expanding privileged group. It includes Communist party leaders, everyone of consequence in the government, artists, writers, doctors, lawyers, teachers, technicians, upper-echelon administrators, and the highest level of office workers.

One has only to acquire lots of the right kind of education, which automatically results in better pay, to ascend to the intelligentsia—a difficult task for a peasant child who does not have what sociologists concede are the advantages of city children, workers' children, and, especially, the intelligentsia's children. But peasant children do make it—if not because of the educational system then because of some special talent such as acting, dancing, or political maneuvering.

Although all of the people in the U.S.S.R. are commonly known in America as "Russians," only those coming from the Russian Republic itself should be called that, strictly speaking. And being Russian is better than being any other nationality in an extremely nationality-conscious country. Being a Communist party member is better than not being one despite the Communists' persistent explanation that "membership never means privileges, only responsibilities." And these are the goals a lot of the upward-bound people set for themselves, consciously or unconsciously.

Admission to the party is by invitation or election, but a well-educated man or woman who has been a good Pioneer and Komsomol can, with continued hard work, devotion to the cause, the right friends, and no political missteps, be reasonably assured of membership at some point in his or her life. It is more difficult to become Russian. "I am Georgian and my wife is Russian," a successful journalist told me. "My daughter will be Russian."

This child, who is being educated in one of Moscow's best schools, is already more Russianized than her father. She lives in Russia. She speaks Russian. When she is asked what nationality she is—and this is a question regularly put to small children as well as adults—she says she is Russian although the father's nationality traditionally determines the answer. And when she grows up and has to elect a nationality for the internal passport required for all Soviet citizens, she will have the choice of being Georgian or Russian. Presumably, she will decide to be Russian with her father's blessing.

"But I shall always be Georgian," the father said proudly. "I could never be anything else." He was born of Georgian parents, who, if not members of the intelligentsia, were certainly on its fringes. Because they were both Georgian, he had no choice of nationality when he came of age.

His father was an engineer. His mother was a doctor. A precocious only child who spoke Georgian first, then Russian, and finally English, he grew up in Tbilisi during the early years of Sovietization.

He had read a lot of the Russian and Georgian classics before he was introduced to them in school, and was well on his way to becoming an Ernest Hemingway and Jack London fan before he was graduated from college. He was too young to serve in the army at the beginning of World War II, but his father went. And when his father was killed, he was so shattered that he had to do something positive about it. "I felt awful," he said. "I had to do something meaningful. Man cannot live by bread alone. I went out immediately and joined the Komsomol."

Ten years later, after studying in Moscow, receiving a degree in international law, and working as a radio commentator and journalist, he became a member of the Communist party.

"I love Georgia," he said wistfully. "It is beautiful there and the people are like me, but I am no longer like them. I look like them. Sometimes I think like them. But I could not live there. Moscow is alive and vital. I could never live anywhere else. In my way, I am Russian."

But not so Russian as to blend into the culture without being noticed. Like most Georgians, who are accustomed to drinking native wines from childhood and who pride themselves on not getting drunk, he has a built-in distaste for bolting vodka and other hard liquors. And drunks disgust him.

Blond or light-brown-haired Russians are physically identifiable among the black-haired Georgians, Armenians, and Azerbaijani, who have olive skins, and among the Central Asians, but they are quick to adapt their ways to the culture in which they live. Ukrainians and Byelorussians adapt well, too. But members of other nationality groups rarely disappear in "Russian" situations, and out in the far-flung republics there are strong efforts not just to preserve the ethnic or national cultures, but also to keep them free of Russianization.

Seclusion for women, which is about the least "Russian" practice one might advocate among a people who only in the 1920's allowed their women to be unveiled, has reappeared in Uzbekistan—not among the "backward" peasants, but among a few well-educated women party members who belong to the intelligentsia. And the idea, a kind of reverse snobbery, has been so appealing that it has spread to women of other ethnic groups that had no tradition of seclusion.

In the meantime, the intelligentsia, which is thought to be less than the 20 per cent shown in the 1959 census, grows because of the immense efforts being put into education. Peasants, who account for 45 per cent of the population, wave good-by to their children, who head for better-paying industrial jobs in the cities and membership in the working class. And the working class, which is the other 35 per cent of the population, is gradually educating itself and its children upward into the intelligentsia.

Whatever else it is, the intelligentsia is better paid, better housed, better fed, and better dressed. No figures are available, but it is generally believed that the intelligentsia owns most of the cars, the refrigerators, what diamonds there are, and perhaps half the dachas. It is they who have the in-comers and the chauffeurs, and the know-how to acquire a good education and more privileges for their children.

But when it comes to the elaborate new wedding ceremonies, all the classes *are* equal. The cost, regardless of income, is one ruble sixty kopecks (about $1.77). These weddings, a far cry from the free love the state sanctioned during the 1920's, are bigger and more ceremonial than anything since the days of the church and the czars, and they are expected to become even more ceremonial.

By the fall of 1967 the motherly women whom the atheistic state has authorized to marry young couples are supposed to have neat black-and-white uniforms for their jobs. Such uniforms, according to Nina Dashchenko, the gray-haired director of the yellow stucco Palace of Weddings on Moscow's Shchepkin Street, will make weddings more beautiful. And more official. "The stronger is the family the stronger is the state," Mrs. Dashchenko said, paraphrasing both Marx and Lenin. "We want our brides and grooms to be sure of what they're doing. We want these marriages to last. We believe the solemn ceremonies have great value."

Solemn ceremonies, as the weddings are called, were introduced in Leningrad in 1959 and are now available throughout the Soviet Union. They were the state's answer to what apparently was a strong desire for something more memorable than merely filling out and signing marriage forms at a registry bureau. Young people so disliked the ZAGS, as the dreary bureaus are called, that they were reverting to thoroughly unsocialist church weddings. But the new ceremonies serve other purposes, too.

The Communist party recognizes a man and woman as husband and wife if they live together, but there is nothing very official about such a union. The nature of the solemn ceremony, with its public exchange of vows before relatives, friends, and such government and party officials as may be invited to attend, dignifies the marriage. It is also strong competition to the religious rites that have persisted.

Solemn civil ceremonies, it is argued, will help to prolong marriages and thus stabilize family life. Mrs. Dashchenko said that only 2 per cent of the thousands of couples married in solemn ceremonies in Moscow had been divorced. The figure is lower than for the population as a whole. But the first of these marriages was performed only eight years ago, so it will be quite a while yet before the ceremonies' value can be properly known.

Solemn ceremonies, available only to couples who have never been married before, are optional. Yet most parents—who had no comparable wedding rites because they would not go to a church, the only place that then offered them—encourage the young people to be married in what is considered to be this new, even glamorous manner. A ceremony lasts perhaps seven minutes.

A month before it is to take place the young couple comes to the Palace of Weddings to fill out the application. In the countryside, where there are no wedding palaces, the couples still register at a bureau. The girls are usually between the ages of nineteen and twenty-two. The men are generally twenty-three to twenty-six. If they are eighteen or older they do not need their parents' permission.

Those couples who fill out their applications at the Shchepkin Street Palace of Weddings—rarely arriving hand in hand and not at all demonstrative by Western standards—are shown into a large, high-ceilinged reception room. On one side is a glass counter and shelves stocked with wedding gifts that are for sale: silver-plated vodka cups, plastic costume jewelry, decorative china pieces, and simple gold or gold-plated wedding rings. Next to this is a counter where couples may check their coats. On the other side are little tables and chairs where the couples sit, two by two, to fill out the necessary forms. While they pore over the papers a loud-speaker system provides allegedly romantic music. "Moscow Nights," which is to the Soviet Union what "Arrivederci Roma" is to Italy, alternates with "Tammy's in Love."

"It is then time for the families to meet each other," Mrs. Dashchenko said, explaining what happens in the next thirty days. "The young couples talk about the marriage with their families and friends. They discuss everything. We like them to meet with some of our older couples. Our first couples have six-year-old children."

The couples also visit special wedding shops to buy their wedding clothes, and the prices obviously separate the reasonably well-to-do from the poor. These shops are only for those who can produce their marriage registration certificates, and they are stocked with a wide range of goods: poorly made short white dresses of cotton or artificial silk (about $27 to $40, although elsewhere they are usually more), shoulder-length tulle veils, men's dark suits (about $67 to $128), gifts, china, linen, and other household items. A bride's white shoes alone can cost $40.

The day of the solemn ceremony itself is rarely solemn. Thirty to forty weddings are held in the Shchepkin Street palace's great hall in a single day, or one about every ten minutes. And there are fluttery brides, nervous bride-grooms, relatives, and friends everywhere. Parents generally do not attend, but wait at home for a family celebration.

The couples have to pass through the reception room, where more prospective brides and grooms are busily registering, and then on into various comfortable waiting rooms. Relatives and friends go into one room, grooms into another, and the brides into a third. The girls' room has big mirrors, and it is not unusual for five or six brides to be primping before a single mirror.

Then everybody waits—occasionally for thirty minutes beyond the appointed time. When their turn comes, friends and relatives line up behind the bride and groom, and the whole party troops into the great hall to a recording of Tchaikovsky's "The Dance of the Sugar Plum Fairy." The hall itself is typical of Soviet elegance. The thirty-foot-high walls are institutional cream in color and are ornamented with heroic moldings that probably antedate the revolution. The windows at one end are draped with bright-yellow silk and shaded by white silk Austrian blinds. Near them are heavy maple desks. The floor is covered with dark-red carpet. Above everyone's head looms a giant chandelier, a modernistic glass-and-brass affair that looks Scandinavian and probably is. There are no chairs, for everyone stands. The three wedding officials behind the desks are women. The one in the center is the wedding director or one of her assistants. At the left is a clerk who is responsible for the wedding records. And on the right is a people's deputy whose job is to make a serious, congratulatory speech and hand the couple their marriage certificate.

"We always ask if it is their 'sincere desire' to marry each other," Mrs. Dashchenko said happily. "They always answer 'Yes.'" The "yesses" are the pledges the couples make—their only pledges—but they kiss (one rarely sees kissing anywhere else except at a railroad station or airport), sometimes exchange rings, sign the registry for the last time, and are then considered man and wife. A recording of "The Blue Danube," which is played softly toward the end of the ceremony, booms out at the finish and ushers the couple out of the hall.

Champagne is optional afterward in a baroque room with heavy Soviet furniture. A photographer takes pictures if the couple wants them. Sometimes the wedding party arrives and departs in big black rented limousines. In rural areas such weddings take place in palaces of culture, if these are available, or in some other public place. And the family celebrations tend to be bigger and longer and involve a lot more food—partly because more food is obtainable.

Divorces are not happy occasions, of course, but they are so much easier to get today than they once were that at times they are almost festive. On December 19, 1917, shortly after the revolution, Lenin signed the first decree on the dissolution of marriage. "A marriage is to be annulled," it said, "when either both parties or one at least appeal for its annulment." In other words, divorce was to be had for the asking, and nobody had to show cause.

At the time, the Bolsheviks considered the family little more than a useless "bourgeois" institution, and couples were supposed to sustain whatever love relationship they might desire by themselves. There was to be no external pressure. And nobody was supposed to have to live with anyone he or she did not want to live with.

In 1926, in its famous Code of Family Law that legalized couples living together without their ever having to register such arrangements with a government agency, the Soviet Union made divorce even simpler. Until then, one had at least to appear in a court. Now all one had to do was apply to a registry office and wait three days for his or her spouse to receive a postcard saying the marriage had ended.

Predictably, this free and romantic system ran into difficulty. The people developed what their increasingly nervous leaders termed "frivolous" attitudes toward marriage and divorce, although the divorce rate was low by Western standards. In 1936 Stalin decided to do something about it.

His new Family Code required the couple to appear at a registry bureau and have their divorce recorded in their internal passports. It also introduced a series of fees: fifty rubles for a first divorce, one hundred and fifty for the second, and three hundred for the third. Responding to this financial pressure, the divorce rate immediately dropped. But there was more to come.

Curbing divorces in a society that still allowed marriages to go unregistered meant that some marriages obviously were being dissolved outside the registry bureau. This, the lagging birth rate, and a desire to do something even more positive about stabilizing family life led in 1944 to yet another, stricter, decree. It abolished unregistered marriage. The 1944 law gave the courts jurisdiction over divorce suits, made the procedure prohibitively complicated, and raised the fees so that there was a hundred-ruble charge merely for making an application for a divorce and then additional fees ranging from 500 to 2,000 rubles. And it was not until after Stalin's death that the laws were re-examined and slightly modified.

Today, because of reforms in 1966, a divorce is faster and cheaper, and several of the pretrial requirements of the 1944 law have been eliminated. One has only to show that a marriage is finished and that it is unlikely to be restored.

Divorce cases are tried in small, district people's courts by a tribunal consisting of an elected judge and two elected jurors. There are no lawyers (although anyone may have one represent him if he or she chooses), no flags, no police officers, no witnesses, no Bibles, and no lawbooks. The proceedings are at once serious and informal, and conducted in layman's language.

Raisa Dmitriyeva, a small, soft-spoken brunette, presides over one such Moscow court. "I talk to the man and wife separately," Mrs. Dmitriyeva said. "I try to get them to patch things up if they can. If there are children, we talk about what this will mean. Sometimes I get them to try again. By the time they come to court the man and wife usually aren't angry with each other. They have already decided to separate. There is a fight only if one of them does not want the divorce. This is rare."

Mrs. Dmitriyeva's experience parallels the government statistics. More than 85 per cent of couples seeking divorce last year had agreed to it beforehand, and about 96 per cent of the requested divorces were granted.

The mother gets custody of the children, Mrs. Dmitriyeva said, unless "she's a drunk or insane." Property is divided evenly, although a pianist usually gets his piano, a writer his typewriter. A father is expected to contribute to the support of his minor children—25 per cent of his salary is automatically deducted for one child, 33 per cent for two, and 50 per cent for three or more. And there is no alimony (unless one of the partners is incapacitated, and then only for one year), because everyone is presumed to be self-supporting.

Nobody knows exactly what the next step will be, but there is talk in Moscow of even more liberal marriage and divorce laws. Some jurists think that when both partners agree to a divorce, the case should not come to court at all, but be arranged through the Bureau of Official Statistics. And it is possible that the new laws, already being considered, would restore common-law marriage as it existed before 1944.

In the meantime, the Soviet woman will persevere. All the signs indicate that once she gets her refrigerator, her vacuum cleaner, her automobile, and her dacha, she may reasonably be expected to think in terms of the air conditioners she is only beginning to hear about. When she gets used to her false eyelashes, somebody will have begun to figure out how to make her hair dye look more natural. And by the seventy-fifth anniversary of the revolution, she probably will not just know about the difference between diamonds and glass, but will care about it.

THE ECONOMIC
MACHINERY

»

H. Erich Heinemann

On Tsvetnoy Boulevard in Moscow, next door to the circus, there is a little island of free enterprise in the world capital of Communism. It is a collective-farm market, one of about 8,000 in the Soviet Union, where peasants are free to bring their produce and sell it for whatever they can get. Prices are consistently higher in the collective-farm markets than in the retail food stores run by the Soviet government, and, according to some Muscovites, if a housewife wants a really good selection of food, she has to get to the market by seven o'clock in the morning.

Yet despite the high prices and the inconvenience—there are only three collective-farm markets in Moscow, a city of more than 6,500,000 people— the customers keep coming. I went by the market numerous times and always saw brisk trade going on, sharp haggling over prices, and crowds of people moving through.

The collective-farm market is clearly an anomaly in the Soviet economy, where practically everything is not only owned by the government, but is tightly controlled as well. But the collective-farm markets continue to flourish, not because of any basic shortage of food (this has not existed for many years), but because the ponderous mechanism of the U.S.S.R.'s economic machine has not yet figured out how to supply its citizens with the kind and quality of perishable fruits, vegetables, and meats they want when they want them.

It did not take long after I arrived in Moscow to discover that anomalies such as the collective-farm market are the rule rather than the exception in the Soviet Union. Right away I could sense that the crowds surging along Gorky Street, which is supposed to be Moscow's Fifth Avenue but is a pretty poor imitation, seemed to have money to spend, yet the man in the street is still shabbily dressed and he still has to devote about half his income to buying food. Americans spend less than 20 per cent of theirs on food.

The stores were well stocked but quality was poor and prices were very high, especially in relation to the average Soviet wage of about one hundred rubles a month. Eggs were well over one ruble a dozen, a pair of fur-lined boots for women was sixty-five rubles, and a man's suit, which looked as though it came straight off the rack of an American Salvation Army depot, was one hundred and thirty-five rubles.

At the official—and highly artificial—exchange rate a dollar is worth only ninety kopecks (90/100ths of a ruble). This exchange rate is rigidly enforced, with criminal penalties for violations, but even the Soviet authorities seem not to take it too seriously. Anyone with dollars can walk into one of several "foreign currency shops" in Moscow and buy the best that the Soviet Union has to offer at roughly a third of the ruble price.

I heard a good deal about the great strides the Soviet Union is making in developing its electric-power industry, but in Leningrad I saw secretaries with their desks shoved over next to a window so that they could see to type. I never once saw a worker in a Soviet factory with a hard hat, a standard safety precaution in American plants, and in Kharkov I saw women without protective respirators spraying paint on metal panels in an air-conditioner factory. The officials who were guiding me around told me blandly that industrial accidents and industrial diseases were "practically unknown." From reading about the Soviet Union I knew that it had computers that were fairly advanced even by United States standards, but I was struck by the fact that the abacus and pen and ink are still the basic computational devices in Soviet industry.

In my opinion, there is no reason to doubt that the Kremlin is at long last showing some interest in improving the quality of daily life in the U.S.S.R. Direct controls over internal travel and place of work have largely disappeared, a five-day week is being introduced, the minimum wage is gradually being raised from forty-five rubles to sixty rubles a month, consumer credit is available, and personal savings have risen so rapidly that laying out 2,000 to 5,000 rubles for a co-operative apartment has become quite the thing in Moscow.

The questions are: how deep is the Kremlin's commitment to the consumer, and how far is it likely to go? The government still gets about 40 per cent of its revenue from a "turnover tax" that is built into the retail-price structure. A Volga passenger car (which looks a bit like a Swedish Volvo) costs the government 1,900 rubles to produce, but it retails for 5,500 rubles, and you may have to wait five years to get one. Housing, too, remains in desperately short supply. Several years' wait is required for accommodations in most parts of the country, and even then the allotment for a family of four is a two-room apartment (plus kitchen and bath).

In busy stores people have to stand in line three times to make each purchase: first to select the goods, then to pay for them, and finally to pick them up. At the meat counter many shops thoughtfully provide a table where the housewife can unwrap her purchase, just to make sure she received what she ordered. The whole thing is so chaotic that I could not help wondering whether the government is deliberately trying to make it hard for people to buy. That might be true. A Soviet mathematician has figured out that the Russian people spend about 70 per cent of their free time waiting in lines.

The authorities tolerate the collective-farm markets and the private agriculture that supports them (which produces roughly a third of the Soviet Union's gross agricultural output and 13 per cent of marketed farm output on some 3 per cent of the cultivated land) because they are at an impasse in food distribution. On a vastly larger scale, the government is also facing serious problems in maintaining the over-all growth rate of the Soviet economy. Since 1960, according to Nikolai K. Baibakov, the Soviet Union's chief economic planner, the economy has been growing at an annual rate of 6 per cent, down from the 8.2 per cent of 1956 through 1960. In Western estimates the drop in the growth rate is similar but the level is lower, from 6 per cent to 4 per cent.

Still more ominous is the fact that the government has found that growth is getting steadily more expensive. Each year more and more rubles are having to be invested in new plants and machinery in order to get a ruble of increased output.

Soviet statisticians do not publish estimates of the value of their country's total output of goods and services (or gross national product) that are comparable with those compiled in the West. However, according to estimates prepared by United States intelligence agencies—estimates that are closely followed by some Soviet economists—the U.S.S.R.'s gross national product was the equivalent of about $335 billion in 1966, or roughly 45 per cent of the American output of $740 billion. In 1960, according to these same sources, the Soviet Union's G.N.P. was equal to about $245 billion, or approximately 44 per cent of the United States output that year (measured in 1966 prices) of $557 billion. Nikita S. Khrushchev's proud boast that by 1970 the Soviet Union would surpass the United States in per-capita output no longer gets publicity in the Soviet press.

Not only is the Soviet economy less than half the size of the American economy, but it is also far less efficient. The civilian work force totaled about 108,000,000 people at the end of 1966, compared with about 74,000,000 in the United States on the same date. Thus the output of the average Soviet worker was about one-third that of his American counterpart. The difference is most glaring in agriculture: despite persistent migration to the cities over the last fifty years, there are still about 38,000,000 farmers in the U.S.S.R. compared with about 4,000,000 in the United States. Accurate comparisons of farm output in the two countries are hard to come by, but Soviet authorities concede that their agricultural production "probably" does not exceed 80 per cent of the American level.

Lately, agriculture, traditionally the soft underbelly of Soviet economic power, has been getting a larger share of the pie—wages have been increased for farm workers, pension coverage has been extended to them, and farm investment has been raised sharply. Western agricultural experts in Moscow believe that these measures will lead to higher output, but it remains to be seen whether they will get at the basic inefficiency of Soviet agriculture.

The decline in the U.S.S.R.'s economic growth can be traced in part to the disastrous crop failures the country experienced in 1963 and 1965, when large amounts of wheat had to be purchased in the West. But the problems are much deeper than that. Premier Aleksei N. Kosygin spelled some of them out in agonizing detail in a landmark speech to the Central Committee of the Soviet Communist party on September 27, 1965. "The advantages and opportunities offered by the socialist system of economy," he said, "are still far from being utilized to the full." "Quite a few errors" had been committed in planning the course of the economy, he added, leading to an "improper balance between the different branches of the economy."

Kosygin went on to say that too little attention had been devoted to agriculture, which in turn had helped to slow the rate of industrial growth, particularly in consumer-goods industries. The planned targets for consumer-goods production had been too low, and "even those plan targets have been systematically underfulfilled." Delays in the construction of new

plants were so long that there was risk that "the equipment installed becomes obsolete even before the plant becomes operational. . . . We are not
satisfied with the results achieved," he remarked, in what was probably the
understatement of the day.

Not unlike the problem that faced the economic high command of the
Kennedy administration when it took office in January, 1961, in the midst
of the nation's fourth postwar recession, the Kremlin has had to grapple
with the necessity of getting the country moving again. In the United States
the response of Kennedy's "new economists" was to cut taxes deliberately
during a period when the federal budget was already running in deficit in
an attempt to release private purchasing power and thus stimulate business
activity.

In a totally different setting, the Soviet government is moving cautiously
to loosen just a bit the rigid controls it exercises over the production of
goods and services. As Gilbert Burck, of *Fortune,* pointed out in his July,
1966, analysis of the Soviet economy, the U.S.S.R.'s leadership has finally
discovered what the management of General Motors learned in the early
1920's when it decentralized operations but kept a firm rein on policy.
"Precisely because the managers at the center have been trying to discharge
too much responsibility," Burck observed, "they have vitiated their control
of their far-flung complex."

Indeed, except for Rumania and tiny Albania (whose Maoist line has
isolated it even within the Communist bloc), all of the nations of Eastern
Europe have introduced reforms designed to make their economies more
responsive to consumer demands and thus reduce some of the inefficiency
and waste inherent in any system of rigid central control. In most of the
countries, in fact, the reforms have gone quite a bit beyond what the
U.S.S.R. has devised.

The current Soviet reforms, announced by Kosygin in his September,
1965, speech but not due to take full effect until next year, are highly complex, but the basic thrust is fairly simple: In place of incredibly detailed
instructions from Moscow on how to conduct their affairs, the managers of
Soviet businesses are now being turned loose, at least in theory, to solve
some of their problems for themselves.

Furthermore, the reforms make a radical revision in the structure of
incentives in Soviet society. Where previously workers and managers had
been rewarded for meeting production targets expressed in physical units of
output (whether pairs of shoes or tons of steel), henceforth the key criterion
of success will be profitability. Salary bonuses will be directly tied to the
profits of an enterprise, and a whole range of social services that Soviet

enterprises provide for their employees—including housing, child-care facilities for working mothers, and paid vacations—will also be financed from funds built up from accumulated profits.

The aim of the reforms, it seems to me, is to make Soviet managers a little less like bureaucrats and a little bit more like entrepreneurs.

The stakes are high in the U.S.S.R.'s drive to spur the growth rate of the economy. The appetite of the long-suffering consumer for a better standard of living has been whetted by steady increases in wages and a gradual improvement in the availability of goods and services. Most Soviet citizens, particularly those living in the major cities, would probably agree with Sasha, a former correspondent for Tass, the government news agency, that "things are normal now," in the sense that there is enough food to eat and clothes to buy. But relief from privation is far from satisfaction with things as they are.

Just as much as any American, Moscow's man in the street wants improved living conditions for himself and his children; he wants to be able to buy refrigerators and television sets that work and clothes that are stylish at reasonable prices; and especially if he is a member of the burgeoning middle class of technicians and engineers who really run Soviet society, he wants the freedom and mobility that come with a private automobile. The department stores in the Soviet Union are always jammed, the people have money with which to buy, but watch them shopping and it is clear that they want quality as well as quantity.

During the last few years the government has started to respond to this demand. Rising wages provide little additional incentive if consumers cannot buy anything with their money. New investment going into consumer industries is being increased, Italian and French auto companies have been called in to help in a massive drive to boost automobile production to 800,000 cars by 1970 (from 230,000 in 1966), and heavy pressure is being brought to bear on manufacturers to improve quality, in design as well as in production.

But the U.S.S.R.'s leadership has also made it plain that the increased attention to consumer needs will not be allowed to divert significant resources from heavy industry or the military establishment, the traditional darlings of Soviet economic planning. If this decision is carried through, the only way that a dent is going to be made in meeting the material needs of an expanding population of about 235,000,000 is by increasing the economic growth rate. Thus the key question, in my opinion, is whether Soviet industry is going to get enough new freedom under the economic reforms to get the growth machine humming again.

Conversations with managers of numerous enterprises—ranging from a hothouse farm growing cucumbers and tomatoes in Moscow to a steel mill in Volgograd—made it plain that the prospect of greater managerial freedom, plus improved opportunity to better one's own lot through one's own efforts, is being greeted with considerable enthusiasm. But persistent questioning also brought out the fact that the scope for individual initiative, even under the reforms, will be quite limited.

I visited Kuzma N. Kolosov at the Marfino State Farm in Moscow. He told me that he hopes to be able to increase his production of cucumbers, which are highly profitable for his enterprise, and cut back on tomatoes and other vegetables, which are less so. But Kolosov was not sure that this would be allowed, and he said that if his farm continues to be required to grow relatively unprofitable products, "then we will have to ask for reimbursement."

In Volgograd I saw Pavel P. Matevosyan, director of the Krasny Oktyabr (Red October) Steel Works, which turns out about 1,300,000 tons of steel annually. He was pleased with new machinery that he had installed to clean steel rods and then inspect them for flaws with ultrasonic waves. Matevosyan, whose managerial exploits have earned him the title of Hero of Socialist Labor, one of the Soviet Union's highest civilian awards, made the decision to acquire this equipment without consulting higher authorities. Yet if Krasny Oktyabr, which has annual sales of almost 200,000,000 rubles, finds it necessary to borrow more than 500,000 rubles for current operating needs, Matevosyan has to go to Moscow for approval.

At the Sverdlov Textile Works in Moscow, Nikolai N. Vasilyev, who runs a plant turning out synthetic fabrics for draperies and women's dresses, was proud of the artistic freedom accorded the fabric designers in his factory. It turned out, however, that before a new design can go into production approximately one hundred and thirty people have to approve it.

The economic reforms currently evolving in the Soviet Union are clearly limited. Even so, widespread debate has developed among Western commentators on Soviet affairs over whether or not on the eve of the fiftieth anniversary of the Communist seizure of power in Russia (and the one hundredth anniversary of the publication of the first volume of Karl Marx's *Das Kapital*) the Soviet Union is starting to experience "creeping capitalism." After all, profits, the wellspring of incentive under capitalism, are to play a key role in the Soviet economy of the future, while Soviet businessmen are to get some freedom for Western-style wheeling and dealing in order to get the economy moving again.

William Blackie, board chairman of the Caterpillar Tractor Company, gave what might be called a typical capitalist view of the Soviet economic reforms in an article published in mid-1967 by the National Industrial Conference Board, a private nonprofit research organization based in New York. "One of the major causes of communist reform," Blackie said, "is undoubtedly the increasing evidence of capitalist success and the growing knowledge of this among the communists. The idea that the capitalist countries are more successful, because they are capitalist, is penetrating through the Iron Curtain." He speculated that it may only be a matter of time until the principal difference in economic organization between East and West is simply one of ownership—"a sort of state capitalism as contrasted with our private capitalism."

Soviet propagandists can scarcely be expected to proclaim that the world's most powerful Communist state is having to adopt wholesale the techniques of capitalism in order to satisfy the needs of its people. The Novosti Press Agency, which in effect functions as the public-relations arm of the Soviet government, dismisses interpretations of the Soviet economic reform such as Blackie's as "another dose of lies and misinformation." "Assertions and 'forecasts' about a 'backslide to capitalism,' " Novosti says, "give no clear idea of the essence of the processes taking place in the Soviet economic system and merely misinform the world public."

Yet, quite apart from the propaganda sphere, I think that predictions of an imminent epidemic of capitalism in Eastern Europe are, much like the celebrated reports of Mark Twain's death, a bit premature. At no time have the Soviet authorities given any indication that they are considering, or even seriously discussing, any modification of the essential character of their system: state ownership and control of all important aspects of the economy. V. A. Fedorovich, an economist on the staff of the Novosti Press Agency, echoed the government line when he told me that "ours is a totally planned economy."

The purpose of the Soviet economic reform, according to Aleksei F. Rumyantsev, the influential editor of the *Ekonomicheskaya Gazeta,* which is published by the Central Committee of the Communist party, is not to move the Soviet Union to a new economic system, but, rather, to make an existing system work more efficiently. State planning (a Soviet euphemism for state control), Rumyantsev told me in the course of a long interview in 1967, has not been weakened by the economic reform, but, on the contrary, has been strengthened, because the state planning agencies will be freed of a great deal of detail work and hence will be able to concentrate on really important items. He pointed out that all major investments in new plant and equipment, the basic composition of the output of an enterprise, and the over-all size of its wage bill, among other items, remain firmly under the wing of the authorities.

I see no reason to quarrel with Rumyantsev. Both in its formal structure and in its informal application, the Soviet economic reform has left the government and the Communist party as firmly in control of the economy as they ever were. As Professor Robert W. Campbell, of Indiana University, commented in 1965 in his book *Soviet Economic Power,* "Despite incessant institutional tinkering, retreat from the distinguishing feature of the Soviet system, that is, its high degree of centralization . . . has been imperceptible."

It is quite true that many features of the current Soviet reform—particularly its emphasis on profits, interest payments, and a poorly disguised form of rent—are very un-Marxian. But, as Campbell notes, trying to understand Soviet developments from the vantage point of Marxist theory "is not a very helpful point of departure." Analysts who start from Marxist theory, Campbell says, "become preoccupied with connecting every act of the Soviet government with some Marxist idea. There is an urge to interpret everything as some logical result of the Marxist heritage or as a perfidious betrayal of Marx's real meaning." The Communist party, he adds, "professes Marxism as its sacred official ideology. Great care is taken to preserve the sanctity of this ideology and to rationalize everything in terms of it or by appeal to it. But in a way this is all a monstrous pretense." The theory and even the spirit of Marxist analysis, he continues, "are largely irrelevant to the conditions and problems of the Soviet situation. Marx's analysis was mainly concerned with the future development of nineteenth-century capitalist countries—not with the task of propelling a peasant society [such as that in prerevolutionary Russia] into the twentieth century."

No one can tell exactly what the future holds, but from everything the Soviet leadership has said and done, I believe that there is no present intention in the U.S.S.R. of abandoning state ownership and control of the economy for anything even remotely resembling Western-style private enterprise. Yet a careful survey of developments elsewhere in the Communist bloc does raise a serious question whether within the Soviet reform there is perhaps the germ of a comparatively new form of economic organization—one that is neither fish nor fowl, neither capitalist nor Communist.

This is market socialism, and it is in Yugoslavia that it has found its most extensive development. A greatly oversimplified description of market socialism is that there is no private ownership of industry, but the role of the government in controlling the economy is vastly different from the traditional Soviet one. In the Soviet Union, for example, all major investment decisions are made by the government, prices are fixed by the government, and there is tight governmental allocation of materials. By contrast, in Yugoslavia the government's role in guiding the economy is much less direct and relies to a large extent on the sort of generalized controls over credit and financial flows that are common in all Western economies. The Yugoslav government has largely surrendered its ownership role in the economy to worker committees and it has turned its enterprises free to take their chances in the rough and tumble of the marketplace. Most importantly, Yugoslav managers, who are elected by their workers for five-year terms, have real authority to make decisions and take business risks.

President Tito has also forced through a crucial political change. As the Yugoslav economic model has slowly evolved in the years since 1948, when the first decisive rift between Moscow and Belgrade occurred, the role of the Communist party in running the domestic economy of the country has been gradually lessened, until at the present time—on the testimony of both Yugoslav and Western observers—it no longer has a decisive voice except on the broadest policy questions. Other Eastern European countries have not gone so far, but the degree of autonomy that has been accorded to enterprises, especially in Hungary and Czechoslovakia, suggests that a transition to full reforms, of the Yugoslav type, may not be long in coming.

In the Soviet Union the case is much harder to make that market socialism is just around the corner. Looking at the intellectual content of the reforms announced by Kosygin in September, 1965, Rush V. Greenslade, Soviet affairs analyst for the United States Central Intelligence Agency, concluded that "the proposals include the first timid steps away from tight central direction of the economy and toward a market socialism." It is amusing, though probably not significant, that Kolosov, the director of the Marfino Farm in Moscow, volunteered at the end of our long conversation that it was his hope that the economic reform would lead eventually to the direct election of managers by their workers, rather than their appointment by the state, as at present. Direct election of managers is one of the key elements in the Yugoslav reform.

But in the real world of Soviet power politics any early move toward a genuine market socialism does not appear likely. Rumyantsev, who, because of his role as economic spokesman for the Central Committee, reflects the conservative views of the Soviet Establishment, takes a condescending attitude toward Yugoslavia's economic reform. He told me a little parable designed, in his words, to show how "the Soviet people felt about the Yugoslav economic system." He was fifty years old, he said, and he felt that it was fair to say that in most matters his judgments about life were probably superior to those of his son, who was only nineteen. But at the same time he felt that he should not impose his judgments on his son, for learning from one's mistakes was an integral part of growing up. The point of his story lies in the fact that the Soviet Union is currently celebrating its fiftieth anniversary, while it is nineteen years since the rift between Belgrade and Moscow.

The fact remains, though, that one of the avowed aims of the Soviet economic reform is to give the nation's business managers more freedom to solve problems on their own, and, once the reform is fully in effect, to free the over-all economy from some of the ills of excessive bureaucratic centralization. Managers are expected to act like entrepreneurs, yet the state is stubbornly holding on tight to all the main levers of economic control: the direction of important investments, the level of wages, and the character of the products that an enterprise turns out.

The position of the Soviet manager is a bit like that of some Czechoslovak officials in a story I heard from an American Sovietologist. These officials were seeking to reduce a high rate of traffic accidents and appointed a committee to make suggestions for improved highway safety. After long deliberations the committee decided that the most effective approach would be to shift to British-style left-hand driving. At first the government was inclined to accept the committee's recommendation, but eventually it was decided that a wholesale shift to left-hand driving would be too radical a departure from the past. So, instead, trucks and buses were to move to the left side of the road, while other vehicles would continue, as before, on the right.

On the east bank of the Volga, where the steppes stretch barren and raw toward Central Asia and the Caspian Sea, a new industrial complex is rising. Where ten years ago there was nothing, today the city of Volzhsky has more than 100,000 people. Started as a camp to house the 30,000 workers involved in the building of the great Volgograd Hydroelectric Power Station, one of the largest in the world, Volzhsky has been turned into a permanent city. Thirty-three industrial plants have sprung up on the dusty plain (construction has started on a thirty-fourth), and they are turning out, among other diverse products, automobile tires, construction equipment, and synthetic rubber and fibers.

In Volzhsky, which is not far from Volgograd, I got a sense of the vigor and dynamism in Soviet life today. There is the headlong rush toward industrial expansion that has characterized the Soviet economy since Stalin consolidated his power in 1928 and 1929. There are plants in place. There are people working. There are products rolling out. But Volzhsky has another side, too. Even to my untrained eye, everything had the unmistakable appearance of a crash program—of buildings, factories, and trolley lines built at breakneck speed, and worry tomorrow about whether the quality is good or the cost was reasonable. In the "old" part of the town, apartment houses that were built less than ten years ago were clearly in need of repair. Their construction had been shoddy; the streets were narrow and dusty. In the newer part of town, where row on row of identical five-story apartment buildings are rising, the residential growth has run far ahead of essential municipal services, shopping facilities, and transportation. When I visited the "temporary" executive offices of the 80,000,000-ruble Volzhsky Synthetic Fibers Plant, I climbed a concrete staircase whose steps are already crumbling, even though the plant itself is far from completion.

The late Oskar Lange, a Polish economist who at one time taught at the University of Chicago and later became a high official in the post-World War II Polish government, once described the Soviet economy as "a *sui generis* war economy." His point was simply that since 1928 in the Soviet Union the overriding goal has been rapid industrialization, to the exclusion of practically everything else. This is not so far different from, say, the United States during World War II, when the nation's entire productive machine was geared to winning the war. "Very rapid industrialization," Lange said in a series of lectures in Belgrade in 1957, "which was necessary in the first socialist countries, particularly in the Soviet Union, as a political requirement of national defense and of the solution of all kinds of political and social problems, due to backwardness [of the prerevolutionary economy], requires centralized disposal of resources. . . . The process of rapid industrialization requires such centralized disposal of resources . . . to concentrate all resources on certain objectives and avoid dissipation of resources on other objectives which would divert resources from the purpose of rapid industrialization."

He gave an excellent description of what is known today as the "Stalinist" economic model. Stalin was obsessed—and, history shows, correctly so—by fear of foreign invasion and was determined to bend the entire effort of the Soviet nation to the construction of an industrial base adequate to support a modern military machine that would insure national survival. The purpose was deliberately to unbalance the Soviet economy. Industry was to come first; almost everything else—consumer goods, agriculture, and housing—was to follow.

Despite tremendous cost to the Soviet people in human suffering and loss of individual liberty, there is no question that the basic aims of Stalin's economic policies were accomplished. Soviet industrial expansion during the 1930's did provide the wherewithal to turn back the Nazi invasion in the 1940's. In the postwar period the vast wartime destruction was repaired, and the Soviet Union went on to build its position as the world's number-two industrial power. At the start of the industrialization drive the Soviet Union had four times the population of Great Britain but only a quarter of the British industrial output; today its output surpasses that of each of the Western European countries by a wide margin. Moreover, in a limited number of high-priority sectors of activity—aircraft design, hydroelectric-power generation, and space exploration are good examples—Soviet technology is among the most advanced in the world.

But as Professor Alec Nove, of the University of Glasgow, pointed out in the 1965 edition of his classic book, *The Soviet Economy,* "this system tends to outgrow itself, to the very extent to which it succeeds in establishing a modern industrialized economy and emerges into a period of relative normality." As the economy becomes more complex, as the number of "priority sectors" slated for rapid expansion multiplies, as it becomes more difficult to draw surplus agricultural labor into the industrial work force, Nove said, "a comparatively unsophisticated system [of the sort devised by Stalin] . . . becomes inadequate for the job."

In a centrally directed economy like the Soviet Union's, party functionaries and government bureaucrats have to allocate the nation's resources among a staggering number of possible end uses. It is not simply a question of making broad divisions between, say, investment in new industry, production of consumer goods, military spending, and spending for social welfare, but also of deciding how many autos, tractors, bobby pins, and television sets to turn out.

As an example, if automobile production is to increase by 10 per cent, the planners have to figure out how much this will increase the need for steel, glass, and rubber and how this in turn will affect all other sectors of the economy that use steel, glass, and rubber. In practice, of course, things never work out the way the planners intend, so over the years Soviet managers have had to resort to all sorts of extralegal devices to fulfill production targets assigned to them. One of the most common is the *tolkach* (literally, "pusher"), whose job it is to find scarce materials and through bribery or cajolery get them for his plant. In the judgment of one of the Soviet Union's leading mathematical economists, Viktor V. Novozhilov, who at seventy-five had just retired as chairman of the Department of Statistics of the Engineering-Economics Institute in Leningrad, the central planning mechanism has simply become "overwhelmed" by the vast number of interrelated choices that have to be made in putting together the annual economic plan. "The whole mechanism has to be more flexible," he told me.

But there is another factor, which has put powerful pressure on Soviet authorities to make their system more responsive, not to the desires of the central planners, but to the demands of the population. This is the very success that the regime has had in raising incomes in the country above the subsistence level. In 1955, for example, the average monthly wage (excluding collective-farm workers) was seventy-one and a half rubles; in 1966 it was ninety-nine rubles. The total spendable income of consumers has risen still more sharply, more than doubling, from 53 billion rubles in 1955 to over 120 billion rubles in 1966. During the same period of time retail prices (which, of course, are controlled by the government) have been roughly stable.

An average monthly wage of ninety-nine rubles ($109.89 at the official exchange rate) does not sound like much in comparison, say, with the average monthly earnings of factory workers in the United States, which were running more than $450 in mid-1967. But direct comparisons between the two countries are difficult, because a number of basic services—including housing, medical care, and local transportation—are furnished in the Soviet Union either at a fraction of cost or entirely without charge. A ride on the Moscow subway (probably the best in the world) costs only five kopecks; rent, including all utilities, is not likely to be more than a dozen or so rubles a month for a family of four; and medical care is free. Besides, in the Soviet Union the working wife is the rule rather than the exception, so in most families there are at least two breadwinners.

The Soviet consumer has shown a twofold reaction to this increasing affluence: first, his spending on goods and services has risen sharply (though less rapidly in recent years than in the first few years after Stalin's death in March, 1953); second, as incomes have pushed well above the subsistence level, he has become increasingly choosy about what he has been willing to buy. Rather than purchase shoddy, poorly constructed, or out-of-style goods, consumers have been quite willing to save their money instead (in accounts that pay 2-per-cent or 3-per-cent interest, depending on the type of account).

This pattern shows quite clearly in a decline in the growth of per-capita consumption, in a sharp increase in inventories of unsold goods, and in an even sharper climb in personal savings accounts. According to a study prepared for the Joint Economic Committee of the United States Congress by two American economists, David W. Bronson and Barbara S. Severin, the growth rate of per-capita consumption in the Soviet Union dropped from an annual average of 6 per cent for the years 1951 through 1955 to 2.5 per cent for 1963 through 1965, in large part because consumers have rebelled against the poor quality of the goods being offered to them for sale. Meanwhile, retail inventories have climbed more than twice as fast as sales. In clothing and other soft goods, for example, sales went up 9 per cent between 1960 and 1964, while inventories jumped 53 per cent, to a total of more than 12.7 billion rubles, or more than half of the total sales in 1964. According to Bronson and Severin, this happened despite "repeated price cuts for various commodities, particularly cloth, [that] have failed to increase the volume of sales significantly."

The behavior of the Soviet saver has been equally interesting. He added 4.2 billion rubles to his savings accounts last year, bringing them to a total of almost 23 billion rubles, up 22 per cent from the year before. According to official figures, there were 61,000,000 savings accounts, which averaged three hundred and seventy-seven rubles per account. In 1960 total savings were only 11 billion rubles and the average balance was two hundred and nine rubles.

The growing unpredictability of the consumer posed problems of crisis proportions for the consumer-goods industries, as massive stocks of unsold (and, in some cases, unsalable) goods piled up in the warehouses. Traditionally, Soviet industry has been geared to production, not to sales, so that if a factory was turning out dresses that nobody wanted to buy, or shoes that did not fit, this did not matter. All that counted was that the plant fulfill its annual production quota.

Professor Marshall I. Goldman, of Wellesley College, an expert in Soviet marketing problems, believes the mismatch between supply and demand in consumer goods has become sufficiently serious so that something like the ups and downs of a Western-style business cycle has started to appear in some Soviet industries.

The economic reform, which gears rewards to profits rather than production, is clearly aimed squarely at this problem. A manufacturer, whether in the Soviet Union or anywhere else, cannot make a profit unless he can sell what he produces. And under the reform Soviet retailers have considerable freedom in ordering the goods they stock. The individual store manager is increasingly replacing a bureaucrat at the Gosplan (the State Planning Committee) as the man who determines what is actually on the shelves. Vasily N. Bukin, the fast-talking thirty-nine-year-old director of the Kirov Department Store in Leningrad, told me that the system works two ways. If he guesses right, and the merchandise moves, then the store's profits will be high and there will be bigger bonuses for everybody. A wrong decision, and a sticky inventory, on the other hand, carries a risk of loss. Bukin would probably have little trouble making the adjustment if he were suddenly transferred from Kirov's in Leningrad to Korvette's on Fifth Avenue in New York City.

A diligent search of Soviet economic literature can turn up muted criticism of rigid central controls over the economy long before Stalin's death in 1953; some articles have been cited as far back as the early 1940's. But it was not until September, 1962, that Professor Yevsei G. Liberman, of

Kharkov State University, published, with at least the tacit blessing of Khrushchev, an article in *Pravda* arguing that the efficiency of the Soviet economy could be raised considerably if industry used profitability rather than production as its main yardstick of success and if, in addition, enterprises were allowed to gear their operations to customer demands rather than central-planning directives.

The Liberman article touched off an intense debate in the Soviet Union that led eventually to an experiment, starting in mid-1964, in which Bolshevichka (Woman Bolshevik) and Mayak (Light Beacon), two major clothing manufacturers, were switched over to a management system similar to that advocated by Liberman. Because of his key role in promoting this experiment, many Western analysts—notably Marshall Goldman—have given Liberman much of the credit not only for the initial test, but also for the far broader economic reforms that eventually followed. In my opinion, after talking to many Soviet economists (but not to Liberman), this greatly overstates the case and badly slights a large number of creative and surprisingly undoctrinaire Soviet economists who did much of the groundwork for the present reform and who seem determined to press for even greater liberalization in the future.

The leaders of this group, all of whom are strongly oriented to the use of mathematical techniques in economic analysis, are Professor Novozhilov, of the Leningrad Engineering-Economics Institute, Leonid V. Kantorovich, director of the Mathematical Economics Institute at Novosibirsk, and Nikolai P. Fedorenko, who heads a similar institute at the Academy of Sciences in Moscow. In 1965 Professors Novozhilov and Kantorovich, with another leading economist, the late Vasily Nemchinov, were awarded the Lenin Prize, despite bitter attacks from conservative Soviet economists, who accused them of all manner of bourgeois heresies.

Briefly put, all of these men had long been arguing—and loudly since the wraps were taken off the economics profession following the death of Stalin—that the Soviet Union had to have an economic system that was responsive to consumer needs and a price system that would reflect the shifting demands of the population. The latter might not be practical in the Soviet Union, they conceded, so they set about devising a mathematical system whereby the working of the marketplace could be imitated inside an electronic computer, which could then spew out hypothetical "shadow prices" that could guide the central planners to a correct or "optimum" allocation of the economy's scarce resources.

In any event the Bolshevichka-Mayak experiment was broadened in January, 1965, to include some four hundred plants in light industry as well as a few in the food industry plus a large number of retailers. Managers were given broad authority to do a great many things that previously had been dictated by the planning authorities in Moscow: they could make arrangements for materials and labor, set the total of their wage payments, decide how many workers to hire in each category, and make contracts directly with customers regarding product design, delivery dates, and details of transportation. Just about the only major power retained by the central authorities was that over wage rates.

Despite the new freedom, the plants had all kinds of problems in carrying out the experiment, largely because the government bureaucracy never fully reconciled itself to the increased independence the firms had gained and kept throwing roadblocks in the way. Shipments of materials were waylaid and diverted to other factories not involved in the experiment, and demands were made that plants meet old production quotas that no longer applied.

Even so, the government clearly was pleased at the way the experiment was going. By late spring of 1965, less than six months after the Bolshevichka-Mayak test was broadened, Moscow was buzzing with rumors that a major economic overhaul was in the wind.

The industry-wide reforms that Kosygin finally spelled out at the end of September (and which were implemented in a long series of directives and decrees published during the following months) had four principal features.

1. The machinery of the Soviet government for controlling the economy was recentralized in Moscow, as it had been originally under Stalin, thus scrapping the system of regional economic councils, abbreviated in Russian as *sovnarkhoz,* that Khrushchev had set up in 1957 in what was billed at that time as an attempt to decentralize the economy. According to the experts I interviewed, the reshuffle in 1957 had turned out to be not a genuine economic reform at all (as the Kosygin reforms are widely assumed to be), but, rather, a political move aimed principally at moving some of Khrushchev's entrenched political opponents out of Moscow. The same old tight government control of industry that characterized the Stalin era continued, with the sole exception that, instead of one agency barking orders, there were twenty or thirty, many of them working at cross-purposes.

2. Kosygin "proposed" a "complete set of measures" to "expand the economic independence and initiative of enterprises and associations [groups of enterprises working in the same or related industries under common control] and to raise the importance of the enterprise as the main economic unit in our economy." To accomplish this, he said, "excessive regulations" of industrial activity would be abolished (the number of centrally prescribed targets for performance would be cut from more than thirty to eight), and enterprises would be given the "necessary means for developing production" (through profits retained in the business or through bank loans).

Finally, funds would be created, also from accumulated profits, to pay special bonuses to the workers and to pay for new housing, "over and above the centralized resources allocated for this purpose," for kindergartens, for Young Pioneer camps, rest homes, sanatoriums, "and for other social and cultural needs."

3. There were to be eight targets, or success indicators, that would continue to be prescribed in Moscow. These indicators, which go to the economic heart of the current reform program, are as follows (in the order in which he named them): the volume of goods to be sold; the main assortment of goods to be produced; the total amount of money available to pay wages; the amount of profits and the level of profitability; payments to and allocations from the state budget; the volume of centralized capital investments; the main assignments for introducing new technology; allocation of materials. "All other indices of economic activity," the Premier said, "will be planned by the enterprise independently, without endorsement by a higher organization. This will relieve the enterprises of excessive control and will permit them to adopt the most economical decisions in the light of actual production conditions." As notable as any of the measures he mentioned was the one that he did not mention: the gross volume of output that generations of Soviet managers had used as their principal yardstick of success.

4. In order for the reform to succeed, there would have to be a general overhaul of the system of wholesale prices, which had not been revised since 1955 and were by that time far out of line with actual production costs. There was, however, to be no change in retail prices. In addition, Kosygin called for a streamlining of the system for supplying materials and equipment to eliminate the supply bottlenecks that traditionally have been endemic in the Soviet economy.

The overhaul of the price system, which went into effect in mid-1967, with wholesale-price increases that averaged about 15 per cent, is regarded by Soviet economists as especially important, for two reasons. First, since economic calculations have to be carried out largely in money terms (how else do you add together shoes, steel, and sulphuric acid?), if prices do not correspond closely to "value," however that is defined, the money yardstick gets rubbery, and the planner who is trying to allocate scarce resources among numerous competing uses has to grope in the dark. Second, the haphazard character of the Soviet price system had resulted over the years in wide disparities in the profitability of Soviet industry, with some sectors operating at profit rates that would make the most hardened capitalist drool and others showing big losses that were subsidized by the state. However, if enterprises were now to carry on a wide range of activities with funds accumulated from profits that formerly had been financed by the state, then prices had to be adjusted so that profits would be roughly constant throughout industry.

In the course of his talk Kosygin made no mention either of rent or of interest. This may have been because the words themselves have unfortunate connotations to the Marxist ear. In the directives that followed his announcement, though, it became clear that both were to be included in the new scheme of things, and, further, that their role was to be important.

Capital, which theretofore had been dispensed by the state as a "free good" (no charge was made for its use), would in the future carry a charge, which apparently would average out to be about 6 per cent. Enterprises in the extractive industries, such as mining or oil, would pay a differential rent charge, calculated to eliminate the possibility of windfall profits accruing to concerns with favorable natural situations. In addition, while the Soviet State Bank (the Gosbank) has traditionally charged interest on its loans, the proportion of new investment to be financed with borrowed money is to rise, so that interest payments are sure to bulk larger in the profit and loss statements of Soviet enterprises than ever before. (Under the reform, interest rates will range from 1 per cent to 8 per cent, depending on the character of the loan and whether or not it is repaid on time.) Moreover, the "net profit" figure from which bonuses are to be paid was to be calculated after payment of capital charges, rent, and interest.

In my opinion, the charges for capital and rent represent the boldest attack in the entire Kosygin reform on the deep-seated Soviet problem of inefficiency in new investments. But only time will tell whether, in the Soviet environment, they will be adequate to root out the waste of resources that for so long has been characteristic of the system.

By and large, the Kosygin reform followed the model that had been established in the Bolshevichka-Mayak experiment. But there were a couple of significant and interesting differences that throw some light on the government's attitude toward the reform and the direction that it is likely to take in the future. First, enterprise managers got a good deal less freedom to run their own businesses than was accorded the heads of the pilot plants. Second, the key concept of profitability—which is really the most important index of the manager's ability as a businessman rather than as a production engineer—was redefined. Where previously profitability had been defined as net profit as a per cent of sales, now it was to be profit as a per cent of total capital investment. It is clear to me that here, too, as in the case of the capital and interest charges, the thrust of the reform is to reward managers for getting a maximum yield from the assets that have been entrusted to them.

As originally scheduled, the reform was to be fully in effect by the beginning of 1968, but this has been considerably delayed. I was told that by mid-1967 only 4,700 enterprises, accounting for about 30 per cent of the Soviet Union's gross industrial output, had been brought under the reform, and the prospects were that it would be late 1968 or early 1969 before the process was complete.

In a sense, the reform starts to bring the Soviet economy full circle. During the first three years following the Bolshevik Revolution—the period known to historians as "War Communism"—the fledgling Soviet economy all but collapsed under the pressure of widespread civil war, foreign military intervention, and domestic mismanagement by untrained revolutionaries. Lenin's answer, starting in March, 1921, was a strategic retreat to the "commanding heights" of the economy. Free enterprise, private initiative, and a considerable measure of capitalism were not only allowed but were actually encouraged, while at the same time the government remained in firm control of basic industry and the financial structure (such as they were). In a burst of enthusiasm, Walter Duranty, then *The New York Times* correspondent in Moscow, reported that "Lenin has thrown communism overboard." This was incorrect, for by the end of the decade the government was as firmly in control of the economy as ever, but the fact remained that only by turning to private initiative were the Bolsheviks able to accomplish the essential job of reconstruction.

I would be the last to argue that there is any direct parallel between the economic crisis that faced Lenin in 1921 and the impasse of a falling economic growth rate with which the U.S.S.R. is trying to struggle today. Yet in both instances individual initiative has proved to be a tantalizing alternative to rigid central controls. I disagree completely with the people who argue that "creeping capitalism" is already evident in the Soviet Union. Still, the seeds of market socialism have been planted, and they may yet flower.

Nikolai Fedorenko told me that he could not understand the paradox between the government's decision to begin to decentralize economic planning and its retention of tight central control over the price structure. "It has been recognized that it is impossible to have central planning of everything down to the tiniest nail," he said, "yet it seems that the price of the nail has to be set from the center." Curious, indeed. I agree with Mr. Fedorenko.

EDUCATION:
THE PRESCHOOL CHILD

»

Fred M. Hechinger

It is difficult to single out any recognizable, distinguishing landmark in describing those semisuburban, residential neighborhoods that ring the "new Moscow." On both sides of the wide main thoroughfares, with their rapid and somewhat chaotic commercial traffic, stand the large, rectangular, sprawling apartment buildings that aim at looking Scandinavian but achieve instead more the appearance of the charmless workingmen's housing complexes of Germany in the 1920's. Once your car veers off the boulevard and into the maze of narrow, unpaved paths and occasional clearings with benches for tired *babushkas* (grandmothers), it is virtually impossible to find any address without the aid of a familiar resident. Even the local folk were arguing among themselves when my driver asked for directions to Kindergarten 67. Not even the added information that it was located on Karbyshev Boulevard, Block 82, Building 118 was much help.

What complicates the search is the fact that kindergartens are liberally sprinkled among the drab newish apartment houses. While they are immediately recognizable by the spacious outdoor playgrounds, with their sedate green-chaired swings, reminiscent of suspended lovers' benches on

Southern back porches, they are as standardized in their two-story construction pattern as are the taller apartment structures they serve.

At last, despite the conflicting advice of some helpful *babushkas,* we found Kindergarten 67, walked past the curious, giggling huddles of youngsters, and soon were watching a game of musical chairs and some pleasantly disorganized efforts at organized dancing to the assertive rhythm of an upright piano. Before long, a group of youngsters, seated on little chairs in a bright, airy, toy-studded classroom, were clapping their hands and, with gay blue and red hair ribbons bobbing up and down, singing a song about the chores little boy Lenin did with good cheer, always helpful, like a good Boy Scout.

Kindergarten 67 had been selected according to my specifications: a school that was in a residential area but not in the center of the city and that represented the general plan of organization and construction now in use. In the Soviet Union as in the United States many kindergartens must get along with makeshift and improvised facilities, but the trend toward the kind of establishment typified by Kindergarten 67 is quite evident. Spot checks in other parts of the city and in Leningrad confirmed this. Naturally, the pattern may change, but since the prototype is relatively inexpensive and easy to build, this is unlikely for the time being.

Later in the morning, I sat in the small, plain, comfortable office of Madame Sofia Borisovna Shvedova, the director of Kindergarten 67, a determined, soft-spoken, plumpish, middle-aged lady with an unruly shock of wiry, almost black hair. A grown-up Lenin looked benignly down from a large picture frame as Madame Shvedova said in polite but unmistakable reproach: "I feel that the United States is neglecting the moral education of children."

Soviet children in nursery school, at the age of three or even younger, begin to be made aware of the importance of a strong and pure character, she said, and this is best accomplished through children's stories and songs about the boyhood life and struggle of Lenin, the national hero.

I suggested that the difference between our two countries' approach to children might not be as great as it appeared across the geographic and ideological distance. After all, American youngsters enjoy the famous story about George Washington, who could not tell a lie about having chopped down the cherry tree. They learn about Jefferson's inventiveness, about Lincoln's boyhood in the log cabin, about the practical Ben Franklin. They study the tenacious idealism of Tom Paine and the persistence of Franklin D. Roosevelt in overcoming the ravages of polio. They learn to admire the courage of Charles Lindbergh. . . .

Madame Shvedova interrupted me with a patient smile. Children need a simple and concrete approach to moral fiber and patriotism, she said, adding that this is best accomplished by focusing on one person, with whom they become thoroughly familiar.

I reminded Madame Shvedova that the American Revolution took place almost two hundred years ago—almost four times as long ago as that of the Bolsheviks—and therefore a great many more national heroes had piled up in our past, making it both difficult and undesirable to single out one person. (It would hardly have been tactful to remind the director of the fact that Lenin happened to be almost the only Soviet national hero whose reputation had not been tarnished since 1917.)

She was not persuaded. "You think we have too much cult of personality," she said, and then insisted that the inculcation of young children with the basic virtues must be made simple and uncomplicated to be effective.

At this point it appeared evident that, given a chance to reform American preschool education, Madame Shvedova would prescribe exactly what the Daughters of the American Revolution would were they empowered to run the nation's schools. Nor is this surprising; for Madame Shvedova is, of course, a daughter of the Russian Revolution.

The fundamental point that emerged from this conversation was that the staunchest defenders of the Soviet revolution, in particular the Communist party, its Central Committee, and its youth organizations (the Young Communist League and the Pioneers), are Soviet Russia's and Soviet education's most conservative force.

It would, however, be misleading to dwell too long on Madame Shvedova's concern with ideology and Lenin's boyhood. For the fact is that she presides over an exemplary venture in early childhood and preschool education—a nursery school and kindergarten for a hundred and fifty children which, though a typical establishment for youngsters from just below two up to seven years of age, is by no means merely a showcase. The daily routine of Kindergarten 67 provides an introduction to Russian ways of bringing up children.

The youngsters are delivered by their parents between seven and eight o'clock in the morning. They are divided into six groups of about twenty-five children each. Breakfast, at 8:15, is the first of three meals served during the day. Each group is supervised by one teacher and an aide, usually an older woman.

Perhaps underscoring the essential class consciousness of Soviet society, the teacher is invariably an upper-class "professional"—fashionably dressed and coiffed—and more often than not young and attractive, while the aide or "upbringer" is a grandmotherly type in a cook's or perhaps a nanny's light-blue apron. While both appear to be equally close to the children and generally work harmoniously together, there is never any doubt as to who is in charge—always the "specialist" and not the servant.

Although the atmosphere is free and easy, the day is organized according to a strict timetable. The younger children almost always work in pairs or in small groups, and there is much stress on developing good speech habits and co-ordination. Each year the work becomes a little more serious, and during the last year (when American children would actually be in first grade) the preparation for school turns more formal, with some stress on counting up to ten, recognition of letters, and tentative experimentation with reading. Some children are taught to play the piano, and in some kindergartens English instruction is offered to four-year-olds.

The general impression, however, is one of greater relaxation and more emphasis on play rather than academic learning than in many American kindergartens. While the "new class" of Soviet parents—the university-educated and education-conscious new upper middle class—is beginning to push for an earlier start (with a premature eye, as in the United States, on university admission), the conservatives among early-childhood educators in the Soviet Union so far have been fairly successful in resisting the pressures. Quite naturally, therefore, Madame Shvedova expressed surprise over my own six-year-old son's kindergarten-level work with numbers and letters.

For those Russian children who attend nursery school and kindergarten —attendance is not compulsory, and the fee ranges from two to twelve rubles a month, according to the parents' income—the experience affects more of their total day and interests than for American children. Most kindergartens have a small dormitory with white metal and white-sheeted cribs. If the parents have jobs which make it difficult to take care of their children, youngsters may board at the school during weekdays, and even nonboarders may be left overnight if the parents want to have a late evening at the theater or visit relatives in the country.

Each school has a well-equipped medical office and the services of a doctor and a nurse. Parents are given monthly health reports, including details of weight and growth.

At 10:30 we went to the kitchen, where the two comfortably fussing cooks spread out a large napkin and insisted that I eat a complete sample of the children's lunch: vegetable soup, diced liver with mashed potatoes, and a liquid fruit gelatin. The director tasted every course and pointed out that this is a requirement to make sure that the youngsters' food is up to par.

A visitor to Russia learns quickly that children enjoy a very special status. Perhaps it is because adult life is, and has always been, so hard and drab that Russians lavish all the care they can afford on their children. It may be that nostalgia for a paradise soon to be lost leads to an almost frantic effort to make the children's lives as happy and carefree as possible. Perhaps, too, in the way of American parents of Depression vintage, Russians are trying to give their children the advantages they themselves have lacked. Finally, in a society which discourages hereditary wealth, it may be especially tempting to lavish goods and comforts on the young. At any rate, in Moscow, where shops and department stores still offer few items of high style and superior quality, there are huge children's stores overflowing with well-made, colorful, and relatively inexpensive toys, from gay inflatable rubber ducks to fine bicycles with training wheels.

While Russia's adults would win few prizes for stylish attire, the youngsters in nursery school and kindergarten look as though they had just emerged from a children's fashion show, with bright reds and blues, manly sport shirts, and very ladylike pleated skirts setting the tone. And the nursery schools are jam-packed with well-made wooden and plastic toys—operational trains and hobby horses as well as boy-size automobiles—and with a seemingly endless variety of individual "sets"—ducks, clowns, and, of course, red stars—for every child.

In a country where living space is still desperately short and where a young couple with one or two small children (the maximum number most urban Soviet families can afford) must often still share the parents' or in-laws' two or three rooms, space seems to be lavished on the preschoolers. In the more recently constructed nurseries, the classrooms are huge and bright, with adjoining washrooms and ample sinks and toilets. The locker rooms are spacious, with a locker for every child. Although Russian workmanship tends to be shabby, the child-size furniture is well made and attractively decorated with colorful formica tops and pictures of little bears and other animals on the backs of the chairs.

The school I visited was set in more than an acre of ground, with small, covered lean-tos which can be used as outdoor classrooms, a small swimming pool and a wading pool, with water spouting from the mouth of a huge clay fish. Inlets of water enabled children to float their small boats.

What are the major ingredients of Soviet preschool child care and child rearing? How does the Russian way of dealing with the young influence adult behavior and attitudes? These questions are crucial to any understanding of life in the Soviet Union.

Current Soviet practices can be understood only in the perspective of history. After the Bolshevik Revolution and in the early 1920's, Russian educators looked for a way to hold out to pedagogy the promise of total freedom that had given political slogans much of their spellbinding power. This, after all, was the moment when breaking the chains of past restraints meant, to theoreticians and the masses alike, absolute freedom—freedom from the ruling autocracy, freedom from hunger and want and even from the laws of economics themselves, freedom from moral and religious taboos, freedom from family dictates, free love, free everything.

Soviet educators did not have far to look for the prescription. The United States was deep in experimentation with progressive education—the classroom in which the teacher became the adviser rather than the dominant authority symbol, the school and family in which permissiveness was to release the youngsters' native talents and creativity.

Quite understandably, therefore, John Dewey and his disciples became the heroes of the Soviet school. Stanislav Shatsky and Pavel Blonsky became the Soviet leaders of the progressive movement, and Nadezhda Krupskaya, Lenin's widow and an eminent educator in her own right, added luster to the movement.

At no time, however, did the Soviet version of the "learning by doing" approach to dealing with children retain the American restraints of educational experimentation and moderation. With characteristic revolutionary zeal, permissiveness was made total.

The abortive political theory of the withering away of the state led to the parallel goal of the withering away of the school. The teacher was not merely demoted to an advisory or guiding position; she was virtually condemned to educational impotence. Schools were run by student committees. Textbooks were abolished and replaced with sloganeering pamphlets. Homework was outlawed. Examinations were denounced as a form of bourgeois exploitation and abolished. Students formed brigades, and the brigade leader, in oral tests, was able to "pass" the entire group, without any check on individual achievements.

The orgy of total freedom was not to last long. By 1930 a serious reaction had set in. In 1931 the Central Committee of the Communist party issued a decree that demanded that the schools do more serious preparation. It called the progressive movement a failure because it had not provided society with the technical skills it needed so desperately if production was to be improved. It conceded that many youngsters had become generally well adjusted but said they lacked "the most elementary knowledge."

In the following year the Central Committee became more specific. The authority of school administrators and teachers was re-established. Textbooks were introduced. The People's Commissar for Education, Andrei S. Bubnov, more renowned as Stalin's lackey than as an educator, said: "Our next task is to re-establish discipline in the schools."

This was only the beginning. By 1936, at the outset of Stalin's great purges, the leaders of Soviet education's first era had disappeared. Anatoly V. Lunacharsky, Lenin's close friend and ideological adviser and the People's Commissar for Education for the first twelve years of the revolution, had died in 1933, and Shatsky the following year. Blonsky was arrested, and died in 1941 in a forced-labor camp. The use of child psychology and intelligence tests was outlawed. Dewey became the symbol of bourgeois, and even imperialist, reaction.

In the years that followed, a new star rose on the educational horizon—Anton Semyonovich Makarenko—and he proved to be a durable educational light, in part because he was singularly adaptable, but also because he tended to be educationally less dogmatic and politically more astute than either the extreme progressives or Bubnov.

Makarenko's background suited him ideally for the task. Following the revolution the Russian countryside was terrorized by roving gangs of children and adolescents, without homes, families, or support. These "wild children" lived by theft, robbery, and worse. Makarenko became the key figure in the establishment of special boarding schools—"colonies"—for delinquents, and while the regular establishment was off on its spree of total permissiveness, Makarenko began to achieve astounding success in the rehabilitation of these brutalized youngsters. His experimental methods leaned heavily on the creation of group-imposed discipline, with self-discipline as the ultimate goal.

In later years Makarenko adamantly denied that his experience and theories were in any way confined to the care and education of delinquents. He became, and has remained, the most popular Soviet writer on problems of bringing up children, at home and in school—a kind of cross between Dr. Benjamin Spock and Dr. James B. Conant. Among his popular writings are *The Road to Life* and *Learning to Live*. In his stress on "the collective"—the Russian equivalent for "the group" in American education—he created the Lincolnesque slogan "In the collective, by the collective, for the collective."

As Stalinist authoritarianism became another discredited chapter in the revolutionary history, the schools sought a more normal way of functioning and of satisfying the demands of a people with a deeply ingrained love of children. And so it is the Makarenko guidelines that today seem to set much of the tone. For example, he warns: "Threats and reprimands are often used to achieve subordination. As a result of this approach children become liars, cowards, rude, and high-strung."

He adds: "Parents avoid direct contact with children and delegate their authority to others, such as grandmothers, nannies, and older siblings. This kind of behavior brings about a break between parents and children; the latter withdraw, become introverted and distrustful, and often easily fall under bad influences."

It is equally wrong, he continues, for parents to "bribe" their children with rewards, with the result that the youngsters "learn how to be calculating and self-centered."

In today's Soviet preschool approach, the three most striking factors are a genuine love for children, a tendency toward extreme protectiveness, and early inculcation of the importance of the group—Makarenko-style—above the individual. Out of these basic attitudes grows Soviet society, with all its facets, good and bad, its sense of family loyalty, its considerable stoicism in the face of hardships, its conformity, and its reliance on orders and instructions.

In the dining room of the Hotel National in Moscow, at the height of the breakfast rush, four waitresses (who generally indicated little interest in the guests' orders or preferences) vied with each other to serve, entertain, and keep happy a pretty little three-year-old American girl. In no time the room appeared to have been turned into a nursery and the waitresses into a cross between nurses and doting grandmothers. One of the European guests, visibly annoyed, said: "In Germany, France, and most civilized countries they would tell the mother that children are not allowed in the dining room."

The driver who had taken me to one of the nursery schools I visited had seemed a particularly dour, noncommunicative type. Yet only minutes after our arrival I looked out of a classroom window and saw the same driver, smiling broadly, dancing around the yard with a laughing child at each hand.

But as obvious as the Russians' love for children is their extreme protectiveness. Youngsters almost invariably seem overdressed—babies wrapped in bottomless layers of blankets and older children still buttoned up in overcoats on warm spring days. An American professor, who with his wife and four children spent a year in Moscow, said that the teachers frequently lectured him and his wife about their apparent neglect in clothing their youngsters. "We were made to feel that we were sending our kids half naked to school," he said.

Fathers carrying their strapping five-year-old sons piggyback through Moscow's streets are a familiar sight.

One woman educator eyed a picture of my two young sons, both of whom are considered well nourished by an American pediatrician's standards, and said: "Send us your baby and we will fatten him up."

During a visit to a kindergarten I noticed that a little boy, who apparently had stubbed his toe, was crying. Within seconds the teacher had thrown her arms around him and was consoling him.

Americans who have had young children accompany them in the Soviet Union report that they have been publicly criticized by strangers if they permitted the youngsters to stray twenty or thirty yards away while playing in the park. Russian women, especially of the older, grandmotherly type, consider this a sign of neglect. Moreover, the official theory, expressed in every manual about child care, is that everybody is responsible for assuring that youngsters are brought up properly. Neglect or mistreatment of any child thus becomes everybody's business. And the theory, reinforced by a demonstrative love of children, is so broadly interpreted that free advice and even criticism, handed out to complete strangers, is considered perfectly normal, when it might be resented as meddling in other people's affairs under similar circumstances in the United States.

While Russians tend to overprotect and overpraise their children, they also use the reverse of this technique of child rearing: as the principal form of discipline they withhold their love and approval. In fact, Russian child-care manuals suggest just such withdrawals of affection—temporarily but demonstratively—as the basic form of punishment, just as they strictly rule out corporal punishment.

Thus the mother disciplines the misbehaving child by not smiling at him and by giving him the silent treatment for several hours, after having delivered an emotion-charged lecture, perhaps with a hint of tears, about the personal disappointment and hurt the disobedience has brought to a mother who has always done so much for the ungrateful offspring. Similarly, a teacher will punish a young pupil by not calling on him or her for the rest of the period and by giving the impression that she is looking straight through the culprit as though the space he occupies were empty.

Apparently, this highly personal, emotion-laden approach is effective. The fact that this is so also documents the closeness of relationships and bonds between young and old. And when the period of temporary "estrangement" is over, there appears to be no lingering resentment. After the penance, the old warmth returns.

Equally important in the Russian approach to rearing children is the early stress on being a member of, and responsible to, the group. In those child-care centers that accept very young infants, the tots are placed into the playpens in twos, threes, and fours rather than by themselves as they are in the United States.

In nursery school, at age three and four, when in the United States the typical effort is to get children used to working in pairs, the Soviet emphasis is already on the larger group. There is a good deal of group dancing and singing.

Whenever possible, the songs and games have a moral. One group of twenty-four five-year-olds, sitting cross-legged on the floor, was enjoying a funny song about a little boy who did everything wrong, and while the youngsters delighted in his problem it was clear that the hidden intent of the verses was to teach children how to do things right.

Professor Urie Bronfenbrenner, of Cornell University, who has been one of the most perceptive commentators on both American and Soviet preschool education, has pointed out that when American three-year-olds are shown pictures and asked to talk about what they see, these "tests" of the children's reactions scrupulously avoid calling for any "right answers." Not so in Russia. "Each of the pictures depicted a child engaged in some clearly desirable or undesirable activity," Professor Bronfenbrenner reported. "On one page, a little boy was shown buttoning a heavy overcoat for his younger brother; in another, a little girl was wiping her still dirty hands on a clean towel."

Subsequently, the children were shown a picture of a little girl who went on playing with her toys while the rest of the group was busy cleaning up the room. The teacher asked whether the children saw anything familiar in this. They quickly responded: "Masha! She doesn't help." When Masha, a pretty youngster in a blue dress, seemed close to tears, the teacher quickly rescued her from the cruelty of such peer censure. "Masha used to do things like that, but she doesn't any longer," she said. "We all see her helping gladly now." End of lesson.

Not long ago in a Moscow public school attended by two American teen-agers—a girl who spoke Russian fluently and a boy who had recently arrived and understood only a little Russian—an incident underlined the Russian emphasis on family and group loyalties. The American boy had amused himself with the time-honored trick of drawing faces on the back of his hand and making them grimace by stretching and contracting the skin. A Russian boy, sitting next to him, copied the trick and was caught doing so by the teacher. The latter scolded him for not paying attention to the lesson, but then raised her voice in emphasis. "Worst of all," she said, "you have corrupted your American neighbor."

The American boy failed to understand what was happening. But the American girl, stung by the injustice done to the Russian classmate, rose to his defense. "It was not the Russian who corrupted his American friend," she told the teacher. "It was the other way around."

For the moment the incident seemed closed. But after class the teacher asked the American girl to see her privately. "You have done a terrible thing," the teacher said. "You were disloyal to your group." It seemed, by Russian standards, wrong not to uphold the honor of the group, the family, the class, et cetera—a far greater failing than letting a boy outside the group be unjustly accused.

This is a crucial lesson, as important an element in Russian child rearing as it is to an understanding of the Russians' extreme clannishness and their readiness to close ranks and defend their and their government's action whenever an outsider questions it.

This explains much that, often mistakenly, is usually attributed to a slavish submission to the official propaganda line. For example, during my stay in Moscow, the news about the defection of Stalin's daughter spread like wildfire. Nothing had yet been printed in the Soviet press, but the British Broadcasting Corporation, the Voice of America, and an effective grapevine had already made the episode the talk of the town. Since the public had, however, not yet been informed by its own government that the event had actually happened, it was clear that no "line" existed on what people ought to think about it. Yet, almost invariably, the reaction was one of antagonism and spontaneously, almost personally, hurt feelings. Apart from the condemnation of a mother leaving her children ("How could she do this?"), there was the equally strong disapproval of disloyalty to the group. "My group—right or wrong" is one of the most fundamental "moral concepts" that are made part of Soviet youngsters' reflexes from early nursery-school age on.

Along with this basic attitude goes the companion concept of giving the peer group great powers over behavior and discipline. The teacher early bows out of the routine role of being the enforcer of the rules. Since violation of group standards and pride is so severely frowned upon, the punitive action can readily be left to peer disapproval. Indeed, since in Russia as elsewhere youngsters tend to be far more unforgiving disciplinarians, the adult role tends to be one—as it was in Masha's case—of reducing the peer-inflicted penalties.

Even in the universities it is the students who are responsible for disciplining offenders, and it is the undergraduates rather than the administration who wield the power of suspension or expulsion. "Usually our task is to veto such stern measures," said a university administrator in Moscow. "Young people, you know, tend to be too cruel toward each other."

Professor Bronfenbrenner described a case in which the leader of one elementary school's Pioneer group and seven of his classmates were caught swimming illegally and without supervision. The offense took on particularly serious proportions because apparently a youngster had drowned under similar circumstances a year before.

But the school's only punitive action was directed at the parents, who were summoned and told about their children's misbehavior. When one mother, by way of excuse, said she had not known where her son was, the principal reacted sternly. "That is exactly the problem. Nothing could be more serious. I would rather be told that your son is getting failing grades, or that he speaks rudely to a teacher. But when it is a matter of endangering his life, that must not be permitted."

The actual punitive action was left to the peers, who summoned a council meeting and, in the course of a long hearing, threatened such severe punishment—including barring the culprits from summer camp—that the adult observer, a Young Communist League representative, eventually suggested an effort to make the punishment fit the crime. Eventually, some special chores and a week's probation were agreed upon.

There is one important similarity in the Soviet and American approaches to bringing up children and young people: the great stress on the peer group. The major difference, however, appears to be that the American tendency, following years of permissiveness, is to regard peer groups as independent "subcultures," governed by standards of their own making. This is especially pronounced in the adolescent or teen-age brackets. By contrast, the Russians, while relying equally strongly on the peer groups, labor mightily to impose on these groups traditional—*i.e.,* adult—standards, mores, and morals. This, of course, begins almost imperceptibly with far greater moralizing in the games and songs in nursery school and the love and withdrawal-of-love penalty within the family.

In its extreme, neither approach is without pitfalls. The excesses of the American subcultures, once the lines of communication between generations have been cut, are too familiar to require documentation. But the too rigidly adult-proscribed and tradition-bound Soviet pattern carries germs of trouble at the other extreme, and not necessarily only in terms of political submissiveness. By imposing adult viewpoints, standards, and techniques on such activities as nursery-school drawing and painting, the Russians may well stifle the children's creativity, originality, and spontaneity.

Excessive American permissiveness and excessive Soviet domination by adult tradition, because they are extremes, lead to some of the same undesired effects of hostility to society. Juvenile delinquency, or, as the Russians call it, hooliganism, with stress on antisocial gang action, is no strange phenomenon in either culture. In fairness, it must be conceded that the American problems on this score seem to be more troublesome than the Soviet Union's.

Professor Bronfenbrenner's conclusion on this vital aspect of Soviet and American attitudes toward early-childhood education bears consideration. He reported: "If the Russians go too far in subjecting both the child and his peer group to conformity with a single set of values imposed by the adult society, perhaps we have reached the point of diminishing returns in allowing excessive autonomy and in failing to utilize the constructive potential of the peer group in developing social responsibility and consideration for others. Moving to counteract this tendency does not mean subscribing to Soviet insistence on the primacy of the collective over the individual or of adopting their practice of shifting major responsibility for upbringing from the family to public institutions. On the contrary, what is called for is greater involvement of parents, and other adults, in the lives of children, and—conversely—greater involvement of children in responsibility in behalf of their own family, community, and society at large."

Makarenko is too shrewd an observer and educational pragmatist to overlook some of these contradictory problems. He wrote: "Only a blending of the individual approach while setting and upholding group standards can bring about positive results. Of course, this delineation is of a very delicate nature and requires great skill on the part of a pedagogue. I often ask myself, where do I set legitimate limits while guiding my pupils? How much advice is desirable, and when does it change to coercion? The right of the pedagogue and his good intentions alone do not qualify him for this task. He has to have tact and sensitivity in dealing with each case individually."

But on one score he has no doubt: the kind of total permissiveness from which both the Soviet and the American child-rearing efforts have learned an unhappy lesson must be avoided. "The logic of our discipline," he said, "places each individual in a position of greater security and freedom. This paradox is easily understood by children, who find it verified in every step of their experience. Discipline in the group is a full guarantee of the rights and potentials of each individual."

Leaving all social and political theories aside, a visit to the Soviet Union's nursery schools and kindergartens underlines the importance of preschool education, which is only just being discovered in the United States.

This is not to say that there are not some Soviet parents who are considerably reluctant to send their children to "school" so early. Such opposition is widespread, and in fact only a minority of children across the country attend the early-childhood preschool classes. (Soviet statistics on this are not reliable, but a fair guess is that perhaps 25 per cent of all children get some preschool education, including 40 per cent in urban areas and 10 per cent in rural areas.)

As in the United States, the gap between those who have had preschool advantages and those who have not has become something of a threat. In a familiar theme, increasing numbers of "new class," educated parents are insisting on an early start in reading—with an eye to the distant future of admission to a high-prestige university, a kind of Russian counterpart to the Ivy League syndrome.

There are strong indications that the traditionalist Soviet educators, who, like their colleagues in the United States, have in the past resisted pressures toward preschool reading, are losing their battle. The Ministry of Education of the Russian Republic, which determines national policies, has authorized a special booklet of guidelines to show parents how to start their preschool children on the road to reading and basic numbers concepts if they are not getting such advantages in kindergarten. And, in large part as a result of the earlier start of learning, high-level Soviet pedagogical planners are hard at work on a new curriculum which would condense the present four-year elementary school into three years, giving extra time and scope to the more advanced instruction in the remaining seven years of the middle and secondary grades.

Meanwhile, there is little question that the role of preschool education is being taken more seriously in Russia than in the United States. Perhaps most important, the Russians have worked hard at overcoming the weakness for which the American preschool and Head Start programs have been most severely criticized—lack of continuity between preschool and school levels. Soviet elementary-school teachers regularly visit the kindergartens from which they will receive their pupils, and the preschool personnel take an active hand in the placement of their youngsters in the schools.

Madame Shvedova, the self-possessed and outspoken director of Moscow's Kindergarten 67, expressed great interest in, and admiration for, some recent experimental practices in American preschool education. She listened to an account of a program which permits youngsters, on their own initiative, to play and "work" in a so-called "numbers room"—a special classroom in which all the games and the decor are related to numbers. She was interested in the kind of physical activities—sports and exercises—engaged in to let children get rid of their aggressions.

But in the end, she said with a tinge of irony: "Now you are beginning to understand preschool education. You always thought we were just mean—locking up the kids and taking them away from their parents."

Yet even this competent educator's "I told you so" must be modified by the opinions and sentiments of that universal force of human doubt and questioning—the parents. Only recently, said Madame Shvedova, she had to call a parents' meeting to deliver a serious lecture to the mothers and fathers. Every evening, she explained, when the parents come to pick up their children they bring them toys and candy bars. "It is because they feel guilty for having left their children with us all day, and to get rid of their guilty conscience they spoil their children," she said.

The conflict between parents and pedagogy, school and home, family and society clearly is not just an American phenomenon.

EDUCATION:
TRIUMPHS AND DOUBTS

»

Fred M. Hechinger

Every weekday, shortly after the noon hour, one of the main lecture halls of the Institute of Foreign Languages is transformed into a motion-picture auditorium. Down ancient staircases and out of adjoining buildings and annexes students wander in, some carrying lunches of sandwiches, candy bars, apples and oranges, to attend the special screening of a foreign feature film, often an avant-garde French, Italian, English, or American picture of the kind not shown in Moscow's movie houses.

It is a fringe benefit as well as a shrewd teaching device—a kind of improve-your-accent-while-you-eat come-on. It is also typical of the atmosphere of modern pragmatic scholarship that belies the institute's outward appearance in its maze of ancient czarist buildings in old Moscow. The buildings may look obsolete, more suitable for the teaching of medieval than modern languages, but, three flights up, the old semiruins house as elaborate an array of electronic language laboratories as any institution in the world. The institute is engaged in computerized analysis of accents, intonations, and linguistic characteristics. Yet its students still spend hours in hair-splitting discussions of grammatical fine points. And few, if any, ordinary Soviet elementary and secondary schools use the devices of modern teaching technology in their foreign-language instruction.

The Soviet Union is proud of the low cost of books, and even the most pro-American Russians shake their heads in disapproval when they spy the price on an American book's dust jacket. At the same time, Russian university students complain bitterly about the difficulty of obtaining many basic books, required in their courses. Because of the lack of communication between the consumers and the officials who decide which books to mass produce, some titles that 300,000 students need annually are run off the presses in editions of 20,000, while others that are in small demand flood the market by the millions.

Higher education is free, and in theory the Soviet Union subscribes to the idea of a classless society. In fact, however, high-prestige universities, such as Moscow's and Leningrad's, the Soviet Union's Ivy League, have a far more middle- and upper-middle-class enrollment than their American equivalents. And the more socially conscious Soviet education leaders are advocating a special program to prepare rural boys and girls for the stiff competition for university admission, in a manner reminiscent of the compensatory education programs for deprived Negro youngsters in the United States.

In theory, the Soviet Union is committed to the proposition that all pupils are created equal and that, if good teaching clears the way, all will be able to benefit from the same curriculum, without any need to separate the bright from the slow. But in practice, more and more of the able students are siphoned off into the most fashionable, high-prestige schools of the system, the specialized schools in which intensive instruction is offered in one field, such as English or physics or mathematics. And the most education-conscious parents—the counterpart of those in America who push their children into the select private schools or into public schools such as the Bronx High School of Science, in New York—leave no stone unturned and no string unpulled to get their children into the special schools. At a parent meeting in a Moscow special school an irate woman disrupted the proceedings and set off a violent floor debate when she demanded to know: "Why was my child refused admission to this school?"

The point of these random observations is that the Soviet education system presents a study in contrasts. The most modern and the most obsolete teaching techniques exist side by side. The ideal of the classless society is hampered by a class-conscious people and by the rapid rise of an educated and education-conscious "new class"—*nouveau riche* in educational rather than in material advantages.

Soviet education, after fifty years of frantic build-up and many zigs and zags in the politico-pedagogical line, presents a picture of a huge, centrally controlled machine, generally successful in specific, often short-term goals, but held back by a deep professional conservatism, reinforced by an iron-clad political preservation of the *status quo*. But while the conservative lid is kept on by old-fashioned pedagogues and political hacks, ferment is ripe. New ideas are demanding to be heard, and there are indications that the system may be on the verge of far-reaching changes.

The accomplishments of the system are remarkable. The Soviet Union inherited a predominantly uneducated peasant country, with an estimated illiteracy rate of about 75 per cent. While the czarist secondary schools were, in the French-German tradition, of creditable quality, they served only a fraction of the population. The intelligentsia was too alienated from society and from the sources of power to constitute more than a separatist island within the total culture. The gulf between educated and ignorant was too wide to be bridged, too wide even to tempt the educational have-nots to try to cross it.

While there had been occasional rumblings of dissatisfaction, even among a few czarist education experts, the general mood was one of continuing restrictions, fed by the fear—entirely justified—that a more educated populace would soon demand more liberal policies. It was quite in character, in the first half of the nineteenth century, for Count Sergei S. Uvarov, Minister of Education under Czar Nicholas I, to demand that the Russian schools dedicate themselves to "the truly Russian conservative principles of orthodoxy, autocracy and nationalism." In 1887 the Ministry of Education warned the secondary schools, which admitted only 2 or 3 per cent of Russia's youths, against opening their doors to "the children of coachmen, lackeys, cooks, washerwomen, small tradesmen and their kind."

In terms of numbers, the story tells itself, although it must be remembered that the education explosion has had considerable impact in all countries that made the transition from an agricultural to an industrialized society. In 1915 Russia had fewer than 10,000,000 pupils enrolled in elementary and secondary schools of all types. The Soviet Union's present total is about 50,000,000, not including about 4,000,000 in the technicums, the vocation-oriented trade and technical schools. In higher education, the last czarist count was 127,000 students. Today it is 4,000,000. Even allowing for the fact that half of this enrollment represents part-time evening and correspondence students, the increase is huge.

American public-school enrollment currently stands at about 44,000,-000, and the combined enrollment of all institutions of higher learning, from junior colleges to graduate schools, is 6,400,000. Private elementary- and secondary-school enrollment would add another 7,000,000.

More important than the enrollment statistics is the output of the educational production line. According to Soviet count, its institutions of higher learning have graduated 6,500,000 since the revolution, and the technicums 10,500,000 technicians.

At present, education is compulsory from first grade, which children enter at seven years of age, through eighth grade. During those years school is organized into four years of elementary school and four years of "incomplete secondary school." Not yet compulsory are the last two years of secondary school, grades nine and ten. (The eleventh year, introduced by Nikita S. Khrushchev in 1958 to make up for time spent by students in required "polytechnic" training in factories, has since been abandoned.) But the newly proclaimed educational policy will make the ten-year school compulsory—with options to continue in the academic secondary school or to switch to vocational training—by 1970. Soviet educators concede that this goal is moderately realistic only in the major cities, with at least another decade required for implementation in the rest of the giant country. (How large the Soviet Union is was driven home to me when, during a bull session in Leningrad, two Soviet students from Vladivostok told me that they were farther from home, though within the Soviet borders, than I was from New York.)

It would be misleading to think of the development of Soviet education since 1918 as one steady, carefully charted march toward universal education. On the contrary, it had to win not only the war against illiteracy, but also a host of conflicting educational and political battles. The first twelve years of Soviet educational history were dominated by a combination of revolutionary fervor—the search for total freedom from authority and tradition—and the progressive movement of American and European education. The blend turned out to be far more extreme, and child-centered, than in nonrevolutionary America. To enthusiastic young Bolsheviks, rejecting the ways of the past was not merely a break with pedagogical tenets; it was war against a hated way of life.

The new Soviet educators, who wanted to create a school dominated by the pupils, with the teachers passively in the background, were sincere. They were confident that psychology and motivation could make up for what the schools lacked in structure and formal requirements.

As for the politicians, many undoubtedly welcomed the destruction of the old school and the defrocking of the pedagogues. This, after all, offered easy assurance that the schools could not become redoubts of counter-revolution. Moreover, by endowing the young with self-importance, a network of youthful agents to watch over, and report on, their elders was easily established. In a less violent way, the Soviet student of this early era took on some functions that the Hitler Youth carried out in Germany's Nazi revolution and that the Red Guard seems more recently to have assumed throughout China. (It is worth noting that some Soviet educators believe Chinese education to have entered a "pragmatic phase." "Pragmatic," it must be understood, is the Soviet code name for progressive education, since the word "progressive" is reserved as a term of praise for forward-looking—*i.e.,* socialist or fellow-traveling—persons, countries, and ideas.)

On the practical side, the progressive era offered a crucial advantage that today is often overlooked by its foes, in both the Soviet Union and the United States. Since the progressive school made relatively slight academic demands, it was possible to pour huge armies of students into the system and bring about an expansion of public education that, by conventional measures, might have taken infinitely longer to accomplish. In both the Soviet Union and the United States the progressive period coincided with unprecedented expansion in public education—in the Soviet Union at the lower levels of the public schools, in the U.S. at the high-school level. Purists in both countries suffered apoplexy as they witnessed the goings-on that masqueraded as education, but the purists had not demonstrated any great commitment to universal education on their own academic terms when the power was theirs.

In the Soviet Union the purists returned to power somewhat sooner than in the United States, and with a vengeance. The Soviet political leaders, in a tone and language reminiscent of American critics fifteen years later, charged that the schools had failed to teach students the "fundamentals." Rector Albert P. Pinkevich, of Moscow State University, one of the leaders of the postrevolutionary education build-up, in 1931 turned against progressivism and what the Russians called the "Dalton Plan"—reliance on practical projects and field trips to let students "learn by doing," as subsequently tested by the Dalton Schools of New York. Pinkevich, who despite his turnabout was soon to be liquidated, said: "Unfortunate results showed that the project method and the Dalton Plan do not provide sound and profound knowledge, and do not train the children to work systematically."

Between 1931 and 1936 the schools once again embraced the three R's and reaffirmed the central authority of the teacher. The utopian dream of the withering away of the school was disrupted by the rude awakening to the demand that the schools furnish the skilled manpower required by a state which, too, instead of withering away, had assumed vast and central powers. Directives from the Communist party's Central Committee rained on the heads of Soviet educators. Stalin spoke of the schools as "the fortress and the arsenal" with which the battles of industrialization and world power must be won.

To be sure, some of the catch phrases were retained. "Polytechnic education," which in the progressive "unified labor schools" of the 1920's meant largely "learning by doing," now was given a quick new interpretation. A 1931 directive of the Central Committee said: "Every attempt to separate the polytechnization of the school from a systematic and firm mastery of the sciences, and of physics, chemistry, and mathematics in particular, constitutes the most flagrant perversion of the ideas of the polytechnical school."

Where the student leaders and Pioneers had been whips to keep the teachers in line, their role, now that most teachers were reliable Communists, was to help the school authorities by encouraging classmates to work harder and by enforcing student discipline.

Only one constant remained: to create the "new Communist man." After the revolution Lenin had insisted: "We must declare openly . . . the political function of the school. While the object of our previous struggle was to overthrow the bourgeoisie, the aim of the new generation is much more complex: It is to construct a Communist society."

The goal of universal public education, which the Soviet Union shared with the United States, never changed. By the beginning of World War II, Soviet school enrollments were four times what they had been before the revolution. The war temporarily halted that march, but it was quickly resumed after victory.

The next major change in educational theory came with Khrushchev. Impulsive, a great tinkerer as well as a somewhat anti-intellectual grassroots politician, he was determined to leave his stamp on the school system. His 1958 school reform aimed at extending public education from ten to eleven years, perhaps as part of his favorite slogan of "catching up with and overtaking the United States." But his deliberate effort to raise the status of the workingman (and to expand the Soviet pool of skilled labor) led to a return to the original polytechnic education—to bring about a closer "link between school and life." Students were made to spend part of their school hours in factories, on the farms, or in other forms of "productive labor." Almost all candidates for admission to the universities were required to have two years' work experience before being admitted to higher education.

The Khrushchev school reform turned out to be singularly unpopular. It is a measure of the changing Soviet scene that public opinion, if related to such a fundamental issue as the education of children, can no longer be ignored. Parents were adamantly hostile to the idea of having their children exposed to the manners and mores of the rough workingmen in factories.

"Instead of taking the school to the factory, the ways of the factory were brought to the schoolchildren," said one angry father. He added that, whatever else the children might have learned at the assembly line, they picked up bad language and premature skills in handling the vodka bottle. Especially among "new class" parents, the already strong undercurrent of anti-blue-collar class consciousness quickly came to the surface. Moreover, middle-class parents, their eyes fixed on their children's eventual entry into prestige universities and higher-education institutes, considered on-the-job labor training a demeaning waste of academic time. "My daughter, who wants to be a mathematician," said a father who lives in a Moscow suburb, "found herself in a school that had only one outlet for polytechnic education—animal husbandry. All she learned was how to run a fox farm."

On the university scene, the academic leaders, especially in the sciences, resented the two-year postponement of university admission. They wanted to get their hands on the mathematical and scientific talent without delay, while it was still hot.

The last two years have been spent erasing the Khrushchev reforms. The eleven-year school has been abandoned, and polytechnic education has again been modified. Today it differs little from the shop requirements of a suburban American high school—wood- or metalwork for the boys and sewing for the girls. Even driver education, that controversial American invention, is accepted in some Moscow schools as a substitute for productive labor in the factory. The girl whose parents complained about her unproductive care and feeding of foxes now spends several hours a week in a telegraph office, learning to operate computers and teletype machines, to the delight of her mathematics-minded father.

Another Khrushchev innovation—the boarding school, or *internat*—appears to be increasingly in disfavor and decline. Perhaps inspired by the exclusive institutions for privileged sons and daughters of Western capitalists, the competitive Premier had envisioned similar advantages for Soviet youths along with a return to greater stress on communal living, so popular in the early days of the revolution. The timing was wrong. Russian parents, increasingly possessive about their children in a society that is not encouraged to be possessive about much else, were lukewarm toward the boarding schools. A man who spent some time with the then Premier and his wife revealed that Mrs. Khrushchev herself had said privately that she sympathized with parents who wanted to keep their adolescent children at home.

In the face of such sentiments, the boarding schools, hampered by excessive costs, have increasingly turned into schools for children from broken or undesirable homes or with serious emotional problems. The exception is a relatively small number of *internats* used to groom gifted students for special skills and careers. A high-prestige boarding school in Moscow is run under the auspices of Moscow State University and under the direct supervision of Academician Andrei N. Kolmogorov, winner of a 1966 Lenin Prize, who presides over the Soviet mathematics reform in much the same manner as Jerrold Zacharias, of the Massachusetts Institute of Technology, has masterminded the physics reform in American schools.

Despite all the historic zigs and zags, visits to Soviet schools today reveal some impressive strengths. The instruction, though old-fashioned in technique, is usually highly competent. The relationship between students and teachers is one of mutual respect tempered by informality. After hours, chatty groups of youngsters and their teachers populate the corridors. Although the old custom persists that students must rise when teachers or visitors enter the room (as it does in most of Europe and in many of New York's better private schools), there is no trace of either the surface subservience or the behind-the-backs hostility that frequently marks German and French schools.

Like much of Russian life, the schools are flavored by a kind of family atmosphere—complete with both its mutual understanding and its frequent flashes of exuberant praise and exaggerated scolding. Totally absent is the rigidity typical of much of the German public-school scene ever since the days of Bismarck.

In a ninth-grade English class, equivalent to the junior year of high school, the teacher asked for volunteers to talk about their career plans. Two girls spoke fluently about their prospects of entering the university and their anxieties over exams. They willingly submitted to questions. "Now, how about the boys?" said the teacher, a slim, youngish woman with a slightly stilted British accent. Nobody volunteered. "Won't you try, Anatoly?" she addressed one of the students. He shook his head. After some unsuccessful coaxing, the teacher, somewhat sheepishly, stood up for the young men. "The boys are always shy and not as brave as the girls," she said. "Besides, they worry more about their mathematics than their English." The attitude was that of the slightly embarrassed mother whose little boy had refused to shake hands with an acquaintance.

In another school I was invited to talk with the students, aged about fourteen, before the bell opened the next class. What was their favorite English book? *Catcher in the Rye* won hands down. One boy, seated next to a pretty girl, had just satisfied the requirement of getting up to greet me and the teacher. Now he barely looked up to enter the conversation. He was busy examining the latest collection of Beatle photographs.

In a tenth-year (senior) English class the lesson had begun with the customary bone-dry discussion of the assigned reading—an essay about food preparation in England. "We are fortunate to have an English-speaking visitor from America with us today," said the matronly teacher. "Why not ask him some questions about food in the United States?" A girl rose to the occasion and dutifully asked about the uses of roasting oven and frying pan. Nobody seemed thrilled about this line of questioning, and before my option expired I suggested that any other queries, even on unrelated topics, would be all right. Hands shot up. A pretty brunette whose yellow tights and ballet slippers contrasted incongruously with the prim, mid-Victorian black-and-brown school uniform and white-lace, high-necked collar, said: "Tell us about modern art in the United States." Even though such art forms are still out of favor in the Soviet Union, the teacher greeted with an amused and understanding smile the subsequent talk about op and pop.

An American scholar who spent a year with his wife and four children in the Soviet Union in 1966 supplemented these observations. His children were enrolled in a Moscow kindergarten and elementary school, and although they began their adventure without any knowledge of Russian, teachers volunteered in the afternoons to help them learn the unfamiliar language. The school attended by these youngsters was one of the so-called "extended-day schools," which permit children of working parents to stay until five o'clock in the afternoon. From one to three, the children engage in supervised play, and for the remaining two hours they do their homework, with teachers available to help them.

Another American youngster, the daughter of a diplomat, after attending a Moscow public school for a few months, startled her parents with the question: "Why do I suddenly want to learn so much?"

Part of the answer is in the effective use of the parents as partners. The parents' meeting, the Russian equivalent of the P.-T.A., is an important supporting force. Typically, the parents are invited to meetings at the beginning of each quarter, in the school's auditorium. Like all Russian meetings, they seem to American observers to go on forever. A four-hour session is not unusual.

The school principal usually opens the meeting with a talk about overall achievement in the school, personal cleanliness, and study habits. A local policeman, speaking about traffic safety, is likely to scare the parents out of their wits with details of accidents caused by carelessness. A member of the local People's Court may depict the dangers of juvenile delinquency. A bemedaled member of the city council—the politicians' voice—will glad-hand the parents with tales of the community's generosity toward the school's budget.

At a recent meeting in Moscow this approach backfired. Irate mothers interrupted the smooth-talking politico with demands for a traffic light in front of the school. The council representative hedged, with talk about the need for an uninterrupted flow of cars. "Then why were you able to do it half a kilometer down the road in front of the new department store?" a mother shouted. When the harassed official mumbled something about the importance of economic progress, a chorus of voices sprang up. "Are our children less important than economic progress?" the women demanded.

After the mass proceedings, the parents are asked to meet their children's teachers in the youngsters' classrooms. It is here that the bond between home and school is established. During these classroom sessions the teachers offer a critique of each child in front of all the parents. Parents may, and do, challenge the teachers, but the over-all effect appears to be one of keeping everybody on his toes.

Although the Soviet Union works hard at creating the public image abroad that it is a society without personal want, it is worth noting that most parents' association chapters also raise funds—not only to buy extra equipment for the classroom, but also to offer financial aid to needy students. A revolving fund, for example, may be used to pay for school uniforms if some of the youngsters' parents cannot afford them. Not long ago an American couple temporarily living in Moscow, who had not yet gotten around to outfitting their teen-age daughter, were surprised to find her properly uniformed when she returned from school. The parents' fund had taken care of the matter.

Other misconceptions exist about the nature of free higher education. While it is true that there are no tuition charges and close to 80 per cent of all university students get a subsistence stipend, averaging about thirty-five rubles a month, the majority of students rely on a continuing subsidy from their parents, ranging anywhere from thirty to eighty rubles a month. Considering the fact that one hundred and fifty rubles constitutes a considerably better than average monthly wage, the sacrifice made by many parents, even through the years of graduate study, is substantial.

The lion's share of the credit for a school atmosphere that is admirably conducive to learning belongs to the teachers. In addition to the natural devotion the Russian teachers bring to the job, the system generates continuing pressure for diligent performance. Quality controls, many of them rather brutal by American standards, are built into the process all along the line. Each school's director has sweeping powers in assembling, supervising, and dismissing his staff. He is given an annual budget, based on enrollment and on the school's special goals. The only operational limitation on the principal's powers as captain of his ship is the authority of the seven-man council of the teachers' union, all members of the school's own faculty.

The forty-three-year-old principal of Moscow's School 84 commands a faculty of fifty for an enrollment of 1,000 pupils ranging from first grade through the final year of high school. He has four assistants, two for academic affairs and two for administration. Together they keep a close tab on the teachers' performance.

"This year I am dismissing two teachers," the principal said. In the case of one teacher, he added, it had taken him two years to persuade the union council to go along with him, but agreement had now been reached. I asked by what criteria he arrived at so drastic a step. "I pay frequent classroom visits," he replied. "I listen to reports from parents. But mainly I can tell easily from the teacher's success and productivity." He explained that if a teacher consistently fails to get a respectable proportion of his students admitted to the universities or if his class always does poorly in the national mathematics competition "he cannot be doing a proper job."

Technically, a dismissed teacher may appeal to the People's Court of the local district, but the principal left little doubt that such an appeal, against the massed testimony of "experts"—the Russians' trademark of superior wisdom—is not likely to be of much avail.

To be dismissed from a teaching assignment is a disastrous penalty. Every Russian, from street cleaner to nuclear physicist, carries a basic personal document—his work book. The dismissal becomes a permanent entry, and a teacher dismissed from a job in Moscow or any other major city must, if he wants to remain in the profession, settle for rural or provincial employment, where standards continue to be low and where the teacher shortage is serious. It should be added, however, that because the penalty is so severe, it is invoked rather sparingly. Nevertheless, it is a constant threat.

Although teachers enjoy considerable status (though by no means on a par with that of university professors), their compensation is not impressive. In their relentlessly pragmatic approach to manpower utilization, the Soviet authorities appear to have licked the worst of the teacher shortage by pegging the basic salaries so low that the majority of teachers "volunteer" to work extra hours for extra pay. (Many schools still operate on double sessions.)

For high-school teachers the basic starting salary is about one hundred rubles ($111) a month, and the maximum for experienced professionals is about one hundred and thirty-five rubles for eighteen hours of classroom instruction a week. (Elementary-school teachers get about twenty to thirty rubles less.) But all teachers are encouraged to work overtime, up to maximum earnings of two hundred rubles per month. The job carries with it a pension of 40 per cent of the salary, after twenty-five years' service.

The Soviet teacher is pretty low on the economic totem pole. Not only does he live in a totally different bracket from that of higher education, where the range is from one hundred rubles for instructors without advanced degrees to five hundred rubles for full professors (and six hundred for top administrators); the bitter fact is that a hard-working taxi driver or waiter may make 50 per cent more than a fully certified high-school teacher, and a skilled worker can easily bring home twice the teacher's pay. (Among professional people, only physicians, who are in plentiful supply, are worse off than teachers.)

Under these circumstances, how can the schools attract teachers—and so many well-trained and devoted ones? Part of the answer lies in the fact that class consciousness offers greater social prestige to the white-collar professional than to the highly paid factory worker.

The Russian schools' basic curriculum is standardized and demanding. During the four years of elementary school the week consists of twenty-four periods of forty-five minutes each, spread over six days. (This is about equal to the American five-day week in those schools that offer five daily instruction periods.) In the subsequent grades the total of weekly classroom periods rises from thirty in fifth grade to thirty-four in ninth and tenth.

The Russian schools, along with the economy at large, are on the point of switching over to a five-day week, with a two-day weekend. While the general labor force is expected to make up for the extra holiday by working one additional hour a day, the problem in the schools is the frequency of double sessions, which will make such a stretching of the academic day difficult.

More important than the hours spent in the classroom, however, is the intensity of instruction in certain fields. For example, mathematics—considered the key to all learning under the Soviet education scheme—is given six classroom periods a week during the entire ten years of public schooling, with the exception of five periods in eighth grade.

All those who complete the academic high school must take physics for five years, chemistry for four years, and a foreign language for five years. Russian language takes up twelve hours in grades one to three, nine hours in fourth grade, five hours in fifth and sixth, three hours in seventh, and two hours in eighth. This does not include literature, which begins with two weekly hours in fifth grade and works up to five hours in the last two years of secondary school. Other required subjects are history, geography, biology, astronomy, drawing, fine arts, music, physical education, and workshop.

Given these impressive standard requirements, it is easy to single out extraordinary strengths in Soviet youngsters' education. Almost invariably Americans who were temporarily enrolled in Soviet schools are able

1917 bread line in Petrograd, Russia's capital, on the eve of large-scale riots
(*Novosti*)

Units of czarist army firing on besieged police in the early days of the February Revolution, 1917, in Petrograd   (*Novosti*)

February, 1917, on Petrograd's Liteiny Prospekt: an artillery unit that has gone over to the revolutionary side   *(Novosti)*

Czar Nicholas II, under arrest at Tsarskoye Selo, after his abdication *(Exclusive News Agency Ltd.)*

Soldiers with banners parading the streets of Petrograd on April 18, 1917
(*Exclusive News Agency Ltd.*)

A Bolshevik military patrol car operating in the Nevsky Prospekt, Petrograd,
during the battle between Lenin's Bolsheviks and Kerensky's followers, 1917
(*Exclusive News Agency Ltd.*)

At the Finland Station in Petrograd, on April 16, 1917, Lenin emerges from his train while a navy band plays the "Marseillaise." In this painting by a Stalinist-era artist, M. Sokolov, Stalin is shown standing behind Lenin, though there is no evidence he really was there.   *(Sovfoto)*

Georgi Lozgachev, *below left,* at the age of six, with his adoptive mother, Anna Yelizarova-Ulyanova, sister of Lenin, 1912; and, *below right,* Georgi standing next to Lenin in Moscow, at Sixth All-Russian Congress of Soviets, November 7, 1918

Shooting during the July demonstrations in Petrograd, 1917   *(Novosti)*

Appeal "To the People of Russia" composed by Lenin announcing advent of the Bolsheviks to power   *(Sovfoto)*

"From the Military-Revolutionary Committee at the Petrograd Soviet of Workers' and Soldiers' Deputies.
"To the Citizens of Russia.

"The Provisional government has been overthrown. State power has passed into the hands of the organ of the Petrograd Soviet of Workers' and Soldiers' Deputies of the Military-Revolutionary Committee, standing at the head of the Petrograd proletariat and garrison.

"The cause for which people struggled: immediate proposal of a democratic peace, abolition of the landlords' ownership of the land, workers' control over production, creation of a Soviet Government—this cause has been insured.

"Long Live the Revolution of Workers, Soldiers and Peasants!"

"Military-Revolutionary Committee at the Petrograd Soviet of Workers' and Soldiers' Deputies.
"25 October 1917, 10 A.M."
November 7, 1917 (new style)

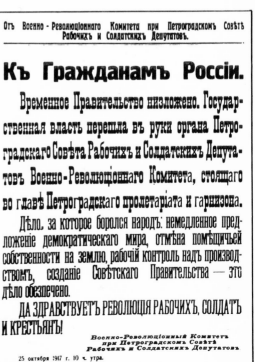

Отъ Военно-Революціоннаго Комитета при Петроградскомъ Совѣтѣ Рабочихъ и Солдатскихъ Депутатовъ.

Къ Гражданамъ Россіи.

Временное Правительство низложено. Государственная власть перешла въ руки органа Петроградскаго Совѣта Рабочихъ и Солдатскихъ Депутатовъ Военно-Революціоннаго Комитета, стоящаго во главѣ Петроградскаго пролетаріата и гарнизона.

Дѣло, за которое боролся народъ: немедленное предложеніе демократическаго мира, отмѣна помѣщичьей собственности на землю, рабочій контроль надъ производствомъ, созданіе Совѣтскаго Правительства — это дѣло обезпечено.

ДА ЗДРАВСТВУЕТЪ РЕВОЛЮЦІЯ РАБОЧИХЪ, СОЛДАТЪ И КРЕСТЬЯНЪ!

Военно-Революціонный Комитетъ
при Петроградскомъ Совѣтѣ
Рабочихъ и Солдатскихъ Депутатовъ.

25 октября 1917 г. 10 ч. утра.

Lenin addressing Red Army troops while Leon Trotsky listens at the foot of the platform, 1919

Trotsky, as Commissar for War, inspecting Soviet troops in Moscow, 1921 *(U.P.I.)*

Registration card of the Political Police Administration of the Province of Baku with a photograph of J. V. Stalin, March, 1910. It reads:

"Apparent age: 30-32 years. *Year and place of birth:* Dec. 21, 1879. *Height:* 1 metre 69 c/m. *Corpulence:* Thin. *Frame:* lean. *Girth:* 70 c.m. 1. *Hair: Color:* Black and wavy. *Thickness:* Thick. *Baldness:* 2. *Beard and mustaches: Color:* Brown. *Shape:* Thin. *Thickness:* Thick. 3. *Face: Color:* Yellow-white. *Sanguinity:* Anaemic. *Face expression:* Gay. Face pockmarked. 4. *Forehead: Height:* Medium. *Slant:* Medium. *Wrinkles:* Horizontal. *Shape of head:* Oval. 5. *Eyebrows:* Black. *Shape:* Arched. *Thickness:* Thin. 6. *Eye sockets: Size:* Medium. *Depth:* Hollow. 7. *Eyes: Color:* Hazel. *Distance between eyes:* Medium. 8. *Nose:* Straight. *Base:* Medium. *Height:* Medium. *Length:* Medium. 9. *Ear: Shape:* Oval. *Protuberance:* Medium. *Size:* Medium. *Helix:* Broad. *Top:* Thick. *Bottom:* Thin. *Lobe: Shape:* Arched. *Attached:* Full attachment. *Lips:* Small mouth. *Chin: Length:* Medium. *Slant:* Vertical. *Shape:* Coarse. *Fullness:* Thin."*

Stalin in 1933 (*The New York Times*)

Victims of the famine of 1921-1922, during which millions starved. The Soviet regime itself may have been saved by the American relief mission directed by Herbert Hoover. *(The New York Times)*

The first American relief train to reach Samara *(The New York Times)*

The first tractor ever seen in Khvalynsk, on the Volga, illustrates the beginning of mechanized agriculture in the mid-1920's   *(The New York Times)*

Workmen installing a giant turbine at the Dnieper River power station, 1930
(The New York Times)

Soviet soldiers mop up remnants of the German Sixth Army in the Battle of Stalingrad, January, 1943   *(Sovfoto)*

Prisoners of war from the German Sixth Army, who surrendered at Stalin-grad, marching to internment, February, 1943   (Sovfoto)

Top: The Teheran Conference, November 28–December 1, 1943: Premier Stalin, President Franklin D. Roosevelt, and Prime Minister Winston Churchill, with their military chiefs, on the portico of the Soviet Embassy *(AP wirephoto from 12th Air Force)   Bottom:* The Potsdam Conference, July 17–August 2, 1945: Premier Stalin, President Harry S. Truman, and Prime Minister Churchill a moment before the start of the first session   *(Official U.S. Navy photograph)*

V-E Day, May 10, 1945, in Red Square, where demonstrations lasted into the night

Memorial meeting held in the Bolshoi Theater, January, 1950, on the twenty-sixth anniversary of the death of Vladimir Ilyich Lenin. *Left to right:* P. N. Pospelov, P. K. Ponomarenko, A. N. Kosygin, Chou En-lai, A. I. Mikoyan, Mao Tse-tung, N. A. Bulganin, J. V. Stalin, L. P. Beria, M. A. Suslov, G. M. Malenkov, M. F. Skiryatov, N. S. Khrushchev, V. M. Molotov, N. M. Shvernik, V. V. Kuznetsov, V. N. Chernousov, K. Y. Voroshilov *(Sovfoto)*

Communist party Secretary Khrushchev addressing the Twentieth Communist party Congress in Moscow in February, 1956, the occasion on which he delivered his famous denunciation of Stalin. In the first row behind him are Presidium members Kirichenko, Suslov, Malenkov, Kaganovich, Bulganin, Voroshilov, Molotov, Mikoyan, Saburov, and Pervukhin. *(Sovfoto)*

Stalin's coffin being carried by Nikolai Shvernik, Lazar M. Kaganovich, Nikolai Bulganin, Vyacheslav M. Molotov, Vasily Stalin, Georgi Malenkov, Lavrenti Beria, Moscow, March, 1953. On the far left is Stalin's daughter Svetlana. *(Sovfoto)*

Nikita Khrushchev at the United Nations on September 29, 1960, with Soviet Foreign Minister Andrei Gromyko. At this session the Soviet Premier attacked colonialism and argued for the replacement of the Secretary General by a three-man directorate while shouting, fist-pounding, and banging his shoe on his desk. *(U.P.I.)*

Anastas Mikoyan in his Kremlin office with Harrison E. Salisbury, 1967 *(The New York Times)*

to drift along without additional effort in mathematics for two to three years after their return to American classrooms.

Penmanship is still taught with rigid pedantry and old-fashioned, clumsy pens (no ball-points or pencils are tolerated!). Yet the instruction is highly effective and leads to levels of legibility that have been lost in the Western Hemisphere.

Reading is given high priority, with impressive results. By contrast, the written word is neglected. Long hours are invested in grammar, in Russian as well as in foreign-language study, but little time is spent on compositions, book reports, or other written assignments. Systematic and rather dull exercises in drawing up outlines often take the place of composition. The result is that written expression suffers, and even at the graduate level students grumble over the occasional assignment of what would be, by American standards, a rather scant requirement. American graduate students at Moscow and Leningrad universities are frequently complimented by their Russian professors on their competence with the written word. The Soviet Union remains a highly verbal society, with long speeches, endless arguments—and four-page newspapers.

On the whole, the Soviet schools represent an impressive educational establishment that has accomplished much but has arrived at a crossroad of doubts and uncertainty. It is a system conscious of the need for change, but held back by a stifling conservatism. The schools have served Soviet society well in the initial build-up of industry, but they must now adapt for a more complex phase of national development and rapid urbanization. Those at the controls appear confused and unsure about how to shift gears.

In its simplest form, Soviet education's conservatism is manifested in the curriculum itself. The requirements have become so deeply rooted in the over-all plan that they are being perpetuated without sufficient critical analysis and review. For example, while a convincing case can be made for the concentration on mathematics—not as a specialized scientific subject, but as a key to modern life and logic—there is little rational justification for the requirement of five years of physics and four years of chemistry, except for future scientists. Where the American schools have long erred by including too little science in their general education, leaving many bright students seriously underexposed, the Soviet schools have piled on too much, too indiscriminately.

Perhaps even more important, the conservatism in teaching methods leads to an unnecessary lengthening of coverage in many fields. Thus the old-fashioned "The pen of my aunt is on the table" approach to foreign languages, with long, repetitive phonetic drills at the start of virtually every lesson, means that most youngsters require five or six years to attain the kind of mastery that could be achieved with modern instruction in little more than half the time.

Many Russian education experts know this. They know what might be done and have kept up with research abroad. In their training of interpreters and of engineers who will serve abroad, they do indeed apply modern-language instruction that compares favorably with the most modern training programs anywhere in the world. Yet the tendency to protect traditional methods in the school curriculum is demonstrated by the fact that the well-staffed and electronically equipped Institute of Foreign Languages operates two separate courses: one for future teachers and the other for those who plan to put their language knowledge to practical use, such as interpreters. A simple move—marriage of the two programs, with greater stress on the linguistic fluency provided by the practical approach—would quickly vitalize language teaching in the schools.

In fairness to the educators, it must be added that national isolation has created problems of its own. Considering the fact that several generations of English teachers have now been trained with little opportunity for study of the language in English-speaking countries, the state of instruction is remarkably good. Nevertheless, the obstacle is formidable. While many of the English classes are competent, few achieve the level of brilliance and conversational liveliness that is often found in German-language classes where continuing contact with East Germany has provided first-hand practice for teachers.

Experts in the central textbook office of the Academy of Pedagogical Sciences have spent years on the preparation of a new series of four English-language texts. The process is meticulous and slow. It involves a nationwide competition for the best manuscripts. Eventually, the winning texts are analyzed, reviewed, and revised. A draft is then printed in a limited edition of perhaps 1,500 copies, distributed among experts and classroom teachers across the country. After consolidation of the comments and criticisms, a revised version is published, this time in an edition of about 20,000, to be used experimentally in a sampling of classrooms in a number of regions. Only when all the returns are in and a new redrafting has been accomplished can a new text be put into mass production and distribution. In the case of the four-year English texts, the time between original manuscript and nationwide use was estimated at ten years. When I suggested that such a lag might be excessive, the director of the project said: "In the same period you will have published a number of poor texts. We will be sure to have published the best possible version."

In another field—the new mathematics—Academician Kolmogorov hinted at a similar criticism of American haste. In his sunny, starkly modern office at Moscow State University, he pointed to an entire shelf of American new-math textbooks and a somewhat smaller collection of British and French versions. "Some of the American books are very good and very attractive," he said. "But most of them introduce too many new and different topics at once."

Russian educators are deeply suspicious of fast-spreading educational fads. They acknowledge that American innovation-mindedness is of great value to them—to avoid costly mistakes. Aleksei I. Markushevich, another mathematician, who is vice president of the Academy of Pedagogical Sciences, in a plea for conservatism, said: "The task of those who develop education is to be careful in selecting the building blocks. It is most dangerous to be under the influence of a fad." It almost seemed like a refrain, repeated by other officials during subsequent discussions. "You must not discard what may be useful," Markushevich added.

Yet it is well to recall that the Soviet authorities are also experts at costly educational mistakes of their own.

Schoolmen all over the world lean toward professional conservatism. Beyond this normal occupational hazard, Soviet educators and theorists are loaded down with the ballast of a political experience that makes it understandably difficult for new ideas and experimentation to get off the ground. Every past school reform has subsequently been denounced as either politically or pedagogically "incorrect." From the progressive phase, through the ultratraditional three-R's revival of Stalinism, to the exuberantly earthy factory- and life-oriented Khrushchev interlude, the nationwide reform proclamations were inexorably followed by renunciations and retreat.

The crucial aspect of this manner of "progress" is that, with the exception of the original progressive experiment, all the school reforms had been invented and proclaimed, not by educators, but by politicians for political reasons. In the end, it fell to the educators, who were not responsible for the original mistakes, to undo the damage and get the educational train back on the tracks. For example, it is unlikely that many educators (especially if their memories went back to the 1920's and the project method) believed with Khrushchev in the magic of the polytechnic-education revival. They simply carried out orders or, at best, tried to slow down their implementation as much as seemed politically safe. The more sophisticated among them knew that their next task would be to lead an orderly retreat and, if possible, make it appear like a legitimate educational march toward new objectives.

Such experiences hardly encourage educational innovation. They lead to a "wait for orders" attitude and, since professional expertise under such a system is used mainly to protect the schools in their periodic withdrawals, conservatism becomes glorified. This deprives pedagogy of innovation-minded leadership. In contrast to the Academy of Sciences, which often is the generator of intellectual and scientific excellence, the Academy of Pedagogical Sciences more regularly gives undeserved prestige to pedagogical opportunists who have their eyes on the main chance of ideological approval from the Kremlin. It is in the Kremlin, or, more specifically, the Central Committee of the Communist party, that the forces of conservatism get their most constant reinforcement.

These forces have had their most damaging impact on the humanities. Although statistically a huge block of school time—officially estimated at 48 per cent—and a substantial part of university enrollment bear the humanities label, ideological considerations have drained life and quality out of that "sensitive" sector.

During a classroom visit in a Moscow secondary school the assistant director pointed with pride to a spirited girl who was challenging her teacher's mathematical theories. "It's in mathematics," the administrator said, "that we have all our best arguments." This is not surprising. Bright students need an escape from the kind of teaching that is prescribed in the latest 1966 official syllabus for history in the eight-year school. "The teaching of history," says the document, "plays an enormous role in the general education and Communist upbringing of the younger generation, which is to take an immediate part in building up Communist society. The course of history at the secondary school must . . . bring home to pupils that the downfall of capitalism and the victory of Communism are inevitable, disclose consistently the role of popular masses as true makers of history. . . . Of particular importance at the present juncture is a thorough study of the current stage of Communist construction, stressing the role of the Communist party as the leading, guiding and directing force of the Soviet society." This limiting prospectus continues: "History and other general subjects must be taught at school in such a way as to bring up the youngsters in the spirit of Communist ideology and ethics, intolerance towards bourgeois ideology. . . ."

In this scheme of things history is the key subject for the reinforcement of dogma, just as mathematics is the key subject for the development of society. As anchor or albatross, depending on the observer's point of view, history begins to be taught informally, with a smattering of important dates, events, and heroic episodes in Russia's past, as early as second and third grade. In fourth grade a complete overview of Russian history is offered, and during the last three years of secondary school—grades eight, nine, and ten—Russian history is studied in greater depth.

But this is only part of the story. During the other years, when ancient and medieval as well as modern European history are on the agenda, the frame of reference is always the "correct" interpretation—the battle of the masses against the oppressive "ruling circles." Just as *Spartacus,* a modern Soviet ballet, becomes a gigantic and rather vulgar tableau of the proletarian struggle against the fascist enemy, so all history is either prelude to or accompaniment of the Soviet era. Wars are either imperialist (bad) or "of liberation" (good), and history thus becomes the permanent instruction manual for every radio and television commentary or newspaper report on every current conflict.

How flexible this approach can be made in the service of official doctrine is clearly shown by the fact that even many of the czars, despite their brutal exploitation of the masses, appear as heroes of the Russian past. Every day long lines of Russians wait to visit Lenin's Tomb in Red Square and troop with equal reverence through the Armory Museum to admire the diamond-studded decadence of czarist extravagance and waste. It is only the American egalitarian who sees in such pomp the cause of the Bolshevik Revolution.

In addition, the Soviet system has perfected the use of priorities as a means of impressing on its citizenry what is and what is not important. Thus the crucial final examinations in history—after years of study of the world-wide scene through the ages and just before the trauma of the university-admissions rat race—virtually ignore all but the current century of the Russian story. Since teachers and students know this, it is a safe bet that the emphasis of learning and teaching is squarely on that part of the human story which, at the risk of sacrificing scholarship, promises to lead to a "correct" understanding of Soviet man's destiny.

The educationally most damaging aspect is not the ritual of indoctrination itself. That process has become so cut and dried that students and teachers take it in their stride, rather like a meaningless methods course in the American study plan. Far more serious is the effect of the omission or exclusion of vast areas of discussion, controversy, and analysis. Students whose education has rushed them through this narrow tunnel, without windows to the real, controversial world of history, economics, and sociology, cannot imagine that anything exists outside the radius of their understanding. They cannot look for new answers—not even answers that the changing nature of their own society requires—because they have been deprived of the ability to ask pertinent questions.

Fred M. Hechinger

As a result, the humanities have assumed a second-rate flavor. The huge thirty-story main complex of Moscow State University, on Lenin Hills, is the exclusive domain of mathematics and the sciences. The humanities are quartered in a labyrinth of old, early nineteenth-century buildings downtown.

Reflecting this symbolic, external downgrading, the humanities attract many rejects and youngsters of lesser talent or ambition, including those who will become tomorrow's conservative party hacks.

Soviet officialdom, of course, denies that this is so. When I asked Vyacheslav P. Yelyutin, a steel engineer, who has been the Minister of Higher Education since 1954, about reports that the humanities, especially at the universities, where most high-school history teachers are trained, are in low repute, he dismissed the statements as "incorrect."

Yet a day later I asked an able secondary-school principal what, if he could bring about any improvement of the Soviet schools, he would single out for first priority. Without hesitation he replied: "Strengthen the humanities." When I told him that the Minister of Higher Education thought all was well in that area of the curriculum, he said with a smile and a shrug: "The Minister does not see what goes on in the classroom."

Others, even prominent educators such as the rector of Moscow State University, describe the subordinate position of the humanities as a temporary phenomenon, something to be readjusted once the needs of production and the demands of the consumer have been satisfied. During a spirited discussion I had with fifteen graduate students in a dormitory of Leningrad State University, a young history scholar justified his own discipline's current lack of prestige. "Science and engineering are needed for production, but what does history produce?" he asked. "Once we are as rich as the United States, we will be able to spend money for the humanities, too."

When I asked a leading Soviet administrator of a university history department why he and his colleagues in the humanities reconcile themselves so readily to their inferiority complex, the interpreter seemed at a loss. But the professor, who understood very little English, waved the linguistic difficulty aside and, with a broad grin, acknowledged both that he understood the meaning of "inferiority complex" and that he was a victim of it. It would be a long time, he thought, before a historian might become rector of a major Soviet university. "The scientists will say: 'They shall not pass,'" he explained.

The lowly station of the humanities is, for the moment, self-perpetuating. Because they cannot attract the best students and are unable to hold out sufficient promise of distinguished careers, they find it difficult to inspire superior effort and scholarship. It is fair to say that most of the research and scholarship in the humanities and social sciences dealing with the last three hundred years is third-rate. The further back in time, the better the scholarship. Experts attest that in so safely remote a field as archeology Soviet scholarship tends to be brilliant.

Freewheeling research in these politically sensitive areas is impossible. Undergraduate libraries are inadequate, and only graduate students are admitted to the excellent libraries of the Academy of Sciences. Library catalogues, which were ideologized, with dogma displacing the alphabet, in the early postrevolutionary fervor and never fully disentangled from their political "reorientation," are a shambles. In Leningrad undergraduate reading space is so scarce that students buy tickets to the nearby Hermitage Museum and study in quiet corners in the galleries.

The mere physical effort of obtaining essential research materials in the humanities is forbidding. By contrast, scientists who want a copy of a recent technical periodical, published anywhere in the world, need merely apply to the Information Section at Moscow State University to receive a reprint, if necessary a translation, within a matter of days.

The humanities' second-class citizenship inevitably affects the quality of the effort. There is little of the excitement that comes with original and unfettered scholarship in the sciences, especially in mathematics and physics. Lectures are frequently dull, before an uninspired audience.

While it is difficult to gain admission to the universities—only about one-fifth of all qualified applicants make the grade—it is next to impossible to be expelled for academic reasons. A clubby family atmosphere prevails, and the general attitude is that any student good enough to get in must be smart enough to be kept in, regardless of performance. As a result, many nonscience students are satisfied with the equivalent of a gentleman's C. Many take examinations over and over again until they finally sneak by. It is not unheard of for indulgent professors to give a passing grade to students who have not done their required reading—on a promise that they will get down to business during the following term.

American graduate students who have spent a year or more studying side by side with Soviet classmates at Moscow or Leningrad quickly rush to their Russian colleagues' defense. They point out that the rigors of academic housekeeping are often such that the students are worn out before they get to the main business of reading and research.

In the winter, for instance, a Russian student may spend hours standing in line at the Lenin Public Library—first, until he is able to check his outer garments in the entrance hall, and then, until he actually is given his book.

Moreover, in a bureaucratic, centrally controlled society, the essential, everyday functionaries move slowly, and if absence or sickness prevents them from moving at all, everything comes to a standstill. One student who had special permission to borrow a book from one of the collections found that the woman in charge of that section would be away for three weeks. Until her return nobody was empowered to hand over the volume.

"Books are not the only problem," said one student. "When the lady in charge of laundry was sick, nobody at Moscow State University washed the shirts for several weeks."

The relaxed family spirit governs the all-important "section meetings"— conferences attended by faculty, graduate students, and undergraduates in each of the many subdivisions of the major disciplines. During these meetings papers are read aloud, often while the professors who will judge them are discussing their own problems and concerns.

At a recent section meeting in Leningrad's history faculty, a flustered girl undergraduate read aloud what was by general consensus an overly long, pedestrian effort, weighted down with sophomoric ideology. The critique by old and young, high and low, was brutally frank, as only members of a defiantly loving family can be with each other. When it was all over the senior professor, who had been just as harsh in his criticism, turned to the luckless coed and, with avuncular sincerity, said: "Do not be discouraged just because nobody has liked your paper. You have done the best you can. Just keep doing your best and all will be well."

At the same time, to shrug off the section meeting as just a friendly ritual misses a vital point. For it is in section meetings that crucial academic decisions are made—what is to be studied and researched, which texts are to be used, and even what dissertations are to be produced. In the course of such deliberations the supremacy of the party is maintained. Every section meeting includes a party representative, usually a rather junior faculty member. If a sensitive book or syllabus is under debate, the party representative, after a decent span of time has been given to the free exchange of views, will make his suggestion. The discussion then continues a little while longer—until the senior professor, now given his cue, quietly submits that "we have all agreed" that such and such a text or topic, as suggested by the party representative, is the favored choice. No vote is taken. The issue is closed.

This procedure is not designed to inspire independence of thought or scholarship. Yet throughout Soviet life and education there are signs of the beginnings of a search for new ways of giving the nation the kind of forward thrust that comes only with greater independence and initiative. Without these, it is impossible to relax the rigidity of the huge bureaucracy, which regulates all the details of Soviet life, and it is becoming increasingly evident that the bureaucracy now blocks rapid economic build-up as well as the road to a more sophisticated social order.

The lack of training for independent decision-making; the pinpointed and narrow, even if frequently highly competent, specialization of all higher and much lower education, and the dearth of generalists, in the sciences as well as in the humanities, to shape cohesive purposes of national and economic development—all these seem to call for far-reaching educational changes and reforms. No final decisions have been made as to the new direction, and the pedagogical conservatives as well as the old guard of the party would undoubtedly like to stem the tide of change. But other forces are pressing against the hardened walls of the mold.

Professor Mikhail A. Prokofiev, Minister of Education of the Russian Republic, has publicly berated schools for permitting substantial numbers of pupils to drop out after eighth grade. His criticism of the curriculum—and its lack of holding power—is reminiscent of similar complaints in the United States a decade or more ago. "The biological disciplines, for instance, hitherto erred on the side of the abundance of facts that had to be learned by heart," Professor Prokofiev said. ". . . In physics, the pupils have been drenched in a flood of old and newly discovered laws, with these laws, moreover, being taught in the schools as originally formulated by their discoverers, and not from the standpoint of present-day science. . . . The number of school hours devoted to compulsory subjects is too great and, furthermore, our curriculum is too rigid. . . . There is no scope for reasonable initiative. . . ."

For over three decades the Soviet schools have been forced to submit to the ideological fiction that inherited abilities count for nothing. Teachers had to forswear all tests of ability and potential, principals were under strict orders to permit neither the selection of gifted pupils nor the grouping of youngsters according to ability. Nothing counted but the students' achievement, and all were expected to master the prescribed curriculum.

Human nature has long clashed with the official theory. But as attendance at secondary school becomes universal, the number of those who lack either scholastic capacity or interest and who prefer seeking a job and the independence of a weekly paycheck is bound to increase.

"We no longer insist that all children are alike," said one veteran educator-psychologist whose career goes back to the days, before 1931, when it was still permissible to think of children's aptitudes.

The need to assess a student's "potential" is now freely talked about. Widespread concern over the increasing number of "dropouts"—a new word in the Russian language—has turned the interest of Soviet educators to the search for better ways of "motivating" students.

In a compromise between outright attention to gifted children and the old denial that they exist, the new fad of Soviet education is the "special school," with stress on one subject, such as a foreign language, mathematics, physics, and occasionally even history. Some of these schools encompass all the grades, from elementary through high school, while others consist of the secondary grades only. The concept is reminiscent of New York's famous Bronx High School of Science. The difference is that, since aptitude tests are, for the moment, still outlawed, selection tends to be haphazard—by teachers' recommendation and guess and, not infrequently, parental pressure. The advantage of such schools for university admission has not been lost on "new class" parents who want their children groomed for prestige universities or institutes.

Unless there is a reversal of present trends, the special schools, however, seem to be an interim solution. Educational psychology—the investigation of how children learn—which had been a forbidden science, outlawed along with Dewey and Freud, is making a gingerly return. Until last year psychology was not given faculty status at Soviet universities, except as a subdivision of philosophy, which is almost entirely confined to the study of Communist party theory. Within the last twelve months, in a major evolution of policy, psychology has been given a life of its own—with the establishment in Leningrad of an Institute of Psychology, and in Moscow of a department of psychology.

Perhaps to justify and legitimize the field, which had previously been ridiculed as a bourgeois pseudo science, the new departments are for the moment dominated by experts in "the psychology of engineering," an apparent effort to use behavioral science to increase productivity. But the educational psychologists are hard at work. They are fully familiar with such American pioneers as Jerome Bruner, at Harvard. They have studied the effect on learning of such revisions of the curriculum as popularized by Professor Zacharias, the physicist at the Massachusetts Institute of Technology. They have translated and issued in limited editions of about 1,500 copies most of the key writings of current American psychologists, not for general use but for high-level parallel study and research. (A good deal of experimental work in psychology, some of it as part of biological study and some as part of medicine, has been carried on in the Soviet Union, much of it similar to Western research, but little, if any, of the outcome has been applied, or even made available, to education.)

So far no orders have been issued that would make such research applicable, but the toe is in the water and the more open-minded school people are eager to take the plunge.

Moreover, in the inner sanctum of the research division of the Academy of Pedagogical Sciences an entire room is newly filled with an impressive collection of American professional literature on guidance—another shunned academic pasture. Highly placed experts predict that within a year guidance counselors will be functioning in the Soviet secondary schools. It is difficult to believe that these advisers will not before long try their hand— openly or in secret—at predicting the aptitudes of their pupils.

Many basic problems remain. While it is true that all ninth and tenth graders for the first time this year were offered four hours of electives a week (and the allotment is to be increased to six hours beginning in eighth grade), it is difficult to make the elective system work under present conditions. As long as teachers are held severely accountable for their pupils' failures, the human tendency will be to say: "You're not doing too well in mathematics. Better 'elect' an extra math course." And as long as the total curriculum remains neatly mapped out, what chance is there to branch out into an unknown territory?

The same limitations hamper the official challenge to let students indulge in independent study. While it is relatively easy for bright science students to forge ahead independently in the laboratory, how safe—and feasible—is independence in history, economics, and sociology?

One Western diplomat, pointing to the omnipresent bureaucracy, said: "It is difficult even for the Russian *émigré* to make his way in an open society until he learns that he cannot just wait to be told what to do and what will be done for him." Students at Leningrad State University echoed this view. They agreed that Soviet life is too tightly centralized, but they blamed the forces of history for the current bureaucratic strictures. "It's the aftermath of the Mongolian yoke," said one history major. "As people become better educated and able to think and shift for themselves, the strings can be relaxed."

This, then, is the immediate issue. How to relax controls so that the schools may teach greater independence—and how to persuade the forces of conservatism in pedagogy and in the party that this must be done, for the good of the country, despite the risks to the Establishment.

Professor Yelyutin, the Minister of Higher Education, in an interview, indicated that, at the highest level of educational leadership, conservatism may be in the process of being replaced by official impatience. He said that while he was not worried about quantity in Soviet education, there was need for greater stress on quality and on "different solutions." He demanded that educational technology be updated, "to bring the teachers into the front line of new methods and to let the students benefit from it."

'The modern engineer must also know the basic humanities," he said. "We can't teach him everything he needs, but we must teach him how to learn."

Professor Yelyutin went on: "I would like to see students develop the ability to use their knowledge better." Instead of the old-fashioned and rigidly prescribed high-school courses in preparation for university admission, he favored the introduction during the senior year of high school of new methods of instruction that resemble university teaching—lectures, seminars, and tutorials.

But the problems are, in fact, more fundamental. In the past, much of the labor force on the level of the highly skilled and the subuniversity category of technicians has come out of the technicums, a special version of specialized secondary schools. But the Soviet Union has become increasingly aware, as has the United States, that modern technological society requires a higher degree of sophistication. Efforts have been made to upgrade the technicums to the higher-education level, not unlike some of the American junior colleges.

This, however, has not solved the problem of status and prestige; "new class" parents want their children to go to the universities or, failing this, to the institutes that enjoy university status. As a result, it becomes increasingly difficult to supply the army of highly skilled technicians and maintenance experts a nation with rapidly developing technological and urban services requires. The Soviet Union has the strange, contradictory appearance of a country that has the basic know-how to construct a modern society but lacks the skilled manpower to prevent deterioration and decay from outpacing the construction.

A second, and even more fundamental, problem arises from the fact that Soviet officialdom regards the universities as a tiny fragment of the whole higher-education scene. Of the total of more than seven hundred and fifty higher-education establishments, only about forty are universities. The remainder are institutes—for languages, agriculture, a host of highly specialized professions from health to cinematography and, of course, teacher training. And while Minister Yelyutin projected a higher-education enrollment of 8,000,000 (about 60 per cent of it full time, the remainder evening and correspondence enrollment), present indications are that the expansion of the universities must still expect to take a back seat to that of the highly specialized institutes.

Even the universities are, by American standards, professional schools rather than institutions of general and broad scholarship and learning. Yet, within the Soviet framework, they are infinitely more far-ranging than the institutes. Thus the broadly educated leadership and managerial echelon, already dangerously thin, is not likely to be reinforced rapidly enough to give the huge country the cohesive planning and thinking it so urgently requires. Under the present plan the base of university graduates—the only representatives of anything approaching more extensive higher education—is likely to be so small as to turn into an elitist group of power and privilege. This will increase the already excessive pressures for university admission, without providing enough alumni. (While college admissions pressures in the United States are severe, too, the alternatives are much broader. Those who fail to gain admission to the universities and institutes in the Soviet Union may pursue their studies by correspondence course, but this is a low-prestige solution. Evening courses carry higher status, and students get four weeks' vacation with full pay, prior to examinations, but the way to a more broadly educated nation may have to come through less restrictive university admission, a more broadly oriented university curriculum, and less narrowly specialized approaches to education in the institutes.)

These challenges come at a difficult and crucial time. Urbanization has reached a crisis that leaves on higher education's doorstep the huge task of assimilating masses of people who are not only poorly educated but have not yet developed the tradition of education-consciousness. Moreover, the rural schools lag seriously behind those in the cities, and few urban teachers want to teach in distant villages and towns.

Not unlike American efforts at upgrading the education of Negro and Puerto Rican children, Russian experts are pushing for the conversion of existing boarding schools into special compensatory institutions in which bright children from the farms may be prepared for higher education.

Underneath the uniformity of the Soviet Union's giant education system and purposely hidden by the smoke screen of official doctrine, the world of school and university is trying to cope with great divisions and conflicts that cry out for debate and resolution.

Perhaps the least complicated of these conflicts are those which arise from the need to reconsider educational methods, to adjust the school to the pace of the modern child. "Tots in kindergarten today know all the dirty jokes we are telling," quipped a Leningrad psychology student. But when she was reminded that American psychologists have already provided considerable research on earlier learning, she replied stiffly: "We must develop our own theorists."

What about the experience of the past, I asked. What about John Dewey and Stanislav Shatsky? "That's just historic; we need what's practical now," she answered.

But not all of those involved in the behind-the-scenes debate are as certain that the past holds no lesson. In Moscow's Experimental School 710, Professor Mikhail A. Melnikov, now in his eightieth year, spends his "retirement" as the school's director. A former vice president of the Academy of Pedagogical Sciences, the heavy-set, fatherly man, whose searching blue eyes have watched children and reforms come and go for sixty professional years, issues no denials about the uses of educational history and experience. His school's experimental program is "based on differentiation and on the students' special interests." Except for the final examinations, there are no tests. Apart from a certain number of basic required courses, the students may select their favorite subjects in each of three divisions—physics and mathematics, biology and chemistry, and the humanities. Even though many traditional educators have scoffed at such excessive freedom, Professor Melnikov reports triumphantly that in the past three years a record 95 per cent of his graduates have entered the institutions of higher learning.

Is the Melnikov liberation of school and mind merely the freak of a distinguished survivor from an earlier, more freewheeling era? Increasing signs of a new sense of searching—and of new pressures—point in a different direction.

One of the clichés of the revolution, perpetuated in every syllabus and textbook, is the creation of "the new Soviet man." But the framers of the cliché failed to contemplate that the new men might not fit the old Bolshevik mold. Slowly, among the institutional and educational leadership, two worlds are emerging: the Old Men, whose minds and reflexes are conditioned by the educational and political party line, and the New Men, who, though loyal members of the apparatus, want to free themselves from the confining formalism of that line.

Professor Ivan G. Petrovsky, rector of Moscow State University, a serious, slightly pedantic, courteous man, bald and with peasant features, represents the Soviet old world. He is a mathematician, and by all accounts a good one, but he has been rector of the Soviet Union's largest and most prestigious university for sixteen years and a faculty member for thirty-seven. Understandably, Professor Petrovsky finds it easier to look to the past than to the future. Just after the revolution, he recalls, a typical class at Moscow University consisted of two hundred students, and out of these only about ten ever graduated. Today 90 per cent of the huge classes of about 3,000 freshmen remain to complete their degrees.

Professor Petrovsky was graduated in 1927. Within three years, at the age of twenty-nine, he was chairman of the Department of Higher Mathematics at a Moscow engineering school. "During these years it is difficult to realize that one has become an old man," he said. The role of the party?

"It is impossible to separate the party from the university," he said. "The history of the party is the history of the university itself."

This prototype of the Old Soviet Man—probably close to the ideal textbook version of orthodoxy—when asked about controversies that trouble the university can think only of a debate over the mathematical views of a French scholar. He allows that, perhaps, "it may have been our fault not to have paid enough attention to the humanities." He pauses. Then—a soft afterthought: "Man does not live by bread alone." In the years ahead, he is sure, interest in the humanities will increase, and as an indication of the growing concern with the arts he cites the creation of the Society for the Preservation of Monuments.

At Leningrad, the country's second university in size and reputation, Professor Kirill Kondratyev, the young, fortyish new rector, belongs to a different world. An atmospheric and space physicist, he was graduated in 1946, after five years of wartime service. All his concern is with the future. His antennae pick up ferment, and he demands change. In the idiom of the American university president, he spreads out the university's huge building program, and defends the controversial plan to move out of the decrepit czarist palaces in the heart of Leningrad to a streamlined campus in suburban Petrodvorets, the historic Peterhof.

Professor Kondratyev, whom the young scientists at Harvard (where he has been a repeated visitor) speak of as a kindred spirit and of their generation, sees and seeks controversy everywhere. He found students overloaded with outmoded requirements, freed half of an incoming class of 50 per cent of their lectures and seminars and proved that the freewheeling group did better than their tradition-bound classmates. He responded to complaints about bright students who fail to pass their entrance requirements by asking the Ministry of Higher Education to let him admit 10 per cent of each year's class on a more intuitive basis.

He said that he has been pressing for a basic reform: election of university rectors by the faculty, for a limited term of administrative office. While this may seem a matter of detail, it would, in fact, snatch the universities from under the direct control of "Moscow," the Ministry of Higher Education, which now appoints rectors and prorectors. It would cut the ties with the political bureaucracy and might—although there is no assurance that this would happen—make it easier for the New Men to take over education's reins.

The tug of war between the old and the new, between the anachronistic forces of the *status-quo*-minded party and the future-oriented "new class," is far from resolved. Through the tight organization of the little seven-year-old Octobrists, the nine-to-fourteen-year-old Pioneers, and the members of the Komsomol (Young Communist League), up to twenty-eight years of age, the party-line conservatives have dug powerful positions. But at present they appear to be more intent on halting the retreat than in leading the advance.

It is difficult to keep a revolution alive—especially when so many of the trappings of the Western middle-class world appear attractive to the growing Russian middle class. During a visit to a high school in Moscow, I was surprised to find a chemistry classroom packed with youngsters under the direction not of a teacher but of a pale and earnest teen-age girl. Two other girls were perched on the laboratory table, acting as recording secretaries. I had stumbled into a membership meeting of the Komsomol.

A bedraggled little boy stood up, flustered and ill at ease. He was asked why he wanted to join the Komsomol. Somewhat despondently, he said that, since only five of his comrades had remained outside the fold, he felt like an outcast. His lame appeal was followed by a good deal of giggling and buzzing, but when a show of hands was requested, he was voted "in" with only a few abstentions. There was no opposing vote.

The impression was clearly one of a ritual that no longer is taken too seriously. To most of the youngsters the business seemed something of a lark—except for the intense girl in front of the room who tried, a little stuffily, to uphold decorum and gravity.

A university student confirmed this impression. Even though the majority of students are members, he said, the leaders tend to be dull, provincial types who have their eyes on political district jobs.

A former student recalled that as recently as 1960 the Komsomol contributed visibly to higher education by plastering the university's walls with posters warning the girls against the bourgeois evils of lipstick, mascara, and stylish dress. It is a measure of the retreat to prepared positions—under strong pressure—that today the Komsomol organizes fashion shows and jazz concerts. Not unlike churches afraid to lose the swinging crowd, the Komsomol is trying to modernize its image.

But the gap remains. Soviet university students show little enthusiasm for slogans and revolutionary rah-rah. They accept such rituals as the occasional week of potato harvesting, but they know and admit that their "productive labor" is of little use to the farmers. They look at the week in the rural hostel as something akin to the freshman mixer on an American campus. "You get to know everybody," said a practical coed in Leningrad.

All in all, party and Komsomol, once the voices of liberation, have become the puritanical watchdogs of manners and morals, and of political conformity. It is the Komsomol that lectures, behind closed doors, any

Russian girl student who is seen too regularly dating an African student.

It is tempting to conclude that, because the Komsomol and the party, in their old-guard posture, appear slightly ridiculous, their power is gone. Yet if the central bureaucracy decided to tighten the controls, the domination of the school and university scene could probably once again become pervasive, rigid, and even oppressive.

But the popular and economic pressures, now and in the long run, appear to be in the opposite direction. For the moment the students' stance is one of massive disinterest in politics and international affairs, apart from international style in music, art, and dress. Like the American student generation of a decade ago, Soviet youth has turned inward, to a mood of privacy. This is Russia's Silent Generation. It is not dissatisfied; on the contrary, it is quite aware of its privileged position and of its nation's growing prosperity. But it appears to sense that, if only the controls could be relaxed, the first pleasant taste of comfort and affluence could lead to a steady diet.

In visiting Russian schools and talking with university students, I sensed a new style and drive alien to the older generation. The teen-age boys and girls, despite their Victorian uniforms, are physically of a new mold—with easier smiles, less inhibited manner, and greater poise. If the revolution, with its powerful drive toward universal education, wanted to achieve this, it has indeed accomplished much. It remains to be seen whether the new generation can be kept faithful to the old dogma.

The latest educational reform call has sounded the alarm for greater independence and personal initiative. More of Russia's youth may be ready to respond than the reformers are bargaining for. Thus education may well become the testing ground for the forces of progress in their contest with the old guard during the first decade of the second half-century of the first Soviet state.

Much of what that second half-century has in store will be determined by the gathering force of new interests, goals, curiosities, and aspirations of that segment of the population which the Soviet state has singled out for special favors, privileges, and powers—the highly educated university alumni. There is every indication that today's university students are bored with the anachronistic trappings of the original revolution. They are more effectively conditioned against active rebellion than are their counterparts in the West, but generational gaps cannot be bridged, much less eliminated, by doctrine or decree. And the plain fact is that the revolution was made by, and for, another generation. The question now is how soon the controls will be relaxed sufficiently for the new generation to assert itself—not as rebels against socialism (for they see much to admire in the socialist state), but as the modern antagonists of restrictive statism and doctrinaire bureaucracy.

Even the relaxing of controls is not, at present, a matter of monolithic decision. In Moscow the controls—real or imagined—are still on everybody's mind. I found it difficult to establish straightforward contact with university students there. Perhaps the very fact that no one is permitted to enter the giant university complex on Lenin Hills without presenting a pass is in itself a deterrent to normal, informal get-togethers. In fact, the consciousness of the barrier appears to encourage semiclandestine contact on the part of the alienated. I hardly ever sat for more than five minutes in the little park outside the downtown humanities center of the university, facing the Kremlin walls, without being joined by one or two Soviet students.

The question "Are you American?" was usually followed by the explanation that it is difficult to practice one's English. Then came the routine nonacademic questions—about American cars, jazz, fashions.

"I am studying journalism," said a tall, handsome youth, who indicated that he was more interested in the swinging side of student life than in scholarship. "Of course, I would like to get a job on the staff of one of the magazines, but the editors would not agree with the stories I would want to write. I do not like everything that happens."

A few days later, after a similar introduction, a nervous youth in a light-beige raincoat—a student of history—said that although he himself had no interest in religious observance, he was attracted by the study of religion. He was conscious of the difficulty of turning this interest into a career, just as he was fully aware of the politics of his family's life. "My father is a government official," he said. "He did well under Khrushchev, and we lived in a nice four-room apartment. Now his job is no longer so important and we only have two rooms." After a moment's silence, he said, with a slight shrug, "My mother is Jewish."

But this is Moscow, and the meetings with students remain peripheral and therefore not typical or satisfactory. Eight hundred kilometers away, in Leningrad, the controls are not as rigid. Nobody guards the gates of the university, and I walked in and out, met the students and, once my presence was made known to them, entered into free-flowing group discussions.

One evening, at seven, I accepted an invitation to a student dormitory. Having left an identifying document—any document bearing the visitor's name, merely to eliminate squatters who might otherwise move in and remain unnoticed—at the concierge's booth next to Lenin's bust, I was free to visit my friends. Crammed into a small room for two students, furnished with two iron beds, a table, some bookshelves and cabinets, twelve to fifteen of us held a bull session, with a few participants drifting in and out.

After a round of introductions—I remember a biologist, two historians, a graduate student of economics, a physicist, a girl psychologist and her graduate-school husband—the discussion at first seemed halting and somewhat strained. But a huge pot of coffee—later in the evening spiked modestly with brandy—warmed the conversation and turned the meeting into an ordinary, nonceremonial occasion.

The students generally were pleased with the powers they enjoy in the administration of the university. The Student Soviet (council) has almost unlimited powers over student affairs, including determination of the amount of student stipends. Students sit on the admissions committee, may ask the administration to add or eliminate courses or lectures, and may bring teachers up on charges of poor instruction.

I asked whether students actually avail themselves of that right. Only recently, I was told, an instructor of statistics who had become so engrossed in his personal research with computers that he failed to prepare his lectures was asked to appear before the student committee, was charged with dull, ill-prepared lectures, and admitted his neglect. "He is doing much better now," said one of the students, satisfied that matters were under control.

"Next to that of the administration itself, ours is the most important power," a student said.

The over-all impression one gains from such discussions is that these young intellectuals are generally pleased with their personal status—they stressed that on completion of their studies all of them are guaranteed job placement—and with their education, but that they generally lack interest in the larger issues of the world and even of their own society. It may have been courtesy to the American visitor, but questions about such issues as Vietnam or the Middle East conflict failed to be broached. (An American student who has been in the Soviet Union long enough not to be entitled to such tactful treatment any longer ascribed such silence to apathy and confusion rather than politeness. After all, anti-Chinese sentiments are powerful, even more so among Russians at large than within the government, and the students thus could hardly be expected to become agitated over a far-away war, fought by Americans.)

One graduate student questioned me on the support that had been given to the National Student Association by the Central Intelligence Agency. I explained that I personally and my newspaper editorially had been indignant about the clandestine financing when it came to light. But I also offered a thumbnail sketch of the period when the flow of secret funds was begun—the conservatism of Congress and the right-wing pressures by Senator Joseph

McCarthy and his supporters in opposition to the expenditure of money for liberal ventures abroad. The student interrupted me. "You misunderstand," he said. "I am not objecting to the money. What does it matter where the money comes from. It is only the use to which it is put that matters. Of course, we would not approve if it were used for spying, but if not —what is the difference?"

The evening passed quickly. It seemed less political and infinitely less argumentative than a similar gathering in an American dormitory. Once, in touching on disagreement with past policies, the subject was dismissed with a resigned reference to the days of the Cult of Personality. Mention of Khrushchev evoked smiles, chuckles, and a not-at-all-disapproving backward glance.

"How do the people in America feel about the Soviet Union?" a student asked. "Why is there not closer contact?" When I suggested that this might be the fault of both governments, the questioner nodded and repeated, as if to underline it, "Yes, both governments." Another student added, "The newspapers, too. The newspapers are always lagging behind the people. They should catch up."

Several students expressed the hope that more Americans would come to the Soviet Union, and when I suggested that this ought to be a two-way affair a young economist replied, "You must realize that we are still relatively poor and don't have the money to travel, while you are the richest nation in the world."

One student, an economics major with an interest in history, said he did not wish to pass judgment on the policies of Khrushchev but thought the former leader had put into words what most people want when he promised that the Soviet Union would "catch up with and overtake the United States." "I am glad that Khrushchev took his trip through the United States," he added. "We have been waiting for your President—first Eisenhower, then Kennedy. I suppose President Johnson will not come now, but if he comes the people will give him a friendly reception."

More than five hours later, well past midnight, I prepared to leave. A young English girl, an exchange student, caught the session as it broke up and invited the hardiest survivors to another room, where, with an American electric skillet and a medley of Russian ingredients, she prepared tea and a Leningrad version of pizza. The guitars took over, the night's festivities went on, but the serious bull session was at an end. An hour later I collected my "document," said good-by, and went on my way.

LITERATURE:
THE RIGHT TO WRITE

»

Harrison E. Salisbury

Maya Borisova is a lovely young woman with reddish hair and Dutch-blue eyes that light up as she talks. She was trying to tell me why the fate of Russian poets has always been so hard and often so tragic. We were talking in the lounge of the old stone house in Leningrad at No. 18 Voinov Street, home of the Writers Union. She is a lyrical poet who sometimes writes of love, of girls in spring, and sometimes of the forty tons of nuclear explosive which hang, in her words, suspended over the head of each person in the world.

I had mentioned the tragedy that seemed to stalk the lives of Russian poets—beginning with Pushkin, Russia's greatest, killed at the height of his genius in 1837 in a duel instigated, it has long been suspected, by Czar Nicholas I, who feared his liberal views. Pushkin's death had been followed by that of his friend and fellow poet Mikhail Lermontov, killed in a duel in the Caucasus. In more recent times there had been the tragic end of Sergei Yesenin, the young revolutionary poet, once married to Isadora Duncan, who cut his wrists and bled to death in 1925 in Leningrad. Vladimir Mayakovsky, idol of a generation of young Russians, shot himself in 1930. Marina Tsvetayeva, the most beautiful of modern Russian poets, hanged herself in 1941, despondent in the dark Volga province where she had been exiled after returning to her motherland on the eve of World War II. Osip Mandelshtam, one of the greatest Russian poets of the twentieth century, died, mad and starving, in one of Stalin's concentration camps (the transit camp at Vladivostok) in 1938. Anna Akhmatova, dean of Russian poetry, was reviled as a cross between a "nun and a whore" in a campaign launched by Andrei Zhdanov in 1946 which robbed her of a livelihood and nearly cost her life. The fate of Boris Pasternak was fresh in every mind—the vituperation heaped upon him when he won the Nobel Prize, and the savagery of the Communist party bullyboys which hastened his life to its end.

Nor, I noted, was the end in sight. Even today, in a period of comparative liberalism, the poets were the center of attack and counterattack. In late 1962 and early 1963 Nikita S. Khrushchev, after earlier giving them his support, turned on the most brilliant of them, Yevgeny Yevtushenko, Andrei Voznesensky, Bella Akhmadulina, Bulat Okudzhava. He said to them and to the young Soviet artists: "We are declaring war on you." For a few months it appeared that these talents—the pride of the new Soviet intelligentsia—might become sacrifices on the altar of Communist party dogmatism.

All this was in our minds as we discussed the fate of poets in Russia. An elderly Leningrad critic, a man who had devoted his life to literary research and who was the author of several respected studies, said that he believed that to be a good poet you must suffer. Russia had always been the home of great poets. This meant, in a word, that they had had to suffer. Otherwise they would not have achieved greatness.

Maya Borisova rejected this thesis with a quick shake of her head. That was not the reason. The reason lay in the Russian concept of a poet's role. The poet must always be ahead, in the vanguard. He must be in the vanguard of thought, of feeling, of philosophy. His poetry must deal with the vital questions of morals, of life, and of creation. He must stir his countrymen to action. If he did not confront the essentials, he was not a true poet. Inevitably, the poet must come into collision with authority, for authority, be it czarist autocracy or Bolshevik Communism, was dedicated to the defense of its own position. The poet was a man who challenged, who questioned, who rejected, who saw that the king wore no clothes and did not keep his silence. How could the poet fail to find himself in conflict and controversy?

Maya Borisova is not one of Russia's great poets, but she is a sensitive writer, a woman of conviction and poetic ideals. Her views on the role of the poet differ only in minor detail from those of others of Russia's younger generation. They argue endlessly among themselves. But they stand together in a single attitude, which, most simply put, is a demand for full, complete, and unrestricted creative freedom. In this the writers have made common cause with the artists. They see their struggle as one and the same. The relationship between the poets and the artists, the writers and the sculptors, is intimate and personal. The sculptor Ernst Neizvestny is Yevtushenko's best friend. Khrushchev once turned on Neizvestny and exclaimed, "Only death will cure the hunchback!" The threat hardly budged the powerfully built Neizvestny, front-line fighter in World War II, a man officially declared dead and posthumously decorated, an accidental survivor of one of Russia's *shtrafny,* or punishment battalions, from which hardly one in a hundred men returned alive.

Because of the Russian tradition of the "civic" poet, stemming from the days of Pushkin, much of the excitement in the post-Stalin days has been centered in poetry, in the struggles of Yevtushenko to decry the horrors of the German massacre of Jews at Babi Yar in the Ukraine and the persisting anti-Semitism which the suppression of the Babi Yar facts implied; in Yevtushenko's warning against the danger of a recidivism of Stalinism (incorporated in his poem "Stalin's Heirs," published after Khrushchev's personal intervention); in his autobiography, with its insights into the savagery of Stalin's purges, life in Stalinist Siberia, and the macabre atmosphere of Stalin's lying-in-state.

Frequent travel abroad by the Russian poets, notably Yevtushenko and Voznesensky, has made their names and faces familiar in the West. The trips, too, have been a source of controversy and scandal, as neo-Stalinist foes of the young liberals comb over their conduct, searching for words and actions that may be used to discredit them.

The poets have become a symbol to Russian youth of their own generation. Poetry readings, always popular in Russia, have become a mass phenomenon; scores of thousands turn out in the streets for recitations on the annual Days of Poetry, and recitals sometimes attract audiences of 30,000 or 40,000 to sports stadiums.

Upon the poets have fallen the sharpest lashes of official reprimand and reprisal. An experimental young poet in Leningrad, Iosif Brodsky, a protégé of Anna Akhmatova, was exiled in 1964 to a northern labor camp for five years on charges that he was a vagrant. In reality he was, and is, one of Leningrad's most talented young writers. His exile drew an angry petition from dozens of writers. Now, after serving two years, he is back in Leningrad, at liberty, devoting himself, as before, to writing. His work has been published in the Leningrad literary almanacs. He is busy working on translations—a familiar device to enable a writer whose original work is not officially approved to support himself while waiting for the political winds to change.

"We are very glad that he is with us, writing again," Maya Borisova said. "He is a very talented poet. I don't always understand him. But we value him very highly."

Other poets have felt the sting. Bella Akhmadulina has been refused permission to travel in the West, although she often is invited and goes to Bulgaria and Hungary. The reason lies not in her talent; she has been regarded by some writers, including Valentin Katayev and the late Ilya Ehrenburg, as the most talented woman poet of her day. Often young Russians speak of her as the heir to the tradition of Akhmatova and Tsvetayeva. She is a poet with a silvery gift of speech, of bell-like imagery, of passionate emotion, and a deft, almost elfin sense of humor. It is not for these qualities that the travel permits for her seem to get lost in Russia's vast bureaucracy. It is because she speaks out in what Mayakovsky called "full voice." In a remarkable poem called "Rain" she set forth her literary articles of faith in a dialogue with a critic who seeks to put her back on the path of safe, solid, somnolescent Socialist Realism. Never! she cries. Never will she write to dictate. Not even with a gun could she be forced to write against her conscience. A gun, responds the critic; yes, a gun is not a bad thing, sometimes.

Images of guns and warfare recur in the speech of the young Soviet poets. And with good reason. They consider themselves on the advance skirmish line of a battle that is not fought with words only. They are well aware of the literary struggles of Russia's past and of the bloody wounds and the mortal sacrifices that litter that past in times not long vanished. They are obsessed by the knowledge that under Stalin the most gifted talents of a deeply creative nation were wiped out. Not only were their works suppressed, not only were they forbidden to write and publish in accordance with their ideals, but they were also physically exterminated or brutalized by the Stalinist system.

The agony of those times hangs over Russia like a bloody fog. Those of the older generation who survived it are scarred indelibly. Some, like Ilya Ehrenburg, have dedicated the last years of their lives to a twin purpose: to re-creating and re-establishing the truth about the dozens, the hundreds of Stalin's victims, and to educating the new Russian generation in artistic traditions, not only Russian but Western, and not only literary but in the whole field of creativity. It is an endless task and one that engaged Ehrenburg to the last of his days. To this purpose he wrote nine volumes of his reminiscences and was engaged, before his death, in writing one or two more volumes "to bring the story up to date—from 1953 to 1964," to cover, in a word, the Khrushchev era.

These are controversial tasks. There is no agreement between any two members of the literary Establishment as to the precise facts of the sad and intricate pattern of relationships between the writers and the Communist regime in the stormy fifty years since 1917.

At the beginning it seemed clear enough. The revolution was a liberating force. There was not a writer of any stature in Russia who had not supported the century-old struggle against the czar's despotism. Gogol, Pushkin, Lermontov, Herzen, Chernyshevsky, Dostoyevsky (before his late conversion into an ardent monarchist), Turgenev, Tolstoy, Chekhov, all had dreamed of a new Russia. The writers of 1917—Maxim Gorky, Vladimir Mayakovsky, Aleksandr Blok, Boris Pasternak, Andrei Bely—many, many greeted the revolution as opening the way to new freedoms, new creative achievements. Some quickly became disillusioned. Blok died in 1921, after having written two great poems commemorating the revolution: "The Scythians" and "The Twelve." Ivan A. Bunin, hostile from the start, went into exile. Others began to lose their zeal. They found that revolution and creative freedom did not necessarily equate. There were violent rows, savage disputes. The poet Nikolai Gumilev, divorced husband of Anna Akhmatova, was shot in 1921 for supposed complicity in a plot against the regime. Bely went into exile in 1921, but came back in 1923 to live on in Russia until his death in 1934. Yevgeny Zamyatin, satirical author of *We* (the precursor of George Orwell's *Nineteen Eighty-four*), stayed in Russia until 1931, when he was permitted to emigrate to Paris, where he died. Aleksandr I. Kuprin left his country in 1917, but came back shortly before his death in 1938.

The figure of Stalin began to tower more and more over the Soviet scene, dominating the world of culture as he did all other spheres of Soviet life. More and more the key questions turned on Stalin, on Stalin's views, on Stalin's relations with Russia's writers. The nature of these relations, the role played by Stalin in the lives of Mayakovsky, Gorky, Pasternak, Ehrenburg, Leonov, Sholokhov, and others now haunts literary Russia.

Maxim Gorky, an early Bolshevik, broke with Lenin and went to Capri to live in 1921. Stalin lured him back to Russia. Did Gorky then use Stalin or did Stalin use Gorky or did each use the other? *Kto kovo?* (Who gets whom?)—as the Russians say. Looking back over the record of the terrible years, different writers give different answers.

"No writer used Stalin," Valentin Katayev told me as we sat eating shashlik in the outdoor garden of Moscow's Uzbekistan Restaurant. "It is ridiculous to think that Gorky used Stalin. Stalin used him. He was Stalin's trophy, his great prize. Stalin valued Gorky precisely because Lenin had lost him and Stalin got him back." In Katayev's view, Stalin made use of Gorky to whip the writers into line, to impose upon them the concept that they must dedicate their every effort to support the Soviet state, that they must become, in his phrase, the "engineers of human souls."

When Gorky died, Stalin elevated him to the rank of a saint in the Stalinist iconography. Many Russians long suspected that Stalin might have poisoned Gorky because Gorky had begun to perceive the basic evil of the Stalin system. Gorky died in 1936, and a year or so later one of Stalin's police chiefs, Henryk Yagoda, was charged with conspiring with a pliant physician to take the lives of Gorky and Gorky's son. Was this at Stalin's order or was the story part of the Grand Guignol atmosphere of those days? The truth may never be known, but the mood of Soviet writers today is to believe that Gorky died a natural death. His health was not good. He drove himself to the extreme. He rose each morning at 6:00 A.M. and wrote like a demon until noon, obsessed with the need to record every thought, each experience. Then he began a whole new day, conferring, talking endlessly, smoking without interruption, sitting and drinking until midnight or later. He had a young wife.

"He probably died a natural death," Katayev concluded.

Konstantin Simonov shared Katayev's opinion. "I didn't like the original story [of poisoning by Yagoda] very much," he said. "I don't like the other versions. I'm inclined to let the old man die a natural death."

Once, Gorky brought young Leonid Leonov to see Stalin. Leonov was introduced, and the company sat down around a table to eat, drink, and talk. Gorky sat next to Stalin. The others at the table were Leonov, Kliment Voroshilov, Abel Yenukidze, and Nikolai Bukharin (the last two later purged by Stalin). Gorky and Stalin were soon engaged in lively conversation. Voroshilov leaned toward Leonov and the two began to speak in low voices so as not to interfere with the Stalin-Gorky talk. Suddenly Stalin broke in. He had heard every word Leonov had spoken to Voroshilov. Stalin looked coldly at Leonov and said to Gorky: "Who is this young man?"

"This young man is speaking for Soviet literature," Gorky said, adding emphatically, "And he has the right to speak."

There was a pause. Stalin lifted his hand to his black mustache and after caressing first the right side and then the left, replied in a low voice, his eyes piercing Leonov's: "I understand."

But what Stalin understood Leonov does not know to this day. Leonov came to see only too clearly the dangers that flowed from Stalin. He still remembers a dinner with five of his writer friends in 1937. They were Boris Pilnyak, Artem Vesely, Isaak Babel, Osip Mandelshtam, and Bruno Yasensky, or Jasienski, a Pole. Each died in a Stalinist concentration camp. Only Leonov survived. "I should have perished with them," Leonov now says. "Why did I live and they die?" Possibly the curious fragment of conversation between Gorky and Stalin in some way protected him from the fate so many others suffered.

The names of Gorky and Mayakovsky are often bracketed because Stalin bracketed them. Five years after Mayakovsky shot himself in April, 1930, Stalin declared: "Mayakovsky has been and will continue to be the best and most talented poet of the Soviet epoch." In Pasternak's words, Stalin began then to popularize Mayakovsky just as "potatoes were popularized during the regime of Catherine the Great." He did not popularize Mayakovsky because of literature, but because of politics, Katayev explained.

The effort to bracket Gorky and Mayakovsky is indignantly rejected by Lila Yuryevna Brik, *grande dame* of Russian letters, an aging but still beautiful woman who lives in an apartment near the Moskva River cluttered with Picassos, Légers, Chagalls, Tatlins, Kandinskys, two or three striking Georgian primitives by Nikko Pirosmanishvili, and many drawings, cartoons, and caricatures by Mayakovsky. Of Mayakovsky Mrs. Brik, in white Courrèges boots, just back from a Paris visit to her sister, Elsa Triolet, wife of Louis Aragon, said simply: "He loved drink and he loved women and he loved me for fifteen years." On a long golden chain around her neck she still wears the ring he gave her and the one she gave him. Mayakovsky had engraved within hers her initials L. Yu. B. repeated over and over in an endless refrain which spells LYUBLYU-BLYU-BLYU (I love, love, love you).

"People coupled Gorky and Mayakovsky," she said, "only because Stalin used them both. But he used Mayakovsky after he was dead. He used Gorky while he was still alive." It had been suggested that Mayakovsky shot himself because of the ideological strait jacket which Stalin and his regime were fashioning. But Mrs. Brik rejected this thesis. "You must know," she said with a passion that has not been cooled by the years, "that Mayakovsky was the most sensitive man in the world. He was a wonderfully simple, wonderfully warm man. But his skin was so thin. He suffered terribly. Why did he kill himself? Well, it was not the first time. He tried to kill himself in 1916. Then, later, he got a revolver from Gorky—or tried to get one. In the spring of 1930 he was upset. He had been thrown over by a very lovely girl. She was twenty-two. He was thirty-three. She thought he was too old for her. All his life he had been afraid of growing old. He was afraid of death. He wanted too much to live. But now he was growing old. So he thought."

Of course, Mrs. Brik conceded, there had been the savage row between Mayakovsky's literary organization, LEF, and the party-sponsored RAPP.

That upset Mayakovsky, and there had been other small problems. But nothing big. "I was not in Moscow," Mrs. Brik said sadly. "Had I been there maybe we would have sat down and played some cards and talked and that would have been the end of it. But I was not there. . . ."

Never in his life had Mayakovsky met Stalin. Then after his death Stalin turned Mayakovsky's reputation to his own uses.

Writers were attracted to Stalin. He was a sinister figure but he was also a magnetic figure. Even such a man as Pasternak felt the attraction. When Stalin's wife, Nadezhda Alliluyeva, shot herself on November 8, 1934, the Writers Union sent Stalin a joint message of sympathy. Pasternak did not sign it. He sent his own message, couched in vague, mysterious terms. He said: "I share the feelings of my comrades. On the evening before I found myself as an artist thinking profoundly and continuously about Stalin for the first time. In the morning I read the news. I was shaken as if I had been on the spot and had lived through and seen everything."

For a generation literary scholars have sought to penetrate the meaning of Pasternak's curious words. What was the relationship between the fearsome Georgian dictator and the dreaming Russian poet? Was there in this message some clue to why Pasternak had survived the scythe which cut down most of his friends and associates in the 1930's and 1940's? Did this bear some relationship to the strange "protector" figure, the half-brother, Yevgraf, who appears at critical moments to save the life of Doctor Zhivago?

Konstantin Simonov believes this may be true. There were, he said, many complexities in the relationship of Pasternak and Stalin. Another respected Russian writer, a close and understanding friend of Pasternak, rejected the idea but suggested that Pasternak's character had been idealized by the younger Soviet generation and in the West. "Pasternak was not a simple, unworldly man as many of you in the West think," he said. "He was a man of contradictions. He had his own character. But he wished to be part of the Establishment, to be recognized, to belong. He could have been a courtier of Stalin—if Stalin had permitted this. He was not really a rebel at all."

Katayev contrasted Pasternak with Mandelshtam. "Mandelshtam was outspoken," said Katayev. "He was a real opponent of Stalin. I remember once he came to our house. It must have been 1936 or 1937. He was shouting against Stalin—what a terrible man Stalin was. We were terrified, my wife and I. We had two small children. We did not know what to do. Pasternak was never like that. He did not denounce Stalin. After all, he wrote a very good poem about Lenin. And he wrote one about Stalin, as well."

Some Soviet writers have criticized Pasternak for not standing up more strongly to Stalin. Some have specifically blamed him in Mandelshtam's death. Stalin telephoned Pasternak (it was the only telephone call he ever made to Pasternak) and asked him about Mandelshtam. Pasternak replied that there was little he could say, for he did not know Mandelshtam well. The critics have said this doomed Mandelshtam to arrest and death.

Katayev does not share this opinion. Stalin and his secretaries frequently telephoned writers, asking for an evaluation of one man or another. You never knew, he said, what was in their mind. Usually it was something innocent. In a few days there would be an announcement of an appointment of some kind. Pasternak did not know Mandelshtam well, Katayev said. His response to the call was perfectly normal and natural.

In the opinion of Galina Serebryakova, who knew Pasternak well in his later years, the suggestion that Pasternak had any connection, mystical or otherwise, with Stalin is gross slander. She believes Pasternak deliberately endangered his life by writing again and again to Stalin and to the Central Committee during the purge years in support of writers and individuals who had fallen into the hands of the secret police. She thinks he was trying to provoke his own arrest. Other friends of Pasternak scoff at this.

Lila Brik boils with indignation when she hears Stalin and Pasternak mentioned in the same breath. As for his letter to Stalin, she says that Pasternak always talked in a mystical fashion. Possibly he made his letter deliberately cloudy so Stalin would not know what he meant. She remembered that in 1936 he went to Paris to attend a writers conference. The purges were on and the atmosphere was tense. Pasternak sat up all night drinking and talking with Aleksandr S. Shcherbakov, head of the Moscow party organization, a man very close to Stalin. The next day Pasternak was in despair. "Why did I tell him everything about myself?" he asked in agony. "What will happen now?" Then he had a second thought. "Well, probably he didn't understand a thing I said." That, Mrs. Brik believes, is possible. "His mind worked in a different way from that of ordinary people," she recalled.

Once, Pasternak wrote a poem in which he spoke of the "beautiful dead apron" and in the next sentence mentioned the pulse beating in the temple. There was great discussion as to Pasternak's meaning. Someone said that the "beautiful dead apron" referred to a woman's drawn eyelids. Mrs. Brik asked Pasternak what he meant. "Well," he said, "I saw this apron. It was beautiful and it was lying on a chair. It wasn't doing the work for which it was designed. It was dead. So I wrote that line in my poem."

The contacts between the older writers and Stalin became a controversial fact in their lives—true especially of Ehrenburg. The neo-Stalinist voices in the Soviet Union charged that if, as he declared, he knew in the mid-1930's of Stalin's crimes, he should have spoken out then. They claimed they did not know and therefore could not raise a hand. They charged that

Ehrenburg himself was an intimate part of the Stalin apparatus, a criticism also directed against Ehrenburg from abroad. His foreign critics contended that he failed to use his special position with Stalin to try to save the Jewish writers and intellectuals who perished in the purge of 1949–52.

Mrs. Serebryakova, acting on what she said was evidence given to her in private conversations with General Poskrebyshev, Stalin's chief of purges, said that Ehrenburg was, in effect, an agent of Stalin. She took the position that she and other good Bolsheviks did not have knowledge of Stalin's crimes, but that Ehrenburg did, and therefore he was as guilty as Stalin. Stalin protected Ehrenburg, Mrs. Serebryakova contends, and it was thus with singular ill grace that Ehrenburg posed as an exposer of Stalin's crimes.

To this, not long before his death, Ehrenburg responded with vigor that belied his seventy-six years. "There is one old lady in Moscow who spreads these stories," he said. "I will not mention her name because she is still living." In all his life he had but one conversation with Stalin. It came at a moment when he was an outcast, unable to get his work published, shunned by his friends, virtually cut off from any source of livelihood, not knowing what lay ahead of him. Most of his closest associates had been arrested or executed. For all he knew, he would be next.

This was in the spring of 1941. Ehrenburg had been in France during the German occupation. He was and remained a passionate Francophile. He had been writing a novel, *The Fall of Paris,* about the tragic events he had witnessed. In those days the German-Soviet pact was in full vigor. Ehrenburg hated the Nazis. He put every bit of his feeling into his novel. No one would publish it.

One day Ehrenburg's telephone rang. It was Stalin's secretary. Would he call such and such a number—Stalin wanted to talk with him. "Not for a moment did I think it was a joke," he recalled. "No one made jokes about Stalin in those days." His daughter's dogs were in the flat, yapping and making a racket. He shut them out of the room and called the number. Stalin answered.

"Excuse me for asking you to call," Stalin said. "I don't know you personally but I know you well by your works." Ehrenburg rejoined that he knew Stalin well by *his* works. The call was about *The Fall of Paris.* Stalin had been reading it. He liked it. Ehrenburg said he had been having trouble getting it published. "Let's work together, you and me," Stalin said, "and see if we can't push it through."

Before the day was over, Ehrenburg's telephone rang a dozen times, with editors calling, wanting the rights to serialize *The Fall of Paris.*

That was his only call from Stalin, Ehrenburg said, and the only personal conversation he ever had with the dictator. True, Stalin showed him some favor. He intervened in April, 1948, to see that Ehrenburg's novel *The Storm* won a Stalin Prize. And he did not take Ehrenburg's life when the other Jewish writers perished. Ehrenburg had, like so many of his compatriots, kept a bag packed ready for the midnight knock of the police in the 1938 purge days. In March, 1949, when he awaited arrest, Ehrenburg did not bother to pack a bag—why, he could not certainly say. Possibly because it seemed to him it had all happened before. Finally the suspense became unbearable. All Moscow buzzed with rumors that he had been or was about to be arrested. Ehrenburg wrote a letter to Stalin. He said, in effect, if he was going to be arrested, let them arrest him. End the suspense. The next day his telephone rang. It was Georgi M. Malenkov, expressing surprise. Why hadn't Ehrenburg reported this before? Ehrenburg said he had but had gotten no response. Hardly had Ehrenburg put down the receiver when his telephone began to buzz. Once again editors wanted him to write for their publications. Trapped in such a situation could Ehrenburg have saved the lives of Itzik Fefer, Peretz Markish, or the others? The guilt, if guilt there was, lies with all the writers of those days. "We were all guilty," says Simonov quietly. "All of us bear part of the blame for what happened in the 'anticosmopolitanism' campaign."

Ehrenburg did not attempt to analyze Stalin in his memoirs. The problem, he thought, was too complex. Possibly the answer lay in Stalin's genes. Genes were not popular under Stalin (in fact, he drove out of scientific life, into exile, and even to death the leaders of Soviet genetics). But now they are in fashion again. Possibly they hold the real answer. In general, Ehrenburg felt, there was real mania behind Stalin's conduct, a pathological condition. Then, too, Stalin was lacking in political education and was confronted with problems he did not understand. Stalin's faults were matched by those of Russia—a country lacking in traditions of political action, possessing a citizenry which had no knowledge of how to counterpose its views to those of authority. In the end it was the tragedy of unlimited power feeding on power, growing more and more dangerous and bizarre.

Once, Ehrenburg recalled, Stalin invited a group of writers to his dacha and the talk was about writers, writing, and traditions in writing. Stalin was in an easy mood and he began to offer his ideas. There were two main traditions, Stalin said. There was that of Shakespeare—broad, deep, complex, and general—and there was that of Chekhov—simple, narrow, and specific. Chekhov wrote on a small scale; Shakespeare, on a grand scale. "If I was a writer," Stalin said, "I think that I would write in the tradition of Chekhov." Imagine, exclaimed Ehrenburg. This man who turned Russia into a savage, histrionic melodrama, a tragedy that out-Shakespeared Shakespeare, this man whose life was a mixture of Hamlet, Macbeth, and Othello thought of himself in terms of Chekhov, the most modest, most simple, most self-effacing man, the man who understood himself and others as no one else. He could not get over the contradiction.

To Leonov the answer was simpler: Stalin was afraid. He was a Georgian who was trying to rule a dangerous country. Russia had never been easy to rule. The dangers obsessed Stalin. And the tragedy of Stalin became the tragedy of Russia.

The older generation does not look upon the younger generation with entire approval—or vice versa. Simonov, Katayev, Aleksandr Tvardovsky (editor of *Novy Mir*), Konstantin Paustovsky (critically ill and near death in the summer of 1967), Kornei Chukovsky, the venerated, eighty-five-year-old writer of fairy tales, defend the right of the younger poets and prose writers to creative freedom but they do not always agree with the use to which the young put it.

Ehrenburg thought the younger poets talked too much and cut too much of a public figure, particularly in the West. He valued them highly, but he recalled the work done by Pasternak, Akhmatova, and Tsvetayeva before they were thirty. Have Yevtushenko, Voznesensky, and Akhmadulina come up to this mark? He doubted it. He did not like to make comparisons, but his favorite contemporary poet was Boris Slutsky, hardly known in the West. No one, Ehrenburg believed, had written more deeply, more profoundly, on the spirit of the Stalin era. Lila Brik joined in this high evaluation. Slutsky was one of five young poets whom she and her husband, Osip Brik, took into their home in the days just before World War II, nourishing them both physically and spiritually. Only Slutsky and one other, Nikolai Kulchitsky, came back from the war.

Leonov had less sympathy for the younger generation. He is a man who talks in periodic sentences (the younger generation says he talks and talks and long ago gave up writing), and as he talks he toys with gadgets— a kind of flat gear which spins like a top, a gleaming metal joint, a delicate little instrument which measures the size of screws. The younger generation, he is convinced, has no sense of history, no sense of experience. "They think that Rossiya [Russia] is the name of a movie theater and, as Stalin's Minister of Education Andrei S. Bubnov once said, they imagine that Napoleon is just the name of a kind of pastry."

It was all very well, he thought, for them to criticize Stalin. But they must get the story into perspective. In World War I when a Russian army was sent into battle without weapons the general wrote a polite and humble letter, suggesting that he might be issued some guns. In World War II Stalin got on the telephone to a factory that was behind on its delivery of tanks. He told the director that if the tanks were not produced on time he would send a squadron of dive bombers to blast the plant off the map. There was the difference. It was not that Leonov thought the young writers had no talent, but there was a saying that when the stars begin to halt their sparkling then life begins and trees begin to grow on the planets. Now, the new young stars are still sparkling and flashing.

"I saw one of the young writers when he was arguing with Khrushchev," said Leonov. "His lips were trembling. What would he have done if he had been up against Stalin?"

The world is not big enough for them any more, Galina Serebryakova says. Yevtushenko is here today, in New York tomorrow, in Siberia the next day. But that isn't enough for him. He wants to go to other planets. They are in such a hurry! But they haven't the experience and they haven't the knowledge. Gorky said a writer must wait twenty years and then write about his experiences. They won't wait. That's why their work lacks depth.

The real critics of the younger generation are not the Leonovs, however. They are the surviving spokesmen of the Stalinist era, the men who believe for a variety of reasons that the clock should and must be turned back. These men constitute a powerful company. They have important political allies within the highest circle of the government. If this political influence now seems somewhat on the wane it is probably because the political neo-Stalinists have overplayed their hands in nonliterary matters. This coalition has twice staged major coups. They organized the disgraceful attack on Pasternak when he was awarded the Nobel Prize and they stage-managed the savage outburst Khrushchev directed against the young writers and painters, and older figures like Ehrenburg, in 1962–63.

The political supporters of the conservative line are headed by Aleksandr Shelepin, onetime head of the Komsomol and the state security apparatus. His allies, among others, have been Vladimir Semichastny, who succeeded him in both the Komsomol and security jobs, and Sergei P. Pavlov, Semichastny's successor in the Komsomol. Leonid F. Ilyichev, once himself a target of Stalinist persecution, masterminded much of the neo-Stalinist strategy (including the Pasternak affair) in the days when he was Khrushchev's chief propagandist. Downgraded and relegated to the post of deputy minister of Foreign Affairs, he changed none of his views and still works and hopes for a conservative comeback. Closely allied to this group is Yuri Zhukov, a powerful editor of *Pravda* who sometimes devotes himself to foreign affairs and then switches to cultural and ideological concerns. Some younger writers characterize Zhukov as their most unprincipled opponent and contend that he deliberately travels abroad, going over the path of their travels and sniffing out any kind of incident or publicity that might be blown up into a scandal in Moscow and used as a weapon against them. The feud between Zhukov and Yevtushenko, for example, has taken on violent personal overtones.

There is no spokesman for the conservatives more articulate and unreconstructed than Vsevolod Kochetov, editor of the magazine *Oktyabr*. He dismisses with a casual wave of his hand the young poets so beloved by the younger generation in Russia and so highly valued by many of the older writers. He thinks Yevtushenko, Voznesensky, and Akhmadulina are hardly worth talking about. "We have had many such groups in the past," he says, airily. "All they say is 'I,' 'I,' 'I,' 'I.' Look up history and you'll see how this has happened before. Will anything come of them? Who knows? Time will tell. But you can't say from what they have done so far. All they do is point to themselves and try to attract attention."

In contrast, he names half a dozen poets who he thinks possess real talent—Yegor Isayev, Yaroslav Smelyakov, Vasily Fedorov, and Boris Ruchyev among them. None of them are bad poets. But only Smelyakov is mentioned by the younger poets as a colleague whom they respect.

Kochetov has an equally low opinion of Yuri Kazakov, who most critics believe is one of Russia's best writers. "He's fired all his bullets," says Kochetov with contempt. "There are no more bullets in his machine gun, and those who are using him to shoot will find this out. His first stories were good; the later ones very uneven. Foreign acclaim and attention have gone to his head."

He dismisses Vasily Aksyonov, author of *Colleagues, Ticket to the Stars,* and a remarkable unpublished novel called *The Steel Bird* (the censors have held this up for more than a year), with the remark, "He seems to have written himself out—this is often the case with young writers."

But his most savage ire is concentrated against Aleksandr Solzhenitsyn, author of *One Day in the Life of Ivan Denisovich,* the classic study of one prisoner's single day in a Stalin concentration camp, a book published in 1962 only after the personal intervention of Premier Khrushchev. "He is a very mediocre talent," Kochetov insists. "He writes the poorest kind of language—full of vulgar Russian words and *mat* [Russian obscenity based on the mother oath], which has no place in literature."

Russia, he insisted, had had many writers similar to Solzhenitsyn in the days before the revolution. No one now remembers them. "Fifty years ago," he said, "there was a writer named [Vlas M.] Doroshevich. He wrote about the prison camps on Sakhalin Island. No one remembers his name today. If we could meet fifty years from now no one would remember the name of Solzhenitsyn, any more than anyone recalls Doroshevich today."

Nothing so aroused the neo-Stalinists as the action by Solzhenitsyn in addressing to the Fourth Congress of the Union of Soviet Writers, held in May, 1967, a letter demanding the end of Soviet internal censorship. Solzhenitsyn pointed out that there was no provision in the Soviet Constitution for censorship, yet, in fact, for years the function had been carried out by the censoring organization called Glavlit.

Nothing may be published in the Soviet Union—no book, no magazine, no newspaper; not even a theater program or a matchbox cover—unless it bears a number, indicating that its publication or printing has been approved by Glavlit. Every Russian publication bears in small type in an inconspicuous place the telltale number.

In addition to the censorship, the government and the party can, of course, bring direct pressure to bear on publishing houses, which are run either directly by government agencies or by quasi-government agencies such as the Writers Union or the Academy of Sciences. A word from the Central Committee may be enough to halt the publication of a book. On the other hand, there is a certain amount of autonomy, independence, and even local variation. A writer may find his book rejected either by a publishing house or by the censor in Moscow. But when he sends it to a Siberian magazine, the Siberian editor, proud to have a contribution from a famous Moscow writer, may get it cleared for publication by the local censor, who may be his personal friend.

Many writers have said frankly that abolition of the Glavlit censorship might confront them with twenty or fifty individual censors in the persons of the directors of publishing houses and magazines. Yet they would far prefer the individuality and possibility for maneuver that abolition of censorship would bring.

"Even Dostoyevsky," Solzhenitsyn declared, "could not at one time be published in our country (even today he is not published in full). . . . For how many years was Yesenin considered a 'counterrevolutionary' (and were not people imprisoned for possessing his books)? Was not Mayakovsky branded an 'anarchist,' a 'political hooligan'? For decades the immortal poems of Akhmatova were considered to be 'anti-Soviet.' "

Pointing out that the work of writers like Tsvetayeva, Bunin, Mikhail Bulgakov, Platonov, Mandelshtam, Voloshin, Gumilev, Klyuyev, Yevgeny Zamyatin, and Aleksei Remizov was suppressed for years, he demanded that the Writers Union defend writers rather than join in their harrassment. He recalled the physical violence and persecution directed against Bulgakov, Akhmatova, Tsvetayeva, Pasternak, Mikhail Zoshchenko, Platonov, Aleksandr Grin, and Vasily Grossman. He cited the deaths of Paul Vasilyev, Mandelshtam, Artem Vesely, Pilnyak, Babel, Tabidze, and Zabolotsky and recalled that after the Twentieth party Congress it was revealed that more than six hundred innocent writers had been sent to prison camps under Yagoda, Yezhov, Beria, and Abakumov.

As for himself, he said that his novel *The First Circle* had been seized by the security police and then circulated without his permission among a limited body of literary and political persons. Many of his personal papers and archives were confiscated by the police. Slander about his military record was being spread, including an allegation that he had betrayed his country or served the Germans. He noted that he had never been a prisoner of war. The fact was that, after having been decorated several times for bravery, he was arrested on almost the last day of the war and sent to prison for criticizing Stalin in letters written from the front to a friend. His novel *The Cancer Ward* had been rejected by both magazines and publishing houses. Theaters were unable to gain permission to present his play *The Stag and the Camp Prostitute*.

"I have a clear conscience because I have fulfilled my duties as a writer in all circumstances," wrote Solzhenitsyn, "and because I will fulfill them even more successfully, more indisputably, when I am dead than I can while I am still alive. Nobody can bar the road to the truth. I am ready to accept death for the sake of the cause but how many lessons do we need to teach us that the writer's pen should not be stopped while he still lives? Never once in our history have we been able to say this is so."

Kochetov said that Solzhenitsyn's letter "is filled with bile." All societies, he said, have their own censorship. There is a censorship in the West, one in the Third World, and one in the Soviet Union. "You have laws against pornography," he told me. "All countries have military censorship. Should there be a literary censorship? Sometimes, perhaps. Where would you be without a law on pornography?"

Nikolai Gribachev, conservative editor of the illustrated monthly *Soviet Union,* spoke more strongly. He called Solzhenitsyn a liar. Take his letter, he said. What a way to act! If he wanted to have the question discussed, all he had to do was send a request to the Presidium of the union. (Solzhenitsyn pointed out in his letter that he had asked and been refused permission to speak.) Instead, Solzhenitsyn sent out two hundred and fifty copies of his letter to members of the union. "He has a very bad nature," said Gribachev. "He is just thinking of himself. There is no censorship, moreover. None at all. Of course, there is a military censorship. A law on state secrets. But you have that in the United States. It is just a matter of editorial judgment. So Solzhenitsyn lied when he raised that question."

Solzhenitsyn, he said, was a member of the Writers Union. But he did not attend the congress. Instead, he sent his statement to the West. "I don't understand," said Gribachev, "why I am called a conservative in the West. So is Kochetov. Why is this? I am just a plain-speaking honest man. I say what I think. I don't try to organize something unclean like Solzhenitsyn. There is no censor in this country. The question which he raised is a lie and he knows it."

Gribachev said that Solzhenitsyn's *One Day in the Life of Ivan Denisovich* was very narrow—it just dealt with the survival of one man who worries about whether he will get a piece of bread in order to live until the next day. Ivan Denisovich, he said, is not a noble character, such as Lermontov created in *A Hero of Our Times*. He is small and narrow, and that is why the novel can't be great. For himself, he liked Alyosha the Baptist better, even though Alyosha was a believer. Alyosha was true to himself and his belief. He was a noble figure. But Solzhenitsyn was a narrow man. Everything revolved around himself. He had no broad philosophy. He was just an opportunist, a man who traded on his situation.

Gribachev was one of the group to whom Solzhenitsyn's novel *The First Circle* had been circulated. He found it a "very bad book," deliberately provocative politically, designed to be used by Western propaganda. "It is political and it is tendentious," said Gribachev, "and it is intended to be. Frankly, I don't like Solzhenitsyn either as a writer or as a person."

Galina Serebryakova is inclined to agree with Gribachev about Solzhenitsyn. Although she survived twenty years in the camps, she did not like *One Day in the Life of Ivan Denisovich*. It only scratched the surface. After all, 1937—when she was arrested—was quite a different thing from the late 1940's—when Solzhenitsyn was arrested. What happened in 1937 was that Russia turned on its own people. It was not just a struggle for a crust of bread, as Solzhenitsyn described it. There are, as Mrs. Serebryakova put it, writers on a world scale and there are writers on a county scale. Solzhenitsyn is a "county" writer, and the danger, she felt, was that by writing a narrow study of prison-camp life he destroyed the chance for a good deep study of the period. Simonov had said that the Stalin period must be studied with a microscope, must be gone over painstakingly, detail by detail, so that the full truth could be known. She agreed with that, and she herself was writing her memoirs—in part, at least. But it was a big subject. It had to be approached carefully. The trouble with Solzhenitsyn and the new generation of writers, in general, was that they lacked "political culture." They did not see their work in relationship to politics, either internal or international. And in that there was danger.

For all her trials and experiences, Mrs. Serebryakova had emerged essentially a conservative. And on questions of censorship and a writer's role in the Soviet world she stood closer to Kochetov, Gribachev, and the

Komsomol group than she did to the Tvardovskys, the Paustovskys, the Ehrenburgs, and the others who were trying to insure a broader canvas and a freer scope for the new Soviet writers.

Among these writers there was no question about the essential justice of Solzhenitsyn's appeal. They supported it. They had no doubt that Solzhenitsyn's talent was the greatest in Russia today. ("The only living classic in Russia," Yevtushenko called him.) One after the other they said that he was the one man writing in Russia about whom there was no question and could be no question. Of course his works, both *The First Circle* and *The Cancer Ward,* should be published.

"They must be published," said Kornei Chukovsky, dean of Russian letters, writer of hundreds of fairy tales and stories for children, who with his own money (200,000 old rubles, about $25,000) built a children's library at his country home in Peredelkino and had it painted with fairy-tale scenes in order to delight the thousands of youngsters who annually make a pilgrimage to see him. A thousand or more turn out for his storytelling sessions around a great bonfire in his woods. It was at Chukovsky's home that Solzhenitsyn spent several weeks in the spring of 1967 preparing his letter to the Writers Congress. "He is a very talented man," said Chukovsky, his eyes sparkling. "You know that when *One Day* was submitted to *Novy Mir,* Tvardovsky gave it to me and I wrote the first criticism of Solzhenitsyn."

In Russian literary matters predictions are always difficult. But in the summer of 1967 there was agreement among the liberals, both young and old, that Solzhenitsyn's letter had produced positive results. Solzhenitsyn was summoned before the Presidium of the Writers Union for a full discussion of his views. The manuscripts and papers seized by the police were returned to him. Agreement was made to publish *The Cancer Ward,* although possibly not without some cuts. There was no decision on *The First Circle.* This was regarded by most as far the stronger of the two Solzhenitsyn works. Based in part on his own experience as a prisoner, it described life in a special police-run scientific laboratory dedicated to research in sound and acoustics. Among other tasks, the institute monitored wire-tapped telephone calls of Russians and foreigners in Moscow. Some of those working in the institution were prisoners, others were free.

On the broader question of abolition of the censorship there was a conviction that it would be quietly abandoned, but probably not until after the fiftieth-anniversary celebration had passed.

The struggle between liberals and conservatives was far from over. But the liberals felt the tide was running in their direction and that it would continue, barring a critical worsening of the international situation. For, all conceded, politics in the Soviet Union is interconnected. Tension on the world scene meant tension reflected internally, even into literary matters. But for the moment the outlook seemed positive. A collected edition of Boris Pasternak's works was in the final editing stage. It was to be in six volumes, the first of which was scheduled to appear early in 1968. Volume Six was to be *Doctor Zhivago.* Its appearance, it was agreed, would cause no uproar and would bring satisfaction even to Nikita Khrushchev, the man who was falsely blamed by many for the row over Pasternak's Nobel Prize. Actually, Khrushchev was far from Moscow, vacationing at the Black Sea resort of Pitsunda, when the Pasternak affair broke. He plaintively told a visitor to his country home one day in 1967 that there were two things he had not succeeded in accomplishing during his rule. He had not persuaded Russia to plant corn, and he had not gotten *Doctor Zhivago* published. There was belief, too, in literary circles that Andrei D. Sinyavsky and Yuli M. Daniel, the two writers who were sent to forced labor in February, 1966, on charges of sending anti-Soviet works to be published abroad would be amnestied in the general pardon that traditionally accompanies great state occasions such as the fiftieth anniversary.

It might be, as Gribachev contended, that Voznesensky was a naïve fool in insisting that "beauty will save the world." Gribachev had an idea that guns and rockets would do more. It might be, as he insisted, that Yevtushenko was like a dog with a can tied to its tail or a calf sucking at the teats of two cows (America and Russia). It might be, as he insisted, that Voznesensky and Yevtushenko were growing old and that no one was interested any longer in their poetry or in the writing of Aksyonov.

It might be that time was on the side of Mikhail Sholokhov, who had employed the platform of the Writers Congress to criticize his "friends," both young and old (Ehrenburg, Yevtushenko, and Voznesensky), for not showing up for the meeting and for what he called "a kind of Fronde," or rebellion of the young against Soviet norms.

But it seemed to many that in the quarrel between the generations of Russian writers the young would have the last word. Already the young admitted cheerfully that they did not read Leonov (except for *The Robbers,* a book of his youth). They admired Ehrenburg (but no longer read him as once they did). They tolerated Simonov. They respected Paustovsky and Tvardovsky. They had not read Konstantin Fedin for years. Jazz, they admitted, not older writers, was their real passion. As for Sholokhov, so alienated were they by his reactionary views that they even challenged his authorship of *And Quiet Flows the Don.* "He couldn't have written it," one intense young writer said. "What happened was that he found the diary of a White Guard officer. He copied it out and passed it off as his own."

"He is a Cossack," snapped Lila Brik, fire in her eyes. "We made the revolution against the Cossacks—men like him." "When I want to hear a clown I go to a circus," said another young man of Sholokhov.

Perhaps the closest bond between young and older generations was that forged by Katayev. He was regarded by the young with affection and toleration. They liked, in particular, a new concept he had half-humorously proposed—what he called "mauvism" from the French word *mauvais,* or bad. Katayev proposed the word to describe what he called the "highest form of Socialist Realism just as Marxism describes Imperialism as the highest form of Capitalism." By mauvism Katayev meant writing that was not prettified, that was completely natural yet artistic at the same time. Bad—yet good.

"I am the world's number-one mauvist," he said with a twinkle in his eye. "Anatoly Gladilin is number two. Aksyonov is very good in this genre. Solzhenitsyn works a little too hard with words and form. Tolstoy was a great mauvist. *War and Peace* has no classical construction. Yet it is great nonetheless. Dostoyevsky was the mauvist par excellence."

Of course, said Katayev, there could be no talk of censorship and art. How could good writing and censorship coexist?

This was a question that for more than a hundred years had troubled the Russian writer. From the time of Gogol and Pushkin the struggle against censorship had gone forward. It was a basic demand of the fervent young reformers and revolutionaries who carried on the long battle against czardom, the battle they thought they had won in 1917.

Now another fifty years have passed—fifty years of the Communist regime which so many in 1917 believed would bring a new era of liberty and freedom to the arts. That hope had proved vain. But there was no sign that the young writers of Russia and their allies in the older generation had lost faith or confidence.

One sunny Sunday my wife and I made a pilgrimage to the village of Peredelkino, a little cluster of houses set in spruce and birch forests around a blue-domed old Orthodox church, fifteen miles from Moscow. The bells in the belfry rang out as we got off the train and walked up the grassy, winding lane to the cemetery. In the warm summer sun many families were planting flowers at the graves of their dear ones. Like all Russian cemeteries, that at Peredelkino is a bit of a maze, with narrow paths that disappear into oddly placed grave plots and tiny iron fences surrounding monuments. Charlotte and I wandered through the maze, gradually moving toward the tall pine under which lay the grave I was seeking. Here and there families were relaxing; some were picnicking in the cool depths of the cemetery. Finally, we emerged at the graveside. The last time I had been there it was marked only by a wooden cross. Now a simple marble shaft stood over the grave with a bas-relief of the leonine profile of Pasternak. As we approached, two Russian women were standing beside the grave, in figured-cotton dresses. "Is this the one?" one woman asked. "Yes," said her companion. "It was him."

Handfuls of flowers lay on the grave, and in a few minutes a number of persons strolled by to pay their respects—middle-aged couples, peasants, a young boy and his girl friend. The spirit of Pasternak, the spirit of truth, it was plain to see, still glowed in Russia. It did not seem likely it would ever die, no matter what the obstacle, what the regime.

THEATER:
THE NAKED TRUTH

»

Harrison E. Salisbury

The Lenin Komsomol Theater in Leningrad is located in a drafty hall, set in a park not far from the Peter and Paul Fortress where so many Russian revolutionaries spent long years during the nineteenth century. The theater was built in the heyday of Stalinesque architecture and is distinguished by vast promenades, imitation marble columns, plaster statues of Stakhanovite workers, and buffets selling soda pop and ice-cream sandwiches. The audience in the theater was made up, for the most part, of sailors, cadets from the naval training stations, their blonde girl friends, young workers from the Leningrad factories, and a sprinkling of older men and women who looked as though they might be attending on tickets passed out in bookkeeping offices or to factory clerks. The acting was on a par with the second-rate house and the third-rate audience—young actors and actresses who made up in vigor what they lacked in experience. There was nothing distinguished about house, audience, or company. Had the evening's entertainment been *The Dollar Princess* or *The Merry Widow* it could have been a duplication of what went on in a hundred provincial Russian theaters in a hundred provincial Russian cities, with decor, audience, and repertoire unchanged for the last thirty years.

Bertolt Brecht's *The Threepenny Opera* was being presented that evening. Poor as the company was, molasses-paced and hardly able to sing, the staging was stylish. There was a fine revolving platform and a dramatic central maze of staircases and landings, which were exciting to watch. It was a long, long way from the Berliner Ensemble's presentation of the Brecht work, but it was even farther from the Soviet stage as it had frozen into a bore during the late Stalin years.

For the first time in a generation of Soviet theatergoing that night I heard the Russian words for "whorehouse" and "prostitute" uttered publicly. I saw eight blowzy "prostitutes," breasts bulging and hips swaying, cavort on the Soviet stage. There were many things about the Komsomol Theater's presentation that might have surprised Brecht: the backdrop of light and signs, looking like Broadway and Forty-second Street; the Nazi helmets and Iron Crosses worn by the beggars' chorus; the Northwest Mounted Police uniform worn by Brecht's leading character, Mr. Brown, and the policemen in costumes that came directly from old Mack Sennett comedies. But if it was difficult for a young Leningrad cadet and his girl to decide whether they were watching a spectacle about eighteenth-century London or twentieth-century New York, there was no doubt that the hands of the Russian theatrical clock no longer stood fixed at March 5, 1953, the date of Stalin's death.

Brecht was not, actually, a very good symbol of this change, although he was part of it. Even the best, the most contemporary, most imaginative companies in Moscow today do not play Brecht as well as he is played in Berlin, in Paris, in London, in New York, or, for that matter, at the Tyrone Guthrie theater in Minneapolis. Nothing to match the explosion of sight, sound, and emotion compressed into the Guthrie presentation of *The Caucasian Chalk Circle* has hit Moscow.

The Threepenny Opera has gradually begun to appear in the repertoire of the Russian companies, much as it has proliferated in the high-school and college theaters of the United States—and usually at the same level of incompetence. "We don't do Brecht very well here," admitted Valentin Pluchek, the director who has made Moscow's Satire Theater one of the most exciting of the post-Stalin epoch. He was first to break the ice by reviving Mayakovsky's *The Bedbug, The Bathhouse,* and *Mystère-Bouffe,* all banned for years under Stalin. The problem with Brecht, Pluchek felt, was the persistence of the Stanislavsky tradition of realism. Outside of a few experimental theaters like his own—the Taganka Theater and the Sovremennik (Contemporary) Theater in Moscow and the Theater of Comedy in Leningrad—the Russian theater was locked in the old methods and old styles. There was nothing like New York's off-Broadway movement to bring experiment to the stage.

The best Brecht was the Taganka Theater's performance of *The Good Woman of Setzuan*. As recently as five years ago hardly a single Brecht production was to be found in all of Russia, and this despite the fact that before his death Brecht had become the most distinguished ornament of the Communist East Berlin stage.

"We have no theater of the absurd here," Pluchek said. "Indeed, we have no young playwrights—or old playwrights—writing in that genre. Ionesco is unknown to Russian audiences. A couple of years ago *Rhinoceros* was prepared for presentation, but it was not put on. I don't know why." The reason was probably to be found in official conservatism, the residual legacy of Stalin's bad taste and the banality of his censors and police. Those of the avant-garde in the Russian theater know about the playwrights of the absurd and admire them. They know about the "angry young men" of England, and have staged a number of John Osborne's plays. They know about Edward Albee, Harold Pinter, and LeRoi Jones.

"The difficulty with Edward Albee," one theater man said, "is that homosexuality doesn't seem to us to be such a pressing problem. His plays appear to be remote from our reality." But *The Ballad of the Sad Café* opened in 1967 at the Sovremennik Theater with a production young Muscovites liked.

The playwright who interested them most, however, was Peter Weiss. Not that they had seen any of his works in Moscow, but they hoped to— when the time was a little more appropriate. "Peter Weiss is a genius of the first order," Pluchek said. "His *Marat/Sade* is amazing."

"Are you going to put it on?" I asked.

Pluchek laughed. "I don't think that in the jubilee year of the revolution we can put on a play in which revolution occurs in a madhouse."

No theater was more dazzling than the Russian stage at the time of the revolution and in the years that followed. Those were the days when Konstantin Stanislavsky and Vladimir Nemirovich-Danchenko were still at the height of their powers and the Moscow Art Theater had not yet become a museum relic of the past, a theatrical fly in amber. Vsevolod Meyerhold was bursting with new ideas, new techniques, which set the pace for the world. There were others: Aleksandr Tairov; Nikolai Okhlopkov, with his revolutionary stage; Mayakovsky, creating new forms, breaking every ikon, smashing every tradition. The explosion was not confined to the theatrical stage. Even before the revolution a fever had raced through the arts. Ballet was being transformed by Diaghilev, Bakst, Nijinsky, Stravinsky; art by Malevich, Kandinsky, Tatlin, and Chagall. Everything new was hailed. The horizons opened outward. The film era of Eisenstein, Vsevolod Pudovkin, and Aleksandr Dovzhenko was at hand. The world came to Moscow to worship at the feet of the brilliant new directors, to study and admire the new staging, the new acting. But all that was long past by 1967. Nowhere had the Stalinist police smashed down harder than on the world of tinsel and light, of poetry and imagination, of grease paint and mascara.

By 1953 there was nothing left but the Art Theater, and that had retired into its past. Stanislavsky and Nemirovich-Danchenko were dead, but the repertoire was hardly changed from prerevolutionary days. It was still Chekhov, Maeterlinck, Gorky, and Tolstoy. Indeed, even the actors had hardly changed. The actresses in *The Three Sisters* had grown old, so old they tottered about the stage. Anna Karenina was middle-aged. The theater had become a caricature of itself. The jewel-like Maly Theater, home of Aleksandr Ostrovsky and traditional Russian plays, a kind of Russian Comédie-Française, went on unchanged. Not even Stalin could find anything ideological or political to complain about there. But the very name of Meyerhold was never mentioned except, perhaps, in whispers. His theater had been liquidated on January 8, 1938.

Whatever may have been the reason, Meyerhold was still alive in the spring of 1939, and there was even gossip in Moscow that he might be given a new directorship. In June, 1939, a Conference of Theatrical Directors was held in Moscow, and Meyerhold was invited to attend. On June 15 he spoke. It was not a very long address, but in it he gave his opinion of the state of the Russian theater. "Without art, there is no theater! Go visiting the theaters of Moscow. Look at their drab and boring presentations that resemble one another and are each worse than the others. . . . Everything is gloomily well-regulated, averagely arithmetical, stupefying and murderous in its lack of talent. Is that your aim? If it is—oh! you have done something monstrous! You have thrown out the baby along with the bath water. In hunting down formalism you have eliminated art."

It was the last open appeal for honesty in art, for creative freedom, that was to be heard in Moscow for nearly twenty years. Two days after delivering his remarks, on the night of June 17–18, there came a knock at the door of Meyerhold's flat. It was the secret police with an order for his arrest. He was led away to vanish in the labyrinth of Stalinist concentration camps, dying, it was said, at the hands of a common murderer in 1942. A few days after Meyerhold's arrest, tragedy was piled on tragedy. His wife, Zinaida Raikh, was brutally murdered in their apartment on Brusovsky Lane—her eyes were gouged out and her body covered with stab wounds.

Meyerhold's critique of the Soviet theater held true for years. Okhlopkov was whipped into line. The last sparks of revolutionary spirit were beaten from his theater. A dozen dramatists, among them Isaak Babel, Artem Vesely, Vladimir Kirshon, and Sergei Tretyakov, vanished into the concentration camps. The playwright Mikhail Bulgakov, whose *Last Days of the Turbins* had been a sensation of the postrevolutionary era, died, a broken, persecuted man. Natalia Sats, gifted founder of the Moscow Children's Theater, disappeared but survived. Aleksandr Tairov tried to carry on with his Kamerny Theater, but it was hopeless. His theater physically survived until the campaign of 1949–50, directed against what was called "cosmopolitanism." This drive, with its strong anti-Semitic overtones, was begun in the field of the theater, and the first victims were theater critics, most of them Jewish. The Kamerny Theater became a central target because it was found to shelter "esthetic formalism [which] serves only as a cloak for anti-patriotic activities." The theater was closed down, and for years a new Kamerny Theater building, which had been commissioned just before the debacle, stood unfinished and gaping. Tairov, sorely beset and depressed, died prematurely.

With this background, the Soviet theater emerged slowly and painfully, with many a hesitant step, after Stalin's death. The first steps were taken by Okhlopkov, in his new Mayakovsky Theater, where he began to experiment with some of Meyerhold's old excitements. He staged a thrilling *Hamlet* and a fairly successful Brechtian *Mother Courage*.

Okhlopkov had made his start as a director at twenty-one, when he commandeered half the population of Irkutsk to present a mass drama on the banks of the Angara River, and his strength had always been in massive concepts. His production in 1961 of Euripides' *Medea* in the Tchaikovsky Hall with a choir of one hundred voices and a Greek chorus of forty women became an epic paean of humanity in the throes of injustice, a kind of theatrical commentary upon the prison camp of body and spirit into which Russia was turned by Stalin.

Okhlopkov dreamed of a new experimental theater that would give free flow to his imagination and his sense of mass spectacle—a circular playhouse with tiers of 3,000 seats and a plexiglass roof that could be opened at night. He died an untimely death in 1966, his dreams and his potentials as a director unfulfilled, in part because of the scars left by the terror.

Nikolai Akimov's Leningrad Theater of Comedy took up in the mid-1950's where Akimov had been forced to leave off by the gathering party pressures in the late 1930's. He began with Yevgeny Shvarts, a playwright who had almost been driven to suicide by the persecutions of 1938 and 1939, when so many of his friends vanished. Shvarts lived to endure the siege of Leningrad, when 1,300,000 of his fellow citizens starved or froze to death or were killed by German shells and bombs. A gentle, unworldly man, he was a writer of children's tales, but the ugliness of the world was more than he could bear. He began to put down some truths in a series of plays—ostensibly fairy stories, but actually social satires—among them *Shadows, The Naked King, The Dragon.* They were created in the 1930's, and while it might be argued that his target was not Stalinist Russia but the horrors of Hitler's Germany, the parallel was too keen, the comparisons too apt. The plays were banned in Stalin's time and have come back into the repertoire only slowly since then, largely at Akimov's instigation. The bite of Shvarts's satire needs a Soviet setting. A Phoenix Theater presentation of *The Dragon* in New York was only mildly successful.

Shvarts had a friend in Leningrad, an eccentric named Daniel Harms, a man who belonged to a little writers' clique called the *"nichevoki,"* which means "nothingists." Nothingists they really were, dedicated to writing stories that had no point—a kind of Russian "shaggy dog" group. Harms perished in the early days of World War II—not from German bombs, but at the hands of the Soviet security police. He was denounced as a German spy, apparently because he wore a floppy hat and walked with a limp. Harms left a small legacy of literary works, among them some pieces for the theater. These, too, in a bizarre way, offered a stinging commentary on the Soviet system. Thus far none of Harms's work has been presented by Akimov, but there is talk that it may be.

Grigory Kozintsev is another survivor of the harshest repressions of the Stalin days. He is the brilliant Soviet film director who made *Don Quixote* (from a scenario prepared by Shvarts) and who won a Lenin Prize for his *Hamlet.* He is a worldly, talented man who lives in a fine apartment in Leningrad with his beautiful wife and seventeen-year-old son. His living room is decorated with an Italian Renaissance carved wooden angel, No masks from Japan, a poster for the original performance of *Mystère-Bouffe* by Mayakovsky, a remarkable seventeenth-century ikon, African masks, a Léger painting, a good Picasso, a cartoon done by Mayakovsky before the revolution (one from a set of which Lila Brik possesses half a dozen), and thousands of books. The books flow out of the shelves and onto the tables and chairs. In a prominent place—as on the tables of many writers in Moscow and Leningrad—is a big new volume called *Meetings with Meyerhold,* a collection of reminiscences about the great director.

"Yes," said Kozintsev, "Meyerhold is the great influence today." In films, he said, Eisenstein was supreme. Eisenstein escaped Meyerhold's fate by a hairsbreadth. He died of a heart attack in 1948. He probably would have been arrested in the "cosmopolitanism" drive had he not thwarted the police by dying.

It was interesting to Kozintsev that Stanislavsky's influence as perpetuated on the Moscow stage and in the artistic council of the Art Theater had become sterile, had led the theater, in effect, to a dead end, whereas in New

York the Stanislavsky method had been elaborated, vitalized, transformed into a living instrument giving the theater new scope and new depth. But then, he conceded, New York was the most exhilarating city in the world. So he had found it on his two visits. Hollywood, on the other hand, he felt was not very interesting.

He was deep in preparation for a new film. He would begin work, he hoped, in December, 1967. He planned to make *King Lear*. Shakespeare, in his view, was a remarkable contemporary, a man who was able to understand the universality of human character and thus foresee the future. He hoped to develop *King Lear* within the terms of that concept—not by any means in modern dress. That he regarded as a cheap trick, a bit of adolescent sensationalism. What he hoped to do was to bring *Lear* to life in today's terms.

"I can't help thinking of Stalin," I told him. "Naturally," he replied.

Soviet film technique, he felt, was beginning to pull abreast of contemporary influences. By far the strongest of these, he considered, was Antonioni. He and most of the leading Soviet film producers thought *Blow-Up* was the most interesting current picture. Like many Soviet writers and workers in artistic fields, he had seen *Doctor Zhivago* in the West. He was not very impressed (although favorable votes far outnumbered unfavorable votes in the small sampling of the intelligentsia which was asked the question). He thought that both *The Bridge on the River Kwai* and *Lawrence of Arabia* were superior to *Zhivago*.

Kozintsev was not seriously disturbed by reports that many of the best films made in recent months by Soviet directors would not be released for showing until after the November jubilee. One estimate put the number of films held up at more than a dozen, among them three important pictures. These were Dostoyevsky's *Skverny Anekdot* (*Boring Tale*), *Asya Khromonozhka* (*Asya the Lame*), and *The Passion of Andrei Rublov*. The reason for the delay was clear. Each film was intensely realistic and cruel in its depiction of life. Each was reminiscent of Bergman's technique. The Dostoyevsky story was characterized by some who saw it as "very pathological." *Asya Khromonozhka* was a collective-farm tale. Only two professional actors, a man and a woman, were used. The rest were ordinary farmers. It was a story of a very ugly girl who wanted love, and the tragic outcome of her passion. *Rublov* contained some of the grimmest scenes ever shot by a Russian film camera—animals being beaten to death and the sadistic treatment of people —as well as reproductions of the great Rublov ikons. The film was done partly in black and white, partly in color.

Regardless of the sadism in them, there was no doubt in anyone's mind that the three pictures were superior, artistically, to the entries the Russians put forward in their 1967 film festival: *Zhurnalist,* a picture deliberately made to include background shots of a dozen cities, and a bland coproduction with the Poles called *Zosya.*

The fact was that the theater had now become interesting to the most creative talents in the Soviet Union. One of Aleksandr Solzhenitsyn's complaints to the Writers Union related not to his novels and short stories, but to his play *The Stag and the Camp Prostitute.* Solzhenitsyn's first love, actually, had been the theater. He studied as an actor under the direction of Yuri Zavadsky, one of Moscow's leading directors in the early 1930's, who was compelled to work four years in Rostov during the purges because of official disfavor. He is now again a leading Moscow director. Solzhenitsyn completed his play in 1954, at a time when he was living as an exile in Kazakhstan. Thirteen years later he still had not been able to get it produced. Although both the Vakhtangov and the Lenin Komsomol theaters in Moscow expressed interest, and the Sovremennik had accepted it in 1962, it had not yet been officially cleared for presentation.

Vasily Aksyonov, working with the Sovremennik Theater, has a project for a modern version of Aristophanes' *The Frogs,* a production that would go forward on two levels—one real, one imaginary; one ancient, one modern; one Aristophanic, one Aksyonovian.

The Sovremennik Theater, led by a young director, Oleg Yefremov, was the first new theater to be founded in Moscow since the 1930's. It sprang up about 1959, formed by young actors, most of whom had been trained at the Art Theater. It set out to create a new repertory, one that would reflect new trends in the Soviet Union and the best of avant-garde theater in the West. For several years every Sovremennik première was surrounded by tensions. Sometimes the shows did not open—they were closed by the government censors. Nothing was harder to get in Moscow than a ticket to a Sovremennik performance.

By 1967 the vanguard role had been seized by a tiny theater around the corner from the Taganka subway station, near a busy shopping center. The director of the Taganka Theater was Yuri Lyubimov, and a visit to the Taganka Theater was the most exciting way to spend an evening in Moscow. Whether this would continue to be true was a question. Lyubimov, whose talent, energy, imagination, and courage had created the theater, was critically ill, and no one knew whether he would ever again be able to take his place in the director's chair. Without him, the Taganka would be like *Hamlet* without Hamlet.

It was the Taganka that created the stage presentation of John Reed's *Ten Days That Shook the World,* a re-creation so vivid that the spectator literally felt propelled back into the days of November, 1917. The Taganka, too, was the theater that created and presented a play about Mayakovsky called *Poslushaite! (Listen!)*. The genre of these works is not easy to describe. Kozintsev, in Leningrad, called them a "mixture of Meyerhold and Brecht," but Pluchek felt that Meyerhold provided more intellectual content, and perhaps less drama, than did Lyubimov at the Taganka. The secret of Lyubimov's production was to make an idea into a spectacle (play is not an appropriate word). He took Mayakovsky, for example, and ripped apart quotations from Mayakovsky, about Mayakovsky, declamations by Mayakovsky, to Mayakovsky. He fashioned this into a scenic collage, mounting it against a battery of lights, of noises, of music, of sound, of pictures, posters, and sensations, which battered the minds of the spectators and the nerves of the actors. He set his company marching through the constantly shifting collage at a pace that caused the audience to grip their chairs. Spotlights jabbed through the auditorium; rows of reversed footlights created a curtain of light through which the actors appeared and disappeared. Through it all the portrait of Mayakovsky as a figure, human but heroic, emerged and his ideas pounded out into an ethos. The comparison with Brecht and Meyerhold was apt but also meaningless, for Lyubimov created his own special world of thought and sensation.

The core of his productions is not, in the end, visual, aural, and tactile impulses, but ideas. As *Poslushaite!* develops, it becomes a raging debate, a flaming argument between Mayakovsky, the free, vital artist, and the sterile forces of banality and party bureaucracy. More and more it becomes apparent why its public première was long delayed, why the rumors swept Moscow that it would never be presented.

In the spectacle, a party meeting is called to criticize Mayakovsky, to denounce him for his original and unconventional ways of thought. "Why don't you make everything beautiful the way they do at the Bolshoi Theater?" a woman party member demands. "You must write so that the workers and peasants can understand you," the party secretary insists. One critic winds up each of his denunciations with an appeal to the party group: "Am I right? *Da ili nyet?*" (Yes or no?) All, sheeplike, shout: *"Da!"* Only Mayakovsky says *"Nyet."* Finally, Mayakovsky is driven from the stage by the eruption of vapid party criticism.

The final scene resembles a funeral meeting. There are ikonlike portraits of Mayakovsky. The oration goes to the crux of the matter. Only truth is important, and only the artist knows what the truth is in his own terms. The Taganka audience bursts into wild applause, and suddenly questions spring to mind. Is Lyubimov saying that Mayakovsky was driven to his death by the party demand for conformity? Or is he presenting, in the guise of a parable about Mayakovsky, the contemporary debate that rages over the role of the young Russian writers like Yevtushenko and Voznesensky?

The questions are not idle. Closely associated with Lyubimov and the Taganka Theater from its beginning has been Andrei Voznesensky. Both Voznesensky and Yevtushenko have been strongly attracted to the theater. In June, 1967, a dramatization of Yevtushenko's "Bratsk Station" was given its première at Riga. And in July, 1967, the Taganka Theater gave its two-hundredth performance of Voznesensky's poetic collection entitled *Antimiry* (*Antiworlds*).

The performance at the Taganka Theater on July 2, 1967, came at a moment when Voznesensky was deeply troubled. He had been to the United States a month or so earlier, and on his return had been subjected to something more than the usual caviling by the party hacks. In part this reflected the tensions on the international scene. In part it reflected the courage and candor of the letter Voznesensky had dispatched to the Writers Union supporting Solzhenitsyn in his plea for abolition of censorship. Voznesensky was invited to return to the United States in late June for a poetry festival at Lincoln Center in New York. He had received tentative permission to go but, as is so often the case in Russia, the project was being reviewed. One day it appeared that he would go, the next that he would not be permitted to. "The worst part about these things," he told me, "is the uncertainty, the indecision. You do not know whether you will go or not, and the decision comes at the last moment. Or is changed at the last moment. It is so boring in this day and age to have people act like this, always mixing politics into whatever you do."

Voznesensky had brought back from the United States a vast collection of buttons, of the type beloved by high-school and college youngsters. But the joke had not been entirely successful. His wife had worn a button with a rude remark on it in Latin. "We thought it was all right, because no one in Russia knows Latin," he said wryly. Then he had to go to the hospital, and the doctors complained in shocked terms about the button. They were among the few people in the country who knew what the button said. "You know," he mused, "life is really still too serious in Russia. We aren't ready for that kind of humor."

I asked him what Soviet youth had to rebel about—they had no Vietnam war to protest against and there was no vital race issue to direct their energies into. "Don't worry," he said. "We still have plenty for them to rebel against. It's no problem."

This conversation was in my mind when I went to the Taganka Theater for the anniversary performance of *Antimiry*. Outside, there were dozens of young people begging for tickets. Inside, every seat was filled. Present were many members of the younger Soviet intelligentsia. There was throughout the auditorium that intangible sense of excitement which proclaims that an event is about to take place.

The play began much in the Taganka tradition. About twenty poems were presented, full of flash and excitement. The first was a jazzy one called "Rock 'n' Roll," set to splashy music, splashy movement, young people frugging and twisting all over the stage. Then came a satire called "Strip Tease," with a shapely Russian girl simulating a sinuous disrobing act. The performance went on, assaulting the mind and the senses in the Lyubimov style. There was no intermission. Tension built to the end. Then Voznesensky emerged, looking like a worn teen-ager—his hair rumpled, face long and serious, hands thrust deep in the pockets of his familiar houndstooth sports jacket. He began to recite. First came a fairly conventional attack on China and the closed minds of the cultural revolution. Then he moved into an excoriation of what the Russians call *"khamstvo"*—stupidity compounded, deliberate rudeness and vulgarity. He recited a verse about a revolt of the strip teasers and one about the death of poetry, the death of Copernicus, the death of Dante. But when all these great men had vanished, their truth remained.

Finally, he began to deliver what he simply called "Monologue." It was not as poetic as his usual style, not so filled with his usual delicate play on words and sounds. It was a poem about truth and about hypocrisy. Speak the truth, Voznesensky said—no more lies. That is all that is important. He spoke of things of which Russia might be proud and things of which it might be ashamed. A face, he said, is not just for shaving; it should be able to blush for shame. He talked of those who bang their shoes on the table at the United Nations and worry not about the consequences of their actions, but whether their feet smell. And he talked of those who play with Vietnam as though it were a game. Vietnam is not, he said, a game of lotto which amuses on an idle afternoon. The people of the world today, he said, had no need for the fig leaf of hypocrisy. They want and need the naked truth.

When he had finished speaking, the audience did not leave; nor did it stop its applause. Voznesensky called upon them to send get-well cards to Lyubimov. "He is a brave man and he wants and needs your support." The applause went on. The lights were switched off. No one moved. Voznesensky poked his head momentarily out from behind the scenery. He made a casual gesture of his hand and withdrew.

A youngster came up to him and said, "I have something to show you." It was a photograph of Voznesensky and Khrushchev at the time of Khrushchev's attack on the poets in 1963.

Later on Voznesensky said sadly, "That was a difficult time, too, but we came through it." Curious things happened, he recalled. In the days of the Khrushchev crisis two young sailors suddenly arrived. They had come down from Leningrad to present him with a flag from their cutter. "If you're in trouble," they told him, "just call on us. We'll come down and support you, just as the sailors did in 1917."

Voznesensky smiled. He did not think he would need the help of the sailors. If there was trouble now, if there was trouble about the trip to the United States and about his frank words at the two-hundredth performance of *Antimiry,* well, perhaps he would not be able to go abroad for a while. The heavens wouldn't fall. He would go up to Riga and do some writing. After all, he was a poet. As for the party critics—he used a word somewhat stronger than "nuts."

Not since the ill-fated speech of Meyerhold in 1939 had the Russian theater heard words so strong, so forceful, so uncompromising as those spoken by Voznesensky at the two-hundredth performance of *Antimiry*. But the year was 1967, not 1939. For all the troubles, all the harassments, all the pressures being put on the Soviet theater, and that would in the future be brought to bear, the forces of creativity—and freedom for the poet to write, the artist to paint, and the stage to portray—would ultimately triumph.

ART:
A RETURN TO MODERNISM

»

Hilton Kramer

A specter is haunting Soviet art—the specter of modernism. Fifty years ago the Bolshevik seizure of power placed artists of the most avant-garde persuasion in a position to transform completely the cultural life of the Russian people. The revolution was indeed the first political event in modern history to accord modernist artists such comprehensive, officially sanctioned power. Within a decade, however, the avant-garde was shattered, its power was lost, and the values of modernism placed under an official ban. Yet today these values, though they have a completely unofficial status and suffer a precarious existence, are again in the ascendancy. Though the newly burgeoning modernist movement remains extremely vulnerable to the ideological, bureaucratic, and penal vagaries of the Soviet state apparatus, the existence of the movement is the most important fact of art life in the Soviet Union at the present time. One can say without hesitation that modernism is once again on the rise and claiming some of the best minds and talents of the younger generation.

The obstacles facing these talents are enormous. There is, first of all, the official esthetic doctrine of the Soviet state. This doctrine is something more than a philosophical position. It is a program of action. Under the banner of

Socialist Realism, a debased populist doctrine dominates not only public taste and public discussion but also the very content of art education as well as art history and most of what passes for art criticism in a situation in which no real criticism of official dogma is permitted. The consumption no less than the production of art is given an ideological definition, and the ideology—stripped of its dialectical refinements and euphemisms—is openly designed to flatter the state, to celebrate its leaders, to mythicize its history, and to romanticize the common life of its people.

Thus the aspiring modernist finds his way blocked, when not overtly and energetically condemned, by a state monopoly on the means of artistic training, production, exhibition, consumption, and discussion. And, as if this were not enough to discourage all but the most determined and robust talents from persisting in their unorthodox ambitions, there is yet another, subtler obstacle. The cultural monopoly that has been in force since the late 1920's has effectively removed from public view the great examples of modernist art—Russian as well as non-Russian—that might have served as an impetus to esthetic innovation and in general provided the cultural context in which significant new expression is most fruitfully conceived.

This policy of suppression is no longer as total as it once was. In the galleries of the great Hermitage Museum in Leningrad, and in Moscow's Pushkin Museum, too, one can now see the numerous paintings by Picasso, Matisse, Bonnard, Derain, and other luminaries of the pre-1917 School of Paris that once belonged to the collections of the millionaire Russian art connoisseurs Ivan Morozov and Sergei Shchukin—collections that were nationalized after the revolution. These paintings, which in the case of Matisse, especially, constitute one of the greatest single collections of this great artist's work in his most significant period, have only lately been placed on public view. Predating the revolution, these pictures constitute the historical limit beyond which official doctrine has drawn a tight curtain. And in the case of Russian modernists who were of the same generation as Matisse, even their pre-1917 works are held in the museums' so-called "reserve collections," where only a privileged few may see them. Thus at the Hermitage one may see a Matisse landscape but not a Kandinsky landscape influenced by Matisse.

Accompanying this suppression of works of art there has been an equally effective program proscribing the literature, including visual reproduction, of the international modern movement. Thus the artist, especially the young artist, who aspires to work in a modernist direction begins his labors in a situation of nearly complete isolation from the examples and ideas that provide his counterparts in other countries with their most solid and immediate artistic sustenance. He is condemned not only to a lonely and politically dangerous vocation, but also to the necessity of meeting the demands of that vocation without easy access to the artistic and intellectual materials generally acknowledged to be indispensable to his enterprise.

And yet, though the obstacles are enormous and the expense of spirit they exact are incalculable, their effectiveness is not complete. Somehow artists contrive to remain in touch with at least some fragment of the materials they need. For one thing, there continues to be a certain amount of private collecting, and these collections are well known to the artists—at least in the big cities. Some of the collections have been assembled over a long span of time and on very little money, for the official ban on modernist art—particularly on the pre-1925 work of such Russian modernists as Kazimir Malevich, Aleksandr Rodchenko, Lyubov Popova, El Lissitzky, Vladimir Tatlin, and others of like persuasion—made it possible for the knowledgeable collector to buy this work for practically nothing. While the state frowned on such art, there was, and is, no barrier to its collection by private individuals. Indeed, through acquaintance with these collections— and with the modern Russian works in the reserve collections of the museums, for those who have access to them—a new generation of Soviet artists is establishing contact with some of the most original and radical achievements in modern art anywhere. And the fact that these achievements are specifically Russian and were hailed in the first years of the revolution as the advance guard of a new Soviet culture gives this new generation a sense, too, of recovering a part of its legitimate cultural patrimony.

Possibly even more important than the private collections, which, after all, are few, are the foreign publications—art books, exhibition catalogues, magazines—which the artists have somehow managed to collect for themselves. The one book most frequently encountered in these artists' studios is *The Great Experiment: Russian Art, 1863–1922,* written by a young English art historian, Camilla Gray, when she was twenty-six, and published five years ago in London and New York. This book, based on research in the Soviet Union as well as in Western collections, is a definitive study, rich in illustrations, of the Russian modernists, and its jealous possession by young Soviet artists is often their only tangible link to the native artistic tradition they regard as their own—the tradition officially consigned to oblivion when Socialist Realism became the established doctrine of the state. There is even said to be a copy of the book in the library of the principal art academy in Leningrad, a stronghold of Socialist Realist instruction, but available only to the faculty, not to students. And the book turns up in some surprising places. In the course of a discussion with Pavel Korin, one of the most gifted and cultivated senior artists of the Soviet Establishment— he is now seventy-five—and a master of heroic illustration, I was suddenly shown the plates in Miss Gray's book to support the view that modernism was a dead end and had long ago been exhausted. Even for this gentle-spoken antagonist of the old Russian avant-garde, who thinks of himself, with more than a touch of vanity, as heir to the great mural painters of the Italian Renaissance, Miss Gray's book was his principal point of contact with this still-controversial chapter of Russian art.

The Great Experiment is not the only foreign publication on Russian art one encounters in the artists' studios. A painter in Leningrad proudly brought out his copy of a monograph on Pavel Filonov, the Russian futurist painter who is a minor figure in Miss Gray's study. This book was written by the Czechoslovak critic Jan Kriz and was published in Prague in 1966. Apparently, a few copies were put on sale in the Soviet Union last year, though the work of Filonov, who designed the decor for Mayakovsky's first play (before the revolution) and conducted his own school of "Analytical Painting" in Petrograd in the 1920's, remains sequestered in the reserve sections of the state museums and is never written about in the Soviet press.

Such are the links—tenuous but determined—with Russia's vanguard past. But far more decisive for the new modernist art in the Soviet Union are the foreign publications devoted to modern art in the West. These include monographs and picture books on particular artists, histories of painting, sculpture, and graphic art, catalogues of recent exhibitions, and current art journals. The traffic in these publications is brisk, and often the entire character of an artist's work—and the eclecticism that is its principal weakness—is determined by the publications that have come to hand. For the artists in question, these foreign art publications constitute an alternative culture—a world of esthetic values remote from the official culture of the Soviet state—at the same time that they hold out the promise of restoring the modernist spirit to the position of authority and respect it occupied, briefly but brilliantly, in the first years of the revolution.

These first years of the revolution constitute a truly amazing period. The most extreme forms of abstraction in painting and sculpture became—overnight, as it were—an official style, dominating the schools, the museums, and the studios. But it was not a period innocent of esthetic conflict or of the political conflicts that came ultimately to determine the course that art would be forced to follow. While the new generation of modernists in the Soviet Union looks back on the art of these years with respect and longing, it is not unaware of the ambiguous political legacy that these years imposed upon Soviet art as a permanent condition.

Most of the stylistic innovations actually preceded the revolution. As early as 1913 Vasily Kandinsky created his first abstract expressionist compositions, while living in Germany. By 1915 Kazimir Malevich, who

had swiftly passed from an impressionist to a fauvist to a cubist style, produced his first suprematist paintings—works of pure geometrical form. By
then Tatlin had already—in 1913–14—executed some abstract reliefs and
constructions composed of found objects, and in 1915 exhibited abstract,
"open" sculptures suspended from the ceiling by wires. By 1915–16 Naum
Gabo had created the first prototypes of his open-form constructivist sculpture. Even Marc Chagall, a more lyrical and conservative talent than any of
these, had, by the time he returned to Russia from Paris in 1914, assimi-
lated the principles of fauvism and cubism and transformed them into a
highly personal mode of fantastic art.

The tumultuous years from 1917 to 1922 saw the consolidation of these
and many other innovations into the beginning of a cultural system, with
full bureaucratic control over schools, museums, publications, and public
decoration. Despite significant differences in esthetic outlook and personal
temperament, the artists of the vanguard welcomed the revolution with
enthusiasm. For a few years of electrifying activity the illusion persisted that
revolutionary politics and advanced art were moving in the same direction.
There was a sense that the esthetic ideals of modernism could at last be
fully implemented under a social system that was a kind of political analogue
to these ideals. As Malevich said: "Cubism and futurism were the revolutionary forms in art foreshadowing the revolution in political and economic
life of 1917." While this proved to be a mistaken interpretation of both
politics and art, it was nonetheless a powerful impetus to radical artistic
activity so long as the illusion of shared ideals remained intact.

The persistence of this illusion owed much to Lenin's appointment of
Anatoly V. Lunacharsky in 1917 as the first Commissar of Education.
Himself a playwright with an interest in modernist esthetics, Lunacharsky
had become well acquainted with the various modern movements in the
arts during his eleven-year exile in Western Europe, and he had formed
many friendships with artists. Under his direction a Department of Fine
Arts was established as part of the Commissariat for People's Education.
He appointed his friend David Sternberg as director. The painter Nathan
Altman became chairman of the Petrograd section, Tatlin chairman of the
Moscow section, and Kandinsky a member of the governing committee.
Though in theory all points of view were to be represented, in fact the
Department of Fine Arts became, in the words of its later enemies, a "leftist
dictatorship of the arts."

Under Lunacharsky's regime the Soviet government spent some
2,000,000 rubles on new museums—thirty-six were actually set up and
twenty-six others planned—and on contemporary modernist works for
their collections. As Camilla Gray points out, "With this chain of galleries,

Russia became the first country in the world to exhibit abstract art officially and on such a wide scale."

Of great importance, too, were the free schools—combination technical schools and art studios, known in Russian abbreviated form as vkhutemas —established under Lunacharsky's authority, because virtually every member of the avant-garde was involved in their teaching program and administration. Chagall, for example, was made director of the school in his native Vitebsk in 1918. And some of the pedagogical programs developed, but not always implemented, in this period—notably Kandinsky's—proved to be of enormous consequence to art education the world over when the avant-garde was dissolved and some of its most illustrious members went into exile. Thus the program that Kandinsky was denied permission to pursue in 1920 later became the basis of his course at the Bauhaus in Germany.

By 1922, however, the honeymoon of the revolution with the avant-garde was over. The unhappy fact is that there was no unanimity among the artists on either esthetic, pedagogical, or social questions, nor was there, despite the efforts of Lunacharsky and others, a political atmosphere really conducive to an understanding of their lofty, often utopian ideals. The artists were divided between those who believed in the complete esthetic autonomy of art—a position that had always held a precarious place in Russian intellectual life—and those who regarded pure esthetic expression, or art in any disinterested form, as socially obsolete, a residue of bourgeois culture that could now at last be jettisoned in favor of new utilitarian art forms serving the needs of the entire society.

Even among the purists there were fierce doctrinal disputes and nasty power grabs. Perhaps the most vulnerable figure was Chagall. First, his school at Vitebsk was taken over, more or less behind his back, by Malevich, who instituted a suprematist program to conform to his, but not to Chagall's, ideas. Then, in Moscow, where he painted murals for the State Jewish Theater, Chagall found himself relegated, by a committee including Kandinsky, to the lowest paid stipend because his work was insufficiently abstract.

These intramural conflicts, while indicative of the corrupting effect that power may have on artists and their work even where they are in a position to control their own destinies, did not ultimately determine the end of the avant-garde era. That was determined by the politics of the Soviet state.

The end came in stages, but by late 1921 the drift of events was clear enough. Official support of the vkhutemas was being withdrawn. Lenin was launching his New Economic Policy, which, with its partial return to capitalism, had the effect of restoring art to the "free market"—which is to say, placing it at the mercy of individual patronage. The great experiment was collapsing, and a new conservatism—new to Soviet art, but with deep roots in the Russian past—would shortly make itself felt. When Lunacharsky organized a huge exhibition of Soviet art for the Van Diemen Gallery in Berlin in the spring of 1922—the first comprehensive showing of suprematism and constructivism in Western Europe—Gabo and his brother, Anton Pevsner, with Kandinsky and Chagall, availed themselves of the opportunity to go into permanent exile.

Meanwhile, as if on cue to supply the market created by the New Economic Policy with goods appropriate to traditional taste, there was a resurgence of the "Wanderers" group, the Peredvizhniki, whose master had been Ilya Repin and which specialized in anecdotal and inspirational painting fully understandable to the masses. Founded in the 1860's with a program of "bringing art to the people," they took as their motto the statement of Nikolai G. Chernyshevsky that "Only the content is able to refute the accusation that art is an empty diversion."

During the "leftist dictatorship of the arts" the Wanderers were in retreat, but now they returned to favor. In 1922 they organized a huge exhibition in Moscow to coincide with the New Economic Policy, and announced: "We mirror the daily life: the life of the Red Army, workers, peasants, revolutionaries and heroes of labor. Our style is 'heroic realism' in a monumental form." The Wanderers then formed the Association of Painters of Revolutionary Russia and mounted an exhibition honoring the fifth anniversary of the Red Army. Works from this exhibition eventually became part of the permanent collection of the Museum of the Revolution, while modernist works in the state museums passed sooner or later into reserve collections or were destroyed.

Remnants of the avant-garde persisted for another few years. The group around Tatlin and Rodchenko, in opposition to purists like Malevich and Kandinsky, had long insisted that the true modern artist should become a kind of technician, and under the New Economic Policy these artists turned to industrial design and applied art. In the theater, the productions of Vsevolod Meyerhold were based on a radical application of constructivist esthetics to acting ("bio-mechanics") and stage design. In 1922 Meyerhold produced his controversial staging of Fernand Crommelynek's *The Magnificent Cuckold* with a set by Lyubov Popova. But such experiments were more and more disapproved, and in 1928 all private art groups, schools, and organizations were dissolved by government fiat. The experiment was over. An American connoisseur of modern art who visited Aleksandr Rodchenko in his studio in 1928 found that all his abstract work had been packed away. As for Tatlin, one can see in certain private collections in the Soviet Union today some of the feeble figurative paintings he turned out in the 1930's, when, as one observer put it, "he was broken in pieces by the regime."

For in 1932 the "heroic realism" of the Wanderers—denounced ten years before by Mayakovsky as "the depths of hideous banality"—was established as the official style of the state. In that year the Communist party ordered "the unification of all existing literary and artistic groups into a single Union of Soviet Artists," with the aim of "uniting all those who support the Soviet system and take an active part in the building of Social-ism." Socialist Realism became the only permissible style, and modernism passed from being a controversial activity to an activity regarded as an attack on the state.

From the vantage point of the 1960's and the current revival of mod-ernism in the Soviet Union, the bureaucratic instrumentality of this change —the creation of the Union of Soviet Artists—was almost as fateful as its ideological content. Thereafter no one could consider himself an artist out-side the union. Membership in the union, with its commissions, exhibi-tions, and stipends, not only assured the artist a livelihood, but also gave him a vested interest in maintaining bureaucratic control over the means of artistic production. Thus, in the controversies over modernism that have been raging in the past few years—sometimes in the Soviet press but more frequently in private—the union has been concerned, at times more vehe-mently than government leaders, to denounce all deviations from esthetic orthodoxy. Having long enjoyed the privileges of a state monopoly, the union is a jealous guardian of its power and shows no sign of relaxing its domination.

Thirty-five years after the founding of the Union of Soviet Artists the Socialist Realist tradition safeguarded by this power still answers, for the most part, to Mayakovsky's description. Nowadays, of course, the paintings and sculptures depicting Stalin in heroic stances are nowhere in evidence, but those of Lenin are ubiquitous. In the course of a day's business in the Soviet capital, a visitor encounters, even outside the museums, some fifty to seventy-five images of Lenin: paintings, photographs, statuettes, heroic monuments, illustrations, all of the most egregious sentimentality and artistic nullity. In museums such as the Tretyakov Gallery in Moscow and the Russian Museum in Leningrad, devoted to the history of Russian art, the twentieth-century sections are likewise dominated by Lenin's image— and with equal artistic effect.

There are, needless to say, a good many other subjects open to mem-bers of the union—the portrayal of Soviet life, memorials to the revolution and to the suffering endured in World War II, and a whole range of Rus-sian historical subjects, Russian culture heroes, and current Soviet eminences—but it is scarcely an exaggeration to say that the depiction of Lenin remains the central task of official Soviet art. So central, indeed, that this summer a special session of the Academy of Fine Arts of the Soviet Union, the counterpart in the field of art of the Academy of Sciences in the science world, has been convened, as part of the official celebration of the fiftieth anniversary of the revolution, to discuss the image of Lenin in Soviet fine arts. Learned philosophers and theoreticians will address themselves to this edifying topic. Lenin's own esthetic views will be expounded at length, and the dimensions of Soviet achievement measured against the specifications of Leninist theory.

In a recent interview the president of the Academy of Fine Arts, Vladimir A. Serov, a veteran painter of the Stalinist era who is now secretary of the Artists Union and the man credited with arranging Nikita Khrushchev's visit to the 1962 exhibition that resulted in the latter's famous attack on the modernists as "pederasts," made it clear to me that the purpose of this special session would be to restate the importance of Lenin as a subject for Soviet artists. Indeed, one had the impression in this interview that the union was preparing to use the big anniversary celebration as a means of further tightening its hold on the artistic life of the country in an effort to ward off any gestures in the direction of modernism. "Realism is our achievement and our force," Serov confidently declared.

When asked if the effects of science and technology, which have decisively transformed Soviet life in so many other respects, might not have given a new generation of artists an altered view of their vocation, he replied: "On this question, two positions are possible. According to the first, scientific knowledge and its technical application have completely changed the basis of art—both its subject matter and its methods. But this view, which leads ultimately to the rejection of realism and encourages abstraction, is one that Soviet artists categorically reject. For art is not a medium of theory, but a medium of feeling. Hence the second position, which is the position of the Artists Union: that since it is the function of science and technology to improve the quality of human life, it remains the function of art to depict in traditional ways the improvements in life. Art does not need to change because of science."

This will no doubt remain the official view of the Artists Union for the foreseeable future—though not necessarily of its younger members, some of whom are known to occupy themselves privately with art of a more advanced persuasion. But it is not the only view that is being entertained, even in the official precincts of the Academy of Fine Arts. In another section of the academy, at the Institute of the History of Art, I found, if not exactly the reverse of Serov's orthodoxy, at least an intelligent and informed awareness that the world had seen some significant changes—artistic and intellectual changes—since the original formulation of the Socialist Realist position.

Thus, in an interview with two eminent members of this institute, the art historians Yuri Kholpinsky and Boris Veimarn, who hold the rank of corresponding members of the academy, I discovered that the official esthetic ideology of the state was considerably leavened, at this intellectual altitude at least, by ideas of a far more freewheeling character. The institute itself is responsible for an immense range of publications and research —from an enormous *General History of Art* (eight volumes) and the even larger *History of Fine Arts of the Soviet People* (nine volumes) to popular booklets and picture albums and textbooks for the schools. One of its current projects is a mammoth *Anthology of World Esthetic Thought* from ancient times to the present; three volumes have already appeared, with two more to come.

While they made it clear that the writings of Marx and Engels together with those of the nineteenth-century Russian critics Vissarion G. Belinsky, Nikolai G. Chernyshevsky, and Aleksandr I. Herzen provide the main ideological guidelines of the institute's work, giving it a distinct social orientation, Kholpinsky spoke with evident admiration of the works of Heinrich Wölfflin, Alois Riegl, and Wilhelm Worringer, the modern German art historians and estheticians who have long had a wide influence on historical studies of art in the West. And not only on historical studies of art: Worringer's important work, *Abstraction and Empathy,* 1908, is known to have played a decisive role in encouraging Kandinsky to paint his first abstract paintings and was clearly a source of the painter's own treatise, *On the Spiritual in Art.*

Moreover, Kholpinsky's special interest at the moment appeared to be contemporary French criticism, particularly the so-called "structuralist" school, comprising the writings of the anthropologist Claude Lévi-Strauss, the literary critic Roland Barthes, and their associates. While careful to note his disagreements with a point of view so "unhistorical" in its method and so "formalist" in its abiding concerns, Kholpinsky nonetheless defended the work of these writers, especially of Lévi-Strauss, as having great importance for the future study of art history. He pointed out that the structuralists had been anticipated in many of their ideas by the Russian formalist critics of the early twentieth century—a group long held in official contempt but soon, one senses, due for rehabilitation.

The relevance of all this to the revival of modernist art in the Soviet Union is not difficult to divine. When, and if, that revival comes finally to receive official recognition—a distant but not hopeless possibility—the academicians of the Institute of the History of Art will not be unequipped to deal with it. On the contrary, one has the impression that the way is being prepared for a specifically Russian interpretation of the history of modernism—and there will be no shortage of Russian materials when the time comes.

But it is one thing to pursue such elevated philosophical issues within the confines of a Marxist-oriented academic institute. It is quite another to produce the actual works of art upon which the current revival of modernism will ultimately depend. What, then, does this art consist of?

In answering this question, a foreign visitor to the Soviet Union cannot claim to offer more than fragmentary impressions. When it comes to unofficial work—that is, all art produced outside the jurisdiction of the Artists Union—one is dealing with a very scattered art scene, some of whose inhabitants are not even known to each other. Private art galleries do not exist. Private collections are sometimes difficult to see, at least in their entirety, because of their owners' confined living space. The artists themselves differ in their willingness to expose their work to outsiders. Yet even fragmentary impressions sometimes reveal a good deal.

Let us begin with the two painters whose work seems to me the most accomplished that I have seen in the Soviet Union.

Dmitri Krasnopevtsev, who is forty-two and lives in Moscow, is a painter of still life. There is nothing radical or aggressively vanguard about his work, which is extremely subdued, even in its use of color, generally limited to blacks, whites, and grays. The motifs of Krasnopevtsev's paintings are, moreover, rather commonplace—tree trunks and branches, vases, flowers, bottles, a dish of eggs, table tops, and all manner of ordinary objects. Yet his pictures are not in any sense realistic. They are at once mysterious and very pure, imparting an aura of delicate melancholy. His draftsmanship is impeccable but very personal; the rendering of every object is given a specific emotional density. In feeling, these paintings remind one at times of the early Chirico, but a Chirico shorn of symbolism, the dreamlike quality made more objective. One thinks, too, of certain classical still lifes of Derain. The structure of these pictures is lean and taut, and they inhabit a kind of metaphysical silence far removed from the noisy rhetoric of the workaday world.

This is indeed the artist's intention, for he has said about his work: "Our noisy and dynamic age, above all else, needs silence and the opportunity for concentration during interludes of silence. We need more than ever a silent kind of art." This suggests an affinity for abstraction, but Krasnopevtsev is not an abstract painter. In a sense, he accomplishes the purposes of classical abstraction while remaining committed to the representation of objects.

At an opposite extreme of temperament and style is the Leningrad painter Yevgeny Mechnov-Voitenko. Unlike Krasnopevtsev, who, like many other modernist painters in Moscow, shows his work from time to time in unofficial exhibitions improvised in clubrooms or private apartments and occasionally sells pictures to private collectors, Mechnov-Voitenko has never sold or exhibited a single painting. He is thirty-seven, and the tiny, crowded room in which he lives and works contains all the work he has ever produced—dozens of large abstract paintings and hundreds of small charcoal and pen drawings, also mainly abstract.

Of the new modernist paintings I saw in the Soviet Union, Mechnov-Voitenko's exhibited the surest grasp of abstraction. He is in possession not only of enormous natural abilities, but also of a keen understanding of what recent developments in abstract painting have meant. His first abstractions, dating from around 1957, are cubist in design, but closer to a precise rendering of a well-made cubist sculpture than to traditional cubist painting. One of these is entitled "Homage to Miró." The bulk of his work dates from the early 1960's, and in this the traces of cubist design give way to all-over patterns evidently influenced by Jackson Pollock and Mark Tobey. The artist himself is evasive on this point, at once insisting that his only masters have been Mikhail Vrubel (1856–1910) and Valentin Serov (1865–1911), the much-admired precursors of the original Russian avant-garde, and yet admitting to having seen reproductions of Pollock and Tobey in the pages of the magazine *Art in America*. In any event, it is undeniable that these American abstractionists have figured importantly in his development. Like Pollock, Mechnov-Voitenko often uses enamel, which is dripped onto the picture surface at great speed, and, like Tobey, he sometimes favors an almost Oriental calligraphic touch. The influence of Paul Klee, too, is sometimes detectable.

He handles these sources with great skill and intelligence, and is by no means confined to their example. A picture called "Homage to Rilke" (1962) is a very dark, thickly textured, almost black all-over monochromatic work of no evident derivation. His masterpiece—an untitled work of 1960—is a large (I would guess about ten by five and a half feet) all-over abstraction on a white ground in which drips, calligraphic touches, and expressionistic texture are nowhere in evidence. Instead, there is a painstaking design of small, precise, keylike interlocking shapes of many colors deployed with great skill and pictorial tact. It is surely a picture that would have found its way into a museum collection in the West had conditions been propitious.

Both of these artists are professionally trained—Mechnov-Voitenko as a theatrical designer, a profession he has not followed—and the training shows. There is nothing in their work of that near-amateur technical gaucherie that sometimes disfigures the work of others of like persuasion. In addition, Mechnov-Voitenko has a background in the study of foreign languages and literature. Both artists have already produced sizable *oeuvres* of remarkable quality and consistency.

Impressive, too, are two other Leningrad artists—Yevgeny Ruchin and Aleksei Khvostenko. Ruchin, now in his late twenties, was trained as a geologist and is mainly self-taught as an artist. He is amazingly cognizant of every up-to-date artistic development the world over, and this, combined with an evident enthusiasm for what is new and fresh, leads him to attempt more styles and ideas than he has yet mastered. Nonetheless, he has produced some solid work—austerely designed landscapes that recall, to an American eye, the work of Marsden Hartley, a series of views from his studio window that suggest something of the early Matisse, highly decorative expressionist pictures of the old Russian Orthodox churches in Novgorod (perhaps his most successful work to date), and various forms of assemblage and abstraction. Even where the style may not be radical, the use of unusual materials gives it a pointed energy and verve. He has had several unofficial exhibitions in Leningrad.

Khvostenko is also self-taught, his education being mainly literary; he is a poet (though unpublished) as well as a painter. He, too, is in his twenties. Though he has produced a small number of respectable abstract paintings, his forte is collage; and in this genre he has been much influenced by Robert Rauschenberg and the earlier dadaists. There is in his collages an extraordinary nervous momentum in which images from magazines, newspapers, and other printed materials, either pasted or transferred to the page by the technique known as frottage, generate a sense of speed and disaster. Often these collages are combined with actual writing, and his collages are really a species of visual poetry. He has followed the logic of his talents in this respect by producing a number of handmade portfolios in which fragments of poems, themselves embellished with visual elements, alternate with collages. He is a man of intense sensibility, and one has the impression that, although already accomplished, he is only at the beginning of an important career at a boundary where literary and visual art meet.

In Moscow, besides Krasnopevtsev's work, the most interesting paintings I saw were by Aleksandr Poteshkin, Sergei Yesayan, and Anatoly Zverev.

Poteshkin continues the line of Russian geometrical abstraction, a surprisingly rare direction among the new painters. He, too, is a complete professional. He might best be described as belonging to the "romantic" school of geometrical painting. His pictures do not appear to be based on a fixed principle of design, but are clearly improvised within the limits of his chosen repertory of geometrical shapes. He is a striking colorist, romantic in this respect as well.

Yesayan, an Armenian, is an artist of a quite different outlook. Even his technique—he works exclusively in egg tempera—sets him apart from his contemporaries. He is a fantasist, and the succession of small pictures he has produced in recent years have a quality of ancient lore about them. Mainly, they are interior scenes with figures, set in some unidentifiable historical or mythological past—scenes of ritual and spiritual grandeur. Even his few still lifes have this same aura. Strictly speaking, such pictures are not really modernist at all, but they are works of total conviction, executed with great technical finesse. They are the output of an artist with a completely personal culture that eschews both the official and the unofficial conventions of his contemporaries.

Zverev, something of a favorite with collectors of the new art in Moscow, is an artist of more familiar sensibility—an expressionist of lyrical temperament with a tendency to be undisciplined. His best works to date are a series of abstract expressionist water-color portraits done in the late 1950's. Clearly an artist of drive and energy, he can also be extremely facile, and is indeed an artist whose development is vulnerable to the influences immediately at hand.

This is true, also, of some of the other painters on the Moscow scene who have already won a certain reputation among the small band of collectors—foreign diplomats and journalists and rising members of the new Soviet bourgeoisie and professional classes—who are the mainstay of these artists. Dmitri Plavinsky, Oskar Rabin, Vladimir Nemukhin, and Lidiya Masterkova, among others, are all expressionists, abstract or figurative, working in stylistic veins that are not especially original or distinctive, though in a private collection in Leningrad I saw a picture by Nemukhin— an oversize abstract still life of a bottle opener—that was outstanding.

Of the sculptors, I saw the work of only two who were notable. The younger, Ernst Neizvestny, forty-two years old, is perhaps the best-known Soviet artist of his generation—at least to the foreign art public—for he has been shown in London and New York and much publicized. He is an artist of surpassing energy and power, grandiose in ambition and rhetoric. His small studio in Moscow, a garage with a sleeping balcony, is crowded to the ceiling with what appears to be hundreds of works, most of them in plaster or stone or bronze, all depicting some heroic, anguished metamorphosis of the figure. On a high shelf one can see some masklike cut-metal heads, more or less on the order of Julio González's cubist heads, but this is a direction apparently abandoned. In addition, Neizvestny is also a prolific graphic artist and has lately been occupied with a voluminous series of etchings to illustrate Dante's *Divine Comedy*.

One can discern a number of foreign influences in this sculpture—that of Henry Moore in the way the figures are "opened," and Jacques Lipchitz, too, the Lipchitz of the late, "heroic," massive baroque figures. Like Moore and Lipchitz in their later phases, Neizvestny aspires to a monumental statement, a kind of heroic humanism. This is a difficult aspiration for a serious artist working in a cultural milieu that has systematically corrupted and debased all forms of public rhetoric and that has seen the complete brutalization of monumental sculpture. Neizvestny's work does not escape the perils of this situation. The enormous hands in dramatic gesture, the twisted mouths, the orotund musculature of his larger-than-life male figures and their altogether massive stance—these and other characteristic features of his sculpture, while clearly the work of a sizable talent, are closer in feeling to the clichés of Socialist Realism than to the more critical spirit of modernist art. In the presence of so many writhing forms, immense shoulders, and clenched fists, one understands the meaning of Krasnopevtsev's appeal for "silence."

Neizvestny handles these matters with somewhat greater tact in his graphic work, where the medium itself appears to act as a brake on his tendency toward overstatement. Yet even there one is struck, as one invariably is with his sculpture, by the distance separating the sheer force of his abilities from their proper realization.

On the Soviet art scene Neizvestny occupies an ambiguous position. Though belonging to the modernist camp, he is yet somehow acceptable to at least some elements of the Establishment. Lately he has received an important state commission for a large work for Artek, the big children's summer colony in the Crimea. One artist in Moscow compared Neizvestny's role to that of the poet Yevgeny Yevtushenko, characterizing both as artists adept at simulating esthetic rebellion while remaining closely allied to easily understandable conventions.

If Soviet sculpture today is largely a wasteland, its immediate past strikes one as even grimmer, and so it was all the more astonishing to encounter a very gifted sculptor who had survived the long years of the Socialist Realist blight with his considerable energies and talents undimmed, a sculptor, moreover, who has been more or less on the fringes of the Establishment for most of his career. It was during my last evening in Moscow that I was taken to the studio, just off Gorky Street, of Dmitri Tsaplin, now in his seventy-seventh year. This sculptor proved to be a master carver of a kind one rarely sees any more. Earlier in his career he lived and worked abroad—in Paris from 1927 to 1932, and in Spain from 1932 to 1935—and had exhibitions in this period in Paris, Madrid, and London before returning to Moscow in 1935. His studio is still filled with most of the work shown in those exhibitions—exquisite stone carvings of animals and fish, and figures and portraits more Egyptian than anything else. Indeed, though I never thought I could stomach still another portrait of Lenin, Tsaplin's were works of a notable sculptural probity. And his current work-in-progress includes large abstract carvings in granite. With some sixty of his works in Soviet museums—mainly portrait heads—he seemed quite prepared to embark on a new direction. Opening a copy of Herbert Read's *Concise History of Modern Sculpture,* Tsaplin pointed to a reproduction of a very pure abstract carving by the English sculptor Barbara Hepworth and confidently declared: "Mine will be better."

Five years have passed since Nikita S. Khrushchev stood in front of a painting by Robert Falk (1886–1958), one of the early modernists who survived the Stalin period, and declared: "I would say that this is just a mess," and then went on to announce to the younger modernists who were present: "Gentlemen, we are declaring war on you." One measure of the change that has taken place since that day is the fact that a large Falk retrospective exhibition, many times postponed, was finally mounted late in 1966. Though the "war" declared by Khrushchev continues, one has the impression that it is nowadays more energetically conducted by entrenched reactionaries within the cultural Establishment than by the government as such. To some extent the old-line Socialist Realists are in the position of the nineteenth-century academicians who resisted the innovations of the impressionists and every succeeding avant-garde generation: their power and position are at stake. But the bureaucratic authority of the Soviet Academy gives it incomparably greater power to enforce its point of view.

Two forthcoming events will do much to indicate the direction in which things are moving. One is the immense retrospective exhibition of the entire history of Soviet art that will take place in 1968 as part of the year-long anniversary celebrations, for there is now a debate taking place in the academy itself about the inclusion of the early modernists—Kandinsky, Chagall, Malevich, *et al.*—in this official survey. Were these artists to be included in an exhibition honoring the revolution, it would indeed be the first step in a total rehabilitation.

The other event will be the opening, at some distant date, of the new gallery now under construction to house special exhibitions for the Tretyakov Gallery, the principal museum of Russian art in Moscow. When this gallery is built, it will release space for the immense reserve collections.

One museum director expressed the hope that the occasion would be used to restore the Russian avant-garde to its proper historical position.

Already something of this sort is being done at the public lecture programs conducted by the Pushkin Museum in Moscow. In this adult-education series, one can hear about the entire history of abstract art—not only about Kandinsky and Malevich, but also about Mondrian and Pollock as well. These lectures are always crowded. As one museum official put it: "The new generation of the sixties cannot hear enough about the abstractionists, and they are yearning to see the Russian leaders of this school."

Certainly the key to the future is that "new generation"—and not only of artists, but of collectors, too. In a real sense the future of Soviet art is in the hands of the enlightened bourgeoisie, which, in the Soviet Union no less than in the Western democracies, looks to art both for spiritual sustenance and for a certification of its own leisured status. Because this class, in the Soviet Union, tends to be young and well educated and distinctly modern in its outlook, if only because of the functions it has been trained to perform in a highly technological society, it is no longer satisfied with the shopworn populism of Socialist Realism—a style fabricated for less sophisticated minds.

There is indeed a tacit alliance between the new bourgeois elite and the new modernists, between the new managers and the new bohemians. And as the position of the former grows in importance, the place of the latter will be assured. In some respects the official events planned for the fiftieth-anniversary celebrations are designed to obscure the importance of both.

I recall dining one evening in Moscow with an artist and a young physicist. The physicist had been invited both because he spoke English, which the artist did not, and because he was an ardent collector of the new art. At the end of the meal an expensive cake was served. The physicist and his wife had brought it. It was called a Sputnik cake, and the design of the icing—circular motifs of various sizes tracing a pattern of interlocking spheres—had a remarkable resemblance to one of Rodchenko's metal constructions of 1920 that we had been looking at in Camilla Gray's book. When I pointed this out, we all laughed, and the physicist declared: "Well, perhaps when the anniversary is over, we shall be able to have our art in the museums again instead of in the bakeries." Like so many of the observations of this new generation, it was an expression not of pessimism, but of impatience.

THE WORLD OF MUSIC

»

Harold C. Schonberg

The Leningrad Conservatory of Music is a very large building and it contains a correspondingly large concert hall. To the graduating students the concert hall has special significance. It is there that they audition before a jury of professors. A great deal depends on the impression they make. Indeed, their entire future could very well depend on it. If they impress the jury, it means performances with orchestras, solo concerts, a chance to participate in international competitions. Perhaps even—who knows?—a decent apartment.

I stood outside the door of the auditorium. The sound of Tchaikovsky's B-flat-minor piano concerto could be heard. My guide, an official of the conservatory, put his finger to his lips and motioned me in.

No more than half a dozen people were in the thousand-seat hall. All were grouped in the rear. (I later found out they were competing pianists and their teachers, following the opposition.) As I tiptoed to a seat, a floor board creaked. A woman glared at me. "Sh-h-h!" she whispered. A uniformed guard looked at me and put his finger to his lips. "Sh-h-h!" he whispered.

On stage were two Steinways. The solo part of the Tchaikovsky was being played by a serious, good-looking young man. At the second piano another man was playing the orchestral reduction. From the walls, looking benignly down, were the heroes of Russian music, in mammoth-size paintings—Tchaikovsky, Mussorgsky, Anton Rubinstein, Glinka, Rimsky-Korsakov, and others.

The boy finished. He had played magnificently, with breadth and virtuoso fingers. He left the stage, still serious and unsmiling, and was succeeded by a young lady who played a Bach prelude and fugue, some Scarlatti, some Beethoven, and then a tricky, fast-moving Shostakovich prelude. Halfway through she broke down and stopped. She flushed, gamely started again, and broke down in the same place. Once more—and still another breakdown. She kneaded her fingers and looked despairingly around.

Suddenly an awful, disembodied voice resounded through the hall. It came from one of the judges, who was in the balcony, out of my line of sight. As I think back on it, the voice was kindly enough, but I had identified with the girl on stage, and to me it sounded like Judgment Day. The voice seemed to be telling the pianist to take her time, calm down, try again. She did, and even managed to get through the piece this time, but the initial sparkle of her playing was gone.

My guide was waiting for me when the auditions were over. "Are the kids always that serious?" I asked. "Wouldn't you be?" she answered. Perhaps. But American students often kid around in class and even during examinations. In Russia it seems to be a matter of life and death, and if they have fun in class I never saw it. I dropped into a violin class at the Leningrad Conservatory. Everything was deadly serious. A girl was playing Bach, and the tip of her tongue was stuck out in concentration. She finished and put her violin down. She did not smile. Four or five young people, awaiting their turn, were seated at the rear of the classroom. They did not smile.

A few days later, in Moscow, I visited the Central Music School, where gifted children are taught. In one class two children were playing some two-piano pieces by Shostakovich. One was a boy, about ten years old, a thin child with a serious face. The other was a girl, about the same age, a chubby kid with a serious face. They sat on the edge of their chairs. Otherwise their feet would not have reached the pedals. They played well. There was no groping for notes, no faltering rhythms, no letup in the smooth, well-schooled, perfectly drilled playing.

They finished. They turned around to face the visitor, serious, unsmiling. I looked back at them and smiled. They did not smile back. There was a long pause. I felt I had to do *something,* and so I stuck out my tongue at them. That did it. The boy grinned, and the girl started to giggle. Once the ice was broken they turned out to be delightful, well-adjusted children. But they have been taught to take their music seriously.

At the Central Music School I sat in the auditorium and listened to a succession of brilliant youngsters. In they came and out they went, anywhere from thirteen to seventeen years old. Each played the piano or violin with amazing strength and confidence.

"These children are typical of our school," said the principal. I looked at him in blank disbelief. If the Central Music School had classes full of this kind of talent, it houses a collection of potential geniuses unparalleled under one roof. I pressed the point.

"Well," said the principal, with just the trace of a smile, "of course we have made an effort to show you our most talented pupils." I felt a little better.

These days qualified visitors are welcome at music schools and conservatories throughout the Soviet Union. It was different not too long ago. I first visited Russia in 1961, and it was a frustrating experience. Few people were willing to talk. Foreigners, especially Americans, were almost never asked to Soviet homes, nor were there many Russians who would accept an invitation to have dinner with an American. Conversations with Russian musicians would produce only pious official doctrine about the glory (and historical inevitability) of Socialist Realism and the sterility of decadent capitalistic bourgeois formalism. It was hard to get close to a Russian. All seemed to be suspicious or frightened.

I remember, in 1961, trying to get into Russian conservatories outside Moscow. I was especially eager, in Odessa, to visit the conservatory and have a talk with the head of the violin department. For out of Odessa, for some reason, has come an unusually high proportion of the great violinists of the century—Mischa Elman, Nathan Milstein, Toscha Seidel, David Oistrakh. (The Russians joke about it. They say it is something in the climate of Odessa.) I made my request for a visit known to the proper authorities.

"Yes, yes, of course. Come back in three hours. We shall have an introduction to the director for you." I came back in three hours. "We are sorry, but today there are entrance examinations. Come back tomorrow." I came back the next day. "We are sorry, but the school is closed today. The students are out in the fields helping the farmers reap the collective harvest." I gave up. That afternoon I walked to the conservatory and stood outside, listening to some very classy violin playing drifting from the windows, feeling something like an excommunicated monk. I never did get in.

Today things are different. Everything in the Soviet Union is different.

People are talking, anxious to exchange ideas. To the average Russian the West is no longer The Enemy. The country has, for the most part, shucked off the monumental inferiority complex it used to have, and vast changes seem to be in process. The changes apply to music, too, for within the last few years Soviet music has been changing as much as Soviet literature, and in some respects even more. There are few, if any, genuine avant-gardists in Soviet literature, whereas there now decidedly are in music. For the first time since the early 1930's Russia is making a move to enter the international musical community.

The most astonishing esthetic phenomenon of the Soviet Union in the last few years, and one worthy of a great deal of attention, is the existence of a musical avant-garde unmistakably derived from the West. It had to be derived, for there was no precedent for any kind of avant-garde musical movement in Russia. Using scores, studying records and tapes of such international avant-garde musical heroes as Pierre Boulez in France, Luciano Berio in Italy, Yannis Xenakis in Greece, John Cage and Lukas Foss in the United States, a handful of Russian composers began to work out the principles of serial technique, aleatory and other devices that the West had enthusiastically adopted after World War II ended.

Of these devices the most important is serial technique, a sequel to the twelve-tone system worked out by Arnold Schoenberg around 1923. The twelve-tone system was built around an ordered sequence of all the individual notes of the scale. These twelve notes were immediately presented as a "row" and then subjected to specified manipulations. Serialism, especially as developed by Boulez and by Milton Babbitt in the United States, extended the Schoenberg idea to all aspects of composition. Not only were the notes "ordered," but also timbre, rests, silences, articulation and duration of notes. In the process tonality was destroyed. There was no home key; pieces were no longer in C major or D minor. Indeed, there was no key at all. The result, to conventional listeners, was excruciating dissonance.

Quite the opposite is aleatoric music, an even more recent development. Aleatory is a term used to describe random elements in music. In aleatoric music a composer will surrender control to a performer, who can do what he wants to do, within certain limits—or, sometimes, no limits at all. Or a composer might write a piece according to a roll of the dice, or the way ink dots are scattered on paper. Just as serial music is the most controlled kind of music ever composed, and is often under attack for being too rigid and "intellectual," so aleatoric music is the least controlled and is often under attack for being anarchic and formless. Both kinds of music are almost always abstract, in the sense that a Mondrian (controlled) or Pollock (random) painting is abstract. Up to now the Russians have always been the most nationalistic of composers. From Glinka on, all Russian musicians drew nourishment from their heritage of folk music. But most avant-garde music, being abstract, has nothing to do with folk elements. This alone made it anathema to Russian estheticians and ideologues. The very fact that now a group of Russian avant-gardists, and even some adventurous composers not of the avant-garde, are beginning to write music that dispenses with nationalistic elements is a momentous step in Russian music, and one not yet sufficiently realized by the West.

In the entire Soviet Union there are not more than a dozen or so avant-garde composers, but they are a determined group of youngsters, most of them under thirty years of age, who work under handicaps but produce serial and even a form of electronic music. It is a music that is as little liked and understood by the Russian public as it is in the West, being athematic, pointillistic, dissonant, and a complete break with the past. The avant-garde composers in the Soviet Union work pretty much by themselves. Very little of their music is published, and performances come seldom. In Leningrad, however, a young conductor named Igor Blashkov has adopted some of the modernists and presents their music in public. Some of the avant-garde Russian composers are not even members of the all-powerful Union of Composers. They exist much as avant-garde composers in the West exist— by teaching or doing hack work. They do not live very well. But the point is that while so big a country as the Soviet Union has only about a dozen avant-garde composers, it is a dozen more than existed only a few years ago.

Of course the conservatives, the Establishment, do not like the new music. They do not stop the younger composers from writing it, but they certainly will not go out of their way to help their radical young colleagues. The Establishment is bothered, really bothered, by the attention visitors give the modernists. Most Establishment composers are middle-aged or old. They have grown up on a Socialist Realism kind of music and they cannot understand the squeals, blips, glissandi, tonal ruptures, and wild clumps of jagged sound that the modernists are producing. They are intellectually aware that the new music has taken root all over the West, but emotionally they refuse to believe it. They *cannot* believe it.

And they become terribly upset when a visitor wants to hear the new Russian music and not theirs. "But you will be getting the wrong idea of what our composers are producing. . . ." I heard this cry from the Establishment everywhere, and my experience in Kiev was typical.

I had gone to Kiev expressly to hear the music of the four resident avant-gardists—Leonid Silvestrov, Leonid Grabovsky, Vladimir Zagortsev, and Vitali Godziatsky. In Moscow I had emphasized the fact that for once I did not want to meet any of the Establishment group. I wanted to meet only those four youngsters, hear their music, have dinner and a talk with them if they were so inclined. *Da, da.* All would be arranged.

So when I checked into the Union of Composers building at Kiev, I was greeted by about twenty old-school composers. Where were Silvestrov & Co.? "They will be here later." How much later? "They will be here later. What music of ours would you like to hear?" I explained that I was sure their music was very beautiful. But we in the United States, I said, were familiar with their type of music, whereas the Russian avant-garde was an unknown quantity to us. That was why I was especially interested in hearing the new kind of Russian music. Looks were exchanged. Somebody went to a telephone. "They will be here," said the spokesman of the group. "In the meantime, can you tell us about the latest developments in American music?"

Presently Grabovsky and Silvestrov turned up. Then Zagortsev. Then Godziatsky. They sat in the rear, four nice-looking, slim, intense boys, attentively listening to the discussion but contributing nothing. The point that the older composers tried to make was that great music not only stemmed from a folk tradition but that it also had to have "heart" and "soul." "Do you really like this new kind of music?" one of them wanted to know. I said that like or dislike had nothing to do with it, in view of the fact that virtually every young composer of any importance in the world today was writing in this idiom. In the meantime, here were the young composers. Would it be possible to hear their music?

Once the youngsters got the idea that I had really come to Kiev just to hear their music they moved in and took over. They rushed to get tapes, and they volubly explained what they were trying to do. The older men listened to the tapes with sour faces and, one by one, drifted away. At the end only the four boys, a girl, and two or three of the Establishment group were on hand. The girl desperately wanted me to hear one of her scores. "But if you like *their* music, I am afraid you will not like mine." I did listen to one of her pieces, a ballet. It was virtually a rewrite of *Le Sacre du Printemps.*

Would the boys have dinner with me? *Da! Da!* The five of us and my translator went to that monstrosity known as the Hotel Dnipro. We followed protocol by offering toast after toast in vodka, Georgian wines, and Ukrainian pepper brandy. The brandy was mine, because I had a cold and a sore throat. "We in the Ukraine," Silvestrov said, "believe that the best cure for a cold is pepper brandy." That interesting potable tastes like Tabasco sauce diluted with nitric acid. It grows on one.

I wanted to ask questions. Instead, I was on the receiving end. How did composers manage in America? How good were the performances? What kind of audience? How much money could a successful composer make?

What were living conditions like? Does everybody in America have a car?

The questions were typical. Soviet musicians and, indeed, all Soviet intellectuals who have not been abroad have a burning lust to know what is going on. They want all the information they can get, and they want books, records, tapes, scores, newspapers, magazines (art magazines especially)—everything.

Finally I managed to get a question in. "Just how many of you are there in the Soviet Union?"

Grabovsky grinned. "Give me a piece of paper," he said. He wrote down his name and those of his friends; Sergei Slonimsky and Boris Tishchenko, in Leningrad; Andrei Volkonsky, Edison Denisov, and Alfred Schnitke, in Moscow; Arvo Pärt and Culdar Sink in Tallinn; and Nodar Mamisashvili, in Tbilisi. "Here," Grabovsky said, giving me the list. "This is all of us."

Grabovsky and his friends were quite honest in estimating their own music. They are searching for new means of expression and admit they are feeling their way. Lacking instruction in serial technique, removed from the more cosmopolitan centers of Moscow and Leningrad, they have had to work things out for themselves, using Western texts they managed to locate, studying and analyzing contemporary music in score, on records, and on tape. While their music may be somewhat crude, it has vitality and enthusiasm. It is also a mishmash. Everything is jumbled together—serial technique, aleatory, extramusical sounds (such as rappings on the cello with knuckle or bow), explosive tonal outbursts, extreme dissonance, an exploitation of extreme and uncomfortable instrumental registers.

Godziatsky is the only one of the four who experiments with electronic music. He does not have any equipment—there is no studio of electronic music anywhere in the Soviet Union, just as no conservatory gives any course in post-Webern techniques—and so he uses a tape recorder, working with man-made sounds somewhat in the style of the early musique-concrète school in Paris. He also favors Satie-like titles: "Rupture of Flatness," "Emancipated Suitcase," "Anti-Piano." His music is rather primitive, and he knows it, but he feels compelled to use electronic media and had to make the best of his inadequate tools.

Indeed, the entire Kiev group could possibly be described as modern primitives, in the art-history sense of the word. The music of the Moscow and Leningrad avant-garde groups is more polished, closer to Western models. All Russian avant-gardists are in close contact with the experimental Polish group headed by Krzysztof Penderecki. The avant-garde festivals in Warsaw attract many Western musicians, and some of the Russian avant-gardists have been able to get to Warsaw and meet leading practitioners of the new music from the United States and Europe. Avant-gardists all over the world keep in close touch with each other, and the Russian group knows exactly what is happening in Cologne, in Baden-Baden, in Milan, New York, and Buffalo.

Most Russian musicians, even the conservatives, seem to agree that the two most talented of the avant-gardists are Boris Tishchenko and Sergei Slonimsky, in Leningrad. Tishchenko is a fine pianist who plays his own music in public. His piano sonata is a wild piece, full of clusters played by palm and forearm, and with ferocious rhythms alternating with slow-moving serial textures. The sonata is overlong and overserious, but clearly the work of a major talent. Tishchenko's Third Symphony, which had its première in Leningrad in April, 1967, is a better work: surer, more concise, less dependent on formula. It is fully in the post-Webern (Tishchenko says "post-serial") world, makes use of aleatory, and is undoctrinaire enough to include a touch of folk flavor.

Slonimsky also is a "post-serialist" who handles his materials in a highly personal manner. He is not afraid to mix textures, and his music has more style and elegance than is commonly associated with the medium. One of his pieces, a tiny song cycle for soprano and flute, achieves an unusual degree of intensity.

The Moscow avant-gardists are, on the whole, a polished and careful group without the strength or profile of the Leningrad or Kiev composers. A score like Alfred Schnitke's Music for Piano and Chamber Orchestra is very much in the international style, even to the use of jazz elements. Andrei Volkonsky and Edison Denisov stem from the Boulez-Berio axis, and their competent music illustrates a modern kind of academism.

These are the composers who, in the next decade, will be attracting attention in the West. In the meantime the big man of Russian music is, of course, the shy, slim, nervous, chain-smoking Dmitri Shostakovich. Shostakovich these days makes few public appearances. He has been ill, and, in any case, he has always loathed the spotlight. He is a revered figure in Russia, and everybody loves him as a human being as well as a composer. But few see him. The Union of Composers did make a tentative appointment for me. "He is not feeling very well this week but will see you next week." But the following week: "He still does not feel well. You will understand."

The career of Shostakovich illustrates the ups and downs of Russian music since the 1917 revolution. In many respects it has been a sad and unfulfilled career. Many observers in the West feel that he has been crushed by events; and it was most interesting to hear some of the younger Soviet composers admit that Shostakovich has not lived up to his extraordinary potential. They blame it all on Stalin, and for good reason. If ever a career was ruined by a superimposed esthetic and the tastes of a dictator, it has been that of Shostakovich.

By rights he should have been a creator in the line that extends from Glinka through Mussorgsky, Tchaikovsky, and Prokofiev. Russian music begins with Glinka (1804–1857), who showed Europe the first fruits of Russian musical nationalism. Glinka traveled in the West, studied its music, and then superimposed a Russian framework on it. He had many followers. The nineteenth century saw a powerful Slavophilism in all of the Russian creators. Musically, the century culminated in two composers. Tchaikovsky was and is the more popular, but it was Mussorgsky who had the greater influence. Tchaikovsky, with all of his Russian nationalism, tended to think in cosmopolitan terms. Mussorgsky was much more a Mother Russia type of composer; and he, with the other members of the famous Russian Five (Balakirev, Borodin, Cui, and Rimsky-Korsakov), consciously set out to express a specific Russian tradition in music.

That was typical of the times. There always has been a didactic element in the Russian creative mind. Marc Slonim, in his study of Russian litera-ture, makes the point that all factions of nineteenth-century Russian society, Populists and Marxists, liberals and conservatives, "took it for granted that literature should instruct and make readers conscious of social and political problems." Similarly, the nationalist group of composers tried to create a music that stemmed from the people. Many decades later this was to develop into official Communist policy.

The Russian nationalist composers held sway for much of the century, and not until the 1890's or thereabouts was there an esthetic shift. "As the decade of 1830–40 forged the national consciousness," Slonim writes, "and that of 1860–70 the social and political consciousness of educated society, the 'nineties attempted to mold its esthetic credo." The period from about 1890 to 1914 in Russian music saw the beginnings of close liaison with the West, resulting in an art strongly influenced by the then current European movements. Sparked by such publications as Serge Diaghilev's *World of Art* magazine, by such groups as the Moscow Art Theater and the Evenings of Contemporary Music, Russian creators displayed a fertilization by the West —but on Russian artistic terms. Symbolism, decadence, futurism, impres-sionism, primitivism—all were mingled. Those were the years when Stra-vinsky startled the world with his three great ballets for the Ballet Russe and when Prokofiev was just trying his wings.

Shostakovich, born in 1906, was a child of the revolution. He attended the Leningrad Conservatory and composed his remarkable First Symphony as a graduation piece. When it was first performed, in 1926, it immediately attracted international attention, and so did such following works as *The*

Nose (an opera based on a Gogol story), the "May Day" Symphony, the First Piano Concerto, and several ballets. In some of this music the influence of Prokofiev could be felt, but there also was a quality of wit and irony, a *joie de vivre,* an exultant athleticism and imagination, that marked it as something special. It was new, it was exciting.

And this was a period when the new, the exciting, the experimental were encouraged in Russia. The years immediately following the 1917 revolution saw complete freedom for any creator. By the late 1920's, however, the cult of Socialist Realism and music for the proletariat began to make itself felt. Lenin's statement "Art belongs to the people" suddenly was made to condition the entire Soviet esthetic. Stalin, whose intense dictatorship gathered in the arts as a vehicle for propaganda and socialist instruction, saw to it that the freedom of any creator was chopped down. He also saw to it that the pure ears of Communist musicians should not be contaminated. Any foreign music in any way advanced was banned—all of the twelve-tone music of Schoenberg and his school, all of Bartók and Hindemith, all of Stravinsky after *Petrouchka,* virtually all of the significant music that was shaping the destiny of the West. The curtain descended, leaving not a crack of light. Any music within the Soviet Union not based on conventional harmonies and/or folk material was condemned as "decadent," "imperialistic," or "formalistic."

A weird jargon of critical invective was developed. Thus Yuri Keldysh, in his *History of Russian Music,* published during the Stalin era, described Stravinsky's music as the "reactionary essence of modernism as an anti-folk end in art, reflecting the decadent ideology of the imperialist bourgeoisie." A trained Russian critic could rattle off this kind of nonsense with the ease of Joan Sutherland taking a high C. For decades this kind of double talk and doublethink was drummed into creators' heads as official doctrine. No wonder many of them worked in actual fear, never knowing when winds of policy might change, leaving them high and dry; never knowing when they would be accused of formalism.

Nobody could give an exact definition of formalism, but it was the dirtiest and most fearsome word in the lexicon. "Formalism," sneered Prokofiev, "is the name given to music not understood on first hearing," and it is as good a definition as any. Several times Prokofiev himself was attacked for formalism. It was in 1936 that Shostakovich first was exposed to the dread word, by none other than Stalin himself. The occasion was a Moscow performance of *Lady Macbeth of Mtzensk,* an opera based on a story of the nineteenth-century Russian writer Leskov, dealing with adultery, murder, and suicide. Stalin became furious at the grim subject matter and the lack of any kind of melody with which he could identify. In those days Shosta-kovich was one of the world's leading modernists, and he did not spare the dissonances. Stalin is said to have stormed from the theater in a fury after the first act. Immediately the opera was withdrawn and its composer attacked. Stalin then postulated three criteria for Soviet opera: subjects should have a socialist theme, the musical language should be realistic, and the plot should be "positive."

Shostakovich was able to rehabilitate himself with his Fifth Symphony, composed the following year. But he was running scared and was not going to take any chances. Many Western observers felt that after *Lady Macbeth of Mtzensk* Shostakovich was composing, in essence, nothing but safe music, falling back on workable formulas and on subject matter that extolled the Soviet system. But in 1948 he got into trouble again. He was strongly attacked, along with a group of the most important Soviet composers, Pro-kofiev, Aram Khachaturian, Vissarion Shebalin, and Vano Muradeli among them. It was a work by Muradeli that sparked the assault. On November 7, 1947, his opera *Great Friendship* received its première at the Bolshoi Theater and was immediately withdrawn after an official criticism called it historically and ideologically incorrect, with "inexpressive, poor, unhar-monious, muddled music." A few months later the Central Committee of the Communist party held a meeting at which specific charges were proffered against Soviet composers. The date was February 10, 1948, and the Polit-buro spokesman for cultural ideology, Andrei A. Zhdanov, was responsible for the substance of the attack. He also made the speech. Hence the pro-ceedings have come to be known as the Zhdanov Decree.

The most serious charge against the composers was that of formalism. And it was not only the composers who were in trouble. *The New York Times* reported that one important critic and his family were arrested and imprisoned. Each composer was forced to beat his breast and apologize. "How could it have happened that I failed to introduce a single folk song into the score of my opera?" Muradeli wailed. He told the Central Com-mittee that such a fact "can be explained only as a manifestation of my inherent snobbishness." Shostakovich said that the party was right. "I am deeply grateful to it and for all the criticism contained in the Resolution. . . . I shall try again and again to create symphonic works close to the spirit of the people from the standpoint of ideological subject matter, musi-cal language and form."

Whatever adventure any Soviet composer may have had was killed after 1948. A period of even greater sterility set in. Only Prokofiev had the genius to work within the limitations of Soviet doctrine, and even he had to compose music that was second-rate compared with his previous scores. As for Shostakovich, he simply surrendered. He turned out skillful, careful, and uncontroversial scores, most of them slick products with little of the power and individuality of his early music.

After Stalin died, voices were raised for a more liberal cultural policy, and the second All-Union Congress of Composers in 1957 actually spoke up for more freedom. Little was forthcoming. Premier Khrushchev turned out to be an artistic low-brow. He insisted on cows being painted as cows, and in music he liked tunes one could whistle. Thus he discouraged experimentation in the arts. "We are opposed to peaceful coexistence in matters of ideology," he stated, and the Russian estheticians promptly followed his line. Russian publications were full of articles about the necessity for a Soviet composer to write music that represented the Soviet traditions and the reservoir of folk material. These articles constituted official policy, to be disobeyed at a composer's peril.

It was not until the duumvirate of Kosygin and Brezhnev that Russian intellectuals began to achieve a limited amount of freedom. Kosygin and Brezhnev seemed determined to avoid low-brow esthetics and the cult of personality. Neither has made any significant pronouncement on the arts. No longer are Russian magazines full of exhortations and warnings about the necessity of pursuing the goals of Socialist Realism. All of a sudden, Russian creators had more freedom than they hitherto had thought possible. In the process certain writers and composers, or specific works of art, were rehabilitated. A party decree of May 28, 1958, exonerated Muradeli and other composers of charges of formalism. *Lady Macbeth of Mtzensk* is now considered a Russian classic. A film has even been made of the opera. It now has the title *Katerina Izmailova* and has been revised, but the revisions are minor and the score is heard pretty much as it existed in 1936. Muradeli's *Great Friendship* is no longer on the official black list, though it is not in the active repertory of any Russian opera house. Presumably, it could be staged if a producer was interested in the score.

Shostakovich's Symphony No. 13, nicknamed "Babi Yar," ran into trouble during the Khrushchev era but is now rehabilitated. It is a long work for soloists, chorus, and orchestra set to five poems by Yevgeny Yevtushenko. One of those poems, "Babi Yar," is about the massacre of Jews in Kiev during World War II. It was this subject matter that caused the trouble. Khrushchev objected to the poem about the Jews. He said that there was no anti-Semitism in the Soviet Union. But he added that it was better for Jews not to hold high posts in government, saying that in his opinion the unrest in Poland and Hungary in 1956 had been caused by the large number of Jews in high places. Khrushchev told Ilya Ehrenburg, the

Jewish journalist, that his remarks were not anti-Semitic. "You must understand that as a professional politician I have to take things as I find them and warn against dangers."

Shostakovich and Yevtushenko went ahead with the preparations for the world première of "Babi Yar," which took place on December 18, 1962. It was not the gala occasion that a large-scale Shostakovich work normally would have evoked. The government box was empty. Yevtushenko had to plead with the chorus to appear at the concert. Shostakovich was apprehensive. "When Shostakovich and Yevtushenko rose to take their bows at the end," wrote Priscilla Johnson in *Khrushchev and the Arts,* "the thunderous applause that greeted them was homage not only to the music but to a signal act of political courage." But after a second performance on December 20 all future performances were cancelled. On February 10, 1963, the symphony was again presented, in revised form. Some say that it was Shostakovich who first yielded to demands that the controversial sections of the symphony be rewritten, and that Yevtushenko then agreed.

Musicians in Russia say that the revisions were minor. Today the score is in favor. As yet it has not been performed in the United States. Big, ambitious, very much in Shostakovich's national style, the "Babi Yar" Symphony is nevertheless not a complete success. Some of it comes uncomfortably close to poster music, some is pure Shostakovich formula, and all of it is old-style Socialist Realism. My guess is that it will not emerge as one of Shostakovich's important scores.

In any case, Shostakovich and Prokofiev were the strongest influence on twentieth-century Russian music—at least until the last few years. From about 1930 to 1960 Russian composers, without exception, were busy writing music that was little more than direct imitation of Shostakovich and Prokofiev. It was bad derivative music, and not a single composer of stature emerged. Not one. Russian instrumentalists may have conquered the world, but Russian composers had absolutely nothing to offer the international community. Only recently have there been indications that Russian music is beginning to make an effort to catch up with Western music.

The catching-up process began in embryo shortly after the war, though not until the post-Khrushchev era did things begin to move with any speed. When the full history of contemporary Russian music is written, one of the major events of the period following World War II will be the impact of the cultural interchange after the death of Stalin in 1953. Before that, Russia was a closed, suspicious, provincial society. But shortly after 1955 Russia began to send its cultural figures all over the world. Word-of-mouth reports about the West penetrated the big Soviet cities. In a country like the Soviet Union, where the press is under rigid control, word-of-mouth reporting has developed into a high art. It used to be said that when a Russian ballet company or symphony orchestra returned to Moscow after an American tour, the next day the entire city knew the quality of lingerie the girls had purchased or the number of drip-dry shirts the musicians had picked up.

Despite official doctrine, the Russian intellectuals developed a great admiration for America and things American. In 1959 one Russian musician, a dedicated Communist, visited New York for the first time, walked along Fifth Avenue, and returned to the hotel in a thoughtful mood. "We in Russia," the musician said to an acquaintance, "have been told all about American capitalism and the exploitation of the workers. Now I have seen with my own eyes, and let me tell you that we in Russia could stand a bit of this decadent American capitalism."

One concrete result of the interchange was a strengthening of Russian musical standards and a reconsideration of performance practice. The Russians had been inclined to be smug, confident that their musical training was unsurpassed. But when the Boston Symphony Orchestra visited Russia in 1959—it was the first American orchestra to appear there—the Russians heard a quality of playing previously unknown to them. They still shake their heads about it. "It was a blow to our pride," a Russian musician told me. "The difference between Boston and our orchestras was so great it was insulting. We had meetings and decided to do something about it—about the caliber of playing, about the caliber of the instruments themselves." Since then the standard of the major Russian orchestras has been lifted.

Just as orchestras were provincial, musicians, even such great ones as Emil Gilels and David Oistrakh, came out of Russia with somewhat provincial ideas. Violinists, for instance, would play Mozart much as Leopold Auer had taught in the 1890's, complete with slides and a romantic vibrato. That no longer happens. (The process worked two ways. Western musicians, listening to the handsome and unneurotic way the Russians played romantic music, began to modify some of *their* ideas.)

Another facet in the increase of musical sophistication has been the cessation of radio jamming by the Soviet authorities. Until a few years ago Russians could listen only to local broadcasts; all others were jammed. Thus the musicians had only a sketchy idea of the new music in the West, although a fortunate few did have a handful of recordings. Since jamming ceased, a short-wave radio set and a tape recorder are primary tools of all Russian composers. They listen to broadcasts from the West and tape the music they find interesting. The result is that the average Russian musician is now quite well informed about what is happening on the international musical scene. It may be secondhand information, but it is generally accurate. In any case, enough Western musicians have come to Russia to give the information-hungry musicians plenty of data.

Today the Russian musicians are in the process of absorbing the immediate past and catching up with the present. The majority, instead of writing music that echoes Prokofiev and Shostakovich, are writing music that echoes Bartók, Hindemith, or the Stravinsky of *Le Sacre du Printemps*. A few are even attracted by the music of Webern, Boulez, and Stockhausen. All of these major twentieth-century figures were condemned only a short time back, but all of a sudden composers like Stravinsky and Bartók are major influences on current Soviet music. Bartók has turned out to be the most important, except to the avant-garde, and one guesses as a possible reason—aside from the composer's musical power—his constant use of folk elements. Any edition of a Bartók score or any recording of a Bartók work is soon sold out. The one work that seems to have made the most profound impression on the younger Soviet composers is Bartók's Music for Strings, Percussion and Celesta. Virtually every second Soviet score I came across has echoes of that powerful work. It is part of the new Soviet musical subconscious.

The influence of Bartók and other modernists is not noticeable in the music of the composers of the older generation. Composers like Shostakovich, Kabalevsky, Khachaturian, Khrennikov, and the other veterans of the 1930's are not going to change. These composers are traditionalists, their style has long been solidified, and their roots are in Socialist Realism. Shostakovich, revered as he is, exerts little influence on the course of the new Russian music. As for the others, the younger composers look on them as quaint antiques.

This cleavage between younger and older composers has been happening since Orpheus played his lyre. In the United States, for example, the music of Piston, Harris, and Schuman, important figures of the 1930's, means nothing at all to today's younger composers, who follow different gods. But Russian composers are apt to be a little touchy about hints that they are discarding the tradition of their elders. I had a round-table discussion with several Soviet musicians on this subject. One of them got the idea I was trying to use them as a whip to lash the Kabalevsky-Khrennikov school of composition. "It is natural for young musicians to be impatient with their elders," he said quietly and pleasantly, but with a glint in his eye. "For instance, what does the young school of critics and musicians in America think of *you*?" And he indeed did have a point.

By far the largest amount of present-day Russian music comes from a middle group that is trying to make a synthesis of old and new techniques. They are not avant-gardists. They are reluctant to give up their tradition of using folk material. At the same time they would not think of using folk material in the old-fashioned, posterlike, primary-colored way of an Aram Khachaturian. All of them write tonal music, generally with a good deal of the kind of dissonance that puts one back in the 1930's. Some of them even flirt with aleatory or serial technique. Their attitude is that all music should be expressive, even twelve-tone music, and that there is no good reason why any technique cannot be combined with nationalism or a tonal way of writing. In short, these composers are cautiously feeling their way into the international idiom of the West.

In this they now have official sanction. The official line is expressed by Tikhon Khrennikov, head of the Union of Composers. "Anybody in the Soviet Union is free to compose any kind of music he wants to compose," Khrennikov grandly says. "The Union of Composers will make no obstacles." But to this permissive statement he adds a barb. "While a revolutionary may compose anything, that does not mean he is necessarily entitled to the benefits of the Union of Composers."

The Union of Composers controls publishing, performance, and salary, and any composer not in favor is not going to go very far. As the center of Soviet musical life, the Union of Composers comes in for a good deal of quiet criticism, though it would be worth a composer's career to make his criticism public. It is felt by many young composers (and not necessarily the avant-gardists) that the Union of Composers is too powerful; that it is interested in preserving a comfortable *status quo,* rewarding the obedient boys with plenty of performances and good housing, letting the more rebellious ones live in miserable flats and ignoring their music completely.

Khrennikov and his group may be the Establishment today, but the stronger representatives of the new middle group are in the process of pushing hard and will be the Establishment tomorrow. Most talked about of this group is Rodion Shchedrin, sometimes described as the "official modernist" of the Soviet Union. He is a skillful musician who already is beginning to get performances in the West, including a commission from the New York Philharmonic. Typical of his recent work is his Piano Concerto No. 2, a score with strong Bartókian dissonances, a touch of Hindemithian baroque, a leaping melodic line, a pointed avoidance of nationalism, and, here and there, some avant-garde devices. One movement has a section of aleatory, carefully arranged and very mild, apparently inserted just to let the world know that the composer knows what is going on. The effect is not very convincing, but it is there, and it would not have been there a few years back. Shchedrin would appear to be an eclectic.

Many of the official modernists use folk materials in a new and rather daring way. Kara Karayev, from Baku, delights in exotic instruments and

neo-Stravinsky rhythms. Arno Babadzhanian, an Armenian, writes successful popular songs and then turns around to compose cryptic-sounding piano
pieces in a neo-Scriabin idiom. Then he comes up with an old-fashioned,
traditional cello concerto. Another eclectic, Nodar Gabunia, from Georgia,
has a real shocker in such a piece as his "Fables." Using authentic native
instruments and a pared-down, Bartókian kind of folk purity to a point at
which the music sounds almost like African chant, Gabunia has composed
a really impressive score. It is nationalistic, but with an inner strength, resource, and excitement far removed from the pretty-pretty nationalistic
vapidities of the previous generation.

Quite a few of the Russian composers are using elements of jazz, and
thereby hangs a tale. Jazz in the Soviet Union has only recently again been
sanctioned. A few years back there was, officially, no such thing as jazz, and
this despite the fact that every restaurant in Moscow had a combo and
what passed for a blues singer ("St. Lou-ees vooman, wid her diemoond
rings . . ."). And also despite the fact that the bootlegging of old X-ray
plates bearing recordings of the latest jazz seemed for a while to be one of
the Soviet Union's more thriving industries, more thriving even than the
stealing of windshield wipers from automobiles.

In 1926 two small American jazz bands appeared in the Soviet Union.
Sidney Bechet and Tommy Ladnier were among the players. For a time,
a Soviet brand of jazz developed, led by Alexander Tsfasman, Isaak Du-
nayevsky, and Leonid Utyosov. Then the Stalin era set solid, and jazz was
represented as an example of everything evil in decadent capitalism. Utyosov
had to change the name of his group from "The All-Union State Jazz
Orchestra" to the "All-Union State Variety Orchestra." Not until 1962 did
an American group again appear in Russia. That year Benny Goodman
brought a band over. In 1966 the Earl Hines Orchestra toured. But for
years American jazz could have been found in any Russian record collection. More recently, tapes have been copied from Voice of America broadcasts. European youth, and the Russians are no exception, has always been
wild about jazz.

The performance of real jazz, as contrasted with pop and dance music,
started in Russia around 1955. In addition to large orchestras, one still led
by Utyosov, small jazz combos began to spring up, and officials turned
their heads away, pretending the groups did not exist. The new wave of
Soviet jazz was at first influenced by Dixieland, and one of the original
Soviet Dixieland combos, the Vladimir Grachev Sextet, is still alive. Dizzy
Gillespie and Charley Parker then became strong influences. From that
emerged a group of Soviet jazz modernists, developing along their own lines.

Many Russian jazzmen try to combine American jazz with Slavic folk elements. The new wave takes itself very seriously as a concert form. Russia has a large group of dedicated jazz musicians who look on jazz as a new art form and have thoroughly studied the history of jazz and its performance. Some are conservatory-trained and experiment with music of such Renaissance composers as Josquin des Prés, trying to translate it into contemporary jazz. Some are outright modernists, such as the Gevorgian brothers (Eugene on piano, Andrei on bass), who compose and play only their own music and use everything from twelve-tone techniques to Indian raga. Many jazz musicians are entirely self-taught. There are jazz festivals in Tallinn and elsewhere, and even a children's jazz festival. In every large city there are one or more (Moscow has five) youth clubs where jazz can be heard and where there are weekly jazz sessions.

These jazzmen do not normally play hotel dates. That is reserved for the dance bands. There is one or more in every large hotel, and the young people of Moscow have picked up all the latest dances. One of the great experiences of Moscow is to stand outside the café of the Hotel National, which fronts on Manezhnaya Square and gives a view of Red Square, and watch elderly folk looking at the dancing within. The kids can be seen through the plate glass, writhing in ecstasy, some of the girls wearing miniskirts, some of the young men in beards. The elderly people outside press their noses against the glass and then look at each other in perplexity, with woeful shakes of the head. "What is the world coming to?" They watch with disturbed fascination, completely ignored by the youngsters.

As a matter of fact, many of the youngsters have adopted Western habits. Girls wear slacks and let their hair grow long. Boys grow beards, put on dungarees, sling their guitars on their back, and stroll through Red Square or Gorky Street in the best established beatnik tradition. Some of the old-timers do not like it. "Five years ago," growled one, watching such a noisy group, which had had perhaps a bit too much vodka, "we would have grabbed those boys and cut their hair in public."

Russia has its pop music. As in the West, it is a commercial enterprise, and the artistic results in Russia are just as bad as anywhere else. Hit songs come and go, with a built-in life of a few months before everybody gets tired of the insipidities. And, as in the West, consistently successful entrepreneurs of hit material are rewarded by success and all that goes with it—money, cars, country houses, big city apartments.

Virtually all Russian musicians, from pop to classic, are conservatory-trained. The various conservatories and music schools play a prominent part in Soviet musical life. The Soviet Union has over 2,000 children's music schools, 187 specialized music schools, 22 Central Music Schools for gifted children, and 23 conservatories. Musical education in the Soviet

Union is much better organized than in the United States. It is not that there is more of it. As a matter of fact, there probably is not. American conservatories of music are spread through the country, and in addition every American college and university offers comprehensive courses in music for those interested. Many universities have music departments on the level of a conservatory. In the Soviet Union musical education is confined to special schools only. Those schools, however, take any gifted student through basic training to the upper echelons of a conservatory. They offer, free of charge, comprehensive training, with the student a ward of the state. Russian musical educators describe the system as a pyramid, with the children's music schools at the base and the conservatories at the top.

The two conservatories with the greatest reputation are the one in Leningrad, founded in 1862 by Anton Rubinstein (it was then, of course, the St. Petersburg Conservatory), and the Moscow Conservatory, founded in 1864 by Anton's brother, Nicholas. Considerable rivalry exists between the two.

Originally, the conservatories received some funds from the imperial treasury, but never enough. Students before the revolution had to pay higher fees than equivalent university students. But Russia always has had a great respect for talent, and gifted but penniless children always managed to find rich sponsors. If a child was brilliant enough, even his religion did not matter. The Rubinsteins were Jews, and in the early years of the century there came from the ghettos a great procession of Jewish violinists, headed by Mischa Elman and Jascha Heifetz.

Each of the conservatories has its profile. The big figures at the Moscow Conservatory were Tchaikovsky (who had graduated from St. Petersburg but went on to teach at the Moscow Conservatory), Sergei Taneyev, and Rachmaninoff. They represented a more European point of view than St. Petersburg, which was run for many years by Rimsky-Korsakov, an outstanding representative of the nationalistic tradition, and Alexander Glazunov, the conservatory's director until 1928. Prokofiev and Shostakovich are among eminent St. Petersburg/Leningrad graduates.

Both Moscow and Leningrad are outstanding conservatories and both draw upon the best students in the Soviet Union. Most of the students come by way of the Central Music School system, where gifted children are scouted much as American colleges scout high schools for likely football prospects. Musically gifted children in the Soviet Union have nothing else to do but develop. Their needs have been taken care of, they have had the benefit of some of the best and most intense preparation offered anywhere in the world, and they can spend their lives practicing. The glowing result can be seen in such phenomenal instrumentalists as Oistrakh, Gilels,

Harold C. Schonberg

Richter, Rostropovich, and Kogan and in so brilliant an orchestra as the Leningrad Philharmonic.

It is only in singing that Russia is weak. Russia has never been a major contributor to the international operatic stage, despite a handful of great vocalists, headed by Feodor Chaliapin. One expert explains the situation by saying that singing in Russia before World War I was taught largely by Italians. They fled the country when war was declared, leaving Russia without trained vocal teachers. And it is a fact that such fine turn-of-the-century Russian singers as the tenor Leonid Sobinov display on their recordings a decidedly Italianate type of production.

Whatever did happen, it played havoc with the new generation of singers. Russian tenors and sopranos today, for the most part, demonstrate inferior schooling. They sing in a squeezed, unsupported manner, with a persistent tremolo, and they appear frightened to death when engaging high notes. It is a problem about which the conservatories are greatly concerned. "Why should we engage one of our old bad singers to teach young singers their bad vocal habits?" one conservatory official said to me. Recently, the Soviet government has been sending some of its best young singers to Italy for training.

Otherwise, Russian musical training, from elementary school to conservatory, is excellent in its traditional, conservative way. It represents a continuity of tradition extending back to the romantic period, and Russian musicians do have more of an affinity for romantic music than musicians trained elsewhere.

Visitors to Soviet conservatories and music schools are constantly being asked how Russian training compares with American. The question is not hard to answer. Standards are high in both countries. Russian training is, on the whole, more intense but narrower. American training is more eclectic, with an intermix of French, German, and Russian elements. Russian players tend to "get into" their instruments more than Americans do. Their approach is emotional, and they like to highlight the drama or poetry of a piece of music. Americans tend to be more literal, more objective and, to many Russians, colder. Russians are always talking about American efficiency, but distrust it in music when it begins to override what they consider to be the legitimate emotional end of interpretation.

Americans have the great advantage of being exposed to all manifestations of international culture, and are much more familiar than are the Russians with the latest trends in composition and musicology. In recent years, however, the Russians have been catching up. The cultural interchange has seen a kind of fertilization in which Russian and American performing artists have been taking the best from each other. In the process they have become close in many ways, even to the point where they give concerts together, as the pianists Malcolm Frager and Vladimir Ashkenazy have been doing.

So far, it is interesting to note, no Russian conductor has made the kind of international impact that the great Russian instrumentalists have made. When such Russian conductors as Kirill Kondrashin, Yevgeny Mravinsky, and Gennady Rozhdestvensky appear in the West, they are respectfully received and reviewed, but the general feeling is that they lack imagination and color. Often this is an unjust estimate. The West is used to flamboyant virtuoso conductors with mountain-sized egos and choreographic movements on the podium. Russian conductors are not taught that way. They conduct from the wrist and arm, with few body motions and with an air of sobriety. In the overheated musical world of the West, audiences tend to take such sobriety as an indication of inhibition or pedanticism. As a matter of fact, Russian musicians have as much spirit as the next man. The West has not been exposed to the best Russian conductors for any length of time, and judgment must therefore be deferred. But in technique, preparation, background, and knowledge, it is clear that the best Russian conductors are strong and accomplished, and it would be interesting to see several of them in charge of a Western orchestra for a season or two.

With musicians of such high quality coming out of Moscow and Leningrad, the admirable performance standards in those two cities should come as no surprise. Both cities have fine symphony orchestras (Moscow has five), ballet companies of international fame, and the cream of native and foreign soloists. The two opera companies—the Kirov in Leningrad and the Bolshoi in Moscow—are equally famous. Both go in for large-scale opera with stupendous stage effects. In Yuri Shaporin's *The Decembrists,* regiments— no, armies—of soldiers fight on the stage, and die so realistically that live ammunition must surely be used. In Rimsky-Korsakov's *Sadko* a fully manned ship is tossed on a stormy sea. In the same composer's *Legend of the Invisible City of Kitezh,* the Tatars raid a village, kill everybody in sight, and put the village to the torch. The entire stage seems enveloped in smoke and flames. All of this may be naïve, but it is effective. The Russian stage technicians need bow to nobody. Audiences wait impatiently for these spectacular effects and go ooh and aah when they happen. Top ticket price at the Bolshoi or Kirov opera houses is about $3.50.

The operatic repertory, which is much the same all over the Soviet Union, consists of standard Italian operas, with a concentration on Verdi and Puccini; a few French operas; hardly any German opera, and, of course, Russian opera from Glinka to Prokofiev. To a foreigner *Madame Butterfly* (called *Cio-Cio-San* in Russia) takes some getting used to in Russian (all operas are sung in Russian). But once *Boris Godunov* and *Prince Igor* are heard in the original language, any other version sounds pallid.

Moscow, during the music season, is extraordinarily active, easily as much as any major capital in the world. Opera, ballet, concerts, operetta, and musical comedy flourish in at least a dozen large theaters, and most performances are sold out. Moscow these days is full of traffic jams, and the jam is compounded when the Bolshoi Opera, which in addition to its own theater also uses the Kremlin's Palace of Congresses, is presenting a favorite work. The traffic backup is unbelievable. And what is going to happen when a new Fiat plant produces its promised 600,000 automobiles a year for internal consumption? The imagination stops dead. One thing is certain: the face of Russia will be changed.

Outside of Moscow and Leningrad, things take a sharp drop. Performances in other cities, such as Kiev or Odessa, are provincial, with much lower standards and a style of stage presentation that has long since departed from the West. Seeing an opera like *Faust* in Kiev may be a delightful experience, but not for reasons that would please the management. It is delightful because everything is so old-fashioned and run-down. A Mephistopheles who wears a black doublet and a cap with feathers, and who slinks through the opera with a red light permanently focused on him, has not been seen since the days of Pol Plançon, the French basso, who was regarded as unrivaled in that role in the late nineteenth century.

Few Russian musicians, except for the international celebrities, are handsomely paid. The top artists live in luxury. But the majority live under conditions that most of their opposite numbers in the West would regard as deprivation—one- or two-room apartments, no automobile, broken-down pianos, few of the amenities that any working musician in the West takes for granted. An active orchestra musician in the Soviet Union might make $150 a month. Of course, as has been pointed out many times, it is not easy to equate Russian with American salaries. Russians pay very little for housing and nothing at all for medicine and education. On the other hand, they pay a great deal for clothing, cars, luxury items. Housing is a sore point with many Russian intellectuals, and they are extremely sensitive about it. By now they have a good idea of how Westerners live, and one reason many still hesitate to invite foreigners into their homes is because they are ashamed of their living conditions.

While Russian musical training at its best is universally admired, there is less to praise in other facets of the Russian musical establishment. The system has always been plagued by problems of distribution. Looking for sheet music or phonograph records in the Soviet Union can be a frustrating experience. Music is inexpensive—if you can find what you are looking for.

The full score of Glinka's *Ivan Susanin,* in three volumes and on fairly good paper, runs to 1,048 pages and sells for about $20 at the official rate of exchange. In this country the price would be closer to $70. The trouble is that whatever I happened to be looking for was not available or was out of print. I was not interested in Beethoven sonatas or Tchaikovsky symphonies. Those can be purchased anywhere in the world. I was, instead, looking for music not available anywhere else—a complete edition of the Scriabin piano music, for instance, or Shostakovich's *The Nose.* No music store in Moscow or Leningrad had them.

Those looking for records encounter the same difficulties. Russia produces 180,000,000 records a year, about half of them classical. The catalogue of soloists is rather full. Tchaikovsky's popular B-flat-minor piano concerto has been recorded in Russia by Gilels, Ogdon, Cliburn, Richter, Sokolov, Ashkenazy, and Serebryakov. But try to find them. A spot check in three Moscow record stores turned up only the Gilels and the Richter. In all fairness, it should be mentioned that few American record stores carry complete stocks, especially of older recordings. But an American determined to get a specific record can, by hook, crook, or writing directly to the record company, manage to get his hands on a copy. In Russia that is next to impossible.

Because of a 1966 arrangement between Capitol Records and the Russian recording industry, the Russians are now beginning to pay close attention to their product. Under the provisions of a three-year contract, Capitol has the rights of first refusal to any record made in the Soviet Union. Capitol also is required to select a minimum number of records and guarantee sales to a certain point. Naturally, the Russian technicians want to produce a product that is equal to any in the world. Most Russian records until recently have been technically inferior. Now the Russian technicians are recording in four-channel stereo on high-speed tapes, using the best foreign equipment. But few Russians will be able to enjoy these sparkling new recordings. Russian-made playback equipment is, to put it mildly, wretched. There is no such thing as buying component parts, as so many American collectors do. Russians have to use what the industry brings out. That means low-powered amplifiers, shoddily built speakers with built-in distortion, and cartridges guaranteed to plow through the grooves of a record after two dozen plays. The Russian technicians admit this and merely say that they hope in a few years to get better equipment on the market.

The future? The Russian musical scene a generation from now? The next ten years should show a consolidation in Russian composition, with avant-garde textures and techniques entering the musical language as they have entered the musical language of the West. The chances are that where there now are only a dozen avant-gardists, the next decade will see hundreds. But the chances also are that the avant-garde movement will establish even less of a following among Soviet audiences than it has in the West. One can look forward to a kind of music in which the nationalism that has persisted since Glinka will be colored by a kind of modernism that uses everything from Stravinsky to serial technique, with infusions of jazz. At the moment a new musical language is being forged, just as it was forged by Glinka and his followers. The parallel is close. Russia in the first decades of the nineteenth century was just coming out of a long period of isolation, just as Russia today is coming out of a long period of isolation. Most Russian composers, avant-gardists and conservatives alike, now feel that their future depends on the freedom to write the way they want to write. "If they try to stop us," one composer told me, "we'll go underground." And a veteran observer states that in his opinion a major shift in policy would be unthinkable.

"The young creators," he says, "now know what is going on in the world, and they want to be part of it."

FIFTY YEARS OF SOVIET BALLET

»

Clive Barnes

Galina Ulanova, sitting on a sofa in a room at the top of the Bolshoi Theater, did not look at all like a legend. Very youthful, exquisitely dressed, she looked serious yet hardly forbidding, even though the warmth of her smile was tinged with a certain gravity. "Today, I think"—and she measured the words carefully to the translator—"today, Soviet ballet has never been more interesting. It is changing and developing, and while the old traditions are being kept, new traditions are being formed. The young dancer is very lucky, very privileged. It is an interesting time in Soviet ballet."

The Bolshoi Theater is both a fortress and a cathedral—it is difficult to penetrate and the rituals within its walls demand total dedication from their celebrants. It is a world within a world and yet not apart from the world. Leave the Bolshoi by the stage door, go out into the street, look at the people and look at the shops, listen to the town and watch its face. There is an eagerness to it. There is an eagerness, too, in Soviet ballet, a feeling that things are changing.

In the solemn pages of *Pravda* and the hardly less solemn pages of the literary weekly *Literaturnaya Gazeta,* controversy raged this summer over the future of ballet, and to the outsider it would seem that some great and bloody battle was in progress between Old Faith and New Faith with terrible blows being dealt on both sides. Not a bit of it. The battle has been effectively over for some time. The leader of the progressive movement, forty-year-old Yuri Grigorovich, is installed as director of the Bolshoi Ballet. The impressive tirades appearing in the press are nothing more than the exercise of the old Russian tradition of artistic polemics, perhaps with a feeling on both sides that the Old Guard and the New Guard (the latter being, as befits victors, far less talkative) should put down their attitudes for posterity—and in case anyone makes a mistake in the immediate future.

What, then, was the battle about? There is a wonderful Mussorgsky opera, *Khovanshchina*. It is about the struggle of Peter the Great (or Peter I, as you soon learn to call him in Russia) with the boyars and, crucial to this struggle, the religious controversy between adherents of the Old Faith and the New Faith. With an imperfect command of the history of Russian theology, it is slightly difficult to know the precise ideological differences between the two. I was once told that the basic disagreement was on the number of fingers that should be employed in making the sign of the cross, and I found this explanation so satisfying in its irony that I resolved never to look further. However, I suspect that the religious aspects of that war had more to do with the relationship of church and state than with any number of fingers. The answer would presumably lie in history, and, in the same way, to understand Soviet ballet today and its present dissensions it is necessary to look at the past.

The Russians are a political people. The exercise of politics is of interest to them, rather like it is to the English, almost as an end in itself. They enjoy argument, they seem to love dialectic. Now, Russians apart, dancers the world over are born politicians. Perhaps it is because they are never allowed to speak on stage that off stage they spend quite an amount of time in what might be called "artistic organizational discussion," although the dancers call it "gossip" and it might be best thought of as "ballet politics." There are no ballet politics like Russian ballet politics. This, even to a greater extent than in most countries, appears to complicate the whole history of Russian ballet, not least the history of the past fifty years.

There is, of course, a continuity to that history. Soviet ballet is Russian ballet. The first professional Russian ballet took place in 1742 during the coronation festivities of Elizabeth, daughter of Peter the Great. The first important Russian ballet school was founded in Moscow in 1773. It was the beginning of the Bolshoi Ballet School. All the pupils were orphans, and an Italian dancing master, Filippo Beccari, started with sixty-two children. It was a three-year course, and twenty-four of the aspirants became

Ukrainian Republic Kindergarten No. 142 in the city of Zaporozhye (*Novosti*)

A singing class   (*Charlotte Curtis, The New York Times*)

Boys working out on a trampolin and in a science class at Moscow's
Pioneer Palace   *(Novosti)*

A second-grade German class in Moscow   *(Novosti)*

A graduate student in the phonetics lab of the Moscow Institute of Oriental
Languages   (*Novosti*)

offee break on the Leningrad University
mpus   (*Novosti*)

Soviet teen-agers enjoying one of the latest
dances   (*Magnum*)

Cyclists start off in front of Moscow State University for the annual long-distance race between Moscow and Smolensk. *(Camera Press-Pix)*

Learning the fine points of soccer at a Pioneer camp outside Kiev *(Robert Lipsyte, The New York Times)*

Lidiya Skoblikova, speed skater, in 1964. She is the first athlete ever to win four gold medals in the winter Olympic Games. *(A.P.)*

Galina Baksheyeva, a leading tennis player, at a Davis Cup match with Chile in Moscow's Luzhniki sports complex *(Robert Lipsyte, The New York Times)*

Girls off on a camping trip to one of the Volga islands *(H. Erich Heine-mann, The New York Times)*

Babushkas, or Russian grandmothers, who typically wear head scarf, non-descript clothes, and flat-heeled slippers *(Harrison E. Salisbury, The New York Times)*

Yelena Ryabinkina, who is with the Bolshoi Ballet, and her younger sister, Ksana. They are what most women would like to be—beautiful, young, fashionable, and successful. *(Charlotte Curtis, The New York Times)*

A family on a collective farm near Pavlovsk, in Siberia, cheerily celebrating a church festival holiday, in 1954 *(Harrison E. Salisbury, The New York Times)*

A *babushka* and her daughter cleaning up after dinner in their Moscow apartment   *(Marc Riboud, Magnum)*

A young girl assembling electric equipment on the Zaporozhets car, produced at an auto factory in Zaporozhye, Ukraine   *(Pictorial Parade)*

A waitress in a Tbilisi restaurant   (*Charlotte Curtis, The New York Times*)

Tatyana Fyodorova, now an official of the Moscow Metro, the subway system, who helped build the subway with her own hands in the 1930's   (*Charlotte Curtis, The New York Times*)

A woman tending a textile machine in a factory in Tashkent   (*Charlotte Curtis, The New York Times*)

Radiant bride being congratulated after her marriage at the Palace of Weddings in Moscow   *(Charlotte Curtis, The New York Times)*

Vyacheslav Zaitsev, the Soviet Union's foremost fashion designer   *(Charlotte Curtis, The New York Times)*

A cream-and-black wool suit designed by the Moscow House of Fashion, for which Zaitsev works   *(Charlotte Curtis, The New York Times)*

Alexius, Patriarch of All Russia, at vespers service on Twelfth Night in the Moscow Epiphany Cathedral   *(Tass)*

Members of Baptist congregation in Leningrad's Kalinin district during a weekday service   *(Elliott Erwitt, Magnum)*

The Torah being presented in the only synagogue in Odessa   *(Elliott Erwitt, Magnum)*

A procession around the Moscow Yelokhov Cathedral at Eastertime   *(Novosti)*

Fresco at ancient Trinity Monastery at Zagorsk, the seat of the Orthodox patriarch in Russia   *(Harrison E. Salisbury, The New York Times)*

Eighteenth-century Preobrazhenskaya (Transfiguration) Church in Kizhi, built without a single nail, one of the finest examples extant of early Russian church architecture *(Novosti)*

A pleasure boat on the Moskva River, with the Kremlin in the background
(*British European Airways*)

In Moscow, a growing modern city, new buildings like the headquarters of
East Europe's Council of Mutual Economic Assistance (Comecon) present
a vivid contrast with older ornate buildings like the Hotel Ukraina.   (*U.P.I.*)

Traditional Siberian home, decorated with elaborate wood filigree *(Walter Sullivan, The New York Times)*

A mass-produced, prefabricated, prestressed, reinforced-concrete room unit being lowered into place *(Novosti)*

A prefabricated building going up in Pitsunda, a new resort on the Black Sea *(Garth Huxtable, The New York Times)*

A model of a rest-house hotel for the Crimea, a design on a par with what is now being done in the West   *(Novosti)*

Ada Louise Huxtable, architecture critic of *The New York Times,* and Peter Grose, chief of the *Times* bureau in Moscow from 1965 to June, 1967, on Moscow's Kalinin Prospekt   *(The New York Times)*

Charlotte Curtis, women's news editor of *The New York Times,* near Red Square with the Kremlin and St. Basil's Cathedral in the background   *(The New York Times)*

soloists, which was just as well for Signor Beccari, because he received, at the end of the course, two hundred and fifty rubles each for the soloists, but only one hundred and fifty for the rest.

By 1917 Russian ballet was the most important in the world. Indeed, Russia was the only country (apart from Denmark, then regarded balletically as a provincial backwater) in which ballet had not fallen into decadence. Russia's dominance began around the 1880's, although at that time most of its ballet masters and even its star dancers were either French or Italian, and Christian Johansson, the founder of the true Russian style, was a Danish-trained Swede. Yet very soon Russian dancers became pre-eminent. The Russians have always had a feel for dance—they dance like the Italians sing and the birds fly. At the turn of the century the two principal Russian companies, the Maryinsky in St. Petersburg and the far less significant Bolshoi in Moscow, were unquestionably the only companies, apart from the then unknown Danish Ballet, treating ballet as a fine art.

Yet it was fine art attached to the court. It was fine art where certain of the young ladies who had influential friends were permitted to display their jewels, or trophies, on stage. It was fine art where the motives of its appreciators varied enormously. The famous balletomanes of St. Petersburg, sitting in the front row of the Maryinsky with their enormous opera glasses trained upon the *corps de ballet,* were indisputably connoisseurs, but, looking back, one wonders, connoisseurs of what?

Into this scene, with its pretty chandeliers and colorful uniforms, came revolution. It came with Michel Fokine, Aleksandr Benois, and other now lesser-known dancers, choreographers, and designers. Fokine and Benois believed that dance was more expressive than was then accepted. They believed in a new dance, and, unable to give their ideas wide acceptance in Russia, in association with an impresario of genius, Serge Diaghilev, they made their greatest impact in Western Europe. In 1909 the Diaghilev Ballet Russe stormed Paris, and two years later London fell. But it is important to remember that these Diaghilev dancers were all Russians and that the theories of Fokine were those current in St. Petersburg at that time, even though Fokine was admittedly their principal proponent.

Everyone seems to be agreed that during all the fantastic events of 1917 in St. Petersburg, by then renamed Petrograd, the Maryinsky Ballet acted almost as if nothing was happening. Lenin might be addressing the crowds at the Finland Station, but Tamara Karsavina was dancing at the Maryinsky. The very night the Bolsheviks seized power, the Maryinsky Ballet danced, although only about a fifth of the cast appeared and the theater itself was far from full. After the performance Karsavina went to a supper party at Edward Cunard's. She wrote: "At supper we could hardly hear ourselves speak—field-guns, machine-guns, rifle-fire were deafening." And so the ballet greeted the revolution.

The position of the ballet immediately after the revolution was not altogether easy. After all, it had been intimately associated with the Czar. They were the imperial dancers, and in the first revolutionary fervor there were certainly those who regarded the ballet as a czarist plaything as expendable as Fabergé jewelry. Luckily for the Soviet Union and the world, other counsels prevailed. Lenin himself insisted on the protection of the arts, which were henceforward to be for the proletariat. The theaters were organized under various committees and, because of what seems to have been the enlightened guidance of the first Commissar for Education, Anatoly Lunacharsky, they continued with scarcely a break in continuity.

For the ballet, the situation was an interesting one. Many of Russia's finest artists were out of the country at the time, appearing with the Diaghilev Ballet. A few returned to Russia; others who wanted to return were prevented by wartime conditions. Few could guess what was going to happen to ballet in Russia, and while some were hopeful that a new artistic dawn was breaking, others were nervous at the thought that such frivolous things as the performing arts would suffer in the stringent times ahead.

During the first few years of the revolution most of the dancers stayed, but quite a few either left for the West or remained in the West. The losses to Russian ballet were grievous. Michel Fokine, the leader of choreographic revolution, went. So did the most famous dancers: Anna Pavlova, Tamara Karsavina, Vaslav Nijinsky (although, in fact, his career was already ended by madness), Adolf Bolm, Pierre Vladimiroff, Vera Trefilova, Olga Preobrajenska, Alexander Volinine, later Olga Spessivtseva—the list could be greatly extended, for it encompassed probably the most notable of Russia's dancers, its choreographers, and its teachers. The lifeblood of Russian ballet was being drained away.

Fortunately, it had more lifeblood than anyone could have expected. The departure of dancers such as Pavlova and Karsavina left a void, but there were other dancers. Fokine, then the hero of everything progressive in Russian dance, was a disastrous loss, but his elder, Aleksandr Gorsky, remained in Moscow, and soon other ballet masters emerged to take Fokine's place. Western dance historians have always written as if everyone who was anyone deserted Soviet ballet at this time, but this is far from the case. Certainly most of those dancers who had *international* reputations cashed in on those reputations and chose the artistic security the West appeared to offer. But there were many others left in Russia.

For many of the dancers, particularly the intellectuals among them, the revolution appeared to be a heaven-sent chance to express their artistic ideals. Remember, in the arts Fokine and his group had been revolution-aries. Thus it seemed natural to the younger dancers that the social revolution would encompass an artistic upheaval, during which time they would have full opportunity for that very self-expression the formalized Imperial Ballet did not permit. And during most of the 1920's this appeared to be so.

This decade was a time of experiment in Soviet ballet, the time of Kasyan Goleizovsky and, more particularly, Feodor Lopukhov. The theater was at its most vital, and experiment was the very oxygen in its lungs. In Petro-grad (called Leningrad after Lenin's death in 1924) and Moscow, Golei-zovsky and Lopukhov, who worked at various times in both cities, experi-mented assiduously.

Goleizovsky ran the full gamut of experimentation with his specially formed Moscow Chamber Ballet and at other times with a group in Petro-grad. He tried his hand at pure dance, acrobatic dance, erotic dance, and barefoot dance. He was the complete iconoclast. He had worked with both of Russia's dance reformers, Fokine and Gorsky, and he, too, rejected much of the convention of the old classic ballet. He soon became admired and detested—the most controversial choreographer of his day.

Lopukhov also experimented, but with rather more discretion and per-haps to more lasting effect. To meet him today is to meet Russian ballet. Born in 1886, he has known triumph, years and years in the artistic wilder-ness, and then, finally, triumph again, until now he is the idol of the young and creative generation in Soviet ballet. Lopukhov, Lopukhov—the name is on their lips like a symbol or a promise.

He lives in an apartment in the Ballet School in Leningrad. He is still as active as ever, teaching, working, and inspiring. We talked in his apartment, in a room whose walls were covered with ornamental trays that he had obviously spent a lifetime collecting. It was a strange setting, but Lopukhov seemed shyly at ease and talked with simplicity about his beliefs. Chiefly, these were an assertion of the power of classic dance.

Sometimes his statements have a kind of gnomic poetry, such as when he says "The human body is like lace." But more often he is a fountain of wisdom, expounding simple truths, such as "I like to see a technique that is natural," or, perhaps more philosophically, "From nothing you can do nothing."

He gives great credit to Lunacharsky, whom he had first met in Paris in 1908. It was, he says, Lunacharsky's decision to adhere to the classical tradition and only build upon the past.

Lopukhov in the 1920's seems to have been everywhere in Soviet ballet. He revived some of the old nineteenth-century classics; in fact, he is credited with having created the Lilac Fairy solo in *The Sleeping Beauty,* often regarded as one of Marius Petipa's finest variations. But his main task was the formulation of the Soviet style of dancing.

The new Soviet school of dancing was closely based upon the old Maryinsky method, but, as Ulanova puts it, "There is more plastique to the dancing, more inherent feeling." There were also a number of technical innovations, some inspired by the new generation of dancers, including Asaf Messerer and Aleksei Yermolayev, others more the result of the pushing forward of the choreographers. It was Lopukhov, it seems, who first used the new Soviet style of partnering, with the ballerinas carried high above the heads of the male dancers, which has now, during the last decade, passed into international usage. When it began, Pyotr Gusev, then a principal dancer, now one of Russia's leading artistic administrators, told me, a critic suggested that "it was more gynecology than ballet."

Lopukhov believes that most people in the Soviet theatrical world opposed him during the 1920's. "Both Meyerhold and Mayakovsky supported Goleizovsky, never me. But I continued to work wherever I could." Toward the middle of that decade both Lopukhov and Goleizovsky fell out of favor, and this whole period was regarded as one of artistic decadence, being "formalistic and out of touch with the Soviet people." As Lopukhov says today: "I have always believed that Soviet art needs *all* aspects of *all* art." At the end of the 1920's such an attitude was not popular.

Talking to people in Soviet ballet I put to many of them the question: What was achieved by the 1920's? In restrospect most agreed that the period had produced a great deal of value in terms of inspiration to the present generation. Two of the most distinguished, however, were more specific. They both answered with the single word "Balanchine."

George Balanchine, present director of the New York City Ballet and founder of American classic dance, studied in Petrograd during the 1920's. In 1924 he left Russia for the West and soon joined Diaghilev's Ballet Russe, which was then an expatriate company based in Monte Carlo. But before he left he had come under the influence of Goleizovsky and Lopukhov. "Goleizovsky," he once told me, "was never a direct influence, but seeing his work inspired me to try my own hand at choreography." The influence of Lopukhov, whose student Balanchine was, has proved perhaps more enduring.

Lopukhov regards the creation of *Dance Symphony* in 1922 as his greatest achievement in all this period. Set to Beethoven's Fourth Symphony and subtitled "Magnificence of the Universe," this was an essentially plotless work even though its elevated theme was reflected in the reported grandeur of the choreography. Among the dancers who appeared in it were Alexandra Danilova, Leonid Lavrovsky, and George Balanchine. Here, early in his career, Balanchine was given a taste of the neoclassic dance. And this respect for classicism and interest in experimentation was what Balanchine took with him to the West. And forty years later he brought it back from the West to Russia.

Soviet art is politically orientated; art is an instrument of the state, or, to be more charitable, one of the prime concerns of the state. It should be remembered that the state not only governs art, but also pays for it—and, like most payers of pipers, it wishes to call the tunes. This is not ideal, yet neither is the American system whereby an arts patron buys with his money influence his talents could not command. In the West there is also the influence of the box office, the need to be popular, loved, successful, and financially solvent. There is a narrow path between these two extremes, where some all-but-disinterested body, such as Britain's Arts Council, provided with so many checks and balances that every time it moves it practically rattles, is able to give money without wishing to wield political influence. But the Soviet Union is no nearer such an ideal than is the United States. Both have their problems.

During the late 1920's and the 1930's, and even the 1940's, the political climate for the arts in Russia changed markedly. The era of Stalin was not conducive to artistic achievement, and far too many irrelevancies entered the arena of artistic judgment like enormous maverick bulls out to gore even the most stylish of matadors. Just why Lopukhov and Goleizovsky passed out of favor at this time is a question to which probably they themselves do not know the answer. Goleizovsky all but faded away. Indeed, a few years ago, when he was invited out of his semiretirement and started to work with the Bolshoi, it was almost a Rip Van Winkle situation. Lopukhov continued, but on a very small scale and without the outward distinction his innate distinction deserved.

So far as I know, there were no specific charges leveled at these two. Yet the kind of charges they experienced were similar to those leveled at Dmitri Shostakovich by Andrei A. Zhdanov, first in 1936 and later following the Decree on Music issued by the Central Committee of the Communist party in February, 1948. Shostakovich and other prominent Soviet composers were accused of numerous "artistic crimes," including that of having "persistently adhered to formalism and anti-people practices." The statement ended with the peremptory request that the artists "liquidate their faults and become more conscious of their duties to the Soviet people." Lopukhov, choreographer of Shostakovich's ballet about a collective farm, *The Bright Source,* was implicated in the "artistic crimes."

Whether or not it was to escape the deadly embrace of "formalism," certainly ballet started to take a different line in the 1930's. The move was

Clive Barnes

toward the literary ballet, the ultimate triumph of which was Prokofiev's *Romeo and Juliet,* choreographed by Leonid Lavrovsky in Leningrad in 1940. Lavrovsky expressed to me his belief in this period of choreographic work, suggesting that it represented "a decision to show the human being, the man, his feelings and emotions."

It was in their efforts to accomplish this that the choreographers and librettists of the 1930's moved toward the great works of literature. During this period ballets were inspired by Pushkin, Balzac, Gogol, Lope de Vega, and Shakespeare, and great efforts were made to insure that the ballets were both serious in content and moral in tone.

The doctrine of Socialist Realism, with its emphasis upon characterization, storytelling, and human expression, was not out of keeping with the ballet reforms instituted by Fokine at the beginning of the century. As a reaction to the classical ballet that preceded it, the typical Fokine ballet was a dance-drama, where the drama might be as important as the dance, but, in any event, both were perfectly fused. This Fokine-style ballet finds its fullest expression in *Romeo and Juliet,* which complies with all of Fokine's rules for the reform of ballet and the establishment of expressive dance.

Today the period of the 1930's and 1940's in Soviet ballet is under a cloud. I asked many people to nominate ballets created at that time which they thought would survive in the permanent Soviet repertory. Some people replied: None at all. One distinguished critic said: "*Romeo and Juliet,* of course, but not in the Lavrovsky version—with new choreography." Even the period's warmest admirers could not extend the list beyond *Romeo and Juliet,* Vasily Vainonen's *Flames of Paris,* Rotislav Zakharov's *The Fountains of Bakhchisarai,* and Vakhtang Chabukiani's *Laurencia.*

As this present rejection of the ballets of the 1930's and 1940's has been, so far as one can now see, the turning point in Soviet dance, it is worth looking at in some detail. In the first place, the introduction of established literary themes into ballet was not a new development. *Romeo and Juliet,* for example, had often been used before by ballet, the first recorded occasion being as long ago as 1811, when the Italian choreographer Vincenzo Galeotti created a *Romeo and Juliet* for the Royal Danish Ballet in Copenhagen. But it was the seriousness and purpose that the Soviet ballet masters brought to their work that was new.

The intention, of course, was to break with the classic ballet of the nineteenth century. In this Lavrovsky and Zakharov were following the path of Fokine, a fact that recently Lavrovsky acknowledged. Much earlier, writing about his original version of Prokofiev's *Romeo and Juliet,* he suggested: "Ballet, particularly tragic ballet, demands noble, plastic, and heartfelt pantomime, which arises from the dance and constitutes its most significant element. Ballet is a choreographic play in which dance must appear as the sequel to the pantomime, and pantomime as the logical sequence to the dance. . . ." That was the nub of the argument: "Ballet is a choreographic play." Is it? Should it be?

Romeo and Juliet enjoyed a world-wide triumph. From its first production in Leningrad in 1940 and its revival by the Bolshoi Ballet in Moscow in 1946, the music of Prokofiev, the choreography of Lavrovsky, and the unforgettable performance of Galina Ulanova as Juliet came together to produce one of the high points of dance history. It is no wonder that when the Bolshoi Ballet first appeared outside Russia, at London's Royal Opera House, Covent Gardens, in 1956, the ballet chosen for the première was *Romeo and Juliet* with Ulanova. Three years later, when the Bolshoi made its North American debut at New York's Metropolitan Opera House, *Romeo and Juliet* and Ulanova were again chosen. The ballet still stands as a monument to a certain kind of ballet-making. Unfortunately, as time went on it became obvious that it was going to have few, if any, successors. Far from being a new development in Soviet art, *Romeo and Juliet* started to look as if it were the end of a line.

Polemics, as we have already said, appear to be an essential part of Soviet ballet. A few years ago, for example, most of the principal dancers of the Kirov Ballet signed a letter to *Pravda* complaining about the company's artistic management. In similar circumstances in the West, either the dancers or the management would be almost honor-bound to resign. But in Russia nothing happened, for it all apparently was regarded as honest, useful criticism and good, clean fun. On the other hand, the battle between the Old Guard choreographers of the 1930's and 1940's and the latest generation of Soviet choreographers has brought its full number of literary skirmishes, and, to an outsider at least, they look both bitter and bloody.

The first public shot was fired by Igor Moiseyev, a choreographer himself and founder of the Moiseyev Ensemble, the first and still foremost folk-dance company in Russia. In the *Literaturnaya Gazeta* of April 24, 1952, he wrote an article called "The Ballet and Reality." In it he said that "there is much stagnation and conservatism in our midst. A fear of the new is making itself more and more apparent in ballet: as an art form it has hardly any links with contemporary reality, it is far removed from life."

This kind of attack was fairly conventional, but where Moiseyev was more deadly in his strictures was in accusations that the dance element in Soviet ballet had become neglected. He wrote: "Our repertoire is monotonous because it lacks variety of style . . . all our latest productions suffer from a common fault, the poverty of dance form; the striving after content and the depiction of it are taken as a denial of the leading role of the dance. . . . Nobody would think of belittling the significance of clever miming in ballet. But the most expressive, most emotional, most poetic language of ballet is the dance." In one deadly shaft he said: "We have justly criticized many old ballets because they did not combine the dance with healthy thought, but we cannot permit new ballets to have healthy thought uncombined with the dance."

Nor did Moiseyev flinch from attacking by name the leading Soviet choreographers of the time, Lavrovsky and Zakharov. Even *Romeo and Juliet* did not escape; he wrote: "Unfortunately, even in a production of such great stature as 'Romeo and Juliet,' a ballet that profoundly depicts the Shakespearean tragedy, the choreographer, L. Lavrovsky, gives undue weight to the element of mime, as if distrustful of the language of the dance."

Zakharov fares even worse, for Moiseyev takes two of his most famous ballets and writes contemptuously: "To change the dance until it becomes the dullest part of the ballet, as for example is done in 'Cinderella' and 'The Bronze Horseman,' to convert ballet into a selection of technical stage effects in which everything is demonstrated except the abilities of the ballet company and the powers of the choreographer, in which scenery undergoes a more complex evolution than the dancers themselves and in which the confusion of styles leads to the worst possible eclecticism, is to discard the best traditions of the classical ballets without infusing anything new into them. The classical ballet in its time knew the fairy-story ballet, but that was dance plus fairy story and not fairy story minus dance, as is the case with the Bolshoi Theater productions of 'Cinderella' and 'The Bronze Horseman.' "

Probably this article marked the end of an era in Soviet ballet—not because Moiseyev had written it, but because what he had written summed up what so many other people at that time were thinking. At first the dramatic choreographers of the 1930's, notably Lavrovsky and Zakharov, were apparently not affected. They still had considerable triumphs ahead of them in the Western world—and, as Lavrovsky has only recently been justly claiming, the very first success of the Bolshoi Ballet in England and the United States did, at least to some extent, depend upon his *Romeo and Juliet*. But by this time the writing was on the wall.

Zakharov himself replied to Moiseyev in *Literaturnaya Gazeta* a couple of months after the original article. He complained that Moiseyev "unjustly underestimates the successes of Soviet ballet" and he could not agree that it was "standing aside from the tempestuous development of reality." He contended: "The new quality that distinguishes Soviet ballet qualitatively from the prerevolutionary court ballet is the creation of a whole range of ballet plays, as against empty ballet-divertissements which were characteristic of the Imperial Ballet. Thought, content and expressiveness have really been embodied in the best Soviet ballet."

However Zakharov imagined reality to be tempestuously developing, the next development was perhaps the unexpected, almost unnoticed, return of a prodigal. It was a return by proxy. George Balanchine had left Russia in 1924. Before his departure he had conducted a few scandalous choreographic experiments in Petrograd and for his pains had been critically rapped on the knuckles, by no less than the important critic Akim Volynsky. But in June, 1958, his first full ballet was seen at the Bolshoi Theater.

It is ironical that the first Western ballet company to penetrate the Soviet Union was not one of the major troupes, not the New York City Ballet or the Royal Ballet. (The latter was scheduled to go in 1956, but canceled on political grounds following the Hungarian uprising.) It was, instead, the little-regarded Paris Opéra Ballet. It went to Moscow with a full complement of works by Serge Lifar and Harald Lander, but the ballet that caused the real stir was George Balanchine's *Le Palais de Cristal,* better known elsewhere as *Symphony in C.*

Knowing the Parisian dancers, one would assume that it was deplorably danced, but it came as a revelation to some people, even though the official critical reaction was slightly guarded. One young Soviet choreographer told me: "When I saw *Palais de Cristal* it was a new world opening to me. I knew that Balanchine's way was not my way, but I also knew what I had to do." Presumably Zakharov would have called *Palais de Cristal* a modern version of one of those imperial "empty ballet-divertissements." But for the younger generation it was a liberation. Here in Russia were the most highly trained technicians in the ballet world—and they longed to dance.

There was one other result of the Moiseyev article—or, if it was not a result, it proved an interesting coincidence. In 1957 Igor Moiseyev was invited to return to the Bolshoi Ballet and to choreograph a new production of Aram Khachaturian's ballet *Spartacus.* In December, 1956, Leonid Jacobson, a quite distinguished Leningrad-based choreographer with a bent toward experimentation, had mounted another version of the score for the Kirov Ballet. The Moiseyev version had its première in March, 1958. Although, in the words of the fine Soviet critic Natalia Roslavleva, "Moiseyev's version was in some parts superior to that of Jacobson . . . apparently classical technique was unable to offset the lack of action."

The ballet did not survive in the repertory, and when the Bolshoi company wanted to mount it again, in 1962, it revived, in a modified version, Jacobson's monumental Leningrad production, where dance plays second fiddle to spectacle while Rome burns. It was the Jacobson version that the Bolshoi Ballet danced in New York.

To dance or not to dance, that was becoming the question. Of course there was always the classic repertory—*Swan Lake, The Sleeping Beauty, Giselle* (which was, during the 1940's, accused of "mysticism" but later forgiven), *Don Quixote, The Nutcracker, Raymonda*. No, there was no lack of things to dance. But the young dancers, first in Moscow and Leningrad and later throughout the Soviet Union, longed for new ballets that would exploit dancing.

During the first part of the 1950's Lavrovsky, as artistic director of the Bolshoi Ballet, was in an unassailable position. He had in fact produced only one work which by common consent, first in Russia and later outside, was a masterpiece, his *Romeo and Juliet,* and even this had been planned by Zakharov in its first stages, and the famous Shakespearean director Sergei Radlov had played a certain part in the production. But the real credit was Lavrovsky's, and this *Romeo* was the epitome of the Fokine ballet. But before *Romeo,* even after *Romeo,* Lavrovsky's successes looked a little thin on the ground.

Prokofiev, the Soviet Union's greatest ballet composer, was not altogether happy with Lavrovsky when the choreographer started to mount *Romeo,* but Lavrovsky, with his skill and good sense, won him over, and Prokofiev was pleased with the result, more pleased, I am told, than he was with Zakharov's production of his *Cinderella.* It was therefore natural that he should entrust what proved to be his last ballet, *The Stone Flower,* to Lavrovsky, who, with the composer's wife, was responsible for the libretto. Prokofiev wrote the music for *The Stone Flower* in 1949 and 1950, but it was not until early in 1953 that Lavrovsky began work on it. Prokofiev died soon after the beginning of rehearsals, and Lavrovsky's ballet was produced at the Bolshoi Theater the following year. It failed and was quickly withdrawn.

In 1957 *The Stone Flower* was mounted for the Kirov Ballet by Yuri Grigorovich; it was a marked success, and two years later it was reproduced by the Bolshoi Ballet. Grigorovich, a character dancer with the Leningrad company, had been interested in choreography for many years and even as a student would prepare short dances. His first ambitious effort came in 1956 when he was invited to produce the choreography for the school's graduation performance, which he set to Glinka's "Valse-Fantasia." Other ballets at the Leningrad Maxim Gorky Palace of Culture followed, before his first major success with the Prokofiev ballet.

Soon additional works came forth. His second ballet, *Legend of Love,* to music by a young composer, Arif Melikov, of Azerbaijan, was also first produced at the Kirov and later at the Bolshoi. Invited to become acting leader of the Kirov and later acting leader of the Bolshoi, his position in the latter capacity was confirmed as a permanent appointment, and in 1965 Yuri Grigorovich became artistic director of the Bolshoi Ballet, the most important position in Soviet ballet. Since that time he has produced a completely new and highly successful version of Tchaikovsky's *The Nutcracker* and revised the traditional Petipa version of *The Sleeping Beauty*. He has also started work on a new production of *Spartacus,* which is being envisioned far more in terms of pure dance than hitherto, and he is proposing to rearrange Khachaturian's score quite considerably.

The contrast between Yuri Grigorovich and Leonid Lavrovsky could hardly be more marked. Grigorovich is a very youthful forty, ebullient, confident, expansive, a rapid and decisive talker, a very fast worker, and a man uninhibited almost to the point of indiscretion; in some ways he is an almost unlikely man to have as a leader, because he is, oddly, a private face in a public place—there is nothing, even superficially, of the official about him. But his explosive energy, his eagerness for every single aspect of the dance, and his talent make the respect that his colleagues and even audiences feel for him readily understandable.

Lavrovsky is the more statesmanlike figure, agreeable, sensible, and tactful. He clearly realizes that the esthetic balance has shifted against him but feels that such shifts are inevitable in the development of any art form. He told me: "Soviet ballet is changing less than you might imagine. Forms of expression can be changed—but these are relatively unimportant when the content remains the same. And the content of Soviet ballet, the purpose of Soviet ballet, does not vary." He may be right.

What Grigorovich has achieved is a new emphasis on dance as such. His master is Feodor Lopukhov, and he admits to a considerable admiration for what he has seen of Balanchine. Through Lopukhov, Grigorovich claims kinship with the classical heritage of Petipa, in fact kinship with those same "empty ballet-divertissements characteristic of the Imperial Ballet" so haughtily rejected a few years previously by Zakharov.

The new interest in dance is not only apparent in Grigorovich but is shared by virtually all of the young Soviet choreographers whose work I know or have discussed. The senior of them, together with Grigorovich, is Igor Belsky, who is director of the Maly Ballet, Leningrad's second company. Belsky, who, incidentally, was better informed regarding Western ballet than anyone, apart from a few critics, I met in Russia, was typical of the new attitude. While accepting the value of some things achieved in the 1930's, he felt that ballet based on literature was in danger of being mere illustration. He was happy enough to retain the old content, but insisted that this be expressed through the language of the dance.

Belsky was interested in "symphonic dance," and not only saw choreography as being far more orientated to music than drama, but also regarded choreography, ideally, as on the same level as a score, a commonplace in the West but much more unusual in the Soviet Union. Yet Belsky was as far from rejecting the necessity of a theme and fully accepting that dance might be an end in itself.

This is an apparent division between Soviet ballet and dance in the West. We accept that some of our ballets can be "plotless" (not abstract, for nothing involving human beings in a stage performance can be properly called abstract), and this the Russians find uninteresting or even impracticable. It is not for nothing that in the announcements of future repertory at the Bolshoi Theater the names of the composer and librettist are both given, but that of the choreographer is nowhere to be seen.

Yuri Slonimsky, Russia's leading dance historian and critic and also a well-known ballet librettist, was convinced that ballets without a readily recognizable content would never prove acceptable to Soviet artists or audiences, and Slonimsky is in the vanguard of the progressive movement in Russian dance. However, I later discovered that some young choreographers are actually producing plotless ballets in Leningrad. Georgi Aleksidze and Nikolai Markaradzhants have done so for a chamber ballet they have founded in association with the Leningrad Philharmonic Orchestra. In addition, Konstantin Boyarsky has created a plotless work for the Maly Ballet. And on all sides it was agreed that the interest in pure dance works began with the visit to Russia of George Balanchine and the New York City Ballet in 1962.

Of course, as Aleksidze was quick to point out, plotless ballet had started in Russia, and both he and Markaradzhants were pupils of Lopukhov, just as Balanchine had been more than forty years ago. Also, as with Balanchine, neither of these young men wish to produce only plotless works. One agreed with the other, who said, "We are merely extending the range of Soviet ballet—we make realistic ballets and will always continue to do so, but also we will make ballets that do nothing but interpret the music. Soviet ballet is now absorbing all tendencies, and this is something we have learned from the 1920's."

The presence of so many new choreographers is partly what Ulanova meant when she stressed the new developments in Soviet ballet. Certainly the activity is considerable. Gone are the days when she could write angrily in the *Literaturnaya Gazeta* about the lack of enterprise shown by the

Bolshoi Ballet, which now, under Grigorovich, is trying hard to give chances to young choreographers. Aleksandr Lapauri, in association with Olga Tarasova, produced *Lieutenant Kije,* before the Grigorovich regime, and another pair of choreographers, the husband and wife team of Vladimir Vasilyov and Natalia Kasatkina, have now created three works for the Bolshoi, and have others in active preparation.

Vasilyov and Kasatkina are typical of Soviet ballet's younger generation of creative artists. They are widely traveled, extremely knowledgeable, and deeply committed to their art. Another even younger choreographer of reputation is Oleg Vinogradov, whom I have not met, although I have seen two of his ballets, *Cinderella,* for the Novosibirsk Ballet, and *Asel,* for the Bolshoi. Neither was a complete success, but both showed a great potential talent. Just as with Vasilyov and Kasatkina, Vinogradov makes the mistakes and the errors of judgment of the genuinely talented. They are not mediocre.

In one particular sense, *Asel* proved unusually interesting: it is a modern-dress ballet with a truck driver as its antihero and a heroine torn between the love of two husbands. It has helped to answer the constant Soviet plea for ballets on contemporary subjects, and it won the praise of Igor Moiseyev, who used it this summer as the springboard for another attack in *Pravda* upon Lavrovsky. Unfortunately, Vinogradov has yet to find a modern idiom to match his modern subject matter, but the attempt itself is no small matter for praise.

Almost equal emphasis must be put upon the administrative and pedagogical advances in Russian ballet over the past fifty years as on its creative development.

In the West, when we speak of Soviet ballet we tend to mean only the Bolshoi Ballet and the Kirov Ballet, perhaps with a few of the more celebrated folk-dance ensembles. In fact, there are now thirty-six ballet companies in the Soviet Union.

The quality of these classic-ballet companies varies widely. The leading ones, apart from the Bolshoi and the Kirov, are the company of the Stanislavsky and Nemirovich-Danchenko Theater in Moscow, that of the Maly Theater in Leningrad, and the companies of Kiev, Novosibirsk, and Tbilisi. All these have appeared in the West, and their standards are high indeed. But not all Soviet companies achieve such a level. Appearing during the recent White Nights Festival in Leningrad was the Novgorod Ballet, which was very provincial. It was vastly inferior, not only in manner of presentation but even in actual dancers, to Western companies such as, say, the Cologne Opera Ballet or the Pennsylvania Ballet Company. Perhaps Novgorod is unusually unfortunate (although the company's selection to appear at a festival would suggest that at least someone is proud of it) but, on the other hand, seeing this troupe perform does act as a corrective to any thoughts that all Soviet ballet companies are of value. Novgorod is not—and there may be one or two other inferior ones.

However, Soviet ballet has reached a point in its development where it has a unified style of its own. There is such a thing as a Soviet dancer, who is different in style and technique from dancers found anywhere else in the world. In 1917 there were two important schools in Russia. The school based on the Maryinsky Theater (today the Kirov Theater) in Petrograd and that of the Bolshoi Theater in Moscow. The Maryinsky School was by far the more important, and the style of its dancers was quite different from that of their Muscovite colleagues.

The Maryinsky was the major company because Petrograd was then the capital. When the Bolsheviks made Moscow the capital it became inevitable that the Bolshoi Ballet would become the first company of the country, but this could not be achieved overnight. Throughout Russian dance history it was the Maryinsky School that produced the leading dancers, and this tradition continued almost until the present generation.

So many of the leaders of Soviet ballet have emerged from the Kirov School that it is almost embarrassing to list them. But undeniably the Bolshoi Ballet has benefited enormously from the acquisition of Rostislav Zakharov, Leonid Lavrovsky, Galina Ulanova, and, most recently of all, Yuri Grigorovich. The difference between the ballet schools in Leningrad and Moscow is today considerably less. Many Leningrad teachers have worked in Moscow, and the entire Russian training method is based upon that of Leningrad's most famous teacher, Agrippina Vaganova, who helped to codify the Soviet system.

The Soviet style is, naturally enough, a development of the old imperial style, yet it, too, has undergone development. At the beginning of the 1920's Lopukhov in his ballets introduced the high partnering lifts, which were then unknown. There has also been an advance in male technique, in part encouraged by the dancing of Aleksei Yermolayev in Leningrad and Asaf Messerer in Moscow. It was Messerer who was also at least partly responsible for the abandonment of conventional mime gestures in Soviet ballet.

Over the past fifty years the Soviet Union has produced a formidable and beautiful machine for the training of dancers. The work of the schools speaks for itself. In part, of course, it is because they have rather more people to choose from than do Western schools. For a male dancer, in particular, it seems likely that a ballet career is regarded more highly in the U.S.S.R. than in the West and as a result the competition to enter ballet school is stronger. The West has a great deal to learn in this respect. Also, Soviet schools are state schools, whereas the West has few state ballet schools. To be sure, scholarships are available to such institutions as the School of American Ballet, in New York, and the Royal Ballet School, in London, but the parents of most children have to pay—and to pay quite heavily.

Once Russian dancers graduate from the schools (where, incidentally, if they finish the course they are guaranteed a job in ballet) and join the companies, they are treated rather differently from Western dancers. They are regarded as responsible artists, and the strict classroom discipline typical of Western ballet is abandoned. If a dancer in professional class does not wish to do a certain exercise, he will not do it, and dancers appear to come and go as they please. External discipline has been replaced by the inner discipline of the artist himself.

Soviet ballet derives a considerable strength from its abiding traditions, and in the classroom such traditions are naturally inculcated. Talking about Rudolf Nureyev (the former Kirov dancer who left for the West), a few of his former colleagues mentioned, in a rather shocked fashion, that when Nureyev was in Leningrad and the junior member of Aleksandr Pushkin's class, he had bluntly refused the task of running over the floor with the watering can to lay the dust, the traditional chore of the young dancer. And yet at the same time, while tradition at that level is revered, on certain more significant levels it too often seems disregarded.

The Soviet ballet repertory must give considerable cause for concern, and this is not merely because so many ballets of the period have failed to stand the test of time, for this would be true of all countries and all times. What is more significant is the erosion of the Russian classical repertory, the wastage of ballet's actual substance over the last fifty years.

Swan Lake is one of the greatest of all Russian ballets, yet nowhere in Russia can it be seen in its original version. The Bolshoi *Swan Lake* is a national catastrophe rather than a national monument. Even in Leningrad, where Konstantin Sergeyev, a ballet director of great sensibility, is in charge, the Petipa and Tchaikovsky masterpiece *The Sleeping Beauty* has been amended by Sergeyev himself, so that, while it is produced with consummate style, much of the original work has been knocked away to make room for the new.

The present Soviet attitude to choreography differs enormously from that in the West, and it is an attitude unwittingly symbolized by the absence, mentioned earlier, of the choreographer's name from the forthcoming announcements. In Russia the choreographer is not regarded as the equal, or, properly speaking, superior, partner of the composer. Often one imagines that his role is envisaged as no more or no less than that of the director of a play or opera. As a result, it seems as strange to the Russians to maintain

Swan Lake intact for seventy years as it would to us to maintain a fossilized production of Shakespeare for the same length of time.

Consequently, some of the most perfect examples of nineteenth-century ballet are in the process of being lost. Some people in Russia oppose this process heartily. Lopukhov and Gusev, two of the most enlightened men in world ballet, wish to see the works of Marius Petipa, Lev Ivanov, and Michel Fokine restored and preserved, but it sometimes seems that they are fighting a lonely battle. It is, however, a battle in which Leningrad is a great deal more concerned than Moscow is. Sergeyev and his wife, the former ballerina and great teacher Natalia Dudinskaya, have the liveliest regard for the continuity of tradition, and the Kirov even maintains in its current repertory such a wonder from the past as Petipa's *La Bayadère*. One could wish, though, that Sergeyev would apply his great skill at creatively direct-ing old choreography to the production of classic versions that are as closely authentic as possible or, rather, as is reasonable. The latter qualification is necessary because certain aspects of the original versions—Siegfried with a shield-bearer in *Swan Lake;* no solos for either the Prince or the Lilac Fairy in *The Sleeping Beauty*—were expedients forced upon Petipa and would be insupportable today.

Strangely enough, Russia and the Bolshoi provide one of the most strik-ing examples of the way in which a ballet classic can be properly main-tained; this is Leonid Lavrovsky's production of *Giselle*. While keeping the old choreography virtually intact, Lavrovsky has re-examined the work's dramatic basis and contrived to make the ballet meaningful for modern audiences. This intelligent approach is at a far remove from the action of the choreographer who feels it incumbent upon himself to rechoreograph the entire ballet.

The physical conditions under which the Soviet dancer works are en-viable. At the Bolshoi, and probably the Kirov, there is a certain amount of natural friction between the opera and the ballet companies, although a good deal less than at London's Covent Garden. But apart from this diffi-culty of two organizations sharing the same home, everything that can be done for Soviet dance and the Soviet dancer apparently has been done.

The dancers themselves are well paid. A great many dancers own cars, the ones I know live in pleasant, well-furnished, and well-equipped apart-ments, and they seem in much the same income bracket as dancers in the West. They do also have more security. They all receive a pension, some-thing rare in Western ballet generally and actually unknown in the United States and England.

The classes offered dancers are excellent, and rehearsal conditions are good. The Bolshoi, for example, has built a rehearsal theater just beneath its roof, with the stage exactly the same size as the main Bolshoi stage, although the proscenium arch is naturally low and the auditorium only holds about one hundred people. This is a kind of luxury unknown in Western ballet.

A dancer's education in Russia does not necessarily terminate when he joins a ballet company, for there are various forms of further choreographic education available that are designed to help him become a teacher, régisseur, or choreographer. In both Moscow and Leningrad there are courses given in choreography—courses that recently have incurred the scorn of Igor Moiseyev. Yet the courses themselves, well planned and intelligently conceived, can presumably do nothing but assist the apprentice choreographer to fulfill to the maximum such innate ability as he may possess. The gift of choreography is rare indeed, and is as rare in Russia as anywhere else. Choreography, as such, cannot be taught, any more than musical composition as such; in fact, rather less, because musical composition, through the advantage of an established musical notation, has set rules which at least can be studied. Choreography has no rules—but no one ever suffered from a few informal precepts.

There is one respect, however, in which at least the Bolshoi dancer is not to be envied—the matter of his audience. Perhaps the essence of repertory theater is the presence of a regular audience, to act as a friend, guide, and stimulus, and this is particularly true of the ballet audience. In Moscow (the situation does not appear to obtain in Leningrad) the ballet has become a tourist attraction. Muscovites find tickets for the Bolshoi almost impossible to get, and as a result the Bolshoi Ballet has been cut off from a regular—and informed—audience.

For foreign tourists, getting tickets for the Bolshoi—the best seats cost a little more than three dollars—is ludicrously easy, and even Russian tourists, a rather less privileged class, find it moderately easy to obtain tickets. Thus the Bolshoi in Moscow is dancing to audiences who are not well acquainted with ballet, do not attend ballet performances in their home towns, and have no standards.

Officially, the dancers enjoy playing before these unsophisticated virgin groups, and each trade-union party sends a song through their hearts as they dance for a true people's audience. Unofficially, with all the best will in the world, it disturbs them. They are not snobs and they genuinely do enjoy playing before uncommitted audiences of, say, factory workers or children (dancers all over the world will agree that in some respects such audiences are most responsive), but at the same time they recognize the need for the serious dance audience that exists in Leningrad, New York, and London.

A dancer can maintain his standard for just so long, particularly when helped by the intelligent criticism of his colleagues. But the audience, as the French aptly say, does assist. If you get the same applause, uncritical and loving, every night, whether you dance your variation very well, well, or simply atrociously, there comes a point when even the most dedicated artist is going to say: "So what! Who cares? Who knows?" The dancers are at present behaving with great sincerity, but I did see one or two performances in Moscow that I suspect the artists in question would not have given in New York or London.

Another aspect of the Bolshoi Ballet's wide tourist appeal is its appearances in the Kremlin Palace of Congresses. This is an enormous hall seating 6,000 people that was built specifically for conferences. Most of the time it is used as a theater, and the results are disastrous. The stage is huge and, unlike normal Russian stages, unraked. It therefore is difficult to dance on. As a dancer put it to me: "You dance twice as hard for half the effect." Then there is the matter of communication. Although the Bolshoi is a large theater, it is rather like Lincoln Center's New York State Theater in that it contrives to give the effect of intimacy. The Kremlin hall is a barn, and the dancers are gesturing out to infinity with the hopelessness of drowning sailors on a stormy night. They cannot act, only gesticulate. Of course, the theater's existence means that many more people see the Bolshoi Ballet than would otherwise have done so. But they are not seeing the company under favorable conditions.

There is one other respect in which the Russian dancer and choreographer feel deprived: they seem, and the proposition is so basically unlikely that I put it forward with all due diffidence, to want Western-style criticism in the Soviet Union. Just at the time when we in the West are feeling guilty, or, if not guilty, at least a little defensive around the edges, about our seemingly barbarous habit of serving our newspaper criticism with bacon and eggs for breakfast the morning after the artistic night before, the Russians find themselves wanting just that.

During almost all my conversations in Russia I found that Western critical processes, if not always Western critical practices, were admired, and this feeling appeared so widespread that its expression could not be put down solely to hostlike courtesy. Some of the younger critics feel frustrated at the limited opportunities for criticism in the Soviet Union. The national newspapers are too small to carry proper criticism, and, remarkably enough, the U.S.S.R., of all countries, does not possess a national ballet magazine.

Igor Moiseyev, always blunt and always to the point, said, "Look, in America and England you have *Dance and Dancers, Dance News,* and *Dance Magazine,* but do you have that number of dance companies?" Certainly Russians are longing for a dance magazine of their own which could act as a platform for professional criticism and a general clearinghouse for ideas and arguments. They also want more general criticism and more criticism of specific performances, the latter being virtually unknown in the Soviet Union.

It would not be just, however, to leave the subject of criticism without saying how high are the standards of Soviet dance criticism. Yuri Slonimsky has placed the world in his debt as one of the most perceptive dance historians of our century. His works urgently need translation in the West; shockingly little of his writing is available. And among others are Natalia Roslavleva and Vera Krasovskaya, both notably erudite and, better still, sensible. Unfortunately, one of Russia's best critics—on day-to-day performances probably *the* best—Mikhail Gabovich, director of the Bolshoi Ballet School and before that Ulanova's partner, died tragically young. His critical comments are much missed.

Regarding the esthetic of Soviet ballet I find myself remembering—at least, I *think* I am remembering, but I have a poor memory for literature— a Greek confectioner in Chekhov's one-act play *The Wedding.* In this he declaims, with notable forcefulness, "There is Russia and there is Greece . . . there is Greece and there is Russia. . . ." A short speech, yet a speech not without significance, for the Russian way of doing things, the Russian approach to art, has always differed from that of the West, and never more so than now.

One merely has to walk around a Russian picture gallery and look at the contemporary Soviet paintings on view to be aware that some enormous barrier divides us from Russia. Russian paintings tell stories; the paintings of the rest of the world attempt to transfix a vision. The situation is the same with Soviet ballet—the same with understandable modifications.

There were choreographers and musicians in Russia with whom I talked about John Cage and Merce Cunningham. They wanted information and they were interested, but the Soviet Union is not about to spawn a Merce Cunningham. Looking at Soviet ballet—and the confectioner's words ring ironically in my ears—I fear that it courts mass popularity a little too assiduously. The arts are for all the people, and this is admirable, but does it not disregard the fact that the people are not for all the arts?

I wonder whether the Soviet ballet master has that most important freedom of all: the freedom to fail. American ballet has suffered under the whiplash of the box office. Yet artists could choose to disregard it and starve to death—and, moreover, starve with a certain dignity. I have a feeling that the Russian choreographer needs to be popular. There are times when the artist should have the opportunity to meet his need to be unpopular.

Is a minority art necessarily a bad thing? If the selection of the minority is based solely upon privilege or wealth, this may be undesirable, although even here one must mention parenthetically the great art patrons of the past whose enlightened connoisseurship left us no small heritage. Then again, both in Soviet and Western society, we accept the principle of unequal education (together with some degree of equal educational opportunity, which is a different thing), and it may prove that a system of unequal recreational pleasures will also prove desirable.

In the United States we have one pure people's art, called television, and the public's lightest whim is catered to by entrepreneurs struggling like mad tigers to get, on any terms whatsoever, the largest possible audience for their product. The results are not edifying, but they offer a lesson to everyone concerned with the future of the performing arts.

Looking back on the achievements of Soviet ballet since the Bolshevik Revolution, two things strike me particularly: first, the sheer quality and quantity of dancers that have been produced and are being produced, and, second, Soviet ballet's new-found apparent flexibility of purpose.

The dancers are remarkable. More almost than the performances I saw on stage (which, after all, were no different from the many Soviet performances I have seen on Western stages), it was the classrooms that impressed me. At the Bolshoi to watch the girls' class of Yelizaveta Gerdt, or the men's classes taken by Asaf Messerer or Aleksei Yermolayev, is to be made aware of both the power of Russian dance traditions and the almost limitless potentiality of the dancers. Watching these classes, like observing those of Natalia Dudinskaya and Aleksandr Pushkin in Leningrad, was an education and a delight in itself.

It would be possible to put some of them on stage, and, indeed, with certain natural modifications, that is virtually what the Bolshoi Ballet did when it produced Messerer's *School of Ballet,* which is a stylized version of a Messerer ballet class, and, incidentally, the closest thing to a plotless ballet the Bolshoi has yet reached.

The flexibility of Soviet ballet, the willingness to absorb influences from outside, is perhaps part of the eagerness I noted in the Russian people generally. I remember the Bolshoi Ballet on its first visit to the West at Covent Garden in 1956. After the initial performance there was an enormous party on the Covent Garden stage for British and Russian ballet to make contact. The Russians were perfectly polite but on guard and nervous. When I saw them later in class they were dressed in old-fashioned formal practice clothes, the girls wore no make-up, and the whole scene could have been photographed at the beginning of the century.

In 1967 I watched the girls in Dudinskaya's class in Leningrad. From the way they were attired (in Western-style practice dress, many of them in bright colors), the make-up they wore, and, more indefinably, their general manner, I could have been in a classroom in New York or London. The contrast makes a small but, I think, significant point.

THE RESOURCES OF A NATION

»

Theodore Shabad

The small auditorium of Moscow's Architectural Institute was crowded with faculty members and students. The occasion was the public defense of academic dissertations, a ritual required before the granting of scholarly degrees to postgraduate students. On that day a young Chinese, one of the last students from his country still remaining in Moscow during the deepening Soviet-Chinese rift, was presenting his plans for apartment buildings of the future. A Russian graduate student offered a thesis on town planning in the Siberian Arctic.

As usual on such occasions, lively discussions developed. The Chinese student's designs for future apartments seemed straightforward, but one point gave pause to the examiners. Little kitchen space had been provided. Instead, the future architect had envisioned communal kitchens and canteens on every floor. It was evident from the Russians' comments that while such arrangements might suit the Chinese, they would never do for future Soviet housing. The Russians had had their fill of communal kitchens under the cramped conditions forced upon them by a stringent housing shortage. Now that they were slowly acquiring small but private apartments they were in no mood to return to communal services. "Suppose you have guests in and want to prepare food for them?" a woman professor said. "Who wants to bother with a communal kitchen at such a time?" The Chinese conceded that a small kitchenette might be provided for these occasions. Finally the dissertation was approved, with the understanding that the architectural ideas it incorporated were not likely to apply to Soviet conditions.

It was now the turn of the future Arctic town planner. His thesis was that new mining towns, about the only type of settlement required in the rigorous far-northern reaches of Siberia, should have architectural protection against the severe cold and blizzards of the eight-month winter. He presented several concepts. Again a spirited discussion ensued, revolving around the height of buildings and whether the entire town should be covered by a vast plastic dome or structures should be linked with one another and a central shopping center by enclosed passages that would keep out the prevailing winter temperatures of forty and fifty degrees below zero. After several persons had commented, a middle-aged man asked for permission to speak.

"I may be somewhat out of line," he began, "but I represent the Institute of Design of the Nonferrous Metals Industry. We plan the development of those remote mineral resources, gold, tin, diamonds, and we are in a sense the potential users of the fancy covered settlements you're discussing here. I may be a little blunt, but it seems to me that you are talking in a vacuum. You act as if the principal problem in these northern latitudes of Siberia is to make it as cozy as possible for the housewife to go from her home to the grocery store. I would say that you are missing the point. Our problem is not to attract people to settle in those inhospitable areas. If we could help it, we would not want to send anyone there. For one thing, it costs too much just to maintain people. Everything has to be flown in—food, fuel, equipment, materials, supplies. We are looking forward not to the settling of miners under air-conditioned plastic domes but to increasing mechanization and automation that will reduce the required manpower to a minimum."

An embarrassed silence followed. Finally a professor explained somewhat apologetically that the dissertation was not concerned with industrial planning in Siberia and the distribution of manpower, but was, basically, just an exercise in architectural planning of a settlement under rigorous climatic conditions. The candidate was relieved to hear that the results of his research had been approved, purely on architectural merit, of course.

To me, after listening to the rambling discussions for several hours, the remarks of the nonferrous metals man were an eye opener. A foreign correspondent in Moscow rarely penetrates below the glossy veneer of government documents and approved policy speeches to hear arguments pro and con on disputed issues, to delve into the intricacies of decision-making that show where the country is going and why. It was in search of this additional insight that I had got into the habit of attending academic dissertations whenever the announced topic was not forbiddingly abstract or technical. Sometimes the effort was rewarded.

The remarks of the nonferrous metals man were revealing on several grounds. In the first place, they suggested once again how important the cost factor had become in Soviet economic planning and development. For decades under Stalin, ever since the first five-year plan (1928–32), political, strategic, and other noneconomic considerations had guided Soviet planners in listing priorities for the opening up of the nation's vast resources. Political motives entered into the early policy of developing industry in outlying regions of the Soviet Union, inhabited mainly by non-Russian minorities, even if local resources for a particular industry were entirely lacking and had to be shipped in over long distances at high cost. The results of this policy are still evident in widely scattered small steel plants around the periphery of the Soviet Union that were built in the late 1930's and the 1940's only because the existence of a steel plant, a basic element in a modern economy, lent prestige to the area in which it was situated. In most cases, these outlying plants were distant from economical sources of iron ore and coking coals, the two basic ingredients of iron and steel production.

Strategic considerations also played a vital role at a time when the Soviet Union considered itself to be in a "capitalistic encirclement." To lessen strategic vulnerability of industry through a pattern of decentralization, the Soviet planners adopted a policy of developing so-called local resources, especially widely found lignite (an inferior type of coal), peat, oil shale, and other mineral fuels, even if some of these resources were of low grade and had to be developed at high cost. A related policy was the development of heavy industry deep in the nation's interior so that it would be less exposed to a potential invader than the older industrial districts of European Russia that were a relatively short distance from the border. Probably the most famous example of this early development of the Soviet Union's interior was the so-called Urals-Kuznetsk combine, twin iron-and-steel complexes constructed in the 1930's. The combine encompassed two great plants, the Magnitogorsk mill of the Urals, on the site of a high-grade iron ore deposit, and the Novo-Kuznetsk mill, in Siberia's Kuznetsk Basin, which produced coking coal. The two complexes were 1,400 miles apart, and their operation depended on a costly rail shuttle system that carried coal from the Siberian mines to the Urals mill and iron ore from the Magnitogorsk mine back to the Kuznetsk.

The project was the subject of great controversy as early cost-conscious planners argued with those who were more concerned with the development of an industrial reserve base deep in the Soviet interior. As it turned out, the project paid off, for in World War II, when German armies occupied the exposed heavy-industry centers of the Donets Basin in the Ukraine, it was the newly developed industry in the Urals and in Siberia that became the base of the Soviet war effort.

Disregard for economic accounting may have saved the Soviet Union in World War II by providing the industrial rear area necessary for defense, but after the war arbitrary considerations in planning and economic development were no longer adequate to insure a continued rapid rate of growth. The turning point came in the middle 1950's, after Stalin's death, when a series of far-reaching decisions were taken, altering the previous priorities in resource development. These decisions were designed to give greater weight to cost considerations and to transform the economy into a more efficient mechanism.

The discussion in the Architectural Institute also focused on the manpower problem. The desire of the nonferrous metals man to keep Siberia's population to a minimum seemed like a complete turnabout from earlier calls to young Russians to go east and help develop the vast resources of that part of the country. This did not mean that the Siberian resources were no longer needed. It meant that ways had to be found to develop those resources with as few people as possible. To understand this new attitude toward human settlement in Siberia, one must go back to the twenty-year period, from the middle 1930's to the middle 1950's, when millions of Soviet citizens served in forced-labor camps under Stalin. Although the vast majority of the camp inmates were ostensibly found politically suspect during the era of the great Stalinist purges, it was a practical fact, whether intended or not, that the forced laborers constituted a great pool of cheap manpower that could be used by the Soviet regime in economic development and construction projects in areas where conditions were too harsh to attract ordinary wage-earning labor. Many of the Soviet Union's great railroad projects, power dams, gold and tin mines, and other industries were built and operated for two decades by forced labor. These projects were often far from populated areas, in remote parts of Siberia, where a severe climate and poor living conditions took their toll.

Although economists have found forced labor, with its lack of incentive and low productivity, to be a highly uneconomical form of manpower, the fact remains that the Soviet economic planners were long able to use this reservoir of virtually unpaid labor for the opening up of key resources. This manpower pool disappeared in the middle 1950's after the amnesties that followed Stalin's death, when most of those exiled were found to have been unjustly accused and were rehabilitated. Although the great majority by far returned to their homes in European Russia, many former camp inmates remained in the eastern areas, henceforth as normal wage earners. The Soviet authorities soon discovered that the change from forced labor to the use of paid labor enormously increased the cost of labor, and thus the cost of operation, for mines and industry in remote parts of the country where wage scales had to be inflated by incentive payments to attract workers. In addition, the Soviet planners found that the housing and other services needed to keep workers in Siberia were more expensive than their equivalents in European Russia because of the added construction costs in severe climatic conditions and the greater transportation costs involved in hauling goods and materials.

Since Soviet university graduates must serve three years in a job determined by the government in return for the free education they have received, it has become a widespread practice for planners to assign young engineers and technicians to hardship posts in remote areas that cannot normally be staffed because of a lack of applicants. After the three years of compulsory service are up, most young people are drawn back to the more comfortable jobs and living conditions of European Russia. The resulting turnover has become a major problem in the economic development of Siberia.

The difficulties of keeping people settled in Siberia have been a direct result of the increasing liberalization of life. For years, under Stalin, the strictest kind of labor legislation controlled employment practices. Under a 1940 law that was repealed only in 1956, three years after Stalin's death, no Soviet citizen working in the government-run sector of the economy— and that included almost all enterprises outside of collective farms—had the right to change jobs without his employer's permission. The abolition of these controls led to the present impasse over the peopling of Siberia. The government was no longer able to commandeer workers for areas that offered inferior working and living conditions. The authorities began to use other methods, such as wage incentives and longer vacations, to induce people to move to Siberian industry. So concerned has the government become with this problem that one of Siberia's research institutes, the Institute of the Economics and Organization of Production, in Novosibirsk, devoted several years to manpower surveys in Siberia to determine why people would not settle down. The investigators found that the higher wages paid in Siberia, compared with European Russia, were not enough to attract newcomers or to keep people from leaving. More important considerations, according to these surveys, were inferior housing, services, and other amenities compared with the more developed parts of European Russia.

The authorities discovered to their chagrin that in some years more people were leaving Siberia than arrived there, resulting in a net out-migration that was just barely balanced by the natural population increase within Siberia.

This is borne out by official Soviet statistics. In the seven-year period 1959–65, for example, the nation's total population rose by 11 per cent, from 209,000,000 people at the beginning of 1959 to 232,000,000 at the end of 1965. Since there is no significant migration across the Soviet Union's borders, this increase was entirely the result of the excess of births over deaths, or the natural rate of increase. During the same period the population of Siberia also rose by 11 per cent, from 22,500,000 to 25,000,000. The rate of natural increase in Siberia, with a relatively young population, is higher than the national average, so the increase over the seven-year period could have been expected to be higher than 11 per cent. The logical explanation is that whatever additional natural increase resulted from Siberia's young settlers was canceled out by an excess of departures over arrivals.

Why all this concern with the settlement of Siberia and the use of its resources? A good way to put that question in perspective is to examine briefly the physical geography of the Soviet Union and the factors that inhibit or promote its economic development. A vast country, three times the size of the continental United States and stretching almost halfway around the world through eleven time zones, the Soviet Union has large areas that are either too cold, like the Siberian forest, or too dry, like the Central Asian deserts, for agriculture. And it is agricultural settlement that basically determines the limits of human occupancy except for small industrial population clusters around outlying mines, lumber camps, and other nonfarming facilities. In the simplest terms, this crucial area of agricultural settlement in the Soviet Union takes the form of an elongated wedge that has its broad base on the western borders of the Soviet Union and extends eastward across the Ural Mountains into Siberia, where its point is pinched out between the Siberian forest in the north and the Central Asian deserts in the south. It is this settlement wedge that contains most of the nation's population, farms, and manufacturing, with some of the greatest concentrations in central European Russia, around Moscow, the historical core area of the country.

Politically, the Soviet Union is divided into fifteen so-called union republics, each of which has its own government, capital, and legislature, much like an American state or a Canadian province. The largest and most populous is the Russian Republic, which includes European Russia, west of the Ural Mountains, and Siberia, to the east. Around the Russian Republic are grouped fourteen republics of minority nationalities. They are the three Baltic republics (Lithuania, Latvia, Estonia) in the northwest, Byelorussia in the west, the Ukraine and Moldavia in the southwest, the three Trans-caucasian republics (Armenia, Azerbaijan, Georgia), and the five Central Asian republics (Kazakhstan, Uzbekistan, Kirghizia, Turkmenia, Tad-zhikistan).

The population core and agricultural wedge that make up the economic heart of the Soviet Union include the Baltic republics, Byelorussia, the Ukraine and Moldavia in addition to European Russia and then extend into Siberia to include the northern agricultural belt of Kazakhstan known as the virgin lands.

The industrial-resource problem and its relevance to Siberia arise in the following way: Although the European part of the Soviet Union ac-counts for most of the farm output and incorporates most of the population and manufacturing, it is, with a few exceptions, poor in the mineral fuels, energy resources, metals, and other raw materials that are the essentials of a modern economy based on heavy industry. Many of the resources lacking in European Russia are found in abundance in Siberia, where development and utilization are impeded by problems of human settlement. To over-simplify, the Soviet Union thus consists of two great regions: the thickly populated European Russia in the west, with the bulk of agriculture and industry but few basic resources, and the hostile Siberian environment in the east, with sparse population but valuable resources that are essential for continued industrial growth. The Soviet Union has now adopted policies to bring these resources into play effectively and economically. In discussing those policies, one is dealing with the basic resources that make a nation an economic power: mineral fuels like coal, oil, and natural gas; electrical energy, without which no modern economy can operate; iron and steel and other metals, the basic building blocks of machines, equipment, vehicles, and appliances; and chemicals, particularly petrochemicals and synthetics, which have been late starters in the Soviet Union.

One of the most dramatic upheavals in the U.S.S.R.'s use of resources took place in the 1950's in the area of mineral fuels as the economy shifted gears from a predominant use of coal to the utilization of cheaper and more efficient oil and natural gas. For more than two decades, ever since the Soviet authorities embarked upon their ambitious program of all-out in-dustrialization in the first five-year plan, the nation's complex economy had run almost exclusively on coal. The railroads, equipped almost entirely with steam locomotives, used coal; power plants burned coal to produce elec-trical energy; the modest chemical industry was based on the use of coal.

This reliance on coal stemmed from a number of factors. For one thing, coal deposits, though not always of the best quality, were widely distributed through the vast land and had been far better explored than the country's oil or gas resources. A second consideration was strategic. Encircled by a hostile world and anticipating, sooner or later, an armed attack, the Soviet authorities were concerned with decentralization of industry based on the use of local fuels and other resources. Since coal was the fuel most commonly found, it was the first to be marshaled for industrial use. Finally, the long preservation of the coal era stemmed also from the rigidity of the Soviet economic planning system. Influenced by early concepts of the Industrial Revolution that attributed a key role in economic development to coal, iron, and steel, Soviet decision makers of the 1930's and 1940's were slow to respond to technological innovations that brought the more flexible and transportable oil and gas to the forefront elsewhere in the world. While the United States, for example, was busily developing the oil and gas resources of its Gulf Coast by building refineries and pipeline systems, the Soviet Union continued to haul hundreds of millions of tons of coal over huge distances, adding greatly to the burden of an overloaded rail system and burning up one-sixth of the coal in transport alone. In the U.S.S.R. coal remained king through World War II and into the early postwar period.

Meanwhile, other developments were slowly laying the basis for a new age. Before World War II the only significant oil-production centers were the old Caucasus fields of Baku and Grozny, in operation since the late nineteenth century. These centers supplied refined products to the Soviet economy, then a modest consumer of petroleum derivatives, and even had a surplus for export. In 1942, when German armies drove into the Caucasus and threatened to seize the oil fields, geological-exploration teams shifted their attention to a promising region between the Volga and the Ural Mountains. As oil exploration was intensified there during the wartime emergency and after the war, productive field after productive field was uncovered, opening up new vistas for Soviet economic planners. The new Volga-Urals fields, at first dubbed the "Second Baku," soon far exceeded the output of the "first" Baku, which, though never reached by the Germans, had been seriously set back by a wartime production decline. Soaring output in the new fields enabled the Soviet Union to regain its prewar level by 1950, to double it by 1954, and to quadruple it by 1959. Two years later the U.S.S.R. was second among the world's oil producers, after the United States and ahead of Venezuela.

The fuel structure of the Soviet economy was completely transformed. Great pipeline systems, laid eastward from the Volga into Siberia and westward into European Russia, carried crude oil cheaply and efficiently over thousands of miles to newly built refineries, eliminating the expensive long hauls of coal. In addition to increasing domestic consumption of petroleum products by shifting power stations to the use of residual fuel oil and railroads to diesel locomotives, the soaring Soviet output left an increasingly large surplus for export, making a substantial dent in world markets. Out of total domestic production of 243,000,000 metric tons (1.7 billion barrels) in 1965, the Soviet Union exported 66,000,000 tons, two-thirds in the form of crude oil and one-third as refined products. Most of the exports went to other Communist countries in East Europe and to Cuba, but substantial quantities also moved to Italy, Scandinavia, West Germany, Japan, India, and even Brazil. Although the great Volga fields continue to dominate the Soviet oil scene, new rivals began to emerge in the middle 1960's. Vast reserves were discovered and began to be utilized in the remote Siberian forests of the Ob River Basin and in the arid desert of the Mangyshlak Peninsula on the Caspian Sea. In both cases, inhospitable natural environment is expected to slow development, but after power lines, railroads, and adequate housing and services have been provided, the newly discovered deposits should provide additional oil for the expanding Soviet economy.

The oil era also ushered in a gas era. Natural gas production, virtually non-existent before World War II, slowly picked up in the 1940's as geologists uncovered gas fields in their search for petroleum. The first pipelines from the fields discovered at Saratov, on the Volga, and from the Carpathian foothills in the Ukraine supplied the new fuel to Moscow for use only by the Soviet capital's domestic consumers. Economic planners were still too dedicated to coal to think about the wide range of industrial applications for gas.

It was only in the 1950's, when intensive exploration yielded vast reserves in many parts of the country, that natural gas began to be used for power generation, for improving the performance of iron and steel furnaces, and as a chemical raw material. Some of the gas fields were situated in European Russia, close to consuming centers. Other great reserves were found thousands of miles away in the deserts of Central Asia and the arctic tundra of northwestern Siberia. To transport the valuable gas to European Russia, the Soviet authorities drew up a program for the laying of mighty transmission mains using pipe of forty-inch diameter or more over thousands of miles of desert and forest, across streams and mountain ranges. The first gas main from the Central Asian fields near Bukhara to the industrial region of the Urals was completed in 1963 and was followed by a parallel line two years later. As the fiftieth anniversary of the Bolshevik Revolution approached, pipeline-construction teams were completing the first of a series of transmission mains from the deserts of Central Asia to Moscow and preparations were under way for a pipeline system from the new arctic fields to Leningrad, the Baltic republics, and Byelorussia.

The coming of oil and gas had far-reaching results. The use of coal, though still high in absolute terms (590,000,000 metric tons in 1967), declined sharply relative to oil and gas. Coal accounted for two-thirds of all Soviet fuels in its heyday in the 1940's, when an item like firewood was still as important as oil (15 per cent each), a low-quality fuel such as peat contributed 5 per cent, and gas a negligible 2 per cent. In 1967 the share of coal in fuel production had dropped to about 40 per cent, and oil and gas combined accounted for 55 per cent. Fuel oil and natural gas assumed an increasingly important role in power generation; petrochemicals and natural gas created an entirely new basis for the chemical industry, replacing the costly and less efficient coal-based chemicals. A broad program of dieselization and electrification of the Soviet rail system that began in the middle 1950's reduced the role of steam traction to 15 per cent by 1965, cutting coal consumption on the railroads. In addition, the Russians made more efficient use of coal, particularly of surface coal accessible by strip-mining operations, by burning it in huge pit-head electric generating plants and transmitting the power by long-distance lines to consumers. Uneconomical underground mines were shut down, and for the first time in the history of Soviet economic planning the authorities had to concern themselves with the development of alternative industries in the old coal-mining towns to provide employment for the former miners.

In the electric-power industry, too, a revolution took place in the 1950's. Under the previous policy of industrial decentralization, motivated in part by the desire to lessen strategic vulnerability, Soviet planners had encouraged the construction of small power stations, each serving a single industrial plant or a limited area within a radius of fifty to one hundred miles. This pattern of development, while adequate in the early stages of industrialization, no longer suited the requirements of an increasingly complex economy after World War II.

On the eve of the war the Soviet Union produced about as much electricity as is now being generated by Norway or Sweden (48,000,000 kilowatt-hours a year). Although the Russians doubled their power output by 1950, after the postwar recovery, it was still short of the needs of a modern economy. It was primarily to meet those needs that the small-stations policy was abandoned in the middle 1950's for a system of huge generating centers that would burn cheap fuels and be linked by high-voltage transmission lines to industrial consumers. This change in policy was made possible by a number of factors. First, there was the new availability of oil and natural gas, low-cost, efficient fuels that could be transported cheaply by pipeline to power-station sites. Secondly, there had been a decision in the coal industry to develop previously untouched deposits of low-grade brown coal in Siberia for use in big power complexes at the mine sites. Thirdly, there were advances in technology that enabled Soviet industry to manufacture the huge turbines and generators needed for the big power stations and the high-voltage lines required for economical long-distance transmission of large amounts of electricity.

Just as Siberia offered rich resources of oil and natural gas for transmission by pipeline to the manufacturing and population centers of European Russia, Siberia was also looked upon as a storehouse of electric power for the western part of the country. In addition to the accessible brown-coal deposits for use in steam-electric stations, Siberia offered rivers with the greatest hydroelectric potential in the Soviet Union. Foremost among them were the Yenisei, flowing through the entire breadth of Siberia to the Arctic Ocean, and its tributary the Angara. The latter was particularly suitable for water-power development because it was the outlet of Lake Baikal, a natural storage reservoir that insured year-round flow without the seasonal stream-level fluctuations that often interfere with a regular power supply from hydroelectric stations.

Before the Russians tackled the development of the tremendous water-power potential of the Siberian streams, they had already made use of water resources in European Russia, particularly along the Volga and Dnieper rivers. The construction of a whole series of power dams along these two rivers began in the 1930's, but except for the well-known 560,000-kilowatt Dnieper station, inaugurated in 1932 with American assistance, the early stations were relatively small installations. It was only after World War II that increased industrial capacity enabled the Russians to attempt bigger projects. Two giant stations on the Volga River, ordered built by Stalin in 1950, exceeded the size of the Grand Coulee project, the largest water-power complex in the United States. The first big Volga station, at Kuibyshev, with a generating capacity of 2,300,000 kilowatts, began operations in 1955, followed three years later by the Volgograd dam, with a capacity of 2,500,000 kilowatts.

However, it remained for the great Siberian streams to generate even more electric power. After a relatively small hydro station had been completed at Irkutsk, on the Angara River, in 1956, with a capacity of only 660,000 kilowatts, the Russians proceeded to build the largest water-power-producing complex yet attempted. This was the Bratsk dam, situated farther downstream along the Angara River. With a planned capacity of 4,500,000 kilowatts, it is twice the size of the big Volga stations. The first generators at Bratsk began producing power in 1961, and by 1967 all but the last two had been installed, providing a total capacity of 4,050,000 kilowatts. By the fiftieth anniversary of Soviet rule, the Bratsk dam builders had already moved downstream to begin work on the next project, at Ust-Ilim, where another big dam the size of Bratsk is under construction.

Meanwhile, other teams were busy on the Yenisei River at even larger power projects. At the Krasnoyarsk dam, just above the Trans-Siberian rail city of the same name, workers were planning to celebrate the anniversary of the Bolshevik Revolution by installing the first two 500,000-kilowatt generators, the world's largest power-producing units. (The Bratsk dam used 225,000-kilowatt generators.) The great generators, of which twelve are ultimately to be mounted at Krasnoyarsk, for a total capacity of 6,000,000 kilowatts, had to be shipped to the dam site during the brief ice-free summer navigation season on specially constructed barges that carried them from the manufacturing plants in Leningrad up into the Arctic and along the Siberian coast to the Yenisei River. On the Yenisei, too, even before the completion of the Krasnoyarsk project, preparations were under way to build a second power complex of equal size upstream near Shushenskoye, where Lenin was once exiled, at a natural hydroelectric site where the mighty stream comes rushing out of a gorge cut through the Sayan Mountains.

It is to these great power projects that planners are now looking for a major Siberian contribution to the Soviet economy. The power stations are expected to supply vast amounts of cheap electricity for so-called energy-oriented industries that are economical only where low-cost power is available. These power-hungry industries include the electrolytic refining of aluminum, magnesium, and titanium—lightweight metals with a growing role in aerospace development—and a number of synthetic chemical processes. Because of the low cost of Siberia's hydroelectric power and the large amounts required in these industries, Soviet planners find it economical to ship raw materials thousands of miles eastward to this electrical workshop of the Soviet Union and then ship the finished products back thousands of miles for consumption in European Russia. In the long run, Siberia's power plants are expected to have a surplus of electricity that must be transmitted westward to European Russia.

Because of this, Soviet power technologists have been in the forefront of research and experimentation on economical extra-long-distance transmission lines. They have done pioneer work in particular with the use of direct-current systems, which are more economical than the traditional high-voltage alternating-current lines for transmitting very large amounts of electricity over very long distances. In 1962, while serving as a correspondent of *The New York Times* in Moscow, I accompanied a delegation of United States power officials, led by Stewart L. Udall, Secretary of the Interior, on an inspection tour of the Soviet Union's big dams and transmission lines. The Americans expressed particular interest in Soviet development of the D.C. transmission system, which also has grid-interconnection applications in the United States—for example, between the hydroelectric-power producers of the Pacific Northwest and the consuming centers of California. At the Volga River dam at Volgograd (formerly Stalingrad), the United States officials bombarded their hosts with technical questions about an experimental eight-hundred-kilovolt D.C. line that was about to be inaugurated between Volgograd and the heavy-industry district of the Donets Basin, several hundred miles to the west. This experimental line serves as a testing device for future systems that are expected to carry Siberian power westward to European Russia at even higher voltages and over considerably greater distances.

While the Soviet Union was struggling to convert its antiquated coal-dominated economy to the use of more efficient oil and gas, a transition made twenty to twenty-five years earlier in the United States, developments in its iron and steel industry did not show a similar lag. In both the United States and the U.S.S.R., the two leading steel-producing nations, high-grade iron resources, the so-called direct-shipping ores that can go from mine directly to blast furnace, approached depletion during World War II and in the early postwar period, and ways had to be found to make use of lower-grade materials.

In the United States the best ores of the Lake Superior iron ranges had been mined, and a technology was developed in the 1950's to start mining limitless reserves of an iron-bearing rock called taconite that required upgrading for blast-furnace use. Similarly, in the Soviet Union, the richest and most accessible ores of the Krivoi Rog Basin of the Ukraine had been gradually exhausted, and as mining operations penetrated more deeply underground the ore was found to be of increasingly lower quality. Like the Mesabi Range of the Lake Superior district, the Ukrainian iron basin also had tremendous reserves of lower-grade iron-bearing rock, in this case iron quartzites, which could be mined by open-pit operations but needed upgrading. Again, like the Americans, the Russians found that modern technology was a match for the problem and that ores once regarded as valueless could provide an economical basis for a major expansion of the iron and steel industry.

In fact, the Krivoi Rog Basin was selected as the site for one of the nation's largest mills. It will be second only to the Magnitogorsk plant in the Urals, which now produces about 10,000,000 tons of pig iron a year following the installation of a tenth blast furnace in 1966. With the shift

[234]

to low-grade iron ores, which are being upgraded at five huge concentrating plants, the Krivoi Rog Basin is expected to continue to supply about half of the Soviet Union's iron and steel industry with ore. The mill in the Krivoi Rog Basin is scheduled to reach a capacity of 8,000,000 tons of pig iron in the late 1960's, and in addition Krivoi Rog iron ore will continue to move to mills along the Dnieper River and, farther east, to iron and steel plants in the Donets Basin, the principal producer of that other ingredient of the iron and steel industry—coking coal.

In the Urals, too, rich iron ores have become increasingly depleted, including the "magnetic mountain" that gave its name to Magnitogorsk, and Soviet planners have had to look to other sources to feed the ravenous furnaces not only at Magnitogorsk but also at Chelyabinsk and Nizhni Tagil to the north. Low-grade ores and upgrading were again the answer. At Kachkanar, near Nizhni Tagil, a vast deposit of iron ore that contains vanadium, an important steel alloy, was developed, and open-pit operations began in 1963. Another low-grade deposit, put into production in the late 1950's at Rudny (Ore-town) in the adjoining steppe of Kazakhstan, was already shipping usable concentrate to the Magnitogorsk and Chelyabinsk mills. An ore supply for the Urals iron and steel industry, which accounts for about one-third of the country's output, was assured. Lesser iron and steel centers have been constructed in the Kuznetsk Basin of Siberia, the Karaganda Basin of Kazakhstan, Cherepovets in northern European Russia, and Lipetsk in the central industrial region south of Moscow, but the Ukraine and the Urals are expected to continue to provide the bulk of the Soviet Union's iron and steel. Productivity is being increased not only by greater use of raw materials but also by larger blast furnaces; the U.S.S.R. was completing the world's biggest, with a working volume of 95,000 cubic feet, in the Krivoi Rog mill in time for the fiftieth anniversary of the revolution. Additional aids are the use of natural gas and oxygen blast to speed smelting and save coke and the increasing introduction of continuous casting machines, which bypass several stages of the traditional steel-making process.

Although technological improvements have often been introduced more or less simultaneously in the United States and the Soviet Union, the resource-development policies of the two nations have been far apart in one respect. The United States has found it cheaper in many cases to import essential minerals from abroad than to develop low-grade domestic resources. Stockpiles of strategic commodities are being maintained for emergencies, but basically the United States relies on foreign sources for many key minerals. In the security-conscious Soviet Union the emphasis has been on domestic resources, both to develop the country industrially and to avoid reliance on foreign sources. Although virtually every mineral with industrial applications can be found in one form or another in the vast territory of the U.S.S.R., many deposits are of low grade and require costly processing. Because of this the Russians have often been leaders in developing the required technology, as in the case of iron ore. Even when some minerals were imported—for example, tin and tungsten, from China—an all-out effort was made to develop domestic supplies. In the case of tin and gold, this often meant opening up mining complexes under the most adverse natural conditions, as in northeasternmost Siberia, near the Bering Strait, where the winter lasts eight and nine months and bitter cold frequently prevents all outdoor work. As the Soviet-Chinese rift deepened in the 1960's, Peking's shipments of some strategic commodities to the Soviet Union were cut back sharply, and the Russians had reason to congratulate themselves on their foresight in developing their own resources, even if at a high cost.

An essential group of metals in steelmaking are the so-called alloying elements, which impart special qualities like strength, toughness, or resistance to corrosion to the steels with which they are alloyed. In two of these metals, manganese and chromium, the Soviet Union leads the world, possessing more than enough for its own needs. Manganese, mined in Soviet Georgia and the Ukraine, used to be shipped from Black Sea ports to the United States until the Cold War sharply reduced Soviet-American trade in the late 1940's. The United States has since met its needs by importing manganese from a number of sources—Brazil, India, Ghana, South Africa —and the Soviet Union has become less important in the world's manganese trade. It ships about 1,000,000 tons a year, out of a total production of 7,000,000 to 8,000,000 tons, mainly to its allies in Eastern Europe and some of the steelmaking nations of Western Europe. Soviet chromium, which accounts for about one-third of world production, still moves to the United States. In the middle 1960's the United States has been purchasing more than 200,000 tons a year from the Soviet Union, or about one-third of Soviet chromium exports. In the case of other alloying materials— nickel, molybdenum, cobalt, vanadium—the Soviet Union is less abundantly endowed but has been meeting its basic needs, even if this means mining and smelting low-grade ores in harsh environments, as in the nickel-cobalt area of Norilsk in northern Siberia, where a city of 150,000 people has been built in the arctic tundra.

In the base metals—copper, lead, and zinc—the U.S.S.R. has also succeeded in meeting its needs and has, in fact, an exportable surplus for its allies in Eastern Europe. Emphasis has been placed on the production of aluminum, magnesium, and titanium. In aluminum the Soviet Union has pioneered the use of raw materials other than bauxite, the traditional ore, of which it has a relatively low supply. The Russians are now producing alumina, the intermediate product in aluminum-making, from lower-grade ores such as nephelite and alunite, compensating for the higher cost of processing these ores by recovering useful by-products like cement, soda, and potash. Total production of aluminum, estimated at more than 1,000,-000 tons, appears to be substantially in excess of needs, judging from exports equal to one-fifth of total production in 1965. For its nuclear-energy and weapons programs the Soviet Union has developed an adequate supply of uranium since the early 1950's, with producing centers concentrated in the Tien Shan mountain system of Central Asia. Uranium is also recovered from the Krivoi Rog iron basin of the Ukraine and from oil-shale deposits in Estonia.

The Russians have been late starters in the chemical field, largely because of the lag in developing their oil and gas resources as a basis for the modern production of petrochemicals, synthetic rubber, synthetic fibers, and plastics. The changes that resulted from the increased use of oil and gas can best be illustrated by the synthetic-rubber industry. Lacking natural rubber, which requires a tropical climate nonexistent in the Soviet Union, and reluctant to rely on imports, the Russians were among the first to develop the manufacture of synthetic rubber. To produce the industrial alcohol required to make butadiene, one of the components of synthetic rubber, the Soviet planners had to rely on potatoes and grain. The diversion of many millions of tons of potential food and animal feed to produce alcohol for synthetic rubber ate into the grain supply, already tight because of the low productivity of agriculture. It was only the expansion of the petrochemical industry and the associated production of synthetic alcohol from oil-refinery gases that gradually freed millions of tons of grain for use as livestock feed. By 1965 no more edible farm products were being diverted into the making of synthetic rubber. This not only helped ease the farm situation, but also lowered production costs.

The chemical revolution linked to the new oil and gas age also had a direct bearing on the increasingly consumer-oriented economy. While modern chemicals have a key role to play in heavy industry—for example, as a substitute for metals in short supply—they also make possible a substantial increase in the production of consumer goods through the use of synthetic fibers and plastics. The production of man-made fibers quadrupled in the decade 1955–65, offering a wider range of cheap raw materials for the expanding consumer market. The new emphasis on chemicals also resulted in the expansion of fertilizers, which had been in short supply in the early decades of the Soviet regime. The newly available natural gas provided a cheaper and more efficient raw material for ammonia synthesis and the production of nitrogenous fertilizers, which increased fourfold from 1958 to 1965. And improved manufacturing techniques increased the concentration and effectiveness of fertilizers.

In the fiftieth year of Soviet rule, the U.S.S.R., more intent on spending its rubles wisely, was thus on its way to a more modern economy. An exaggerated dependence on coal as the wherewithal of industry was giving way to a more sophisticated use of mineral fuels, especially oil and natural gas. Big central power stations linked by an increasingly intricate grid system made it possible to use energy resources more efficiently, shifting blocks of power from one area to another as needed. Technological advances permitted the economical use of low-grade resources for an expanding industrial capacity. The resources of Siberia—gas, oil, low-cost hydroelectric power—were being marshaled increasingly to supplement the poor supply of fuels and energy in the great manufacturing centers of European Russia. And, perhaps most important, a rational population pattern was being achieved by keeping the manpower in Siberia and other hostile environments to the minimum needed for resource development and concentrating labor-oriented manufacturing in the densely inhabited economic core areas of European Russia.

POPULATION OF THE SOVIET UNION AND ITS REPUBLICS
(in millions)

	1913*	Jan. 1, 1940		Jan. 1, 1967	
Russian Republic	89.9	110.1		127.3	
European Russia	n.d.		82.4		86.6
Urals	n.d.		10.5		15.4
Siberia	n.d.		17.2		25.3
Ukraine	35.2	41.3		46.0	
Byelorussia	6.9	9.1		8.7	
Moldavia	2.1	2.5		3.4	
Baltic Republics					
Estonia	1.0	1.1		1.3	
Latvia	2.5	1.9		2.3	
Lithuania	2.8	2.9		3.0	
Transcaucasian Republics					
Armenia	1.0	1.3		2.3	
Azerbaijan	2.3	3.3		4.8	
Georgia	2.6	3.6		4.6	
Central Asian Republics					
Kazakhstan	5.6	6.1		12.4	
Uzbekistan	4.4	6.6		10.9	
Kirghizia	0.9	1.5		2.8	
Tadzhikistan	1.0	1.5		2.7	
Turkmenia	1.0	1.3		2.0	
TOTAL FOR U.S.S.R.	159.2	194.1		234.4	

* Figures for 1913, the last peacetime year before World War I and the Bolshevik Revolution, are for territory now occupied by the Soviet republics.

n.d. means no data.

Totals are not exact because the figures have been rounded off.

POPULATION OF MAJOR SOVIET CITIES (OVER 500,000)
(*in thousands*)

City	Description	1939	1967
Moscow	Capital of U.S.S.R.	4,137	6,507
Leningrad	Capital of the czars	3,385	3,665
Kiev	Ukrainian capital	847	1,417
Tashkent	Uzbek capital	550	1,241
Baku	Azerbaijan oil city	775	1,196
Kharkov	Ukrainian industrial hub	833	1,125
Gorky	Russia's "Detroit"	644	1,120
Novosibirsk	Biggest city in Siberia	404	1,064
Kuibyshev	Volga oil center	390	992
Sverdlovsk	Industrial city in Urals	423	961
Tbilisi	Capital of Georgia	519	842
Donetsk	Coal-mining center	466	841
Chelyabinsk	Industrial city in Urals	273	835
Kazan	Capital of Volga Tatars	398	821
Dnepropetrovsk	Ukrainian industrial hub	527	817
Perm	Industrial city in Urals	306	796
Odessa	Black Sea port	602	776
Omsk	Siberian industrial city	289	774
Minsk	Capital of Byelorussia	237	772
Rostov-on-Don	South Russian city	510	756
Volgograd	The former Stalingrad	445	743
Saratov	Volga River city	372	720
Ufa	Urals oil center	258	704
Riga	Capital of Latvia	348	680
Yerevan	Armenian capital	204	665
Alma-Ata	Capital of Kazakhstan	222	653
Voronezh	Central Russian city	344	611
Zaporozhye	Dnieper dam city	282	596
Krasnoyarsk	Siberian industrial hub	190	576
Lvov	West Ukrainian city	340	512
Krivoi Rog	Ukrainian steel center	189	511

The following republic capitals have fewer than 500,000 population

City	Description	1939	1967
Frunze	Kirghizia	93	396
Tallinn	Estonia	160	340
Dushanbe	Tadzhikistan	83	332
Vilnius	Lithuania	215	317
Kishinev	Moldavia	112	302
Ashkhabad	Turkmenia	127	238

BUILDING THE SOVIET SOCIETY: HOUSING AND PLANNING

»

Ada Louise Huxtable

"When you are trying desperately to clothe people, you don't worry about sewing all the buttons on." That was the way a Soviet housing official characterized the Gargantuan construction program that has turned the open fields around Moscow and other Soviet cities into a white expanse of standardized residential blocks and created new urban centers from Siberia to the Black Sea. He was describing the most concentrated, large-scale attack on the housing problem and on the industrialization of building anywhere in the world at any time in history.

A purely Soviet phenomenon, and a direct result of the Soviet system, this building program has no parallel of any kind in the United States. In size, scope, and boldness, with all of its daring experiments and all-too-obvious flaws (construction has frequently been quick, crude, and untrained), it is undoubtedly one of the most significant undertakings of the twentieth century. It has already reshaped one-sixth of the world's inhabited land surface, the third most populous country, and one of the two great powers of the modern world.

I faced the Soviet official, Nikolai F. Yevstratov, head of the Institute of the General Plan of Moscow, across the inevitable T-shaped arrangement of desk and conference table on a recent visit to Moscow, sharing the usual bottles of fruit soda, under the ritual portrait of Lenin. (The portraits vary from rigid realism to sophisticated sketches, a clue to the taste of the office's occupant grasped eagerly by the Western visitor.) We were in one of the city's uncountable government buildings, shabby, musty, with a precarious lift and peeling walls, the decaying entrance guarded by a little old lady in kerchief and carpet slippers. Almost all of these buildings are slated for demolition in the "reconstruction" of the city.

Yevstratov was right. Buttons are off all over the Soviet Union. Construction has left a trail of popping tiles and falling cornices. Even in nearly new buildings, the finishes flake, the joints leak, and the edges meet haphazardly. Western observers report it all. What they fail to report is the story behind the flaws: a remarkable advance in building technology in an incredibly short time—the last decade, to be exact—on a scale that is leaving other countries far behind, and the significance of a fifty-year experiment in turning an agricultural country into an industrial country. This has meant an urban society and cities—instant cities and instant housing.

Starting from virtually nothing, the job has been done. It has been delayed by war, defense and military spending, and the emphasis on heavy industrialization of the Soviet Union's first forty years, which pushed housing and consumer needs to a back burner. Little was built that did not serve direct state purposes. What simmered, chiefly, were shortages. If today the architectural norm is considerably less than Western and, to the Western eye, skills are still lacking, the results of the postwar Soviet building boom are no less important. The Soviet experiment in constructing a society physically as well as socially and economically is a fascinating chapter in the history of man's struggle with his environment.

What I found, in the fiftieth year of the Bolshevik Revolution, was a startling breakthrough in Soviet building. The products of the new technology are not only better built, but are moving rapidly toward stylistic sophistication. These results have been exactly ten years in the making. Since 1957, with the release of more state resources to the building industry and the assignment of top priority to housing construction, there has been a concentrated development of design and production techniques. Much has been trial and error, and the errors are visible all over the Soviet landscape. But what has been achieved is the industrialization of building on a national scale. There is now country-wide mass production of standardized, precast, prestressed, reinforced-concrete elements that can be preassembled in the factory and erected on any site in minimum time with minimum labor. The means are co-ordinated factories and site assembly. The spur has been need, limited building skills, and a state-directed program.

In much of the rest of the world, and notably in the United States, construction is still in the handicraft age. The significance of quickly, cheaply, and industrially produced building in a time of universal housing shortages and the spread of urban slums should not be underestimated. Neither should the Soviet advances in this field. They constitute a kind of architectural Sputnik.

This is not apparent to the casual observer of Moscow's new sky line. But even the untrained eye can instantly see that modern architecture has come to the Soviet Union. It is doubly surprising because the popular image of Soviet building has been formed by the familiar pictures of the crumbling five-story walk-ups of the 1950's and those identical, pompous, neoclassical skyscrapers, seven out of the same giant cake mold, that dominated the Stalin-era Moscow view. They are rather funny now, those pretentious all-purpose mock-Roman wedding cakes, accommodating with equal ludicrousness the university, the Hotel Ukraina, the Soviet Foreign Ministry, apartments, or whatever; they are acquiring the status of period pieces. One is amused, rather than outraged, partly because the balance of the sky line is changing so radically.

The wedding cakes face striking competition today: the new Kalinin Prospekt, at least a third of a mile of dramatic modern skyscrapers in a co-ordinated urban design; the svelte, thirty-two-story Council of Mutual Economic Assistance Building, being put up jointly by the U.S.S.R. and Eastern European countries; a slender, 1,745-foot-high reinforced-concrete television tower; the nearly completed new headquarters of Gosplan, the state planning agency that directs all aspects of Soviet life, soaring behind Gorky Street's traditional façades. Sixteen-story apartment houses are now standard. The steel, glass, and marble Palace of Congresses, the first indication of this radical change of architectural course, has stood inside the historic Kremlin since 1961. Its break with the past is still a subject of lively controversy.

The new buildings are increasingly sleek, assured, uncompromisingly contemporary versions of the international style. Reactionary Soviet pseudo-classicism is a thing of the past. Finishes, although still far from Western standards, are improving noticeably. More important, with a few exceptions the distinctive style of the new work is the result of the Soviet system of large-scale prefabrication.

By Soviet count, 393,000,000 square meters (about 4 billion square feet) of new housing space was constructed in cities and towns in the five-year period 1961–65. With the usual optimistic upgrading, 1966–70 is expected to produce 480,000,000 square meters. Two million houses were built in rural areas from 1961 to 1965.

In Moscow, a city of 6,500,000, 230,000 new apartments are completed every year. The new southwest district, begun on the city's outskirts fifteen years ago, already accommodates one and a half million residents. The newest section, Novye Cheryomushki, occupies 1,500 hectares (about 3,700 acres) and houses 170,000 people. The buildings rise like a scaleless white mirage out of the flat green fields. Across the sixty-eight-mile ring road that now marks the city limits of Moscow, a new 220,000-hectare (543,620-acre) district is planned. It will contain five neighborhood units of 1,000 apartments each, called "living groups," with social, educational, cultural, and commercial services for each group, in a mixture of low and high-rise buildings.

Leningrad claims 50,000 new apartments annually. Tbilisi, the former Tiflis, capital of the Georgian Republic, gives a 9,500 figure and aims for 10,000. Similar statistics are at every city Soviet's finger tips.

The importance of what is being done is summed up by an American, not a Soviet, official. Dr. A. Allan Bates, chief of the office of industrial standards of the United States Bureau of Standards, who has watched the experiment closely, said: "The Russians can now produce a four-room apartment of acceptable quality for the equivalent of $3,000 to $3,500. It would cost $10,000 here. What the Soviet Union has done is to develop the only technology in the world to produce acceptable low-cost housing on a large scale."

I brought two standard preconceptions about this housing to the Soviet Union. In addition to the image of styleless buildings falling apart virtually on completion, I had been primed for the well-advertised monotony of the new housing developments. I learned quickly, because it soon becomes so obvious, that things are measured differently by the Russians, and what is sterility to us is bliss to them. Comparing their present standard of living with the immediate past, and against still-existing conditions, this is quite understandable. It is pointless to measure against the American way of life. There is no meaningful basis of comparison. This does not mean that what they have does not need to be vastly improved (they know it), or to deny that the American standard of living is infinitely better. It means that judgments must be made in perspective.

That perspective can be quickly and painfully established by a fairly typical Moscow example. A middle-class apartment of six rooms, built about 1910, might have been occupied by a single family of a mother, father, and two children as late as 1920. In the early 1920's, with the influx of population to the cities and the deterioration of the housing stock, that family would have been reduced to three rooms. The other three rooms would have been shared, at first by relatives. By the mid-1920's, as housing shortages increased, the six rooms were occupied by six families, using the communal kitchen and bathroom. After World War II, with its mass destruction of housing, there were thirty-five people in these same six rooms. Fragments of families shared rooms; all shared the one inadequate, refrigeratorless kitchen and antiquated bath and toilet. Waiting for the single stove, some cooked all night for the next day's meals. Conditions were unspeakable; maintenance was a losing battle; it was a nightmare existence.

Against this background, it is no wonder that the Soviet concept of paradise is still the dated public-housing ideal of the 1930's: a home for all—in what continues to be the most critical housing shortage to be found anywhere—in rigidly regular, wide-spaced residential rows with lots of trees and green space between. Buildings are lined up on very broad, straight, bowling-alley streets, with more grass and trees down the middle.

Each "neighborhood" is uniformly predictable. About 20,000 people are serviced by kindergartens, schools, a laundry, nursery, commercial center, cinema, and café. There are "experimental" neighborhoods, and when they have proved themselves they will be predictable, too. (In all fairness, it should be said that American mass suburbia is equally predictable and equally monotonous.) The clean but uniform results in Soviet residential neighborhoods make Western visitors miserable and Soviet citizens ecstatic. There are complaints about far-from-perfect accommodations, but there are few sophisticated criticisms of planning. At least the mistake was never made of eliminating shops from the ground floors, as was done in New York public housing, even when the Russians had little to put in them.

This lifeless model of public planning is admittedly no longer adequate. It is certainly inadequate for an advanced, affluent country like the United States, where such developments, often with less design merit but more spacious apartments, form the hard core for the underprivileged and the alienated. In Russia, in the newest accommodations, the lucky families, who were previously doubled and tripled in communal quarters, are as happy as clams. The standard will be obsolete once the acute housing crisis begins to ease and living conditions improve. Housing in preparation now for 1970 has larger rooms and better layouts. Neighborhoods are being more carefully studied, although still with doctrinaire formality. Architects and planners are aware that their biggest future problem—creating a more varied and enriched environment with their standardized, industrialized buildings—is already outlined with alarming clarity. At least one architect spoke feelingly of the new districts as "dead."

On the other hand, there is a surprising pleasure in conformity, a contentment with regimentation in the Soviet system and philosophy, that militates against the variety, human scale, and individualism that are desirable to the Western mind. There is also a surprising pride—so much has been struggled for, so much is hard won—that makes Soviet cities and public spaces, in spite of monotony or shabbiness, well kept. Perhaps rubbish is a by-product of the affluent society. Or perhaps New York needs a thousand little women with twig brooms, a common sight in Moscow. But Russians love and respect things big, new, and standardized, and in mass multiples of thousands—the biggest swimming pools, the biggest stadiums, the biggest housing developments, and, now, the biggest theaters and hotels. In one of those curious paradoxes that pop up all over the Soviet Union, the enchantment with size has a peculiarly American ring.

Russia is rich in paradoxes. The new skyscrapers are within spitting distance of those small wooden houses with fretwork window decoration that foreigners find so picturesque and Russians find so shameful. The Russians know the interior conditions of these houses and the foreigners do not. Still, some are gems of the art of building in wood, and their eradication will be a severe architectural loss.

While some workers may not be able to get a fascia straight on Moscow's new Rossiya Hotel (an air-conditioned nightmare for 6,000), others are masters of the delicate application of gold leaf in the preservation of historic monuments. At the same time that leaky joints in new buildings are caulked with what looks like massive doses of bubble gum, the most painstaking reconstruction of the war-damaged czarist palace proceeds at Peterhof, now called Petrodvorets, and Leningrad's classic eighteenth-century monuments are surrounded by restoration scaffolding by the mile. The very limited building skills of a nation devoted to the improvement of the worker's lot are going into the upkeep of czarist treasures, which, the people are reminded daily, belong to them. The fact that even with a continuing severe housing crisis preservation of a magnificent historic heritage has top priority is another paradox, and one overwhelmingly to the country's credit.

The paradoxes sometimes border on black humor, which one suspects may have been a "Russian" invention that they have not yet claimed. Luxury hotels have no sink stoppers. In vast prerevolutionary dining rooms the rhythm of twenty-foot marble columns is punctuated by a parade of naked white 1935-type refrigerators marching down the room between them in solemn kitchen splendor. Linen and menus are permanent. Triple sets of formal cut-glass stemware stand at every place, suggesting Lucullan banquets, while the customer plays a waiting game. The waiter outwaits him. Strangers sit and starve together, cafeteria style. Misery needs company.

The most modern aircraft appear to have interiors run up by home dressmakers inspired by a 1930 Greyhound bus, sprinkled with the rose petals of farewell bouquets. The slim, elegant, richly costumed dancers on the Bolshoi or Kirov stages seem of a race different from the stolid, square-cut pedestrians outside. Favorite performances re-create a fairy tale of larger than life czarist splendor. In the dedicated pursuit of equality for all there are privileges for many—and a class consciousness surprising to Americans.

It is often an upside-down world to the Western eye. But it is a world that must be understood, and to learn how it is being built and who conceives, designs, and executes it and controls its form and structure I spoke to the heads of many government agencies.

The prime shapers inhabit the huge administrative complex of Gosstroy, the State Construction Committee, which unites construction, architecture, and the building industry for the whole country. They range from the State Committee for Civil Construction and Architecture, at the top of the design pyramid, to a legion of special institutes for special tasks. Of particular interest are the Institute of Town Planning, which locates and lays out all new communities in the Soviet Union; the Scientific Research and Design Institute of Standard and Experimental Design, which devotes much of its attention to the development of housing, and the Research Institute of Concrete and Reinforced Concrete, dedicated to the technology of concrete manufacture and production of building elements. There is, naturally, no obstacle to government research in the building field, except for the juggling of fund allocations that must be done in any national budget. Since the state not only does the research but also builds, the application of developments is assured. The conditions for rationally planned building are optimum. To date, unfortunately, the results are not, although current construction progress is impressive. The planning of communities is desolate to Western eyes, and has a long way to go.

Each city has its building and planning administrations under the city Soviet. In Moscow, for example, there are organizations with names like the Central Department of Planning and Design, the Central Department of Building Materials, and the Central Department for Moscow Construction. Each department has many subdepartments and all are co-ordinated at the top.

The Central Department of Planning and Design takes care of the studies of the future of Moscow (the Institute of the General Plan of Moscow bases its work on that framework), the city's housing design, special building design, and the design of parks, street furniture, restaurants, shops, and so on. It is the heaviest in concentration of architects. The Central

Department of Building Materials controls production of building supplies. The Central Department for Moscow Construction is the most interesting to the outsider, for it deals with the special construction practices that have been developed to control and co-ordinate everything from prefabrication of building parts in the factory to erection of the building on the site. Approximately 300,000 people are said to work in these three main departments concerned with Moscow planning and building.

For rough comparative purposes, approximately 19,000 people work in New York City's Planning, Housing and Redevelopment, Public Housing, and Public Works departments, which handle public construction only. These are the main agencies, although some public work filters out through other departments. Public construction amounts to about 30 per cent of the city's building total, with the rest done by the private sector.

It is sometimes hard for the visitor to the Soviet Union to grasp the obvious: the state does all building, everywhere, with one significant exception. About 20 per cent of Soviet housing is now constructed as co-operatives, undertaken by labor groups or professional unions, using government loans. The advantages of this are shortened waiting time for apartments, some stepping up of the housing supply, and a few more amenities inside. The houses are frequently of conventional construction, because the state prefabrication factories are greatly tied up in national production. With these, one has a "personal" apartment, as one may have "personal" savings or a "personal" automobile, or a dacha, a "personal" country house. The word "private" is studiously avoided. The country houses, still a privilege of the better-paid or otherwise favored, are also frequently co-operatively constructed. One Moscow group is importing Finnish prefabs for them.

Aside from the aforementioned, all construction is state controlled. It has brought standardization to such places as fabled Ashkhabad and Tashkent, hard hit by earthquakes, to mountain tribes of the republic of Georgia, who have been moved out of picturesque poverty to lower elevations and state housing, and to the permafrost areas of Siberia. Some of the more amusing effects, once one's eye has been reoriented to the facts of Soviet building life, are the quasi-Miesian glass boxes that are "prototype" ladies' hairdressing salons, the standardized kiosks run by rampantly individualistic female small-produce vendors on all city streets, and the automatic way in which standardized laundries, schools, and markets can be identified. One must remind oneself that even the red mineral-water vending machines, completely mechanical except for a community glass rather than disposable cups, are not the property of some enterprising vending-machine king but of co-operatives. The street shoeshine concessions, traditional bastion of vest-pocket capitalism, are . . . what? Sometimes the mind boggles.

Smaller cities have less complex planning and building arrangements than Moscow. In Tbilisi, for example, a city of 842,000 that is the capital of the republic of Georgia, planning and construction are executed directly by departmental and management divisions of the city Soviet.

In such an immense bureaucracy the red-tape traps are legion and many have been fallen into. At the same time there is still the real and virtually unparalleled chance for co-ordinated, large-scale effort. In some cases, such as building technology, the opportunity is paying off. In others, such as city planning, the process appears to have eliminated creative experimentation. The need now, openly acknowledged, is for quality as well as quantity solutions.

I visited the chief architect of the Soviet Union, Mikhail V. Posokhin, who, as head of the State Committee for Civil Construction and Architecture, is the country's top architectural decision maker. He is a man of obvious talent, diplomacy, and reserve, and, as a practicing architect as well as administrator, a taste maker to be reckoned with. Posokhin's committee reviews all projects and plans of national importance. His preferences are clearly demonstrated in the clean, cool, contemporary buildings and projects with which his name has been associated: the Palace of Congresses, the redesign of Kalinin Prospekt, a new resort at Pitsunda, on the Black Sea. The committee's headquarters are not in one of the many decaying Moscow office buildings; they occupy the high-ceilinged rooms of a prerevolutionary wine merchant's mansion. The fine wood doors are immensely tall and heavy, there are meaningful moldings, and the dignity of architecture is clear. The fruit soda is the same.

I investigated the operation of some of the special institutes, headed by lively, intelligent men who ranged from an architect who could double as a Madison Avenue executive, complete with matching foulard tie and handkerchief, to the classic Bolshevik of rugged features, leonine gray hair, open shirt, declamatory style, and immaculately manicured nails. All were knowledgeable men, familiar with developments in the rest of the world; many had had firsthand observations through travel.

Interviews were reinforced by field work, marathon trips through endless new residential districts in Moscow, Leningrad, and Tbilisi, and a jolting ride through Caucasian splendors to the newest construction on the Black Sea. What I saw, in this immense country, was only a sampling. I sought exceptional examples, since the standardized ones were omnipresent. It was, necessarily, a carefully chosen itinerary for a limited time, stressing the newest developments. I saw a great deal that had been seen before and some things that had not yet been seen by outsiders, such as the carefully planned resort at Pitsunda, thanks to the chief architect's understandable pride in the country's best new work and the promise of a professional, rather than a less-trained journalistic, eye.

Pitsunda is the current Soviet showpiece of prefabrication and planning. It stands for all that the Russians consider best and most progressive in their recent work. It was a revelation of new architectural standards—standards still little known beyond Soviet borders—and the increasingly sophisticated design use of prefabricated building systems. It is a resort built from scratch on a sheltered cape east of Sochi along the beautiful stretch of Black Sea coast known as the Caucasian Riviera. Second to none of the better-known rivieras in the splendor of its setting, it is famous chiefly as the area where Nikita S. Khrushchev vacationed and demonstrated fun and games to the press.

When Pitsunda is finished, it will consist of seven fourteen- and fifteen-story towers sweeping around the edge of a one-hundred-and-eighty-five-yard crescent beach bordered by a primeval pine forest and a theatrical backdrop of Caucasian mountains plunging to the sea. There are two combination restaurant-cinema buildings between the towers, one for nine hundred people in either restaurant or theater, the other for 1,300. A heated pool for winter use is under construction. All buildings are joined by a continuous beach-front promenade. The resort will accommodate 3,000.

The towers are made of completely prefabricated units, from frames to facing panels. They are handsome, clearly modern buildings, with full-façade balconies, glass-enclosed stairs, roof cafés, and solariums, showing considerable attention to proportion and detail. The exterior panels are faced with a creamy mosaic, finished at the factory. The restaurant-cinemas are of special design—interlocking glass-walled rectangles finished in white marble or ceramic panels. The connecting promenade is of random-laid Georgian marble, grading from chalky white to beige. The only color will be in interior Venetian blinds in the towers, with different hues on their two sides for random accents.

The plan of Pitsunda has been conceived and carried out as a dual exercise in development and conservation. One stipulation was that not a single one of the ancient pine trees should be cut. Pitsunda has been designed by the chief architect of the Soviet Union because it is considered an undertaking of national rather than of local importance. The site is ranked as a national trust. The result is a quite striking version of international modern, with some debt to Le Corbusier's towers in greenery, that would rank high on any international design scale.

Pitsunda's engineers are particularly concerned about finishes, and special measures are being taken to insure a technical level related to the design level. Even so, the completed buildings will probably lack Western technical polish. But they are a far cry from the classical cake molds and crumbling walk-ups that constitute the popular cliché image of Soviet building.

Although the effect of the towers, pools, restaurants, and promenade will be as *soigné* as in any Western resort, the similarity ends there. Pitsunda is a resort Soviet style, a concept hard for Americans to grasp. It is being built by the All-Union Council of Trade Unions, the national trade-union organization with headquarters in Moscow. Many vacation facilities are controlled by the trade unions. Like other seashore and mountain retreats, Pitsunda is a "people's resort," and its hotels are "rest homes" for the workers. Space is allocated to the various unions for the annual "rest, recreation and treatment" arranged for workers and their families on a sliding scale of subsidized costs. Food, lodging, and medical care are provided.

The "rest home" towers have single rooms with shared bath facilities for single workers and one-to-three-room-and-bath arrangements for families. The rooms are about ten by twelve feet, but glass walls can be opened to balconies and breath-taking views. Utilities throughout will be all electric. Total cost, including furnishings, will be 35,000,000 rubles, or $38,850,000, but United States and Soviet costs defy comparison.

A debate is already under way about future expansion. The feeling at present is that the natural self-contained beauty of the site makes expansion undesirable. This, in itself, is a departure in design philosophy in a society that tends to think of building in mass multiples of thousands. At the construction site, kerchiefed women in cotton print dresses mix mortar and run skeleton elevators, and bronzed men take swimming breaks on the gray-pebbled beach. A sign on one of the towers, one letter to a balcony, proclaims GLORY TO THE WORKERS. The jet set will have to look somewhere else for its next playground.

The ride to Pitsunda was along hairpin turns of spectacular Caucasian roads favored by strolling mountain cows and trucks carrying prefabricated elements to building sites. The sheer, lush green hills were wreathed in mist, and milky mountain streams coursed through chalky stone beds. An army of Lenins, arms upraised, guarded small mountain villages, and open charabancs of Soviet tourists hurtled along under the midday sun. The Black Sea was Mediterranean blue. There were stretches of fairyland, settings for ballet with mountain scrim behind, swan lakes, gingerbread pavilions, tenth-century Byzantine churches, and white-painted statues of basketball players and Olympic swimmers at Gagra, Novy Afon, and Sukhumi along the coast. Shabby rather than chic, with rest homes instead of casinos, the small towns could not have been more beautiful or beckoned more seductively to the visitor.

It was one of Russia's loveliest springs. Back in Moscow, hedges of lilacs faced the Bolshoi Theater, tulips were fluorescent in the Alexander Gardens, and parks quickly became jungle green. Even the brusque earnestness of rushing Muscovites was touched by the pleasure of warm sun and clear skies. Food displays in store windows were imaginative and plentiful; there were enough consumer goods of the costume-jewelry and fancy-shoe variety to make the streetscape less bare; kiosks on every avenue sold oranges and ice cream (some of the best in the world), and queues lined up for itinerant tanks of kvass, a refreshing thin beer made from fermented rye, and sudden deliveries of popcorn. The girls wore beehive hairdos of various artificial colors, tentatively short skirts, and eye make-up often ingeniously improvised with East European drawing pencils found in art-supply stores.

Beyond the vastnesses of Red Square and Revolution Square and the treasures of the Kremlin, the characteristic post-Napoleonic streets of the 1820's, with their uniform, small classic buildings finished in umber-toned plaster, wait quietly for demolition. Some can be glimpsed through the Stalin-era arches of Gorky Street. Rich, rugged late-nineteenth-century buildings put conventional Victoriana to shame, making stunning streetscapes of strident chiaroscuro that are seldom photographed. They, too, exist on sufferance. Moscow is an intriguing and often handsome city. It showed its best face in the spring sunshine.

All this almost, but not quite, compensates for the fact that there is no real style, and no *joie de vivre* in Moscow yet. On the street, or catching an eye, few smile. There is little grace. Whatever concessions have been made to the pursuit of "the good life," the Russians have succeeded in avoiding "bourgeois decadence"—the overt pleasure in the splendid delights of living and that shiny bauble called civilization. Culture, pursued unremittingly, is a strange, deflowered ritual that stresses body and mind building according to scouts' rules and state morality. Everything is relative, of course, and Moscow is decadent compared to Peking. But the grayness of the city is more of the spirit than of the environment.

The talk at the conference tables, over the fruit drinks, was seldom tinged with ideology. Communication, even through interpreters, was direct, on a familiar professional level, concerned primarily with the universal problems of building and rebuilding cities and housing for as many people as quickly as possible. The results are a phenomenon that can only be explained by the Soviet past.

Prerevolutionary Russia was 80 per cent rural and agricultural. Communism, according to Lenin, required an industrialized society. The new Soviet leaders believed that it was necessary to create that industrialized society as quickly as possible to make Communism viable, to prove that its theories worked, and to resist what they considered to be the pressure of outside dangers to their existence.

Industrial strength is urban strength. It means factories and cities. Between the two wars Soviet effort went into the development of heavy industry as the basis of the Communist economy, and housing was neglected. The economy, in fact, supported little else except the massive industrialization program and military spending. All resources were channeled to these ends; agriculture, housing, and consumer needs waited. Serious housing shortages grew worse.

Soviet cities show comparatively little building from the 1930's and 1940's. The main push was going into power plants, steel mills, and armaments, an emphasis intensified under Stalin, and World War II interrupted construction of all kinds. Living standards that were bad became more critical with the war. An incredible amount of the already insufficient housing stock was wiped out. The Institute of Town Planning lists 1,700 cities and towns that were 50 per cent to 100 per cent destroyed. Minsk and Stalingrad (now Volgograd) for example, had to be totally rebuilt. The initial postwar effort went into the reconstruction of destroyed and damaged cities. By the 1950's the housing crisis, always bad, had become a top-priority item. The country mobilized its efforts to meet it.

The situation was made worse by other problems. Millions of people had been lost in the war, many of them young men or trained workers. There were shortages of manpower, skills, and materials. Transportation was poor. An immense amount of building had to be done in a single generation, and it became quite apparent that it could not possibly be done by traditional means.

Any solution had to minimize labor and transportation and stress local materials. The only universal local materials were the ingredients of concrete—sand, gravel, and water. The logical answer, decided on as early as the 1930's but never implemented until the 1950's, was the manufacture of prefabricated, reinforced-concrete building elements, with skills concentrated in the factories. To use less reinforcing steel, and to make lighter, more manageable units, the program emphasized prestressed concrete.

To produce enough buildings to meet the need and do it economically meant mass production—the manufacture of standardized building parts on a very large scale. The Russians bought and borrowed some techniques, developed others. Whole factories were purchased from France, bits of technology were taken from Sweden and Denmark. The only significant debt to the United States is to Henry Ford, for the assembly line. To co-ordinate prefabrication and construction in unprecedented volume, the factory combine was developed to unite manufacture and site erection. In a country with the extreme climatic conditions of the Soviet Union, factory prefabrication meant year-round production and employment. Otherwise, the building season, with its "wet" on-site operations, must be limited to temperate times of the year, which also cuts the volume of production.

Scandinavia has excellent methods of prefabrication and unit construction, but it has not faced anything remotely resembling Russia's problems of scope and scale. The Scandinavian countries have been able, comparatively, to work with small, jewel-like solutions. The United States has not faced its problems of blight and large-scale building with any unified emphasis on industrialized building processes at all. But today, after ten years of work, the Soviet Union has the largest cement manufacture and the most progressive reinforced-concrete building technology in the world. There was no preoccupation with design finesse, as explained earlier, just with mass production. Only now are design and manufacturing reaching a point of more sophisticated co-ordination that approaches the Western idea of architecture. This is what the visitor is beginning to see in the new Soviet buildings.

When the serious assault on Soviet housing began, standard blocks of apartments were first built out of standard materials. The original sector of Moscow's new southwest residential district was begun in 1952–53. This area, accommodating one and a half million people today, is covered with five-story brick buildings faced with cream-yellow ceramic tile. Characteristically, the tiles froze and thawed and rained to the ground. Nets were spread to catch them. Muscovites delight in telling how Moscow's population jumped one million on one August day in 1960. It was the day that five surrounding towns were annexed to create Greater Moscow and to lay the groundwork for further expansion of the city's outlying regions.

Those early southwest buildings on the perimeter of the city stretch on identically, in parallel straight lines, bordering uniform wide avenues. There is no scale, no variety, no surprise. It is monotony with light, air, sun, and greenery in season, and, in sum, that effect is no worse and even sometimes a good deal better than a lot of the construction on the outskirts of large American cities. The outlying landscape of free enterprise is sordid and chaotic; of a state-planned society, clean and regimented. It is not a choice that offers many pluses in either case beyond a greater or lesser roof over one's head. If the Soviet planning results are sterile, the American nonplanning results are rapaciously and hideously destructive.

The story goes that Khrushchev did not approve of anything higher than five-story walk-ups and that high-rise housing was virtually blocked in his time. True or false, what was constructed as the first prefabricated buildings produced by the experimental technology of the late 1950's were five-story walk-ups. The houses looked terrible, but they had the first prefabricated reinforced-concrete panels as interior load-bearing walls. Their exterior walls were non-load-bearing room-size panels, also of prefabricated reinforced concrete. These panels measured approximately ten by twelve feet. Windows were set in at the plant, and the preassembled unit was hoisted into place by specially developed cranes.

Houses went up fast and shoddily. Moscow's extreme climate, with winter temperatures of thirty-one to thirty-five degrees below zero, played havoc with joints. Walls leaked and were caulked with ugly ribbons of sloppy black sealant. Soundproofing was inadequate. This wobbly blackline checkerboard model is all over the Soviet landscape.

Better joints and lighter, sandwich panels were developed. After 1957 small experimental plants in the field were replaced by the combine, with centralized manufacture of all building elements, including factories specializing in different parts, co-ordinated right down to the process of assembly on the site. The objective, since skills were so scarce, was to make the largest possible parts, in the factory, on the largest scale, and to cut down cost, construction time, and the number of workers on the site. Skills were to be trained and concentrated in the industrialized process.

According to the Moscow Scientific Research and Design Institute of Standard and Experimental Design, the first combine developed for Moscow now produces 30,000 apartments a year. There are three combines in the Moscow area, using various techniques, working at different capacities. One method makes the prefabricated panels by pouring the concrete into vertical steel forms. (Plastic can sometimes produce better shapes and finishes, but it is still scarce, and steel stands up to continuous use.) With another system, called "vibro-rolling," forms containing reinforcing, windows, doors, et cetera, are placed on a continuous vibrating conveyor belt. This system is said to produce 15,000 apartments a year. An average prefabricated panel now weighs five to ten metric tons. It must be remembered, always, that the total objective of every aspect of the system is low-cost building.

In 1962 the switch was made from five- to nine-story houses. The reasons were undoubtedly as much technological as any change in taste. The Russians were also working toward the obvious fact that high-rise buildings are more economical in mechanical services and the utilization of urban land. They claim that nine- or ten-story buildings can be completed in two

months with the industrialized processes. With height, the load-bearing interior panels have given way to prefabricated reinforced-concrete frames.
In 1964 the model apartment house rose to twelve stories. In the same year
plans were made for the sixteen-story houses appearing now. Computers
are used to schedule manufacture and erection. The objective is to deliver
units to the housing in construction and have them swung immediately into
place. There are no stockpiles at building sites. Moscow officials claim to
produce one apartment every five minutes from a Moscow combine.

Each new model is constructed experimentally and checked out for a
period before going into mass production. Such matters as vertical align-
ment of prefabricated units in a tall building have been a subject of close
study. A fact to be remembered is that the 1957–67 period brought Soviet
housing virtually from huts to high rise. It has been a little like inventing
the umbrella.

The newest experimental model is a seventeen-story apartment house of
considerably altered design. Built in the spring of 1966, it is on Prospekt
Mira, a broad street in northern Moscow. When I saw it, tenants had occupied it for only three months, and some had just moved in.

This is a big-city building, in familiar Western style. It is a block-long
high-rise apartment house of the type that New Yorkers are accustomed to.
Prefabricated exterior wall panels alternate with angled, ribbed balconies
for an effect of very acceptable proportion and scale. From the outside, as
façade architecture, it is a good deal better-looking than most of what New
York gets. Entrances and halls, however, are still minimal-institutional,
almost penal, in their stripped-down bareness and Spartan detail.

The apartments are pleasant. I visited two at Prospekt Mira, and was
given a warm reception by their proud inhabitants. Theoretically, there is
no favoritism. You get the latest and best apartment if your name on the
waiting list and the available accommodations coincide. In a kind of additional point system, it helps if you are a good producer or have otherwise
proved your value to the state.

The tenant of one apartment was an editor, a Jewish war veteran who
lived with his mother. He was working on a quiet Sunday morning in a room
furnished as a study with still-scarce, small-scale, vaguely Scandinavian-style
modern furniture. The furnishings throughout the apartment were as new
and modern as the accommodations, an ideal seldom realized though much
desired by the new buildings' tenants. In the other apartment, a round Russian
couple sat in front of a new television set in a tidy little living room. A family
of three, they had three rooms. (Four people to three rooms is par under
current government standards of space allotment, and two to a room is more
common. One to a room is the present ideal.) An equally small bedroom was

a compact marvel of older furniture of massive, mirror-polished wood and blue crushed velvet. Kitchens, which will receive design attention after 1970, were about the same size as the other rooms. They had stoves but no refrigerators or cabinets. (Refrigerators must be bought and are still hard to get.) Invariably, there was a table against a balconied window. Both tenants showed, with great pride, one closet and one set of bookshelves, built in. (Another fact that Americans must keep in mind is that basic plumbing is still a basic triumph. First things first.)

Rooms are small but airy and light, with large windows. This building had one- to three-room apartments. In Soviet figures, kitchens and baths are not counted as rooms, or "living space." At present each person is allotted nine square meters of "living space," or about ninety-seven square feet, excluding kitchen and bath. An extra four square meters, or about forty-three square feet, is added for a family. Plans in preparation for 1970 increase this to twelve square meters, or about one hundred and twenty-nine square feet per person. The Prospekt Mira apartment house appeared to be of the new norm. Inevitably, all rooms serve as bedrooms in one form or another. There are exceptions, of course, at both ends of the scale. Those privileged by position, productivity, or importance to the state can live comparatively luxuriously. Others are still crowded into substandard dwellings.

Rents are never more than 4 to 5 per cent of income. The standard rent is thirteen and a half kopecks a month, or fifteen cents, per square meter of living space. That is ten and three-quarters square feet. The allotment of nine square meters per person works out to one ruble and twenty-five kopecks, or about $1.40 a month. A family multiplies this by the number of persons, plus about forty cents for the extra family allotment. A family of four would pay about $6.00 a month for an apartment of two small rooms plus a bath and kitchen. Additional space, for anyone lucky enough to have it, costs three times more, or about forty-five cents per square meter.

The most widely publicized experiment in recent Soviet prefabricated building has been the development of a boxlike, room-size unit. These complete rooms, with doors and windows, or identical units containing combinations of stairs, halls, baths, or kitchens, are stacked up like blocks for almost instant housing. A small, five-story building of these units, requiring on-site work only for connection of plumbing, wiring, and services, can be put up in two days.

Technologically, this is a bold, intriguing idea, and one five-story experiment can be seen in Moscow. Many more of this type have been constructed in Minsk. Architecturally, it is disappointingly dull, since it is treated in the simplest, most standardized form possible. (Another prefabricated "box" experiment, Habitat, at Montreal's Expo 67, by the young Israeli architect Moshe Safdie, is startlingly different in its spectacular design approach to a similar idea. Habitat emphasizes variety, rather than uniformity.)

The advantages of the box system are appealing. In respect to the rapid construction of whole new towns around new industries or for the development of natural resources, the potential speed and efficiency of the system stagger the mind. Photographs of units being swung into place by huge cranes are provocative and dramatic. The disadvantages, however, are very real. The huge units are harder to transport than smaller ones, although large trailer trucks have been produced to carry four or five at a time; damage, not uncommon in transport, is more serious than in smaller units; and there is little possibility of variety in design. While the technicians are intellectually in love with the idea of the system, architects prefer more flexible units, which are generally admitted to be of wider practicality.

The latest system divides the standard ten-by-twelve-foot panel into two five-by-twelve-foot units—one a prestressed concrete panel, the other for glazing or other prefab inserts, including color and decoration. The newest buildings in Moscow, using a combination of the large and small panel systems, show a felicitous union of design and technology for the first time. Mosaic tile surfaces, factory bonded to the panel, are replacing painted concrete. Full-balconied façades further vary the pattern in regions with hot climates, such as the republic of Georgia. Prefabrication is now almost universal except in special cases, as in earthquake areas, which use poured-in-place concrete frames rather than prefabricated ones. There is considerable preoccupation, if still limited success, with details.

Standardized industrial construction in the Soviet Union now goes far beyond housing. The enlarged significance of the development of this design technology is that it is being used for all large-scale building. Moscow's Kalinin Prospekt, for example, has housing on one side and administration buildings on the other side, using the same units and systems, but in different designs.

The only important buildings that are not prefabricated today are special structures, such as the Palace of Congresses in the Kremlin; Pioneer palaces, which are used for a combination of culture and indoctrination for children on the Brownie and Scout level; palaces of culture, or community centers, in major cities; memorials, and all singular projects of particular status or symbolism. These designs are usually chosen through competitions, which play a large role in the Soviet Union. The competitions are judged by juries set up by the Union of Architects, the state professional organization, to which all practicing architects belong. National projects will have juries on the state committee or national level. The State Committee for Civil Construction and Architecture must approve all designs considered to be of national importance, or over a specified cost, even when a competition is conducted locally, and whether or not a competition is involved.

Sometimes a special building is the work of the chief architect of a particular city, as in the case of the new concert hall in Tbilisi. Chief architects head city design departments when a city is large enough or historic enough, or the volume of new construction warrants it. They are appointed by the city Soviets. The chief architect of the Soviet Union, as head man of design, also draws certain plums. Thus, Posokhin, working with other architects, has been responsible for projects of top national status.

Results in the special building field, both competitively and by direct commission, are interesting. They all seem to fit into an identical style bracket. The decade of the 1960's is as monolithically modern as the 1950's were neoclassical. Variety in competition entries is almost all within this same idiom. The stadium under construction in Leningrad, a steel-framed, glass-walled drum by Sergei Speransky, head of the Leningrad department of the Union of Soviet Architects the new concert hall by Tbilisi's chief architect, Ivan N. Chkhenkeli; plans for a large department store and remodeled stadium by architects of Tbilproyekt, the Tbilisi design department, and projects for the new Tretyakov Art Gallery and an Electronics Center of the Academy of Sciences in Moscow are all coolly, correctly, slightly *retardataire* international style.

With the Soviet emphasis on the use of concrete, there is no "brutalism," no sophisticated superplay with surfaces and volumes, no romantic projections and recesses, no suggestions of modern medievalism or flying saucers. It is the smooth face of the 1930's international style, the movement that made the world modern, in 1960's dress.

The buildings could all have come from the same office. In a sense, of course, they do, although architects stress their independence of design. When architecture is state-run, and all major projects are state-approved, there is an understandable tendency to work in the state-sanctioned style. Considering the fact that this style has broken with the dead, derivative neoclassicism of the 1950's that was the nadir of Soviet architecture and probably of architecture anywhere, the new buildings can only be praised as a giant step forward. The current official style is progressive, rational, and often agreeably handsome.

The disquieting fact, of course, is that it is an official style. It is not called that, and the suggestion is frequently denied. But in the Soviet Union there has always been only one style in practice and ascendancy at a time. Where creativity is involved, this is unnatural and distressing. It is also an inevitable and obvious result of an art and industry under state control. My personal reactions are peculiarly mixed, because I find the process bad and the best of the present product good. I deplore the lack of freedom and variety, of invention and experiment, the loss of the innovative character of an art that is almost a guaranteed casualty of nationalization of design and construction. On the other hand, I cannot deplore the lack of esthetic exhibitionism and atrocious architectural acrobatics, the cheap tricks and squalid waste of resources, which, like freedom of speech, are a guarantee of free creativity.

In addition, it is impossible to avoid the comparison of the official Soviet style with what would be the equivalent official style in the United States—the reactionary atrocities being constructed in Washington on Capitol Hill, the country's symbolic focus, under the totalitarian powers of the Architect of the Capitol. The thought of what it would be like if J. George Stewart controlled all major building in the United States chills the blood. What would happen, of course, would be a repetition of building in the Soviet Union in the 1950's. To complete the comparison and the anachronism, if Posokhin were the Architect of the Capitol, Washington would be getting some suitable additions. (It would be less than kind to suggest a cultural exchange.) In fairness, other government building, under the United States General Services Administration, has been moving toward a better contemporary standard.

Now that rational professionals are in control of building in the Soviet Union, the results, whatever the all-too-clear faults and dangers of the system, are promising. Under any system controls and co-ordination are always the most sensitive areas of planning and design. Without some controls, there is chaos; with too many, sterility. Ultimately, everything depends on the quality of their administration and of the talent that carries them through. There are no easy answers, Soviet or American.

The Russians, right now, are establishing a commendable design standard. This judgment is made, as it must be, against the existing and past history of building in the Soviet Union: lack of skills, tradition, practice, and, until recently, of contact with the developments in the rest of the world. Under these conditions, the current product is remarkable. Any simple, modern style, however, is dependent for excellence on quality of finish, details, and materials, and here Soviet architecture still has a long way to go.

The building that has become symbolic of change and aroused the most interest and curiosity in the outside world is the Palace of Congresses, completed in 1961. Probably the single most important structure built in the Soviet Union in recent years, it not only demonstrated the break with classicism, but also exhibited an even bolder policy—the decision to put a completely contemporary building inside the Kremlin walls as a twentieth-century addition to its progression of historical architectural styles. This was a daring step, completely in tune with the most advanced architectural philosophy. It took double courage; there was, first, the rupture with stylistic conservatism, and, second, the challenge of a conspicuous structure that would have to be extremely well built with little or no experience in style or construction to draw on.

The results, architecturally, are quite good. It must be said immediately, however, that a 6,000-seat theater, no matter how well engineered, is a disaster for performer-audience contact, and the building's success is less for the performing arts than for the meetings and party events that it is meant to accommodate.

It is, essentially, a conservative modern building, but one marked by straightforward design and a fair degree of simple elegance. The design is sophisticated for Moscow, not for New York. The immediate resemblance to Lincoln Center has one important difference: it lacks Lincoln Center's pretentious and mannered pomposity. The interior lobby spaces are notable. As for details, carpet wrinkles but marble and parquet floors are well laid, glass and metal window junctures are clean and tight, the immense restaurant area that occupies the entire "penthouse" floor is pure Russian in its echoing vastness and military ranks of tables. Furnishings in the building do it less than justice, although they are tastefully selected from what is obviously available. They have a "throwback" modern look, emphasizing highly varnished woods.

The building was constructed largely by the Russians, with some imported help, as elsewhere. Italian contractors, for example, put up the Soviet Pavilion at Expo 67, and there has been a tradition of foreign design and labor in Russia since the eighteenth century. To the objective historian, there is less of a claim to native architectural greatness than seems so to the Soviet citizen. The Palace of Congresses is a surprisingly sensitive addition to the Kremlin and an appropriate manifesto of modern Soviet architecture.

If the manifesto seems a little late and slightly dated to Western eyes, it is necessary to see it against the curious history of Soviet architecture in the last fifty years.

Architecture joined the revolution early. In the 1920's Soviet architects believed that they would build a radical new world. Their buildings would be as progressive and unfettered, as free from the shackles of bourgeois tradition, as everything else in the Communist state. With the artists, the architects joined in a brief adventure called "constructivism," which is one of the most interesting chapters in the history of modern art. In painting it was pure abstraction—elementary shapes, floating, locking, interpenetrating, in patterns of studied geometric simplicity. The vocabulary of abstraction was carried over into the design forms of architecture. Among the architects were Konstantin S. Melnikov, Panteleimon A. Golosov, and Vladimir Tatlin.

Modern architecture, led by such men as Le Corbusier in France, was a revolutionary movement throughout Europe in the 1920's. Le Corbusier was welcomed in Moscow; he designed the Centrosoyuz building on Kirov Street, built from 1928 to 1934, currently the Central Statistics Agency. It is in active use and appears to have had relatively recent attention in paint and repairs. This is an important and handsome historic structure, denounced during the period of Soviet classicism, and admired now by the intellectually alert. It has come back into historical perspective.

The constructivist product of the 1920's and early 1930's, with its interlocking cubes, circles, and rectangles in asymmetrical compositions, is as easily identifiable today as seventeenth-century Italian mannerism, and just as intriguing. This was the work of superior talent harnessed to a kind of esthetic revolutionary spirit. At least one or two buildings in this style and of this period can be found in many Soviet cities. To the visiting historian they make up one of the most fascinating episodes in twentieth-century architecture.

In Moscow, in addition to the Le Corbusier building, there is the Zuyev Club, by Golosov, of about 1928, with a remarkable glass cylinder pushing through a right-angled wraparound projection of a solid wall. The Rusakov Club, built in 1926 as a workers' club by Melnikov, is now a movie theater. Melnikov was the architect of the sensationally successful constructivist Russian pavilion at the Paris Exposition of 1925. ("They carried me on their shoulders," he says today.) His own house still stands, half hidden by a high fence and overgrown lilac bushes. A shabby concrete double cylinder, it is made of two interlocking forms, the rear pierced by a pattern of small lozenge-shaped studio windows. At the top, proudly incised in the concrete, are his name and the date, 1928. These buildings are the subject of quiet architectural pilgrimages by foreign visitors.

Konstantin Melnikov is now in his eighties. I visited him in Moscow's Central Hospital one warm May evening. He was an ambulatory patient, and we met on a path lined with bushes laden with sweet-smelling white blossoms. Courtly, blue-eyed, with thin white hair and mustache, in a bathrobe over a hospital suit of green cotton, he broke off a flowering branch and presented it to me with gentle dignity. We spoke through a student interpreter. It was an evening—with the hospital hush and the fading light and an old man's memories—that will remain with me like a dream; a strange excursion into the past.

Central Hospital is a huge, forbidding neoclassic pile of undiluted grayness, and its location, in a distant suburb of the city, belies its name. In front, a once-formal classical garden with a dry, neglected fountain has long gone to shaggy jungle growth. The outdoor promenade route is a straight path that goes squarely around the hospital grounds. Where it relented in back, softened by the bushes that made a kind of natural arbor over wooden benches, we sat and talked.

He spoke of the early days after the revolution, of the ardor that filled every heart and led the hand of the architect to new ideas and forms. He told how easy it was then to find an answering ardor in the officials of the party, of how he went to the leaders, a young man with sketches under his arm, and received immediate approvals without reviews or delays. His face saddened as he spoke of the changes in the 1930's, of burgeoning bureaucracy and the increasing difficulties of getting the new work built. He had been an innovator, a creative force, and the force was cut off abruptly with the government's turn to academic classicism as the approved Soviet style. He would not speak unkindly of the men who embraced the change and who built the pompous, empty monuments of the late 1940's and early 1950's. His involvement in architecture was personal, not polemical. He was not interested in issues, past or present. He cared only about architecture as an art. In the soft spring evening air, as the sun went down, he spoke of old enthusiasms and old triumphs. "There were men of talent in my day, and there are men of talent now," he reminded me. He was not bitter that Soviet history had passed him by.

At his house his daughter did not answer the door. The bell rang and a dog barked and a hand pushed the curtains aside momentarily on the second floor. A passer-by said no one would come; the neighborhood children bothered them.

Those early dreams of architectural revolution were short-lived. Most of the daring schemes never got off the drawing board. Vladimir Tatlin's bold projects for extraordinary constructivist structures were paper tigers. It is all in the archives now. The new regime, even when it favored the new designs, had neither the resources nor the skills to build them. Money and technology were in tight supply.

By the mid-1930's the cultural freeze had set in with a vengeance. The work of the avant-garde was denounced as decadent, bourgeois, and unsuited to the system's aims and ideologies. The innovators were supplanted by the academicians: Socialist Realism in the arts, neoclassicism in architecture. With the first general plan of Moscow in 1935, "reconstruction" of the city began from the center to the Sadovoye Ring boulevard. Huge squares were cleared of old buildings and avenues widened to hold troops and tanks. Later, the unrelieved asphalt was softened with parks and planting. New blocks, first of utilitarian plainness, and later embellished with the details of a sterile classical eclecticism, began to make their appearance between old mansions and prerevolutionary construction. Building was stopped by the war.

The turning point for Soviet architecture was actually the international competition for the Palace of the Soviets for Moscow. In 1939 a classical solution was chosen, and the architectural die was cast for the next fifteen years. The winning design would have elevated a supercolossal Lenin on a colonnaded pile that would have been the ultimate Communist wedding cake. Fortunately, the foundation conditions, it is said, would not support it and the war intervened. Today the site accommodates one of the biggest outdoor swimming pools in the world.

After the war, in the late 1940's and early 1950's, Roman skyscrapers and block-long *palazzi* rose on all of Moscow's major streets, framing new avenues and plazas. The formula was repeated in every large Soviet city and the satellite capitals. One vigorous architect, highly placed in Moscow design and building, spoke so rationally of the kind of modern building going on today that I asked him what he had been doing during the neoclassical period. "I will not tell you the street," he said, "but I designed one of the largest *palazzi* with one of the biggest, most useless cornices you ever saw!"

With Moscow's prewar population on the way to being doubled, a new circle of growth extended far beyond Sadovoye Ring. Broad avenues were cut through the city. The need for new housing became intense.

In the mid-1950's the architectural thaw came, as in other fields, after the death of Stalin. The neoclassical mold was broken. Khrushchev denounced the style publicly. All this, plus a new generation of architects and pressure for huge quantities of construction, led to a new kind of building. The pattern was utilitarian; the preoccupation was with speed and economy. There were no more cornices or pilasters; new buildings went up without classical ornament.

The five-story walk-ups appeared, row on row, on the outskirts of Moscow and every other city, lining vast new boulevards, and designed to save costs and avoid the expense of elevators. Classicism had been routed by pragmatism. By 1955, one architect explained, "they had cleaned it all up and left nothing." The results were generally unpopular with architects, administrators, and the people—except those lucky enough to get the new apartments.

By 1957 the concentrated push for industrialized construction was on. The further expansion of Moscow's city limits came in 1960 and encompassed another huge circle, now bounded by the new Moscow ring highway. Today Moscow is ringed with suburbs: the southwest, Cheryomushki, Nagatino, Fili-Mazilovo, Khoroshovo-Mnevniki, Khimki-Khovrino, Medvedkovo, Severnoye Izmailovo, Cherkizovo, Noviye Kuzminki. None of them are like any suburb that any American has ever known. These are not the little houses with handkerchief yards, the split-level "developments," the colonial salt-boxes with two-car garages, or even the "garden apartments" that have become the American suburban way of life. They are blocks and blocks of unrelieved identical apartment houses, punctuated by standardized service and recreational buildings. Five- and nine-story structures are now being complemented by twelve- and sixteen-story buildings. All are arranged with the relentless regularity and the uniform open spaces of what Americans know and denigrate as public housing. This is Soviet planning.

As with most things in the Soviet Union, planning is not exactly what it seems to be to the Western eye. It can be understood only in terms of that cultural readjustment that the foreign visitor must make to comprehend most of what he sees.

The planned city in the United States, for example, is primarily a sociological and functional concept. It is the ultimate American dream of the good life. This description oversimplifies the complex economic and political factors involved, but it is the guiding ideal.

The planned city in the Soviet Union serves a completely different purpose: it is a vehicle for the location of industry. "Under conditions existing in our country the building of towns constitutes a part of the national economic plan," reads a report prepared for an international planning seminar in 1966. Planning is primarily economic. New cities are placed according to the programs of central industrial agencies, not according to planners' theories or the claims of climate or ecology, for certainly the climate in northern Siberia is not ideal and the industrial pollution of Lake Baikal is already a problem. However, industrial cities distribute jobs and population, which are other Soviet concerns. The aforementioned "conditions existing in our country" include the vast undeveloped resources and unpopulated sections of the Soviet Union east of the Urals and in Siberia.

There is no debate over whether a new town should have its own economic base or not, or whether it should serve as a satellite community to provide greater living amenities for an older city, a discussion heard often in the West. In the Soviet Union the industry is chosen and located and the town is planned around it. Except for this important difference, planners everywhere aim for the same thing—the good life. Where Soviet planning is inextricably tied up with the Soviet system is in its basic economic premise—state ownership of land and state control of building and resources and population movement. This means centralized state planning, a fundamental Communist concept. The results are neither as bad as those who fear centralized planning contend nor as good as that kind of planning *carte blanche* should make them.

By the count of the Town Planning Institute of the U.S.S.R., a part of Gosstroy since 1954, nine hundred new Soviet cities have been built in the fifty years since the revolution. These cities have all followed a carefully specified pattern. They are "zoned" communities, with areas set aside for industrial, residential, and recreational purposes. These functions are referred to as "labor, mode of life, and rest." (The Russians rest as seriously as they work.) A population of 100,000 to 150,000 is the norm. This supports smaller industries, such as tool production or chemical plants; cities of 300,000 are planned for heavy industry, such as steel.

Generally, as in all things, the Russians think big. They are planning cities for 500,000 now. The new Fiat plant, scheduled to open in 1971, will be in a city called Togliatti after the late Italian Communist leader, which already has several chemical plants. Its goal is 500,000; it had a population of 150,000 in 1966. For comparison, the privately undertaken new town developments in the United States aim, on the average, for a population of 60,000 to 100,000; some of the postwar British new towns, planned originally for about 75,000, have been doubling that figure; Scandinavian new towns run 100,000 to 200,000 and are largely satellite communities.

One of the more interesting developments in the Soviet Union is at the other end of the scale. This is the "scientific" town, for only 20,000 to 40,000 inhabitants, built to bring scientists together in a planned research community. The notable example is the Akademgorodok that is a southern suburb of Novosibirsk housing the Siberian branch of the Academy of Sciences. Scientific centers in the Moscow region are Dubna, Obninsk, and Pushchino. Typically, there is a "zone" of research institutes, a "residential zone," and a "network of rest zones."

Another kind of new town is the resort, such as Pitsunda. The best description is straight from the Russian text: "These new towns arise in health resort regions where they serve as centers of mass rest, tourism and medical treatment." There is something stunningly and distinctively Russian about the idea of mass rest. One suspects that when Togliatti produces automobiles in sufficient quantity, mass rest may turn into mass movement. On such all-too-human factors do planners' principles founder.

Siberia is a prime area of new towns. Along the Angara River, the outlet of the largest fresh-water lake in the world, Lake Baikal, are a series of planned new settlements developed as part of an immense hydroelectric system. The new city of Bratsk, which reached a population of 250,000 in less than a decade of existence, is at the site of the Bratsk dam and power plant, the world's biggest power installation. The city is surrounded by dense Siberian forests. A wooden town, built first of the lumber from the cleared land, is being systematically replaced with prefabricated concrete structures. All of these new towns are fully electrified.

The rich resources of Siberia—lumber, minerals, diamonds, power— are being developed. In the far north of Siberia there is Norilsk, developed in the 1950's and 1960's; the new towns of Mirny, Aikhal, and Deputatsky are in various stages of planning and execution. Construction is on permafrost at great expense in areas of extreme climatic severity. The planners' theoretical studies show dome-enclosed communities with covered *gallerias* and gardens that defy Siberian storms, drifting snows, and howling winds. This is the place for the Buckminster Fuller world of geodesic domes and microclimates, which unfortunately are beyond current Soviet economic resources. Instead, the Russians construct immensely long, straight buildings with all utility lines in the basements, connected by covered passages and arranged in the most severely utilitarian and economical patterns. The model of a north Siberian new town is a remote abstraction of cool white slabs lined up in military formation in white snow. The buildings are on piles, and basements are ventilated to avoid the curious hazard of melting permafrost and having the structure sink suddenly and surrealistically into the ground.

The new Siberian towns are admirable technically. The skill of the planning engineers under such conditions can only be praised. But Norilsk, on the sixty-ninth parallel, in the frozen north, has met the challenge of the city of the future with the banalities of the past. Although nine-story structures have been set skillfully on hostile, icy soil, there is the sterile neoclassicism of streets and buildings in the approved 1950's style, with its vacuous squares, conventional residential quarters, and a main thoroughfare, Lenin Prospekt, of barren pomposity. If the engineering challenge was accepted, the design challenge was not.

I did not visit the far north but I did see another new town, Rustavi, a steel center for 100,000 in the republic of Georgia. Rustavi, begun in the 1940's and still under construction, is divided into the approved industrial, residential, and rest zones, with careful preservation of wooded land between old and new sections. If visual ennui was not its objective, everything contributes to the effect. Among rolling Caucasian hills it is set on a vast, flat plain. Its layout is a rigid gridiron of streets and avenues lined with uniform buildings. In the older sections, trees and plantings have matured for a softening effect. The straight line, right angle, and almost unvaried height and dusty color are totally without appeal to the senses. Rustavi is not even interesting from a distance; it is as dull panoramically, in this otherwise dramatic part of the country, as it is close up. According to the planning, it is explained, prevailing winds blow industrial smoke and smog away from the residential sections; the smog, however, is environmental.

A new town is designed by the republic in which it is to be situated in accordance with guidelines and standards provided by the state Town Planning Institute. If it is large and important enough, it must have design approval from the State Committee on Civil Construction and Architecture. The Town Planning Institute puts out a brochure called *Building Norms and Rules Concerning Design and Construction of Towns and Cities*. The latest version attempts to encourage design interpretation of the standards given rather than the prevalent rubber-stamp planning.

Although there is considerable talk in planning offices about varying the new towns to fit local conditions from tundra to desert, this still appears to be largely wishful thinking. Standard layouts and standard buildings are used over and over again. Seeing one new town is not seeing them all, but it is close to it. Economics, industrial production, and the pressing need to build quickly have dictated this uniformity to a large extent. Monotonous results are due to these factors rather than to any sinister ideology. This is also true for the sameness of the new neighborhoods of the older cities.

The new residential districts, in new towns or old cities, are divided into neighborhood units. Since 1958 the emphasis has been on an officially approved unit called a "microdistrict," which is simply a self-contained neighborhood with apartments and social services for 5,000 to 20,000 people. The social services include a standard cinema, café, hairdressing salon, shops, kindergartens, and schools. For the larger residential zone or district, which has a number of microdistricts, there are larger shopping centers, including a branch department store, cultural and recreational facilities, and a clinic. The Russians do not seem to like the word "microdistrict" now; they prefer to translate it simply as "neighborhood."

Like the housing, the neighborhoods are created experimentally. A single one is built, studied, and then standardized. In Moscow an experimental neighborhood for 8,000 was built in 1957. Another experimental neighborhood for 8,000 was constructed in 1966. Now a new residential district has been designed, which will contain five experimental neighborhoods of a totally different kind. Construction is about to begin on the far side of the city's ring-road boundary.

For the first time the neighborhood units will be further broken down into "living groups." These are smaller, more intimate divisions of 1,000 apartments each, intended to bring services closer to home for a closer-knit community. A shopping and cultural center will be at the subway station. The services for each "living group" will be branches of the larger, residential district service center, and each one will have its own kindergarten, nurseries, schools, and health service.

The latest experimental Soviet housing concept has been developed for this project: two sixteen-story wing-shaped buildings joined by a central service block. These twin buildings will have a restaurant as well as shops, and canteens on each floor. There will be guest rooms for relatives and other visitors, laundry rooms, and a small dispensary for medical care to relieve the larger polyclinics. Planners refer to this design as "a dwelling house with extended social services" and speak of it as a prototype. In appearance it has a bit of the severe stylishness of Brazilian work of the late 1940's crossed with the clean, large-scale simplicity of some of the better American commercial work of the last decade. It is designed, of course, with mass-produced prefabricated elements.

The concept of inexpensive, industrialized housing combined with extended community services is a progressive one by any measurement. It is also a basic need in every country, East or West. That it is being developed in the Soviet Union and that the result shows a heightened design consciousness—the preoccupation with the style of these buildings is clearly evident —are two giant steps forward.

Measured against this kind of progress, over-all urban planning seems strangely retarded—another Soviet paradox. Soviet planning has the curious quality of a time machine; here are the planning theories and pet practices of thirty years ago, perfectly preserved, as if no lessons had been learned. Actually, planners have been beaten bloody by their own ideas since then; no profession has had a more complete and chastening metamorphosis. But as with many things in the Soviet Union, there is a cultural gap.

Here are the immaculate models with their orderly arrangements of buildings, looking so clean and Utopian on a tiny scale, that enchanted planners of the prewar generation. Subsequent construction at full size has proved that they produce a limbo of scalelessness, inhumanity, and miscalculated expanses and voids. Here are the repeated slabs, so elegant on a table top, so monotonous in execution. The buildings are modern in style now, but they are still arranged in rigid patterns on the kind of Beaux-Arts boulevards with *grande allée* vistas that planners once loved and that people shun. Those vast, desolate areas on the ground are measured ultimately by weary human footsteps rather than by the one inch to one hundred feet of a scale rule. The Soviet plan is the big plan—dated, doctrinaire, sterile, lifeless when built—that the profession in other countries now knows is not the answer for livable new communities.

Some younger Soviet professionals, like the architect who called the new neighborhoods "dead," also know this. There has been criticism of Norilsk, for example, in the Soviet press. But there are still legions of planners who consider those vast avenues and overspaced housing blocks an ideal answer to crowded, reeking, substandard buildings on shabby streets. There is little interest in the picturesque among those to whom it means no plumbing and the decay and discomforts of worn-out buildings. To them, sterile planning is a beautiful alternative.

This does not mean that there is no appreciation of the old in the Soviet Union. National monuments and fine old buildings are universally protected and preserved. The Kremlin is obviously such a treasure, as is the city of Leningrad, and extraordinary care is expended on the maintenance and restoration of all monuments in this category. Leningrad has an annual restoration budget of 9,000,000 to 10,000,000 rubles just for its major historic buildings; additional funds are given to unions and societies for maintenance of many individual structures that rank as landmarks. There are special schools for restorers, and the best Soviet building skills are employed in the preservation of the old rather than in the construction of the new.

In Moscow dozens of churches are under repair. Their clustered onion domes are all that are left of old Moscow around the new Rossiya Hotel, for example, silhouetted provocatively against its vast commercial façade. But the debate about preservation is widening now as the planning and "reconstruction" of Moscow move from the new neighborhoods on the city's outskirts back toward its historic center. Moscow is rich in felicitous streets of small-scale post-Napoleonic classicism and a magnificently rugged nineteenth-century Russo-baroque. I have the feeling that all this will be relentlessly "reconstructed" out of existence. There are preservationists, however, who want to keep parts of the past, and they argue violently with those who favor new construction. The Institute of the General Plan of Moscow takes the position that the old buildings should be demolished eventually and many of them replaced with parks. Parks are a Soviet planning obsession.

I was asked by an official of the institute what I thought about GUM, the great Victorian-baroque *galleria* of the 1890's that serves as the state department store and is a particularly effective, richly plastic closure for the far side of Red Square. From the off-with-its-head look in the official's eye, it was clear that my plea for the building's preservation on esthetic and urban grounds came as something of a surprise.

The decision about what stays and what goes, however, is made by the Administration for the Preservation of Historic and Architectural Monuments under the Council of Ministers. Branches of this official Soviet preservation body exist in each republic. The group or its branches must give permission to demolish to the Moscow Soviet or to any other city Soviet under which the planners work. In Moscow 3,000 buildings are Registered Landmarks listed for preservation. (The New York Landmarks Law now protects one hundred and eighty-three buildings and six historic districts.) Recently transportation planners in Moscow were summarily denied the right to destroy a sixteenth-century building restored in the nineteenth century and part of an old wall behind the 25th of October Street to build an automobile overpass between Revolution and Sverdlov squares. Robert Moses could not have been more frustrated. History and architecture won.

In Tbilisi, the old city of Tiflis, the old town has just been put under government protection. This is particularly significant because it does not consist of great monuments but of small, shabby houses with iron balconies almost touching across tortuously hilly, narrow, stone-paved streets. It is as handsome as any French or Italian hill town. In the United States the urban-renewal bulldozer goes instinctively and relentlessly to the old heart of a city. Only the most intense battle and the greatest good fortune might get it designated, if an enabling law exists, as a historic district. In the Soviet Union, which is understandably preoccupied with the critical need for new housing and enamored of new construction, one would not expect the degree of cultivated concern that Tbilisi has demonstrated. Georgia, of course, is one of the Soviet Union's most tradition-rich areas.

The Tbilisi branch of the Union of Architects made the preservation proposal to the Tbilisi Soviet, which in turn presented it to the republic's government. The mayor of Tbilisi is a dark-eyed, sharp-minded, dynamic man whose well-designed modern office sets an immediate tone of cultural sophistication. The Lenin portrait matches. (Among his gifts to me was a miniature volume of the works of the Georgian poet Shota Rustaveli.) The republic approved the proposal and has allocated funds for design study.

This would be something like the New York Chapter of the American Institute of Architects proposing a historic district in Manhattan to the mayor and City Council, which would okay it and then get immediate funds and approval from the state legislature. Since the Union of Architects also staffs Tbilproyekt, the designing and building agency for the Tbilisi Soviet, the proposing architects are the disposing architects, and their studies will go full steam ahead. The plans are for rehabilitation, with relocation of some tenants into new housing and some to be moved back on completion of the renovated apartments. The ground floors will be used for cafés, restaurants, and shops. There are three old city districts and it is estimated that it will take ten years to do the whole job.

In twenty years the new city of Tbilisi is expected to expand on an outward curve within its long, narrow valley to embrace both sides of an artificial lake that was built for irrigation about fifteen years ago. Called the Tbilisi Sea, it is thirteen square kilometers in size and four kilometers from the banks of the Kura River, which winds through the center of the city.

I drove there, with several of the Tbilproyekt architects, on a fair May evening. First they showed me the old city, which they had saved, and then they took me to the site of the new city, of which they dream. But it is no dream; the master plan is made and approved, the path of expansion is set. I found myself hoping, in the light of what I had seen, that the quality of the planning would meet the challenge of the landscape. The evening was warm and luminous, the sky translucent, the lake pearly and still. The green hills around, they told me, had been sere and brown before the irrigation project. With splendid enthusiasm they sketched the future city in the air. We celebrated, appropriately, at an outdoor restaurant overlooking the lake, with champagne corks popping toward it over the railing like Fourth of July firecrackers and the toasts relayed around the table in Russian, Georgian, and English growing warmer and more elaborate as the sky faded and night descended softly and quickly, as it does in the south. An endless stream of Georgian delicacies appeared: shashlik, chicken Tabaka, sauces of garlic and green plum, fresh tarragon and a peppery watercress to eat by the handful. The Soviet champagne was as bottomless as the lake.

After five hours it was suggested that we finish with tea at one of the architect's homes. Our host was a youthful man, a war amputee, intense, intelligent, dark in coloring and mood. A widower, he has three young children. He was engaged in several special projects: a luxurious government guest house for top Soviet officials and a group of nonstandard apartment houses designed for the center of the city. His mother, a small, sweet woman, whose concern for our pleasure needed no English translation, appeared as hostess, although it was after midnight. The table had been pre-set elaborately with cheeses and cakes, and more champagne and cognac were brought. Eventually, and mercifully, there was tea.

The apartment was in a house of the architect's own design. A comfortable foyer opened into a studio at one side, with the drawing table, books, magazines, prints, sketches, and photographs common to architectural workrooms all over the world. I was immediately at home. A large living room directly through the foyer had the good, simple modern furnishings that are the architect's international cachet. On a wall-length Grundig stereo, Charles Aznavour records played. A bedroom off the living room was spacious and balconied. The dining room was on the opposite side of the living room. A kitchen could be glimpsed; the children's quarters were out of sight. As in all Tbilisi apartments, north and south windows provided through-ventilation for the summer heat. Except for the exotic assortment of languages, the intensity and durability of the famous Georgian hospitality, and the periodically solemn toasts to world peace, it could have been an architect's home in any city of the world. There were all the familiar touchstones of the educated esthetic tastes of a successful middle-class professional in the arts. It was not a typical home, of course, and I knew it. But it is increasingly typical for the Soviet Union's productive and privileged intellectuals.

At the top level, the architect in the Soviet Union is increasingly privileged today. He is traveling more widely and developing more international references; the itinerary is no longer to the East European countries and back. He is enthusiastic and understanding about what he sees in other parts of the world. On the student level, there is now liberal access in architectural libraries to a complete range of professional periodicals, including those from the United States, although stock in architectural bookstores, even in large cities, is pathetic. Since the Soviet culture and esthetic are still developing, some of the more far-out Western efforts have little meaning in the Soviet context. But it is quite obvious that the process of learning and assimilation, as in every other field, is going on at a steady rate. Interpretations that are limited or naïve are owing to a natural cultural lag between a country that began its industrialization fifty years ago and major countries that were already sophisticated industrial powers at that time. Standards that are still crude are the result largely of the extreme newness of a genuinely remarkable building technology plus the severe shortage of skills and the lack of any tradition of construction refinement in the close-enough past to set examples of finish or finesse.

The major barrier to Soviet architecture is, again paradoxically, the system that has made its technological progress possible. With state control of materials, processes, and design, there is little opportunity for free experimentation. There might be if critical building shortages were not so severe, but as long as that condition continues the situation is not likely to change.

On the other hand, as long as we in the United States cannot co-ordinate resources and production, cannot achieve a national building code, continue to legislate against prefabrication, continue to permit curious practices such as the disassembly and reassembly of factory-assembled parts on the site by union workers, we will never achieve mass-produced, low-cost housing. This need is at the heart of all social and urban problems.

Technologically, Soviet building now leaves much of the world behind. While others talk of the need for a way to meet the fantastic building projections of the next fifty years, the Russians have developed the techniques of mass production. They are already exporting them to areas of need, such as Cuba. The West has emphasized the exploration of other esthetic and urban problems—of human scale and community coherence, for example, and the quality of the environment. Comparatively, these Western solutions are one-of-a-kind, art collectors' items rather than practical answers to the superscale of today and tomorrow. They are indicative of another deep division between Soviet and American architecture: one of philosophy.

The United States is the bastion of creative individualism, or architecture for art's sake. Creative individualism is "the cult of the personality" in the Soviet Union; its probing and frequently critical explorations are considered to be against the general interests of the state. Art is warped into ideological service. The two fields that are the most purely creative and individualistic, art and literature, have suffered most.

Architecture, since it has legitimate, intrinsic social purpose, has not suffered in the same way. Soviet architects agree that their primary task is the development of housing to alleviate a desperate social need. In their common preoccupation with this social role they are less concerned with the fact that architecture has been repressed as an art in the past, as it was when constructivism lost official favor in the 1930's and during the later Stalinist period. It has since been released from those restraints with a totality unknown to painting or sculpture. The fact that it is now moving toward a new esthetic level—in a sense coming full circle from the aborted modernism of the 1920's to the modernism of the 1960's—and that this new style is based on Soviet technological achievements has a genuine significance.

But there are no stunning virtuoso performances, and if there are avant-garde "underground" sketches by young architects they are of little significance in these circumstances. You do not give a starving man caviar, even in Russia. He gets bread, or basic housing. The work is being done by talented men; they are no longer suppressed by the academicians. They are simply dealing realistically with an emergency condition.

Certainly, architecture for art's sake, or the virtuoso performance, has its proper and essential place as a testing ground for ideas, a breaker of barriers and customs, an exploration of values. As yet it has no place in the U.S.S.R. The question remains whether a bureaucracy can be sold a new idea as easily as a private client. One might predict that this could logically be a future development, that once shortages ease taste at the top might encourage exploration, but only a fool would predict anything about the Soviet Union.

The fact remains that today's architect, anywhere, virtuoso or not, is effective only if he faces today's building on its own terms: on an unprecedented scale, in unprecedented quantities, and for unprecedented needs. The taste and talent, the sense of social form that are his equipment and training are more important than ever for shaping an environment in crisis. Without technology, and the scope and kind of solutions that it offers, his work is without impact or meaning.

The architecture of the 1960's, therefore, is no longer to be pigeonholed with art and culture. It is an art form re-fused in the fires of technology for the most urgent contemporary uses. The Soviet Union knows this, even when the product comes apart at the seams. What it has produced depresses the Western visitor with its uniformity. But its present norm is better than much of Western production, particularly technologically, even if it is still below the best Western design. Esthetically, it is improving all the time. The U.S.S.R. is moving faster than any other nation on one of modern building's most important frontiers. It has helped redefine architecture in the twentieth century.

THE DEATH AND REBIRTH
OF A SCIENCE

»

Walter Sullivan

It must have been obvious to the fifty or so Russians and Americans crowded into the room that the ceremony about to take place represented a milestone. The scene was the Moscow office of Nikolai N. Blokhin, president of the Academy of Medical Sciences of the U.S.S.R. The date was March 31, 1967.

Representing the National Academy of Sciences of the United States, George Bogdan Kistiakowsky rose from his seat at the conference table, shuffling his papers, and all stood, including the man to be honored, Nikolai V. Timofeyev-Ressovsky. Kistiakowsky, a chemist, designer of the explosion that fired the first atomic bomb, former adviser to President Eisenhower, former member of the White Russian army, stood with a lean, erect bearing derived from his Cossack origins. He read:

"In the name of the Council of the National Academy of Sciences of the U.S.A. I am honored to present to you the Kimber Genetics Award. This Award reflects the high regard of your American colleagues for your distinguished accomplishments in genetics over a lifetime of research. . . .

"Your outstanding scientific investigations have placed you in the distinguished line of Charles Darwin, Gregor Mendel, William Bateson and

Thomas Hunt Morgan, whose likenesses appear on the Medal of the Kimber Award. . . ."

Kistiakowsky went on to name some of the previous recipients. He spoke in English, and Timofeyev-Ressovsky responded in English, apologizing for his poor command of the language, derived chiefly, he said, "from scientific periodicals and American detective stories."

Blokhin was about to end the ceremony when a woman pressed forward and asked if she could speak. "Of course, of course," said Blokhin, looking rather startled. There was a tight group of scientists at one end of the room, many of them women and all obviously from Timofeyev-Ressovsky's laboratory at Obninsk, a science research city southwest of Moscow.

The speaker was one of them. She launched into an emotional eulogy, describing what a wonderful leader Timofeyev-Ressovsky was and what great things he had accomplished despite much suffering. Then another girl thrust a bouquet into his hands. Timofeyev-Ressovsky clutched it a moment, then pulled out flowers, handing one to each of the visiting Americans.

Suddenly the visitors noticed that tears were pouring down the cheeks of several of the Russians. A tray of champagne glasses appeared, and the tears were soon hidden behind the bubbling wine.

Why tears on this joyous occasion? They were for the personal tragedy of Timofeyev-Ressovsky and the national tragedy of Soviet genetics—a period of scientific history on which the curtain, it was hoped, had been rung down forever.

Timofeyev-Ressovsky had left Soviet Russia in the 1920's and eventually joined the Max Planck Institute for Brain Research in Berlin, where he became one of Europe's leading geneticists. He discovered that heredity is more complicated than his predecessors Bateson and Morgan had believed. To be sure, heredity is transmitted from parent to offspring in discrete particles, or genes, but he found that these particles interact in some way. In other words, if you reach into the hereditary material of, say, a fruit fly and change the bit of information that controls eye color in future generations, the effect of that alteration depends on other information in the message—a complication that is still not fully understood.

Timofeyev-Ressovsky stayed at the Max Planck Institute even as the Red armies at the end of World War II were pounding at Berlin's gates. His colleagues pleaded with him to flee, but with the political naïveté typical of many scientists he remained, hoping to build a new life in his old homeland. According to former colleagues, he was seized, tried, and sent to Siberia. In 1947 word came to his wife, still in Berlin, that she could join him in the U.S.S.R. She found that he had been allowed to join the staff of an institute in the Urals.

The choice of Timofeyev-Ressovsky for the Kimber Award was reported to the Academy of Sciences of the U.S.S.R. in December, 1965, but he could not leave the country to receive it. The presentation had to wait for one of the periodic journeys to Moscow of delegates from the National Academy of Sciences in Washington. Even then, arrangements for the ceremony were made only at the last minute.

As is so often the case with tears, those shed at the ceremony were partially in rejoicing, for Soviet genetics had at last returned to the mainstream of modern science. Already the Russians were making important contributions in this field, so vital to the relief of human suffering, to the conquest of cancer, to agriculture, to the future of the human race itself. Back from intellectual limbo had come brilliant scientists nurtured in the revolutionary idea that genetics could remake mankind and all other life forms on earth into superior species such as the world has never known.

So discredited did Soviet genetics become during the heyday of the notorious Trofim D. Lysenko from 1948 to 1954 that many have forgotten the surge of intensive, and sometimes brilliant, research in that field during the early years of the Soviet regime. Typical of the earliest and most sensational phase were the ideas of Yuri A. Filipchenko, who believed genetics should be used to improve the genetic quality of mankind. He founded the Soviet Bureau of Eugenics and undertook a genealogical study of the Soviet intelligentsia, where he expected to find the richest genetic material for his project.

The idea of controlling human reproduction as one controls cattle breeding did not hold for long, and meanwhile, with the terrible famine that came in 1920, on the heels of the revolution, Lenin looked to genetics for superior strains of domestic crops and animals. As he put it on a visit to Petrograd: "The famine to prevent is the next one and the time to begin is now." A portion of the famine-relief funds, he insisted, should be diverted to seed selection and plant breeding.

He did not have to look far for the man to head this vital project. A young botanist named Nikolai I. Vavilov had electrified a meeting of plant breeders in Saratov, where he was a professor at the university, by announcing his "law of homologous series." He had arranged the plants of the world in a manner that seemed to show their common hereditary material, much as Dmitri I. Mendeleyev, with his periodic table of elements, had shown the atomic structure common to all matter. It seemed as though it should now be possible to design new plants, just as chemists create new chemical compounds. As Vavilov himself put it with unrestrained enthusiasm in a Kremlin speech: "Biological synthesis is becoming as much a reality as chemical." The breeders at the Saratov conference exclaimed exultantly in a telegram to the government: "Biology has found its Mendeleyev."

Thus, at thirty-six, Vavilov was chosen to head what became the Lenin All-Union Academy of Agricultural Sciences. He brought with him the most advanced ideas on genetics and plant breeding, for he had studied in Cambridge, England, with William Bateson, who gave genetics its name. It was Bateson, in 1900, who saw the significance of the work done a generation earlier by Gregor Mendel. He recognized that the stuff of heredity is not an amorphous mixture of characteristics contributed by the two parents, but consists of particles, or "genes," contributed by each. One or the other of these genes (from the father or mother) would determine, for example, eye color or whether one's hair is curly. The study of heredity, as carried by genes, was christened by Bateson "genetics."

Early in the 1930's a representative of another leading stream of research in this field, Hermann J. Muller, came to work in Moscow. Muller had been at Columbia University doing research under Thomas Hunt Morgan, who used the fast-breeding fruit fly, *Drosophila melanogaster,* as his tool. Morgan had first been skeptical of Bateson's claim that hereditary characteristics—that is, genes—tend to be inherited in batches. He later confirmed this and found the explanation, namely that the genes are implanted at fixed points on the visible units of genetic material, known as chromosomes.

In 1933 Morgan won a Nobel Prize for his work, and his student Muller did so, too, after returning from his stint in Moscow. Muller was honored for his discovery, while working with fruit flies, that radiation (X rays) can alter the genes.

It was, however, Vavilov's work that drew world attention to genetics in the U.S.S.R. Ever since his return from England at the start of World War I he had felt that the secret to improved crops lay in seeking out their places of origin, when first domesticated, thus uncovering varieties that could be used to breed supervarieties of wheat, corn, and other crops. His travels in search of such plants began before the revolution and took him to the Andean Highlands of South America (the source of potatoes), Mexico and Central America (for corn), the Ethiopian Highlands (where barley still grows wild), and the Mediterranean region from Portugal and Morocco to Syria and what is now Jordan. High in the Caucasus Mountains of the southern U.S.S.R. he sought out the homeland of wheat.

The scope of his effort is indicated by the fact that 25,000 living samples of wheat were collected for testing in experiment stations established across the vast width of the Soviet Union under his direction. By 1934 the combined staffs of the agricultural research institutes had reached 20,000.

When not tramping foreign fields in his early days, Vavilov lived in his office at the Institute of Applied Botany (later the Lenin All-Union Academy of Agricultural Sciences). He slept on a leather couch and ate meals prepared by the janitor's wife, who was of poor repute as a cook. Most of his salary was set aside to aid his scientific colleagues. As described by Theodosius Dobzhansky, a former colleague who left Russia and became one of the world's leading population geneticists, "Vavilov was first and foremost a man of action. His energy, forcefulness and working ability were marvelous. He was actually able to get along on between four and six hours of sleep per day, and appeared to neither need nor desire any rest or recreation. No wonder that his collaborators considered it something less than a privilege to travel or live in his company for many days in succession."

The high point of Vavilov's career was the Congress of Genetics, Plant and Animal Breeding, held in Leningrad in 1929 with himself as president. Among the three hundred and forty-eight papers presented was one co-authored by a man of whom few at the meeting had ever heard. His name: Trofim D. Lysenko. Speaking with a strong Ukrainian accent and a vocabulary that gave away his lack of a university education, Lysenko told of his experiments with the temperature treatment of plants. Their growing pattern could be radically altered, he said, if proper temperature was applied at an early stage in the plant's life. He said that the treatment of sprouting seeds of winter wheat with moisture and cold made it possible to sow this wheat in spring instead of fall, its normal planting time, and still have it ripen quickly for a late summer harvest.

The prospect held out by Lysenko would have been of great value for the Soviet Union, where most of the potential wheatlands have too cold a winter and too short a growing season for ordinary winter wheat and must resort to spring wheat varieties that are less productive and yield less grain per acre. By virtually simulating the germination process that winter wheat normally undergoes in the ground in areas with a relatively mild, wet winter, Lysenko's conditioning treatment, called "vernalization," was intended to produce a transformed winter wheat that would mature after spring planting in regions with a short growing season and yield larger crops than ordinary spring wheat.

Little did Vavilov and the other leaders of Soviet genetics realize that this young man, with deep-set burning eyes and quasi-religious fervor, would become the "Savonarola of Soviet science," demanding blind faith in his ideas and bringing, indirectly, death to a number of his adversaries. In fact, Vavilov championed his cause. When he came to the International Congress of Genetics at Cornell University in 1932, he said that Lysenko's conditioning of plants might make it possible to raise alligator pears in New York and lemons in New England.

He made a similar quip to the geneticist S. C. Harland while showing him Lysenko's experiment station in Odessa a year later. He said that environmental influences in evolution were not well understood and that Lysenko might even discover how to grow bananas in Moscow. He pictured Lysenko as "an angry species" and said that great advances were usually made by angry men. Harland was not impressed. He wrote later: "I interviewed Lysenko for nearly three hours. I found him completely ignorant of elementary principles of genetics and plant physiology. I myself have worked on genetics and plant-breeding for some thirty-five years, and I can quite honestly say that to talk to Lysenko was like trying to explain the differential calculus to a man who did not know his twelve times table."

Lysenko's impact might have been negligible had it not been for the fact that his appearance on the scene coincided with a severe agricultural crisis. In the words of David Joravsky, of Northwestern University, "the newly collectivized farms were too primitive and chaotic to use the recommendations of scientists."

Lysenko formed an alliance with I. I. Prezent, a specialist in Communist ideology, or dialectical materialism, who, while not a scientist, was an effective speaker and writer. In 1935 and 1936 they issued a barrage of popular articles and speeches declaring genetics to be a manifestation of bourgeois decadence inconsistent with Darwinism and dialectical materialism. Men like Vavilov were accused of frittering away the government's precious funds on meaningless research while the Soviet population hungered for more abundant food. They claimed that Lysenko's discoveries relating to such staples as wheat, corn, and potatoes could bring about enormous leaps in production.

As Mikhail D. Millionshchikov, vice president of the Academy of Sciences of the U.S.S.R. and chairman of the Soviet of Nationalities, one of two chambers in the Supreme Soviet, told me in a reminiscent talk, Lysenko and his followers made lavish promises—promises that related to a most vital problem, food production. The classical geneticists, he said, failed to make any promises.

Not only did Lysenko's noisy claims excite Soviet leaders because they professed to open a route of escape from the squeeze in agricultural production, but they also had an ideological appeal. Marx and Engels had been great admirers of Darwin, who believed that hereditary characteristics could be altered, during the lifetime of an individual, by the environment, but the two theoreticians of Communism died before the significance of Mendel's discoveries was recognized. Modern genetics—the genetics practiced by Vavilov and others—says that hereditary information is printed into the reproductive cells from the outset of life and cannot be changed except by mutation—that is, through alteration of the genetic material by radiation, chemical insult, or some other such influence. Mutations may be helpful or harmful to the individual. If harmful, they are weeded out by Darwin's principle: survival of the fittest. If helpful, they contribute to the slow process of evolution.

But some of the best-known agronomists and plant breeders of Russia had not been schooled in the new genetics. Such men as Kliment A. Timiryazev and Ivan V. Michurin clung to the belief that characteristics acquired in an organism's lifetime could be passed on to future generations, and their followers regarded modern genetics, rooted in the work of a monk, Gregor Mendel, as "clerical reaction" against pure Darwinism.

Lysenko's attack on genetics was given further ammunition by the racist theories of Hitler. The idea that the German people are genetically superior to all others in an intrinsic, immutable manner led to demands in the Soviet Union for a "progressive" genetics to counter that of the Nazis.

The more heavily the government became committed to Lysenko and his ideas, the blinder it became to their deficiencies. Lysenko's alleged discovery of wheat vernalization proved to have been practiced in the United States in the mid-nineteenth century only to be abandoned in favor of new strains that did even better when planted in the spring. (Apparently, vernalization has now also been abandoned in the Soviet Union.)

Modern genetic theory had enabled American agronomists during the 1920's to inbreed corn, producing strains that were stunted but "pure." They did not carry extraneous genes, only those for certain desirable features. These were then crossbred with pure strains displaying other desirable features. The resulting hybrids were extraordinarily strong and fruitful.

For example, it was possible to dissect out of the hodgepodge of genes in an ordinary crop of corn the one that gives some plants enormous ears. Likewise, by inbreeding, it was possible to isolate the gene that makes corn ripen early or the one that renders it resistant to disease. Because inbreeding tends to produce stunted plants, all such purified strains are measly-looking, but, when combined, the result can be a stalwart plant with many superior qualities. The new American hybrids were producing yields 25 to 35 per cent greater than those of ordinary corn, but to sustain such yields new seed had to be obtained each year.

Lysenko and his followers, on the other hand, scoffed at the genetic basis of hybrid production. They regarded inbreeding as the chief cause of poor crops and sent peasants through the fields with pieces of rabbit fur to pick up pollen from the tassels of as many corn plants as possible and transfer it to the silks of many plants to avoid inbreeding.

Another factor that aided Lysenko was the opposition to annual replenishment of hybrid seed. The view was deep-rooted in Russia, as it had been in the United States, that it is an improvident farmer who must acquire new seed every year. In Russia, difficulties of transport and distribution also stood in the way of hybrid utilization.

Lysenko's unscientific ideas crippled the production of another basic source of starch for the Soviet people—the lowly potato. At the start of the century a Russian, Dmitri I. Ivanovsky, discovered the first plant virus— that which produces the mosaic disease of tobacco plants—but despite the fact that virology was born in Russia, the study of plant viruses had largely been ignored in the Soviet Union, and Lysenko had no faith in the discovery that a virus disease accounted for the failure of potatoes to thrive in a hot, dry climate.

Long before this finding it was known that potatoes grown in a cold climate were largely free of the disease. If such potatoes were sent south to be cut up and planted as seed potatoes, incidence of the disease in the southern planting was low. If southern-grown potatoes were used for this, within a few seasons the virus disease was rampant.

In the hungry 1930's the Soviet government tried to push potato growing to ever more southern latitudes. Transport problems made it difficult to import seed potatoes from northern farms, and officials rejoiced in Lysenko's claim that this was unnecessary. The so-called potato disease, he said, was simply premature "aging" that occurred when the weather was hot during tuber-forming time. If potatoes in southern regions were planted in midsummer instead of spring, he said, full crops could be expected.

The climax came at the Second Congress of Collective Farm Shock-Brigade Workers, early in 1935. Lysenko declared that through summer planting the southern region of the U.S.S.R. could become completely self-sufficient in potatoes within two years. "Bravo, Comrade Lysenko!" cried Stalin from his place of honor at the meeting.

Actually, summer planting had long been a practice of potato farmers in certain regions, including Oklahoma, France, and even Lysenko's home country in the Ukraine. Its usefulness has proven limited. The practice seems largely to have been abandoned in the Soviet Union during World War II, and attempts to reinstate it after the war crumbled as Lysenko's star began to set.

By the time the Soviet genetics congress met in 1936, Vavilov had been ousted as president of the Lenin All-Union Academy of Agricultural Sciences and had been made a vice president. The powerful Soviet propaganda apparatus had been mobilized to demand a genetics based on dialectical materialism. Vavilov apparently still hoped to avoid a showdown and was mild in replying to the Lysenkoists. It was Hermann Muller, the American, working since 1933 at the Institute of Genetics of the Academy of Sciences in Moscow, who rose in fierce defense of his science. Shortly thereafter, Muller returned to the United States, where, in 1946, he won his Nobel Prize.

The crisis in Soviet genetics came to the attention of the world through a dispatch published in *The New York Times* of December 13, 1936. It reported that the Soviet government had ordered cancellation of the Seventh International Congress of Genetics, scheduled to be held in Moscow the following August. (The congress was held in Edinburgh instead.) The dispatch attributed the cancellation to the attacks of Lysenko, who was quoted as saying: "Genetics is merely an amusement, like chess or football." The report also said there were rumors in Moscow that Vavilov and Israel I. Agol, a leading researcher on fruit fly genetics, had been arrested.

Pravda denied Vavilov's arrest—the report apparently arose from an error in transmitting the news from Moscow—but it confirmed that Agol had been seized for association with "Trotskyist murderers." Vavilov himself sent a long statement to the *Times* bureau in Moscow, angrily attacking the report of his arrest and defending the achievements of his institutes (although ousted as head of the Academy of Agricultural Sciences, he still headed the institutes of Plant Industry and of Genetics). The Institute of Plant Industry, which he had led since the revolution, "has grown," he said, "to a most important organization, having few equals in size among the institutes of the world. Its staff has increased from 65 people in czarist times to 1,700 at present, including all of its subsidiary divisions." "Furthermore," he said, "the new building of the Institute of Genetics of the Academy of Sciences of the U.S.S.R. is nearing completion, an additional evidence of the status of genetics in our country. . . . As a true son of the U.S.S.R. I consider it my duty and good fortune to work for the benefit of my fatherland and to give all of myself to science in the U.S.S.R.

"I want to say that the statement about me in your paper and the fabrications by Science Service [an American news service] indicating that in the U.S.S.R. there is no intellectual freedom are totally untrue, and must come from hidden sources, and I want this telegram to appear in your paper."

It is an ironic footnote to this statement to recall that within a few years Lysenko had taken over Vavilov's job as head of the newly constructed Institute of Genetics, of which Vavilov was so proud.

Vavilov had, in fact, been persuaded that the Soviet Union, despite its harsh treatment of those it considered its enemies, offered more opportunity to its scientists than any other nation. He had expressed this view while walking through Sequoia National Park, six years earlier, with Theodosius Dobzhansky, the geneticist who in 1927 left Russia to practice his art in the greater freedom of Columbia and Rockefeller universities.

Now, however, Vavilov was fighting for his life, as well as for the life of his science. Several leading geneticists, including Sergei S. Chetverikov, whom some consider the founder of population genetics, had already been banished from Moscow. Not until 1939 did Vavilov finally speak out strongly against the Lysenkoists. By then it was too late.

When the Nazi armies marched into Poland that year, Soviet forces occupied the southeastern Polish district of Galicia. Vavilov was eager to collect plants from that region before crops introduced by the newly arrived Russians got mixed up with the local strains. His party, so the story goes, split up into small groups, which combed the countryside. Suddenly Vavilov, whom Sir Julian Huxley described as "one of the best scientists that Russia has ever produced," saw a band of sinister-looking men approaching across the fields. "Moscow wants you to answer some questions on the phone," he was reported to have been told. Vavilov walked away, never to be seen again by his colleagues, although it is said that they ultimately received his briefcase, crammed with withered plants. At the top— the last specimen he plucked before his arrest—was a previously unknown variety, the most important find of his expedition. He reportedly died at a labor camp at Magadan, on the frigid Sea of Okhotsk, in 1943.

Nevertheless, genetics was not dead in the Soviet Union. Work being done by Nikolai P. Dubinin in the laboratory of cytogenetics at the Institute of Cytology, Histology and Embryology had excited interest abroad, and there were those in the Academy of Sciences of the U.S.S.R. who thought a new genetics institute should be set up under Dubinin to counterbalance the one headed by Lysenko (and formerly under Vavilov). This was blocked by Lysenko's pervading influence, and the final showdown came at an eight-day session of the Academy of Agricultural Sciences held in the summer of 1948. Joravsky has called it "the most spectacular conference biologists have ever seen or are ever likely to see." It was the nadir of Soviet science. The transcript is reminiscent of the McCarthy hearings in Washington.

At the opening meeting Lysenko tore into genetics. "Progressive" biologists, he said, were defending Darwinism "against the church and against Bateson's scientific obscurantism." The fact that Lysenko found the statistical and mathematical arguments of Bateson "obscure" was, to some, an index of his mental ability. Lysenko also denounced the argument of geneticists that the germ plasm is, in a sense, immortal. That is, the genetic information—the "seed"—passed on from generation to generation in ever-changing combinations survives as long as there is continuity in the flow of life. This view, now generally accepted by all biologists, was described by Lysenko as pure "mysticism."

He also ridiculed Dubinin's study of the effect, on fruit fly chromosome structure, of catastrophic changes in environment brought about by the wartime fighting in and around Voronezh as a "pseudoscientific" project with no practical benefits. To classical geneticists such work opened windows on some of the basic laws governing evolution, but to Lysenko it was a fit subject for ridicule.

There was a strong note of anti-intellectualism in the speeches of Lysenko's adherents. As one of those at the meeting said exuberantly of the Lysenko team: "They are all men of action, we have heard them here, we know their deeds, they are not bookworms. . . ."

Several geneticists stood up to defend their science, attempting at the same time to pacify their prosecutors by denouncing various classical geneticists by name. They gained nothing from their compromises. When Lysenko rose to make his final summation, he said he had been asked what was the attitude of the Communist party toward his views. The transcript then reads as follows: "I answer, the Central Committee of the Party examined my report and approved it. (Stormy applause. Ovation. All rise.)"

That was the *coup de grâce*. Classical genetics had, in effect, been outlawed, and Lysenko had known it all through the turbulent meeting. He had allowed his enemies to hang themselves in public. Now five of them, like Galileo during the Inquisition, sought to escape by recanting. Their statements make painful reading today.

On August 27, *Pravda* published a letter from the Academy of Sciences of the U.S.S.R. to Stalin. "The Presidium of the Academy of Sciences promises you, dear Iosif Vissarionovich," it said in part, "and through you, our Party and Government, determinedly to rectify the errors we permitted, to reorganize the work of the Division of Biological Sciences and its institutes, and to develop biological science in a true materialistic Michurinist direction."

In the same issue of *Pravda* the academy also published a resolution which, among other things, abolished various institutes in the field of genetics, including that headed by Dubinin. It resolved to revise the program of biological research and purge from the institutes and the editorial boards of biological journals those opposed to the Lysenko view.

Thus the entire science of biology was oppressed. Research in genetics came almost to a complete halt, and those in the field who valued their skins vanished into obscurity as fast as possible. Agricultural research hit an all-time low, and Soviet soil science, which had led the world, according to a survey by the United States Department of Commerce, also went into a decline.

When I visited the Soviet Union in 1967 everything had changed. Dubinin and his colleagues were on top. Lysenko was living in relative obscurity in his dacha near Moscow. He was the only scientist who, in so many words, refused to see me.

How had the tables turned so completely? What was happening in Soviet genetics and biology now that freedom of inquiry had largely been restored? A number of those involved in the revolt told me their parts of the story. I found Dubinin installed as head of a new Institute of General Genetics much like the one envisioned for him by the Soviet Academy of Sciences twenty years earlier. He sat in the temporary quarters of his new institute, barely a year old, in a suburb of Moscow torn up by the construction of new apartments and laboratories. His conference table was heaped with current issues of the American journal *Science* and other American, European, and Soviet magazines. He ticked off the recent developments. He knew them well, for he is now president of the Scientific Council on Genetic Problems of the Academy of Sciences—a co-ordinative panel on which various research and health agencies are represented.

He pointed to a new Soviet journal, *Genetika*. "It is our first review on genetic questions. We began monthly publication in 1965. During the past two years," he continued, "ten new laboratories have been organized in the Institute of Biological Problems. In the Byelorussian Academy of Sciences, at Minsk, an Institute of Genetics was formed a year and a half ago under Turbin, who is working on hybrids of corn and wheat. In Kiev, at the Ukrainian Academy of Sciences, there is a department of genetics with several new laboratories doing experimental work on mutagenesis and radiation chemistry. In the Academy of Medical Sciences there will soon be an Institute of Human Genetics. And in Obninsk there is Timofeyev-Ressovsky. He heads the department of radiation genetics in the new Institute of Radiobiology."

A special source of pride to Dubinin is the Institute of Cytology and Genetics that he himself established near Novosibirsk, in the heart of Siberia. At the time when Nikita S. Khrushchev still retained some loyalty to Lysenko, he is reported to have asked why if Dubinin was a "bad scientist" in Moscow he was not also a bad scientist in Novosibirsk.

The first stirring of public criticism of Lysenko came in 1952, close to the end of the Stalin era. But it was the death of Lysenko's chief sponsor, Stalin himself, that turned the tide. The next year, 1954, the party organ *Kommunist* encouraged free scientific discussion (although calling for it to be based on dialectical materialism) and it opposed the suppression of divergent views. It was evident to the new leader, Khrushchev, that Soviet agriculture was in a sorry state. The Central Committee of the Communist party decreed the intensive development of hybrid corn, and this offered to the bolder geneticists a chance to strike back.

Foremost among them was Dubinin, who had been out of sight since his institute was abolished in 1948. In a 1955 article he laid it on the line: "T. D. Lysenko caused the stoppage of work at the critical moment when hybrid corn began to emerge from the experiments in the fields of our kolkhozes and sovkhozes [collective farms and state farms]. Now 20 years later, after the U.S.A., using the very same methods which were worked out in our country, has achieved the introduction of hybrid corn and the establishment of the foundation for production of animal fodder, the U.S.S.R. faces the problem of catching up in a very short space of time on that which we let slip."

Soon the method of crossing inbred lines to achieve superior hybrids—the Dubinin brand of genetics—was being practiced across the width of the Soviet Union. In 1959 Khrushchev made his famous visit to the corn country of Iowa and saw for himself how hybrid corn, used as fodder, can provide a country with abundant meat.

Meanwhile, the word began to get around that the U.S.S.R.'s leading nuclear physicists had helped keep Soviet genetics alive by quietly sheltering some of its most able practitioners in their closely guarded laboratories. The great physicist Igor V. Kurchatov (who died in 1960) played a central role in providing the Soviet Union with its first atomic weapons. His Institute of Theoretical Physics in Moscow was almost sacrosanct, as far as government interference was concerned. Since radiation, such as that from X rays or radioactive materials, can cause hereditary changes, there was some logic to the conduct of genetic research at the institute.

Thus in the 1950's there was a large department of genetics in the Kurchatov institute, and a Laboratory of Radiation Genetics was quietly organized by Dubinin at the Institute of Biophysics of the Academy of Sciences in 1958. It was this laboratory which evolved into the full-fledged institute that he now heads—an institute that itself has a dozen laboratories devoted to such problems as evolutionary genetics, space genetics, viral genetics, immunogenetics, and so forth.

After my talk with Dubinin I visited a couple of the laboratories in his institute. In one of them I was told that the research has, as its starting point, discoveries reported by Richard F. Kimball at the Oak Ridge National Laboratory in Tennessee. Kimball has been studying the manner in which the living cell can sometimes repair genetic damage caused by radiation. In Moscow the work is concentrated on repair processes where the genetic damage, or mutation, has been caused by a chemical, such as mustard gas or ethylenimine. The experimental material includes Chlorella algae and rat liver cells growing in glass containers.

In another equally sophisticated line of research, David M. Goldfarb is investigating the manner in which bacterial cells protect themselves against incorrect genetic information that might be infiltrated into them by foreign DNA. (DNA, or deoxyribonucleic acid, is the long, twisted molecule that carries the hereditary information needed for the continuity of life, much as magnetic tape can store an entire television program.) Apparently the enzymes that unwind the DNA molecule, making it active, "know" the DNA native to that cell and do not act on foreign DNA.

There remains a strong practical element in Soviet genetic research. When I visited the Institute of Cytology and Genetics that Dubinin had founded near Novosibirsk, its director, Dmitri K. Belyayev, stressed the economic benefits deriving from the work there, much as an American scientist might do in testifying before Congress in behalf of his program.

Belyayev said it had been found that, contrary to earlier belief, mutations, or heredity changes, induced by radiation are not always predominantly harmful. In fact, with at least some plants there seems to be an optimum dosage that produces mutations as many as half of which may be beneficial. As an example he cited wheat, for which the best dosage lies between 5,000 and 10,000 roentgens. Treatment with such dosages has generated strains that have short, thick stems, making them resistant to wind, yet have good baking qualities.

At the institute there is also a Laboratory of Polyploidy—a field that was anathema to the Lysenkoists, because it was firmly rooted in classical genetics. Polyploidy is the occurrence of plants (and in some cases animals) that have unusual multiples of a basic number of chromosomes. Thus the sugar beet normally has eighteen chromosomes (nine kinds, occurring in pairs, one set contributed by each parent plant). But by treatment with a chemical, colchicine, it is possible to produce plants that have four of each kind, instead of two; that is, thirty-six chromosomes. These are "tetraploids." By crossing them with ordinary sugar beets it is possible to obtain an odd strain—a "triploid"—with three of each chromosome type; that is, with a total of twenty-seven. Such a strain, according to Belyayev and his colleagues, has been developed by this institute with dramatic results. Sugar production per acre, they say, is 15 per cent higher than with ordinary beets. The new strain has been in use for three years and is now growing on many farms in southern regions of the U.S.S.R.

Another line of practical research looks to the development of hybrid corn whose seeds can be used for subsequent crops, freeing the farm from the need to order new seed each year. Hybrids now in general use deteriorate after a generation or two, but Belyayev reported that new strains developed by his institute were good for three, four, and even five generations.

Belyayev specializes in the genetics of fur-bearing animals. He has been interested, for example, in the fact that female silver foxes on fur farms have several periods of heat in a year whereas wild foxes have only one. He has found evidence that there is a genetic relationship between multiple periods of heat and docility. The genes seem to be linked. Foxes that are docile are the most likely to be caught and the least likely to escape or die young in captivity. This has led to a fox-farm population that has the twin characteristics of docility and multiple periods of heat.

Belyayev predicted that in the "near future" scientists would decipher the manner in which genetic information wrapped up in the nucleus of the cell actually controls development of the individual. "We are trying to direct as much as possible of the work in our laboratories toward that goal," he said. Thus the institute, besides breeding new strains of domestic plants and animals, is also doing basic work on chromosomes and DNA molecules. Julius Kerkis, who worked with Muller in the early days and now heads the institute's Laboratory of Radiation Genetics, explained how he has been studying outside influences (including hormonal balance) on the sensitivity of hereditary material to radiation. His subject matter includes tissue cultured in glass. He explained that his work is related to the basic question of aging. If the cells of our bodies duplicated themselves faithfully throughout life we should not change. Hence some believe aging involves damage, from radiation or other sources, to the hereditary material of the cells.

In the lobby of the institute I saw an extensive exhibit of books, scientific papers, and other documents surmounted by a black-rimmed photograph. Beneath it, in Russian lettering, was the name H. J. Muller. The great American geneticist, who had fought vigorously though in vain against Lysenkoism, had died a few days before.

Closely linked to the eruption of genetic research in the Soviet Union has been the explosive growth of molecular biology. As with genetics, this had its birth—at least to a large extent—in the concern of Soviet nuclear physicists with the deplorable state of biology in the U.S.S.R. The disastrous extent to which the country had fallen behind became evident as windows to the West began opening after Stalin's death.

The situation was a frequent subject of discussion at the weekly seminars known as "Kapishniks" because Pyotr Kapitsa was their central figure. Kapitsa had been one of the most brilliant pupils of Ernest Rutherford, the great British physicist. He had devised a way to generate extremely intense magnetic fields as well as an economical method of producing liquid helium. The latter is so cold that it makes it possible to study materials at extreme low temperatures (close to absolute zero, or the absence of all heat). Britain's Royal Society, at considerable expense, built a special laboratory for Kapitsa, equipped with his new devices, so that he could study the behavior of extremely cold materials under powerful magnetism. He was about to embark on experiments that, Rutherford said, "would add markedly to our knowledge of the structure of matter."

In the summer of 1934 he made one of his periodic visits to the Soviet Union, lecturing and attending a scientific congress. Suddenly he was told that he could not return to England. The Soviet Embassy in London said that because of the urgent need for scientific talent in the U.S.S.R. the "Soviet government has found it necessary to utilize for scientific activities within the country the services of Soviet scientists hitherto working abroad. Professor Kapitsa belongs to this category." Rutherford was furious, pointing out in a letter to the London *Times* the heartbreak of a scientist denied access to his laboratory just when he was about to cash in on his long efforts.

When it became obvious that Kapitsa would not return, Rutherford saw to it that equipment from the new low-temperature laboratory was shipped to the Soviet Union so that the Russian physicist could continue his work. Not until 1966 did Kapitsa return to England, and then only for a visit. He promptly returned to Mother Russia, where he had become a potent force for the freedom of discussion that is so vital a part of the scientific process.

It was this freedom that dominated the Kapishniks, and the participants included such figures as Igor E. Tamm and Lev D. Landau, both Nobel laureates in physics. Tamm, a robust figure who wore the emblem of Master of Sport in mountaineering, gave a lecture in about 1956 that added fuel to the fire. Speaking in the biology department of the Kurchatov institute, he told of exciting new developments in Britain and the United States.

It was evident that by analysis of DNA Western scientists were zeroing in on the chemical mechanism of heredity. J. D. Watson, at Harvard, and F. H. C. Crick, at Cambridge, had delineated the structure of the molecule, and it was only a matter of time before the "code of life"—the precise manner in which the information was encoded into the molecule—would be unraveled.

The prospects for genetics, for biology, for the future of mankind were awesome, for there now loomed the possibility of engineering heredity, not by Lysenko's manipulation of the environment, but by ingeniously controlled mutations. It was obvious to men like Tamm that Soviet science would be hopelessly left behind unless they moved vigorously into this new area. Research in molecular biology was therefore encouraged at the atomic centers.

Meanwhile, one of the more venerable opponents of Lysenkoism had quietly moved into the field. He was Vladimir A. Engelgardt, who, in the 1930's, pioneered in muscle chemistry. This won him an international reputation, and ultimately he became the Soviet representative on the board of the International Council of Scientific Unions—the global scientific body that had operated the International Geophysical Year of 1957–58. In recent years his interest has shifted to the nucleic acids (such as DNA and RNA) and their role in genetics. About 1958 (which seems to have been a critical turning point) it was decided to form an Institute of Radiational and Physical-Chemical Biology, with Engelgardt as director. This cumbersome title served as a camouflage for the real thrust of the work there.

I visited him in his institute and found him spry and overflowing with enthusiasm despite his seventy-two years. He explained that at his request the name of his establishment had been changed to the Institute of Molecular Biology—which more accurately reflects the nature of its research.

At his side was Aleksandr Y. Braunshtein, his prize pupil and perhaps the best-known biochemist in the Soviet Union. Braunshtein told of his current studies of vitamin B_6 chemistry, an enormously complicated—and vital—problem. The vitamin, in its various forms, joins with more than sixty different enzymes to catalyze, or stimulate, reactions in the life process. Some of the antibiotics inhibit certain of these reactions, and so a three-dimensional understanding of how the molecules twist and turn in their interactions with one another has important medical implications. To achieve this understanding, Braunshtein is using ultraviolet, visible, and fluorescence spectra. He explained how his work was related to that of Max F. Perutz and John C. Kendrew, at Cambridge University, who won a Nobel Prize for first mapping the structure of a protein, and that of David C. Phillips, at the Royal Institution in London, who charted the complex structure of lysozyme, an enzyme that breaks down cell walls.

Engelgardt broke in to point out that a man in his institute, A. A. Bayev, had just deciphered the structure of another key substance—the transfer-RNA (ribonucleic acid) that carries the code for the synthesis of valine. The latter is one of the twenty components (amino acids) that are linked in an almost infinite variety of sequences to form the giant protein molecules. The transfer-RNA picks up a molecule of valine and sees to it that it slips into the correct slot in the formation of a protein. The only other transfer-RNA charted so far is that for alanine—a feat completed in 1965 by Robert W. Holley, at Cornell University. It involved charting the correct sequence of the seventy-seven chemical units forming that molecule.

It took Bayev five years to do the job, Engelgardt said. Now, he added, Bayev is seeking out the structural features common to all the transfer-RNA's (some fifty in number).

American specialists who have toured Engelgardt's institute consider it well equipped by Western standards, with automatic spectrophotometers, ultracentrifuges, and other analytical devices. They have also remarked on a practice that they found somewhat quaint and that is based on the belief that those working with poisonous or radioactive substances should drink milk. Every day there is a pause while milk is taken from the laboratory refrigerators and distributed to the researchers—a half-liter apiece.

One of the novel features of Engelgardt's institute is its role as headquarters of the Chromosome Service of the Soviet Union. This is conducting an inventory of chromosome patterns in the population as a way of attacking congenital diseases. Human cells characteristically contain forty-six chromosomes (twenty-three paired packages of hereditary information). Cows have sixty, and fruit flies eight. However, abnormal chromosome counts have been observed in several congenital conditions. For example, it has recently been found that most Mongoloid children, instead of having two versions of the number 21 chromosome (one derived from each parent), have three. In another disorder the child is born with three, instead of two, of the number 18 chromosome. The chromosome inventory, under A. A. Prokofieva-Belgovskaya, of Engelgardt's institute, is being done in the course of routine blood tests in various regions of the country. Those with abnormal chromosome complements will be warned if there appears to be a danger that they will produce deficient offspring.

Engelgardt said that, as with genetics, there is a new journal, *Molekularnaya Biologiya,* whose first issue came out early in 1967, and an interdepartmental council has been formed to co-ordinate research in this field. In a crash training program, he added, a "Winter School" is held each January at Dubna, the atomic-research center on the Volga River. Some two hundred promising youngsters are brought together to hear talks by leading men in the field. "Actually," he said, "there is more discussion than lecturing. And after the sessions they go skiing."

"I tried to get physicists and biologists into the program to avoid compartmentalization, although at first the physicists were not very enthusiastic." However, he added, a new brand of scientist is appearing on the scene—a sort of Renaissance man in the scientific sense, grounded in many fields: chemistry, physics, biology, statistics. A major source of such talent is the new Physical-Technical Institute, established near Moscow by a group of leading scientists including Kapitsa and Nikolai N. Semenov, the Nobel laureate in chemistry.

A visit to Semenov's department in the Academy of Sciences of the U.S.S.R. and to various Moscow institutes showed many signs of the Soviet race to catch up with the West in genetics, molecular biology, and biochemistry. Semenov explained that the Academy of Sciences—a giant organization that towers over Soviet science—was now divided into three sections, one of which, dealing with chemistry and biology, is under his direction. Another deals with the physical and mathematical sciences, and the third is concerned with the social sciences.

Semenov, at seventy-one, was full of energy and humor. In founding the Institute of Chemical Physics in 1931 he had brought about a certain synthesis of chemistry and physics, emphasizing application of the new discoveries in physics to the construction of theories to account for chemical reaction rates and energy releases, including those of explosions. It was for such work that he won his Nobel Prize.

"My goal, since 1950, has been to achieve a marriage between biology and chemistry," he said. "At first it was slowed by the difficulties of the time—the Lysenko problem. However, five years ago [in 1962] I was able to form a new Division of Biophysics, Biochemistry and Physiologically Active Compounds within the academy." He found, as Engelgardt had, that physicists, biologists, and chemists, trained to limited fields of interest, did not mix easily. Of his new unit in the institute he said with a grin: "At first it was a mechanical mixture, but now it is nearly a chemical compound!"

He spelled out the proliferation of new institutes in the field: those of Engelgardt and Dubinin, a new Institute of the Biology of Development ("It is really genetics") headed by Boris Astaurov, a long-suppressed geneticist, and an Institute of Ecology, the last two in Moscow.

"Academician Imanuel Rappoport, who discovered chemical mutagenesis [hereditary changes caused by chemicals] is here in my institute. The agricultural stations are now using Rappoport's results. Spirin is organizing a new Protein Institute where the biosynthesis of proteins will be studied. He has invited four or five colleagues—young men of thirty-five and thirty-six years—to join him there. He is a biologist, and his associates will be physicists and chemists. It will be in the new science city of Pushchino."

I had heard American scientists speak of Aleksandr S. Spirin as one of the most promising young biochemists in the Soviet Union and made a point of visiting him at the Bakh Institute of Biochemistry, headed by Aleksandr I. Oparin, father of modern scientific thinking on the origin of life. Oparin told me of his recent thoughts concerning the manner in which the complex chemistry of life became organized into living cells. (He believes it was analogous to the formation of coated droplets known as coacervates.) Then I was closeted with Spirin, a dark-haired diminutive man who reminded me of Frank Sinatra. He told of his efforts to dissect and reconstruct ribosomes. These are tiny structures within the cell, so small that they cannot be studied in any detail even under the most powerful electron microscope. The ribosomes are thought to be the site where the essence of the life process—the assembly of amino acids into proteins—is carried out, following genetic instructions stored in the DNA of the nucleus and carried to the ribosomes by RNA.

Spirin explained that knowledge of ribosome structure could be of major medical importance, because many antibiotics, such as the tetracyclines, alter the mechanism of protein synthesis in the ribosomes of bacteria, thus interfering with their life process. Such drugs can be used to fight bacteria because they affect bacterial ribosomes, but, apparently, not those of human cells. Intimate knowledge of this process and of ribosomal structure could make it possible to design antibiotics against ailments now beyond reach—even, Spirin said, against cancer.

He explained that each ribosome is formed of two rounded structures of unequal size. These were separated by American researchers in the late 1950's, and then Spirin, in 1963, managed to unfold both the large and small component into a tiny filament. It was then possible to do what he called in English a "strip tease" of each filament, to see what it was made of. It turned out that the large component consisted of an RNA molecule enveloped in thirty different protein molecules, whereas the other was an RNA molecule wrapped in fifteen proteins.

In 1966 the components were reassembled into ribosomes by both his laboratory and American workers. Now he is trying other ways to reassemble the ribosomes into bodies that act normally in the life process. In this way it may be possible to learn more about details of their invisible structure. The work, he said, has features in common with that of the 1950's in which the tobacco mosaic virus was disassembled and then put back together again by Wendell M. Stanley and his colleagues at the University of California.

Spirin complained that American reports on new developments in this field rarely acknowledge Soviet achievements. He keeps in close touch with American work because he regularly attends the Gordon Research Conferences. These are held each summer in New Hampshire as a forum for off-the-record exchanges between leaders in various frontier regions of science.

The current explosion in molecular biology is also evident at Moscow State University—the giant "wedding cake" structure overlooking Moscow from the Lenin Hills. A whole new building was constructed in 1967 for those in this field. Sergei Y. Severin, head of the biochemistry department of the university, and his colleagues described their efforts to unravel the chemistry of energy storage within the mitochondria—bodies within the cell that are far larger than ribosomes. The storage process (known as oxidative phosphorylation) can be blocked so that the energy, instead of being stored, generates heat. It has been found at the university that such animals as pigeons and mice live longer under conditions of extreme cold when treated with a substance that blocks energy storage and thus releases heat.

Today Soviet science has largely shaken off the shackles of Lysenkoism, although the final big step was taken only three years ago, when Lysenko was ousted from Vavilov's former post as head of the old Institute of Genetics. Could it happen again, could another Savonarola, another man of passionate, arrogant, and intolerant views, impose his will on science in the U.S.S.R.?

To assess this possibility one must examine the causes of the past episode. A number of factors were involved, no one of which alone could have accounted for what occurred. They can be summarized as follows:

1. The ideological attraction of Lysenko's ideas as presented by his more rhetorical backers.

2. The existence of a strong national tradition in empirical plant breeding.

3. The agricultural crisis of the 1930's that made the party and government responsive to extravagant promises.

4. The existence of a dictator deaf to the logic of Lysenko's opponents and powerful enough to impose his will without challenge.

In talking to those in the current mainstream of Soviet science one is reminded at every hand of their awareness of the disastrous sequence of events behind them. As early as 1957 this was spelled out by Aleksandr N.

Boris Pasternak in 1958 *(The New York Times)*

Pasternak's grave in Peredelkino *(Harrison E. Salisbury, The New York Times)*

Andrei Voznesensky, Soviet poet and admirer of Pasternak, whose poetic collection *Antiworlds* has been given over two hundred performances at the Taganka Theater in Moscow *(Novosti from Sovfoto)*

Yevgeny Yevtushenko reading Pasternak   *(Black Star)*

Bella Akhmadulina, a poet "with a silvery gift of speech and a deft sense of humor" *(Harrison E. Salisbury, The New York Times)*

Aleksandr Solzhenitsyn, author of *One Day in the Life of Ivan Denisovich* and center of a literary storm in Moscow over suppression of his works   *(Sovfoto)*

Valentin Katayev, prominent author, one of the leaders of the liberal group fighting for greater creative freedom   *(Harrison E. Salisbury, The New York Times)*

Yuri Nagibin, famous for his realistic short stories, at his country house in June, 1967 *(Harrison E. Salisbury, The New York Times)*

Andrei Sinyavsky (with beard) and Yuli Daniel on trial in Moscow for publishing works secretly in the West, before they were sentenced to prison camps   *(Camera Press-Pix)*

Vasily Kandinsky's "Black Lines, No. 189," painted in 1913, before he went into permanent exile, in 1922, when modern art began to be attacked in Russia *(The Solomon R. Guggenheim Museum)*

Left: "Houses under Construction," painted in 1914 by cubist Kazimir Malevich, a major influence on the current revival of abstract art *(Collection, The Museum of Modern Art, New York) Right:* Abstract relief of found objects, 1914, by Vladimir Tatlin, who led a number of Soviet artists into industrial design and applied art

Naum Gabo's "Head of a Woman," 1916-17, an early example of his open-form constructivist sculpture *(Collection, The Museum of Modern Art, New York)*

Kazimir Malevich's "Suprematist Composition: White on White," 1918 *(Collection, The Museum of Modern Art, New York)*

Design for a frieze for the State Jewish Theater in Moscow, 1919-20, by Marc Chagall, who was more lyrical and conservative than the other early modernists

"Hanging Construction," 1920, wood, by Aleksandr Rodchenko
(*Photograph courtesy of Alfred H. Barr, Jr.*)

Opposite: Ernst Neizvestny, at forty
two perhaps Russia's best-known ar
ist of his generation, who has ha
successful shows in London and Ne
York   (*Harrison E. Salisbury, Th
New York Times*)

Ilya Repin's "They Did Not Expec
Him," 1884, an example of paintin
fully understandable to the masse
that came back into vogue when th
brief official support given to moc
ernism after the revolution was witk
drawn in late 1921   (*Tretyakov Ga
lery, Moscow*)

Stage set by Lyubov Popova for Vsevolod Meyerhold's controversial 1922 staging of Crommelynek's "The Magnificent Cuckold"

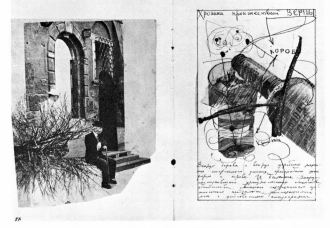

ad of a Faun, carved from stone
1947 by Dmitri Tsaplin, who, at
enty-seven, is one of the few gifted
lptors working in the Soviet Union
ay *(The New York Times)*

Facing pages from a portfolio of collage-poems, 1965, by Aleksei Khvostenko, a self-taught artist from Leningrad, still in his twenties and "only at the beginning of an important career at a boundary where literary and visual art meet" *(The New York Times)*

A class of three-year-olds in Podolsk: Russians believe in catching them
young   *(Novosti)*

Lyuba Timofeyeva, of the Central Music School in Moscow, as soloist in a
work by Dmitri Kabalevsky, who is conducting   *(Novosti)*

David Oistrakh, one of the world's leading violinists, instructing one of his postgraduate students at the Moscow Conservatory *(Novosti)*

Mstislav Rostropovich, who in 1967 played an eight-evening concerto cycle in New York City *(Novosti)*

Pianist Emil Gilels, Lenin Prize winner of 1962 *(Novosti)*

Dmitri Shostakovich, dean of Soviet composers, whose career, many feel, has been thwarted by political interference *(Novosti)*

Aram Khachaturian, from Armenia, one of the leading exponents of Soviet nationalism, whose music was popular in the West in the 1940's and early 1950's *(Novosti)*

Scene from Rimsky-Korsakov's opera *The Tale of the Invisible City of Kitezh,* which, based on a mixture of Russian paganism and Christianity, has been described as the Russian *Parsifal* *(Novosti)*

Students of the Bolshoi Ballet school rehearsing at the bar   *(Cornell Capa, Magnum)*

Opposite: Galina Ulanova, reigning star of the Bolshoi Ballet for two decades, at the height of her career in 1950   *(Sovfoto)*

Irina Kolpakova and Vladilen Semenov, stars of Leningrad's Kirov Ballet, in Tchaikovsky's classic *Sleeping Beauty*   *(Anthony Crickmay)*

Maya Plisetskaya, premier ballerina of the Bolshoi Ballet company, as Odette in Tchaikovsky's *Swan Lake*   *(Anthony Crickmay)*

The Moscow Art Theater in the 1930's, when Stanislavsky and Nemirovich-Danchenko were still alive   *(Morris Gest)*

A. Y. Tairov, whose theater was closed by Soviet authorities in 1950, Gordon Craig, who designed productions for many Soviet directors, and Vsevolod Meyerhold in 1935

Vsevolod Meyerhold, famous Moscow director, photographed in 1938 shortly before his arrest and dispatch to a Siberian concentration camp, where he died

A scene from Mayakovsky's long-suppressed *Banya (Bathhouse)* at Moscow's Satire Theater

Mayakovsky's *Mystère-Bouffe,* a poetic fantasy long suppressed under Stalin, now being presented at the Satire Theater

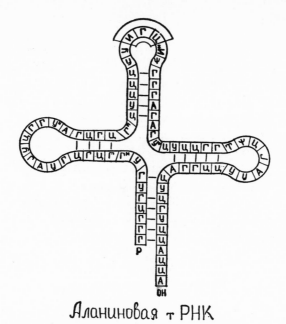

Аланиновая т РНК

Holley's decipherment of the transfer-RNA for alanine. The "anti-codon" or active triplet at the top is the segment that picks up the proper amino acid (alanine) and sees that it is properly positioned in the newly made protein.

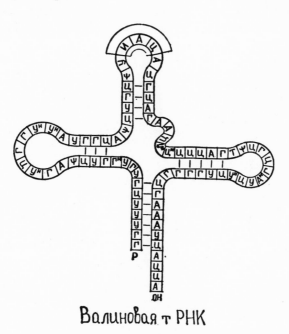

Валиновая т РНК

Bayev's reconstruction of the transfer-RNA for valine. As with Holley's chart, the active triplet is at the top.

Nesmeyanov, then president of the Academy of Sciences, when he said: "We must frankly state that our biology had been acquiring the bad habit of solving debated scientific problems through the pressuring and suppression of scientific opponents, the use of disparaging labels, and other unscientific means. All this has had a negative effect on the development of a number of branches of biological science. . . . In general, it must be stated that one-sided evaluation and attempts at arriving at official evaluations in science by a majority of votes or more vocal behavior are not fruitful."

Such candor is now commonplace. One is left with the impression that the Soviet Establishment has learned its lesson and that a recurrence of suppressive tyranny in the physical or biological sciences is unlikely.

THE AKADEMGORODOK: A NEW LOOK IN SOVIET SCIENCE

»

Walter Sullivan

"It is like something right out of *Alice in Wonderland*," said an American physicist after seeing plans for the machine projected by Gersh I. Budker at the new Academic City, or Akademgorodok, near Novosibirsk. It would generate a cloud of antimatter over a day's time, accelerate it almost to the speed of light, then smash it head on into a comparable cloud of matter traveling in the opposite direction at the same speed. The resulting particle collisions would be at energies far above those achieved in any laboratory in existence or under construction.

"In the United States," the American said, "I don't know where you would get the money for such a wild scheme."

In the Soviet Union, fortress of Communism, Budker has obtained part of his money by going into business. His Institute of Nuclear Physics manufactures accelerators for the blossoming industry of Siberia and uses the profits to swell its own budget.

Budker's operation is but one of many examples of the freewheeling developments taking place in the new "academic cities" springing up here and there in open meadows or forests of birch and pine far from the old scientific centers of Moscow and Leningrad. This decentralization is closely linked to the effort to spread the industrial base of the Soviet Union to remote parts of the country and, at the same time, to exploit talent in those regions.

Certain of the new science centers are also remote by necessity. On a summit in the northern Caucasus preparations are nearing completion for the installation of a fifty-ton mirror, twenty feet in diameter, that is the key element in what will be the world's largest telescope. It must be remote to escape the glowing lights of human habitation. Preferably it would have been farther from the rainy climate of the Black Sea, but the problem of transporting, into the drier regions of Soviet Central Asia, a mirror too wide to ride a railroad made that impractical.

Perforce remote as well is the giant accelerator ring that I visited in a pine forest near the ancient town of Serpukhov. It is designed to produce a beam of protons more than twice as energetic as those in any existing atom smasher, and while the device, more than five hundred yards in radius, is buried in tunnels and concrete revetments reminiscent of the Maginot Line, it still will raise formidable radiation problems. Well separated from the accelerator ring is the new community of apartments and blackboard-paneled offices for researchers at the center.

Already well established is another atomic "city" on the Volga River at Dubna. It is an international research center designed to accommodate Soviet-bloc scientists. On my visit there I saw on the wall of one office a chart showing, in terms of their nuclear structure, all the atoms that have been observed or projected by theoreticians. At the top, in terms of their atomic weight, were such short-lived, laboratory-made elements as Californium, Einsteinium, Fermium, Mendelevium, Nobelium, and Kurchatovium. The Russians explained that Kurchatovium had recently been synthesized in the Soviet Union. Its proposed name (already in use in some American laboratories) would honor the late Igor Kurchatov, a major figure in Soviet physics.

All by themselves, above these elements on the chart, were two of extremely great weight that some scientists have predicted can be manufactured and would survive a comparatively long time—estimates range from seconds to years. The nucleus of one would be composed of 126 protons and 184 neutrons. The other would contain 114 protons and 175 neutrons. These two hypothetical elements hang there on the chart, a constant reminder of an unattained goal, much as maps on the wall of an explorer at the turn of the century would have shown the then unconquered North and South poles.

Of all these rural academic centers the most stimulating, in the view of many visitors, is the Akademgorodok an hour's drive from Novosibirsk.

And to me the most exciting thing there was Budker's "Alice in Wonderland" machine.

Budker, a 1967 Lenin Prize winner, had for some years been interested in colliding beams as a tool for probing the basic properties of matter. In an ordinary atom smasher, particles such as electrons or protons (the hydrogen atom consists of one proton, as the nucleus, and one electron) are accelerated to very high speeds and energies. They are then directed into a target, such as metal foil or a chamber of liquid gas. There they smash into atoms of known identity (metal atoms in the foil or atoms of hydrogen or helium in the chamber). Much of what is known about the composition of the atomic nucleus, short-range forces that act within it, and the properties of the many fragments in the debris of such collisions has been derived from these experiments.

Budker explained that the idea of aiming two beams of high-energy particles at each other had been proposed by American physicists at a Geneva conference in 1956 but was not immediately carried out. Because of the peculiar effects of relativity, when beams of particles that, in both cases, are moving at nearly the speed of light meet head on, they generate collisions of incredibly high energy. This can be explained in terms of one of the better-known aspects of relativity, namely that nothing seen from a particular frame of reference, such as our world, can be observed traveling at more than the speed of light (186,000 miles a second). In an accelerator this means that, once the machine has boosted particles to almost the speed of light, any additional acceleration does not substantially increase their speed but does increase their energy. In a colliding-beam machine the particles of both beams are traveling at more than 99 per cent of the speed of light, as observed by those watching the experiment. Hence one would expect that an observer no bigger than Tiny Alice, in Edward Albee's play of that name, riding one of the particles would see particles of the other beam approaching at almost twice light's speed. Yet because of relativity that is impossible. Instead, he sees particles approaching at just under the speed of light but with enormous energy. This energy is manifest not only to our mythical observer, but also in what happens when the particles collide or otherwise interact.

The effect, in colliding-beam machines, is that the energy is equal not merely to the sum of the beam energies, but to the square of their sum. Thus impinging protons each carrying 10 billion electron volts of energy (10 BEV) would generate an impact of 400 BEV.

The two most powerful proton accelerators now in operation produce beams of 25 BEV or more. If such beams collided, the energy would be 2,500 BEV. By contrast the huge atom smasher to be built at Weston, near

Chicago, will produce only 200 BEV. However, it will be far more versatile than any colliding-beam machine now in sight.

Budker, in 1956, decided to shoot for a more modest goal: colliding beams of electrons, rather than protons. The big problem was to produce enough electrons to have a workable number of collisions. While the proton is terribly small, the effective cross section of an electron is at least 10,000 times smaller. He had started work on two machines, the larger of which would produce half a BEV in each of the beams, when he met Wolfgang K. H. Panofsky, of Stanford University.

After hearing of the work at Budker's institute, Panofsky is reported to have said: "Maybe we should move Stanford to Alaska!" He told Budker that Stanford was well along on a similar colliding-beam project.

"Electron-electron collisions are only good for one or two experiments," Budker told me, "and so we decided to build an electron-positron system, even though it seemed very fantastic at that time."

The positron is the antimatter counterpart of the electron. In fact, it was the first particle of antimatter discovered. Since then it has been found that every kind of particle of matter—electron, proton, meson, et cetera— has an antimatter counterpart. The latter is identical to its sister particle in weight, but it is of opposite electric charge, spin, or other such property. In other words, the realm of antimatter is a looking-glass world.

Antimatter interacts and vanishes as soon as it encounters matter, and since our world is filled with matter (there are many atoms adrift in even the deepest vacuum), antimatter cannot exist for any length of time. Invisible cosmic rays, raining on our bodies and the air about us, constantly smash atoms and often generate bits of antimatter, but only for a split second.

Hence, until recently, no one had ever "seen" a collection of antimatter. Budker's idea for colliding beams of electrons and positrons seemed hare-brained. To generate one positron in his machine would require 100,000 electrons. The co-ordinative scientific council in physics frowned on the scheme, but Kurchatov dissented. He was an impressive man, with a trailing beard like that of Ivan the Great. His prestige rested heavily on his role in producing the first Soviet atomic bomb. Budker had been working in his institute, and Kurchatov reminded him of an old Russian saying: "Ask your wife for advice and then do the opposite." He gave Budker the green light.

That was in 1958. During the years that followed, storage rings for electrons or positrons were constructed by a Princeton-Stanford group in California and by a French-Italian team at Frascati, Italy. At Budker's institute two machines were built: one capable of generating electron-electron collisions and the other to fire electrons and positrons at one another. In 1965 he and the California group reported first results on colliding electron beams, and in the spring of 1967, at a meeting at CERN, the international atomic research center near Geneva, Budker was able to present concrete results from interactions between beams of matter and antimatter.

He also displayed photographs showing the glow of antimatter (positrons) stored in his machine. When electrons or positrons are accelerated around a ring, they try to fly off in a straight line, as does a car on a circular race course. The electrons are kept in the ring by magnets placed around the ring. As the electrons spin around the circle they shed energy in the form of light (known as synchrotron radiation) that shoots off tangentially. To see this light the cameras or television monitors must be aimed toward the oncoming electrons, just as one would have to look at oncoming racing cars to see their headlights.

Because of instabilities in the beam of antimatter, its shape, as seen in cross section, keeps changing. This was evident in films of the beam that Budker showed on a visit to Stanford University. As he tells the story, someone in the darkened hall said, "It looks like an amoeba," whereupon another voice cut in: "You mean an antiamoeba!"

Meanwhile, Budker told me, he and his right-hand man, Stanislav N. Rodionov, had been toying with an even wilder scheme than banging electrons into their antimatter counterpart (positrons). This was to fire protons into antiprotons. Since the proton is 1,836 times heavier than the electron, this would produce collisions far more energetic than any hitherto possible. This was to become their "Alice in Wonderland" machine.

Budker and Rodionov make a contrasting pair. Budker is balding, rotund, strongly self-assured. Rodionov is high-strung, slender, with a shock of dark hair and a gentle manner of speech. Budker pours forth his ideas in an unbroken stream of words. His associates, schooled in scientific terminology (where a milligram is a thousandth of a gram, a millicurie is a thousandth of a curie, and so forth) congratulate one another when they achieve "one millibudker"—meaning they got in one word to his thousand.

However, one vital evening in 1960 Rodionov held his own. He and Budker had flown to Novosibirsk from Moscow and had taken a hotel room. Locally, it was bedtime, but in Moscow it was three hours earlier, and they had no interest in sleep. They puzzled over the projected "Alice in Wonderland" machine for an hour. Then Rodionov pulled out a copy of Agatha Christie's *Cards on the Table*—a story involving eight bridge players and four murderers. He read it aloud for an hour; then, refreshed, he and Budker returned to the proton-antiproton project. Throughout the night they alternated between the intricacies of Agatha Christie and those of particle physics.

The scheme that they worked out was as follows: A batch, or "pulse," of protons will be accelerated in a small machine to 0.4 BEV and injected into the main ring for acceleration to 25 BEV. The protons will then be directed onto a target, producing a shower of atomic fragments, including a certain number of antiprotons. Those antiprotons "fortunate enough" to travel down the tube without hitting the walls will then be directed, with a residual energy of 3 or 4 BEV, into a smaller storage ring and a new batch of protons will be accelerated in the main ring.

Because it is expected that it will take 10,000,000 impacting protons to contribute each antiproton to the storage ring, it should take twenty-four hours, or roughly 1,000 pulses, each with 100,000 billion protons, to fill the storage ring with a stream of 10 billion antiprotons.

When that is achieved, a final batch of protons in the main ring will be accelerated to 3 BEV. Then the stored antiprotons, likewise at 3 BEV, will be switched back into the main ring, traveling in a direction opposite to that of the protons. Some 150 radio-frequency accelerators around the ring will then start to build up the energy of the two counterrotating beams, like fields of race horses galloping around a track in opposite directions, constantly in danger of head-on collision. When both beams are traveling at 25 BEV (which means at more than 99.9 per cent of the speed of light), observations will begin to see what happens when protons and antiprotons meet—that is, when the race horses sometimes collide head on or graze enough to knock each other out of the track.

Budker and Rodionov knew that the chief pitfall in their scheme was the instability that both they and the Stanford group had begun to observe as their storage rings moved to higher energies. The particles, instead of whirling around the rings indefinitely in smooth circles, started to waver, weaving in and out until they began hitting the walls of the ring chamber.

The particles in all accelerators travel through a tube, or "chamber," from which as much air as possible has been evacuated. The deeper the vacuum, the fewer particles are lost from the beam by striking atoms of air. In the machine projected by Budker and Rodionov the chamber would be extremely narrow (1.2 by 2.4 inches). This would make for great economies in construction, because magnets wrapped around the chamber to hold the protons on course could be correspondingly small. Budker pointed out that the 10 BEV machine at Dubna, with a chamber so big two men could crawl through it abreast, required 36,000 tons of magnets. His machine will need only 300 tons. However, to store the precious antiprotons

THE "ALICE IN WONDERLAND" MACHINE

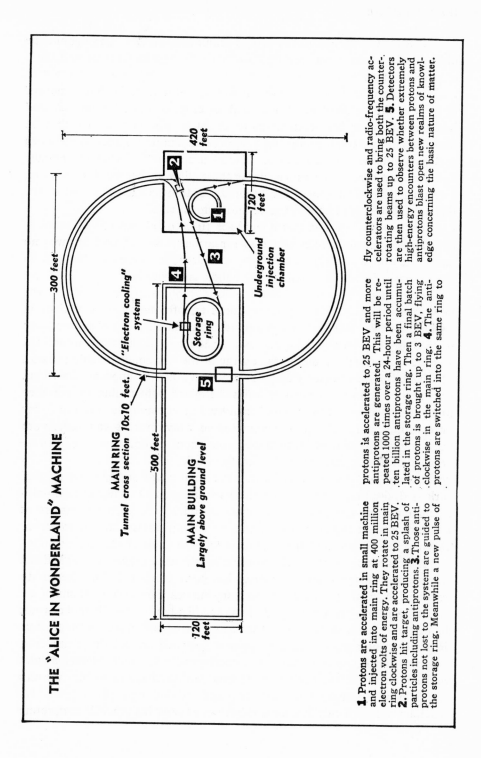

MAIN RING
Tunnel cross section 10x10 feet.

300 feet

420 feet

120 feet

2

1

Underground injection chamber

3

4

"Electron cooling" system

Storage ring

5

500 feet

120 feet

MAIN BUILDING
Largely above ground level

1. Protons are accelerated in small machine and injected into main ring at 400 million electron volts of energy. They rotate in main ring clockwise and are accelerated to 25 BEV. **2.** Protons hit target, producing a splash of particles including antiprotons. **3.** Those antiprotons not lost to the system are guided to the storage ring. Meanwhile a new pulse of protons is accelerated to 25 BEV and more antiprotons are generated. This will be repeated 1000 times over a 24-hour period until ten billion antiprotons have been accumulated in the storage ring. Then a final batch of protons is brought up to 3 BEV, flying clockwise in the main ring. **4.** The antiprotons are switched into the same ring to fly counterclockwise and radio-frequency accelerators are used to bring both the counterrotating beams up to 25 BEV. **5.** Detectors are then used to observe whether extremely high-energy encounters between protons and antiprotons blast open new realms of knowledge concerning the basic nature of matter.

for any length of time in such a narrow chamber it was vital to damp their oscillations.

The solution that came to Budker and Rodionov, after they had laid aside Agatha Christie and dawn was breaking over the taiga, or forests, of Siberia, was a trick that they christened "electron cooling." They explained it to me this way: The oscillations of antiprotons as they spin around in the chamber can be likened to the thermal motions of atoms and molecules that constitute what we call "heat." If electrons are injected into the storage ring at the same energy as the antiprotons, thus flying along with them, much of the antiproton "heat" should be transferred to the electrons through electrical interactions. The antiprotons would then settle into nice round orbits along the center line of the tube, or chamber.

The antiprotons could then spin for a year, as long as there was no failure of the vacuum or electric-power supply. What with human and mechanical fallibility, though, the two Russians do not look for storage times of more than a few days.

Furthermore, they are quick to admit that the whole idea of electron cooling is new and untried. The project is a gamble—one that is costing some $10,000,000, which is far less than the cost of the big conventional accelerators in the United States and the Soviet Union. The projected cost of the machine at Weston, Illinois, is $375,000,000. "If you have to get your money from the government," said Budker, "then other people have to tell the government your machine will work. But if you can ride on your own reputation, if you have the money in your own pocket—and if you are brave enough—then more possibilities are open to you."

Rodionov showed me the shop that has helped put money into Budker's institutional pocket. Workmen were assembling low-energy accelerators of various designs for industrial use. He explained, as an example, that polyethylene normally melts at 230 degrees Fahrenheit, but that after treatment with an accelerator beam it can withstand temperatures twice that high. The accelerators are sold for $100,000 or more.

Then we looked into a hall where experiments in the "bottling" of hot plasmas with magnetic fields were under way. Such bottling is essential to achieve the high temperature needed to harness the hydrogen bomb, but, to date, bottled plasmas in none of the world's laboratories have been hot enough, long-lived enough, or dense enough to provide a workable source of power. The hall echoed to pistol-crack sounds as plasma bottles were formed, then collapsed a fraction of a second later—a process that was witnessed by visitors to the General Electric exhibit at the 1964–65 World's Fair in New York.

After I had seen the comparatively small machines used to generate electron-electron and electron-positron collisions, Budker led the way into a cavernous hall where magnets were being made for the new "Alice in Wonderland" machine. Siberia is a long way from the industrial centers of European Russia, and so the institute makes most of its own equipment.

The shop was generously endowed with machine tools. The plant's center aisle was flanked for its full length by rows of potted palms, their fronds waving over the heads of the busy workmen. From there we passed into another giant hall, five hundred feet long, that sits astride the new machine. The latter, under construction, covers an area of two city blocks. Its main accelerator ring is shaped like a race track most of which is in a tunnel, as a precaution against stray radiation. It will probably be 1970 or 1971 before this machine is in operation.

Another institute that I visited at the Novosibirsk science city was also in business for itself. This was the Computation Center, headed by Guri I. Marchuk, a well-known computer specialist. He explained that the center performs two functions: it is a research institute and it serves as a "computational factory" for Siberian industry. The industrial work is done for a fee, which helps sustain the institute's budget. My tour of the center gave me my most extensive glimpse of Soviet computer technology and the current surge of interest in cybernetics.

The center was four years old, and its staff had grown to four hundred, including thirty "candidates" (equivalent to Americans with doctorates) and eight "doctors" (a higher academic rank, with no American counterpart). There are five computers: three of them are old-fashioned vacuum-tube types, the fourth is a Minsk-22 with some semiconductors, and the fifth is a BESM-6, the most advanced model now in general use in the U.S.S.R. I got the impression that Soviet specialists agree with their American counterparts that Soviet computer technology is five to ten years behind that of the United States. However, the Russians have a special mathematical genius (which helps to account for their leadership in chess), and they seem to be making good use of the machines they have.

Marchuk said the BESM-6 handles a million operations a second. This, he added, puts it between the 3600 and 6600 computers of the Control Data Corporation in the United States. His machine had been operating "a few months," I was told, and it was not running when I saw it. Whereas input to the Minsk-22 is by either punched card or magnetic tape, the fast-working BESM-6 receives only taped input. Its computer "language" is Alpha, closely related to the Algol-60 widely used in the West, but with Russian words and Greek letters in its vocabulary.

Because of Marchuk's interest in meteorology, one of the chief lines of research at the center is in numerical weather forecasting and analysis.

Walter Sullivan

Shortly after World War I, a British mathematician, Lewis R. Richardson, proposed that, with sufficient information on the state of the earth's atmosphere at any one time and adequate knowledge of the physical laws controlling the weather's behavior, it should be possible to calculate, mathematically, what it would do next. The trouble was that he figured it would take 64,000 mathematicians to do the job. Then John von Neumann, one of the founders of computer technology and cybernetics, pointed out after World War II that the new computing machines might make it possible for Richardson's dream to come true. As observational techniques, with rockets, weather balloons, earth satellites, and other devices, have improved, so have the chances that weather phenomena can be described and understood—and hence predicted—numerically.

At the Novosibirsk center they are studying tornadoes and other localized phenomena, and at the same time they are analyzing weather reports from 2,000 stations in an effort to produce three-day forecasts for the region from Moscow to Tokyo. Marchuk said the computer method developed in his institute for these forecasts had now been adopted by the central weather bureau in Moscow.

The Novosibirsk center also does computer analysis for other research institutes. It was trying to fit into a comprehensive picture the observations —magnetic, seismic, and gravitational—made by an expedition surveying the top three or four miles of the earth's crust in Kazakhstan. It was also developing methods for quantitative solution of catalysis problems in industrial chemistry, previously solved only qualitatively.

At the institute industrial representatives are taught, at no cost, how to program their problems themselves. The center then charges for punching the business-machine cards as well as for time on the computers. So far there is no time-sharing system whereby other institutions, via landline, can feed their problems into the computer simultaneously. However, Marchuk said the BESM-6 can handle such traffic and he hopes a time-sharing system will eventually be installed.

While the BESM-6 displayed the banks of flashing lights, spinning wheels of magnetic tape, and neatly packaged electronic units typical of a modern computer, I noticed that the stacks of electronic memory units not in current use were stored on the floor in rough wooden boxes. The National Center for Atmospheric Research in Boulder, Colorado, which I had visited a few weeks before, inevitably came to mind. Dramatic architecturally, it stands on a high mesa with the Flatiron Mountains as a backdrop. Like the central forecasting center of the United States Weather Bureau, in Suitland, Maryland, it has one of the world's most advanced computers—a Control Data Corporation 6600, which handles some 4,000,-

[308]

000 operations per second. Its home is a gleaming wonderland of auxiliary units designed to channel a broad river of problems into the machine at high speed and extract the results with equal dispatch.

It is, of course, results and not frills that count, and the contrast with memory stacks in wooden crates was not necessarily an index of competence. Nevertheless, modern computers seem much scarcer in the Soviet Union than in the United States—particularly those used for research and for analysis of marketing and transportation problems. The new science city that I visited on the outskirts of Irkutsk, farther to the east, was slated to receive a BESM-6 but did not have one yet.

The Computing Center of the Academy of Sciences in Moscow is being used to keep Moscow's stores supplied with certain commodities. Each Friday the shops and depots of Moscow report their needs for the next week. At the same time an inventory of stock piles in warehouses and production centers is pumped into the computer, which then calculates the most economical way to supply each center of demand. It has been reported that savings of 10 to 40 per cent in transportation costs have been achieved by this system.

In the early days of cybernetics—the science of control systems in machines and living organisms—Soviet theoreticians dismissed the subject as a capitalist scheme to replace troublesome workers with machines. There was also objection to the concept of Norbert Wiener, father of cybernetics, that it could become a universal science, helping man solve his social as well as his material problems. This was seen by Communist theoreticians as an attempt to usurp the role of the Communist dogma, dialectical materialism. As one Soviet writer said of the goals of men like Wiener: "Does this not mean that cybernetics opposes dialectics, that it is attempting to take its place as a new ideology?"

Also, as with genetics, the postwar years saw a Soviet reaction against anything "made in the U.S.A." Cybernetics had been developed largely by men in the United States, including Wiener, at the Massachusetts Institute of Technology, and von Neumann, at the Institute for Advanced Study in Princeton.

But by the 1950's it became apparent that unless the Soviet Union delegated some of its control operations to machines, it would be paralyzed by its own bureaucracy. An academician in Moscow predicted that if the then current trend continued, by 1980 the entire population of the U.S.S.R. would be involved in planning and administration.

A turning point, in 1954, was a talk given by Ernest Kolman, a prominent Czech-born mathematician and Marxist philosopher, before the Academy of Social Sciences of the Central Committee of the Soviet Communist party. Cybernetics, he said, was a development that could be compared in importance to the invention of printing and of the decimal system. In 1958 the Academy of Sciences set up a Scientific Council on Cybernetics, headed by Aksel I. Berg, a well-known electronics specialist, and a new journal, *Problemy Kibernetiki* (*Problems of Cybernetics*), made its appearance. In the words of Loren R. Graham, specialist in Soviet science at Columbia University, "the movement towards cybernetics became a landslide." He believes the subject is now more highly regarded in Russia than in any other country. The old Communist dreams of genuine scientific planning and decision making, which had proven elusive because of human limitations, now seemed within reach. There was even talk that the self-organizing manifestations of cybernetics would come into play in ordering human society when the government "withered away" in the manner set as the ultimate Communist goal.

However, a major obstacle to rapid development of cybernetics in the Soviet Union has been the absence of an electronics industry as broadly based, competitive, and diversified as that of the United States. The Russians' successes in the launching and control of spacecraft and missiles have shown that they can perform in a first-rate manner with computers, but, as with many aspects of the Soviet scientific and technological scene, they have had to ration their resources and only activities with top priority have the benefit of such sophisticated aids.

It was evident in Novosibirsk and Moscow that an intensive effort is under way to push Soviet mathematics into a position of world leadership. Fields in which Americans have led the way, such as approximation by polynomials and by rational functions in several complex variables, are now being pursued vigorously in the U.S.S.R. Visiting American mathematicians have seen plenty of lackluster work, particularly in the efforts of mathematical "collectives" and in the old European patronage system where students work under a single master and are tied to his pet lines of research, often repetitive. Yet there are also exciting phases of Soviet mathematics: the world-famous seminar of Izrail M. Gelfand at Moscow State University; the Steklov Institute, which some consider one of the chief concentrations of mathematical talent in the world, and the new boarding school for promising young mathematicians founded outside Moscow by Andrei N. Kolmogorov, best known of the Russians in the field. The school has some three hundred pupils, including a score of girls.

In the view of a leading American mathematician, the best men in Russia are marching forward side by side with their American counterparts. New findings and new ideas fly back and forth across the Atlantic in a matter of weeks. It is no longer appropriate to talk about "Soviet" science, he says. It is "world" science.

One of the best-known authorities on complex variables is the Soviet mathematician Mikhail A. Lavrentyev, who founded the Akademgorodok at Novosibirsk. His Institute of Hydrodynamics there has been working on computer programs for predicting river floods and a study of the oscillations of ships that are being carried around hydroelectric dams in movable tanks.

Lavrentyev told me how he had conceived the idea of this scientific community, which has become a model for a number of others projected or building in the Soviet Union. From the days of Peter the Great, Russian science had evolved chiefly around St. Petersburg. When the capital shifted to Moscow after the Bolshevik Revolution, many institutions and scientists followed the move. In some fields, such as mathematics, Soviet talent became as much concentrated in Moscow as French mathematics is centered in Paris. "There were attempts at decentralization here and in France," said Lavrentyev, "but they were small-scale and never came off. The best people always came back to Moscow or Paris." "It is said," he added, "that the first man sent to the moon should be a Muscovite, because then we can be sure he'll come back!

"What we needed, therefore, was a critical mass, so to speak. We had to get something going that was big enough and attractive enough to hold the best people. We looked around for good men with an entourage of young scientists who could not find a home in any Moscow institute.

"Ten and a half years ago I flew alone to Novosibirsk and Irkutsk. I spoke to the savants. It was obvious that our center should not be inside an industrial city. We wanted an attractive site, railroad connections, and plenty of electric power. Up the Ob River from Novosibirsk a big hydroelectric dam was being built. It would offer ample power and the dam was impounding what is now the Ob Sea [a lake one hundred and twenty-five miles long set in low rolling country of heavy pine and birch]. Sobolev [Sergei L. Sobolev, a fellow mathematician and one of those who had fought for the acceptance of cybernetics] and I called on the government with our scheme and won all-out backing for it."

Now I understood better why Budker's shops were so elaborately equipped. When the government decides something is important, it goes all out for it.

Lavrentyev noted that in recent years Soviet education and research had been almost completely isolated from each other. Universities were for teaching, institutes for research, and there was little or no interchange of faculty or young researchers. Lavrentyev set as one of the conditions for the new academic city that he have a free hand to experiment in education and in organization.

Spartak T. Belyayev, the dynamic forty-three-year-old rector of Novosibirsk University, forming part of the Akademgorodok complex, told me that of eighty or ninety full professors on his faculty, only six have full-time jobs there. The rest divide their time between the university and one of the community's research institutes. The students, after their first two or three years, spend much of their time in the institutes, helping in real research instead of dabbling in make-believe research in the instructional labs.

"We have three tasks here of equal importance—*un ménage à trois*," said Lavrentyev—"education, research, and help to industry." Experimental factories have already been set up near other centers of research in cybernetics and automation, as in Kiev, and Lavrentyev said he hoped the same could be done near his center—"three, four, or five kilometers away, as at Stanford."

Lavrentyev is particularly proud of the recruiting program, called an Olympiad, that he has organized in Siberia, the best known of such schemes in the Soviet Union. Each October, youth magazines, newspapers, and posters display a list of problems in mathematics, physics, and chemistry. Those who send in the best, and most "original," answers are invited in the spring to visit one of twenty or thirty centers east of the Urals for interviews and examinations. About 10,000 or 12,000 reach this stage, and some two hundred research associates, graduate students, and other scholars are dispatched to conduct the examinations.

In this way about seven hundred students are chosen to spend the month of August at the Akademgorodok. Their way is paid to the campus. In the morning they hear lectures, take part in seminars, and visit the laboratories. In the afternoon they engage in sports, hike, or swim at the newly made beach on the Ob Sea, a few minutes' drive from the campus.

The last week of this period is devoted to examinations, and approximately two hundred and fifty students are chosen from these and other candidates to take the intensive preparatory course at the Physical-Mathematical School on the campus. The course lasts from one to three years, depending on the academic level of the incoming student.

In describing this system, the university rector, Belyayev, conceded that it tipped the scales heavily toward physics. However, he pointed out that chemistry had been added to the program three years ago (the Olympiad has been in existence six years), and some biology is being included in 1967.

Lavrentyev, as chairman of the Siberian Department of the Academy of Sciences of the U.S.S.R., could be called mayor of the Akademgorodok at Novosibirsk. All of its institutes come under his branch of the academy, although the university itself is attached to the Ministry of Higher Education in Moscow.

He spoke with pride of the way in which his academic city is being imitated in other parts of the Soviet Union and of plans for additional such centers in his own region. The Ukrainian Academy of Sciences has set one up at Donetsk, in the Donets Basin. Its university is two years old, and various research institutes are being built.

I visited the Akademgorodok across the Angara River from Irkutsk, in a region that is booming because of a series of huge hydroelectric projects. The institutes of the Irkutsk Akademgorodok, which come under Lavrentyev's branch of the Academy of Sciences, specialize in subjects that are closer to the earth than those of Novosibirsk: study of the earth's crust, geochemistry, the physiology and biochemistry of plants, and so forth. The community is being built on the edge of the city's industrial belt and lacks the scenic beauty of the center near Novosibirsk. The university at Irkutsk is slated to move to the new site, as is an institute of mining technology now in the city, but promoters of the new, young look in academic communities are confronted with the fact that the University of Irkutsk is set in its traditional ways and committed to a well-established hierarchy. The University of Novosibirsk was built from scratch to the model of its present leaders.

While the Akademgorodok at Irkutsk is little concerned with the humanities, the Angara River, which flows nearby, is a major center of Soviet archeology. Man-made objects found at the Buryat and Malta sites along the river are estimated, from radioactive carbon measurements, to be 23,000 years old, making those sites the most ancient known human habitations in Siberia.

During my visit to the Akademgorodok at Novosibirsk, Vitaly Y. Larichev and his wife, Inna P. Laricheva, told me of the perplexity of Soviet archeologists at the absence of older sites in Siberia. They pointed out that during the past decade sites have been found in the southwestern United States that seem to be 30,000 to 40,000 years old. It is widely believed that these early Americans came from Siberia via the land bridge that connected Asia and America when much of the world's water was locked in ice sheets and oceans were one hundred or two hundred feet lower than they are today.

The material left along the Angara by those who lived there 23,000 years ago does not resemble the artifacts left by Americans of the Southwest at that time. Hence Mrs. Laricheva, who specializes in the search for evidence of the migrations that populated the Americas, believes the two continents were not in contact at that time. She proposes that there were two movements across the Bering land bridge: roughly 40,000 and 10,000 years ago. She points out that Siberian and American implements that are 10,000 years old bear strong resemblances to one another. It has been proposed, she said, that the first migration may have by-passed Siberia, which was uninhabitable, moving up from China along a coastal plain that was flooded when the oceans rose to their present level.

Other science centers, besides those at Irkutsk and Novosibirsk, are projected for Siberia. Lavrentyev, originator of the idea, told me of his hope for such communities in Krasnoyarsk and Omsk, and he said there is talk of moving an oceanographic institute to the Pacific coast at Vladivostok. He spoke with special enthusiasm of plans for a new Akademgorodok at Shushenskoye, a village near the Mongolian border. It lies south of Abakan on the rushing Yenisei River. Lenin was exiled there as a young man and wrote that it was "not a bad place." Impounding of the river will furnish 6,000,000 kilowatts of power within a few years, and a new rail line to Taishet, on the Trans-Siberian Railway, provides a transport link.

Lavrentyev does not regard all the new science centers as being in a class with his own. Obninsk, for example, is so close to Moscow, he said, that some of those working there live in the city and commute. An important attribute of an Akademgorodok, in his view, is that the researchers work together, live together, and play together. The hoped-for result is constant cross-fertilization of ideas, although I found that some of those with whom I spoke in one field were quite unaware of interesting work in another area of science being done only a few hundred yards away.

Obninsk, home of the Institute of Radiobiology, where Timofeyev-Ressovsky is doing his genetics, is also the seat of a nuclear-reactor development center, a meteorological institute, and a large seismic array, said to be comparable in size to the one built in Montana with Defense Department funds to study the problem of distinguishing underground nuclear blasts from earthquakes.

Equidistant from Moscow, in the opposite direction, is the remarkable new Institute of Theoretical Physics at Chernogolovka. It is apparently an offshoot of Pyotr L. Kapitsa's Institute of Physical Problems in Moscow, formed by a group of bright young theoreticians who were working with Lev D. Landau when he was incapacitated in an automobile accident. Both the director, L. M. Khalatnikov, and his deputy, A. A. Abrikosov, are highly regarded by American solid-state physicists.

While the new theoretical institute has been "out of bounds" to Americans working as exchange scholars in Moscow, enough is known of its output to indicate that some of the best brains in Soviet physics are at work there. It is thought that the work on such subjects as the one-dimensional superconductivity of oriented molecules may prove to have important biological implications. The most promising young men have drifted into such theoretical work, it is said, because laboratory facilities are still not adequate to compete with the rapid pace of American experimental advances. At the same time, I was told, the theoreticians look down their noses at experimenters even more haughtily than do their counterparts in Western Europe.

Another of the academic centers within seventy miles of Moscow is the biological Akademgorodok being built at Pushchino in lush country on the south bank of the Oka River, on the opposite side of Serpukhov from the giant atom smasher. Among the institutes being organized there is one that will study the chemistry of protein synthesis (presumably the one to be headed by Aleksandr S. Spirin) and an Institute of the Biochemistry and Physiology of Microorganisms, which will investigate ways in which bacteria and yeasts can be used to convert petroleum products and similar hydrocarbons into organic matter. There will also be institutes specializing in photosynthesis, brain research, and biophysics. The director of the last-named, Academician Gleb M. Frank, is the scientific director of this new Akademgorodok.

Near Pushchino is one of the world's largest radio telescopes, operated by the Lebedev Institute of Physics in Moscow. Its two antennas form a cross. Its north-south arm is 3,215 feet long and is fixed. The east-west arm is a cylindrical parabola 3,307 feet long mounted on thirty-seven towers, each of which has a motor so that on command the cylinder, more than a half-mile in length, can be rocked to aim at some particular region of the sky.

Also near Moscow is the Akademgorodok being developed at Krasnaya Pakhra, long the seat of NIZMIR, the Institute of Earth Magnetism, Ionosphere and Radio Wave Propagation. Joining it now are the Institute of High Pressure Physics, which is moving out from Moscow, and other institutes dealing with earth physics. According to Academician Leonid F. Vereshchagin, head of the Institute of High Pressure Physics, who is in charge of the new center, the population of this Akademgorodok will grow from 3,000 to 12,000 by 1970.

There is nothing quite like these science cities in the United States. Perhaps the closest analogue is in the communities that have sprung up at remote sites, such as Oak Ridge, Tennessee, in connection with making nuclear weapons or conducting nuclear research. The Soviet centers also have elements in common with American university towns—even to an atmosphere of greater intellectual freedom and creativity than one finds in a run-of-the-mill community. In the Soviet Union this is in part related to remoteness from the stern eye of the central party and government hierarchies. In touring one science-oriented university, far from Moscow, I noticed on one door a sign saying that this was the classroom for instruction in the history of the Communist party of the Soviet Union.

I asked how much time was spent in ideological studies, and my informant immediately saw the drift of my thinking. "Here it is absolutely unique," he said. "The courses are taught by young men who have gone through this university." I was reminded that in church schools in the United States the Bible can be taught in many ways.

As is true everywhere, the greatest display of independence is by the young people. Someone from an American campus might feel almost startlingly at home in one of the student clubs, such as the Integral at Novosibirsk, even to the point of hearing an American folk song sung by a bearded guitar player. While portraits of Lenin and Marx are standard fixtures in the offices of institute directors, here and there, placed inconspicuously, one sees pictures of John F. Kennedy on the wall.

These pictures are not gestures of disloyalty. But to many in the academic community Kennedy has become almost a folk hero, symbolizing the start of a movement toward reconciliation with the West—and consequently greater freedom and a better life at home. In the same context, the only persons in the academic communities who raised, in conversations with me, the question of America's role in Vietnam—and argued passionately on the subject—were those who obviously were the most pro-Western and concerned lest the Vietnam war lead, in the U.S.S.R., to a reversion to the "bad times" of former years.

I was told that twist lessons are being given in the student club of a certain Moscow institute (they have not yet come to the frug). In Leningrad, walking along the Neva River at midnight on one of the white nights, when it never becomes dark, I saw a tight crowd of Soviet sailors, naval cadets, and university students. Curious to know what drew them together, I mounted the Admiralty Bridge, over their heads, and found a young sailor in the center of the group frantically strumming a guitar. The entire crowd was singing with him, but the words were obviously not Russian. Suddenly I realized it was English; they were singing one of the Beatles' songs with great gusto, bobbing up and down like any crowd of American teen-agers.

The sight of these bright young men in Soviet military uniform singing that song (and probably not understanding a word of it) was the most remarkable memory I brought home from Russia. How did they know the words and music? I was told later that in such cases a single record or BBC broadcast is all that Leningrad or Moscow needs. Within a week thousands of copies have been tape recorded and are being memorized.

Despite these hopeful signs, I could not forget that it was not always so. Ideological and political considerations have intruded into Soviet science in more fields than genetics, and throughout my tour of the Soviet Union I sought to assess such intrusions, past and present.

The most serious ideological invasion dates from a speech given by Andrei A. Zhdanov of the Politburo on June 24, 1947. This policy statement, part of a period of repression known as the "Zhdanovshchina," set the tone for what followed, including the grim meeting of 1948 at which Lysenko delivered the *coup de grâce* to his adversaries.

It is ironic that two of the most prominent Western scientists denounced as corrupting modern, materialist science with bourgeois "idealism" were Bertrand Russell and Linus Pauling, who were later to champion the Soviet point of view on such questions as the Vietnam war and nuclear-weapons testing. Early in 1950 Russell and his co-worker Alfred North Whitehead were denounced for their trail-blazing role in the development of symbolic logic and of the mathematical precursors of cybernetics. Pauling was found guilty of inventing the resonance theory of chemical bonds.

In both cases those attacked had made use of symbols or descriptions of things that did not necessarily exist. This was heretical to adherents of Lenin's teaching. Lenin had written an entire book to refute what he considered errors in the physics of his day, particularly the ideas of Ernst Mach, an Austrian physicist and philosopher. Although Mach did most of his important work late in the nineteenth century, his influence on contemporary science has only recently been widely recognized. In fact, to laymen his name is still chiefly familiar because of its use in expressing the speed of a supersonic aircraft: a vehicle flying at Mach 2 is traveling at twice the speed of sound in that medium.

Mach demanded the most rigorous experimental criteria in determining the reality of what he considered abstract concepts, such as "atoms," "molecules," "space," and "time." He thus brushed cobwebby concepts from the minds of scientists and helped clear the way for Einstein's relativity theory. His parallel belief that all existence is sensation led to Lenin's rebuttal in 1909. Lenin dismissed this view as idealism and said that concepts were meaningful only if they represented something with a material existence. Furthermore, he said, matter can exist quite independently from mental processes.

Apparently, the symbolic logic of Russell and Whitehead was too remote from real things to suit the most faithful disciples of Lenin. Pauling's concept of resonance was also admittedly an abstract description, rather than a precise picture of the molecules in question. He sought to present a workable method of dealing with a special problem in chemistry:

Molecules are held together by electrical "bonds" between their atoms. The bonds occur, typically, where an atom's electrons are positioned, on the outer edge of the atom, so that they can be shared by neighboring atoms. A hydrogen atom has one potential bond, like a one-armed dancer. An oxygen atom has two bonds (two arms), and a carbon atom has four. Thus oxygen, the two-armed dancer, can hold two hydrogen atoms, forming a water molecule. Carbon can hold two hydrogen atoms and with its other two arms can hold both bonds of an oxygen atom. That is a formaldehyde molecule, and the link between its carbon and oxygen atoms is called a "double bond." It would appear that all through chemistry there should be such integral bonds. A "bond and a half" would seem to be preposterous, but there are substances that seem to be intermediate between one or more of the integral bond structures. Benzene appears to be a combination of five alternate structures.

Pauling and G. W. Wheland, who expanded the resonance theory, emphasized that they do not believe the molecule is constantly jumping from one configuration to another, even though this was how some chemists interpreted their formulation. Rather, their description was offered as an intellectual device which, through the mathematics of modern physics (quantum mechanics), could be used successfully to predict what would occur in chemical reactions.

Loren Graham, who spent an academic year at Moscow State University in 1960–61, has pieced together the history of what happened in Soviet chemistry and physics after Zhdanov's speech denouncing "bourgeois" science. In the case of chemistry, the outcome was quite different from that in genetics and biology as a whole.

As in the other sciences, there was an All-Union conference to diagnose the "ideological diseases" of Soviet chemistry, with particular reference to the resonance theory. Held in June, 1951, it was marked by the frantic maneuvers of Gennadi V. Chelintsev, a professor of chemical warfare at the Voroshilov Military Academy. He had written a book on organic chemistry that offered an alternate explanation for the resonance phenomenon.

As pointed out by one of the conference speakers, according to Chelintsev's own admission he was "assuming the role in chemistry of T. D. Lysenko. . . ." Chelintsev charged that twenty-six of the Soviet Union's leading chemists, including the president of the Soviet Academy of Sciences, Aleksandr N. Nesmeyanov, were apologists for the resonance theory. Indeed, a report had been prepared for the meeting by a commission of the academy which rejected resonance and substituted for it a theory of "mutual influences" that was very similar. However, it avoided the emphasis on artificiality in Pauling's version. The meeting accepted this report with only one dissenting voice—that of Chelintsev.

By 1961 Pauling was lecturing on his theory to an audience of 1,200 at the Institute for Organic Chemistry in Moscow. But, as Graham points out, the subject is still handled gingerly in Soviet scientific articles.

The controversy in physics followed parallel lines, but it was also intertwined with a world-wide debate on the meaning of quantum theory, with roots in one of the basic paradoxes of science: the seemingly contradictory evidence that light consists of waves and that it is formed of discrete particles. In a sense the same paradox is applicable to atomic particles. A mathematical method, known as quantum mechanics, has been devised to account for the behavior of light and atomic particles, but what is its meaning with regard to the actual nature of those phenomena?

Twin concepts, advanced by Niels Bohr, of Denmark, and Werner Heisenberg, of Germany, prior to World War II, sought to resolve the problem. They said that no observable property of a particle, whether it refers to its wavelike characteristics or its manifestations as a particle, has any reality until that property is measured. This came to be called "complementarity." Likewise, Heisenberg's uncertainty principle said that any such measurement intruded into the situation in a manner that made it possible to measure, with precision, only one property of the particle.

This "Copenhagen interpretation" of quantum theory had been accepted by a number of Soviet physicists by the time Zhdanov made the 1947 speech, in which he said: "The Kantian vagaries of modern bourgeois atomic physicists lead them to inferences about the electron's possessing 'free will,' to attempts to describe matter as only a certain conjunction of waves, and to other devilish tricks."

Soon thereafter Moisei A. Markov, a leading theoretician on relativity as it affects elementary particles, published a strong defense of the Copenhagen interpretation, possibly because he hoped that if an "official" theory was to be established, as was clearly happening in genetics, it should be a good one. His article was attacked by Aleksandr A. Maksimov, who was the closest counterpart of Lysenko in the field of physics. Maksimov called the article a departure from materialism toward "idealism and agnosticism."

According to Graham, the period from 1948 to 1960 can be called "the age of the banishment of complementarity" from Soviet discussions of quantum mechanics. The great physicist Dmitri I. Blokhintsev, who for a time headed the Joint Institute of Nuclear Research at Dubna, published Russia's authoritative university text on quantum dynamics in 1944, but in 1949 he came out with a revised edition. ". . . the clarity of the discussion of the uncertainty relationship has been improved," he wrote. "In the new edition of the book ideological questions connected with quantum mechanics are also considered, and the idealistic conceptions of quantum mechanics which are now widespread abroad are subjected to criticism."

Since Stalin's death the situation has relaxed to a considerable degree. I was interested to find that Belyayev, the rector of Novosibirsk University, had been a pupil of Bohr's at Copenhagen. In Graham's view the debates on quantum theory in Russia today largely parallel those in the rest of the world of physics and are not dominated by ideological considerations.

It is also clear that ideological issues did not handicap Soviet physics in any manner comparable to the throttling of biology by the Lysenko affair. One of the West's leading theoreticians in quantum electronics, in Moscow as a visiting lecturer, told me that the Russians are now challenging American leadership in this field. The most dramatic product of quantum electronics is the laser—a device that produces an intense and narrow beam of light, and which has already figured as a weapon in a James Bond motion picture. It is noteworthy that the Nobel Prize given in 1964 to the inventors of this device was shared by one American and two Russians. The Russians are now working on ultraviolet lasers that could have industrial applications in the synthesis of complex chemicals.

Another field into which party-line thinking intruded was astronomy and its sister sciences, cosmology and cosmogony. Cosmology is the study of the nature of the universe. Cosmogony is concerned with its origin. As an aftermath of Zhdanov's speech, conferences on the ideological state of astronomy were held in December, 1948, and April, 1951.

In particular there was opposition to the "big bang" concept of the origin of the universe as proposed by the Belgian priest Abbé Georges Lemaître and others. Telescopic observations indicate that all of the distant galaxies are flying away from us. The dimmer, and hence more distant, a galaxy of a particular type, the faster is its motion away. This is consistent with a universe that is expanding uniformly in all directions, like an expanding cloud of gas. Lemaître believed this expansion was evidence of the birth of the universe in a primordial explosion. As he once explained his theory to me, the universe was originally a single "atom" that flew apart to form all the galaxies, their stars, and the worlds in orbit around them. Was this an attempt to bring cosmogony into line with religious concepts of creation? He emphatically said "No." But to Communist theoreticians the big bang theory had overtones of clericalism.

Soviet nationalism also affected the lines of astronomical inquiry during this period. The Russians were defensive about the achievements of Soviet science and technology. They made exaggerated claims as to what they had invented or discovered and were extremely sensitive to disregard of Russian accomplishments by Western scientists. There was a rush to build the biggest of everything: the world's tallest building (planned but never executed), the most powerful hydroelectric plant, the biggest atom smasher, largest telescope, heaviest spacecraft. There were sound scientific or economic reasons for some of these feats, but the Russians share with their American rivals an admiration for bigness.

This national pride affected astronomy because the data needed for studies of stellar structure could be obtained only with big telescopes that were largely a monopoly of the United States. Hence theoretical discussions of the subject in Soviet journals were followed by long lists of references to American publications. In the atmosphere of the Soviet Union at that time, this left the author of such a paper open to charges of being "a lackey of Western science."

I found at least some of today's Soviet astronomers willing to talk with candor of what they call "the bad time," with the implication that it is now sufficiently remote to be a safe subject of conversation with an American journalist.

Landmarks along the road back included a 1958 All-Union conference overtly designed to explain to "certain philosophers" (that is, party theoreticians) the achievements of science in relativity, cosmogony, cybernetics, biology, and quantum mechanics. Some of the Soviet Union's most distinguished scientists took part. In 1962 Kapitsa, who had become one of the country's leading protagonists of free expression, published in the newspaper *Ekonomicheskaya Gazeta* an article attacking those who had sought to wrap the chains of dogma around these same subjects, including Heisenberg's indeterminacy principle.

In 1967 in an interview that, it should be emphasized, was published in the Soviet press, Kapitsa argued that controversy and debate are the only way to truth, not only in science but also in social questions. He pointed to a reproduction of Picasso's "Don Quixote" on his wall and told how Pavel Korin, a Russian painter of the traditional school, had seen a Picasso at the Guggenheim Museum in New York. Korin's attitude toward the abstract French painter was suddenly changed; he became a convert. "That is very interesting," said Kapitsa, "because Korin is absolutely sincere, and in painting is absolutely orthodox, yet suddenly a Picasso makes this impression on him! It is perfectly obvious that the clash of artistic styles and creeds is just as important for the development of art as the struggle of opposites is for scientific purposes."

Kapitsa told of his happy years at Cambridge University. "In these years I became a scientist. And throughout these years I lived in an atmosphere of debate which was both public and behind the scenes; most often these debates were scientific, but sometimes they were social. It is difficult to overestimate their value. After all, discussion is in itself dialectic. The truth is born in the clash of opposites. Whenever in science there are no opposites, no struggles, then it is on the road to the cemetery, it is going to bury itself. It is easier to ignore your opponent than to argue with him, but to turn away from him, not to know him, to 'close him down' means to damage science, truth, and society. . . .

"Young people must learn skillful polemics from their grandfathers who made the revolution. At that time oratory was a lofty art, because at times everything depended on the word. I think that young people must develop frank exchanges of opinion to the full, and must not be afraid of conflict."

This eloquent expression of the value of freedom, born of Kapitsa's early experience in the West, also has meaning for those living in lands that consider themselves democratic.

Graham wrote in one of his analyses: "While in the 1930's we could speak of the Bolshevization of science, we can now speak of the scientization of Bolshevism." Despite the new freedom—and there is still a considerable way to go, as implied by Kapitsa's plea—the Bolshevism is still there. No one publicly challenges the basic philosophy of dialectical materialism, although many in the physical and biological sciences are able to ignore it.

It must also be remembered that philosophy can never be fully removed from science. A man's concept of the nature of things plays an inescapable role as he pushes into new territory. His choice of where to look next, of how to formulate an explanation of what he finds, is controlled in large measure by his philosophy. All we can ask is that he be allowed to choose his own.

KEEPING THE RUSSIANS
HEALTHY AND HAPPY

»

Walter Sullivan

The surgeon was a woman and she worked with skill and speed. However, the visiting American surgeon at her elbow was fascinated less by her performance than by the earrings that protruded through her sterile cap and mask, wiggling as she cut and manipulated. They hung perilously over the open body cavity of the patient, and he thought: "What if one of them drops!"

He told me, too, of seeing flies in the supposedly sterile section of an operating theater. Yet he was greatly impressed by the competence of the surgeons and by the highly specialized stapling machines developed for a variety of tasks, from sewing blood vessels end to end to the repair of a damaged eye. Like other visitors from the West, he found many wards over-crowded with beds, yet the atmosphere of what American doctors call T.L.C. (tender, loving care) was remarkable.

On three trips to the Soviet Union in recent years, I encountered comparable contrasts. I watched the blood being drained from a newly deceased woman for use in living patients. I interviewed a researcher who has developed a technique whereby human muscle tissue is minced, then stuffed into wounds, where it allegedly reorganizes itself into new muscle of the proper configuration. I saw giant freezers filled with human spare parts removed from cadavers—bone, tendon, skin, and nerve tissue.

Thus Soviet medicine presents an enormously diverse picture—one that is truly meaningful only when viewed against the background of the past. When the Soviet state was formed there was a gross lack of public-health facilities. The need to develop, as fast as possible, a health service that would bring at least moderately professional care to the vast country demanded special measures, such as the training of feldshers—men and women with less than a full medical education who could deal with routine problems.

World War II left its mark in the numerical dominance of Soviet medicine by women. The war not only decimated the male population, but also diverted from medicine the men who today would have been the more experienced physicians and surgeons.

The practice of medicine and public health is so diverse and specialized that one must depend on the views of specialists in making any assessment. And even for the specialist, assessment is difficult because, in any reasonable length of time, he can see only a small fraction of the medical establishment. Furthermore, his hosts naturally show him their best. Dr. Robert Roaf, Professor of Orthopedic Surgery at the University of Liverpool, has toured Soviet hospitals and research institutes on at least four occasions and has pointed out the difficulties in evaluating patient treatment.

In industry, for example, one can look at production figures, but vital statistics, such as life expectancy and death rates from various ailments, are probably more dependent on economic, social, and hygienic conditions than on medical care. A number of visitors have commented that not much emphasis is placed on medical record-keeping, which has become a science of its own in Western countries. There are exceptions—as in certain aspects of the cancer program—but I suspect that when I was told that national statistics on abortions were unavailable, there was more truth to the reply than evasion.

The organization of Soviet medicine still reflects its early goal of broadening the lowest common denominator of service. The basic treatment center is the polyclinic. It may be in a factory, a school, or a large block of apartment houses. Every citizen, from birth, is supposed to have a medical card and is assigned a physician at his local polyclinic. He apparently can change doctors if he wishes, but must submit a request in writing. The more well-to-do can seek out a physician of high repute and pay him a private fee. Otherwise medical care is free, apart from drugs purchased for home use from the drugstores.

Up to the age of sixteen, the resident of a large city goes to a pediatric clinic. Then he is issued a new medical card and is referred to an adult polyclinic. The staff of a city polyclinic consists, typically, of four specialists in internal medicine, two surgeons, two gynecologists, a pathologist, a radiologist, and a specialist in disorders of eyes, ears, nose, throat, and skin, plus various auxiliaries. There are no hospital beds. If a patient needs bed care he is sent to a hospital or specialized institute.

The hospitals, unlike those in the West, do not usually handle outpatients. Once someone has been discharged from a hospital he is referred to his local polyclinic for follow-up treatment and surveillance. While there are general hospitals that handle all types of cases, the remarkable feature of the Soviet system is the emphasis on specialized institutes—and on specialization in general.

When I interviewed Aleksandr R. Luria, the internationally known researcher on brain function, he explained that his work was made possible by the fact that brain tumor cases from all over the Soviet Union were flown to Moscow for treatment at a specialized institute there. The Russians have a program of "sanitary aviation" to bring patients to the doctor or vice versa. At the Moscow institute several brain tumors are removed each day, whereas such operations are comparatively rare in any single American institution.

Luria has been exploring the detailed function of various parts of the brain by systematically testing patients before the operation to bring to light abnormal aspects of brain function. He then makes careful note, from the surgical results, of that part of the brain affected by the tumor.

In *Survey,* a British journal of Soviet and East European studies, Roaf tells of visiting the Central Institute for Trauma and Orthopedics in Moscow. Trauma is injury of the body, as by an accident. Orthopedics is the correction of deformities. In a single room he found seven patients with a rare congenital condition: the absence of the radius, or heavy bone of the forearm.

The ten departments of the institute's hospital are a commentary on the hazards of Soviet life. They included such titles as: Sport Trauma, Ballet Trauma, Electric Burns, Tumors, Arthritis, Hand Surgery, Neurosurgery, and Children's Orthopedics. Each had its own corridor with small rooms serving as wards of three to six beds each. At least some of the beds were equipped with earphones (presumably for music and radio programs) and a bell to summon aid. There were six operating theaters in the building.

"We saw many cases of difficult tumors treated by widespread resection [removal] of bone and replacement by whole sections of preserved frozen cadaveric bone," Roaf reported. As with live bone transplants, the inserted bone serves as a matrix which is gradually replaced by the patient's own bone tissue.

It was on a visit to the Sklifosovsky Institute in Moscow that I saw freezers filled with frozen human parts. The institute is in a handsome old building constructed in neoclassic style at the end of the eighteenth century by Count Sheremetyev as a memorial to his wife. It has a gracefully curving façade and is surmounted by a central dome. When French troops occupied Moscow in 1812 they used the building as a military hospital. The institute's specialty is trauma, and a fleet of ambulances, resembling miniature station wagons and marked *"Skoraya Pomoshch"* (literally: "Swift Help"), stands outside in readiness to bring in those struck by cars or otherwise injured. About three hundred patients are brought to the institute daily, or come on their own, and roughly a third are kept for extended treatment.

It is here that the pioneering work on recovery of cadaver blood has been carried out. Thousands of Soviet citizens are now walking the streets with the blood of deceased fellow citizens coursing through their veins. I was invited to witness the removal of blood from a newly deceased patient and found it interesting, though a bit grisly. The "donor," head down on a tilt table, was swathed in anonymity by a winding sheet that covered all but an attachment to the jugular vein. My interpreter, a lady of delicate disposition, asked to be excused. The advantages of the procedure were outlined. After removal of the blood, the liver and other internal organs of the donor can be examined for evidence of hepatitis or cancer, which is impossible with a live donor. Hepatitis transmitted by blood transfusion is frequently fatal, and a live donor, though asked, may not know that he has had the disease. Furthermore, enough blood is obtained from a single cadaver to provide a massive infusion where necessary. In conventional practice such infusions carry a mixture of blood from many donors, increasing the danger of infection.

Each year the institute draws some 3,000 pints of blood. Roughly a third of it is rejected because of danger signs in examination of the donor. The withdrawal is done within two or three hours of death. If the blood has not been used within a few months, it is broken down into its components for other medical purposes.

In addition to the transfusion of blood and transplantation of organs, several Russian researchers have for many years been exploring the processes of regeneration. When a claw is torn from a crab it can grow a new one. When a salamander or its larval form (an axolotl) loses a leg, a new one sprouts in its place. What prevents a higher animal from doing the same, and might the impediment be overcome, enabling a man to grow a new leg or a new kidney?

One of those working in this field is Aleksandr N. Studitsky, at the Institute of Animal Morphology in Moscow. It is he who has been experimenting with the use of minced muscle to replace tissue lost in accidents. Muscle tissue does not regenerate to any extent. If an alligator bites a piece from someone's thigh, the lost muscle is replaced by scar tissue and other nonfunctional material, leaving an unsightly cavity. In his experiments Studitsky takes the thigh muscle of a rat, chops it fine, and puts it back in the rat's leg, coupling it with the nerves and blood vessels of the leg. "Within three weeks," he told me, "there is a normal muscle with its net of capillaries, nerve endings, and functional activity." The technique has also been successfully tried in human beings, he said, with muscle taken from one part of the body, minced, and stuffed into a wound elsewhere in the same individual. He said he is now experimenting with the transplantation of intact muscle. However, he believes that the muscle must be coaxed— or shocked—into a "plastic" state (comparable to the disorganization of minced muscle), before, under the influence of neighboring tissues, it adapts itself to its new role in the body.

Studitsky's muscle-mincing technique is not yet in general clinical use. He has raised scientific eyebrows in his country with a variety of unorthodox proposals. For example, he argues that the higher animals, including man, are more efficient at regeneration than lower animals such as crabs, salamanders, and axolotls. The latter have evolved an ability to grow new appendages because they keep losing them, but they cannot regenerate internal organs. On the other hand, man, according to Studitsky, can grow a new liver even if 90 per cent of the existing one is removed. Furthermore, he believes, one's ability to regenerate increases with age. Since advancing years carry us further and further from the time when we first grew our arms, legs, and other organs, most researchers in the field believe the ability to replace lost tissue declines with age.

Studitsky says the growth and health of muscle and bone are dependent on their interactions with neighboring tissue. In this, too, he is unorthodox, for most biologists believe the development of a cell is essentially governed by its own archive of genetic information—its store of DNA. Studitsky has interposed barriers of cellophane or metal foil between muscle and neighboring tissue and finds that tumors develop in the muscle even though, so far as he can tell, there has been no interference with blood and nerve connections. He believes that in the healing of bone an essential role is played by interactions between the "skin" of the bone, or periosteum, the cartilage, and the ends of the bone. He has repeatedly removed, from a living animal, all of a leg bone except its ends, its cartilage, and its periosteum and has found that the bone regenerates promptly.

To demonstrate his point, on my visit to his laboratory Studitsky reached into a cabinet and pulled out a large, liquid-filled jar containing a preserved axolotl with three legs. The animal had been white, but the leg of a dark axolotl had been grafted onto it. At the time of its death and preservation, its other legs had begun to turn dark, too, demonstrating, Studitsky said, the exchange of "genetic" or control information between organs of the body.

Bruce Carlson, at the University of Michigan Medical School, who has verified some of Studitsky's findings with minced muscle and has himself been exploring the mechanisms of regeneration, points out that most of Studitsky's work has been with small volumes of muscle. If his mincing technique (which seems to work better than an intact transplant) is to replace large chunks of muscle, a way must be found to restore the main blood vessels needed to supply such tissue. According to Carlson, a Russian at the start of this century proposed that leukocytes (white blood cells) might be able to transform themselves to replace cells that are destroyed. Many Russians still believe this, and since the details of bodily repair have so far eluded experimenters, the hypothesis has never been disproved.

Carlson himself worked for five months in the laboratory of L. V. Polezhayev, who for more than thirty-five years has been trying to stimulate regeneration in various kinds of tissue. This research, which like that of Studitsky is at the Institute of Animal Morphology, is currently focusing on heart muscle. When a person has a "heart attack," it typically involves the blocking of blood flow through a coronary artery that supplies the heart muscle. As a result, part of the muscle "dies"—what is known as an infarct. If the person survives the attack, he is handicapped for life to a degree dependent on the extent of the damage. If a way could be found to stimulate regeneration of the heart muscle, it would become possible to rehabilitate such cases.

Polezhayev's experiments with rats, dogs, and rabbits involve the inducing of artificial "heart attacks" followed by the injection of substances to stimulate muscle fiber growth and inhibit the formation of scar tissue. So far, although there has been some regeneration, the scar tissue has always won out. He has also tried to find ways to "turn on" regeneration by exposing axolotls to X-ray doses sufficient to block their growth of a new limb, then attempting to discover methods of reviving such regrowth. In parallel work at Obninsk, A. A. Voitkevich is trying to find out how frogs can be stimulated to grow a third leg, as some of them do spontaneously.

In each of the larger cities there are specialized institutes in such fields as cancer and neurosurgery. In the whole of the Soviet Union, for example, there are eighteen institutes of orthopedics and traumatology, all under the central one in Moscow. The Moscow institute renders advice and relays new techniques to the provincial institutes, which in turn help out the general hospitals of their region. Routine cases tend to be handled in the general hospitals, with only those of special interest referred to the specialized institutes.

Many persons who have toured Soviet hospitals and clinics are amazed at the high ratio of doctors and nurses to patients. Roaf tells of an adult polyclinic with forty-five doctors for a population of 10,000 (one for every 222 people compared with one per 630 in the United States as a whole). At a 1,300-bed children's polyclinic in Tbilisi there are said to be 250 doctors and 600 nurses. The large rosters may, in part, be related to short working hours. Some physicians do a four-hour shift, then work another four hours at some other clinic. The pay for ordinary practitioners is low, even by Soviet standards. Roaf likens it to that of a moderately skilled worker. Student nurses are taken on at the age of seventeen or eighteen and live at home. They earn about twenty rubles a month, or $22.20. Nurses are often trained to do a single job—give diathermy treatment, for example —and concentrate on this alone.

Because Russia came out of the war with large numbers of maimed citizens, it has emphasized the development of artificial limbs, particularly during the last decade or so. The best known of these is an arm attached in such a manner that electrical impulses are picked up from the patient's own muscles. These are amplified by a tiny transistorized unit, and a small electric motor responds to the impulses by moving forearm and hand. The battery power supply has to be recharged every three days.

It is reported that more than one hundred and fifty of these limbs are in use. Electrically controlled hands, driven by electric power or compressed carbon dioxide, have been tried in the United States, but American rehabilitation specialists believe they are too complex and difficult to maintain for general use. The conventional hooklike device is far simpler. The more natural-looking Soviet hand, however, is favored in certain cases, such as when both of a person's hands have been lost.

A feature of Soviet medicine that has its roots in nineteenth-century European practice is the virtuoso surgeon, emulated by students who carry his technique to operating rooms in remote parts of the country. Roaf tells of watching Vasily D. Chaklin, "the doyen of Soviet orthopedic surgeons," perform an operation that he had developed for treating lumbar lordosis, or in-curving of the lower back. It involves removing a wedge from the vertebrae. Roaf reported being "much impressed" by the technique of the theater team. "Almost as soon as the skin had been sewn up," he said, "we were shown frozen sections of the material removed at operation: the sections were excellent and were prepared by a technician who, we were told, had only had one year's training."

The treatment of cancer in the Soviet Union has been organized on a national scale that is probably unique in medicine. Known as the Oncology Service, it comes directly under the Ministry of Health in Moscow and is responsible not only for cancer treatment throughout the country, but also for treatment of all tumors, benign or malignant, and for propaganda—by posters, briefings of physicians, and health lectures at the polyclinic—designed to achieve early diagnosis.

D. W. Smithers, Professor of Radiotherapy at the University of London, has visited nine cancer-treating hospitals and their associated research institutes in Leningrad and Moscow. His report appears in the same issue of *Survey* as that by Roaf. Specialized institutes under the Academy of Medical Sciences are "highly privileged research establishments," he says, staffed by "the best brains available." Each concentrates on one area of research concerning the treatment or causes of cancer.

A special role is played by the Herzen Institute in Moscow, which comes directly under the Ministry of Health. In addition to its programs of basic and clinical research, it gives postgraduate training and directs more than two hundred oncological (tumor-treating) clinics throughout the country. Those wishing to join the Oncology Service usually must have spent three years in general practice. As in other fields of medicine in the U.S.S.R., competition is keen for posts in the research institutes—particularly those in the most desirable locations, such as Moscow and Leningrad. The top-ranking trainees get these jobs. Those at the bottom may end up in the more remote stations.

The Herzen Institute advises oncological clinics of the latest treatments. One man from each clinic must do postgraduate work at the institute each year, and every oncologist must come back for a refresher course of a few months once in five years. Much of the surgery at the institute is apparently done by these returnees under the watchful eye of a professor, just as surgery is done by "residents" in American teaching hospitals. Here, too, specialization is the order of the day. A man may specialize in tumors of a single organ, such as the esophagus.

According to Smithers, the polyclinics have responded so assiduously to the order to send doubtful cases to the Oncology Service that more than half those appearing at the latter turn out to have no tumors at all.

Statistical studies of cancer incidence have shown regional differences and trends that could throw light on causes of the disease. Hence the Herzen Institute is conducting a demographic tumor survey through its far-flung dispensaries, some of them in areas with unusual environmental conditions. In some parts of the country it has been found that the rates of primary liver tumors or tumors of the upper digestive tract are unusually high. In big cities, such as Moscow, there is a central registry of tumor cases under treatment by the Oncology Service. Whenever a research institute needs cases of a special type, it can seek them out through this registry. While Smithers was there, a request came in for two patients with peripheral tumors suitable for treatment by chemical perfusion—where the blood circulatory system is used locally to carry an anticancer substance through the tumor area. A check of the files revealed the location of two such patients, and they were presumably moved to the institute for such special treatment.

This raises the question of drug screening. How are new medical procedures tested in the Soviet Union? The rate at which new drugs are introduced seems considerably lower than in the United States and Western Europe, probably in part for lack of a highly competitive pharmaceutical industry. On a visit to the Ministry of Health I was told that drug screening and approval are the responsibility of the ministry's State Committee on the Pharmacopeia. To achieve objectivity, a drug developed by one institute is allocated to another for testing, and the State Committee decides, on the basis of the reported results, whether or not to include it in the next list of approved treatments.

One drug widely used in the West is not approved for general use in the U.S.S.R. That is "the pill," used as a female contraceptive. I discussed the subject with Lidiya K. Skornyakova, a motherly-looking former gynecologist who now heads the Department of Maternal and Child Care in the Ministry of Health. The ministry is worried, she said, about the cumulative effect of the use, throughout a woman's childbearing years, of a drug that simulates the body's hormonal balance during pregnancy. This is how the pill works. It makes the body "think" it is pregnant and thus curbs the formation of fertile eggs. "In particular," she said, "we are concerned at what effect it may have on a woman's climacteric [change of life, or menopause]."

Before many years have passed there will be thousands of women in the West who have used the pill virtually from puberty to menopause. I asked Mrs. Skornyakova whether the attitude of the ministry would change if at that time there was still no evidence of ill effect. "Of course," she replied. Some polyclinics in factories and elsewhere prescribe the pill, she said, but only in special cases, where alteration of the hormonal balance is called for.

Walter Sullivan

Meanwhile, she said, various mechanical means of birth control are being used. I had heard that male contraceptives could be purchased at public vending machines and that diaphragms for female use were sold across the counter by drugstores. I had been told, too, that such devices were expensive, ill-fitting, and of poor quality.

Mrs. Skornyakova pointed out that devices which must be applied as a prelude to intercourse have an inherent drawback. She said considerable emphasis is now being placed on intrauterine devices, two of which she pulled from a drawer. One was the size and shape of a small corkscrew, made from a hollow tube of flexible plastic. The other, made of similar material, resembled a miniature umbrella stick with several arms radiating from one end. Both devices could be squeezed into an apparatus resembling a hypodermic needle but larger and of plastic. With this instrument it is possible to inject one of the devices into the uterus in seconds. As long as it remains in the uterus, pregnancy does not occur. However, Mrs. Skornyakova said that, as in other countries, it had been found that a certain percentage of women cannot retain such a device in the uterus for any length of time.

The devices are hollow, so that a fine wire or other material that shows up in X rays can be inserted to help locate the device within the uterus. When the woman decides she wishes to start childbearing, the device is removed. The umbrellalike model carries a hairlike thread, making it easy to pull it out. These devices are being administered at various polyclinics to women who ask for them. Mrs. Skornyakova said, however, that they have not proven popular with the younger girls.

I pressed her on this point because several Soviet women had complained to me about the difficulty of achieving adequate birth control. A privileged few got the pill from foreigners, but the high abortion rate testifies to the need for more effective and accessible birth-control methods. It was Mrs. Skornyakova who said abortion figures were not available, but she added pointedly that the number is "not a few." (In the United States the Planned Parenthood Federation has estimated that almost a million women have illegal abortions each year, of which a thousand are fatal.)

Mrs. Skornyakova described in detail a new abortion technique that has excited the interest of American obstetricians. It eliminates the traditional D and C method (dilatation and curettage), in which the cervix is dilated and a spoonlike instrument, or curette, is used to scrape the uterus. The new instrument is a tube attached to a suction pump. It is inserted into the uterus with minimum dilatation and sucks out what is removed surgically by the other method. No cutting is done except inside the tube, where tiny whirling blades make the material pass through more easily. The technique, Mrs.

Skornyakova said, can be used through the third month of pregnancy. It greatly reduces the danger of infection or damage to the uterus, she added, and can be completed in thirty seconds. She said the new device is being used in a number of clinics—but not all. Some obstetricians are clinging to the traditional D and C.

Mrs. Skornyakova pointed out that abortions were outlawed in 1936, but that by 1956 criminal abortions had reached such a level that it was decided to repeal the law. Now, she added, the rate of illegal abortions is "very low." I wondered why there were any at all, until students explained that unmarried girls were fearful of having one or more abortions on their medical records lest this handicap their job-seeking. In a society that retains elements of puritanism, the same fear probably inhibits unwed girls from seeking contraceptive aid from their polyclinics. I sensed here a dichotomy between generations. Mrs. Skornyakova and others of her age shrugged off the problem, indicating that "nice" girls have no worries and that public censure by the Komsomol, the Communist youth organization, of girls who are promiscuous takes care of the rest. Yet fear of such censure obviously encourages those who do become pregnant to seek "black market" abortions. I was told that girls who had had three such operations were not rare but that the abortions were not necessarily dangerous in that they might be done, for a fee, by a regular practitioner.

In the case of legal abortions, an effort is first made to persuade the girl that she should have her child. She is shown a film designed to influence her in this respect, warning that an abortion may lead to sterility. The symbol common to these movies is the breaking of a tulip stem. However, if she persists in her purpose, only the approval of a physician is needed to authorize the procedure.

Since Mrs. Skornyakova was responsible for Soviet child care, I asked her about baby swaddling, so often cited by Americans during the height of the Cold War as helping to account for "why the Russians act the way they do." It was said that the Russian babies, wrapped as tightly as mummies, could not kick or otherwise work off energy and thus grew up in a state of frustration. Mrs. Skornyakova laughed. For years now, she said, parents have been advised to cover the legs loosely, so the baby can kick, and to leave the hands free, covering them with mittens lest the baby scratch itself.

As in the United States, sex education is one of the much-discussed novelties of the Soviet Union. In one of the institutes at Novosibirsk I saw a bulletin board covered with enlarged snapshots of faculty members. Beneath each photograph was a caption that put facetious words into the mouths of those shown. My hosts explained with an embarrassed grin that a traveling expert had just given a sex lecture there and these photographs, as shown by a banner caption above them, purported to be candid shots of the audience. Beneath a picture of one worried-looking young professor was the caption: "Should I ask my question?" Under another, of two men looking at each other in surprise, were the words: "Why, we're not so bad after all!" Sex education in the schools begins at fourteen or fifteen, according to Mrs. Skornyakova. Special films are used as well as lectures on physiology, given to the two sexes separately.

Among the fields of medical research considered most important by the Soviet Union are psychology and its sister subject, neurophysiology. Americans often dismiss Soviet work in psychology by equating it with the teaching of a dog, in Pavlovian fashion, to salivate when you ring a bell. (Ivan P. Pavlov had found that if he rang a bell every time food was presented to a dog, the dog would ultimately drool whenever the bell was rung, even if no food appeared.) Yet O. L. Zangwill, Professor of Experimental Psychology at Cambridge University, wrote after an inspection of Soviet activity in this field: "In educational psychology . . . the Soviet Union leads the world."

As with genetics, the Communists, immediately after the revolution, saw in a better understanding of the brain and its learning processes a short cut to the building of the society that was their ideal. Some of Pavlov's ideas on conditioning seemed ready-made for this project. Pavlov was respected throughout the world for his work in physiology. He had won a Nobel Prize in 1904, not for his research on conditioned reflexes, but for his discoveries regarding the physiology of digestion.

He had also found in his conditioning experiments that he could induce "experimental neuroses" in dogs and was exploring the possibility of treating human mental disorders by conditioning methods, a line pursued further by his successor in Leningrad, Anatoly G. Ivanov-Smolensky. Pavlov himself resisted the temptation to develop a general theory of behavior based on his findings. Yet his ideas had a special appeal to the Communists because they were "materialist." That is, he considered the workings of the brain to be as much a part of physiology, or body function, as digestion. This was in contrast to the view of old-fashioned psychologists who believed mind and body were separate realms.

Pavlov also dismissed Sigmund Freud's approach to psychology as misconceived. He examined, for example, the famous case of Elizabeth von Ritter, whom Freud treated for progressive paralysis—an episode recently dramatized on Broadway in the play *A Far Country*. Freud believed he cured her through psychoanalysis, showing her that she was troubled by suppressed feelings of guilt. According to Pavlov, her trouble was a conflict of reflexes—those of inhibition and excitation.

To the dialectical materialist the Freudian concepts, not, strictly speaking, being subject to experimental confirmation, were "idealistic," founded on meaningless dreams instead of solid (materialist) fact. Hence there has emerged a Pavlovian treatment of mental illness which depends on education rather than psychoanalysis. In recent years, however, there has been some recognition of the value of opening up a person's consciousness. For example, Vladimir N. Myasishchev, director of the Bekhterev Institute of Psychoneurology in Leningrad and a Pavlov disciple, has rejected psychoanalysis, yet he has written: "The psychiatrist, by his skilled approach to the patient, helps him to disentangle the history of his life—the complicated and tangled non-understandable or incorrectly understood circumstances of the past and present."

From those working in Soviet laboratories I learned that Soviet research on the brain and its functions is sharply divided between the fields of psychology and neurophysiology. In contrast with American psychological research, with its heavy dependence on rats and other experimental animals, one sees virtually no animals in the Soviet psychology laboratories. The subjects are human. Experiments with animals are classed as neurophysiology, and it is here that Western specialists see the most rapid progress. The research has escaped from narrow Pavlovian lines even though Pavlov's classic discoveries are regarded as the starting point, as they are in the West.

The history of Soviet psychology parallels that of other sciences. There was a meeting after World War II, organized by the Academy of Sciences and the Academy of Medical Sciences and reported to have been sponsored by Stalin himself, which explored the ideological state of psychology. There followed a period when ideological considerations permeated the literature in this field; references to Western work were minimal and obeisance was paid to Pavlov in ways that, in Western eyes, bordered on the ridiculous. Then, with Stalin's death the trend changed. An examination of fifty-two articles in recent issues of *Voprosy Psikhologii* (Problems of Psychology) shows only three with ideological content. The rest cover such subjects as an experimental study of the development of personality in children, information theory and data processing from a mathematical and statistical point of view, and a study of discrimination of objects of varying degrees of complexity against a complex background. In one of the articles there were eighteen references to British or American works.

Zangwill, after his return from the Soviet Union, said that an experimental psychologist from the West "may well find himself more at home in a Soviet psychological laboratory than in the psychiatric clinic of his own home town!" The reason is the gulf that exists between the practice of psychiatry, with its emphasis on analysis, and psychological research, with its systematic study of behavior based on experiment and statistical analysis. It is true, however, that a number of visitors have found Soviet experiments in psychology lacking in rigorous statistical safeguards against various forms of bias (as, for example, in choosing the subjects for a study).

Two men, in particular, have influenced Soviet educational psychology. One was Anton S. Makarenko, who set up a school to train the homeless youths who, in the aftermath of the revolution, roamed the countryside, living by theft and banditry. By social pressure, exploitation of competitive instincts, and the use of activists among the boys, he achieved remarkable successes in remolding them. His common-sense views on child-rearing were incorporated into a text, *A Book for Parents,* that is in almost every Soviet home, a counterpart of Benjamin Spock's *Baby and Child Care.*

On a more theoretical level the work of Lev S. Vygotsky still has a profound influence. Vygotsky was interested in the role that the development of speech plays in a child's evolution of conceptual thought—to what extent are words needed for the reasoning process? In this respect he was apparently influenced by Jean Piaget, the great Swiss psychologist who led the way into this field. Vygotsky died in 1934, when he was only thirty-eight years old, but his colleague Aleksandr Luria carried on his line of research. Because of Luria's command of English and his brilliance on the lecture platform, his influence has extended to Britain and the United States, where he has been a frequent visitor. The work that he was doing on the effects of brain tumors, when I saw him in Moscow, was a direct outgrowth of his wartime experience with those who, because of head injuries, had lost the ability to employ words as symbols of ideas—a condition known as aphasia. Luria had studied such cases to seek out the speech centers of the brain and explore their interrelationships.

Ideas on mental information-processing derived from cybernetics have invaded psychology in the Soviet Union, as they have in the West. Moscow State University recently etsablished a "programmed learning" unit operated jointly by the departments of Psychology and Probability Theory. The use of information theory to achieve a better understanding of mental processes has also been pushed by Aleksei N. Leontyev, who received part of his training in Paris. Leontyev has attacked the view of Western psychologists that individuals are endowed with unequal and inalterable abilities. He says that one's skill at a particular task is determined by many contributing capabilities. Two students may be equally good at algebra, but one may be good because certain aspects of his mental machinery are superior, while the other may profit from a completely different combination of abilities. These various abilities are the fruit of each individual's life experience as well as his inborn characteristics. The fact that even seemingly innate abilities are affected by one's life history is shown, Leontyev says, by laboratory experiments. Animals with experience in problem-solving can solve new problems faster than those new to such tasks. The modification of their mental processes by experience thus outweighs the inherited differences between individuals.

These ideas are ideologically attractive to the Communists because they support the argument that there is no scientific basis for an aristocracy. It was such reasoning, too, that led to Soviet disenchantment with intelligence tests, which were abolished by the education decree of 1936.

Among the experiments that have grown out of the current interest in cybernetics is one relating to the way in which an animal with no language tools solves a problem. A chimpanzee was given a stick and a long tube with a juicy piece of orange inside it. The ape quickly learned to push the orange out with the stick. Then the experiment was repeated, but this time the stick was too big to fit into the tube. The scientists recorded carefully the manner in which the chimpanzee examined the situation and finally chewed enough wood off the stick so that it would fit.

Much of Soviet research with apes and monkeys is done at its famous monkey colony at Sukhumi on the Black Sea. The emphasis there, however, is on hypertension and circulatory diseases rather than on psychology.

Recent Soviet work includes a study of the way in which blind people use their hands to examine objects. Right-handed people tend to hold an object in the left hand and explore it with the right. The question under study is whether this means the portions of the brain associated with each hand play different roles in thought processes. Research in learning psychology has shown that a simultaneous visual experience can increase one's sensitivity to an aural stimulus. Discrimination of musical pitch is greatly increased if the subject has been taught by seeing the note as well as hearing it.

At the Institute of Higher Nervous Activity and Neurophysiology in Moscow, experiments are being conducted with direct chemical stimulation of animal brains. Substances are injected via hollow needles to stimulate a score of brain cells at one time. Apparently some cells are activated by one chemical and some by another, as though the circuitry of the brain was like that of a complex electronic device packed with colored wires, each color representing a different part of the circuitry. In the brain the circuits, instead of being colored, are chemically distinct.

In a recent analysis of Soviet psychology, Neil O'Connor, of Britain's Medical Research Council, describes American psychology as chiefly concerned with behavior rather than with internal workings of the brain, which are attributed to a "black box" beyond experimental reach. "Never far from the mind of any Russian psychologist," he says, "is the question of exactly how the animal he is studying is constructed." He concludes that Soviet psychology "is comparable to American psychology in its expertise and although somewhat smaller in volume is growing rapidly and already equals any other psychology in quality."

Until recently, Soviet psychologists have steered clear of such subjects as motivation, which were alleged to be the private province of the Communist party. The same was true of sociology, but in 1967 an All-Union conference on the subject was held at Sukhumi at which Soviet weakness in the field was spelled out bluntly. A group at the Akademgorodok in Novosibirsk has been agitating for a crash program to develop sociology as rapidly as possible, lest the lack of workable data on manpower, skills, consumer habits, population changes, and the like stand in the way of the more sophisticated economic planning now being attempted.

When I visited the Institute of the Geography of Siberia and the Far East in Irkutsk I met some of those engaged in planning for the vast region east of the Urals. They included a specialist in "medical geography" studying what factors affect the habitability of various parts of Siberia. For example, can the habitable zone be pushed farther north by means of warmer clothing, warmer homes, or a higher calorie diet?

One of the institute's tasks is to project the effects on climate, wildlife, and regional economy of the large lakes being formed by the new hydroelectric dams. The largest such project in existence, at Bratsk, down the Angara River from Irkutsk, has created a lake of more than 2,100 square miles. Autumn and spring both come later to the surrounding countryside because of this lake's effect on the climate. A dam proposed near the mouth of the Ob River, which is longer than the Mississippi, would flood almost 44,000 square miles, compared with the 31,820 square miles of Lake Superior, which now has the largest surface area of fresh water in the world. The Ob dam would also convert a large portion of the arctic tundra into marsh, and its effect on wildlife and climate would probably be radical, I was told by the geographers around the institute conference table. They seemed unanimous in their opposition to the project. Their arguments reminded me of those opposing the Rampart Dam, which would flood 10,500 square miles of the Yukon Basin in central Alaska. The projects have much in common, including their remoteness from present centers of industrial activity. And it was interesting to find that Soviet conservationists are battling Soviet economic developers just as similar camps do battle in the United States.

This was even more evident when I visited Lake Baikal, lying in a great north-south rift that slices the earth's crust in eastern Siberia. Because parts of the lake are more than a mile deep, and the lake itself is three hundred and ninety-five miles long, it holds roughly one-fifth of all the world's lake water. I was driven to a small summit, above a sanatorium with sweeping views of the lake, whose shores are walled by mountains on both sides. It was May, and the peaks on the far side were still snow-clad. The sanatorium was much like a resort hotel. I was told that the young people I saw there had paid a lump sum, plus their round-trip air fare, to have a vacation there. While the lake is extraordinarily beautiful, it is also the home of the most remarkable fresh-water life in the world. More than 1,000 species of plant, shellfish, and vertebrate are unique to its waters.

This is in part because of its great antiquity. Baikal was formed some 25,000,000 years ago and has remained intact ever since. Other lakes come and go as mountain-building processes, glaciers, erosion, sedimentation, and climate change alter the landscape—but not Baikal. Hence it has evolved a particularly distinctive flora and fauna. Furthermore, the species that live there could not survive anywhere else, because the water itself is unique. Not only is it unusually cold and deep for lake water, but it is also extraordinarily free of dissolved minerals. Grigory I. Galazy, who is Baikal's "man for all seasons," says the water is so pure that anyone who drowns there vanishes completely. The little shrimplike crustaceans of the lake quickly eat the flesh, and the skeleton is dissolved away by the mineral-free water.

Galazy heads the Institute of Limnology operated on the lake by the Siberian Department of the Academy of Sciences. Limnology is to bodies of fresh water what oceanography is to the study of the sea. When I saw Galazy, he was championing, without regard to possible personal repercussions, what to some is a lost cause—the saving of Baikal.

A few weeks earlier, G. Evelyn Hutchinson, Sterling Professor of Zoology at Yale University, had cited the farsighted decision of the Soviet government to preserve Baikal as an example of what the United States and Britain should do to save Aldabra Island, in the Indian Ocean. Aldabra, the last home of the giant land tortoise of that region, is the projected site of an air base to be built by Britain, allegedly with American backing. Hutchinson, as president of the International Limnological Society, had pleaded with the Soviet Academy of Sciences to block pollution of Baikal by a giant pulp mill at the town of Baikalsk on the south shore. Such plants, which reduce lumber to the pulp needed for making paper and other cellulose products, typically discharge large amounts of sulphurous wastes into a nearby lake or stream and raise its temperature.

Word came through that the lake had been saved; the plant project had been abandoned. I asked Galazy about it. "There the plant is," he said, grimly pointing across the lake. On the far side a plume of smoke soared into the sky. It had, in fact, begun operating and was already discharging waste into the lake. It was evident that the life of the lake could not tolerate any substantial change, in either the temperature or the chemical content of the water. While elaborate purification methods were being used, there was no practical way to cleanse the water of dissolved chemicals. The only solution was to build a forty-two-mile pipeline to carry the waste water to a stream that empties into the Angara below the lake, but the industrial managers in control of the situation said that would be too expensive.

How much, then, is the unique life of Baikal worth to the Soviet Union —and the rest of the world? Are more than 1,000 unique products of nature's infinite patience over 25,000,000 years not worth the cost of forty-two miles of pipe and a few pumping stations? This is the kind of issue that, in the past, could only be discussed privately in the Soviet Union. Now men like Galazy speak out—as did such prominent figures as Pyotr Kapitsa, the physicist, and Mikhail Sholokhov, the author of *And Quiet Flows the Don,* who brought the Soviet Union a Nobel Prize in literature. In 1966 he addressed the Twenty-third Congress of the Communist party on the importance of saving Baikal, and a large part of one issue of *Soviet Life,* a pictorial magazine designed for English-speaking audiences, was devoted to the debate, with excerpts from statements pro and con. They sounded much like the arguments over pollution of the Great Lakes.

I came away from the Soviet Union impressed by the extent to which our problems are alike. It seems as though complex, highly industrialized societies, like those of the United States and the Soviet Union, are forced to evolve along parallel—perhaps, more properly, converging—lines. Probably the most important man that I saw, politically speaking, was Mikhail D. Millionshchikov, vice president of the Academy of Sciences and president of the Council of Nationalities in the Supreme Soviet. I asked him about this phenomenon of convergence when I interviewed him in the sumptuous executive offices of the academy. His office is a twin of that occupied by the president, Mstislav V. Keldysh, both opening off a cavernous central hall with doors fifteen feet high and walls of marble lined with fabulous chairs whose arms are gilded eagles. The building had been constructed in the eighteenth century as the palace of a son of Nikita Demidov, an industrialist who introduced an early form of mass production in making munitions for Peter the Great.

Millionshchikov agreed that, in a superficial sense, the American and

Soviet societies are converging. More and more, he said, we are confronted by similar problems: pollution, the need for better surface transport, more abundant energy sources, aircraft development, and exploration of the cosmos. In all these fields, as also in the building of atom smashers even larger than those now projected, it will be more economical, he said, for the two nations to work together (once the Vietnam war has been resolved). But as a faithful party member he argued that basically the two societies are as far apart as ever: one capitalist and the other socialist.

Certainly the two countries are still very different in many respects, but I left convinced that, after fifty years of striving toward Communism, the Soviet Union was never more like its American rival than it is today.

FIRST INTO SPACE, THEN THE RACE

»

John Noble Wilford

Four years after the Bolshevik Revolution, Lenin is supposed to have foreseen another day in the twentieth century when Russia would again shake the world. Although the exact language may be apocryphal, the Russians now quote Lenin as saying in 1921 to a prominent rocket engineer: "You must not be upset if some comrades do not believe in the remarkable future of cosmonautics. As for myself I believe in it; I believe firmly that twenty or thirty years will pass, or perhaps even fifty, and a Soviet man—he will certainly be Soviet—will carry out that fairy-tale voyage."

Through economic disorder, internal struggle, and enemy invasion, Lenin's vision must have seemed unbelievably fanciful to even the most optimistic Russian. Man might fly in space. But a Russian first? As for the rest of the world, it paid the prophecy little heed—until October 4, 1957.

On that day a decade ago, with one spectacular stroke, the Soviet Union thrust man into the space age and threw the United States into a sudden race for supremacy in a new arena of the Cold War. It was the day the earth got its first of many man-made moons. The Russians called it Sputnik, meaning satellite or traveling companion. Little bigger than a basketball, Sputnik circled the earth every hour and thirty-five minutes at an altitude of as much as five hundred and sixty miles. People around the world could look up and see the faint, starlike light of Sputnik move across the night sky. The beep-beep-beep of its tiny radio could be heard on every continent and in every land, beaming an awesome message of what man had wrought.

The first Sputnik was soon followed by others, which were larger and more complex. The United States, trying to catch up, rushed to orbit its own spacecraft in January, 1958. Then, on April 12, 1961, a young Soviet man named Yuri A. Gagarin made the "fairy-tale voyage" beyond earth's atmosphere to fulfill Lenin's prophecy.

In 1967, the tenth-anniversary year of Sputnik, the Soviet space program stands between its great triumphs of the past and the realization of its undisclosed but presumably even more ambitious goals for the future.

With their pioneering flights, the Russians set the initial pace and fixed the major directions for the first decade of the space age. They could hardly have picked a more dramatic way to call the world's attention to the technological progress they had made since the days of Lenin and the revolution and to their growing potential for power. The ebullient Nikita S. Khrushchev, when he was premier, could not resist making the point often and in the earthiest terms. "Bourgeois statesmen," Khrushchev told a Polish audience in 1963, "used to poke fun at us, saying that we Russians were running around in bark sandals and lapping up cabbage soup with those sandals. They used to make fun of our culture, the culture of a people considered, so to say, to be the last among the civilized Western countries. Then suddenly, you understand, those who they thought lapped up cabbage soup with bark sandals got into outer space earlier than the so-called civilized ones."

No longer does the Soviet Union dominate space. The early Russian superiority has been matched and in some ways surpassed by the United States, with its manned Gemini rendezvous missions and its successful unmanned flights to the moon and the planets. The last successful manned flight by Russians came in March, 1965. And the death of a cosmonaut in the Soyuz spacecraft crash in April, 1967—like the Apollo spacecraft fire in the United States—sent engineers back to their drawing boards. Nevertheless, the Russians pledged no letup in their space program. Their rate of unmanned launchings was, in fact, stepped up during 1967. According to Westerners who make it their business to analyze Soviet space activities, the evidence suggests that space still enjoys a high priority in the Soviet scheme of things—perhaps even higher than in the United States.

But how high? Russian secrecy about their capabilities and future plans was never tighter. I had wanted to visit the Soviet Union to interview Russian space officials and see their launching sites and laboratories. France's president, Charles de Gaulle, is the only Westerner known to have watched the lift-off of a Soviet craft, an unmanned weather satellite. But perhaps the spirit of a Sputnik anniversary would bring about some relaxation of the ban on newsmen. My application for a visa was rejected, however, at the last moment and without explanation. I was reminded of what a leading Russian space scientist had told me a few months earlier. During the International Astronautics Federation meeting at Madrid in October, 1966, I asked Professor Leonid I. Sedov, head of the Russian delegation, why Western newsmen had never been allowed to visit a Russian launching site. "This rocket project is very important to us," Sedov replied. "We can open all our works only when the international situation is better." The international situation, I was left now to assume, had not improved.

Even so, during the first space decade, the main characteristics of the Soviet space program have gradually unfolded. These have been disclosed in part by the Russians themselves at international scientific meetings and aerospace exhibits, through the speeches of cosmonauts on good-will tours, and in the announcements Russians make after successful flights. Other details are pieced together by Western observers from reports by tracking stations that chart Russian launchings and flights and from the educated guesses of scientists and engineers. Presumably, United States intelligence agencies, with their military reconnaissance satellites and assorted monitoring devices, have accumulated even more revealing information about Soviet space activities. But they do not choose to publicize any detailed assessments.

From what is known, Russian successes are substantial and varied, indicating a serious attempt to explore as much of space as possible and to do it with a logical sequence of preparatory steps. A monument in Moscow recounts the string of early successes. It is a massive titanium structure that rises three hundred and fifteen feet in the shape of a rocket climbing into the sky. Inscribed on it are many of the Soviet "firsts" in space:

> *First earth satellite, Sputnik 1*
> *First satellite to carry an animal, Sputnik 2*
> *First photographs of the hidden side of the moon, Luna 3*
> *First man in space, Yuri Gagarin*
> *First and only woman in space, Valentina Tereshkova*
> *First three-man satellite, Voskhod 1*
> *First "walk" in space, Aleksei Leonov on Voskhod 2*

Other impressive achievements could be added to the list. A Soviet craft, Luna 1, was the first to overcome the earth's gravitational pull, and Luna 2 was the first to hit the moon. Soviet unmanned spacecraft were the first to land softly on the moon and to orbit the moon. Soviet spacecraft have focused cameras and sophisticated sensing devices on nearly every inch of the earth's surface. They have flown to Venus and to the vicinity of Mars. And from time to time, without committing themselves to any timetables, Soviet scientists and cosmonauts predict the journeys of Soviet men to the moon and planets.

Russian determination and persistence are impressive. They tried at least five times before they finally succeeded in soft-landing on the moon a vehicle capable of returning pictures. They tried at least six times to launch probes to Mars, only two of which came close—and those two failed to return data. Despite repeated failures or only partial successes, the Russians have dispatched probes to Venus at every opportunity when the planet was within range.

Their approach to manned flight is conservative, even though this is the area with greatest propaganda potential. Animals were subjected to more than one hundred orbits in the Vostok craft before Major Gagarin made his flight. At least two or three test flights of the new Soyuz spacecraft are believed to have been made before the ill-fated Colonel Vladimir Komarov was launched. (Contrary to persistent rumors, Western observers say they can find no evidence of other cosmonaut casualties in space prior to the Soyuz accident.) On the other hand, and to some extent accounting for the long hiatus in Russian manned flights, Soviet space officials believe it is wasteful to duplicate missions. Several of the later American Gemini flights were essentially reruns of the proven rendezvous-and-docking technique. But the Russians generally do something once and, if it works, go on to the next step.

The scientific results of their space operations are slight. Nothing the Russians have reported compares in importance to the discovery by the first American spacecraft, Explorer 1, of radiation belts around earth—the Van Allen belts. Sir Bernard Lovell, director of Britain's Jodrell Bank Observatory, is probably the only man who has inspected both American and Soviet space installations. He concluded after a visit to Russia in 1963: "Although the Russians may have superiority purely in the sense of rocketry, the Americans have tremendous superiority over the Russians in their ability to instrument their space vehicles and in the extraction of space information."

The Russian commitment to space exploration appears to be deep and abiding. Russians speak movingly of man's destiny to explore the solar system. Their cosmonauts have said they want to be the first men to land on the moon and Mars. As the showcase of Soviet science, space exploration has been primarily responsible for a fivefold increase in Soviet science and research spending since 1957. About 1,500,000 Russians are said to be involved directly in the planning, production, and operation of the space program. The Russians spend more for space in proportion to their resources than the United States does. According to estimates made by Leon M. Herman, senior specialist in Soviet economics for the Library of Congress, the Soviet space budget apparently runs about $4.5 billion annually. This would be only slightly less than the American civilian space agency's annual $5 billion budget, but the American gross national product is roughly twice the Russian.

One of the most studious and cautious of the American experts who keep watch on Soviet space activities is Dr. Charles S. Sheldon II. A former staff member of the National Aeronautics and Space Council, Dr. Sheldon now is acting chief of the Library of Congress science and policy research division. He emphasizes that his observations are all based on public information, not on secret data gathered by intelligence agencies. Summing up the Soviet program to date he has said: "Over-all, the Soviet program seems to have almost as much variety as our own. They have flown a smaller number of spacecraft but have consistently held a strong lead in total weight of net payload." "My feeling," he added, "is that the so-called space race is anything but over, even though with the passage of time it is changing in character."

In the earlier days of the space decade, he said in explanation, it was relatively easy to score spectacular but isolated successes—a spacecraft slightly larger and holding more men, a crude package landed on the moon. Now both the Russian and the American space programs are more involved in proving reliability of complicated systems for longer flights, less interested in a flight just for the sake of headlines. Even the objective of landing men on the moon, as spectacular as that would be, is not considered a gimmick, but a goal requiring a mobilization of technology never before seen in peacetime.

The American scientist who perhaps has had the most direct dealings with Russian scientists is Dr. Richard W. Porter, an engineer and physicist at General Electric. He was chairman of the United States technical committee on earth satellites for the International Geophysical Year (1957–58), during which Sputnik was launched. He now is the chief United States representative to COSPAR (the Committee on Space Research of the International Council of Scientific Unions), which is the leading international group of space scientists. "I'm only guessing, like anybody else," he said when asked for impressions of Russian space aims and priorities. "But they seem to have the same basic objectives as we have, with only minor differences in terms of priorities. These objectives include missions for the military, for science, for practical applications such as communications and weather forecasting and for exploration for the sake of exploration."

He also observed that the Russian space-science program lacks the variety of the American effort. The impression is accentuated, he said, because the Russians, apparently lacking sufficient electronic computer capability, have been slow to analyze and report the data their spacecraft have collected.

"Their manned program," he continued, "seems to have the same aim as ours, including earth-orbiting missions, lunar flights, and, eventually, planetary missions. There's no question that some of their people are working on all three. I can tell from the questions they ask and the interest they show at our meetings and from the papers they present. And there's no question about their interest in the moon. They've said so."

Dr. Porter and other American scientists enjoy cordial relationships with their Russian counterparts at international meetings and correspond frequently between times. Propaganda is seldom heard at their meetings. Russian scientists, of course, are more circumspect about what they say. They will talk with Western scientists about their families and hobbies, food and wines, the conversion rate of rubles into pesetas, or an arcane problem of second-order linear differential equations. But for reasons of military security, certain space subjects—radar tracking, guidance and control, rocket design and capabilities, and spacecraft engineering—are never discussed. No reports along these lines are delivered. Faced with questions in one of these fields, a Soviet scientist will give an answer he knows is either overly general or misleading or try to avoid answering at all by changing the subject.

Dr. Porter suggests that, in addition to secrecy, taste may sometimes dictate the Russian silence. "In the Soviet Union," he says, "it is not considered good taste to talk about what you're going to do, except in the most general terms. It's considered unseemly bragging. And they also consider it a tremendous loss of face if you fail to do something you had bragged about doing."

If the Russians have been coy about their short-range goals, they have repeated time and again their long-range aims: to place into earth orbit large manned space stations; to land men on the moon and establish scientific bases there; to explore the planets, starting with Venus and Mars.

The Russians set out to conquer space with a commanding advantage in at least one important area of technology—the brute force of rocketry.

Though the world suddenly became conscious of it in 1957, Russian interest in rocketry dates back to the turn of the twentieth century and a deaf teacher of mathematics and physics in the provincial city of Kaluga. Konstantin E. Tsiolkovsky, who was born in 1857 and died in 1935, not only wrote fantasies about voyages to the moon, but also wrestled with the practical problems of getting there. He is credited with being the first man to point out the necessity of liquid-propellant rockets for such flights, with making some of the initial mathematical calculations for lunar voyages, and with conceiving the idea of multistage rockets, which he called "rocket trains." The Russians honor Tsiolkovsky as their "founding father of cosmonautics." His grave at Kaluga is a shrine to which returning cosmonauts make well-publicized pilgrimages.

The Russians, in close step with the Americans and the Germans, organized their first amateur rocket society in 1928, and in the 1930's established a military rocket-research program that led to several experimental firings. But not until after World War II did the Russians begin looking at space in earnest.

As in the United States, German engineers and V-2 rockets served as the nucleus for their early efforts. About 1,000 V-2 rockets were built in Russia after the war. The Germans drew the designs and helped with the testing. When the Germans were sent home between 1950 and 1952, the Russians diligently began to apply what they had learned by building and testing their first military missiles and the forerunner of their first space rocket.

The first public indication of what the Russians were up to was a comment in 1953 by Aleksandr N. Nesmeyanov, then president of the Soviet Academy of Sciences. "Science," he declared confidently at an international meeting, "has reached a state when it is feasible to send a stratoplane to the moon, to create an artificial satellite of the earth."

It now appears that, ironically, a certain Russian shortsightedness may have been the deciding factor in giving them an early superiority in space rocketry. The first three Sputniks, it has become known, were launched by a converted intercontinental ballistic missile that had apparently been designed for delivering heavier and, by 1957, obsolete atomic warheads. Hydrogen warheads, by then developed and operational, were more compact and potent, permitting the use of smaller missiles. The United States had already scaled down the original design of its Atlas ICBM to arrive at a more efficient missile, especially adapted for hydrogen warheads and easier to deploy and conceal. But for reasons that are not clear, the Russians stuck to their earlier missile. The result was an inefficient weapon, military experts say, but a giant ready to lift great loads into space.

The Russians apparently have used three basic generations of rockets to launch their spacecraft, both manned and unmanned. The first generation, the converted ICBM, started as a one-and-a-half-stage rocket with four booster engines clustered in the primary stage and an additional engine (half-stage) on top to give the final push into orbit. The rocket was capable of placing 2,900 pounds into orbit. With the addition of a full upper stage, it could lift the 10,400-pound manned Vostoks in which six cosmonauts flew orbital missions—from Gagarin's one-orbit flight in 1961 through the flight of Valentina Tereshkova in 1963. She and Valery Bykovsky, in separate Vostoks, were launched two days apart, but failed to achieve what they apparently set out to do—rendezvous. Miss Tereshkova was later married to a fellow cosmonaut, Andrian Nikolayev, in a union that cleared up doubt about the genetic effects of weightlessness and radiation and produced normal, healthy children.

With the addition of a twin-engine upper stage to the first-generation rocket, the Russians began in 1963 their two-flight Voskhod project. The Voskhod spacecraft weighed 11,700 pounds. (At the time, the American Titan 2 was being prepared to boost Geminis of no more than 8,000 pounds.) Launched in October, 1964, the first Voskhod carried three men, including a doctor, on a sixteen-orbit mission. This was followed, in March, 1965, by the Voskhod flight during which Lieutenant Colonel Leonov stepped through a submarine-like air-lock hatch for a ten-minute walk in airless space. The first-generation rockets, with various modifications and upper-stage engine clusters, were also used to launch the Russian probes to the moon, Venus, and Mars.

After tests in the Pacific in about 1960 and 1961, a second-generation rocket was put into operation. First it was deployed as a missile, and in 1962 it was used as a launching vehicle with either two or three stages. So far, it has been used for launching a number of unmanned vehicles, including reconnaissance craft, a couple of radiation-monitoring satellites called Elektrons, and the Molniya communications satellites. Molniya has brought for the first time a direct television tie between Moscow and far-off Vladivostok. A three-stage version of the same rocket is believed to have launched the two Polet (Polyot) spacecraft, in 1963 and 1964, for what the Russians described as tests of in-space propulsion systems.

In February, 1964, the Russians produced a mysterious third-generation rocket. With a radically new first stage, it is three times more powerful than the Vostok launcher and slightly more powerful than the Titan 3-C and Saturn 1—the tested giants of the American launching arsenal. The Russian rocket was fired in 1965 to launch a 26,900-pound unmanned Proton satellite into orbit. The nature of neither the Proton nor the rocket has been disclosed.

The Soviet space project bearing the label "Cosmos" is in many ways the most interesting and puzzling. From what the Russians say and Westerners infer, the series is really a mixed bag of secret surveillance vehicles, test runs of new equipment (such as a new manned vehicle), navigation and weather satellites, and planetary craft that never got into orbit. Cosmos launchings have come at a rate of sixty a year; in 1966, twenty-one of them were secret reconnaissance satellites. Evidence is persuasive that the Cosmos label has often been used to cover up failures, though there is no evidence that the Russians have had significantly more failures than has the United States. In any event, more than one hundred and seventy-five satellites, launched by both first- and second-generation rockets, are described by the Russians as being part of the Cosmos project.

After more than two years had elapsed, the Russians resumed manned-flight testing with the launching on April 23, 1967, of the new Soyuz space-craft. It was a "new piloted spacecraft," the official announcement said, with veteran cosmonaut Vladimir M. Komarov in the pilot's seat. The air of mystery was thick. How big was Soyuz? Was it to be the first ship in a dual launching? Was a rendezvous and link-up anticipated, or some other form of space acrobatics? The world was not to know. After eighteen orbits, Komarov suddenly was ordered to aim his spacecraft for a landing in the Soviet Union. According to official accounts, the parachute that was to help brake the final descent failed to deploy properly. The vehicle tumbled, spun, caught fire, and crashed, killing Komarov. Thus tragedy struck twice in 1967—first in the United States, when the three Apollo astronauts were killed in their spacecraft on the launching pad at Cape Kennedy, and then when the Russian cosmonaut died during his as yet unexplained mission.

Behind such Soviet operations is a largely unseen space establishment. The Russians are known to have three launching sites, called cosmodromes. The oldest is at Kapustin Yar, southeast of Volgograd, in a semiarid region. This is where the German scientists from Peenemünde worked on the early Russian versions of the V-2 and where the first Sputniks were launched. The U.S.S.R.'s Cape Kennedy lies on a sandy stretch of land in Kazakhstan, at the end of a railroad spur running from Tyuratam. Russians call it Baikonur, which is actually three hundred miles to the north. But trajectories plotted by Western tracking stations indicate the rockets must be fired from the Tyuratam area. This is the lift-off point for all manned flights, missions to the moon, and other experimental satellites. The newest site has been pinpointed near the town of Plesetsk, not far from Archangel and near the Arctic Circle.

Previously a deep secret, the new cosmodrome was first identified for the world in late 1966 by a group of space kibitzers from the Kettering Grammar School near London. Using a World War II radio receiver, a tape recorder, and their wits, the schoolboys plotted the orbital paths of recent Russian flights. They seemed different. By figuring the trajectories and launching times from the data they had collected, the Kettering boys homed in on the new site, the position of which has since been confirmed by official Western observers. The new site appears to be used primarily for the launching of flights that go over the polar region, instead of going around the earth in the vicinity of its equator. Many of the Cosmos satellites blast off from Plesetsk.

There seem to be two Russian space organizations—one open and science-oriented, the other secret and technology-oriented. The Council for the Exploration and Utilization of Space, an arm of the Soviet Academy of Sciences, appears to direct many of the scientific operations. Its functions include the "initiation, organization, co-ordination and popularization of the problems of space flight." Members of this group are the ones who usually attend international meetings. But the real power, it is assumed, is held by a centralized agency under the Council of Ministers and the Communist party. This is the way the Russians have handled other high-priority projects. The secret organization, sometimes referred to as a "state commission," probably directs the design and construction of rockets and spacecraft and the operations of launchings and flights.

Though these are believed to be civilian agencies, a number of air force officers hold high positions. Even the Academy of Sciences has an indirect military tie. Mstislav V. Keldysh, president of the academy, is a general as well as a respected scientist.

Except for some of the scientists and cosmonauts, the men who run the space program remain anonymous. Why? Khrushchev once declared, "Enemy agents might be sent in to destroy these outstanding people, our valuable cadres." Only his death in January, 1966, at the age of fifty-nine, liberated Sergei P. Korolev from that imposed obscurity. He turned out to be the man responsible for designing the Vostok and Voskhod manned vehicles and the various moon craft. His title was chief designer. As such, he held great power and responsibility for the planning and execution of the space program, perhaps greater than any single technical person in the American program. But Korolev was never mentioned publicly until his death. An engineer named Mikhail K. Yangel has been identified as probably Korolev's successor.

Comparisons between the space programs of the U.S.S.R. and the United States are inevitable, even though both countries deny officially that they are in a race. Who's ahead? The question comes up with each launching, Russian or American, with each success or failure. Though experts shy away from drawing up precise balance sheets, saying it is impossible, some of the strengths and shortcomings of the two programs have become apparent.

Rocketry has long been the Russian forte, giving them an advantage by giving their engineers a greater weight-lifting capability to work with. This enabled the Russians to provide their cosmonauts with a two-gas system—breathing air of nitrogen and oxygen much like normal earth atmosphere—instead of the simpler but more hazardous pure-oxygen environment provided for American astronauts. The pure-oxygen environment was a contributing factor to the rapid spread of the Apollo fire.

The greater pay-load capability also enabled Russian designers to introduce the double-hatch "air lock" for the space walks. The air lock, much like the egress and ingress passage in submarines, allowed cosmonauts to leave and return without decompressing the air inside the cabin. To leave the spacecraft the cosmonaut would open the inner hatch to the air lock, step into the chamber, close the hatch behind him, and then open the outer hatch to climb out into space. The system is much heavier than the American system of direct egress into space, but it is considered safer because no decompression is necessary.

At this time, the Russian and the American rockets appear to have comparable weight-lifting capabilities. The Russians offer no hints that they have in the works a rocket capable of matching the Saturn 5's designed boosting power for putting some 95,000 pounds into earth orbit. There have been, to be sure, some unexplained Russian rocket tests in the Pacific, and a lot of rumors. But Westerners profess to have no knowledge of what the tests have involved.

The Russians appear to be stymied by some bothersome problems. Professor Sedov conceded in an interview in 1966 that his country must investigate and solve a number of "difficult problems" before it can send men on a round trip to the moon. These difficulties, he said, involved operations to place men in a lunar orbit, land them safely on the moon's surface, and bring them back to earth. In other words, the Russians could get men to the vicinity of the moon, but there begin the uncertainties. Khrushchev once said that the question was not "mooning man, but de-mooning him." Sedov said the problems are all theoretically soluble but still must pass the test of flight experience. If the Soyuz flight, the only manned mission since the interview, was intended as part of such a test, it apparently was of little help.

Western engineers, some of them non-American, have concluded that the Russians are lagging primarily in electronics and in-space propulsion. They have, these experts say, yet to demonstrate that they possess an on-board computer comparable to the hatbox-sized one on Gemini that proved invaluable for rendezvous calculations and re-entry guidance. The Russians, according to these experts, have not yet shown that they have developed maneuvering rockets as advanced as those sixteen little jets on the Gemini. This, too, could explain the Russian failure so far to rendezvous—a maneuver necessary for moon flight and for the assembling of large laboratories in space.

As a result, some American space officials and scientists have reached the conclusion that Russian space leadership, except in the early Sputnik days, was more apparent than real. They point to American accomplishments as proof. American spacecraft, with what Sir Bernard Lovell calls more sophisticated instrumentation, discovered the radiation belts encircling earth and the pear shape of earth, made the first successful flights to the vicinity of Venus and Mars, returned superior photographs from the moon, took the first cloud-formation pictures for weather forecasting, and made the first use of space for transmitting the human voice, television, and teletype across oceans and continents.

Russian interplanetary vehicles have been plagued with communications blackouts and failures of upper-stage engines to restart in space. And the U.S.S.R. was slow to enter such fields as communications satellites and weather forecasting from space.

The Russians, in one of their successes, revealed to outside engineers the rather crude methods of technology that made it possible. Their Luna 9, in February, 1966, was the first vehicle to land softly on the moon, using radar-guided braking rockets. It is now fairly certain that the Luna landed less than softly, and, when it did, its petal-like covering sprang open and out popped the instrument package. The U.S.'s three-legged Surveyor, on the other hand, made a feather-bed landing on the moon the following June, leading engineers to believe that American guidance and braking technology may be more sophisticated than the Russian system.

If the scientific return is any measure, the United States has surpassed the Soviet Union. A study made in 1967 by Dr. Robert Jastrow, director of the Goddard Institute for Space Studies, in New York City, concluded that Soviet research in space science has contributed "less in originality and quality" than American research has.

Despite the enormous expense of space programs and the inevitable duplication of effort brought about by Soviet-American competition, little has been accomplished to achieve even a modest form of co-operation between the two powers. At their Vienna conference in 1961, President Kennedy suggested to Premier Khrushchev, "Let's go to the moon together." The United States had just announced its Apollo lunar-landing project, designed to put men on the moon by the end of the decade. The President reiterated his appeal in a speech before the United Nations General Assembly in 1963. The Soviet Union never so much as officially acknowledged the invitation to co-operate. The United States, for its part, appeared none too eager, either. Reacting to Kennedy's U.N. speech, Congress attached an amendment to the space budget for that year, restricting the use of funds for a joint lunar mission without Congressional consent.

The two nations did agree in 1966 on a United Nations treaty to bar the use of outer space for military purposes of an offensive nature and forbid any national claims of sovereignty in space. There have also been agreements to exchange medical and biological data obtained in space experiments and to exchange photographs taken by weather satellites. But the information exchanged thus far has been meager.

"I'm not very sanguine about success in co-operation," Dr. Porter has said. "In the long run we may have some co-operation after we've reached the moon, something on the order of that in Antarctica—sharing of certain facilities, visits to each other's stations, that sort of thing."

Professor Sedov in 1966 conceded that such co-operation "would make sense economically and from the standpoint of research." "But," he added, "we don't have any plans for joint launchings. The situation is not technical, but political, and I think the international situation in these days cannot change this."

It seems likely that for years to come the two countries will continue to compete and to maintain their separate space programs.

The United States, with its $23-billion Apollo project, is concentrating its efforts on landing men on the moon as soon as possible. Beyond that, plans involve mammoth earth-orbiting laboratories, practical applications of space for communications, development of nuclear rockets, unmanned flights to Mars, and continued interplanetary scientific probes.

The Russians give no such clear indications of their plans for the immediate future. If they are mounting a project comparable to Apollo, they are not saying so. True, it would be hard to conceal the necessary build-up of new launching pads, assembly plants, and tracking installations. But if the United States knows anything, it is not telling, either. "We can only say we have no public evidence of larger future programs," Sheldon has said.

The Russians have dropped a number of tantalizing hints, however. They usually concern possible preparations for flying spacecraft much larger than anything the United States contemplates at this time. The recurring implication is that the Soviet Union may be concentrating more on developing greater earth-orbiting capabilities than on going to the moon. Late in 1966, for example, cosmonauts on a good-will tour told audiences in Bulgaria, Cuba, and Hungary that the Soviet Union was planning a "new and improved spacecraft capable of carrying more than five men." The cosmonauts even suggested that perhaps one of the passengers would be a "brother" from one of the Soviet-bloc countries.

This was later denied by Lieutenant General Nikolai P. Kamanin, commander of the cosmonaut training center near Moscow. He said the Soviet Union had no such capability. If the cosmonauts had chosen to make an issue of it, they could have reminded Kamanin that on August 5, 1963, Tass, the official Soviet press agency, had quoted him as saying: "The time is not far off when big stations and spaceships will be assembled in outer space."

The Soyuz spacecraft that crashed may well have been part of Soviet preparations for a new generation of vehicles intended for such operations. If that is the case, these vehicles would be designed for rendezvous and docking. Rumors in Moscow at the time had it that a second spacecraft was in fact standing ready to be launched for just such a feat. These rumors may, however, have been inspired in part by the spacecraft's name—Soyuz means "union."

Orbiting laboratories could be put to both scientific and military uses. Telescopes mounted on them could be aimed at the stars for observations undistorted by earth's atmosphere. Sensors could be aimed at the earth for more accurate mapping, detailed surveys of mineral resources, and studies of geological formations. These stations could serve as orbiting weather-forecasting stations and as command posts to direct fishing fleets to large congregations of fish. In much the same way, they could help direct naval and air operations during warfare and serve as spies in the skies over enemy territory.

For such uses to be practical, the men and vehicles must be able to stay in orbit for weeks or months. The Russians, though they have yet to match Gemini 7's fourteen-day endurance test, have shown considerable interest in the effects of long-duration flight on man. In early 1967, it was reported that Boris Yegorov, the physician-cosmonaut, was conducting ground simulation experiments to determine the biomedical effects of "a particularly long flight." A year earlier, the Russians launched two dogs on a twenty-two-day orbital flight to test the effects of prolonged weightlessness and cosmic radiation on living organisms. At last year's astronautical conference in Madrid, Dr. Vasily V. Parin, Russia's leading space medicine expert, reported that the dogs showed no noticeable pathological changes in the heart and arteries. Their reactions in space, he said, were almost as quick as on the ground.

The apparently mounting interest in earth-orbital and long-duration missions has led some Western observers to conclude that the Russians may have dropped out of the moon race, if they had ever seriously entered it.

These observers base their argument on the Russians' slowness to demon-strate a capability to rendezvous in space and their apparent lack of a rocket comparable to the American Saturn 5 moon rocket.

Intelligence sources in Washington, however, have insisted for more than a year that the Soviet Union was developing a more powerful rocket. And a number of American space officials, always braced for Soviet surprises, say they would not be surprised if one of the next Soviet "spectaculars" was a manned flight around the moon. A circumlunar flight without a landing, they believe, could be accomplished as an outgrowth of present Soviet capabilities in rocketry and spacecraft. Meanwhile, whatever its manned-flight intentions, the Soviet Union has stepped up its launchings of earth-orbiting satellites under the Cosmos label, satellites for reconnaissance and weather forecasting, for scientific investigation and for the testing of new systems. And there has been no apparent slackening of efforts to explore the moon and the planets with unmanned spacecraft.

Aleksandr P. Vinogradov, a vice president of the Soviet Academy of Sciences and a leading geochemist, told a visitor to Moscow in 1967 of the results of Russian gamma ray studies to determine the composition of the moon's surface. He conceded that his observations were preliminary and that more definitive studies would be necessary. "We will not have to wait long," he said with a knowing look.

Man, whether Russian or American, has only begun to explore and exploit the new frontier that was opened to him a decade ago by the Soviet Union. For the Russians, in particular, the history of their space program still arouses tremendous pride and stands as the symbol of national accom-plishment. Visitors to Moscow see toyshop windows filled with displays of celluloid spacemen and parchesi-like games whose prizes are imaginary trips to Mars and Venus. Suspended across Gorky Street, Moscow's Fifth Avenue, is a large model of a rocket with a string of lights forming what appears to be its tail of shooting exhaust. Nearly every major space feat, whether unmanned or manned, is commemorated with large multicolored postage stamps. From time to time fences glow with flaming red-and-yellow posters showing a cosmonaut in a heroic pose, captioned: GLORY TO THE SOVIET PEOPLE!

"The success of the Soviet people in this field," Leonid I. Brezhnev, General Secretary of the Communist party, once said, "is a concentrated expression of our growth. In it the economic might of the Soviet power, the level to which our technology has risen, the creativity of the Soviet society are embodied."

The nation that was true to Lenin's vision thus shows every sign of making a strong bid to fulfill another, bolder prophecy. Konstantin Tsiolkovsky, the bearded father of Russian rocketry, once told of a dream of his in which new airlines were being inaugurated from Moscow to the moon and from his home town of Kaluga to the planet Mars. The obelisk over his grave at Kaluga bears his vision of man's destiny in the space age:

Man will not stay on earth forever, but in the pursuit of light and space will first emerge timidly from the bounds of the atmosphere and then advance until he has conquered the whole of circumsolar space.

MOSCOW'S MILITARY CAPABILITIES

»

Hanson W. Baldwin

Born in the ruck of defeat and out of the chaos of decay and revolution, the Soviet armed forces have developed in half a century into a military power second only to their American counterpart.

In the last months of 1917 the Imperial Russian Army of the czars died slowly and ingloriously, raddled by dissidence and mass desertions, exhausted by almost 7,000,000 casualties in the three years of war against the Central Powers. Twice in little more than a decade—in the Russo-Japanese War of 1904–05 and again in World War I—the Russian armed forces had fought bravely but ineptly, weakened by bumbling administration, inadequate supplies and training, and, with some brilliant exceptions, poor leadership. The Russian muzhik was sacrificed as "cannon fodder" to his foes, and for Russia the history of World War I led across a pile of corpses to dissolution and revolution—the end of the House of Romanov, the interim Kerensky regime, and the ultimate triumph of the Bolsheviks.

Little will to fight for the old regime was left in the old Russian army in the fall of 1917. In the Winter Palace fighting in Petrograd when the Bolsheviks came to power, the only element that remained loyal unto death to the Kerensky regime, the legal inheritor of czarist power, was a battalion of women. The last commander-in-chief of the old army, General N. N. Dukhonin, was murdered in December as terror stalked the land. Ranks and its badges were eliminated, the past suppressed, and in February, 1918, the remaining units of what was left of the once vaunted Russian "steam roller," the huge mass armies of the czars, were demobilized, and the military power of Russia, the nemesis of Charles XII of Sweden and of Napoleon, and for long the terror of Europe, faded away.

But in the five intervening decades, out of the ashes of yesterday, the renaissance of Russian military power has altered the geopolitical map of the globe. Today, fifty years later, the world is witnessing an amazing "across the board" development and expansion of Soviet power that is threatening in many elements—strategic missiles, maritime supremacy, military utilization of space, army weapons technology—the comfortable primacy enjoyed since World War II by the United States.

Russia, the nation that depended in World War I and World War II primarily upon mass—the "Big Battalions"—for its defense and fielded gigantic armies that could in many respects be described only as "armed hordes," has now become a modern military power, its forces animated by the old pre-Bolshevik love for "Mother Russia" but also drilled and disciplined in stern Communist ideology.

In 1917—and, indeed, until Nikita S. Khrushchev assumed unchallenged power in 1957—Soviet military concepts were dominated by the ideas of the ground generals; war meant the mass movements of great armies and the taking, or holding, of strategic terrain features—for Russia was and remains the largest national land mass on earth, and invasion had always come to Russia by land. Today the ground marshals have yielded some of their past supremacy to the march of modern technology; the "missile marshals," the airmen, and the admirals share their power. From a nation intent in the past upon guarding its land borders, a nation essentially keyed to the strategic defensive, the Soviet Union has become in fifty years a military power that sails the seven seas, sends Cosmos "spy" satellites at regular intervals across the United States, and has a capability of strong offensive action in most parts of the world.

Thus the past explains the present; the checkered history of the Soviet armed forces has been marked by ambivalence and influenced by conflicting factors:

• Intense patriotism and nationalist traditions, the heritage of ancient Mother Russia, and the revolutionary fervor of international Communism.

• The General and the Commissar: *i.e.,* the two-channel system of command and control in the Soviet armed forces—one military, the other political.

• Geography and Technology: *i.e.,* the influence of geography upon strategic concepts—the sweeping Russian "heartland" extending across two continents and the bordering landlocked or frozen seas—now modified by the technological capabilities of nuclear-powered submarines and aerospace missiles and weapons.

In a sense, the history of the Soviet armed forces has been a series of accommodations between these conflicting factors, with one or the other now and again dominant.

The development of the military power of the Union of Soviet Socialist Republics has passed through many distinct phases.

Initially, the Red Army—reflecting the egalitarian ideas and revolutionary experience of Lenin and Trotsky—was a voluntary militia with elected leaders. It was a political army, with its former czarist officers utilized, but in most cases not trusted, and strictly circumscribed by the vigilant guardians of political morality, the commissars. This army, an impromptu one, hastily organized, loosely disciplined, born out of bloodshed, was weaned in the civil wars. From 1918 to 1922 this makeshift army grew in numbers and skills as more and more of the Russian people, persuaded by the mistakes of Allied intervention and of the White counterrevolutionaries and by clever Bolshevik propaganda, rallied to the Reds. Out of this period of civil war, which consolidated Communist power in Russia, the Red Army got its revolutionary legends and its revolutionary heroes, such as Mikhail Frunze, who distinguished himself in the battles against Kolchak and Wrangel and for whom a Soviet military college is named today.

The period from the end of the civil wars until the great purges of 1937 was one of consolidation and reorganization and growth for the Red Army, following Lenin's death, the exile of Trotsky, and the rise of Stalin. From the beginning the Communist hierarchy was acutely aware of what it termed the dangers of Bonapartism—a counterrevolution staged by the military—and the slowly maturing army was carefully subordinated to the Communist party, supervised by political commissars, and infiltrated by the secret police and an informer system. But gradually the incompatibility of complete egalitarianism and military effectiveness became apparent. In 1929 a field order defined clearly the respective roles of the military commander and his political assistant, or commissar, and made it clear that the commander was to be solely responsible, at least in theory, for the operational control of the troops under his command.

In 1935 ranks were reintroduced, and the Red Army, as D. Fedotoff White put it in his *The Growth of the Red Army,* "became officially professionalized." During this period the ground forces were by far the dominant arm; the navy was largely neglected, although the beginnings of modern air power were developed. At the same time the industrialization of Russia, essential to support modern military power, made considerable strides, and the Communists, still fearful of former czarist officers, began to create a proletarian officer corps of men risen from the ranks or graduated from the new Communist military schools.

Little noticed by the West, the Red Army gradually became more and more powerful until its progress was suddenly terminated in the bloody, sweeping purges of 1937–38. The purges, which decimated the Communist party in Russia and eliminated many of the old-line Bolsheviks, have been variously viewed by historians as part of the unending struggle for power that has intermittently recurred in violent form in Communist dictatorships or as a manifestation of Stalin's psychopathic personality. In any case, thousands of Red Army officers, including many former czarist officers and heroes of the civil wars, were executed, imprisoned, or sent to concentration camps.

Among those liquidated or imprisoned were most of Russia's senior officers, including Marshal M. N. Tukhachevsky, Deputy Commissar for Defense. Forged papers, leaked to the Kremlin by the German Gestapo, were apparently utilized by Stalin as part of the justification for the execution of Marshal Tukhachevsky and other senior officers. The purge was sweeping. It extended, in Khrushchev's later words, down to the level of battalions and even companies. In less than a year, as John Erickson described it in *The Soviet High Command,* "the entire command of military districts had been changed." Among the victims of the purge were Marshal Vasily K. Bluecher, who commanded in the Far East, the two senior naval commanders, every officer who commanded an army corps and almost every commander of an army division. In addition, thousands of junior officers were jailed, dismissed, or persecuted. The resultant shake-up led to a crisis of fear that materially reduced the morale and the effectiveness of the armed forces.

With the political commissars once again in the ascendancy, the results of the purges were apparent in the Finnish "Winter War" of 1939–40, when, in the words of Michel Garder in his *History of the Soviet Army,* a "soulless herd [of Russian soldiers] led by timorous nonentities . . . were massacred by a handful of Finns." They were apparent, too, in the first phases of the German invasion of the Soviet Union in World War II, when the Red Army suffered huge casualties, due in considerable measure to poor leadership, and even greater defections by thousands of men whose loyalties to Moscow had been weakened by the excesses of the secret police, the "knock on the door" at night, and the regime of terror which Communism then meant to many Russians.

Nevertheless, as Garder notes, "Hitler's madness more than compensated for Stalin's madness," and again the pendulum swung. Officers with the welts of police whips still scarring their backs were released from prison camps, and the necessities of war dictated a stirring and successful appeal to Mother Russia's nationalist past rather than to Communist ideology, and insured, at least for a time, the dominance of the commander as opposed to the commissar. Men like Marshal Georgi K. Zhukov, who had always opposed too rigid a party control of the details of military operations, emerged from the war as the new heroes of Russia, and despite huge losses —an estimated 13,600,000 military casualties—the Soviet armed services of 1945 were stronger than ever, bloodied by many battles, and fear was replaced by exultation. "The heroic legend of the Great Patriotic War," Garder notes, "was henceforth part of the heritage of the Soviet Army—a fusion of the classical and revolutionary heritages."

It might be said that the modern Soviet army was born in the rubble and ruins of Stalingrad. Until that battle, Soviet military leadership had displayed, at best, limited distinction, and Soviet successes had been won by mass alone, but from defeat and retreat the Russians rebounded to new strengths, new vitality, and victory.

Indeed, the power of mass, of numbers, continued to be *the* decisive factor in the Soviet struggle against Germany during all of World War II, and it is today a major factor in assessing Soviet capabilities. But the impressive beginnings of modern technology were apparent then in the tanks, the rockets, and the artillery that were available for Moscow's armies in such great numbers.

The Red Army of World War II was, however, essentially an army of foot soldiers, with some elite and well-equipped mechanized and armored divisions, but over-all an "armed horde," composed of a few excellent professionals and many hastily trained armed peasants, moving overland like army ants and utilizing any and every type of transportation and supply vehicle available, chiefly horse-drawn.

The Soviet Union's naval power, even though Moscow controlled the world's largest submarine fleet, accomplished nothing of importance during the war; it was never able until the last to interrupt German traffic in the Baltic or Black seas or even to guard successfully its coasts. Its air power, keyed to the support of ground troops, was eventually successfully used for close air support and in a transport role, but there were grave weaknesses in air defense and a Soviet long-range, or strategic, bombing effort was nonexistent.

Since World War II the Soviet armed forces have completed their metamorphosis; they have become modern and professional in nearly every sense of both words. In this period, until Stalin's death in 1953, political control of the army increased at the expense of military command; then, with Marshal Zhukov's assumption of high responsibilities, the military gained in stature and influence at the expense of the commissar; with Zhukov's downfall in 1957 and the ascendancy of Khrushchev the political apparatus again was paramount.

Today, under the collective rule of Kosygin and Brezhnev, there seems to have been a mutual accommodation between party and army and army and party. The marshals wield great behind-the-scenes power, but there is no one man who can command the loyalties of the entire Soviet army; there is no single marshal on active service with Zhukov's reputation or popularity, and there appears to be no danger of Bonapartism. More important to army morale has been the decline in power of the secret police—not only in the Soviet Union as a whole, but also in the services in particular. At the same time the postwar years have witnessed a blending, skillfully aided by the Soviet interpretation of history, of the national and ideological content of the army's traditions.

But most important from the point of view of power have been the rapid technological developments of the postwar years and the changes in strategic concept these developments have brought about. Khrushchev recognized that the age of nuclear weapons, supersonic planes, and missiles must cause a major change in the Soviet Union's military policies. His efforts to reduce the size of the ground army and to build up the air and missile forces, though partly blocked by events and massive opposition from the ground marshals, nevertheless led to a new chapter in Soviet technology. A great variety of nuclear weapons, including the most destructive bombs and warheads on earth, was manufactured, and a powerful and modern air force, capable of projecting the Soviet Union's might far beyond its frontiers, was created. Khrushchev was somewhat contemptuous of the navy; nevertheless he spurred its submarine-construction program.

Beginning with the Cuban missile crisis in 1962 and following Khrushchev's ouster in 1964, another major acceleration of Soviet military development occurred. Perhaps in part because of its humiliating backdown during the Cuban crisis, the Soviet Union has redoubled its efforts to match the

United States in strategic missiles and nuclear-delivery systems; in the last two to three years it has made, relative to the United States, great quantitative, and some qualitative, gains.

Thus, as a half-century of Communist control of the Soviet Union ends, its military power is approaching an apogee, absolutely and relatively. Its weaknesses of World War II have been partly remedied: it now has a global and offensive rather than a parochial and defensive capability; its mass army has been equipped with perhaps the best assault rifle and some of the best modern equipment on earth and it rides in tanks, on wheels, and in planes instead of slogging by foot; it has created the most extensive and probably the most formidable air defense system on earth against both planes and missiles; it is attempting to achieve parity with the United States in nuclear-delivery capabilities; it has the world's largest submarine fleet, including more than forty nuclear-powered submarines and thirty to forty capable of firing ballistic missiles, and its warships cruise all the waters of the earth.

Soviet military power in 1967—and the important technological-industrial base upon which it depends—is clearly second to that of the United States. But the size of the Soviet military budget, the emphasis upon military research and development, and the very considerable strides of the last few years indicate that Moscow is intent upon nothing less than military parity.

The Soviet supreme command operates on a committee system, with the military always a part of, and strictly subordinate to, the political. Normally, in peacetime, there is no one "commander-in-chief"; Premier Khrushchev was the only Soviet politician to claim the title during peacetime, although Stalin used the term and exercised the prerogatives during World War II.

During that war—which the Russians call the "Great Patriotic War"—a committee of high-ranking officers and Communist party leaders, called the "Stavka," acted as the Soviet Supreme Command or General Headquarters, directly subordinate to Stalin and the State Defense Committee. The latter formulated basic war policies; the Stavka developed strategic and military plans and implemented the policies of the State Defense Committee. Presumably, the same type of organization would control the Soviet armed forces in another war.

In peacetime the ruling Politburo of the Communist party's Central Committee exercises control over the Ministry of Defense and the armed forces. The Minister of Defense is nearly always—though both Trotsky and Stalin assumed the office for a time—an active duty officer. Marshal Andrei A. Grechko was appointed to this post to replace Marshal Rodion Y. Malinovsky, who died on March 31, 1967. He represents little change and can be regarded as a kind of bridge between the "Old Marshals" and the newer, younger officers with a global outlook.

The Soviet armed forces are organized in five service components and various operational commands. Policy and control are exercised at the top level of the ministry through the General Staff of the army and navy, with subsections for operations, intelligence, mobilization, and so on; a main political administration; an inspectorate, and a main directorate of the rear services, for supply, logistics, and administration.

The five service components to which members of the armed forces are assigned are the ground forces, the air force, the air defense forces, the navy (including naval aviation), and the strategic rocket forces (established in 1961). The commands of these five services are primarily administrative rather than operational and are concerned chiefly with training, organization, and doctrine.

The fighting forces themselves are divided and subdivided into various echelons of command. In peacetime the U.S.S.R. is organized in eighteen military districts, each comparable in some ways to an army area in the United States; in World War II the Soviet army organized its divisions and armies into "fronts," the equivalent of a Western army group. There are distinct air defense districts, as in the United States, and the Soviet navy maintains four principal fleets: the Northern fleet, based on the Archangel-Murmansk area, the Baltic fleet, the Black Sea fleet, and the Pacific fleet.

One of the weaknesses of the Red Army in World War II was its inability to maintain sustained offensives for long periods of time. In the wide-ranging offensive operations against the Germans which finally led to Berlin, it was capable, after long preparation, of heavy—indeed, crushing—assault with masses of tanks, concentrated artillery, mortar and rocket fire, and air support. But its somewhat primitive supply and communications system and the Soviet Union's inadequate road network made dependence upon a limited rail network for any strategic or long-distance supply almost essential. The Russians never really solved during World War II the problem of sustaining and maintaining their mass armies in a prolonged and continuous offensive; there were frequent enforced pauses for consolidation and resupply.

Today, with a much more developed industrial base, a better road network, more air transport, and far better and more plentiful cross-country vehicular capability, the Soviet army has unquestionably materially improved its supply system and hence its capability for sustained combat. But the Soviet Union is lagging in, among other fields, computer technology, and whether the Soviet army is really capable today of supplying, storing, issuing, and keeping track of the vast inventory of spare parts and supplies needed in modern war is uncertain. Its administrative processes, shaky and primitive during World War II, have also improved greatly, but whether they are adequate to the strain of combat is moot.

Nevertheless, the trend is clear; the armed horde of yesterday has gone. During World War II there was frequently no notification to next of kin of casualties below the rank of colonel, and thousands, perhaps hundreds of thousands, of Soviet soldiers were buried, unidentified, in unmarked graves. Today there is an extensive and well-organized casualty-reporting system, and each regiment has a graves-registration system, with burial records maintained at the divisional level.

The Soviet armed forces are commanded by professional, career officers and noncoms, and owing to their long conscription term even the lowest ranks can be well trained and militarily competent. The term of service varies from three years in the army to four in the navy. Something like 2,000,000 youths register annually at the age of eighteen, and about half of this number are inducted into the armed services each year between mid-September and mid-October. Noncommissioned officers are selected from the enlisted ranks and are sent to noncom schools. Incentives for them are not high, and the intelligence and educational level among them is still one of the Soviet army's weak points.

Officers usually are carefully selected and attend officer candidate schools for two to three years. Some, as youngsters of ten to thirteen, first attend a five- to seven-year course at one of the fifteen Suvorov cadet schools. Political reliability is stressed, and a careful background investigation of each officer candidate is made. The potential officer must have fine physical fitness and be between eighteen and twenty-three years of age. An elaborate system of more advanced officer schools, including the Frunze Military Academy, a command and staff school for infantry officers of battalion to divisional level, and the General Staff Academy, for potential general officers, provide thorough professional knowledge. This system of military recruitment, selection, and education has given the Soviet army a well-educated, thoroughly professional officer corps, which is the heart of any military force.

The officer corps occupies a privileged place in Soviet society along with the scientists, artists, ballet dancers, Communist party functionaries, and bureaucrats. The pay scale for career personnel in the armed forces, though proportionately higher in relation to average wages in the U.S.S.R. than in the United States, does not fully reflect the prestige of the Soviet officer. The base pay of a marshal, the highest rank, is only 3,600 rubles a year (the official exchange rate for the ruble is $1.11); for a captain it is 840 rubles. There are additions to this: what the Russians call "assignment pay," an extra 1,080 rubles for a captain who is assigned as a company commander; longevity pay, a percentage of base pay ranging from five for two to five years of service up to forty for more than thirty years of service; a servant allowance; subsistence and quarters allowance, and so-called hardship pay. Career enlisted men also receive many benefits in addition to base pay, which can be as low as thirty-six rubles a year for a private.

But despite the pay, the ruble's purchasing power is low, and there is often not a wide choice of goods to purchase. An automobile is beyond the reach of most Soviet military men, and a recruit making three rubles a month for his first two years of service (the pay increases to five rubles in his third year of conscription) has only enough to buy a couple of packs of cigarettes and a liter of poor-quality vodka.

Nevertheless, the Soviet military man occupies a position of distinction in his homeland, partly because the average Russian identifies the army— in contrast to the Communist party—as "his" army, a part of the Mother Russia tradition.

The Soviet Union's large population, its extensive utilization of women in its work force and for auxiliary and noncombatant services, and its classification of all males between eighteen and fifty as potentially eligible for military duty provide the country with a tremendous manpower pool. This age group contained, it was estimated some years ago, about 35,000,000 males considered eligible by Soviet physical standards.

During World War II the U.S.S.R. put into uniform something like 10 per cent of its population—some 22,000,000 people. Today it has the capability of fielding vast numbers of men; current assessments are that Moscow could send at least one hundred and forty complete divisions into battle within ninety days. The limiting factor in the Soviet order of battle is equipment, material, and support and supply potential—not men.

Only a fraction of the available Soviet military manpower is actually on active duty today. The over-all size of the armed forces is about 3,100,000 to 3,300,000 men. The Soviet ground forces, now numbering about 1,600,000 to 1,800,000 men, were until 1960 a considerably larger force. Khrushchev reduced them then, but, because of internal opposition and external events, by no means to the extent he had planned. The army air forces may number about 500,000, the navy (including naval aviation) about the same, the air defense forces 300,000; the strategic rocket forces about 150,000 to 225,000. In addition to the armed forces, there are 250,000 uniformed border guards under the Committee for State Security. This formidable force is supported by 500,000 to 1,000,000 civilian employees who work for the military establishment. The military budget has been officially estimated by Moscow at about 14.5 billion rubles for the

Hanson W. Baldwin

1967 calendar year, an announced increase of 8.2 per cent as compared with last year's figures. United States experts believe the figure bears little resemblance to the total defense costs, many of which are hidden, and that total defense spending in the Soviet Union in 1967 may approximate 20 billion rubles. At the official exchange rate, this would work out to about $22 billion, but expressed in terms of U.S. military costs and dollar purchasing power, the Soviet military budget would approximate $50 to $60 billion, or 14 to 17 per cent of the estimated Soviet gross national product for the 1967 calendar year. Research and development are emphasized in this budget. Some observers think Soviet expenditures for military research surpass those of the United States. Strategic weapons systems, new tanks, and air defenses of many different types are emphasized.

In the past decade the Soviet Union's most spectacular and most important military developments have been in so-called strategic weapons—nuclear arms, giant rockets, and aerospace vehicles.

The U.S.S.R. surprised the world with the speed with which it developed its first nuclear weapon. Since its first test detonation in 1949, it has conducted at least two hundred and fifty nuclear tests in the atmosphere, in space, under water, and underground. The United States, since it became an atomic power, has conducted an estimated total of four hundred and twenty-five nuclear tests. (Not all of them are announced.)

This comparative numerical yardstick would seem to indicate a comfortable lead in nuclear "know-how" for the United States. But the experts are by no means certain this is true. As James H. McBride pointed out in his book *The Test Ban Treaty,* the surprise series of Soviet nuclear tests in 1961–62, which broke an unofficial test moratorium, resulted in a "quantum jump in nuclear technology" for the Soviet Union, while "the United States lagged far behind." The Russians tested in this series the most powerful device ever exploded on earth, which released the equivalent of fifty-eight megatons, or 58,000,000 tons of TNT. They not only made major advances in the technology of very high-yield weapons of twenty megatons and above, but they also destroyed two incoming missiles with a single explosion, and learned a tremendous amount about the strange effects of nuclear bursts in thin air or above the atmosphere, knowledge important to any antimissile defense system.

Some experts feel, therefore, that the U.S.S.R. assumed a lead in nuclear-weapons technology in 1961–62. It seems unlikely, however, that Moscow was able to overcome the sizable U.S. technological advantage "across the board." There is not much doubt, though, that the Russians, who have conducted four times as many tests with very high-yield weapons as the United States has done, lead the world in huge bombs and rocket warheads of immense power. In intermediate-yield weapons of one to twenty megatons, the United States may be equal or superior qualitatively to the Soviet Union; in small submegaton weapons, chiefly for battlefield or tactical use, the United States would seem to have a clear lead.

The total numbers of nuclear weapons available have little meaning apart from their "carriers"—the missiles, planes, and other devices that "carry" the bombs or warheads to their targets. But the total deliverable megatonnage of the entire nuclear arsenal, or the total weight of nuclear explosive that can be delivered to a target if all available carriers are used, is a militarily significant power factor. The Soviet nuclear arsenal, measured in these terms, is a formidable one—estimated by one source at 12,000 megatons, far more than enough to devastate the United States many times over. The total weight of this deliverable arsenal of nuclear explosives has shown a steady increase, relative to the United States, in the last six years, in part because the Russians, with more powerful rockets than our own, use far larger warheads, in part because they have built bombs of far greater power, in part because the United States has deliberately phased out many of its bombers and the huge bombs they carried.

The Russians have paralleled their nuclear-development program with major advances in rocketry. Their early huge, cumbersome, multistage liquid-fueled rockets, which were expensive and unreliable, have been superseded by smaller, lighter, simpler, more reliable missiles, using so-called storable liquid propellants (chemicals that can be kept in the missile for long periods without deterioration, thus increasing readiness), some solid propellants, and improved guidance mechanisms.

Soviet technology has always enjoyed a solid grounding in rocketry; tactical short-range rockets were employed freely in area bombardment missions during World War II. After the war the U.S.S.R. took over large stocks of the German V-2 rockets that were used to bombard London and employed German rocket scientists and engineers to supplement Soviet technology. The Russians built on this basic foundation so rapidly that by 1957, when they launched the world's first satellite, they had developed the most powerful liquid-fueled rocket engine in the world. Since then their progress, quantitatively and qualitatively, has been so fast that in many categories of short-range, medium-range, intercontinental, and sea-launched missiles they challenge the United States. Since the Cuban missile crisis in 1962, when Premier Khrushchev was forced to back down in an attempt to emplace Soviet missiles in Cuba and thus alter the strategic balance of power, the Russians have been producing long-range missiles at a steadily increasing rate and are now threatening to overtake the numerical advantage of the United States. Many Washington experts believe that the current Soviet missile development and production program is keyed to the attainment by 1970 of numerical parity with the United States, to superiority in defensive missiles, to approximate equality in technology, and to a massive advantage in the weight of nuclear explosives that could be delivered against an enemy target. Soviet strategic weapons—missiles and planes—are operated by the strategic rocket forces, the navy, the air defense forces, and the air forces of the Soviet army.

The strategic rocket forces, with a minimum estimated personnel strength of 150,000, a maximum of 225,000, but still growing rapidly, operate the land-based ICBM's (intercontinental ballistic missiles, with ranges of 6,000 miles or more, capable of reaching the United States from any point in the Soviet Union), the IRBM's (intermediate-range ballistic missiles, with ranges of 1,500 to 2,000 miles), and the MRBM's (medium-range ballistic missiles, with ranges of 700 to 900 miles). The latter two categories do not have sufficient range to reach the United States (except for Alaska) from Soviet soil, but can command virtually all targets in Western Europe, North Africa, and many parts of Asia.

Estimates of the number of Soviet land-based missiles vary widely. The ICBM's are variously put at a minimum of 275 to 325 silos or launchers (some in "hardened" concrete-and-steel emplacements sunk into the ground, some in semihardened sites) and a maximum of more than 500 launchers and 800 missiles, including reloads. These are of two types: large, powerful rockets carrying multimegaton warheads and smaller, lighter missiles with warheads similar to those of the United States Minuteman and Polaris, in the one- to two-megaton range. For the last two to three years the Russians have been adding 150 to 200 ICBM's annually to their inventory.

The land-based IRBM's and MRBM's—a category in which the United States has no comparable missile—number about 700 to 900, some of them transportable within twenty-four hours to alternate prepared firing sites.

The Soviet navy's fleet of about 300 to 350 seagoing submarines operates the sea-based strategic missiles. These are of two general types: a ballistic missile, or giant rocket that follows a parabolic trajectory, and a winged missile, or small pilotless plane, that flies in the atmosphere on a straight and level course. About thirty to forty Soviet submarines, some of them nuclear powered, some converted into missile ships from conventionally powered types, carry some kind of ballistic missiles. Most of these are equipped to launch two or three missiles from tubes built into the submarine's "sail," or midships superstructure. The older missiles have ranges of more than 300 miles; a newer category has a range of 700 to 800 miles. The older missiles, it is believed, must be launched from the surface. However, a new type of submarine, believed to have eight missile-launching tubes (half the number carried by the U.S. Polaris-missile subs) and a capability of launching 700- to 800-mile missiles from beneath the surface, is said to be in production.

The air-breathing surface-launched winged missiles, which are part of the armament of the Soviet nuclear-powered "E" class and of other submarines, are believed to be designed primarily for use against ships, specifically U.S. carrier task forces. These missiles, capable of carrying nuclear weapons, clearly have a secondary strategic bombardment capability. They have a high subsonic speed, ranges of 450 miles, and probably have both inertial and terminal guidance capabilities, but for accuracy at optimum ranges they would require some sort of mid-course checkpoint or guidance system, perhaps furnished by another electronically equipped submarine.

In addition to their thirty to forty ballistic-missile submarines of all types (including newly built ships and conversions), capable of launching a total of perhaps 100 to 150 missiles, the Russians have about forty-five to fifty submarines equipped with a total of 100 to 200 winged missiles.

Despite the tremendous emphasis that has been placed on the strategic rocket forces and on missile technology in the last few years, the Russians have not abandoned the piloted plane as a bomb-delivery vehicle. The long-range aviation of the Soviet army aviation forces corresponds to the United States Strategic Air Command. The Soviet command has about 150 to 200 long-range bombers and a number of medium bombers variously estimated at 700 to 1,200.

Some intelligence officers estimate that only a small number of these—100 plus—have the capability of unrefueled two-way flight to the United States from Soviet bases. But unlike the United States, the Russians show no indication of retiring their medium bombers; in fact, even their new twin-engined bomber, a Tupolev model code-named the Blinder B by the North Atlantic alliance, with a 1.5 Mach speed and a 1,600-mile unrefueled radius, is fitted with in-flight refueling equipment. Aerial refueling was virtually an unknown art in the Soviet air force a decade ago; today its technique has been mastered, and it seems probable that virtually all of the aircraft assigned to the Soviet long-range air command have in-flight refueling.

This strategic bomber force has some old and some newer equipment; as has the United States, the Russians have upgraded bomber capabilities with reworking and new weapons.

No new long-range bombers were displayed at Soviet Aviation Day in 1967, but Marshal Sergei I. Rudenko, Deputy Chief of the Soviet Army Air Force, stressed the continuing role of bombers in the missile age and warned that the Russians possessed thermonuclear bombs with an explosive force equivalent to one hundred megatons, or 100,000,000 tons of TNT.

Most of the Russian bombers are believed to be fitted with various aids to enable them to penetrate enemy air defenses, including electronic countermeasures gear, and some first-generation stand-off missiles, missiles intended to have sufficient range to reach a target when air-launched beyond reach of the enemy's air defenses. Long-range bombing has never been a Soviet specialty, and the United States has a decided edge in over-all capability in this field, but the Russians have made great strides in the past decade.

The Soviet air defense system—for some years past the most extensive and probably the most formidable national system ever built against air-breathing missiles and piloted planes—is now being supplemented by the world's first anti-ballistic-missile defense system.

United States intelligence services differ as to the extent, effectiveness, and even nature of this system, but during 1967 evidence accumulated that the Russians were engaged in an impressive deployment of such a system. It is generally agreed that newly installed missile and radar sites around Moscow, and apparently to a lesser extent around Leningrad, represent a defense against ballistic missiles rather than against planes. Other extensive and far-flung installations that sprawl across the "missile window," or route of missile approach from the United States to the Soviet Union, and, indeed, around most of western Russia, are interpreted by the Central Intelligence Agency as part of a conventional defense system against aircraft or atmospheric missiles, but by the armed services as a new Tallinn system (named for the Estonian capital) for defense against ballistic missiles. The military believe that whether or not a nationwide antimissile system has actually been started is immaterial; the state of the art in the Soviet Union, they contend, makes it certain that such a system soon will be deployed if it is not actually being deployed now.

United States technical experts believe that the Soviet antimissile system is, like the experimental Nike-X, a two-missile system: one long-range missile for area defense outside the atmosphere, and one high-speed short-range missile for point defense in the atmosphere close in to the target. The Soviet missile that bears the NATO code name "Galosh" is believed to be the long-range carrier; the "kill" effect of its large nuclear warhead against incoming missiles still outside the atmosphere is magnified by the vacuum of space. High-intensity X rays, the result of the tremendous burst of energy that occurs in a nuclear detonation, can flash across hundreds of miles of space without being absorbed by atmosphere and can neutralize or destroy the warheads of incoming missiles far away from the point of detonation.

The Soviet antimissile radars are believed to be somewhat less effective than those of the United States. They are mechanically operated rather than electronically phased and hence are not so rapid; the Soviet computers are also slower, and the Soviet "recycling" operation—shifting the radar from one target to another and putting a new missile on the launcher—is slower. Nevertheless, the Soviet antimissile system now being deployed adds more defensive strength to a conventional air defense system, composed of SAM's (surface-to-air missiles), a vast array of radar-controlled antiaircraft guns of many calibers, fast, high-flying fighter interceptors, and perimeter and point radar and ground-control intercept stations, which is probably unparalleled in scope anywhere else in the world.

The formidable nature of North Vietnam's defensive system, designed and furnished by the Soviet Union, is a sufficient index of the U.S.S.R.'s own air defense network. It is, of course (as the North Vietnam system has shown), by no means impregnable; the Soviet Union's territory is so vast that it is impossible to defend everything everywhere. But it can take a heavy toll of an attacker—even in the age when the offensive clearly has a technological advantage over the defensive.

The SAM's deployed in the Soviet Union are of the type familiar from use in North Vietnam—the so-called SAM-II's, a later model than the original SAM-I, now being phased out. The SAM-II's, as a result of the North Vietnamese experience, are apparently being modified to make them less vulnerable to enemy electronic jamming and more useful against aircraft at low altitudes. They are supplemented, in the Soviet defensive system, with SAM-III's, specially designed for use (like our Hawk missile) against low-flying aircraft.

Gaps between missile sites are filled—and important targets are further protected—by radar-controlled antiaircraft guns, up to 130 millimeters in caliber. Large numbers of fighter-interceptor aircraft supplement the ground defenses.

Soviet fighters, like the famous MIG-21, and the later Sukhoi "Fishpot," Yak-28, and Yak-29P, all-weather interceptors designed specifically for air defense, have a relatively short radius of action as compared with U.S. fighters, but are high-speed maneuverable aircraft with a very high rate of climb. They are equipped with both heat-seeking and electronically guided missiles and cannon and are designed for—and are effective as—"bomber killers."

All of this air defense system is tied together and controlled by an elaborate system of manned radar and unmanned gap-filler stations, plus numerous ground-control intercept stations, which vector the defensive fighter planes to their intercepts.

The entire complex of antimissile missiles and antiaircraft missiles, guns, planes, radar, and communications is controlled by the air defense forces, with a total personnel in uniform of about 300,000 men.

Despite their spectacular early achievements in space, the Russians appear to have lagged in the development of military applications. Nevertheless, since 1964 they have emulated the United States in launching weather satellites, geodetic and mapping satellites (important in determining exact geographic co-ordinates and for collating firing data for ballistic missiles), and possibly some navigational satellites. The extensive Cosmos series of satellites, which have crisscrossed the United States and other parts of the world, appears to have provided Moscow with reconnaissance photographs and possibly electronic intelligence.

The renaissance of the Russian navy and of Soviet maritime power in the past decade has been one of the more startling strategic factors of the twentieth century. In the last five years especially, the Russians have demonstrated a new-found naval capability and an understanding of the use of sea power for political, economic, psychological, and diplomatic—as well as military—objectives that were completely lacking in the early years of the Soviet regime.

Unlike the army, the navy emerged from World War II with few achievements; the victory over Germany had been won on land, and the naval forces were purely adjuncts, the extension of the flank of the Red Army to the sea. Even as late as 1956, when General Nathan F. Twining, then Air Force Chief of Staff, visited Moscow for Soviet Aviation Day, Premier Khrushchev pointed to a rowboat manned by Soviet sailors on a Moscow lake and remarked contemptuously: "There's our navy." Cruisers, he said, were "showboats," good for nothing except protocol visits. The navy and Soviet maritime power have made great strides since those days.

The Soviet merchant fleet has increased in tonnage from 3,600,000 dead-weight tons in 1959 to 9,000,000 in 1965. Experts believe that the Soviet Union, which had more ships on order in the world's shipyards as of May 1, 1966 than any other power, is determined to engage competitively in the world's carrying trade, to expand aggressively its own exports, and to exercise major influence on maritime chartering rates. If a merchant marine is a major index of sea power and if the flag follows trade as geopoliticians have often said in the past, then the growing Soviet merchant marine is a portent of tomorrow, a vigorous bid for parity or superiority in total maritime power.

The Soviet fishing fleet, like the Soviet merchant marine, has been expanded and modernized in recent years. This fleet, including trawlers, factory and processing ships, and storage ships, is now regarded as the most modern in the world. Its catch, the fourth largest in 1964, helps to feed the Soviet people and is an export item of importance that earns dollars and other hard currency. The fishing policy is aggressive, scientific, and global.

To provide knowledge of the sea, upon which to base its expanded sea power, the Soviet Union has a large fleet of well-equipped research and oceanographic ships, which gather data of all sorts from the arctic icecap to the Antarctic.

But the most important element of Soviet seagoing power is the navy, now second in size to that of the United States, and particularly the Soviet submarine fleet.

This undersea fleet is still the largest in the world, as it was before World War II, but then, unlike today, it was animated by a defensive spirit and lacked modern technology. Today Soviet submarines cruise in all the seas of the world, and the small, obsolete coastal "coffin boats" that once largely made up this fleet have been replaced by big, modern, long-range ships.

The Soviet submarine fleet numbers 350 to 400 operational vessels, plus a few obsolete types used for training. This represents a considerable reduction in numbers, but an increase in effectiveness, as compared with the 450-to-500-ship fleet of fifteen years ago. Gone are the old, small, limited-purpose submarines with a short cruising radius; gone, too, are some of the older vessels of the "W" class, one of the first of the truly long-range Soviet types. Many of the "W" class have been sold or transferred to foreign navies, including those of the United Arab Republic, China, and Indonesia. In their place is a whole new fleet of modern submarines, most of them—300 to 350—capable of deep-sea, medium-range or long-range cruising, the rest still useful for patrol work in the Baltic and Black seas and relatively close to the Soviet coasts.

Of the total number of Soviet submarines now in commission, probably forty are nuclear powered. The nuclear engine enables a submarine to cruise submerged at high speeds indefinitely and it has no refueling problem on even the longest of voyages. In fact, nuclear power has created the world's first true submersible.

The nuclear submarines include so-called attack types, equipped with torpedoes and other antishipping and antisubmarine weapons and instruments; a group of submarines that carry the winged cruise-type missiles, and others, with ballistic missiles. The Russians are building about ten nuclear submarines annually, and a new nuclear-powered class is expected to make its appearance on the high seas shortly. The total submarine building program may approximate twelve to fifteen craft each year, divided about equally into attack types, cruise-type missile submarines, and ballistic-missile submarines. Newest of the fleet is the "H" class, a nuclear-powered ballistic-missile submarine with at least eight launching tubes for submerged firing and missiles of more than 700-mile range. Expected shortly is a sea-launched missile with a minimum range of 1,000 miles.

Thus the Russians are moving a considerable amount of their nuclear-deterrent capability to sea, where, so far, it cannot be easily found, cannot be pretargeted, and hence is not subject to surprise attack and destruction. At the same time they are maintaining a heavy investment in cruise-type antishipping missiles with a secondary capacity for land bombardment and in attack submarines useful against other submarines or merchant ships.

Appraisals of the effectiveness of this submarine force vary greatly. General United States opinion is that it is about fifteen years behind that of the United States.

The Soviet navy, strong beneath the sea, has some sharp limitations in surface effectiveness. It has no aircraft carriers and hence no ship-based air power, a fact that limits its optimum effectiveness to areas not too far from Soviet land airfields, where air cover can be provided for surface ships. It is decidedly weak in logistical support, and it has a limited and short-range amphibious capability. This latter limitation is, however, eased, though not eliminated, by the large numbers of Soviet merchantmen and fishing vessels which could be used to transport large numbers of men and weapons over long sea distances.

The Soviet Union's naval architects and weapons experts have shown both imagination and soundness, and the country is beginning to compensate for its past naval weaknesses. About 850 naval aircraft for maritime and antisubmarine patrol, long-range reconnaissance, and attack are based at fields near Soviet naval bases. They represent, within close range of those bases, formidable additions to Soviet maritime power. The TU-20 "Bear" turboprop has a protracted endurance capability (7,800-mile range without refueling) useful for convoy protection, scouting, and reconnaissance, and the twin-engined TU-16 "Badger" B is equipped to strike either with air-launched torpedoes or with heat-seeking antishipping missiles of twenty-five-to-seventy-five-mile range.

Curiously, the first Soviet naval attempt to base aircraft aboard ship has taken the form of the helicopter carrier. Two new ships of this type—somewhat similar to the U.S. LPD (a type that carries both helicopters and amphibious landing craft)—have been "shaking down" in the Baltic.

The Soviet navy maintains about twenty cruisers in commission, most of them of the 19,000-ton (full load) Sverdlov class, originally armed with twelve six-inch guns, twelve 100-millimeter antiaircraft guns, and other weapons. One or more have been modernized by replacing some of the guns with antiaircraft guided missiles, and some may have been fitted with surface-to-surface missiles.

There are about 100 to 130 destroyers of various classes now in operation, twenty to thirty of them equipped with surface-to-air or surface-to-surface missiles, a few of them with both. Other destroyers have been modernized with antisubmarine-warfare armament and instruments.

The Soviet Union has the largest fleet of coastal patrol craft, minecraft, motor gunboats, and miscellaneous small types in the world, totaling more than 2,000 vessels. Soviet mining capabilities are regarded with respect by the experts of other powers. This form of sea warfare has always enlisted the Russians' naval interest, and the advanced techniques of the Germans have been added to Soviet technology since World War II.

Patrol craft of the Komar and Osa classes, seventy-five and one hundred and sixty tons respectively, have thirty-to-forty-five-knot speeds and are armed with fifteen-to-twenty-mile-range antishipping winged missiles of considerable accuracy.

Soviet antisubmarine operations have been described by intelligence authorities as "weak but improving." As far as is known, the Russians have never detected a United States Polaris submarine on submerged station in the Norwegian Sea, the Mediterranean, or the Pacific. However, stress has been laid in recent years on modernization of antisubmarine equipment and procedures, and the Soviet navy, in contrast to the World War II period, now utilizes sonar buoys, magnetic airborne detection gear, and other sensors and instruments for submarine detection.

The picture that emerges is a mixed one. The Russians do not maintain what Western nations would consider a "balanced fleet"; there are weaknesses in supply and support or logistics ships, in ship-based naval air power, in long-range amphibious capability, in antisubmarine warfare. But the weaknesses are being remedied; the largest submarine fleet in the world is becoming thoroughly modern, and the U.S.S.R. is looking outward upon the oceans of the world. Indeed, the most striking change in Soviet strategic thought in the last two decades is emphasized by Moscow's maritime development program. The old concepts of heartland sufficiency and self-containment, the utilization of a navy merely to extend the Red Army's land flank to sea, the defensive strategy built around light coastal forces for use in the landlocked seas have gone.

Soviet task forces consisting of six to fourteen ships are now maintained in the Mediterranean; Soviet electronic "snoopers" (trawlers or mine sweepers equipped with special radio and radar antennae, recording devices and instruments) follow United States warships and lurk off United States bases throughout the world; Soviet submarines cruise in the Arctic and the Gulf of Alaska and off both United States coasts, and Soviet sea power— conceived in the terms made famous by Mahan—has become an important factor for future history.

The Red Army is still the soul, if not the heart, of modern Soviet military power. Though the grip of the old ground marshals on Soviet strategy and military posture has weakened somewhat, and the influence of the new missile marshals and of the navy has increased, the army still has a large voice in the size and structure of the military budget. In fact, military influence upon the formulation of Soviet policy is probably greater now than at any time since World War II—a tacit acknowledgment of the unsettled struggle for power in the "palace hierarchy" of the Communist party in Moscow, of the Vietnam war, of the Chinese-Soviet split and the development of China as a nuclear power, and of the Soviet Union's discomfiture because of its forced backdown in the Cuban missile crisis and the catastrophe that befell its Arab protégés in the swift Israeli-Arab war in 1967.

The party is dominant, and part of the strength of the influence of the military can be attributed to the fact that the new breed of Soviet marshals —men like fifty-four-year-old Marshal Ivan I. Yakubovsky, now Warsaw Pact commander—epitomizes the professional soldier rather than the soldier-politician. They are men brought up from babyhood to the concept of Communist party dominance; they are conditioned against Bonapartism. For this reason, and because the Soviet ground forces, inheritor of most Soviet military tradition, are far larger than the other forces, the ground marshals, despite the advent of the technicians, still hold a high place in military and political councils and attention must be paid to their views.

Including its tactical air forces, that portion of Soviet air strength organized and trained to provide air support for the ground units, the army numbers about 2,000,000 men today.

It has available for close air support, defense of its forward airfields, and troop transport and supply about 3,200 aircraft, including MIG-17's, 19's and 21's and Su-7's and Yak-25 "Brewer" ground-attack light bombers. This is a formidable tactical air force, and it has been trained to deliver either conventional or nuclear weapons.

The present order of battle of the Soviet army numbers about one hundred and forty divisions, varying in size from a full wartime strength of about 7,300 men for an air-borne division to 8,000 to 8,700 for a tank division and 10,500 to 11,000 for a motorized rifle division.

Of these divisions about forty to fifty are tank divisions, each with about 300 to 400 tanks and consisting of three medium tank regiments and a motorized rifle regiment. Unlike U.S. armored divisions, these divisions are too small and their infantry and artillery elements and maintenance and support elements are too weak to permit independent operations. They are envisaged as part of a mechanized army or tank corps. The remainder of the divisions, except for seven air-borne divisions (60,000 men), are motorized rifle divisions. Each consists of three motorized rifle regiments and a medium tank regiment transported by wheeled and tracked vehicles and with heavy organic support from self-propelled artillery, antitank guns, antiaircraft, and rockets. There are enough transport and cargo planes organized in a separate air transport command to airlift about two of the seven air-borne divisions (with equipment) over medium and short distances simultaneously.

Many of these one hundred and forty divisions are not maintained at full strength in peacetime; best estimates are that about one hundred of them are at 65-per-cent strength or more, others vary from cadres of about 10 per cent up to 30 per cent. The twenty Soviet divisions in East Germany, totaling, with air support, about 300,000 men, two in Poland and four in Hungary are all maintained at full strength, as are some in the Far East, a few in Central Asia, and a considerable number in western Russia. About one hundred of the one hundred and forty divisions are believed to be west of the Ural Mountains.

Soviet mobilization procedures—in no sense comparable in speed to the lightning timetables of little countries like Switzerland and Israel, which maintain minuscule regular forces—are massive and fairly rapid. Of the one hundred and forty Soviet divisions about sixty, comprising five "fronts," or groups of armies, are maintained in active status, and twenty in reserve, in western Russia and the Eastern European countries. Experts believe all of these eighty divisions could be ready for deployment, but not actually deployed, in four to six weeks. The Russians could probably "flesh out" all of their one hundred and forty divisions to full war strength within ninety days after mobilization.

How many more divisions they could field and in what time span is a matter of debate in the Pentagon. In World War II the U.S.S.R. mobilized about three hundred and fifty divisions, plus several hundred brigades and smaller units, but these were in no sense equivalent to the well-armed, well-trained units of today, and it is doubtful that the Soviet mobilization plan now calls for any such number. Nevertheless, the system of conscription, plus annual reserve training, makes available a vast amount of manpower; the limiting factors in the size of the force that could be mobilized would be the supply capability and arms and equipment.

The Soviet order of battle appears to indicate a lack of full appreciation of the huge problem of supplying and supporting modern ground armies. The U.S. "division slice"—the division plus all supporting, supply and administrative troops necessary to maintain the division in protracted combat—is about 35,000 to 45,000 men; the Russians' "division slice" for their far more austere army in East Germany is only about 15,000. Their capability for sustained ground combat would be affected, as it was during World War II, by this weakness, but there are signs that the new younger marshals are moving toward the creation of more supporting army and corps troops.

The modernization of the Soviet army may, indeed, have affected somewhat adversely the "shank's mare" mobility—the mobility of the foot soldier—of World War II. Like the United States army, today's Soviet army is tied to a P.O.L. (petroleum, oil, lubricants) line.

The Soviet ground-battle doctrine is built around mass, shock, firepower, and rapid movement—and the combined use of all arms—rather than upon sustained combat. Nevertheless, the Russians have the vitality and the capability for improvisation to sustain their armies in a long ground war, although periods of intense combat would have to be punctuated by frequent pauses for resupply.

The modern Soviet army is well trained and professionally officered. It is plentifully equipped and organized to fight either conventional or nuclear war.

The Soviet army became a modern army in the 1950's; for the first time since the Bolshevik Revolution it surpassed the United States army in quantity and quality of modern weapons and equipment. In the last decade the United States army has introduced many new weapons and great quantities of new equipment, but even today the Soviet ground forces are about as well equipped as any in the world. Certain items of Soviet equipment, such as the AK-47 rifle, heavy but probably the most reliable rifle in the world, tanks, and heavy mortars, are outstanding. The new main battle tank—the T-62, first seen in a Moscow parade in 1965—is a thirty-five-ton medium tank, developed from the earlier reliable T-54 and T-55 models, with a crew of four and a 115-millimeter gun. Some reports indicate that the gun is smooth bore and fires fin-stabilized projectiles. This tank, many of the older models, and the T-10 M heavy tank with 122-millimeter gun have gyro-stabilized gun mounts to permit accurate fire while the tank is moving, "button-down" hatches to allow movement through areas contaminated with radioactivity, and snorkeling or other gear to permit fording of deep rivers. The Russians also utilize an amphibious light tank—the PT-76 with a 76-millimeter gun—and an amphibious armored personnel carrier (capacity sixteen men), and have recently put into service a new wire-guided antitank missile—the Snapper.

The Soviet army emphasizes heavy mortars as a supplement to, and sometimes a replacement for, field artillery. Mortars up to 240 millimeters in size are in use, to supplement a great variety of multiple-barreled rocket launchers up to 250 millimeters in size and artillery ranging up to eleven and twelve inches in caliber. The army also employs large numbers of anti-aircraft guns and missiles ranging from small caliber, automatic weapons to some of the largest in the world. Rockets similar to the United States's Honest John, designated "Frogs" (Free, or unguided, Rocket Over Ground), are available in a variety of models and with ranges up to fifty miles. There is no real equivalent to the U.S. Pershing bombardment rocket, with its range of 300 to 500 miles, but the Soviet "Scud" missile can reach out to more than 150 miles. The Scud can carry a nuclear warhead as large as a megaton in size.

The Soviet tactical nuclear weapons appear to be considerably larger in power than many of those available in the United States; the Russians either have not been able to develop or are not interested in the subkiloton, or very small, nuclear warheads designed for the precise elimination of one strongpoint or of a small ground unit. Apparently, the Russians do not have, except in experimental form, any nuclear artillery shells, although it is believed they have the capability of developing shells for their 203- and 152-millimeter guns. The smallest rocket warheads are estimated to have a bursting power equivalent to one or two kilotons (1,000 tons of TNT); any weapon releasing less than 1,000 kilotons is considered a "tactical," or battlefield, weapon.

The Soviet army is keyed, as it has always been, to the primary task of defending its homeland. But, if war comes, it tends to conceive of defense today more in terms of offense than at any period of its history. The trading of space for time, the scorched-earth policy which helped to win the wars against Napoleon and Hitler at great cost to Russia, has little place in current doctrine. The army's might is keyed to mass, but to mechanized mass as well as manpower, and a static defense is no part of its doctrine. It believes in mobility and swift, wide-ranging ground strikes—by armor, mechanized forces, and paratroopers deep into an enemy's rear areas—co-ordinated with political, psychological, aerial, rocket, and naval operations.

Hanson W. Baldwin

:

The modern Soviet armed forces, half a century after the Bolshevik Revolution, are second only to those of the United States in total power, second to none in some aspects of that power. The U.S.S.R.'s nuclear-delivery capability is still second but is increasing rapidly relative to the United States. Its air defenses, against planes and missiles, are the strongest in the world. Its maritime power is still second but is also increasing rapidly relative to the United States. Its ground forces are dominant in Europe. Its weapons and equipment, though not as sophisticated or in many ways as advanced as those of the United States, are highly effective, reliable, simple to produce and maintain. As a half-century of Soviet rule ends, it is clear that Moscow is making a bid for global parity or primacy in total military power.

The Soviet armed forces are guided by, and in some senses are an implement of, Communist political philosophy, which has two primary objectives, in some ways ambivalent. The first and overriding objective is the security and welfare of the Russian heartland. The second is the extension of the Moscow brand of international Communism world-wide—*i.e.,* the creation of a world order guided by, or friendly to, Moscow's programs, policies, and aspirations. The Soviet Union will fight to the death for the former but probably only with limited means for the latter.

War, in Communist terms, means political action and political objectives first and foremost; hence military force must be capable of a spectrum of conflict, a flexibility of effort, which, in the past, the Russian armed forces did not possess.

The advent of the nuclear age, as the book of essays *Soviet Military Strategy,* edited by Marshal Vasily D. Sokolovsky, made clear, shook Soviet military concepts to their foundations. Premier Khrushchev was the first to admit publicly that in the nuclear age the heartland could not be successfully defended. He did not put it so baldly, but he admitted that no one could win a nuclear war, and, in effect, he ruled out such a war as an instrument of policy. At the same time he explicitly justified other forms of military conflict, specifically what he called "wars of national liberation" (wars defined in his terms as similar to the one in Vietnam).

Acceptance of this thesis meant, of course, a great shift in the balance of power within the Soviet armed services, a shift that has now occurred. The ground marshals lost some primacy; the missile marshals replaced them.

But even before Khrushchev spoke another shift in Soviet military thinking—a broadening of the professional horizons of the Soviet soldier—was taking place. After the death of Stalin the gobbledygook of Leninist-Stalinist military theories that posed as "principles of war" was gradually de-emphasized in favor of more professional and realistic concepts. The Soviet armed forces modernized their thought processes along with their equipment.

Today still another shift in Soviet military thinking seems to be occurring. The great swing toward strategic weapons for offense and defense, the concept that any future war would be a missile nuclear war, appears to have been somewhat checked. The first edition of the Sokolovsky book stressed the importance of surprise attack at the start of any war; the second edition concedes that war might start conventionally, without the use of nuclear arms, and hence without surprise. Between the lines the authors of the first edition—with some exceptions—seemed to feel that a nuclear war could be won or lost by missiles, planes, and submarines alone, though lip service was paid to the need for all arms. Today, as even greater realization of the military and political limitations of nuclear weapons in achieving viable political goals permeates the ranks of the Soviet armed forces, and as history demonstrates—in Vietnam, the Middle East, Africa—the requirement for conventional arms, there appears to be some swingback of the pendulum. The capability to fight limited wars with limited means, to fight, in fact, nearly any kind of war anywhere, is now part of Soviet military doctrine.

Even if a nuclear war should come, the current military thinking in the Soviet Union pays at least lip service to the necessity of using all forces and all services against the enemy—the ground forces to overrun enemy troops and territory, to mop up, to occupy and police.

Is Soviet military doctrine keyed, basically, to a defensive strategic concept?

In the first half-century of Communism in Russia the Soviet leaders have made it clear that they will support Communist movements in many areas of the world, with arms, with money, with advisers—but nearly always short of direct Soviet military involvement. There is no doubt that the Russians would like to avoid any personal involvement in war, although their military and political leaders believe that armed conflict is an essential implement for the ultimate triumph of Communism. Nor is there any doubt that defense of Mother Russia and security of the homeland is the first objective of Soviet power.

But the Soviet Union, after a half-century, is re-emphasizing, in a military sense, the Leninist view of the world which held that Communism knew no borders. It is looking outward—not only inward upon itself. Its sea power and aerospace power view strategy in global, and even in exoatmospheric, terms; no longer do the river lines and terrain features of the Russian steppes dominate the Soviet military mind. The pendulum has swung

—and it will not return—from the days when Communist military thought interpreted the battlefield in terms of purely Marxist concepts and Soviet strategy was keyed to a continental ground war. It has swung to the era of today, when the Kremlin looks upon the world in global strategic terms. The U.S.S.R. will enter no war easily; in fact, it will shrink from combat, but if battle is joined, it will fight offensively as well as defensively—on the high seas, in the skies, in space, and on the Eurasian land mass beyond its own frontiers.

COMPARATIVE STRENGTHS

Category	United States	Soviet Union
Men [1]	3,400,000	3,100,000–3,300,000
Divisions [2]	21	140
ICBM's	1,054	500–800
IRBM's and MRBM's	0	700–900
SLBM's [3]	544	100–150
Long-Range Bombers [4]	680	850–1,400
Major Naval Vessels [5]	900–1,000	650–750

[1] Total strengths of uniformed personnel in armed forces. In addition, the U.S.S.R. maintains 250,000 border guards and internal security troops.

[2] Includes, for the U.S., four Marine divisions. Excludes, for both countries, brigades, smaller units, and all reserve units.

[3] U.S. figure for these submarine-launched ballistic missiles excludes seven Polaris submarines, sixteen missiles each, undergoing refit or modification. Soviet figure excludes about 100 to 200 winged missiles.

[4] Figures include all U.S. heavy bombers—B-52's, and 80 B-58's, some of which are to be inactivated—and 150 to 200 Soviet heavy bombers plus 700 to 1,200 medium bombers.

[5] Includes major units in active operating fleets only—principally carriers, cruisers, destroyer types, and submarines—and excludes reserve fleets, decommissioned vessels, coastal and river vessels, and small craft.

THE SPORTING LIFE

»

Robert Lipsyte

June. A misty, wind-swept bluff overlooking the Gulf of Finland. A dozen eleven-year-old boys, damp-faced and red-kneed, churn over a lumpy cinder field, scrabbling to kick a scuffed brown ball at a splintery wooden goal. They might be small boys at play anywhere, except for their intensity and their silence. From a corner of the field a middle-aged man studies them relentlessly.

He has been watching them since January, when they trooped through the snow, nervous and chattery, to a drafty gymnasium owned by an athletic club called Spartak. Beneath crimson banners that read MASS AND QUALITY IS THE SLOGAN OF SOVIET SPORT and GLORY TO THE COMMUNIST PARTY, the boys had been examined by doctors, had been interviewed by teachers, and had been handed soccer balls. There were 512 boys in January, the oldest sixteen, the youngest ten. By late March there were one hundred, ready for the cinder field.

The middle-aged man divided them into groups, by age. The eleven-year-olds would practice from 4:00 to 5:00 P.M., twice a week, until school let out in June. Then it would be three times a week, from 11:00 A.M. to 1:00 P.M. He told them, quite sternly, about the importance of sleep, proper eating habits, moral quality, and collective play. They had heard it all before, in school and around Pioneer campfires, but they listened very carefully. They knew that the middle-aged man, Boris Oreshkin, had once played for the national soccer team. He also told them, gently and with laughter, to forget the little mannerisms, the swaggers, and the shoulder rolls they had picked up watching Class A games on television. There would be time enough for such things when they got to the Lenin Stadium in Moscow and played to the roar of 104,000.

It is not so wild a dream, even for eleven-year-old Leningrad boys in sneakers and hand-me-down spikes racing through a dreary June day in the fiftieth year of Soviet power. If they do well here, if Boris Oreshkin thinks he sees something in the snap of their head shots, the drive in their legs, the world's most structured and supervised sports system will find hands to lift them up.

There would be special summer sports camps and "comradely matches" against the youth teams of other athletic clubs, most of which are operated by labor unions in the Soviet Union. There would be opportunities to represent the club in district, city, republic, and even national tournaments, opportunities to represent the city in a Spartakiad, the quadrennial internal Olympic Games.

A team of cyclists, hunchbacked on their frail machines, eerily buzzes out of the mist, circles the cinder field, and disappears. None of Boris Oreshkin's eleven-year-olds look up. Thirty women in bulging jerseys, their gray hair wrapped in white kerchiefs, trot unsteadily behind a physical-culture instructor. Somewhere beyond the trees a basketball slams against a backboard, then skitters along a winter-cracked concrete court.

Far below the wind-swept bluff, on the edge of the Gulf of Finland, children are scrambling into the little wooden sailboats of the Central Yacht Club. Like the silent soccer players, they are students in a sports school, one of 2,500 such schools in the country. Their Boris Oreshkin, once an M Class sailing champion, is another of the nation's 175,000 athletic and recreation directors. He had spent the winter afternoons lecturing the children on currents and wind beneath a portrait of Peter the Great. It was Czar Peter, after all, he would say ironically, who started us off. In 1718, because he realized that yachting was too much fun for admirals alone, Peter created the Nevsky Amusement Fleet for monarchs and bishops and nobles of consequence.

In fifty years, from nearly a standing start, the Soviet Union has increased sports participation from 50,000 people to 50,000,000 and become a leading athletic power in the world. The race has been run against the backdrop of facilities that are rapidly improving but still inferior by Western standards, and it has been run by a population that only in the last generation has been eating beef and greens in quantity. The reason for Soviet success, of course, is a system that spends more than $2.2 billion annually to fulfill an axiom attributed to Lenin—that a nation cannot be strong unless it is strong in sports.

The system works because the government ultimately controls the construction of paddle-ball courts and 100,000-seat stadiums, the transportation of teams, the curriculum in physical-culture institutes, and the production of ping-pong balls. For the common man, sports participation is inexpensive, easily accessible, and sometimes obligatory. It is also, he is told, in the interests of national purpose, essential for his health, for productivity, for progress toward Communism. For the star athlete there is subsidization, material rewards, and an avenue for the self-expression that is not always easy in a controlled society. There are no professional athletes in the Soviet Union, but the champion amateur can remain in school, or at a nominal job that does not interfere with his training, as long as his legs can carry his weight.

"The games and the equipment are the same the whole world over," says Stanislav Yananis, head of the department of Sports Theory and History at the Lesgaft Institute, in Leningrad, the first and most prestigious of the Soviet Union's sixteen physical-culture institutes of higher education. "But there is a difference between sports here and in a bourgeois society," he adds. "Our system is directed by a socialist state and sports is not an end in itself. We are creating a new man, physically, mentally, morally."

Soviet sport is not always grim, but it is always serious. Because an important athlete is required to be an example to youth and a reflection to the world of socialist vitality, his attitude is under constant scrutiny. The sports columns of *Pravda* reserve their strongest scorn for the athlete who lost through "moral weakness."

On a night in June a crowd of three hundred, many of them carrying university textbooks in string shopping bags and over-the-shoulder duffels, jammed into a vaulted gym owned by Moscow's Wings of the Soviet, the athletic society of the civil aeronautics trade union. It was a minor gymnastics meet but important because it was serving as an early elimination for the Spartakiad to be held later in the summer. It was also important because Mikhail Voronin, a twenty-two-year-old world champion, was making his first appearance after a leg injury. The crowd was tensely impatient through the parades and anthems and exchanges of bouquets that mark every Soviet competition.

Voronin, powerfully built but not as grotesquely muscled as most of the other male gymnasts, approached the high bar with what seemed like forced calm. His close-cropped black hair was damp and flat on his head. The crowd held its breath as he spun and turned on the bar, then screamed "Stop" as he leaped down to the mat. His bad leg faltered, and he stumbled. There was dead silence in the gym as the judges awarded him a low point score, far below his usual performance score, but just high enough to qualify him for the next meet on the ladder up to the Spartakiad. Voronin did not hesitate. He waved away that point score and elected to try again, gambling on a last chance for a worthy score or total elimination. The roar of approval that rattled the gym windows was even louder than the applause, fifteen minutes later, that followed Voronin's near-perfect performance.

Before the revolution, sport was an upper-class activity. Aristocrats hunted, rowed, raced horses, and sailed at the Imperial Yacht Club. Merchants' sons skated and worked out in athletic clubs inspired by German traders. The clubs were expensive, exclusive, and jealous of one another. The ineffectual teams that Russia sent to the Olympic Games of 1908 and 1912 had been selected to balance club representation and skirt the traditional St. Petersburg–Moscow rivalry. Russian athletes won few medals at the Olympics, but competitors found them an extremely genial, relaxed, and well-tailored group.

It was forty years before a Russian again participated in the Olympics. In 1952, in neighboring Helsinki, the Soviet athletes nearly amassed the most points, to win the unofficial team championship, but lost in the last day to an American surge. The impact of the Soviet effort upon international sports was tremendous. The Olympics, which have always been subtly merchandised as a kind of moral equivalent to war, became an arena for the muscle of ideology. In the years that followed, as both East and West charged each other with hypocrisy and professionalism and the use of sports as a political tool, always with some justification, controversy obscured what the Russians considered the basic reason for emphasis on athletics. For the infant Soviet state, sports had been an element in survival.

The physical-culture movement, at first an amalgam of Swedish, Czechoslovak, and German mass exercises, began in the Red Army in 1918 to improve the fitness of recruits. It grew and spread, particularly among workers' groups, military units, and the internal-security forces. Although Lenin is now said to have been a hunter, hiker, skater, and cyclist of note, the Communist party took only an encouraging, advisory role until 1929, when it established a single central government agency to direct all physical culture and sports. The sports organization remained essentially the same until the creation of the present Union of Sports Societies and Organizations in 1959. The Moscow-based union is set up along geographical rather than occupational lines and is a so-called social, or nongovernmental, organization. Of the fifty-nine types of sports played in the Soviet Union, the union directly controls forty-four. The fifteen paramilitary sports, such as parachute jumping, automobile racing, and gliding, are supervised by the Voluntary Society for Assistance to the Army, Air Force and Navy, a group known by its Russian initials, DOSAAF.

The development of Soviet athletics between the revolution and World War II was marked by the state's methodical introduction and encouragement of particular sports at particular times in a pragmatic attack on poor health, faltering production, boredom, and political ignorance. Organized athletics provided exercise, increased efficiency, easy amusement, emotional release, and a handy network of clubs for the dissemination of Communist thought. Even now the prime mover in Soviet sports is the Komsomol, the Young Communist League of fifteen- to twenty-eight-year-olds.

It was a Komsomol brainstorm, in 1931, that gave Soviet sports its biggest prewar boost. The early mass sports—soccer, volleyball, cycling, track and field—were catching hold, but the immediate and future base of the whole system, the physical-culture program, was slipping. It was drudgery. Then the Komsomol invented the Ready for Labor and Defense series, nationwide physical-fitness tests. There were national norms, medals, the spice of competition. Since modified, extended to women and children, and broadened to include sports skills, the tests have become the basic athletic measurements.

After the war the sports classification standards leading to the Master of Sports medal were introduced, bringing a new surge in the program. The rectangular bronze medal symbolizes championship-class proficiency for massive weight lifters, willowy girl runners, and pale, concave-chested checkers players.

Despite party claims on Physical Culture Day and American exaggeration during Olympic-fund drives, the Soviet Union does not spring up at dawn for push-ups and a cold shower. The radio broadcasts fifteen minutes of setting-up exercises, but even Soviet radios have to be turned on. The sports hierarchy has been trying for years to increase the number of gym periods for schoolchildren, but the science and math teachers feel that two hours a week are sufficient. And although not yet in the Western-style epidemic stage, "spectatoritis" is on the rise.

Except at the race track, where his conduct is deplorably universal, the Soviet sports fan is enthusiastic, knowledgeable, and among the best behaved in the world. Once, his enthusiasm could be attributed solely to entertainment-hunger, but now it is more an outgrowth of early exposure to sports. Hundreds are still turned away from volleyball games between Moscow girls' teams, and on a June night when several thousand people climbed a muddy, construction-littered hill in Kiev to see a Greco-Roman wrestling match there were dances, jazz concerts, and lectures in the public parks, the movie houses and television stations were offering a full and varied program, and a lovers' moon hung over the Dnieper River.

The sports fan is never more visible or vocal than when the soccer season is stoking up, and June of the fiftieth year of Soviet rule was no exception. As usual, the blue-and-white-clad squads of Dynamo were leading the two-conference, thirty-nine-team Class A Division, the major league. Formed in 1923 to represent the internal-security forces and strengthened later by the interest of Lavrenti P. Beria, Stalin's secret-police chief, Dynamo is the oldest, richest, and best equipped of the nationwide sports societies. It has lost its secret-police image but not the early advantage that enabled it to build and collect rentals from the first stadiums, establish sports-equipment outlets, and recruit the best young players.

In Moscow and Kiev the success of the local Dynamo teams was being taken for granted, but down south in Tbilisi, the capital of the Georgian Republic, it was a matter of great civic and ethnic pride. On a Friday night 40,000 Georgians, mostly men in white shirts rolled at the cuff and open at the throat, came to see Dynamo play Shakhter, a coal miners' team from the Donets region of the Ukraine.

Swarthy and mustached, the Georgians sat restlessly in the stands, eating the greasy cheese bread called *khachapuri* and popping chocolate-covered nuts into their mouths. A Beatles' soccer song crackled over the loud-speaker, interrupted by an announcement of the postgame subway schedule. The night was warm, and a small boy moved up and down the concrete steps of the circular arena peddling cold water from a chipped teakettle. Georgians called him "little capitalist" and paid a few kopecks for a drink from a community cup.

The talk was desultory. Lev Yashin, the so-called "poet of soccer" and goalkeeper for the national team, must be feeling his thirty-seven years, they said; did you see him miss that easy shot against the Austrians on television last week? Russian players, they said, are plodding but steady, Ukrainians are mechanical and precise, Armenians are tricky, and Georgians are fired by temperament. Then Tbilisi Dynamo trotted out and everyone became a coach.

The first half was "so Georgian," a Western observer was told, that even the statue of Mother Georgia on the mountainside must be waving her sword and her wine bowl. With flair and arrogance the Tbilisi players danced through the Ukrainians' textbook patterns, stopping only to trip flagrantly the big blond miners. Tbilisi scored on a beautifully creative feint and head shot, and the crowd leaped up, roaring and thrusting fists into the air. A moment later the spectators were laughing hysterically. A cunning Georgian player, after tripping a Ukrainian, solicitously helped him to his feet and brushed him off, casually took the ball and threw it to a teammate. There was a little good-natured applause for the alert referee who ran out and snatched the ball back.

The second half, alas, was also "so Georgian." Tbilisi Dynamo relaxed and gloated while Shakhter methodically plugged away. Disaster was imminent, but only the so-called "real commissars of football," the fans in the cheap seats, seemed to sense it. They were still screaming for another goal, a safety margin, when the miners pumped in a goal. Shredded newspapers and clumps of *khachapuri* filled the air. The miners scored again, and 40,000 people stood and whistled derisively until both teams left the field. Then they stalked out into the cobblestoned streets, faces twisted in anger and despair.

The next morning the captain and coach of Tbilisi Dynamo were in the office of the chairman of the Georgian Republic Sports Council, and local newspaper accounts of the game began, "There are nights like that! Despite brilliant play and the passing artistry of . . ."

Much of the intense rivalry between cities and regions is historical and some of it is ethnic, but in sports a great deal of it developed during the long period of Soviet isolation. Between the revolution and World War II, under pressure from governments that did not recognize the new regime, international sports federations would not admit Soviet teams or sanction Soviet records. "It was a sports blockade," says seventy-year-old Aleksandr Toivonen, one of the early wrestling coaches. "We sportsmen only waited for the day when we could compete internationally. We felt that we would never really grow until then. But perhaps in the long run we ended up stronger because we had to turn inward into ourselves."

This turning inward involved the creation of elaborate calendars of internal competitions culminating in the Spartakiad, first held in 1928, and the encouragement of intramural sports rivalries not very different from the quota competitions among factories. Teams and individual sportsmen received cash bonuses and free vacation trips. The relatively few foreign athletes who came to the country were generally members of Socialist trade unions. They were not the best of Europe but their brains were picked vigorously.

The Soviet approach to sports became, and still is, painstakingly academic. Foreign books and photographs were reproduced and studied; observers were sent when possible to shoot movies of champions in action.

Esoteric monographs were prepared on sports minutiae. Valery Brumel's 1963 world record was credited, in part, to a three-hundred-page Soviet high-jumping manual some thirty years in preparation.

This academic approach, so consonant with Marxist science and reason, reaches its peak in the higher education of sportsmen. There is a medical school in Estonia offering a six-year course leading to a doctor-coach certificate. The doctor-coach, it is said, will be able, among other things, to integrate the technical training of an athlete with his individual hormonal development. There are two sports science research institutes where complex machines are being developed to measure the energy patterns of runners and swimmers. Igor Ter-Ovanesyan, the long-jumper, has been working for several years on his postgraduate dissertation, "The Influence of Different Rhythms Upon the Speed with Which Certain Movements, in Jumping and Throwing, Are Executed." Yuri Vlasov, the weight lifter, a former engineering student, has created a racklike machine to develop certain leg muscles that most people never use.

Most coaches and physical-culture leaders have been graduated from one of the sixty university sports departments or one of the sixteen physical-culture institutes. The first institute, Lesgaft, was officially accredited by the Ministry of Higher Education in 1919. It was named after Peter Franz Lesgaft, a "progressive" physiologist who taught that environment and training were more important than heredity. He died in 1909, hounded to the end by the imperial government. Ironically, one of the institute's buildings in Leningrad once contained the apartments of the Czar's sister.

Lesgaft Institute has 3,000 students, one-third of whom are women, in evening, correspondence, and various full-time programs. In the regular four-year institute course students matriculate as general "methodists" or narrow "specialists." The methodist will go on to teach physical culture in a school or factory. The specialist, who has concentrated on a particular sport such as basketball, soccer, swimming, or skiing, will be prepared to join the coaching staff of a national-level team. Even the nonsports classes are slanted toward sportsmen. In psychology courses students explore interpersonal team dynamics and "negative emotions" that cause crippling stress. In biomechanics, the emphasis is on bones and muscles in action. The medicine classes concentrate on the heart, lungs, and endocrine glands in search of keys to hidden reservoirs of energy. In Marxism seminars and Communist-theory classes obscure quotations are made applicable to the ideology and sociology of Soviet sport.

"For us it is not just playing ball games and having high results," says Leonid Khomenkov, the genial, bushy-browed deputy chairman of the national Union of Sports Societies. "We compete against the Americans in

Women laying down a railroad line beside the Dnieper dam   *(James Abbé, The New York Times)*

Giant hydroelectric project on the Dnieper River, completed in 1933   *(A.P.)*

American-made tractors being used to modernize farming in Russia in the 1930's   (*The New York Times*)

Grain being harvested on a collective farm in the Ukraine in the fall of 1940 (*Sovfoto*)

A visit by foreign reporters, wearing white gowns, to a state farm in the Ukraine in June, 1966   (A.P.)

Kuzma Kolosov, director of the Marfino State Farm, inspecting cucumber plants (H. Erich Heinemann, The New York Times)

Collective-farm market in Tashkent, where Uzbek farmers bring in produce grown on their private plots and sell it for whatever the market will bear (Charlotte Curtis, The New York Times)

A Siberian plain being turned into a collective farm by young workers in the summer of 1955   (*The New York Times*)

Woman crane operator, one of many women employed in heavy industry   (*A.B.C.*)

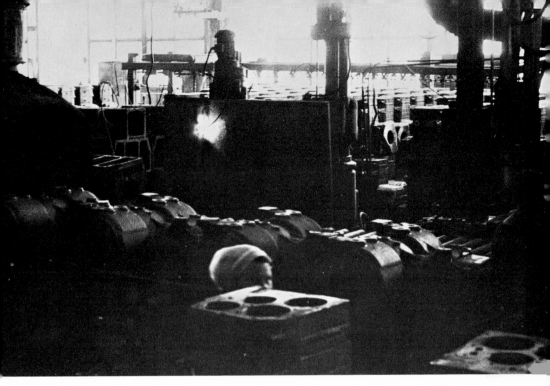

Machines stamping transmission cases in a tractor works in Volgograd first built with American aid in the early 1930's, completely destroyed in the Battle of Stalingrad, and since rebuilt and supplied with automated machines (*H. Erich Heinemann, The New York Times*)

Inna P. Laricheva, an authority on early contacts and migrations between Asia and the Americas, holding "world's oldest spoon," found along the Angara River near Irkutsk   (*Walter Sullivan, The New York Times*)

Vasily Yefremovich Suslov, deputy director of a Leningrad engineering plant now building what the Soviets claim will be the largest hydroelectric turbine in the world, capable of generating more than one-half million kilowatts *(H. Erich Heinemann, The New York Times)*

Aleksei Fedorovich Vasilyev, chief engineer at the Volzhsky Synthetic Fiber Plant, which makes heavy nylon yarn for automobile-tire cords *(H. Erich Heinemann, The New York Times)*

Midday on the Moscow subway, when, unlike rush hours, no one has to stand *(A. Topping, The New York Times)*

The Likhachev automobile factory in Moscow, which produced some of the approximately 230,000 cars made in the Soviet Union in 1966 *(Dan Weiner, The New York Times)*

Left: A Ford-type car leaving a checking ramp in the Gorky automobile plant in 1934 *(Sovfoto) Right:* A customer picking up his auto, one of about 75,000 private passenger cars in the capital, at the only lot in Moscow where new cars are delivered, June, 1967 *(H. Erich Heinemann, The New York Times)*

First of the new "science cities," the Akademgorodok near Novosibirsk—a prototype for several other centers of research and teaching now under construction—with Budker's Institute of Nuclear Physics, flanked by institutes of cytology, genetics, and geology   *(Walter Sullivan, The New York Times)*

Aleksandr P. Vinogradov, a leading geochemist and a vice president of the Academy of Sciences, who interpreted the first gamma ray measurements made near the moon and concluded that that body differs in composition from the earth, standing beside equipment for gaseous analysis of rock samples   *(Walter Sullivan, The New York Times)*

Nikolai N. Semenov, winner of a Nobel Prize in chemistry, now a vice president of the Academy of Sciences and head of the Institute of Chemical Physics, who is admired in his homeland and abroad for the public stand he took against dictatorial rule of Soviet biology during the heyday of Stalinism and Lysenko   *(Walter Sullivan, The New York Times)*

Dr. G. I. Budker, inventor of the "Alice in Wonderland" machine being built at his Institute of Nuclear Physics near Novosibirsk, standing beneath a portrait of Igor V. Kurchatov, "father" of the Soviet atomic bomb *(Walter Sullivan, The New York Times)*

The dynamic young rector of Novosibirsk University, Spartak T. Belyayev, former pupil of Niels Bohr in Copenhagen, who represents one of the most sophisticated schools of modern physics, and who, contrary to traditional Soviet practice, has recruited professors who are also leading researchers in nearby institutes *(Walter Sullivan, The New York Times)*

A cyclotron used for studying nuclear reactions at the atomic-research center established for Soviet-bloc scientists at Dubna, on the Volga River *(Novosti)*

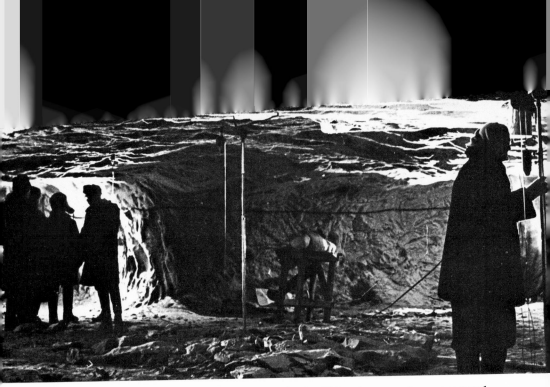

A mine ninety feet below the surface in the Yakutsk area, where structural properties of permafrost are studied   *(Novosti)*

Left: Walter Sullivan with interpreter   *(The New York Times)   Right:* Grigory I. Galazy, head of the Institute of Limnology at Lake Baikal, the most voluminous reservoir of fresh water in the world, whose remarkably diverse life he is trying to preserve   *(Walter Sullivan, The New York Times)*

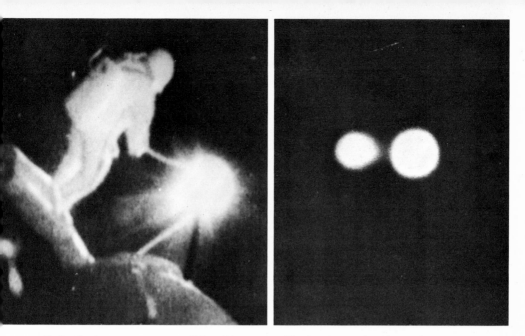

Left: Soviet cosmonaut walking in space   *(Sovfoto)   Right:* One of the first photographs of "antimatter." Positrons, which resemble electrons, but are positive in electric charge instead of negative, were generated at the Institute of Nuclear Physics in Novosibirsk to form a circular beam, part of which is seen here in cross section. The glow is caused by the shedding of energy, known as synchrotron radiation.   *(The New York Times)*

The "Alice in Wonderland" machine under construction at Novosibirsk, in a building five hundred feet long. Concrete forms have just been removed from what will be the inner ring for storage of antiprotons. Once the ring is completed, dirt excavated earlier and heaped in the background will be piled over it to absorb the radiation.   *(Walter Sullivan, The New York Times)*

Soviet Cosmonaut Aleksei Leonov floating away from the Voskhod 2 space-
ship in March, 1965, the first time that man ventured outside an orbiting
spacecraft   *(A.P.)*

ull-scale model of Sputnik III, which was launched in 1958,
precursor of the first manned flight   *(The New York Times)*

Soviet might on display in Moscow's Red Square during the celebration of the forty-ninth anniversary of the Bolshevik Revolution in 1966. The weapons above are intercontinental ballistic missiles; those below are SA-2 anti-aircraft missiles (U.P.I.)

New Mikoyan swing-wing fighter, during the July, 1967, Moscow air show. The wings of this plane—which can fly nearly three times faster than the speed of sound—can be swept fully in four seconds. *(Sovfoto)*

The 315-foot titanium monument to the Space Age near Moscow's Red Square, with, at its base, a statue of Konstantin Tsiolkovsky, a rocket engineer often called the "father of cosmonautics"   *(Sovfoto)*

the Olympics and we want to be first; that is very natural. But we understand that high results and victories have meaning only in that they help
us, scientifically, to explore the potentials of man, to prolong his life and
give that life more rational meaning."

Despite these high ideals, there has been frequent criticism of the postwar Soviet sports program. Such crusty watchdogs as *Pravda, Izvestia,* and
Mikhail Sholokhov have charged that officials are "record happy" to the
detriment of the mass program. At the same time athletes and coaches are
under some pressure, if only psychological, to win international meets. "We
are proud and glad to see proofs of our system," says Khomenkov, "and
when we lose we have to ask ourselves: why did we lose if we have such a
good basis?"

The Soviet Union did not enter the international sports arena until
1946, when it sent a weight-lifting team to the world championships in
Paris. It was a last-minute decision, and the team technically came too late
to be eligible. The French bent the rules, however, realizing that the Soviet
presence would increase the meet's prestige and gate receipts. The mere
announcement that the Russians were coming moved the meet, a relatively
minor event in the sports world, to the front pages of European newspapers.
And strangely but significantly the Russians were immediately installed as
favorites to win.

Reports of prodigious feats of lifting had trickled out of the Soviet
Union through the 1930's, but they had generally been disregarded in the
West, which considered them Communist propaganda. Then World War II
shattered the country, left more than 20,000,000 dead, and claimed the
cream of young sportsmen, ranging from the Lesgaft Battalions that skied
behind enemy lines to the Kiev Dynamo team that whipped the Luftwaffe
All-Stars in a football match the occupation commander had ordered them
to lose. Kiev Dynamo was machine-gunned.

Yet somehow, perhaps through the alchemy of the war, the Russian
lifters were considered the best in the world even before the world saw
them. A characteristic squad arrived in Paris: ten lifters for five events and
more than a dozen coaches, trainers, officials, and cameramen. The previously favored American squad of six lifters and the businessman-coach who
paid their expenses were unable to sleep, endlessly wondering if all that
propaganda had indeed been true.

The details of that meet are still obscured by controversy. Officially, the
Americans won, but the Russians believe that French incompetence and
an unfamiliar point system penalized their athletes. Americans who com-
peted against them insist that the Russians, after finishing second, borrowed
the championship trophy to make a duplicate, which they carried back to

Moscow. The Russians say that is nonsense. The usual fraternalism among athletes was limited by the language barrier and the Russians' insistence on moving around in a group.

Nevertheless, the major patterns that were to emerge in the next twenty years were established. The Russians were box office, an important consideration in the frequently shoestring world of international sports. They were fierce competitors, and they were apparently under pressure to win. They had the system to do it.

The Soviet Union joined the international sports federations one by one. In 1948 the Communist party called for Soviet dominance in international sports as proof of the quality of the mass physical-culture program and the superiority of socialism. The party writers interpreted this to mean "beat bourgeois sports records." International sports, historically marked by controversy and political considerations, began to shake down into a confrontation between two superpowers in a climate of distrust. The Cold War, the Korean War, and McCarthyism created an atmosphere in which the 1952 Olympics became less a sports spectacular and more a so-called "battle for men's minds." To uncommitted nations, it was argued, a sports victory was another plus for either the American Way of Life or the Vitality of the Socialist State. Before the Olympics of 1952, *Izvestia* declared that American sports were a means of "preparing cannon fodder for a new, aggressive war." Before the 1956 Olympics, Senator John Marshall Butler described Soviet teams as "barbaric goon squads" and the Soviet athlete as a "paid propaganda agent of the U.S.S.R., one more slave in the hideous chain of brainwashed individuals slavishly advancing the Communist cause."

Politics played a role in many incidents over the years, from the questionable arrest of a Soviet female discus thrower in London for allegedly stealing about five dollars' worth of hats to the American demand that Soviet athletes be fingerprinted before being admitted to the United States. The Soviet Union, in turn, created turmoil over recognition of teams from Nationalist China and West Germany, scandalized Wimbledon by apparently ordering a tennis player to lose rather than meet a member of the all-white South African team, and withdrew from the 1966 U.S.–U.S.S.R. track meet in protest over the Vietnam war. The track meet was to have been a continuation of the highly successful dual meets begun under the 1958 cultural-exchange agreement. These dual meets, often held at times of great East-West tension, produced enormous paying crowds, stirring performances, and fast friendships among Russian and American athletes. They also focused increased attention on the role of the Soviet athlete in his society.

Without ever losing the comprehensive social security available to the common factory hand, the Soviet athlete can explore the limits of his talent and seek every man's goal of becoming truly accomplished in something fulfilling. He can achieve recognition and respect without ever having to compromise his private visions, as so many writers and painters and film directors must. There is no "slanderous" or "ideologically immature" way of hurling a discus or running the mile. In sports the man and the state both measure the progress of an individual in seconds, meters, and victories.

When a man breaks a record he has a higher priority for a new apartment. This is a major consideration for any young Soviet citizen. Although apartment rentals are relatively inexpensive, it can be years before newlyweds reach the top of a waiting list and "live separate" from in-laws. Jumping farther than anyone else, like painting a picture of "great Socialist reality" or inventing some new technical process, is considered a contribution to the state. Common rewards for achievement in any field are the next available apartment, use of a country home or automobile, a Black Sea vacation.

Most Soviet athletes remain students during their years of peak competition. They are allowed to extend the normal four-year institute or university course to seven years and go on to graduate work that may take them into their early thirties. Since education is free and government stipends are always available, the Russian athlete can marry and raise a family, impossible for many American amateurs.

Most Soviet athletes who work are either teachers or military personnel, the main exceptions being boxers and soccer players, who generally have industrial jobs. The Soviet athlete is never in danger of losing his job because of absences due to training or competition, and his salary continues while he is away. When his playing days are over he is virtually assured of a job of some sort in sports.

In return for all this security he is under absolute state control. The Soviet Union, unlike the United States, never has a problem fielding the best available team. The Soviet Olympic Committee does not have to wheedle funds from private sources; the basketball and soccer federations do not have to watch the cream of each year's talent turn professional. There are no private sources of consequence, no professionals besides circus strongmen.

The Soviet system produces abuses, of course, and areas that cast doubt on protestations of amateur purity. When Nina Stepanova, a twenty-three-year-old runner, took a national championship, her employer, the Skorokhod (Fast Walker) shoe plant of Leningrad, gave her various gifts and a one-hundred-and-five-ruble bonus, equivalent to a month's salary. A Skorokhod official was quite candid about the bonus when asked if he did not think it contradicted the Soviet promise, in 1947, to stop cash prizes to athletes as a prerequisite to Olympic participation. "The bonus came from a trade-union incentive fund," he said, "and although I would not call it a direct investment in factory production, it was a stimulation of labor. Nina will teach and encourage others in sport, and workers will be healthier, more self-controlled, and better organized. It will ultimately mean more pairs of shoes for the Soviet people."

The gross abuses of the Soviet system have been exposed in painful detail by party newspapers. Goalies and forwards have been lured to rival factories and distant cities with cars, sinecures, and cash. Even volleyball players and bike racers have sometimes become "rented legs." The classic horror tale of personal and bureaucratic evil concerns "star sickness" and the degradation of Eduard Streltsov.

In 1958 Streltsov was twenty-one years old. He held a nominal job in a Moscow car plant and was thus eligible to play for Torpedo, the soccer team of the automotive industry's sports society. Moscow Torpedo is major league, and Streltsov was its best player. He was also a frequent drunk, street brawler, and wife beater. He pressured the plant directors for larger cash bonuses, more cars, a better apartment. Fearful that he would go out and get a nominal job in, say, a railroad yard and play for Lokomotiv, or become a construction worker and play for Trud, the officials toadied to Streltsov, bailed him out of trouble, and intervened in his behalf with the courts.

The Young Communist League newspaper, *Komsomolskaya Pravda,* broke the story early in 1958, blaming both the player and the officials. There were stern reproofs, perhaps some moral retraining, and letters of apology. It kept Streltsov straight until that summer, when he raped a woman at a party. The stops were pulled, and Streltsov, in national disgrace, was sent to prison for twelve years. In a country where rape can be punished by death, the sentence was not excessive.

On the night in June, 1967, when Yashin missed the easy shot against the Austrians before 104,000 spectators in the Central Lenin Stadium, it was Streltsov who streaked through the pack to win the game for the U.S.S.R. with a spectacular last-minute goal. He had been pardoned after a few years because he had been, after all, just an "unreasonable youth" who needed rehabilitation. He was also a great player, although soccer fans have grumbled since that his incredible potential was stunted in jail.

Nina Stepanova's bonus was "explainable" and Streltsov is an atypical example, but favoritism toward athletes is real. Among Western purists it amounts to "professionalism"; among party members it is another example of the state's offering of "possibilities" to all men. Soviet officials point out that athletes receive no more than other "contributive specialists," and, in fact, less, because sports competition is only an avocation.

The great Soviet triumphs in European and world championships and in the 1956 and 1960 Olympic Games encouraged and glamorized sports activity at home. Society membership rose, budget strings loosened, and new facilities were constructed. The pride of Soviet sports complexes, built in 1956 on a swamp in Moscow called Luzhniki, is a 17,000-acre microcosm of the entire nation at play. The focal point of Luzhniki is the Central Lenin Stadium, which was erected with the help of volunteer labor in time for the World Youth Festival. The haste with which it was built is reflected in the somewhat crumbly appearance of its yellowing stone façade, but the oval arena, nearly a mile around, holds 104,000 for an important soccer game or track meet.

On a June day when the stadium was being prepared for the 1967 Spartakiad, the Soviet Davis Cup team was playing Chile in the 14,000-seat secondary stadium, where outdoor volleyball and basketball games are also staged. Admission to the tennis matches ranged from the equivalent of about $1.00 to $1.50. On nearby indoor courts Anna Dmitrieva, a pert-faced teacher of French and the country's top woman player, was rallying with Galina Baksheyeva, a university student who is number two and has dyed red hair and long false eyelashes. Anna's year-old daughter watched the women in their last practice session before they went on the European circuit.

At the 12,000-seat outdoor heated pool the city of Astrakhan's water polo team was working out with the Moscow State University team, and eight-year-old divers were hurtling off high boards in a sports-school session. A squealing pack of Pioneers, their red neckerchiefs askew, awaited their turn outside the locker room. They would soon change into bathing suits, jump into indoor pools, and swim along a watery corridor into the main outdoor pool.

In the Sports Palace, the 15,000-seat main indoor arena, an Austrian ice revue was practicing for an evening performance. The arena also is used for basketball, volleyball, indoor track and field, and boxing matches. At a secondary ice-skating rink Moscow mothers in their ubiquitous thin blue raincoats were anxiously watching six-year-old daughters who would all grow up to be Lidiya Skoblikova.

There are twenty-eight gymnasiums in Luzhniki, and almost all were occupied, mostly on a rental basis by sports schools. Lithe young girls spun over Turkomen carpets, weight lifters heaved, and boxers sparred cautiously. Soviet boxers are quite cautious, partly because of their "science," partly because a knockout is followed by a three-month suspension, and a third knockout in a career means banishment from the ring.

On well-tended fields around the main buildings students played tennis, badminton, and soccer. The health clubs—hundreds of women on their lunch hours or after early factory shifts—touched toes and waved small dumbbells.

The Luzhniki complex, which officials hope will someday play host to an Olympics, is owned by the Moscow City Council. Like many other municipal facilities, it is on a self-supporting basis, printing and selling its own programs, administering and paying its nine hundred employees, and dealing with outside unions that supply part-time workers for restaurants and special construction.

Soviet sports administrators like to talk about profits. Some of the profits are kept in the form of 15-per-cent quarterly incentive bonuses, but most are plowed back into new facilities with a resultant extension of the administrators' power and prestige. Some of the profit-motivated schemes seem paradoxical: along the side lines of Lenin Stadium during the Austrian-U.S.S.R. match were billboards advertising West European products. Officials explained that neither the stadium crowd nor the millions watching the game on Soviet television could buy those products. But the Austrians watching at home could, and sponsors were willing to pay the Russians in hard currency.

Some of the profit-motivated schemes would do justice to capitalists. Sergei Budkevich, a thirty-one-year-old Master of Sports in water polo and now vice director of the Moscow open-air swimming pool, the largest heated outdoor pool in Europe, is working on a plan to drill artesian wells that would yield warm water having the mineral content of sea water. According to Budkevich, his pool grosses 1,300,000 rubles a year and nets 400,000 rubles, all from single and group admissions and rentals for mass competition. Almost half of the 900,000-ruble operating expense goes to the city for its tap water and electricity to heat it. But with warm ground water coming up, the water and heat bills would vanish. Net profits would soar, not only from the savings, but also from new customers eager to swim in the equivalent of sea water.

Budkevich's big face becomes dreamy. With all that money he would develop the pool's summer sports camp outside Moscow, which is already a money-maker. He would build sanatoriums, which are sure-fire. Now Budkevich's eyes are far away and his voice drops to a hoarse whisper. In a few years, he says, we'll all be ready for the big one, a domed stadium on top of the pool with seats for 50,000. There would be a sliding floor to cover the pool for indoor soccer and basketball. There will be objections, says Budkevich; the council will say that the dome would spoil the neighborhood's sky line. But there will be help, too. The Pushkin Museum, across the street, hitherto the pool's greatest enemy, will intercede with the council. The museum has been complaining for years that the vapors from the outdoor pool are slowly destroying the treasures of art. Budkevich smacks his hands with glee.

The freedom of sports facilities to get rich is due partly to general measures taken to stimulate the economy and partly to a 1966 Communist party directive that will probably change the face of Soviet sports life more radically than did the organizational decision of 1929 or the international competition decision of 1948.

The Central Committee of the party specifically charged the trade unions, the party units, the government agencies, the Komsomol, and the national athletic union with the responsibility of broadening the physical-culture program in factories, residences, and recreation areas to "improve the productivity of labor, the prevention of disease and the conditions of active rest."

Sports officials had been hoping for such support—and the fresh money and power that went with it—for some time. The response was quite visible in the summer of 1967: new swimming pools, tennis courts, sports palaces, and stadiums were being built at a tremendous rate. Efforts were being made to bring rural areas in Soviet Asia up to large-city standards. State and collective farms, laggards in the physical-culture program, were creating new sports complexes, and plans for urban housing developments were required to include recreation centers.

The methodists were seeing specific results: more bicycles for workers' hostels, better playgrounds for schools, increased attention by factory administrators to the "sports pause," a five-minute calisthenic break taken at midday alongside desks and assembly lines.

The party directive was specifically timed to coincide with a new and crucial phenomenon in Soviet life—the five-day work week. The weekend was coming to the Soviet Union and with it a boom in leisure-time activities. Again in response to the party directive, newspapers began extolling the joys of family sport, and factories were producing modest power boats, many with sleeping quarters and galleys. Sporting-goods stores were featuring new stocks of fishing, camping, and underwater diving gear. More fashionable sports clothes for women were appearing. Electric train service was being established between large cities and ski areas, and the construction of lodges and lifts was being stepped up. Trade unions were building cottages on the shores of artificial seas, and the publishing houses were issuing even more how-to sports books.

The power of the party to galvanize so many agencies for integrated action was awesome. Even the film companies, expected to do their bit, increased their quota of sports feature movies. Among the 1967 releases was a comedy in color called *Royal Regatta,* the hasty work of the usually high-caliber Mosfilm studio. The villain of the film is an opportunistic crew coach, the clown is a runaway sexton, and the hero a handsome scatter-brain who keeps capsizing the shell whenever his girl friend, a chesty Aeroflot stewardess, wings by.

The viability of the Soviet sports system is directly attributable to the inclusion of programmed play in social, economic, and political planning. Critics of the system believe it is overorganized, with a tendency toward stagnation. In the narrow area of international competition this may be true. Expert sports observers have often stated that the capability for crea-tive improvisation is coached out of Soviet teams, that Soviet athletes are disciplined to the point of becoming textbook automatons. Soviet sports officials shrug at the charge and point to the record book. Soviet teams are generally much older than Western teams, but in many sports athletes do not reach their peak until the late twenties. Other critics feel that the Rus-sians have made a particular point of developing minor sports and women's events in an effort to amass Olympic medals. Doubtlessly, the Russians do this, but the foundations were laid many years ago. Volleyball, the number-one participant sport, and wrestling and weight lifting were very early starters in a sports program that needed to include a great mass of people with the least expenditure of land, hard goods, and money. And women have always been a part of Soviet sports, as they have been part of labor and war. A female shot-putter is not a freak in a country that still talks about the "heroic girl sniper of Sevastopol" or the fighter pilot who shot down a German plane in the eighth month of her pregnancy.

As the nation progresses materially, the patterns in sport change. Hiking and cycling are losing popularity to automobile and motorcycle racing. Gymnastics, long a Soviet staple, is too demanding and complicated to compete with basketball, swimming, and "Canadian" hockey, sports for which more and more indoor facilities are being built. But artistic gym-nastics, a kind of athletic ballet, is gaining popularity, especially among figure-conscious young women.

Once isolated internationally, the Soviet Union now maintains sports relations with about eighty countries and receives roughly 10,000 foreign athletes a year, mainly from Communist-bloc and Scandinavian countries. More than 10,000 Soviet athletes go abroad each year. Many physical-culture institutes offer three-month coaching seminars for foreign sports-men, and technical sports advisers are sent out, particularly to young

African nations. Soviet officials call this "sports diplomacy"; Western critics call it propaganda and sports a political tool. To emerging nations Soviet officials offer the record book and history as proof of their system. The socialist state, they say, has given man a second life and filled it with joy and optimism.

In sports, at least, the Soviet Union has made almost incredible advances since the days when *Pravda* called tennis "decadent and bourgeois." The statement is now denied and scorned as "Chinese thinking."

"You must understand this," says Gavriil Korobkov, the national track and field coach. "We had many problems. We didn't have enough food, and tens of millions were living in holes in the ground. Houses come before swimming pools and potato fields before tennis courts. Now we are building those tennis courts and those swimming pools. It's as simple as that. And someday we might even build a golf course. Why not?"

GOD AND COMMUNISM

»

Peter Grose

One pleasant May morning in 1967 I sat in an overcrowded tiny room, the vestry of the Moscow Baptist Church, just a few minutes' walk from the Communist party headquarters building, and heard the staff singing at their morning devotion service—*"Chto za druga mi imeyem, Nas on k zhizni probudil . . ."* It was the old hymn I knew as "What a friend we have in Jesus." On the wall was not a ubiquitous portrait of Lenin, but the old print of Jesus with uplifted face that I used to see in Midwestern farmhouses in the United States.

From the outside, Moscow's Baptist Church looks like a bureaucratic office block. Inside is the sanctuary, clean, white, and square, an island of piety in the noise of everyday materialistic Moscow. Here gentle members of the faith, who crowd into every devotional service, wave farewell to foreign visitors in the pulpit with a flurry of white kerchiefs that suddenly stirs the room like a flock of white pigeons.

Religion is supposed to die out under Communism. Marxist philosophy has "proved" that in a humanistic, scientific society there is no need for the spiritual crutches of the past. Marx called religion an opium; Lenin preferred another figure: "Religion is a sort of spiritual gin in which the slaves of capital drown their human frames." Again and again Communist theorists have demonstrated that as man's intellectual level rises his need for a "God in the unfathomable beyond" will fade away. "That is what ought to happen," a Soviet official hesitantly told some American churchmen, "but I must admit it's doing it very slowly."

Fifty years of Communist rule have not killed religion, and the commissars cannot figure out why. Churches have adapted, evolved, gone underground, or been distorted. Some of them have been persecuted almost unto death, some have flourished. Half a century of temporal pressures has produced schism and unity, phony synods and midnight raids on ancient monasteries. There have been appeals from abroad, defiance from within, surrenders, compromises, exploitation.

Yet, there are scientists and teachers, public-minded citizens, who joined the Communist party but also desire to worship God. I have heard professions of religious faith from a painter, a writer, a translator of technical literature. I sometimes saw small children trying clumsily to cross themselves. A factory worker in the Baltic lands told a Soviet official—not just me: "I believe in God; religion has a deep meaning. If I had no faith, life would be meaningless."

A teen-age member of the Komsomol spoke up at an ideological meeting. "Weren't all those martyrs, especially in the early days of Christianity, touching examples of unselfishness and self-sacrifice for the sake of a cause? Why shouldn't we see in this a close relationship between Christianity and Communism?"

"How is it possible!" asked a party secretary in Byelorussia. "All our young people go through school and there are still believers among the younger generation."

The conflict between the church and the commissar has waxed and waned in a half-century of Communism. Organized religion has not followed the scenario of the Marxist theorists—it has not withered away. The outlook for the next half-century is that it will be the atheist doctrines in Marxism, and not the belief in God, that will be thwarted in Soviet society.

The Communist state has always treated religion gingerly. Lenin warned that "a noisy declaration of war on religion is the best way to enliven interest in it." While atheism is deeply enmeshed in Communist philosophy, it occupies only the periphery of Communist politics, and often has been ignored. The energy and motivation of the fundamentalist Protestants were useful to the early Bolsheviks in constructing a viable economy. Under the pressure of Nazi assaults, Stalin did not hesitate to mobilize the patriotism and resources offered by the Russian Orthodox Church. In 1966 a poll of Soviet young people found that the majority considered belief in God to be among the least of "social evils." The Soviet state has discovered that it can utilize the organized church, though non-Communist, for pro-Communist purposes. With faith lingering on among millions of Soviet citizens, religion seems too serious a matter to be dismissed under the dubious ideology of Marxist atheism.

The ebbs and flows of atheistic militancy have roughly followed the decades of Soviet power. The period of the 1920's was one of uncertainty. The Orthodox Church, under Patriarch Tikhon, was fighting the Soviets, and the church's wealth was appropriated by force.

The 1930's saw the triumph of crude atheism in word and deed, exemplified by the fanatical League of the Militant Godless, a shock force of professional agitators against religion. Arrests, persecutions, executions of clergymen were carried on in the general momentum of Stalin's purges and terror.

This came to an abrupt end with the Nazi attack on Soviet Russia. Stalin sought mass support in the Russian nation wherever he could find it. In 1942 Metropolitan Sergius hailed Stalin as Russia's "divinely anointed leader." On September 4, 1943, Stalin received in his Kremlin office the three leading metropolitans of the Orthodox Church, and a concordat was reached. Four days later the government authorized the church to elect Sergius as its recognized patriarch, and the Holy Synod of ecclesiastical government was granted permission to meet. The publication of a church journal, the opening of theological seminaries and higher church academies, and recognition of the church as a "juridical person" entitled to own property were authorized. The journal of the Godless League was suppressed, and its press and paper turned over to the patriarchy. The League itself vanished.

With the war's end, church leaders fell in with the Cold War demands of Stalin's foreign policy. Metropolitans and bishops were spokesmen for the Soviet line at meetings of the Communist Peace Movement; clergymen graced Kremlin receptions and greeted foreign visitors. Many village churches were reopened.

Religion as an ideological alternate to Communism loomed large in many localities during the 1950's, and the passive co-operation of the hierarchy on temporal matters did not necessarily extend all the way down to the parish priests. Investigators were astonished to discover pockets of strength among a younger generation of believers in an "underground" church, calling itself the True Orthodox Church and reverting to the anti-Soviet utterances of the late Patriarch Tikhon.

Toward the end of the 1950's, believers began to feel another hand at work in the organization of their religious life. The men who succeeded

Stalin stepped up atheist propaganda and, on a more practical level, they invoked administrative measures to cut the church's hold over the population at the lowest levels. The extent of the damage done to the religious structure across the Soviet Union in the five years before 1964 is now becoming apparent. Dissident churchmen in Russia have claimed that 10,000 places of worship were closed down by civil authorities in those years. The figure is probably an exaggeration, but the campaign has been admitted.

A vast bureaucratic structure was evolved to insure that church operations across the land were brought under the effective control of the civil power. This little-known apparatus is directed from an insignificant two-story former town house of a czarist aristocrat on Moscow's Sadovoye Ring boulevard. This is the headquarters of the State Council on Religious Affairs, headed by Vladimir A. Kuroyedov. Originally, there were two such councils: one for the Orthodox Church, in recognition of its pre-eminence in Russian religious life; the other for the "sects," all the other denominations, including Jews, Moslems, and Christian Protestants. Staff and officials were taken over from the ecclesiastical sections of the state security police.

The apparatus consists of delegates, who are regional representatives maintaining close touch with practicing clergymen. They grant the clergy the official registration without which they may not conduct worship services. In effect, the state can name and dismiss church officials. Lists of persons baptized or married in the church are made available to the delegates, who can then direct atheist propagandists to their homes or places of work. Many instances are documented of the harassments that follow. Official instructions to the delegate and his co-workers call for them to "study the constituency of persons attending the church and practicing religious services: baptisms, funerals, marriages, confessions, the measure of influence of religious societies and servants of cults in the winning of youths and children to religion." "Unregistered servants of cults"—illegal clergymen who have lost, or failed to receive, the official registration—are to be exposed and reported.

A special instruction concerns the council of twenty laymen in which the legal authority of each parish church is now vested. "It must be taken into consideration that the existing councils in many communities do not seem reliable," the instructions—given to me by an underground source—said. "You must advise the formation of new councils, out of literate persons who are able to administer the community—not fanatics, but people who would honestly observe Soviet law and your recommendations." From the twenty-man council is chosen an executive body which operates the parish.

"It is desirable that you participate in the selection of the members of the executive body and select persons who will carry out our policies," the government delegates were told.

A group of dissident laymen of the Kirov diocese claimed, in an open letter to the Orthodox hierarchy, that the councils of twenty "exist only on paper." Parish affairs are handled entirely by the executive bodies, these laymen wrote, "which are appointed by the Delegate." They "administer the material affairs of the church without the knowledge of the believers and are fully in obedience to the Delegates." Some clergymen complained that priests had no authority even in their own parishes. The delegate's instructions, they said, are usually given by telephone or personal confrontation, so that no official documents exist to indicate the depth of penetration by civil authority in the affairs of religious organizations.

The efficiency of this apparatus is the key to the present working relationship between church and state, the means by which a non-Communist organization has been adapted for pro-Communist purposes.

The Orthodox Church as an extension of state power in Russia is hardly new. So it was under the czars, and even some party activists of modern times consider the Holy Church something different, less reprehensible than religion in general. "There are some atheist militants," the official press reported, "who believe they have scored a victory if someone is converted from a sect to the Orthodox faith." A pale shadow of what it was before the Bolshevik Revolution, the Orthodox Church is still the most influential and cohesive non-Communist force in Soviet Russia.

There were churchmen who sympathized with the revolution from the start. On February 17, 1918, with the Bolshevik regime hardly installed, the church press contained this expression of grief from a modest Father G. Kazansky: "I write not so much with sadness as with the indignation of a person whose holy of holies, whose soul, was mocked. We have to say that the Orthodox faith had become a weapon in agile and shameless hands for the oppression of younger brethren. We merited the lack of confidence and even anger with which we were met."

In 1945, when Stalin permitted the election of Metropolitan Sergius as patriarch, only nineteen bishops could be gathered from all parts of the Soviet Union, many of them emerging from prisons or labor camps. A remarkable personal diary was found among the papers of the late Bishop Athanasius, an opponent of Metropolitan Sergius. Typed on three legal-sized pages, this document gave almost a month-by-month account of his life in the priesthood after ordination as Bishop of Kovrov in 1921. During his career he spent thirty-three months in active duty in his diocese. For thirty-two months he was at liberty but without a church post. He spent seventy-six months in banishment, and two hundred and fifty-four months in prison or labor camps.

The Orthodox administration in 1967 was organized into seventy-three bishoprics, with most of the posts occupied. The number of theological seminaries was cut from eight to three during the administrative repression of the early 1960's, but those remaining hold some attraction for a new generation of Soviet youth—forty-four were enrolled at the Zagorsk Seminary in 1963.

The atheist journal *Nauka i Religiya* heaped scorn on a letter from a twenty-one-year-old Muscovite who had determined that his chances were slim of gaining admission to Moscow State University and so took a place at a theological seminary. There he could study social sciences, ancient and modern languages, and art. He said: "I just wanted to study—how else could I do it?" The journal also expressed incredulity about highly educated young men who were willing to serve as priests in remote villages. Isn't it boring to live out here? asked a *Nauka i Religiya* reporter, only to hear the reply, "It is not boring to serve God."

The church receives no money from the state directly, though any registered religious congregation is entitled to the land for its church rent-free. The ample budget of the Orthodox Church is met entirely by contributions from believers and from the highly profitable sale of prayer candles made in its own little factories. Church workshops manufacture nearly 18,000,000 candles for the Moscow area alone. The annual income of the Orthodox churches in the Moscow *oblast* has been given as over $6,000,000.

The head of the Orthodox Church today is the Patriarch of All Russia, Alexius, ninety years old, consecrated a bishop before the revolution of 1917. His father had been an equerry to Czar Nicholas II, his grandfather a senator at the court of Nicholas I. Alexius, survivor of the prerevolutionary hierarchy, is now an imposing figurehead, and the decisions of the church are made by a group of younger bishops, churchmen of a new school and generation who are permanent members of the Synod.

There is the Archbishop Alexius, of Tallinn and Estonia, General Manager of the Moscow patriarchy, thirty-eight years old, a man over whose name appear frequent explanations for foreign consumption of the church's role in Soviet society and the solidarity of Soviet believers behind the foreign policy of the Kremlin.

The most dynamic of the younger church leaders is Nikodim, Metropolitan of Leningrad, thirty-nine, the vigorous "foreign minister" for the patriarchy. Father Nikodim appears genial and open; he always expressed annoyance when the church staff around him made me apply to see him through government channels. "I'm no Marxist," he said, nor does he talk in the pedantic lecture style in which Communist officials tend to converse. From his spacious office villa only a short walk from the Stalinist skyscraper that houses the Soviet Foreign Ministry in downtown Moscow, Father Nikodim directs the participation of the Russian church in international organizations. Under his guidance the Orthodox Church emerged from the isolation of Stalinism and entered the world religious community, joining the World Council of Churches and sending observers to the sessions of the ecumenical council Vatican II. Except for his luxuriant full beard and voluminous black robes, which flow around him as he darts from desk to bookshelves to file cabinets while simultaneously barking orders into a telephone, he could be a secular executive. My young Russian secretary, in the office of a churchman for the first time, revealed the outlook engendered by his years of schooling in Marxism. "Isn't it strange," he whispered, "that a man who believes in God uses the telephone just like anyone else?"

Hierarchs of the Orthodox Church live well these days. They are whisked around Moscow in their own long black limousines; their dachas look ordinary from the outside but inside are heavy with art treasures and personal luxuries that few Soviet citizens can amass. Lenin's remark that a wealthy priest poses no challenge to the working-class movement may be taken to heart by today's Communist leaders.

But far from the Moscow patriarchate, among the lean and humble churchmen in the parishes, and among the militant laymen in village homes, there is unrest throbbing through the Russian Orthodox Church.

"The Russian Church is ill, seriously ill. The most serious ailment is the age-old one of caesaropapism, the subjugation of the church to secular authority. In the Church there are bishops who are branches of a dead, sterile and useless fig tree. There are gangrened church members who are playing a pernicious role in its life; they are infecting it with their putrefied exhalations and injecting poison into its most secret depths." The author of these lines was not an atheist propagandist, but a contemporary Russian theologian and historian of the church, a devout believer named Anatoly Y. Levitin, fifty-two years old. Author of numerous books and articles under the pseudonym Krasnov, some of which reached the West only in manuscript, Levitin has been employed for the last few years as a lowly verger in a church in the village of Veshnyaki, on the outskirts of Moscow. He has taken upon himself the role of a spokesman for a rebel movement inside the Orthodox Church. "I am defending the Church because you are failing in your duty," he wrote to the Moscow patriarchy. "I am writing because you are silent."

Parish revolts have a noble tradition in Russian Orthodoxy. The movement that now challenges the Orthodox hierarchy came into the open in

December, 1965, over the signatures of two Moscow priests, both then thirty-five years old, the Reverend Nicholas Eshliman and the Reverend Gleb Yakunin. As Soviet citizens, they wrote a petition to the head of the Soviet state, Nikolai V. Podgorny; as priests, they addressed their patriarch.

Their bold initiative opened the way for further protests, and for disclosures of previous criticisms from clergy and laymen that had gone unheeded and unpublicized. To Podgorny, the two priests complained about state interference in the affairs of the church in violation of Soviet law. Their letter to the Patriarch was of a different character and style, sprinkled with Biblical citations, and containing the sharp charge of clerical participation in atheistic administrative measures. They said in part: "A large group of bishops and clergymen in the Russian Church, under the cover of piety, is knowingly and actively distorting the spirit of Russian Orthodoxy. There are those known for diligently covering up the closing of churches, those who honor any order of local authorities more than the words of the Gospel and the Church canons, those who excommunicate children from the Holy Sacrament, those who abuse the sanctity of holy relics, those who sold out their brothers."

The priests listed specific grievances. Since clergymen are banned from performing services in homes or cemeteries without civil authorization, "no citizen can ask a priest to visit his home to celebrate rites for his sick child or for his deceased parents without putting the priest in danger of losing his registration." About the appointment of clergy, they wrote that "in recent years a practice has been established in the Russian Church whereby not one ordination of a bishop, presbyter or deacon is performed without previous, inevitable interference of a functionary of the Council on Religious Affairs." They said: "Telephone orders, oral instructions, non-registered unofficial agreements—that is the atmosphere of unhealthy secrecy which has enveloped in a dense fog the relations of the Moscow Patriarchate and the State Council."

The priests also criticized the church regulation of 1961 vesting administration of each parish in the council of twenty laymen rather than the clergymen; the latter, therefore, were unable effectively to resist if the council of twenty decided to close the church.

One church official did resist, they wrote. Yermogen, the Archbishop of Kaluga, petitioned the Patriarch in the summer of 1965 for repeal of the 1961 decree. At the request of Alexius, Archbishop of Tallinn, Father Yermogen was dismissed from his diocese. Some time later, according to church sources, Father Yermogen was summoned to the office of the patriarchate and asked to sign the following statement: "In the Soviet Union and abroad there are rumors that I am in opposition to the Patriarch and the Patriarchate. I declare that I fully agree with the actions of the Patriarchate and condemn the letters of the two priests." Father Yermogen was reported to have refused to sign, and wrote, instead, over his signature: "I was discharged from my diocese at a time when we have many vacant dioceses. I think that the best way to prove that I do not belong to the opposition would be to appoint me to one of these." The Archbishop was told he would not be given an assignment.

Emboldened by the protests of Father Eshliman and Father Yakunin, a group of twelve laymen in the Kirov diocese petitioned the Patriarch in an open letter in June, 1966. They recalled the protests that had been made for four years past at the "unclerical" behavior of their bishop, Ioann, a man who, they said, had bluntly informed his priests, "Anyone who disobeys the Delegate [of the State Council on Religious Affairs] will be suspended." In 1965 Bishop Ioann was quoted as threatening a protesting church warden with the words, "I will send you to the secret police." In 1964 he shouted to a parishioner who questioned his actions: "Be damned—you will never be forgiven, neither in this life nor in the future." The twelve laymen described a scene outside their church, St. Seraphim, on August 9, 10, and 11, 1963, when "big detachments of police and civilian monitors surrounded the church and did not let women and children inside. The women fought with the guards, and finally broke through the line."

Levitin and some anonymous laymen joined in the protests, each relating his own experiences. In most cases the texts of the accusations were smuggled abroad for publication; foreign correspondents in Moscow who heard of the documents were given to understand that their positions in the Soviet capital would be endangered if they reported the news. As far as is known, the letter of Father Eshliman and Father Yakunin to Podgorny was never answered; Soviet state authorities preferred to handle the protest through the church mechanism, which would surely respond to the government's wishes.

The two priests were dismissed from their parishes in May, 1966, by the Patriarch; the Synod confirmed the decision formally in October. In June Patriarch Alexius addressed an encyclical to fifty-two diocesan bishops, a broad circulation which gave the best possible indication that the unrest was not considered an isolated or localized act of protest. The encyclical warned of churchmen "who stir suspicion and distrust in church authority and the fatherland." It condemned the use of open letters between priests and their superiors in the hierarchy, and went on: "Persons utilizing this form of open address to their spiritual authority endeavor to spread distrust in our supreme church authority among the clergy and laity, and bring temptation into the quiet stream of church life. If anyone should think he has faith, but does not preserve church unity, such a one not only remains outside the action of the redemptive and all-powerful prayer of God, but even beyond eternal salvation. We see in their activity also an endeavor to cast slander on state organs. The efforts of private persons to step forth in the role of unappointed judges of higher church authority, and their desire to cast slander on state organs, do not serve the interests of the Church, and have the effect of destroying the well-intended relationships between state organs and our Church."

The two priests, like Archbishop Yermogen before them, could thus be disciplined by the church hierarchy. The lay critics posed a more difficult problem. I heard reports of direct state intervention. Levitin related a series of approaches from local party officials, the security police, and the Moscow region delegate of the State Council on Religious Affairs, Aleksei A. Trushin. At one point, he said, he was warned that if he continued writing his articles and letters and distributing them in manuscript form "you will meet with another public body which will confront you with the Soviet Criminal Code concerning the transaction of illegal business."

When I first met Levitin in the autumn of 1966, the air was heavy with melodrama. Through a mutual friend it was suggested that we meet outside the Novo-Devichi Monastery. I took my wife, thinking we would look like casual tourists, a ruse that was spoiled by pouring rain at the appointed hour. As two most unlikely tourists we wandered up and down the path in the rain, passed once or twice a little man with a red nose and misshapen beret who we were sure was Levitin. After several false starts we fell into "casual" conversation. He took us through the cemetery of Novo-Devichi, pointing out the tombs of Gogol and Chekhov with gestures, but his words dealt with the corrupt state of the church hierarchy. We quickly became aware of several men in shabby raincoats who showed an intense interest in the graveyard meeting. A uniformed policeman suddenly appeared. "Let's look at Stanislavsky's grave, over here," our acquaintance said loudly, darting to another row. Under his breath he said, "Why should we walk into their arms?"

The extent of this parish revolt in the Orthodox Church can only be conjectured. Both church and state have excellent means to prevent the formation of any cohesive protest movement. Aside from harassment and threats, no serious action is known to have been taken against the protesters or the Kirov laymen. Levitin is apparently still at uneasy liberty in Moscow. The two priests, long after being dismissed from their jobs, were still living quietly with friends in the Soviet capital.

The dissidence merely confirms the continued existence in Soviet society of believers sufficiently devout and courageous to risk sanctions from church and state, persons who after fifty years still find a regime of atheism obnoxious. For every one who will express his feelings openly, it is reasonable to assume the presence of countless others who would welcome a church reform in Russia. The unrest, moreover, is not confined to the Orthodox Church.

A very strange scene occurred in Moscow one May day in 1966. On the sidewalk in front of the imposing building that houses the Central Committee of the Communist party were crowds of petitioners, maybe four hundred of them, in their kerchiefs and baggy trousers, asking to see Leonid I. Brezhnev, General Secretary of the party. They were dissident Baptists, believers trying to present a grievance at the headquarters of Marxist power. They wanted official recognition for a splinter sect, at odds with the national leadership of the All-Union Council of Evangelical Christians/Baptists. At issue was a feeling among believers that the Baptist leaders had shown themselves too pliable before state authorities.

The demonstration was quiet and intermittent, and came to nothing. Five months later a Soviet newspaper disclosed that five churchmen, agitators for a movement of about 25,000 Baptists which had split from the authorized church over ten years ago, had been tried in court and sentenced to jail for two to three years. Some of the dissenters have now rejoined the national organization.

It is not only in the ranks of the Orthodox that one can find the devout. Much of what has been said about the Russian Orthodox Church applies to other religious hierarchies. The Buddhists of the east Siberian region of Buryatia contend with rapidly depleting numbers in holy orders, the advanced age of the lamas, and, above all, the subservience of Buddhist leaders, who, in echoing Soviet foreign policy, greet fellow Buddhists from abroad with statements about freedom of religion in the Soviet Union.

The four Moslem councils of Central Asia enjoy a favored position in present-day Soviet policy because the Kremlin is eager to solidify friendships with the Moslem lands of the Middle East. Though Islamic culture, notably the limitations on women's role in society, goes against what the Communists of Central Asia are trying to build, the Moslems' religious practice has met less interference from the state than has been felt by other religions. "The mosque still has a strong hold in village life," a Communist newspaper editor in Turkmenia said sadly. A Moslem seminary in Bukhara trains fifty young men for the clergy, and the best students are permitted to go abroad for further theological training in universities of Islam—a privilege denied to young Jews interested in becoming rabbis.

The shrillest noise of the atheists in recent years has been directed toward the once insignificant churches of Protestantism—so-called sects. For many years these localized and tightly knit communities were regarded in a different and less urgent light from that in which the national Orthodox Church was seen. Only in December, 1965, were the two government religious councils—the one for the Orthodox and the other for all else—merged into one apparatus of state control. This seemed to be a tacit recognition that the civil problem of organized religious groups had expanded beyond the once exclusive confines of the Orthodox into new and less familiar areas.

There are many sects in the Soviet Union—Methodists, Lutherans, Seventh-day Adventists, and a dozen others. One stands out for the vigor of its nationwide organization. This is the Evangelical Christians/Baptists. The Baptists appear to be the most dynamic, ambitious, and astute body of believers in Soviet society. Far from suffering through fifty years of state atheism, the Baptist Church is booming. Its baptized membership now totals 545,000, five times its strength in 1917. There are over 5,000 Baptist churches across the Soviet Union.

Protestantism has a history in Russia almost as long as in the lands of Luther and Calvin, and its persecution at the hands of the established Orthodox Church is reminiscent on a small scale of the religious wars of Western Europe. Evangelists from Britain and Germany seized upon native spiritual awakenings in Russia in the nineteenth century, and founded the peasant-based Union of Russian Baptists and the aristocratic Evangelical Christian organization. When the Baptist World Alliance was formed in 1905, both Russian groups were among its early correspondents; the two were formally merged in 1944.

From the beginning of Bolshevik power, these Protestants posed a dilemma. They were believers in God, and dwelt on the happiness in the world to come. Yet they were working-class people and peasants. They had suffered persecution at the hands of the old regime, the Czar and the Orthodox Church. They possessed no land or riches. They could hardly be named among the exploiters of the workingman. Many sectarians rushed to support the Bolshevik regime, for its campaign against the Orthodox Church. The Protestants believed in work and production, just like the Communists, and not in rite and contemplation. With their deep motivation, high morale, and communal spirit, the sectarians threatened to leave the Communists far behind in the quest for almost the same earthly goals.

In 1929 all religious organizations in Russia were placed on a new and restricted footing, the basis still today of their operation in society. The principle was established that the only activity by a religious group to be permitted was the narrowest type of worship. From the start of the Soviet regime, one major church activity had been eliminated—the education of children in Sunday schools or any religious classes. Now everything else

had to go: the communal farms and work teams; the evening classes in reading and writing and the sewing circles under church auspices; above all, the
youth groups for work and recreation, which threatened to deprive the
Young Communist League, the Komsomol, of its monopoly as the ideological inspirer of new Communist generations. The churches existed only
for prayer; there could be no organizational devices to lead Soviet people
to God through work or recreation.

These regulations hit the sects harder than they did the Orthodox
Church, for the worship of God through everyday activity was a character-
istic distinguishing the Protestants from the formalistic Orthodox worship.
Through their work and energy, the sectarians were useful to the Communist state, but their motivation turned them into enemies of Soviet society
because it tended to show up the authorized ideology as somehow lacking.
A Communist party journal recently analyzed the Baptists' appeal to today's
Communists: "What is especially characteristic of Baptist communities?
Discussions about goodness, the human soul, about love—of God toward
people, people toward God and toward each other. They call themselves
brother and sister, as if they were related to each other, kindred souls.
Under such conditions it seems to man that he is not alone, that the community and God are with him. And the believer also has an illusion of comfort for spiritual illness, an illusion of humanity. Our duty [as Communists]
is to replace this illusion in such believers with true humanity, in which
Soviet reality is so rich, and which has not reached the believer who needs
it so much only as a result of someone's inattention, someone's failure to
fulfill his task."

The Baptist leadership has not been accused of undercover co-operation with state authorities. The charge of the Baptist dissidents is, at the
same time, the secret of the church's growing strength and appeal: the
leaders obey the law, precisely and skillfully; they have managed to exploit
to the fullest every loophole in the law to build their cohesive membership.

Sermons from the Baptist pulpits—part of worship services, and hence
permitted—are long and full of instruction and guidance, not stylized ritual.
Baptist parents have resisted quasi-official intimidation and defiantly bring
their children to Sunday services where they can hear religious ideas and
learn, even though the church carefully refrains from any organized religious instruction of the young. A newsletter is sent out regularly and widely,
with a course in the Bible and articles of interest to ordinary families unlike
the heavy theological speculations and hierarchical details contained in the
Journal of the Moscow Patriarchate.

Most impressive are the youth choirs of today's Baptist churches. At a

Sunday service in Moscow's central Baptist church the ground floor is crowded with the usual old people, mostly women, many with their grandchildren. But upstairs in the gallery, gathered around the organ, stand members of the new generation. Their voices are raised in hymns to God. Directing them like an earnest and sensitive orchestra conductor is a Soviet youth in his twenties, an engineer by profession, one of the intellectual elite of Communist society. Asked about their participation in a church choir, these young Russians say they enjoy singing, they like the music and the comradeship. They find it in a Baptist church. "Many of the choir members have not been baptized into the church," said Ilya Orlov, the church's organist and a preacher. "There are probably even Komsomol members in the choir. We never ask anything like that when someone comes to join."

The Baptist organization has been undaunted by the drives of the atheists and the restrictions of the Communist regime. It continues to sponsor a religious purpose in daily life. The Moscow church has recorded a net gain of 1,000 members in the last ten years. Across the Soviet Union in the last two years, about two hundred Baptist churches have been opened or reopened after the collapse of previous antisectarian atheist drives. Baptist leaders insist that they are not interested in gaining new members to present impressive statistics. Applicants for baptism are carefully investigated for sincerity and motivation, and there is a six-month waiting period before any applicant can be admitted.

The Baptist appeal to youth, the vivid sense of conviction, and the energy and skill of the church leadership in the face of administrative frustrations suggest that this band of believers is a candidate for influence in the coming Soviet decades out of all proportion to its numbers and previous role in Russian life.

No Westerner who has not settled down to live for a time under the heavy and all-pervasive air of Communism can fully appreciate the sensation of entering a church in the Soviet Union, of standing in an architectural space given over to the worship of God. The churches are little islands in a vast sea of materialism. There is a silence in the air of a Russian church, be it elegant or shabby, that hangs in startling contrast to the self-consciously activated communal air outside. A church is the only place in Russia where one can choose to be alone.

There is nothing comfortable or physically inviting about a Russian Orthodox Church. There are no pews or chairs, no place to rest. Worshipers stand or kneel on cold stone floors before poorly lit and obscure ikons that make an altar, or, rather, many altars, for Orthodox churches are jumbled and crowded clusters of small chapels. There are few large spaces to elevate the worshiper's gaze as in a great European cathedral. The Orthodox church is dark and tight; it is heavy with gold and incense.

Churches of other denominations and religions are brighter and fresher, more cheerful, less stupefying. Above the pulpit of the main Baptist church in Moscow is a bold slogan in large letters that the most aged worshiper with the feeblest vision could still read: BOG YEST LYUBOV (God is love).

In the first weeks of the revolution churches across Russia were assaulted, pillaged, wrecked, and converted into temples to the new gods of production. Walking along old streets in a Russian town one can hear the whirring of lathes and the scraping of steel coming through former church windows where once the prayers of the faithful were heard. Church buildings were turned into factories and warehouses; their rich mosaics were replaced by an industrial bulletin board. Some of the greater sanctuaries were spared for somewhat more noble purposes—meeting halls, museums (dedicated to atheism, of course, and the historical villainy of the church), or, in the case of the St. Simanis Church of Valmiera, Latvia, a concert hall.

In recent years, however, there has been a change in the official view toward ancient church monuments. An atheist travel writer, pausing at the Cathedral of Sts. Peter and Paul in Vilnius, Lithuania, wrote, "It was so beautiful that even I took off my hat—not before God, of course, but before the human creator of such a panorama of God." Now a walk through Moscow streets will reveal state laborers on scaffoldings around old and derelict churches, regilding the onion-shaped domes, restoring mosaics and artwork in proud tribute to the greatness of the Russian past. Intourist, the state tourist agency, directs foreigners to historical churches that formerly were considered blights on the Communist landscape. When the Soviet Union wanted to convey the Russian spirit to the crowds at Montreal's Expo 67, it included splendid examples of the ikon, that most Russian and worshipful relic of great art.

This is done in the spirit of art and history, not of God. But at the same time the whole doctrine of atheism is undergoing a change as Soviet power reaches its fiftieth year. The professional atheists of the Communist system are acknowledging that they have made a serious mistake. In August, 1965, *Komsomolskaya Pravda* printed this comment, which has now been widely quoted, by G. Kelt, an atheist worker of many years' standing in the western Ukraine: "Today we are once more lulling ourselves: 'Many believers in our country have left the church and religion.' This is self-deception. Only one thing is true: over a large part of the territory of the Soviet Union there are no churches, no cult preachers. But there are believers. If not Orthodox, then sectarians of all possible shades. Because, as has already been indicated, cutting off access does not turn believers into atheists. On the contrary, it strengthens people's leanings toward religion and in addition embitters their hearts."

How can one test the strength of organized religion in the Soviet Union today? As Kuroyedov, the state official charged with religious affairs, said in one of his rare public statements, "No official documents contain indications of whether a person professes religion or not." Spot statistical checks by atheist investigators in various regions showed a two- or threefold increase in the performance of Orthodox rites during the 1950's. In one central Russian district 60 per cent of all children born there in 1960 were baptized, 15 per cent of all marriages and 30 per cent of all funerals were performed in the church.

"Our country conducts no state census of citizens regarding their attitude toward religion," Kuroyedov said. In fact, there *was* such a national census in 1937. About 50,000,000 Soviet citizens declared themselves to be believers, nearly one-third of the population. The census returns that year were destroyed and the census officials arrested; the census of 1939 and the next one, in 1959, omitted all reference to religion.

Every time I visited a Soviet church I came away with the feeling that I was really seeing only a small part of the nation's religious life. There were always shabby old women in their kerchiefs sitting in the dark corners, breathing in the incense, seeming to have lost interest in life around them. If this was all that religion meant, then the builders of Communism should have little cause for concern, about the present or the future.

I found visits to former churches that have now been converted into museums more meaningful. No worship goes on now in such famous churches as St. Basil's in Red Square, but the ikons and priestly raiments are preserved and on display for modern Communists to see without feeling guilty about entering a church. Such museums are usually crowded. One often sees children being led through what were once halls of worship and looking in wonder at objects they have no basis for understanding. A Russian mother told me, with great amusement, of the discovery made by her seven-year-old daughter at the house of a friend. "Mama, you know God does exist!" she said. "I was just at Natasha's, and there on the wall was a real photograph of Him—He has a beard like Grandpa's and He wears a hat that looks like a plate!"

No warm welcome awaits young people in many of the working Orthodox churches today because of the fear felt by the aged worshipers that they come only to cause trouble. In Kiev I watched a group of half a dozen or so Ukrainian youths peer through the doors of a church, curious to see the inside. "You mustn't come in—you're hooligans!" scolded an old woman sitting on the steps. "Why don't you stand up straight"; "Take your hands out of your pockets"; "You should show more respect in here," said other elderly worshipers as the boys wandered quietly through the stuffy sanctuary.

Regular attendance at church is probably not a good index to use for judging religious strength, and the prevalence of middle-aged and elderly worshipers does not mean that religion will die out as the generations pass. For many Soviet citizens, it is only after they have reached their professional peak or retired on pension that their interest can be revealed in a realm that is still dubious in Communist society. At that point, they probably do not care if their superiors at work or social colleagues see them on the way to church. "Sure, it's mostly old people you see in the churches," said one long-time Western resident of Moscow. "I'm willing to bet that fifty years from now those churches will be just as crowded as they are today—and still with old people."

A better guide to the role of religion in public life are the complaints of the atheists themselves. They give countless examples of how religion fills a need in Soviet society even though ideology says it should not. "Once, at the polyclinic I saw the young local priest talking to some women workers," wrote one atheist propagandist. "He chatted with an older woman and her small son, then kissed the boy on the forehead. The doctor came out of his office, spoke to the woman in a displeased tone and refused her something. A few days later I found out that the church members were sending the woman's son to Moscow with their own contributions. The factory committee could have done that! Why didn't it?" An army officer wrote complaining that the location of the church in his village was too attractive, "like a garden"; the club, he said, center of the party's political agitation and propaganda, was remote and dingy. And what about the civil registry rites compared with those of the church? "The same bureaucrat records funerals and births—birth or death, to him it's all the same," he added.

Starting in 1964 the tone of atheist propaganda changed. Gone, and held up for ridicule, was the primitive atheism of the years before. The kind of thinking was abandoned that caused the first Soviet cosmonaut, Yuri Gagarin, to announce that in his journey through the heavens he had not seen God or a single angel.

Nauka i Religiya recently carried a commentary on Teilhard de Chardin, whose loyalties to both church and science would have confounded earlier atheist lecturers. "We atheists and confirmed materialists can read him with interest," the journal said, "to try understanding the secret of his influence over progressive segments of the western intellectual world."

Why did this dramatic change occur?

The old methods of administrative sanctions and brutal persuasion have not worked. Religious faith has outlived them all. And Communist ideology itself has undergone a distinct evolution since the death of Stalin. European Marxists find themselves in a dialogue with Christian thinkers. It fell to the Italian Communist leader, Palmiro Togliatti, the most influential Communist ideologist of the post-Stalin era (outside Communist China), to call for a new, more flexible party attitude toward religious organizations. His ideas began to be accepted in the Kremlin before the fall of Khrushchev, then were quickly taken up by the new leadership. The present head of state, Podgorny, paid a visit to Pope Paul VI. At the same time, the extension of Soviet state controls over church organizations—a political, not an ideological, act—rendered a vehement antireligion campaign less urgent.

Finally, a deeply significant revival of interest in religion, if not total espousal of faith, arose from a quarter far outside the church. The Soviet intelligentsia, freed from the ideological restrictions of Stalinism, began looking beyond Communism for inspiration. The novelist Konstantin Simonov drew a fierce response from *Izvestia* for stating in public that some religious faiths have their "useful side" and seeming to defend Soviet citizens "who find moral beauty and edification in some parts of the Bible."

There are apparently many such citizens. A famous Soviet composer kept a Bible by his bed; "I enjoy it as poetry and art," he told me, then quickly added, "It would probably be better if you did not quote me about that." An Uzbek playwright in Tashkent pointed proudly to two books on his desk, *Das Kapital* and the Koran. Soviet readers plead in letters to newspapers and questions at atheist meetings for the Bible to be sold in bookstores; at present it is not offered for sale, and anyone asking for it at the Lenin Library must put down in writing why he wants to look at it. "An edition could be prepared with atheist commentaries, if necessary," wrote one *Nauka i Religiya* reader. Members of the intellectual elite, of course, have no trouble in obtaining Bibles; they have friends abroad.

The renowned Soviet author of children's books, Kornei I. Chukovsky, was editing an edition of Bible stories for children in 1967. "It seems to me that our Soviet children and teen-agers, who confront Biblical topics constantly in books, galleries, and museums, should finally be able to get acquainted with them directly," the eighty-five-year-old writer said. "They have high artistic value, independent of religious content which will, naturally, be absent in our book."

There is no limit to the interest of liberal Soviet intellectuals in religious themes. A long overlooked novel by Mikhail Bulgakov, who died in disgrace in 1940, was revived by the literary journal *Moskva* this year and became the talk of the Moscow intelligentsia; its topic was the Crucifixion and Christ's encounter with Pontius Pilate. The poet Yevgeny Yevtushenko made a special point of crossing from Spain into Portugal to be at Fatima when Pope Paul made his pilgrimage to the shrine last May. Yevtushenko called it "a very impressive experience." A well-known friend of his in the liberal literary set of Moscow went some steps further: given permission to travel abroad, she went to a church in a Western capital and, far from the eyes of the delegate of the State Council on Religious Affairs, was baptized into the Russian Orthodox faith.

How much of this is really faith? It is possibly just curiosity about the exotic. A student at Moscow State University gaily described the weekend trip she and her friend had taken to the monastery town of Zagorsk over Easter. She raved about the churches, the worshipers, then she suddenly remembered she was a Komsomol member and I was an American, and a reporter. "Of course, we only went there to watch," she said.

Sometimes you see shopgirls in Moscow wearing little gold crosses on chains around their necks. When you ask them, they deny that such jewelry implies a belief in God. Maybe so, but why do they not wear a little gold hammer and sickle?

Curiosity has replaced hostility in the outlook of the present Soviet generation toward religion and its practice. The reason is not difficult to determine. A constant theme of modern Soviet writing is the individual's lack of a sense of purpose in today's society, the old Russian theme of nihilism. Communist society has somehow failed to convince many people of an inherent human decency in the Communist system. Building for the human mind and body, the Communists have ignored the human soul. Religion has appeared in the lives of intellectuals as poetry, as a possible avenue toward the deep morality the Communist system has not supplied to its faithful.

As this discovery penetrates Soviet society, the fact of police controls over one or another church organization fades in historical impact. The church is not the only bearer of religious thought to this intellectual stratum of society, nor do people who accept religion in this way need to come together to worship. Once religion is taken as a source of poetry and morality, rather than as a form of social organization, the strictures of atheism—ineffective and crude as they have been over fifty years—cease to hold value. They need not be denied; they are simply ignored. Then, when a morality is accepted, as philosophers have known over the centuries, faith is not far behind.

Chukovsky tells a favorite story about two small children which may contain the ideology of the Soviet future. He overheard this conversation one day in a Moscow park. "Is there a God?" asked one boy of about seven. "We Communists don't believe so," his slightly older playmate said confidently, "but, of course, maybe He does exist anyway."

THE KREMLIN AND THE JEWS

»

Peter Grose

I went to see Babi Yar one evening in the summer of 1966. The bus drivers in downtown Kiev were most helpful in giving instructions, though I knew only the ominous name of the ravine, not the new names for the streets and residential districts that sprang up after the war in the fresh air of the suburbs. It was the rush hour for homeward-bound office workers, and for this new generation of Kievites the thirty-minute bus ride to Babi Yar was everyday routine. Tired clerks dozed on their feet or read novels taken from battered briefcases, a secretary patted her uneasy hairdo, a young man had eyes only for his date. The rattling bus turned onto Demyan Bedny Street. On the right were modern five-story apartment houses with grocery stores and little repair shops on the ground floors. On the left was Babi Yar. Anatoly Kuznetsov wrote of a different journey to this wild ravine: "With their wailing children, their old and their sick, the Jewish tenants of the kitchen garden spilled out into the street, weeping and quarreling among themselves. They carried rope-tied bundles, battered wooden suitcases, patched carpet-bags and carpentry toolboxes. A great crowd of them ascended toward Lukyanovka, just across the ravine. . . . I hear it distinctly now: the even ra-ta-ta of a machine gun from Babi Yar."

That took place in 1941. In the autumn of 1966 the Soviet Union permitted the true story of Babi Yar to be told at last through Kuznetsov's documentary novel. The publication of this shattering account marked an epic moment for Jews and for humanity.

It is characteristic of modern Soviet society that an event of such magnitude and horror could go publicly unacknowledged for over two decades because it was politically inconvenient for the regime. The poet Yevgeny Yevtushenko wrote of the slaughter in that ravine outside Kiev in a bold poem that was published in 1961, for which he was roundly condemned by officialdom. But until last year, the awesome German massacre at Babi Yar was still shrouded in rumor and obfuscation in the U.S.S.R., and the tens of thousands of Jews who died there went without the tributes and commemorations accorded to those who perished at Auschwitz, Buchenwald, or Dachau.

The ravine is filled in now, to make a broad and rough meadowland. On the evening I visited it there were teen-age boys playing soccer, small children making sand houses. Young couples strolled arm in arm, a factory worker of thirty or so was out for a walk with his three-year-old son. Yes, he knew this open meadow used to be Babi Yar and he knew vaguely what happened there, but that was a long time ago, he said, and now the area meant to him only a new apartment of his own—relief from the crowded housing of the city. Back in Kiev, a middle-aged Ukrainian writer whose memory was longer told me: "I went out to Babi Yar shortly after the war was over. As I walked along I tripped over the torn shoe of a little child—I have never gone back there since."

Why was the story of Babi Yar suppressed? In the first place, as Kuznetsov describes so vividly, there were Ukrainian collaborators alongside the German executioners of Babi Yar. Though renegades, they were Soviet citizens and they shared responsibility for the atrocity. Then, more fundamentally, any tribute to the victims of this ghastly episode was inconvenient to Soviet officialdom simply because the vast majority of the victims were Jews.

The Jew in Soviet society poses a special problem for the U.S.S.R. today. So much has been written in the West with deep emotion and high drama about the sad plight of Soviet Jews that one could assume, wrongly, that the Jews are the only religious, national, or social group with a deep grievance against Soviet power. There are more Jews in the U.S.S.R. than in Israel; only the United States has a larger Jewish population. But there are surely more people outside Soviet frontiers who are deeply concerned about the status of Soviet Jews than there are Jews in the Soviet Union. An international campaign in their defense brings together such strange colleagues as senators from New York State and Bertrand Russell, large American corporations and the British Communist party.

All organized religion in the Soviet Union operates under difficulties—administrative attempts to discourage believers, police penetration, the widening gap between the faith of an older generation and the interests of the young. If this were all there was to the Jewish problem there would be no Jewish problem; it would be the more general question of the dilemmas of all religious faiths under Communism. But Jewry is more than a religion, and the status of Soviet Jews reaches into other problem areas in Soviet society: the status of minorities, the fate of exclusive cultures in a unitary society, the fact of international connections independent of the world Communist cause. There are countless Jewish stories with the theme that whatever happens to a gentile happens more so to a Jew—a gentile sneezes and the Jew catches pneumonia, a gentile makes money and a Jew makes more money, a gentile is reprimanded and a Jew is punished—all of which can be applied to the Soviet Jew today.

It is difficult to form conclusions about the status of Soviet Jewry. There are countless case studies and individual stories on which to base generalizations, but too many of these can be contradicted by the experiences of other Jews. Broad and general information on the Jewish population is sparse—largely because of deliberate efforts by Soviet officials to cloud the issue. The Soviet Communists are on the defensive in this area, and they have much to be defensive about.

Yet some of the world-wide concern is misplaced, for a picture has been created of a community of almost 3,000,000 Jews under persecution, living in daily misery and fearing for their lives. This picture is wrong. One can meet Soviet Jews every day whose reactions to the campaigns in their defense range from total bewilderment to sincere anger. Individuals in the Soviet Union, by and large, are not fearful of being persecuted because they are Jews, though many of them, in common with those in other countries, know well the meaning of discrimination.

What has been persecuted throughout half a century of the Soviet system, persecuted almost unto death, is the Jewish heritage: the religious practices and the culture through which Jews come together to acknowledge a common bond. Soviet pressures for assimilation, general strictures on worship and specific limitations on teaching children about God, geographical dispersion and the traditional, if frowned upon, sentiments of anti-Semitism—all these have dealt a savage blow to the Jewish community in the U.S.S.R.

In 1967 Soviet Jewry has all but ceased to exist as a unity, and in the years to come any hopes for a rebirth of a viable community of Jews must be grounded more on faith than on present reality. Many of those outside the country who express their concern about this situation condemn the present government. However, the breakup of the Jewish community has been a consistent trend throughout the Soviet era, and, against a background of the long, dark decades through which Soviet Jews have lived, the present leadership often seems to offer a fresh breath by its moderation. The story of these decades needs to be retold.

From the start of the Soviet era, the Bolshevik leaders found that there could be no simple "Jewish policy"—the problem cut across too many spheres the revolutionaries were trying to remold. Their underlying purpose was the construction of a unitary state, in which local interests and parochial allegiances were to be surrendered to the primacy of Communism, the society of all the people. The Jewish community, thus, did not fit in from the beginning. It constituted an exclusive society inside what was designed to be a hegemony.

In the first years after the revolution, however, there was no hint of anti-Semitism in the official attitudes of the Bolsheviks. Many of Lenin's closest associates were of Jewish origin, among them Trotsky, Kamenev, and Zinoviev. They had turned their backs on the religious faith of Judaism but they were staunch in their hatred for anti-Semitism, which had been one of the prime weapons of the czarist regime in its policy of dividing and ruling the minorities of the vast Russian empire. The czarist policies had left endemic in the country strong veins of anti-Semitic feeling. This was particularly common in the Ukraine, where it had been encouraged by the czarist police. Indeed, it was in this milieu that the infamous anti-Semitic propaganda pamphlet called *Protocols of the Wise Men of Zion* had its origin.

Middle-aged Soviet citizens of Jewish origin say today that growing up in the early 1920's they were almost literally unaware of anti-Semitism. If their Jewish parents chanced to be staunch Communists, the children could even be completely unaware of their Jewish heritage.

Lenin warned of the dangers of anti-Semitism, and the Communist party conducted an intensive campaign against any manifestations of it in factories and universities. Stalin was quoted in 1931, in an interview for publication outside the Soviet Union, as saying: "Communists, as consistent internationalists, cannot help being the implacable and sworn enemies of anti-Semitism." Vyacheslav M. Molotov was more detailed when he spoke in praise of Jewish culture in November, 1936—almost the last date on which such a statement could be made by a Soviet leader. He said: "Whatever the contemporary cannibals from among the Fascist anti-Semites may say, our fraternal feelings toward the Jewish people are determined by the fact that this people gave birth to Karl Marx, numerous great scientists, technicians and artists, many heroes in the revolutionary struggle."

Less than three years later, Molotov signed a pact of friendship with Hitler's "contemporary cannibals." And in those years the Soviet Union had been scoured by the Great Purge, which numbered among its victims most of Lenin's Jewish associates. Jewish newspapers were suspended, and Yiddish cultural life was sharply restricted.

While the Communist party was resisting outcroppings of anti-Semitism in the first Soviet decades, the authorities were at the same time busy with another aspect of the Jewish problem—the survival of religious practice. Here Bolshevik policy was clear and unequivocal: the Jewish faith, like any other religion, had no place in a Communist society. Judaism held doctrinal beliefs that were particularly hateful to Marxists, notably a belief in the advent of the Messiah, which, according to the Great Soviet Encyclopedia, "was aimed only at breaking the revolutionary activity of the exploited lower classes."

In the heyday of organized atheism, the late 1920's and 1930's, the League of Militant Godless was as active against the Jewish religion as against the Christian. Soviet Jews were harassed if they refused to work on the Sabbath; young Jewish Communists who had already broken with the religious life of their parents made a show of doing menial work—sweeping streets, lugging coal—on Saturdays and Holy Days. Special entertainments, concerts, and other cultural attractions were scheduled by the authorities to attract Jews away from observance of the Passover. Communal meals were provided on the fasting Day of Atonement. Jewish religious schools were closed starting in 1922 in accordance with the general ban on any religious education for children, though an educational network with Yiddish as the language of instruction continued well into the 1930's. A vast campaign to close down synagogues and harass rabbis coincided with similar campaigns during the early Soviet decades against Christian churches. The economic propensities of the Jews gave added sting to the drive after 1928, when the private enterprise of the New Economic Policy (NEP) was halted. Synagogues were branded "clubs of profiteers, of Nepmen," and were categorized as distasteful to loyal Communists not only as places of worship, but also as centers of exploitation and speculation.

At this time, when the Communist party was declaring its "implacable" hostility to anti-Semitism, the following poem was published in a Soviet journal. This translation is quoted by Walter Kolarz in the book *Religion in the Soviet Union,* published in 1962:

> The synagogue: house of the living God . . .
> Gleam, oily eye! Cheek, be suffused with red!
> The pathway to its portals is well trod
> By all the dealers that devoutly treat.
> Within its walls you may with unbowed head
> Glorify God, while joy your being fills;
> Push out your belly, sleek and nobly fed,
> And handsomely discount your notes and bills.
> But for the synagogue, what would avail?
> Elsewhere you'll feel disconsolate, depressed!
> Let ancient talith from your shoulders trail,
> And here, but only here, your soul will rest.
> The synagogue's the place—to get the best
> Of prices, for a coat, a ring, a fake;
> The synagogue is, soberly assessed,
> The best of clubs for nepmen on the make.

The author of this verse, Nikolai Aseyev, was later awarded the Stalin Prize.

The concept of Zionism and of a special Jewish state has always been anathema to the Communists. Lenin opposed it from the beginning. As far back as 1903 he branded the Zionist concept as "politically reactionary." Later on he called demands for a national Jewish culture the "slogan of rabbis and bourgeois." The Communist opposition to Zionism was twofold: the cause of Zionism took the energies of many Jews who otherwise might have devoted themselves to Communism, and the Zionists, although embracing many socialist concepts, were firm supporters of capitalism and bourgeois society.

The antagonism to Zionism and to a political Jewish state has constantly colored the Soviet attitude toward Jews in Russia. Stalin, for example, considered himself a specialist on "minority" questions. He assigned to the Jews the status of a minority nationality. But this posed problems. Whereas the Ukrainian or the Georgian national minority had language, culture, tradition, and a territorial base, the Jews had no territory. They were scattered through the country. In the late 1920's a tentative, but never very successful, effort was made by Soviet authority to give the Jews of Russia a territorial base. An area on the Amur River, in eastern Siberia, just west of Khabarovsk, was set aside for settlement, the beginning of what became Birobidzhan, or the Jewish Autonomous Region.

The experiment tied in with the continuing attraction the Zionist campaign to establish a Jewish homeland in Palestine had for Jews both inside and outside the Soviet Union, including some who sympathized with the

Communist cause. With the creation of Birobidzhan, the Soviet authorities felt they had a competing attraction for Jewish sentiment. The project was launched with great fanfare. Extensive propaganda campaigns were conducted in the 1930's. Much sentiment was generated for it, but, in fact, no great movement of Jewish population to the remote agricultural region ever developed. The purges of the late 1930's hit the Jewish authorities of Birobidzhan as they did all Jews. By 1940 many Jewish cultural institutions had been closed down, including the daily Yiddish papers in Moscow, Kharkov, and Minsk. The Yiddish publishing press had been sharply curtailed, though the twice-a-week *Birobidzhaner Shtern* continued to circulate in Yiddish to about 2,000 subscribers and the Yiddish libraries and theaters of Birobidzhan remained open.

World War II brought new crises to the Jewish community. Stalin had employed harsh measures in the late 1930's to curtail Jewish religious life. His police had charged rabbis with espionage (in behalf of the Nazis!) and had carried out harsh repressive measures against Moscow's Central Synagogue. The Nazis brought into Russia the most virulent kind of anti-Semitism, spreading their propaganda on soil that had by no means been freed of the prejudices encouraged by the czarist regime. Notably in the Ukraine, the arrival of Nazi troops often was a signal for anti-Semitic outrages in which local populations joined the German invaders. In Moscow, anti-Semitism burst out violently, particularly in the autumn of 1941, when the Germans approached the capital. It persisted for months thereafter, encouraged by the complaisant or even approving attitude of Communist party officials. Many believed that anti-Semitic propaganda was deliberately encouraged by Moscow officials to provide a scapegoat for the tragic losses the Red Army was suffering. Anti-Semitism raged in Moscow until high party officials called in their underlings and rebuked them for permitting it to continue, saying in ostentatious indignation that anti-Semitism was not officially sanctioned.

The Jewish Anti-Fascist Committee was then organized by Soviet authorities to carry on pro-Soviet propaganda in Jewish committees of the West, particularly in the United States. The prominent Jewish actor Solomon Mikhoels, a leader in the Jewish Theater, and the Yiddish poet Itzik Fefer traveled from coast to coast in this country enlisting the support and sympathy of the American Jewish community. Paralleling this, there was a relaxation of anti-Jewish activity. Yiddish newspapers, cultural institutions, and publishing activities resumed. The Jewish Anti-Fascist Committee counted in its membership leading writers, including Ilya Ehrenburg, scientists, and Red Army generals.

The committee continued its activity after the war. It issued some reports telling of the anti-Jewish atrocities of the Nazis in the Soviet Union. But in 1948 Stalin cracked down with a savage purge. Almost all members of the committee were executed, as was Deputy Commissar for Foreign Affairs Solomon Lozovsky. They were charged with conspiring to "detach" the Crimea and set up a separate Jewish state. The paranoid origin of this Stalinist suppression apparently lay in a suggestion by Lozovsky that the western Ukraine and Byelorussia might be provided with resettlement areas in the Crimea, from which Stalin had forcibly removed the Tatar inhabitants on charges of disloyalty during the Nazi occupation.

From 1948 to 1953 over four hundred Jewish writers, poets, journalists, scholars, and artists were arrested, exiled, or executed. Anti-Semitism became an official but unacknowledged policy. Quota systems were introduced for the admission of Jews to educational and other institutions. Jews were banned from the top echelons of the Soviet army, the Foreign Ministry, the Communist party. Only in the secret police were they permitted.

The anti-Semitic inclinations of Stalin became clearer and clearer as his life neared its end. In January, 1953, it was announced that a group of Kremlin physicians, most of them Jews, had conspired through the instigation of Zionist organizations—and British and American intelligence agencies—in a plot against Kremlin leadership. Stalin, it was later learned from his heirs, talked wildly of exiling the whole Jewish community in Russia to Siberia.

When Stalin died in 1953, his successors announced that the doctors' plot was a frame-up and called an abrupt halt to the spread of officially encouraged anti-Semitism.

Tension eased in the immediate post-Stalin years, and the old rabbinical dream of a Yeshiva, a seminary for future rabbis, was realized in 1956 when the Moscow Synagogue was authorized to open a small school for higher religious education. A Hebrew prayer book was cleared for publication in an edition of 4,000 copies.

Religious Jews were emboldened by the apparent thaw, and there were reports of new synagogues under construction, new assertions of Jewish community interests. But in 1957 the situation began to revert to what new generations of Jews under Communism had come to accept as normal. Local government authorities were told to adopt a stern attitude toward their Jewish communities, and the administrative measures enacted against the Orthodox Church hit the synagogues with special vigor. Some were closed down by atheist agitators; private prayer meetings were prohibited and propagandists stepped up their "analyses" of the Jewish religion as a particularly reactionary force for exploiting the working people.

A special political factor may have been at work behind this particular suppression of Jewish community life, which coincided with the years of Nikita S. Khrushchev's dominance. Khrushchev's main effort was de-Staliniization, and in his campaign he took serious political risks in riding roughshod over the perpetuators of the Stalinist mentality in the Communist party. Sanctions against the Jewish community were the one aspect of Stalinism that he did not suppress; foreign analysts have speculated that this may have been an attempt by Khrushchev to go at least part way toward pacifying the neo-Stalinists in the party so he could carry on with de-Stalinization in other fields.

Whatever the reason, Jewish religious practice was stultified as effectively as the living cultural heritage had been snuffed out under Stalin. The Yeshiva found itself devoid of students, a new prayer book lay in ineffective manuscript form in a drawer of the Moscow Chief Rabbi's desk, and, as in the 1930's, the ritual requirements for the use of unleavened bread, matzoth, had to be relaxed—there was none to be had.

Through this historical survey one can see the varied pressures against which the world-wide campaign in defense of Soviet Jewry is now mobilized, and the particular sensitivities of Soviet officials in the face of it. If it were simply a matter of religious hostility, that could be explained away in the context of the general policy of atheism. But reinforcing the antireligious moves was the Stalinist policy of cultural suppression, guided by the fear that the Jewish community somehow constituted a more dangerous threat to Soviet power than any other culture. Doubly tainted, the Jews were suspect for their potential sympathies to the "bourgeois" movement of Zionism and its incarnation in the state of Israel—originally welcomed by the Kremlin as an anticolonial development, then gradually blackened with "imperialist" motives as Moscow bid for friendship in the Arab world.

The delicacy of the Jewish question for Communist leaders reverts to the original problem of anti-Semitism. For ideological reasons, and with Lenin's own warnings in hand, the Communist party cannot appear to be authorizing any manifestation of a durable old czarist scourge which then became a Stalinist scourge. The publication of a vicious anti-Semitic book in 1963, *Judaism Without Embellishment,* by T. K. Kichko, was widely noted and condemned abroad. Less noted was the official condemnation of this book as "offensive" by the Ideological Commission of the Communist party.

Politically, there seems to be no room in Communism for a strong Jewish community; ideologically, there is no room for anti-Semitism. The status of the Jew in Soviet society is as much a dilemma for the U.S.S.R.'s Communist leaders as it is a concern for the outside world.

One evening, in the home of a well-to-do Jewish family outside Moscow, I had a long talk about the world concern for the status of Soviet Jewry. The father of the family, a retired actor of about seventy, took one position. "You Americans and foreigners only make it harder for us with all your complaints about the status of Jews," he said. "You only make the authorities more defensive and less likely to make any concessions." Then his son, an engineer still early in his career, spoke up. "I don't think that's right— all those speeches and petitions make the party people know that they won't be able to get away with anything. There are too many people watching. The trouble with your campaigns is you're protesting against the wrong things."

In those two comments are two Jewish attitudes in Russia today, and it is no coincidence that they come from two generations. The representative of the older generation, which remembers the purges and the Stalinist suppressions, is not about to risk new trouble; he would rather plod along with bowed head in the hope that if everything stays quiet something good might yet occur. Young Jews have not suffered enough to turn away from a bolder outlook. They may not know a great deal about their Jewish heritage—how many wise men are there in the Soviet Union to teach them?—but they do not want to let party dogmatism go unchecked. In common with most of their generation, they clearly identify anti-Semitism with Stalinism. Yevtushenko is not a Jew, yet it was he who broke open the Babi Yar story, and he also has warned of the "heirs of Stalin" alive today.

The trouble, according to the young Jewish engineer, is that the foreign critics are looking in the wrong places, and only for anti-Semitism, while there is much more to the Soviet attitude than that.

When the authorities try to discourage Jews from going to synagogue they are denounced as anti-Semitic, but, at the same time they really are trying to discourage anyone from going anywhere to worship God. The closing of synagogues across the country seems less of a specifically anti-Semitic action when one realizes that Russian Orthodox churches also find their doors barred.

A point of criticism among foreigners, and controversy among Soviet citizens, derives from the fact that the word "Jew" appears on the passport or internal identity document of every Soviet Jew. Technically speaking, the nationality at birth of each Soviet citizen is indicated on official documents—be he Russian, Ukrainian, Latvian, Uzbek, or Jew. In this sense the label "Jew" is not understood in the Soviet Union as being a discriminatory designation. It is not, per se, an anti-Semitic label, as is sometimes contended abroad, where it is equated with the Hitlerian designation of "Jew." Foreigners argue that discrimination is made between Soviet Jews and, for example, Soviet Moslems, since the designation "Moslem" does not appear on Soviet passports. But Jews are historically regarded in Russia as a nationality, with, theoretically, the rights and perquisites of a nationality. The designation does not necessarily contain anything derogatory. At the same time, it is a fact that during periods of anti-Semitism in Russia—for example, during the period 1948 to 1953—not a few Soviet Jews deliberately "lost" or destroyed their passports and reapplied for new ones. In many cases in making out the applications for new documents they were able to drop the designation "Jew" because the internal-security police, owing to poor records, did not have their nationality so registered.

Jews complain that there is insufficient cemetery space in Moscow and Leningrad for Jewish burials. In the official view, the granting of such space would violate the equality of all Soviet citizens; it would be an act of favoritism to one segment of the population—and for an "undesirable" religious purpose.

The shortage of matzoth, which stirred an uproar abroad early in the 1960's, coincided with a grain crisis across the country. No Soviet citizens could buy flour for any purpose, so why should rabbis and synagogues be allowed to buy it for their own religious needs? As for Soviet rejection of proposals that American Jews ship matzoth to their coreligionists, these were treated by Moscow as strictly a propaganda gesture.

One of the most tragic personal aspects of the Jewish status is the immense difficulty Soviet Jews experience in attempting to travel abroad, to be reunited, even if only for a visit, with their families in Israel and other countries. Here again, much of the criticism can be aimed at the Soviet system as a whole. Foreign travel is not a right of any Soviet citizen; it is a privilege eagerly sought, a reward conferred by the authorities on those deemed worthy. The Jews are not alone in being frustrated in their dreams of foreign travel, but the restrictions, characteristically, hit the Jews more poignantly, for they are more apt to have relatives abroad than are other Soviet citizens.

There is good evidence that today's Soviet leaders have been stung by the charges of anti-Semitism. For the past two years, matzoth has been available at the large synagogues, even though the average Soviet housewife is still not permitted to buy flour for her own baking purposes. This seems to be a specific gesture to the foreign critics, who watch the matzoth situation so carefully, for in the official view making matzoth available is a special privilege accorded to one group of citizens.

Premier Aleksei N. Kosygin gave heart to many foreigners and Soviet Jews when he said at a news conference in Paris on December 3, 1966, that the Soviet government "would do everything possible, if some families want to meet, or even if some among them would like to leave us, to open the road for them." This seemed a signal that foreign-travel restrictions would be relaxed, and across the Soviet Union Jews submitted applications for passports—often with the Premier's remarks, clipped from Soviet newspapers, attached to their requests. Long-standing policies are not changed by one man's statement, under the present Soviet leadership, so there were disappointments and instances of the old-style harassment of Jews whose wishes to emigrate became known. But diplomatic sources confirmed that the level of Jewish emigration, to Israel, Canada, and other countries, rose sharply during the first part of 1967, reaching the equivalent of an annual rate of several thousand. Then this flow of emigration was abruptly cut off, with dozens of families packed and on the point of departure, when the Kremlin severed diplomatic relations with Israel during the Arab-Israeli war in June, 1967.

Premier Kosygin, incidentally, gave new evidence of how sensitive Jewish issues are to the Kremlin at news conferences subsequent to his Paris statement. During his visit to Britain in February, 1967, he pointedly refrained from any comment on the status of Soviet Jews, though protests were ringing all around him. In New York, at his United Nations news conference, he was asked directly about anti-Semitism and gave the traditional response of a Communist leader: "There has never been and there is no anti-Semitism in the Soviet Union." The new tactics of persuasion by atheist authorities show up on Jewish religious questions. When Jewish religious leaders in Leningrad made a formal approach to local officials in early 1967 for more cemetery space they were greeted with the argument: "Show me in the five books of the Torah where it says that a Jew has to be buried in a special place." But 1967 saw signs of movement on the long-stalled project for a new Hebrew prayer book. Aron Vergelis, the Communist chief editor of the Yiddish literary journal *Sovetish Heimland,* offered to make his printing plant available to the Central Synagogue for an edition of "reasonable" size. "Let them send us the material and we will print it," he said. "We won't even open the manuscript or try to negotiate about it—if our God-believing comrades want a prayer book, we'll try to help them." But relations are frigid between the synagogue and Vergelis, long a spokesman for the Soviet authorities on Jewish matters, and the offer was not instantly taken up. It certainly would not have been made if the chief editor of *Sovetish Heimland* did not feel it would be acceptable to the party leadership.

There are still two striking and clear-cut instances of discrimination in official policies toward the Jewish religion as compared with other authorized religious organizations. First, though the land and the building are intact, the Yeshiva founded after a long struggle in 1956 is still without students. Officials claim there are no young people who wish to study to become rabbis; the synagogue authorities speak of "temporary" difficulties in obtaining the residence permits that any citizen from outside Moscow must have to live in the capital. But there is no institution known to operate in the Soviet Union where rabbis of the future are being trained. With fewer than a dozen rabbis now guiding the religious activity of Soviet Jews, and all of them over sixty, the time could soon come when the world's second-largest Jewish population would be without a single native rabbi. Even the stunted Orthodox Church is authorized to operate three theological seminaries to prepare its future priests.

The second instance of discrimination lies in the fact that the Jewish religious leaders find themselves virtually cut off from Jewish organizations outside the Soviet Union. But here again it is more than anti-Semitism; it is a fear of what international Judaism represents in the world—a pro-Israel policy, if not militant Zionism, the old specter of divided loyalties.

Russian Orthodox clergymen regularly leave the Soviet Union to attend international conferences and commune with their foreign brethren. Bibles, hymnals, and prayer books are exchanged among church organizations; newsletters and bulletins circulate back and forth across the Soviet border. But not among Jews. The relaxation of the last few years has enabled foreign rabbis to visit the Soviet Union, confer with Soviet rabbis and church officials, even address congregations from the pulpits of the synagogues. Each tourist season now brings rabbis, singly and in delegations, to encourage Soviet Jews and gather information. But no Soviet rabbis ever go abroad, no Soviet religious officials ever attend Jewish congresses. Only once, during World War II, did a Jewish religious delegation leave the Soviet Union, to visit the United States. No religious delegation of Soviet Jews has ever visited Israel. Offers of prayer books, or even paper on which Soviet Jews could print their own prayer books, have been firmly refused.

These matters are of deep concern to religious Jews and believers in other faiths around the world. But to that young Jewish engineer they are still the wrong issues.

The secularization of Judaism is taking place in the Soviet Union, just as it is in other Jewish communities, though in the U.S.S.R., of course, it is bolstered by state policy. Like many Jews of the Reform Synagogue in the United States, young Soviet Jews are not particularly interested in the ritual use of matzoth, nor do they express the concern voiced abroad at the dwindling supply of rabbis. Traditional religious practices seem no more valid to young Soviet Jews than they do to young Israelis who are resentful that the buses of Tel Aviv do not operate on Saturdays. A new generation of Soviet Jews is concerned about social distinctions and discrimination in jobs and schooling. They are not the only ones who resent this discrimination. Svetlana Alliluyeva, daughter of Stalin, a man who knew a great deal about anti-Semitism in his time, had this to say to a Jewish reporter in New York: "I know about restrictions in universities and the institutes when very talented Jewish young people sometimes are not taken, and instead of them people of other nationalities are taken, but who are less talented."

Official statistics about the number of Jews in high places go only part way toward alleviating this most intangible of traditional Jewish fears. Per capita, there are many more Jews in so-called "specialist" job categories, requiring advanced education and training, than there are those of any other nationality group of the Soviet Union, including those of specifically Russian nationality. As Kosygin said, "Many of them occupy very high, responsible posts—one of my deputies [Veniamin E. Dymshits], a deputy premier of the Soviet Union, is a Jew."

So what is one to say when confronted with a story such as this? It was told to me by a gentle Jewish woman in her seventies, whose late husband was one of those cultural figures sent to hard labor by Stalin. Though our mutual friends overseas were close and she wanted to see me, she could not hide her desperate nervousness. As we exchanged news about families and friends, she told me of her son-in-law and his twin brother. Their parentage was mixed. The son-in-law declared himself a Jew; the brother chose the Russian nationality of his other parent. The brother is now director of the plant in which he started work as a specialist; her son-in-law is in the same job he has held for the last fifteen years.

No official assurances that Jews are not being discriminated against can convince the individual Jew who sees the Russian or the Ukrainian promoted ahead of him or who is refused a place at a university. These are the issues the young engineer wishes the outside world would raise in discussions of anti-Semitism in the Soviet Union. Perhaps he knew that Americans would find it difficult, in clear conscience, to complain too loudly about social and professional discrimination against Jews in the U.S.S.R.

Let anyone be warned who wishes to go to the Soviet Union to find the Jewish community, the old and traditional Jewish life of the Sholom Aleichem tales and hundreds of other stories. A depressing experience awaits him. The spirit of tragicomedy, of self-deprecation, of deep Jewish pride under a veneer of mock humility and belittlement—all this has completely escaped hundreds of thousands of young Jews now growing up in Soviet society.

The Jewish community is devoid of energetic leadership. I always came away from meetings with the Chief Rabbi of Moscow, Yehuda Leib Levin, with a feeling of sadness and pity for an old and tired man who has been beaten down by a lifetime of religious oppression. Instead of jumping at the offer of a Jewish atheist to publish the prayer book on which he has labored for years past, the Chief Rabbi seemed suspicious, almost frightened that there must be a trick somewhere. It also was impossible to come away with any accurate idea of Rabbi Levin's views, for in his tiny, overcrowded office behind the synagogue he is invariably surrounded by lay officials of the congregation who carefully recite Soviet policy to foreign visitors while the old rabbi just nods. As the father in one of the rare young families of religious Jews told a visiting American rabbi, "Our rabbis have given up too easily."

One seldom sees young Jews in a synagogue, and there seems to be little in the air of the congregation to encourage their participation. If elderly Christians are wary of youthful visitors, because they might be "hooligans" out to mock the believers, the aged Jews one sees in a synagogue seem frightened of any stranger. They appear on the defensive when confronted by foreigners, except when it is clear that a foreigner has been "approved" by the officials. When a visiting rabbi is allowed to speak from the pulpit, they are emotional and enraptured in their welcome, in the comfort they derive from knowing that they are not forgotten.

The happy Jew is found among the ranks of those who have been Sovietized, those who long not at all for the religion of their heritage or the sense of community their grandparents knew. They are the products of fifty years of Soviet power—they are Soviet citizens first, Jews only secondarily. If they are young enough, still early in their twenties, they will not display the same sense of fear that is so painfully evident in their parents' generation, for they did not experience what their forebears have known. They feel a certain confidence that the prevailing atmosphere of public life will not permit serious manifestations of the old anti-Semitism, for that is tainted with Stalinism and there are plenty of articulate gentiles in public life who will resist any part of Stalinism.

Recent years have seen a renewed interest in Jewry among this younger generation, a curiosity—among Jews and gentiles alike—about what being a Jew means. Perhaps the Jewish heritage appears as something exciting and exotic to a generation that finds it boring to be a homogeneous product of the unitary Communist society. From its low starting point in the early 1960's, Yiddish culture now shows signs of an upsurge. *Sovetish Heimland* grew from a bimonthly to a monthly in 1964, and in 1968 the editors hope to enlarge it from one hundred and sixty pages to two hundred pages.

Yiddish folk singers regularly perform in Moscow and other cities with large Jewish communities, and traveling dramatic companies present Yiddish productions, including Sholom Aleichem stories, even though the permanent Yiddish Theater in Moscow, closed by Stalin, still has not been reopened.

Stalin's Great Soviet Encyclopedia commented in 1952, with a finality that turned out to be only wishful thinking, "in the past the Jews of Russia spoke Yiddish." Among the 3,000 letters received by the editors of *Sovetish Heimland* last year were many from young Jews, eager to learn or study Yiddish. "I suspect that there are more young Jews studying or reading Yiddish in the Soviet Union now than there are in the United States," said Vergelis.

The religion of Judaism is carefully excluded from this authorized cultural activity. Do you print any religious articles? Vergelis was asked. "No, we print very few articles against religion," he replied, with the ideological instincts of a Soviet editor. He laughed when I explained that I meant the question to refer to articles favorable to religion. "The interests of the synagogue don't concern us at all," he said.

It is a religious occasion, nevertheless, which now brings the most vivid display each year of young Jews eager to identify with a tradition of which they know so little—the festival of Simchat Torah. On that night in the autumn, youthful crowds throng to the street outside the Central Synagogue; they sing old Jewish songs, many of which are accepted as part of Russian culture, or any other happy songs as they dance in circles and pairs under the eyes of the police, who, far from hampering the festivities, assist in directing traffic away from the throbbing street.

And whatever the Soviet Union's foreign policy may be, Jewish pride is not completely dead. During the week of Israeli-Arab fighting in June, 1967, a young Armenian friend came rushing to tell me how a total stranger nudged him on a Moscow bus, apparently taking him for a fellow Jew. "We're really thumping them, aren't we!" the stranger said with evident glee. The reply came, "Excuse me, I am an Armenian." "That's all right," said the Jew, "you'll do the same to the Turks!"

The old Jewish community may exist no more, but there are young Soviet citizens who know they are Jewish as well as Soviet. Attempts to swallow up the culture and tradition of the Jewish community into a homogenized Soviet culture are not without historical precedent. As Stalinist anti-Jewish measures were gaining steam in 1948 a Jewish poet, Menakhem Bereisha, wrote: "We Jews, who have no desire for national suicide, cannot fail to recall that throughout our history we have reacted to those who have suppressed our souls in the same way as to those who have murdered our people. Inevitably we ask whether now we have not encountered merely a new form of anti-Semitism, which, indeed, does not wish to declare itself as such, but which nevertheless remains anti-Semitism. This is by no means something new. Antioch also wanted nothing but good for the Jews when it attempted to convert them to its God. The Roman Emperors also wanted nothing less. And did not the Catholic Inquisition merely wish to save Jewish souls? At first glance the parallel may appear somewhat strange, but perhaps it is not so strange at all."

Judaism is not exactly inexperienced in the art of survival. Though fifty years of Soviet power have succeeded in the purpose of wiping out a cohesive Jewish way of life, there is enough faith remaining in the Jewish soul to suggest that the community has not gone for good.

DIPLOMACY:
THE INDIVISIBLE PEACE

»

Harrison E. Salisbury

A curious note survives in the collection of Lenin's papers in the Institute of Marxism-Leninism in Moscow, a response Lenin made to the secretary of the Third International (the Comintern), who had reported the death of the American John Reed.

Under date of October 18, 1920, Lenin replied:

"Comrade Kobetsky:

"1. Your report (that is the report of the physician you sent me) and the note should be sent abroad.

"2. Who is in charge of the Hotel Lux? Its remodeling for the Comintern? The management part?

"Lenin."

The Hotel Lux, a medium-class hostelry located a block north of the Moscow City Soviet building (the former Palace of the Governor-General) on Tversky Boulevard (now Gorky Street) soon thereafter became what can best be described as the headquarters of the world revolution. To no building in Moscow was access more difficult. Only holders of special passes, vetted by the secretariat of the Third International and the Soviet security apparatus, could gain entry. In the memoirs of German Communists, underground Polish party members, secret emissaries from the fledgling American Communist party, and Chinese revolutionaries—all those who constituted the general staff and cadres of the Communist revolutionary movement from 1920 to the purge years of the 1930's—references to the Hotel Lux abound. Here it was that bearers of coded communications from Indochina checked in. Here English party members under double or triple *noms de guerre* slipped into Moscow. Here no one asked his fellow's name even though he knew the name that would be spoken would be false. Here old Communists showed no surprise when a friend of twenty years coolly looked through them. Here no one spoke to another unless, by a flicker of an eye or an almost invisible gesture, a sign was conveyed that communication was not forbidden.

Today 10,000 people daily walk past the Hotel Lux and do not know it exists. There is no sign to mark its historic role in Communist party affairs. Not one of the two hundred or more persons who sit behind lace curtains in the Hotel Lux dining room of an evening and look out on the traffic moving in Gorky Street knows or has ever been told what the building once was. Indeed, its very name has vanished. There is no Hotel Lux in Moscow today, no more than there is a Third International. The physical structure survives. It is now, and has for many years been, the Hotel Central, a plebeian institution catering to Soviet engineers summoned to Moscow for dealings with their ministries, or public-health employees coming in for the annual conference on epidemiology.

The vanishing of the Third International epitomizes the distance that separates the Russia of Bolshevism's jubilee year from the Russia that took the first faltering steps toward Communism under Lenin in the autumn of 1917.

No aspect of the Soviet state was more precarious in Lenin's day than relations with the rest of the world. In part this stemmed from its nature. Born in revolution, it was dedicated to the proposition that the whole world would follow in its steps. Indeed, Lenin hardly thought revolutionary Russia could survive without a revolutionary world or at least a revolutionary Europe.

In keeping with this posture, all normal diplomatic relations were broken. Contact with the Western powers was smashed when Russia declared itself out of World War I. The Western powers then supported anti-Bolshevism, and the isolation of Communist Russia became virtually complete.

The Third International, the world organization of Communist and Communist-influenced or Communist-inspired parties, sprang up partly to fill this void, partly to try by revolutionary means to swing the world around toward Russia.

Those days seemed far distant in the summer of 1967 when Anastas I. Mikoyan sat in the Kremlin one afternoon musing about what the world looked like in 1924, when Lenin died. "Before 1924," he said, "we believed that the world revolution would be victorious in Western Europe quite soon." In fact, he said, there were some who thought that the whole world would soon be Communist. But history took a different course. The revolution was not successful, although, he recalled, Bavaria went Communist for a while in April, 1919, and a Communist regime was established in Hungary under Béla Kun about the same time. In the end, the European bourgeoisie proved too strong or too clever, and Europe did not go Communist.

Certainly no one in the Hotel Lux recognized that a historic crossroads had been reached and that the cause of international revolution as they understood it had suffered a death blow. But, in fact, this was precisely what had happened. The Third International (and the Lux) lived on for years. The International even survived the bloody purges of the late 1930's, although whole cadres of its international Communists (most of the non-Spaniards associated with the civil war in Spain, almost all of the staff of the Polish Communist party, key figures in the German, the Hungarian, the Finnish, and other Communist parties) were liquidated. Most were shot, but a few minor members and many wives were sent to the camps of Siberia.

Stalin killed the Third International during World War II, in 1943, dismantling it formally—although maintaining its remnants as an espionage organization—as a gesture to his Western allies. It was briefly revived in another form, as the Communist Information Bureau (Cominform), in 1947, but after an erratic and futile course, largely in the hands of Stalin's international security agents, it fell apart with his death.

The Third International and the international Communist apparatus under Stalin played a more and more obsequious role as he subordinated the cause of revolution to the foreign-policy and security interests of the Soviet state. Thus, when Mikoyan reminisced about Soviet foreign relations, he did not talk in terms of international revolution, or the Third International. He talked, as every Soviet statesman has for nearly thirty years, in terms of great-power diplomacy—of the basic problems that confront the Soviet Union as a superpower. He talked not of revolution, but of the United States, of the Cold War, of the issues that confound and confront both nations.

The story of the United States and the Soviet Union is much longer, more intricate, more entangled than either country usually realizes. It goes back to the times of the revolution itself. The United States was far from unsympathetic to the Russian Revolution. It hailed the March revolution and the downfall of the Czar. It was not unfriendly to Lenin and his Bolsheviks, although worried about Lenin's peace policy and Russian continuance in the war. President Woodrow Wilson held back, against the efforts of his British, French, and Japanese allies, on intervention against the Bolsheviks, but finally yielded, largely to provide a counterbalance against the Japanese in Siberia.

Today's Communist history books blacken the United States and try to give the leading role in intervention to America. But Old Bolsheviks who actually remember those days tell a different story. Moisei Izrailevich Gubelman, an Old Bolshevik of impeccable standing, brother of the late Yemelyan M. Yaroslavsky, a lieutenant of both Lenin and Stalin, had high praise for General William S. Graves, who commanded the American expeditionary force in Siberia. Gubelman was in Siberia in those days and saw action on all the critical fronts. "I knew Graves," he said. "He was not a bad man. We had good relations with him."

The revolution attracted American sympathizers as well, radicals and liberals. John Reed was not the only American who was caught up in the revolution. American anarchists came to Russia—but most of them, like Emma Goldman, were quickly disillusioned. Leaders of the Industrial Workers of the World—William (Big Bill) Haywood among them—came to Moscow. Haywood died there in 1928 and was buried in the Kremlin wall.

Gubelman knew one of the leading American I.W.W.'s, a man famous in his day, now forgotten—Bill Shatov, a leader with Gubelman in the Far Eastern Republic, a short-lived Soviet buffer state in Siberia. "Shatov was a strong man. He negotiated with the Japanese for us after the American expeditionary force left," Gubelman recalled. Shatov was a railroad worker by profession, and he rebuilt fifty-four bridges destroyed by the Japanese on the Trans-Siberian. In the early 1930's he helped to build the Turk-Sib railroad, connecting Turkestan with Siberia. "Shatov was enormously fat," Gubelman said. "He had his own cook. Every year he went into the hospital and had an operation for the removal of his fat."

"What happened to him?" I asked. "I have been unable to find any trace of him." Gubelman pondered. "I don't know," he said. "Along about 1934 I lost track of him. Never heard of him again. I think he died his own death." By that he meant that he thought Shatov had not died in prison or been executed, but he did not seem sure.

American industry played a major role in the early industrialization of the Soviet Union—a role seldom mentioned in Russia today. Ford, Packard, International Harvester, General Electric, and a dozen other big firms, along with British and German concerns, built many of the plants in the first five-year plan. An American, Colonel Hugh Cooper, directed the construction of the Dneprostroi hydroelectric plant, the first great Soviet hydroelectric project and for long the largest in the country. Thomas Campbell, the millionaire Montana wheat farmer, established the first big Soviet state farm—the Gigant farm in the north Caucasus, a huge wheat project on semiarid land.

Most of this activity occurred long before the United States and Russia had diplomatic relations. In that period the Soviet regime itself was probably saved by Herbert Hoover, who directed the American relief mission that fed millions of Russians during the terrible famine years of 1921 and 1922—an operation so vast and so humanitarian that it is still remembered by survivors of those days.

The great architect of pre-World War II Soviet-American *rapprochement* is dead. Maxim Litvinov, who, as People's Commissar for Foreign Affairs, signed the recognition agreement in 1933 with President Franklin D. Roosevelt, died at the age of seventy-five on the last day of 1951. Long alienated from Stalin (he had slept with a gun on his night table during the purges, prepared to take his life rather than submit to arrest by the secret police), his policy of mutual security and collaboration with the West had been abandoned for years. Litvinov's death caused hardly a ripple in the Moscow of the late Stalin epoch.

Litvinov was a symbol of a Westernized Soviet diplomacy which did not survive the 1930's. He was a man who had lived for years in the West, was at home in London, Berlin, Paris, and Washington. His mentor had been the first Soviet Commissar for Foreign Affairs, Georgi V. Chicherin, whom Litvinov succeeded in 1930. Litvinov held the world's attention during the early 1930's with his eloquent demands in the League of Nations for collective security, his impassioned orations on the theme "peace is indivisible."

Litvinov created a whole school of Soviet diplomats—intelligent, clever, highly educated representatives who not only knew their own country, but also were at ease in the complicated milieu of interwar Europe. By the fiftieth anniversary of the revolution only one of this group survived—Ivan M. Maisky. A tough, self-reliant, endlessly able diplomatist, he spent eighteen years in London, eleven of them as Russia's ambassador at the Court of St. James's. He was a man who perceived long before his colleagues the tragic inadequacies of Stalin, the fateful errors he was making in his dealings with Hitler, and who warned again and again—always vainly—

of the coming German attack on Russia. For his pains Maisky was paid with arrest and imprisonment, from which he was freed only by Stalin's death. But his fate was brighter than that of most of his colleagues. Except for a few who took their own lives or chanced to die natural deaths, almost all fell victim to one Stalin purge or another.

In his eighty-fourth year, comfortably working over his memoirs, as he has since Stalin's death restored him to normal activity, Maisky looked back over the past with some warmth. "My mind is fine," he said. "My heart is all right. I have a bit of a paralysis on my left side from a stroke I suffered a year and a half ago. But I consider myself very lucky. I am, I suppose, an optimist. I have lived through many things. I have seen many things. Things are better now than they were. I think they will improve."

He characterized Litvinov as the greatest of Soviet diplomats, the greatest of his day and perhaps the greatest diplomatist of the twentieth century. Unfortunately, Litvinov had ignored the advice of his friends. He had never written his memoirs. There had been some talk of publishing his correspondence, and Mrs. Litvinov, the former Ivy Low, who was still in good health, had been interested in this. But Maisky did not think it would come about. Tradition was against it. Maisky did not mention political objections, but these also existed. Even Maisky has had difficulty. His sharp criticisms of Stalin's failures on the eve of the war and his frank revelations that Stalin fell into a pathological depression on the day the Germans attacked, locked himself in his room, and refused to talk to anyone or make any decisions, were softened down between the publication of his memoirs in the magazine *Novy Mir* and their appearance in book form.

To Maisky's way of thinking, Stalin's psychology led him into the fateful delusion that he could outsmart Hitler. As for Hitler and his attack on Russia, Maisky was inclined to believe that the failure of the discussions between Hitler, Ribbentrop, and Molotov in Berlin in November, 1940, played a major role in the decision in December to order Operation Barbarossa into action. The Berlin talks, Maisky said, convinced Hitler that he could not count on dividing the world with Russia. Therefore, Russia must be destroyed. According to Maisky, Hitler was also infuriated by the Yugoslav crisis in March of 1941, when the overthrow of a pro-Axis government in Belgrade triggered the German invasion of Yugoslavia. Maisky said he did not believe Moscow had deliberately sought to turn Yugoslavia against Berlin and toward Moscow, but certainly Russia had tried to utilize the situation to its advantage.

Vyacheslav M. Molotov, who succeeded Litvinov as Foreign Commissar in 1939, was not a simple yes man for Stalin, in Maisky's view. "You know Molotov," he said. "He is a very strong-minded man. He played a definite role in the evolution of Soviet policy. Our policy was an amalgam of many factors, and Molotov's ideas were one of them."

The tragedy of World War II, in Maisky's opinion, was the division that arose at the end, the split between the United States and Russia, the start of the Cold War. The cause for this, he felt, was very complicated, but the principal factor seemed to him to be the death of President Roosevelt. "Roosevelt," he said, "had a very positive idea of the world and its relations. His death changed many things." Another great factor was Winston Churchill. Churchill had sought to limit assistance to Russia from the start, Maisky said. He had opposed an early second front and influenced Roosevelt against it. But Roosevelt had begun to turn against Churchill before his death. Then, with Roosevelt dead, Churchill regained influence with the accession of President Harry S. Truman. "There is no doubt," said Maisky, "that Churchill had a major role in harshening relations at the end of the war."

There were other factors, too, he conceded. Neither he nor Litvinov had any hand in the direction of Soviet foreign affairs after the war. Litvinov had been recalled as ambassador to Washington and Maisky as ambassador to London in 1943 as a gesture of protest against the failure to win a second front. As deputy foreign commissars, neither of them had much to do with policy after that. In 1946 Maisky left the Foreign Ministry and joined the Academy of Sciences. Litvinov was retired. Their friends and associates were being arrested. Solomon Lozovsky, another deputy foreign commissar, who was close to them, was shot in the 1949–52 purge directed at Jews. It was at this time that Maisky was arrested, along with Mikhail B. Borodin, the famous Bolshevik agent who advised the Chinese in the 1920's, Molotov's wife, and others. The Cold War ruled in foreign policy. Russia was almost more isolated than it had been in the days just after the revolution. Crisis succeeded crisis—northern Iran, Greece and Turkey, Berlin, Korea. The Iron Curtain clanked down. The only relations the Soviet Union possessed in those years were with the Communist countries of Eastern Europe, which were dominated by the clandestine manipulations of the Soviet secret police. The Chinese Communists came into power in 1949, but relations between Stalin and Mao Tse-tung were cold and formal.

Maisky did not attempt to analyze how a Russia ruled by so paranoid an individual as Stalin and dedicated to the proposition of expanding Communist influence and Soviet territory could possibly have lived in amity with the West. The problem of the Cold War involved factors far deeper than the death of Roosevelt or the machinations of Churchill. Soviet postwar policy—aggressive, conspiratorial, antagonistic to the West—almost certainly would have produced the Cold War regardless of what attitude had been assumed by the United States.

Not even Stalin's death in March, 1953, brought immediate change. Relations with the United States remained frozen despite the negotiation of an armistice in the Korean War, the signing of the Austrian State Treaty, and a notable easing of personal diplomatic relations in Moscow. For the first time since the mid-1930's, Russians (outside of a handful of carefully supervised top officials) began to show up for cocktail parties and receptions. No longer did the American ambassador invite twenty Russians for dinner in the hope that two might come. With the emergence of Nikita S. Khrushchev and his temporary traveling companion, Nikolai A. Bulganin, the outward image of Moscow began to change. Khrushchev and Bulganin ranged over the world, visiting Belgrade, London, New Delhi, Geneva. Everywhere the image they presented was a contrast with Stalin—outgoing, unrehearsed, sometimes tipsy, relaxed. Police and secret-service details were reduced or abandoned. By conduct and example Stalin's heirs sought to demonstrate to the world that a new era in Russia's relations with the world had dawned.

But the ice of Stalinism melted slowly. Even after Khrushchev's denunciation of Stalin in 1956 and the practical destruction of the Iron Curtain there was no real relaxation between the United States and the Soviet Union.

Then, in the winter of 1959, Mikoyan suddenly revealed that he was going to spend his "vacation" in the United States, visiting his old friend Mikhail A. Menshikov, Soviet Ambassador to the United States. What ensued was not exactly a "vacation," but by the time Mikoyan's month-long travel in the United States ended, the international atmosphere had radically changed.

The Cold War temperatures greatly improved, Mikoyan recalls. He pays high tribute to the Americans he met on his journey—the businessmen, the political leaders, the newspapermen. He met ordinary Americans in the street and talked for hours with journalists, bank presidents, and "even trade-union leaders." He had long talks with President Dwight D. Eisenhower and Vice President Richard Nixon. The expedition, in his words, "helped us to present to the Americans our political views and to find out what the Americans thought about us." Moscow regarded the Mikoyan trip as a great success, and no small part of the positive evaluation resulted from the discovery that—contrary to what Soviet propagandists had long insisted—the American press could be relied upon to give honest and objective coverage of Soviet affairs.

Unfortunately, Mikoyan conceded, the good effects did not last long.

The hopes for a basic improvement of relations with the United States, of the establishment of a *détente* between the two great world powers, flickered. Khrushchev made his famous trip to the United States, but the reciprocal trip of Eisenhower in 1960 to seal the "spirit of Camp David" was canceled in the diplomatic ruckus that followed the shooting down over Russia of the U-2 plane piloted by Francis Gary Powers on May 1, 1960.

American-Soviet relations bounced back and forth in the years that followed. They warmed with the election of President John F. Kennedy, cooled with the failure of the Kennedy-Khrushchev meeting at Vienna and the subsequent Berlin crisis, came to the verge of nuclear confrontation during the Cuban missile crisis, and then emerged onto what most Russians, official and unofficial, now remember as a sunny plateau in the last months of Kennedy's life.

The assassination of Kennedy came as stark tragedy to the Russian public. It is so regarded by Soviet officials. They tend to idealize him and what they recall as the comparatively untroubled state of relations at that time between the world's two superpowers.

Ilya Ehrenburg, the late Soviet writer and journalist, who was close to the center of Soviet power for forty years, analyzed the role of Kennedy one afternoon in mid-1967. "Only recently," he said, "did I begin to realize the terrible loss to the whole world of Kennedy's death. He was a real American, an intelligent man who knew the world. His contribution not just to his own country but to everyone was so great. He understood international relations and he understood the problems between the United States and Russia."

What brought on Ehrenburg's musings was the general state of United States–Soviet relations, particularly the ulcerous effect of the Vietnam war. To no official in Moscow in mid-1967 did it seem possible that genuine progress back toward a *détente* between the United States and the Soviet Union could be made without a resolution of the Vietnam war. That conflict was seen in Moscow from a specifically Russian viewpoint—as a roadblock in the effort to move toward the hegemony of the two superpowers that they felt was in sight under Khrushchev and Kennedy. They saw it as a dangerous source of world tensions, which involved not only the United States and Russia, but also the desperately complex relationships of China.

It was difficult to find a Russian in 1967 who did not speak of China in terms of apprehension. "Who knows what is going on in China?" Ehrenburg asked. "It is another world, another philosophy."

He told of a friendship he developed in China with Kuo Mo-jo, a famous Chinese writer and scientist. He visited in Kuo's home, became acquainted with his wife. Later on Kuo came to Moscow. Ehrenburg could not understand him. He criticized the Russians for building the new modernistic

Kremlin Palace of Congresses instead of sending more aid to China. Ehrenburg asked Kuo about his wife. Oh, said Kuo, she is ill. Then he gave a peal of laughter. What's the matter with her, Ehrenburg inquired. She's in an insane asylum, Kuo responded, laughing hilariously. "How can you understand people like that?" Ehrenburg remarked.

The question raised by the Russians was how the United States could continue to prosecute the war in Vietnam in the face of the enormous problems with China. "It seems insane for the United States to be bombing Vietnam with the situation so tense with China," one highly placed Soviet official said. Another Russian said he could make no sense out of the policies of either China or the United States.

Analyzing the world situation as it appeared from the windows of *Pravda*'s sprawling plant on the outskirts of Moscow, Yuri Zhukov, a veteran specialist in foreign affairs, said that the great problem of the future was nationalism. It was no accident, he felt, that Lenin in his very last writings devoted himself to this thorny problem, to the quarrel that had arisen between himself and Stalin over the question of Georgian nationalism. In the Soviet Union, Zhukov said, the national question had been pretty well worked out. But in the rest of the world it had become a great issue, *the* great issue.

Zhukov's view of nationalism was echoed by a colleague, a Soviet official who is at the extreme liberal edge of the spectrum. He believed that no issue had been so badly handled by the Bolsheviks as nationalism. "We simply underestimated its force," this man said. "We underestimated it in Europe—in East Europe, for example. And we did not begin to understand its force in Asia. Or in China, for that matter."

Zhukov drew the picture in even broader terms. He talked of the future of the world in Asia, in Africa, in Latin America, and even in Europe. Nationalism was the moving force. It was involved in the Israeli crisis in the Middle East. It was deeply involved in the Vietnam problem. The major error of the United States, as he saw it, was in not properly estimating the force of nationalism in Southeast Asia. Many Russians held the view that North Vietnam would have been, and might still be, a stalwart opponent of Communist China, simply because of the deep force of Vietnamese nationalism.

By implication Zhukov seemed to be suggesting that the Soviet Union had learned its lesson in its attempt to impose its will on the Eastern European countries and now was prepared to permit them to evolve their policies more and more on their own. He implied that Moscow appreciated the danger of manipulating nationalist forces, for example, in the Middle East. He did not touch on the contrasting experience of the United States in Europe, where, after putting economic foundations under the states of Western Europe through the Marshall Plan, Washington acquiesced in the normal evolution of independent policy in those states allied with the United States.

The great problem of the future, said Zhukov, is, on the one hand, to avoid the policy of trying to smash the forces of emerging nationalism and, on the other, to see that these forces are not employed for adventurist games. The danger, he felt, was that the United States might try to smash nationalism. This would not work. It would only give rise to more dangerous consequences, to the multiplication of wars on the pattern of that in Vietnam. The danger of using nationalism for adventurist ends had also confronted the Soviet Union, but, in his view, it had turned against this course. Only China followed such a perilous path. Indeed, this very view of nationalism and how it should be treated lay, he felt, at the root of the desperate conflict between Soviet Communism and Maoism.

The great hazard of the future centered on China. This hazard should not be underestimated. True, China was supposed to be racked by internal division, by the enormous quarrels over the cultural revolution, the Red Guards, and the thought of Chairman Mao. Yet, in the face of all this, China had produced the H-bomb.

Of course, Chinese standards were very low. Zhukov had been to China. They had showed him one of their best collective farms. The people had three meals a day and two blankets apiece. "You see," the Chinese told their Russian guests, "we have already achieved Communism." No one in Europe or America would think that this was Communism, that it was a great achievement to have three meals a day. But for the Chinese it was. Previously, they had had only one meal a day, or perhaps not even that. Now they had made a great advance.

The key to the China problem, most Soviet officials thought, was population. How many people did China have? Possibly 750,000,000. Possibly 850,000,000. Soon there would be a billion Chinese. These were clever, able, intelligent, skillful people. They were well organized. They were led by a powerful government. The world was going to have to cope with the force they represented, a force already sending shock waves out over the whole of the Eurasian continent.

As Moscow approached the fiftieth anniversary of Soviet power this titanic problem—the problem of how to establish a safe and secure world; of how to live with China in the face of Chinese nationalism, Chinese intransigence, and Chinese power—seemed to occupy the central ground on the horizon of the future. No longer was the Kremlin desperately concerned with internal issues of domestic economy. It felt confident that these could be met. But the dilemma of China seemed intractable, unresolvable. Possibly the death of Mao might bring great changes. Possibly this might make it practical, at least for a time, to weld the Communist world back into one again. But even of this there was no great assurance.

In such a situation the statesmen of the day under the leadership of Leonid I. Brezhnev and Aleksei N. Kosygin clung to the policy of attempting to steer the U.S.S.R. and the United States again onto parallel courses. It was not an easy task. The Russians, perhaps, placed too much emphasis on a two-power world, upon the United States and the Soviet Union joining in a kind of global overlordship. They did not always evaluate accurately the rapid rise of a European force which might act as a balancing and stabilizing influence within the superpower orbit. And they seemed to see no real role in the direction of world affairs for the new nationalist states on the rise in Africa and Asia.

The conflicts and clashes between the Soviet and the American power systems were multiple. And within the Soviet Union, even within the Central Committee of the Communist party and the Politburo itself, there were varying dictums. There was a persistent and aggressive young group which wanted to cut loose from the objective of a *détente* with the United States, which wanted Moscow to go it alone, abandon any effort at *rapprochement* with Washington. The advocates of this policy wanted to free Moscow to move the world balance of power in Russia's favor, making it easier to cope with the rising forces in the Asian and African world. This, they felt, would enable Russia to compete effectively with China for the leadership role among the emerging peoples of the backward continents. They saw in this an effective answer to Washington strategists who, they were convinced, were trying to score gains over Moscow by trading on the difficult Soviet-Chinese situation. This Soviet faction took the line that the United States actually was seeking to make a deal with China at Russia's expense, and that if such a manuever was not actually under way it would be if Washington could get any sign of encouragement from Peking.

It did not seem likely that Kosygin and Brezhnev would be driven from Soviet leadership on the issue of Soviet foreign policy. But the division in Soviet opinion emphasized the stress and strain that the sharpening world situation was placing upon the Kremlin and its policies.

After fifty years of rule, the successors to Lenin had accomplished much. They had made Russia the number-two power in the world. They had given the Soviet people a new and higher standard of living and culture. They had placed Russia firmly in the mainstream of world politics. Not that everything had changed. The influence of the secret police had been diminished—but not eliminated. Easy relations between Russian and

Russian were now possible, but there were still barriers to completely comfortable associations between Russians and foreigners. Russians could not yet travel at will abroad. Russians still might get a nasty call from the police after visiting with a foreigner. The differences between the semirestricted Soviet society and the freewheeling West were still big enough to constitute a brake upon the achievement of relaxed, self-confident, secure relations between the United States and the Soviet Union. But time and age and growing comfort almost certainly were beginning to tip the Soviet scales toward the Establishment side on the international scene, toward the duo-power concept of world balance, toward the developed European (and capitalist) system and away from the dangerous, dark, swirling (and revolutionary) forces coming up out of Asia, out of the East, out of the new areas of the world. No one on the podium atop Lenin's tomb on November 7, 1967, would dare to admit it, but the plain honest truth was that Russia, in its philosophy, in its domestic goals, in its foreign policy, was becoming more and more middle-aged, more and more middle class.

The phrase Maxim Litvinov made so popular in his debates at Geneva in the League of Nations days, "peace is indivisible," no longer was heard. It had no place in the lexicon of Foreign Minister Andrei A. Gromyko or his chiefs in the Kremlin. The language of 1967 was different. But no one in the Soviet leadership would in the jubilee year challenge the fundamental and universal validity of the basic Litvinov concept: that world peace could only be maintained by the joint action of the responsible powers.

About the Contributors

Harrison E. Salisbury, an assistant managing editor of *The New York Times,* is one of the country's most knowledgeable experts on Russian affairs. Born in Minneapolis, he received his A.B. from the University of Minnesota. He started his newspaper career with the *Minneapolis Journal* and then joined the United Press, eventually becoming its foreign news editor. He came to the *Times* in 1949 as Moscow correspondent, remaining in that post until 1955. In 1959, in 1961, and again in 1966, he made extensive tours of Russia, Siberia, and Central Asia. His reporting from the Soviet Union has won several awards, including a Pulitzer Prize in 1955. Mr. Salisbury is the author of *Russia on the Way, American in Russia, The Shook-up Generation, To Moscow—and Beyond, Moscow Journal— The End of Stalin, The Northern Palmyra Affair, A New Russia?, Orbit of China,* and *Behind the Lines—Hanoi.*

Lee Foster has been an associate editor in the Book and Educational Division of *The New York Times* since February, 1966. Prior to this assignment, most of his career at the *Times*—which began in 1946—has been in two areas: make-up of the editorial page and editing foreign news. Mr.

Foster was born in New York City on July 22, 1922. He received a Bachelor of Arts degree from the City College of New York in 1943.

Charlotte Curtis, women's news editor of *The New York Times,* is a graduate of Vassar College. She has traveled widely in the United States, Europe, and the South Seas, covering society news and general reporting assignments. She is the author of *First Lady,* and has won news writing awards in 1963 and 1965 from the Newspaper Women's Club of New York.

H. Erich Heinemann, a business and financial reporter of *The New York Times,* joined *Business Week* as a reporter-writer on finance shortly after graduation from Harvard and the Columbia Graduate School of Business Administration, worked as a security analyst in Wall Street and with Morgan Guaranty as an economist before joining the *Times.* He has earned wide respect for his knowledge of banking and money markets and for his ferreting tactics.

Fred M. Hechinger, education editor of *The New York Times,* is a Phi Beta Kappa graduate of the City College of New York who has been writing about education for newspapers and magazines since 1946, following graduate work at the University of London. He holds honorary degrees from Bard, Bates, and Kenyon colleges and from the University of Notre Dame, is the author of a book on Soviet education called *The Big Red Schoolhouse.* His other books include *Teen-Age Tyranny,* which he co-authored with his wife, and *Preschool Education Today.* He received the Education Writers Association Award for outstanding writing in 1948, 1949, 1964; the George Polk Memorial Award 1950–1951; the Fairbanks Award, 1952.

Hilton Kramer, art news editor of *The New York Times,* is a Phi Beta Kappa graduate of Syracuse University and did graduate study in literature and philosophy at Columbia, Harvard, Indiana University, and the New School for Social Research. He is a frequent contributor to periodicals and has taught at Bennington College and the University of Colorado.

Harold C. Schonberg, senior music critic of *The New York Times,* was graduated from Brooklyn College and received his M.A. from New York University. He served as a first lieutenant in the United States Army for four years with the glider and parachute troops. A contributor to many magazines, he is the author of *The Great Pianists* and *The Great Conductors.*

Clive Barnes, drama and dance critic of *The New York Times,* was born in London and was graduated from St. Catherine's College, Oxford University, with honors in English. He has written reviews and criticism on music, the dance, theater, films, and television for many British newspapers and magazines, and is the author of three books, *Ballet in Britain Since the War, Frederick Ashton and His Ballet,* and *Ballet Here and Now.*

Theodore Shabad joined *The New York Times* during World War II, when he drafted the daily war maps of the Russian front for the paper. He returned to the *Times* in 1953 as a member of the Foreign News Desk. From 1961 to 1966 he served as a correspondent in the *Times* Moscow bureau. He is the author of two books, *Geography of the USSR* and *China's Changing Map,* and editor of *Soviet Geography.*

Ada Louise Huxtable, architecture critic of *The New York Times,* is a graduate of Hunter College and did graduate work in architectural history at New York University's Institute of Fine Arts. She is a recipient of both a Fulbright scholarship and a Guggenheim fellowship for studies in design and architecture and has received awards from the Municipal Art Society of New York and the New York State Council on the Arts. She is the author of *Pier Luigi Nervi* and *Classic New York.*

Walter Sullivan, science editor of *The New York Times,* has been a correspondent reporting from the Pacific, Alaska, the Antarctic, China, Germany, and Russia. In 1959 he won the George Polk Memorial Award, and in 1963 the Westinghouse Award of the American Association for the Advancement of Science. His books include *Quest for a Continent, Assault on the Unknown,* and *We Are Not Alone,* winner of the International Non-Fiction Book Prize.

John Noble Wilford, aerospace reporter for *The New York Times,* started his newspaper career while still in school, received his B.S. from the University of Tennessee and an M.S. in political science from Syracuse University. He has served on the staffs of *The Wall Street Journal* and *Time* magazine, and had a two-year military leave with the United States Army's Counter-Intelligence Corps.

Hanson W. Baldwin, military editor of *The New York Times,* was graduated from the United States Naval Academy in 1924 and resigned from the Navy in 1927 to travel and write. He is the recipient of many honorary degrees and awards, including the Pulitzer Prize in 1942 for his reporting of the war in the South Pacific. In 1965 he won a Certificate of Appreciation from the Association of the United States Army.

Robert Lipsyte, sports writer, joined *The New York Times* two weeks after graduation from Columbia University and two years later received his M.S. from the Columbia Graduate School of Journalism. He has written two books, many magazine articles, and won two Dutton Best Sports Story of the Year awards and the Mike Berger Award from Columbia University for "distinguished reporting in the Meyer Berger tradition."

Peter Grose, Moscow bureau chief of *The New York Times* from May, 1965, to June, 1967, was graduated from Yale University, spent two years at Oxford University, and has since then spent all of his career as a foreign correspondent. In January, 1965, he finished a year's tour of duty covering the war in South Vietnam. He is now assigned to the *Times* Washington bureau.

Index

Abakumov, Viktor S., 140
abortion, 35, 51, 332–333
Abrikosov, A. A., 314
Abstraction and Empathy (Worringer), 167
abstractionism, 161, 164, 166, 168, 169, 170, 171, 173, 174, 262
Academy of Agricultural Sciences, 284, 285
Academy of Fine Arts, 166, 173
Academy of Medical Sciences, 276, 287, 330, 335
Academy of Pedagogical Sciences, 106, 107, 108, 115, 118
Academy of Sciences, 74, 108, 111, 139, 166, 266, 278, 285, 286, 287, 294, 309, 310, 312, 315, 335, 339, 351, 444
Academy of Social Sciences, 309

accelerators, 299, 300, 301
Administration for the Preservation of Historic and Architectural Monuments, 271
Agol, Israel I., 284
agriculture, 13, 14–15, 61, 62, 70, 227, 228, 237, 253, 279–281, 287–288, 290, 296
Aikhal, 267
air-borne divisions, army, 379
air defense, 368, 372, 373–374, 382; districts, 365; forces, 363, 364, 365, 367, 374
air force, 362–363, 365, 367, 371–372, 384
airplanes: MIG-17, 378; MIG-19, 378; MIG-21, 373, 378; Blinder B, 371; Su-7, 378; Sukhoi "Fishpot," 373; "Badger" B, 376; TU-20

Index

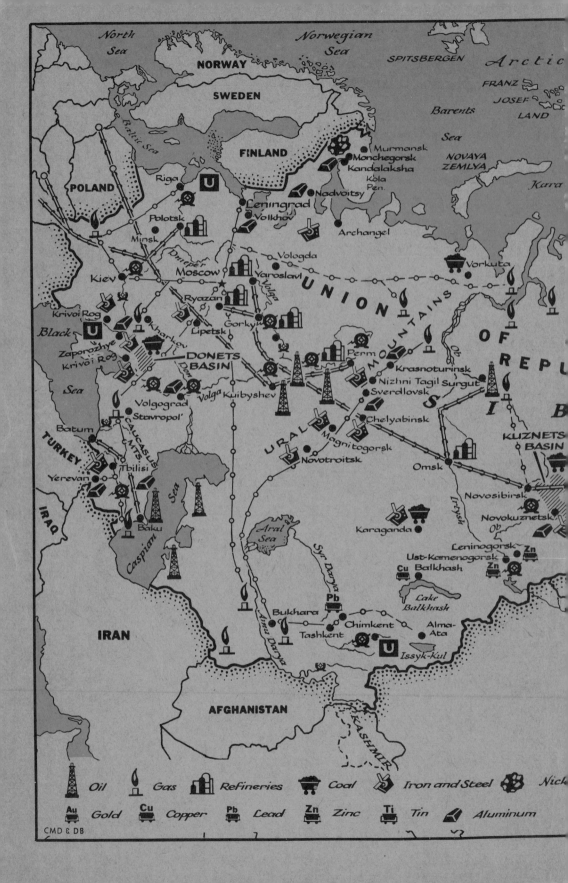

North Sea

NORWAY

SWEDEN

FINLAND

Norwegian Sea

SPITSBERGEN

Arctic

FRANZ JOSEF LAND

Barents Sea

NOVAYA ZEMLYA

Kara

POLAND

Baltic Sea

Riga

Minsk

Polotsk

Leningrad

Volkhov

Murmansk

Monchegorsk

Kandalaksha

Kola Pen.

Nadvoitsy

Archangel

Vologda

Moscow

Ryazan

Yaroslavl

Volga

UNION

Vorkuta

Kiev

Dnieper

Krivoi Rog

Black

Zaporozhye

Krivoi Rog

Kharkov

Lipetsk

Gorky

DONETS BASIN

Don

Volgograd

Stavropol'

Batum

CAUCASUS MTS.

Yerevan

Tbilisi

Sea

Baku

Caspian Sea

Perm

MOUNTAINS

Ob

Krasnoturinsk

Nizhni Tagil

Sverdlovsk

Surgut

URAL

Magnitogorsk

Novotroitsk

Chelyabinsk

Omsk

Irtysh

OF

REPU

KUZNETS BASIN

Novosibirsk

Ob

Novokuznetsk

S I B

TURKEY

IRAQ

IRAN

Volga

Kuibyshev

Aral Sea

Syr Darya

Amu Darya

Bukhara

Tashkent

Karaganda

Pb

Chimkent

Ust-Kamenogorsk

Cu

Balkhash

Lake Balkhash

Alma-Ata

Leninogorsk

Zn

Zn

Novokuznetsk

U

Issyk-Kul

AFGHANISTAN

KASHMIR

CMD & DB

Oil

Gas

Refineries

Coal

Iron and Steel

Nick

Au Gold

Cu Copper

Pb Lead

Zn Zinc

Ti Tin

Aluminum